FLASH/IMPULSE: RUNS IN THE FAMILY

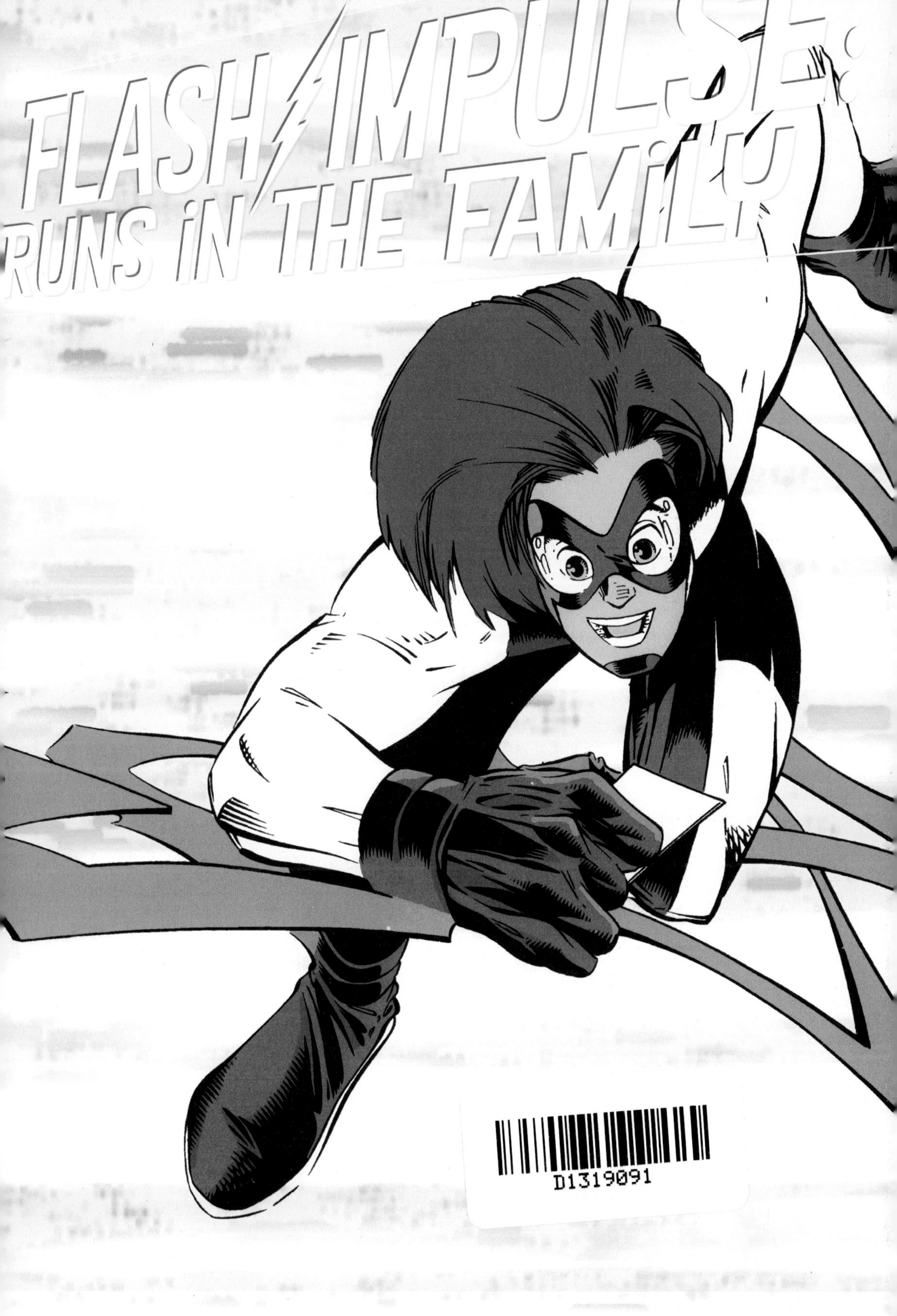

MARK WAID
MARTIN PASKO
writers

HUMBERTO RAMOS
OSCAR JIMENEZ
NICK GNAZZO
pencillers

WAYNE FAUCHER
JOSÉ MARZÁN JR.
BRAD VANCATA
MARK STEGBAUER
inkers

TOM McCRAW
colorist

CHRIS ELIOPOULOS
GASPAR SALADINO
KEVIN CUNNINGHAM
PHILIP FELIX
letterers

HUMBERTO RAMOS, WAYNE FAUCHER, AND TOM McCRAW
collection cover artists

IMPULSE CREATED BY MARK WAID AND MIKE WIERINGO

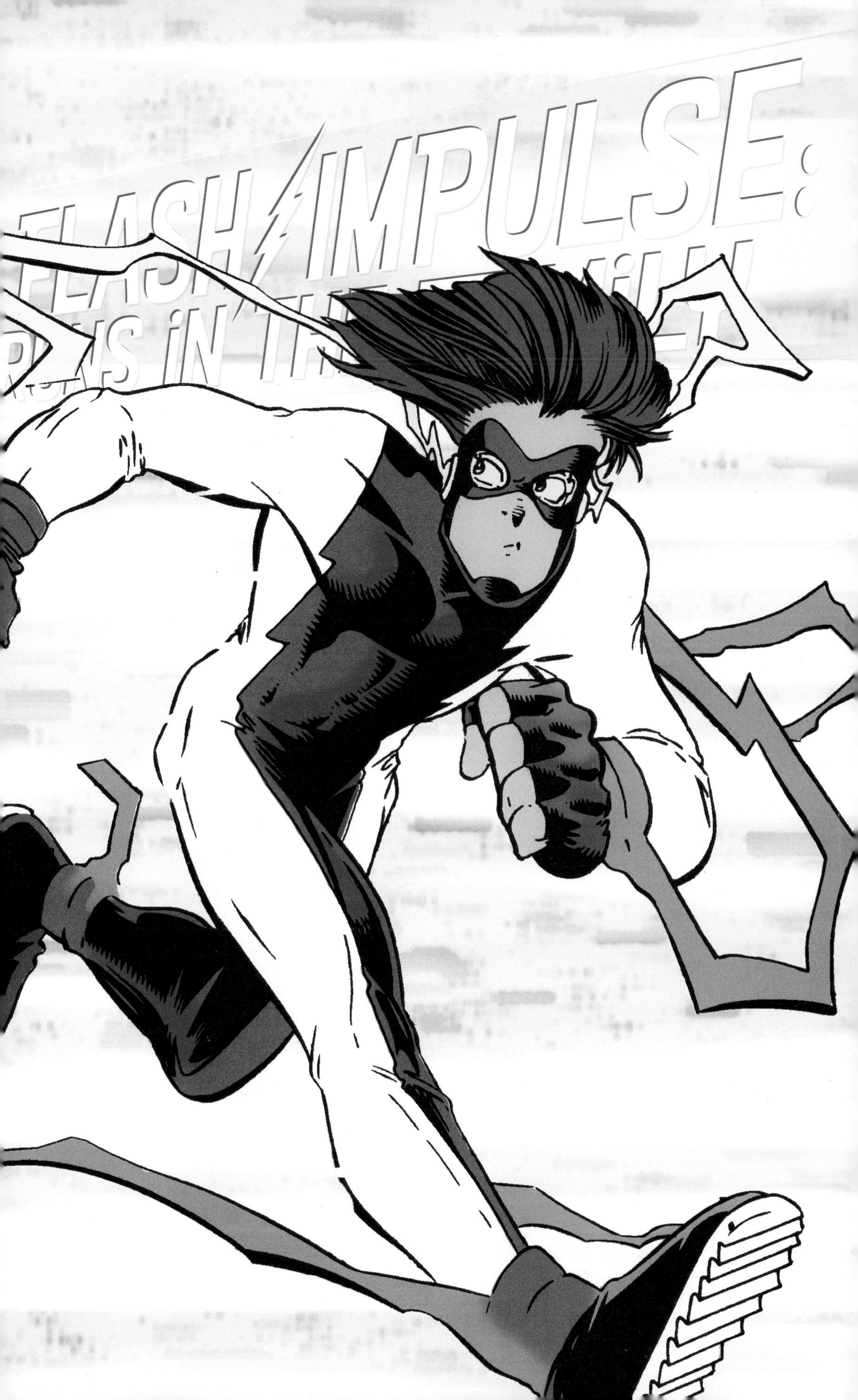
FLASH/IMPULSE:

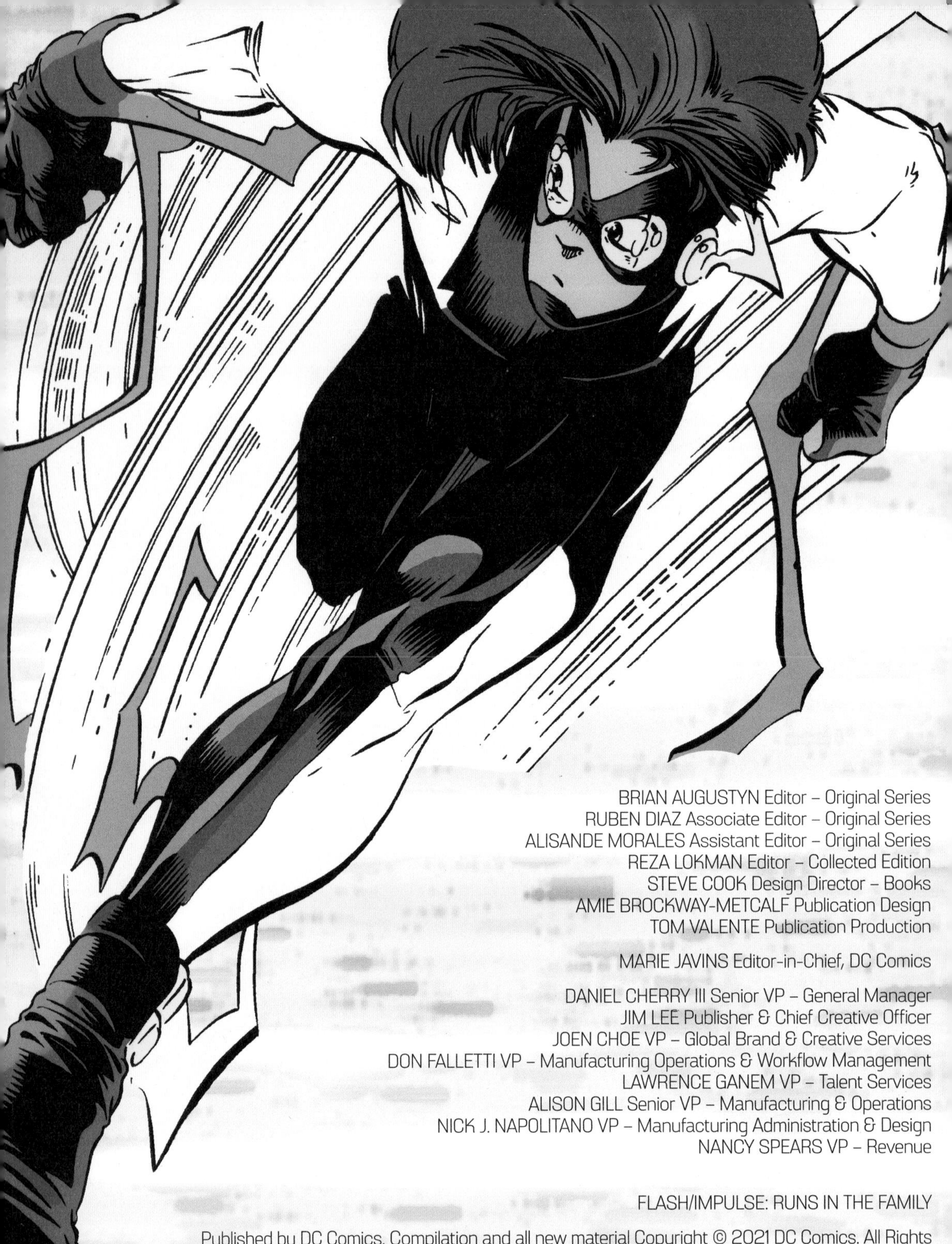

BRIAN AUGUSTYN Editor – Original Series
RUBEN DIAZ Associate Editor – Original Series
ALISANDE MORALES Assistant Editor – Original Series
REZA LOKMAN Editor – Collected Edition
STEVE COOK Design Director – Books
AMIE BROCKWAY-METCALF Publication Design
TOM VALENTE Publication Production

MARIE JAVINS Editor-in-Chief, DC Comics

DANIEL CHERRY III Senior VP – General Manager
JIM LEE Publisher & Chief Creative Officer
JOEN CHOE VP – Global Brand & Creative Services
DON FALLETTI VP – Manufacturing Operations & Workflow Management
LAWRENCE GANEM VP – Talent Services
ALISON GILL Senior VP – Manufacturing & Operations
NICK J. NAPOLITANO VP – Manufacturing Administration & Design
NANCY SPEARS VP – Revenue

FLASH/IMPULSE: RUNS IN THE FAMILY

DC Comics, 2900 West Alameda Ave., Burbank, CA 91505
Printed by Solisco Printers, Scott, QC, Canada. 4/16/21. First Printing.
ISBN: 978-1-77950-948-2

Library of Congress Cataloging-in-Publication Data is available.

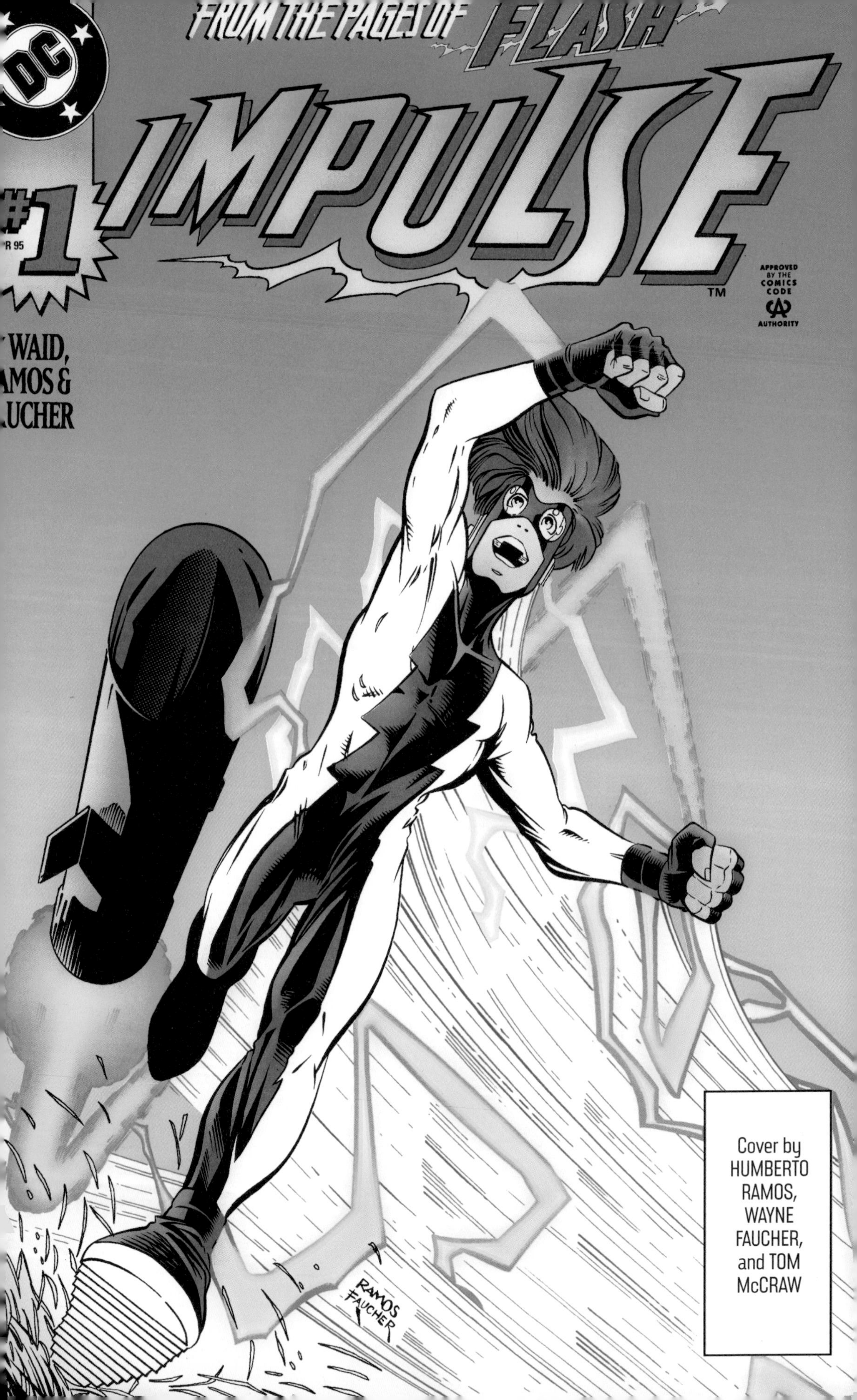
FROM THE PAGES OF FLASH
DC
IMPULSE
TM
#1
PR 95
WAID,
AMOS &
UCHER
APPROVED BY THE COMICS CODE AUTHORITY
RAMOS FAUCHER

Cover by HUMBERTO RAMOS, WAYNE FAUCHER, and TOM McCRAW

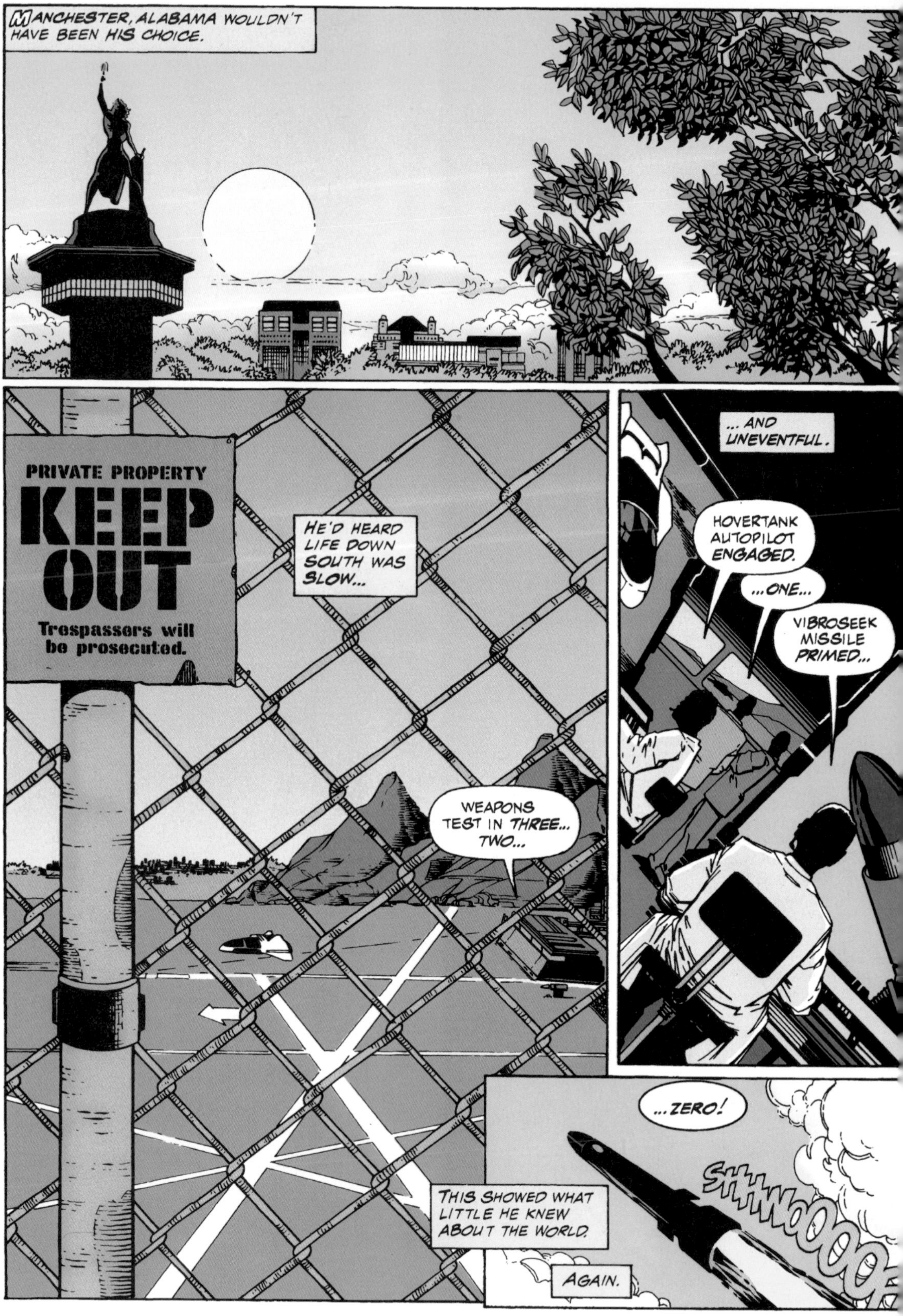
MANCHESTER, ALABAMA WOULDN'T HAVE BEEN HIS CHOICE.
PRIVATE PROPERTY KEEP OUT Trespassers will be prosecuted.
HE'D HEARD LIFE DOWN SOUTH WAS SLOW...
WEAPONS TEST IN THREE... TWO...
... AND UNEVENTFUL.
HOVERTANK AUTOPILOT ENGAGED.
...ONE...
VIBROSEEK MISSILE PRIMED...
...ZERO!
SHHWOOOOOF
THIS SHOWED WHAT LITTLE HE KNEW ABOUT THE WORLD.
AGAIN.

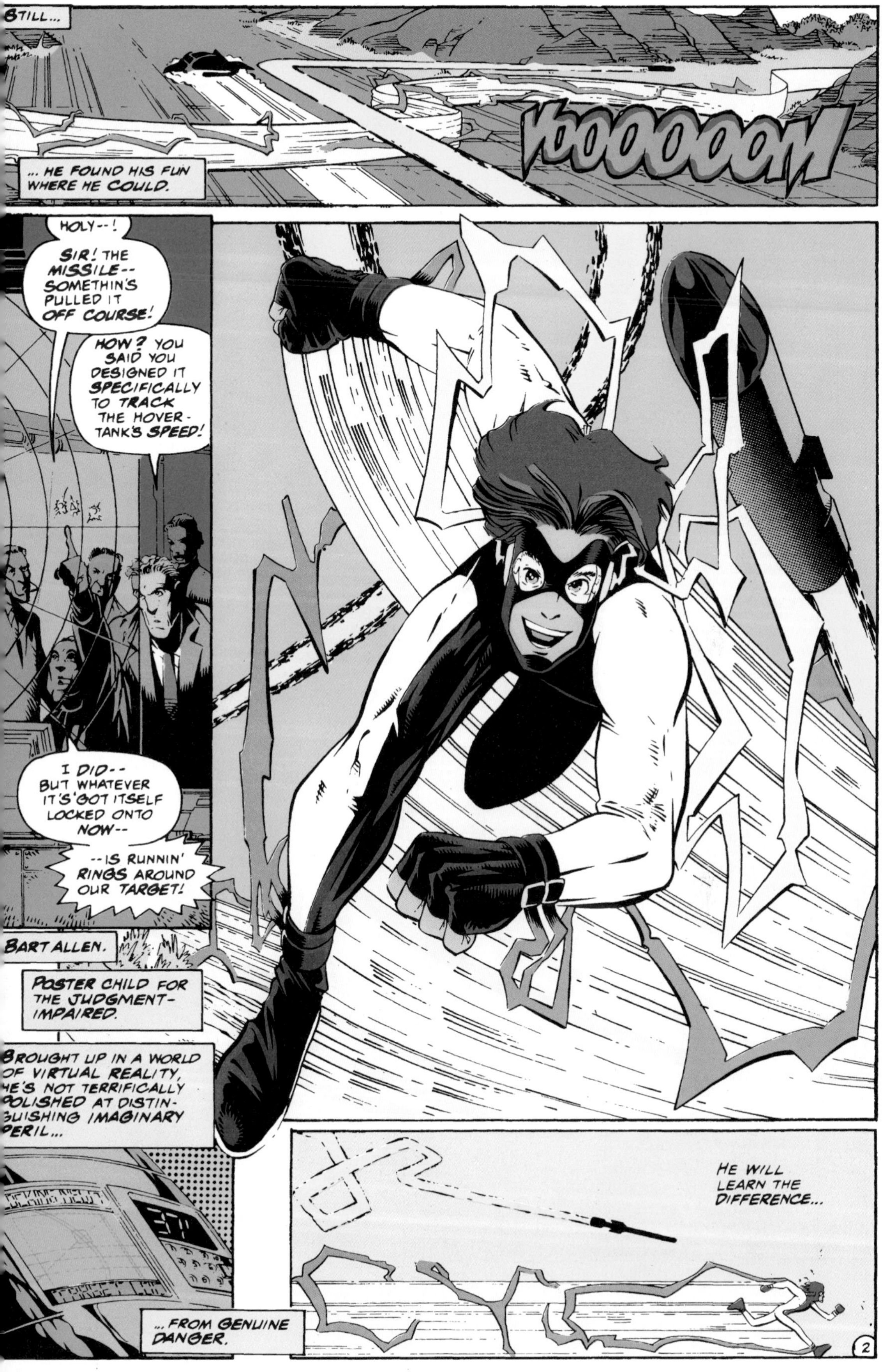
STILL...
VOOOOOOM
... HE FOUND HIS FUN WHERE HE COULD.
HOLY--!
SIR! THE MISSILE-- SOMETHIN'S PULLED IT OFF COURSE!
HOW? YOU SAID YOU DESIGNED IT SPECIFICALLY TO TRACK THE HOVER-TANK'S SPEED!
I DID-- BUT WHATEVER IT'S GOT ITSELF LOCKED ONTO NOW--
--IS RUNNIN' RINGS AROUND OUR TARGET!
BART ALLEN.
POSTER CHILD FOR THE JUDGMENT-IMPAIRED.
BROUGHT UP IN A WORLD OF VIRTUAL REALITY, HE'S NOT TERRIFICALLY POLISHED AT DISTIN-GUISHING IMAGINARY PERIL...
HE WILL LEARN THE DIFFERENCE...
...FROM GENUINE DANGER.

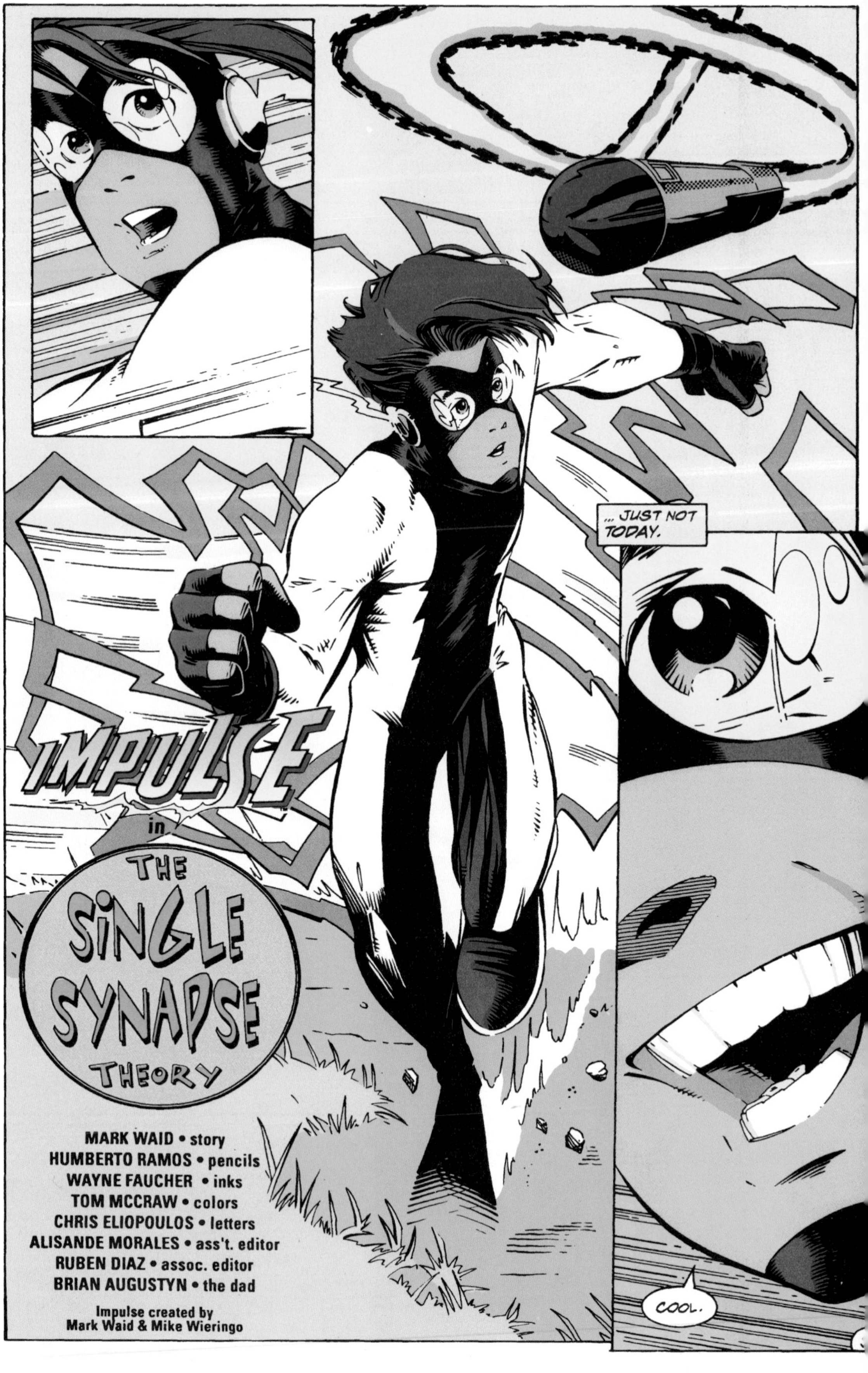
...JUST NOT TODAY.
COOL.
IMPULSE
in
THE SINGLE SYNAPSE THEORY
MARK WAID • story
HUMBERTO RAMOS • pencils
WAYNE FAUCHER • inks
TOM McCRAW • colors
CHRIS ELIOPOULOS • letters
ALISANDE MORALES • ass't. editor
RUBEN DIAZ • assoc. editor
BRIAN AUGUSTYN • the dad
Impulse created by
Mark Waid & Mike Wieringo

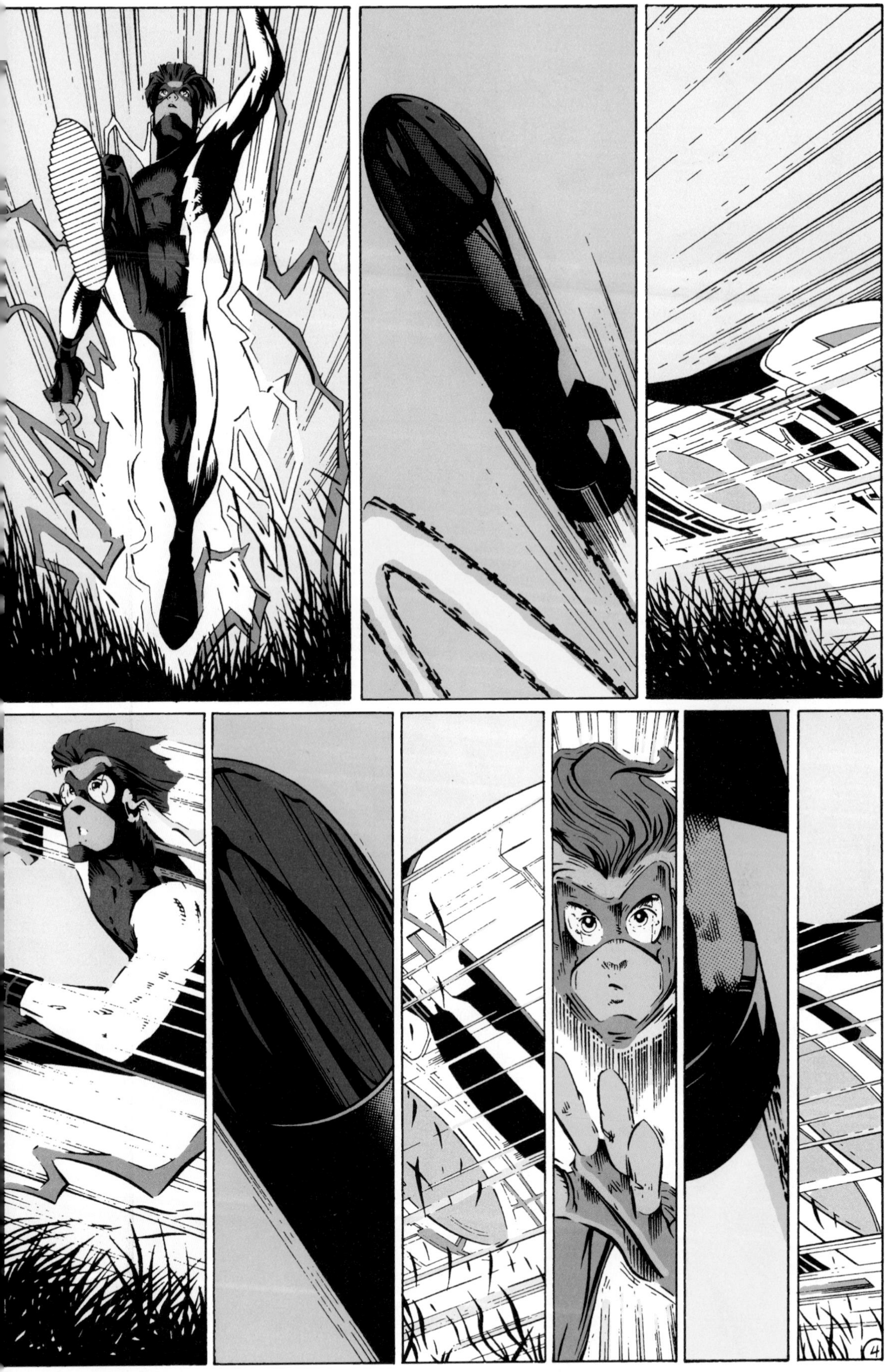

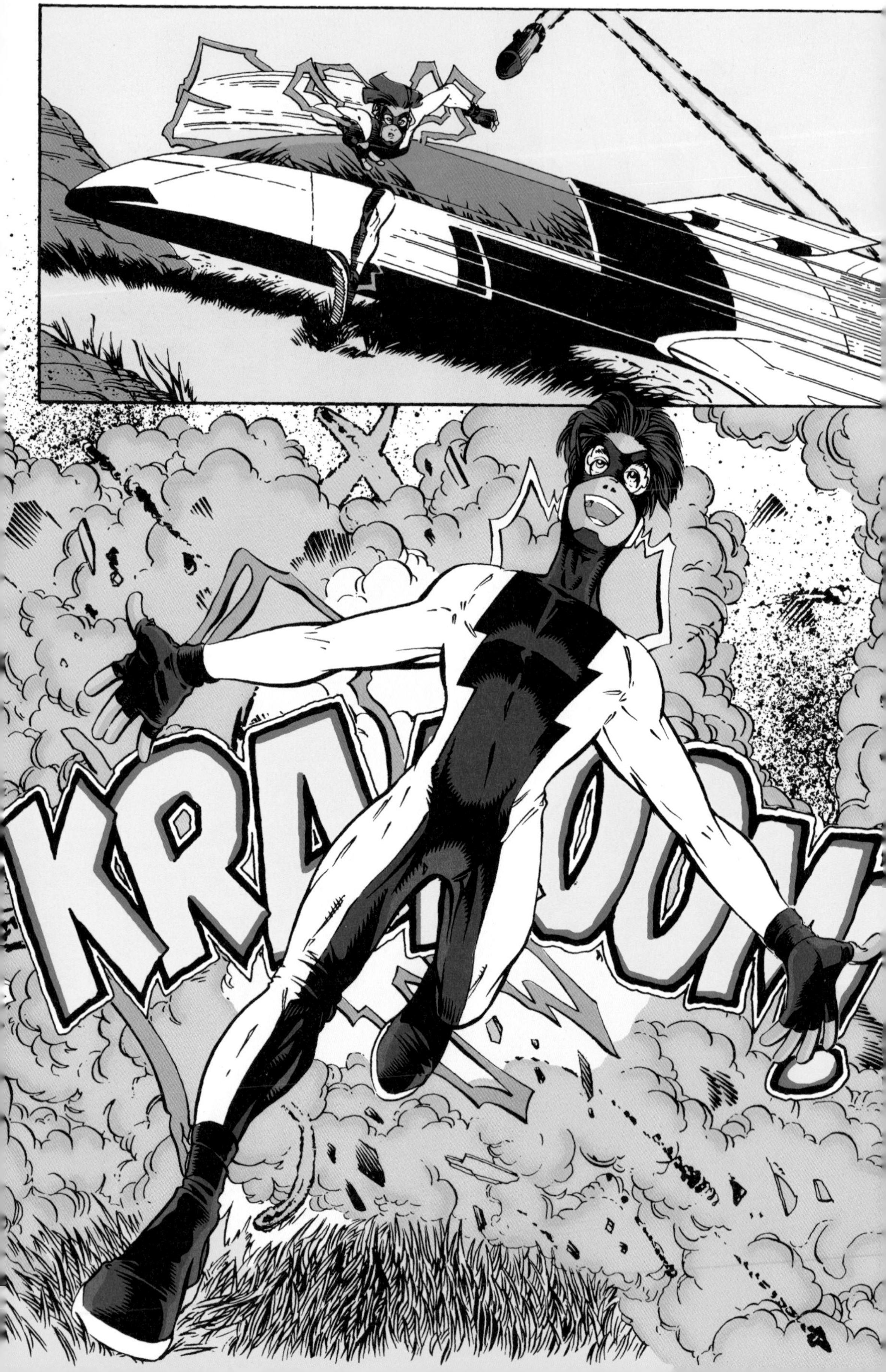
KRA
OOM

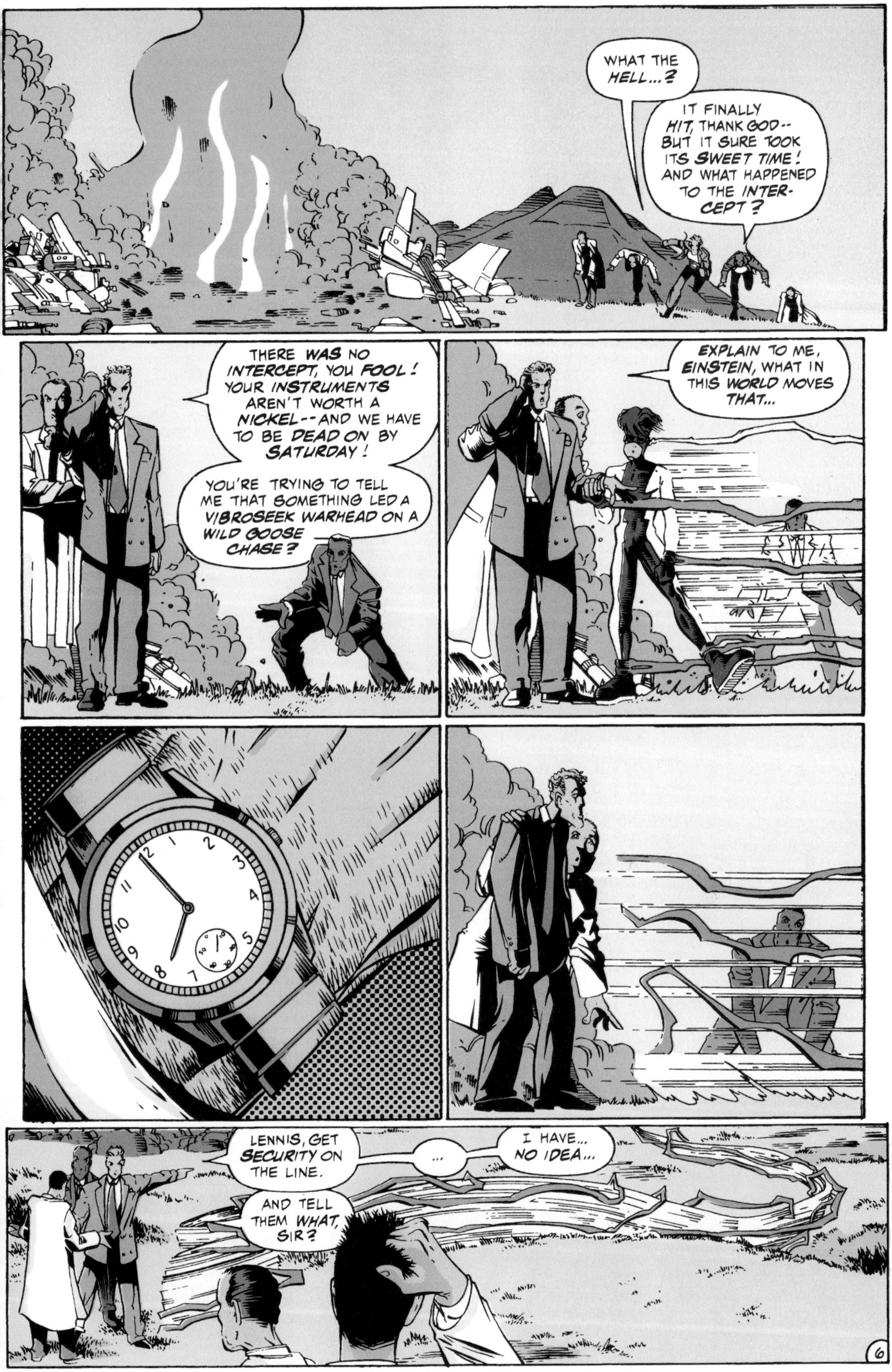
WHAT THE HELL...?
IT FINALLY HIT, THANK GOD-- BUT IT SURE TOOK ITS SWEET TIME! AND WHAT HAPPENED TO THE INTER-CEPT?
THERE WAS NO INTERCEPT, YOU FOOL! YOUR INSTRUMENTS AREN'T WORTH A NICKEL--AND WE HAVE TO BE DEAD ON BY SATURDAY!
YOU'RE TRYING TO TELL ME THAT SOMETHING LED A VIBROSEEK WARHEAD ON A WILD GOOSE CHASE?
EXPLAIN TO ME, EINSTEIN, WHAT IN THIS WORLD MOVES THAT...
LENNIS, GET SECURITY ON THE LINE.
AND TELL THEM WHAT, SIR?
...
I HAVE... NO IDEA...

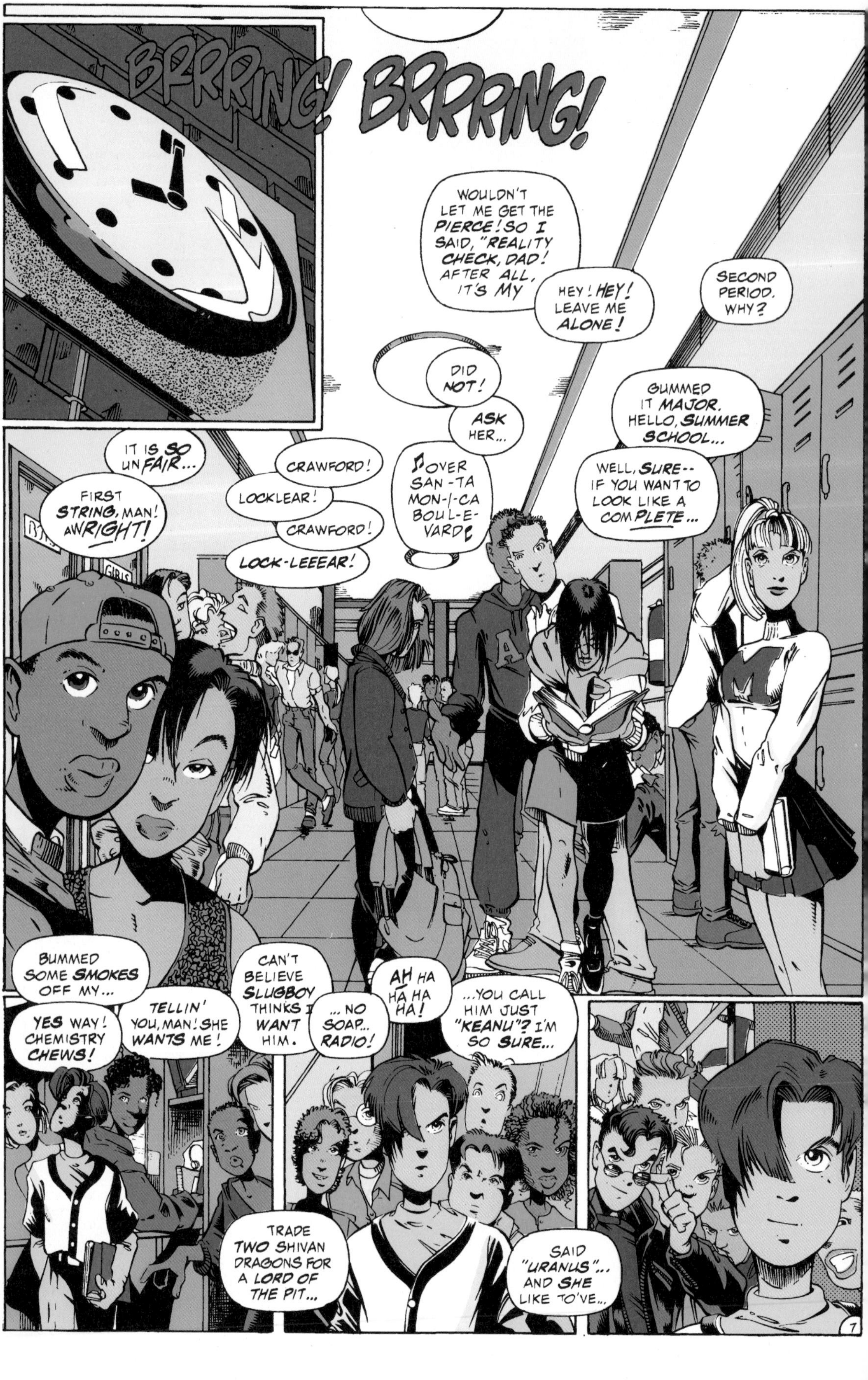

BRRRING! BRRRING!
WOULDN'T LET ME GET THE PIERCE! SO I SAID, "REALITY CHECK, DAD! AFTER ALL, IT'S MY
HEY! HEY! LEAVE ME ALONE!
SECOND PERIOD. WHY?
DID NOT!
ASK HER...
GUMMED IT MAJOR. HELLO, SUMMER SCHOOL...
IT IS SO UNFAIR...
FIRST STRING, MAN! AWRIGHT!
CRAWFORD!
LOCKLEAR!
CRAWFORD!
LOCK-LEEEAR!
♪OVER SAN-TA MON-I-CA BOUL-E-VARD
WELL, SURE-- IF YOU WANT TO LOOK LIKE A COMPLETE...
BUMMED SOME SMOKES OFF MY...
YES WAY! CHEMISTRY CHEWS!
TELLIN' YOU, MAN! SHE WANTS ME!
CAN'T BELIEVE SLUGBOY THINKS I WANT HIM.
...NO SOAP... RADIO!
AH HA HA HA HA!
...YOU CALL HIM JUST "KEANU"? I'M SO SURE...
TRADE TWO SHIVAN DRAGONS FOR A LORD OF THE PIT...
SAID "URANUS"... AND SHE LIKE TO'VE...

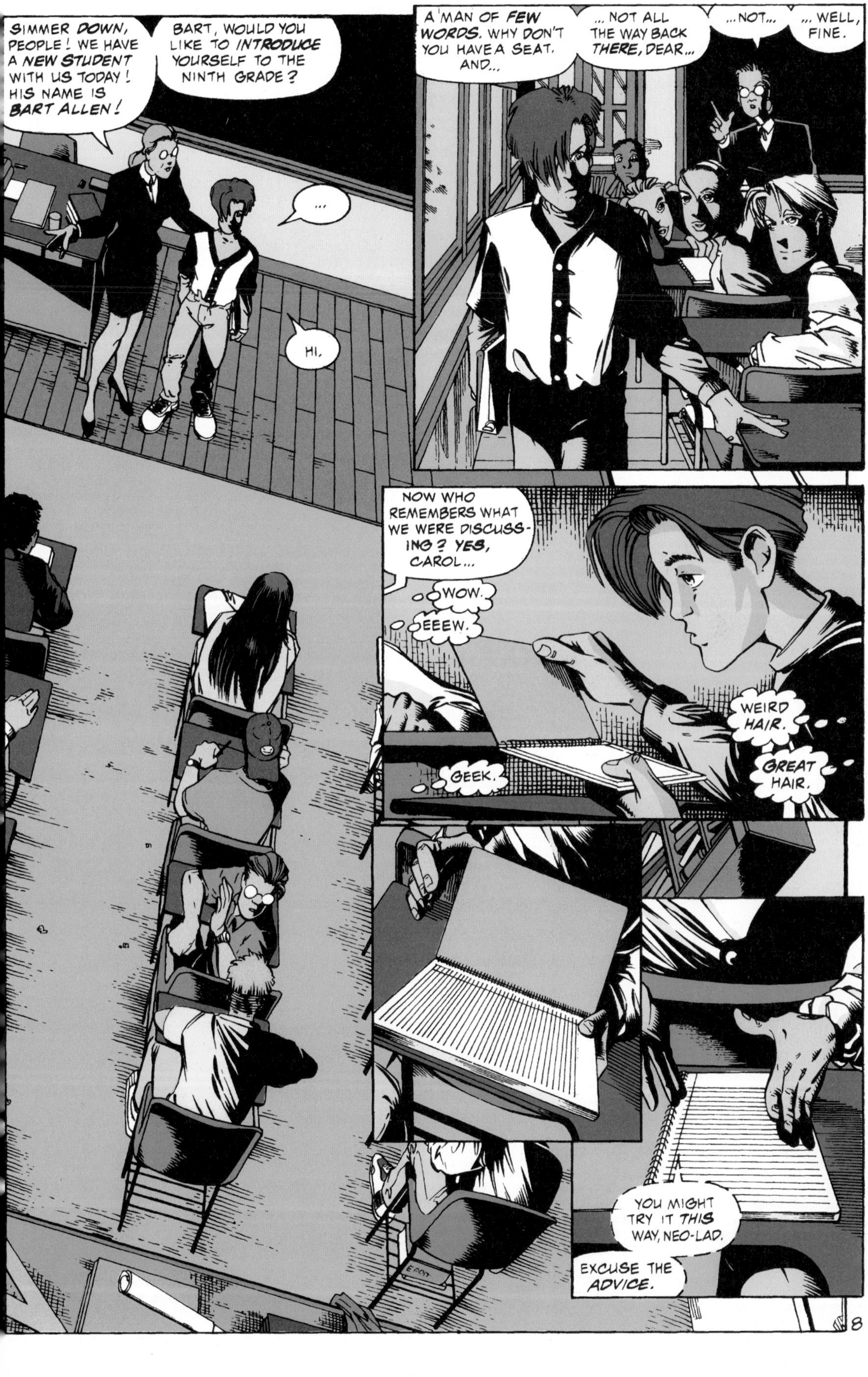
SIMMER DOWN, PEOPLE! WE HAVE A NEW STUDENT WITH US TODAY! HIS NAME IS BART ALLEN!
BART, WOULD YOU LIKE TO INTRODUCE YOURSELF TO THE NINTH GRADE?
...
HI.
A MAN OF FEW WORDS. WHY DON'T YOU HAVE A SEAT. AND...
...NOT ALL THE WAY BACK THERE, DEAR...
...NOT...
...WELL, FINE.
NOW WHO REMEMBERS WHAT WE WERE DISCUSSING? YES, CAROL...
WOW.
EEEW.
WEIRD HAIR.
GREAT HAIR.
GEEK.
YOU MIGHT TRY IT THIS WAY, NEO-LAD.
EXCUSE THE ADVICE.

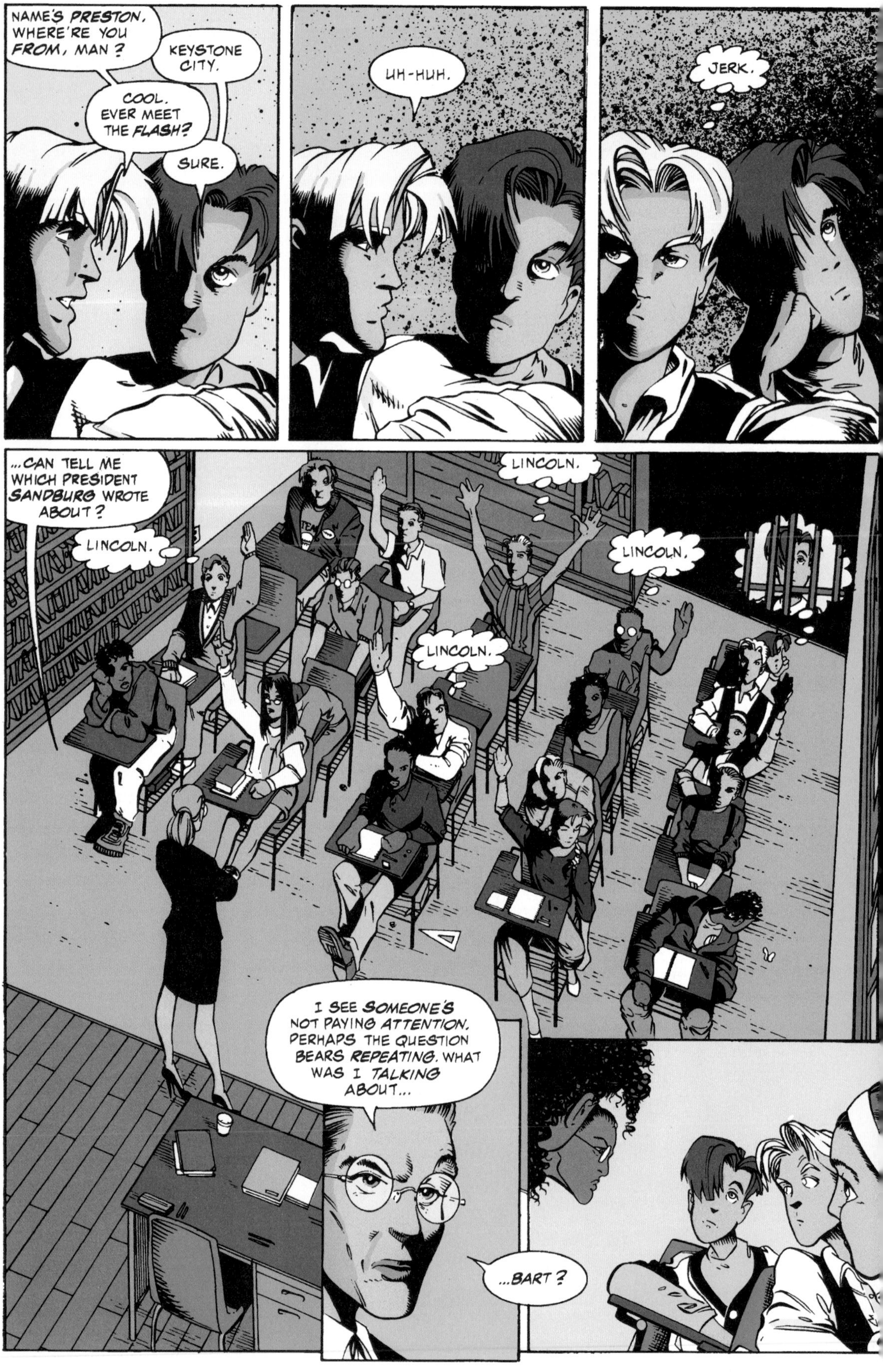
NAME'S PRESTON, WHERE'RE YOU FROM, MAN?
KEYSTONE CITY.
COOL. EVER MEET THE FLASH?
SURE.
UH-HUH.
JERK.
...CAN TELL ME WHICH PRESIDENT SANDBURG WROTE ABOUT?
LINCOLN.
LINCOLN.
LINCOLN.
LINCOLN.
I SEE SOMEONE'S NOT PAYING ATTENTION. PERHAPS THE QUESTION BEARS REPEATING. WHAT WAS I TALKING ABOUT...
...BART?

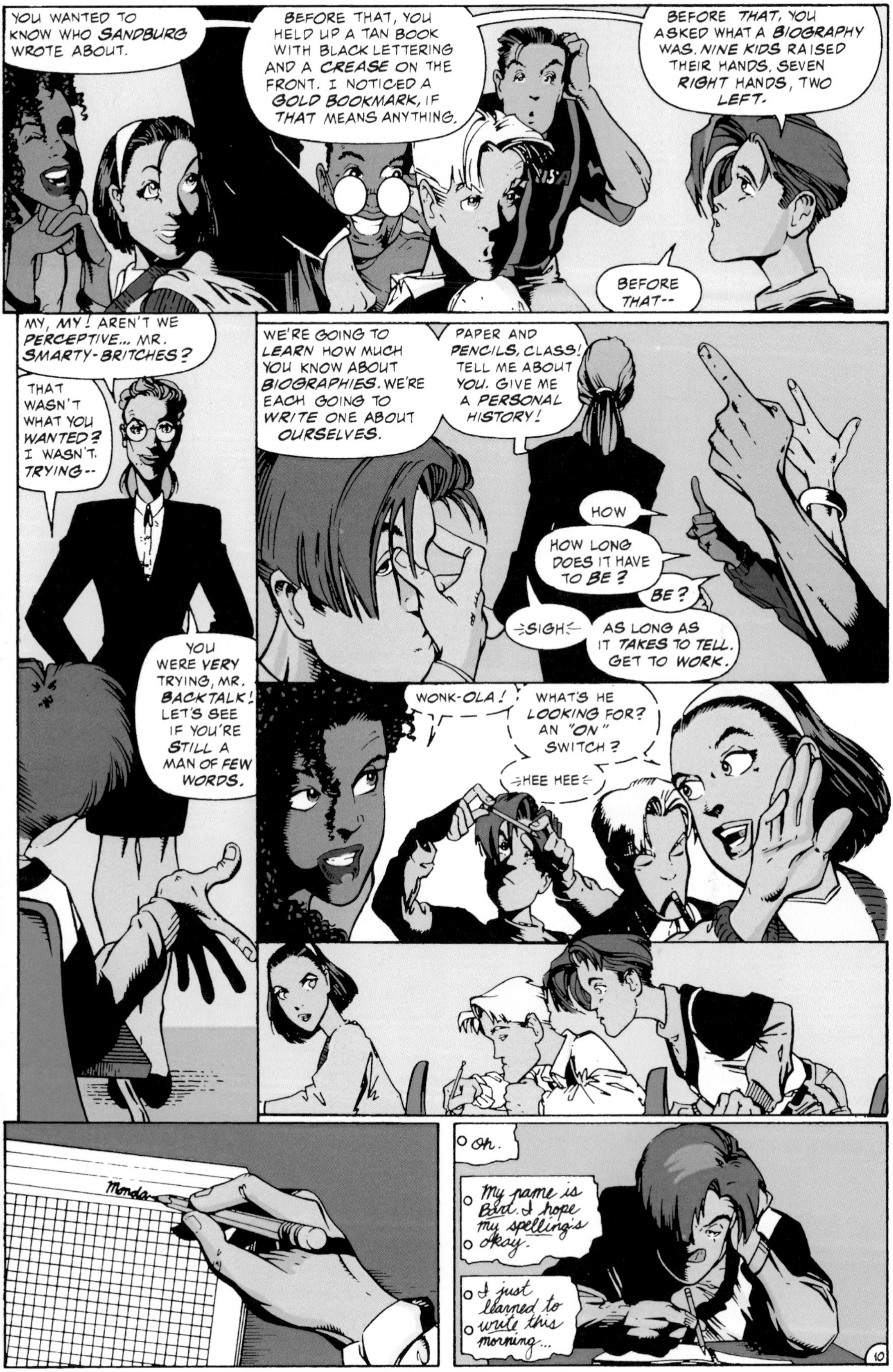
YOU WANTED TO KNOW WHO SANDBURG WROTE ABOUT.
BEFORE THAT, YOU HELD UP A TAN BOOK WITH BLACK LETTERING AND A CREASE ON THE FRONT. I NOTICED A GOLD BOOKMARK, IF THAT MEANS ANYTHING.
BEFORE THAT, YOU ASKED WHAT A BIOGRAPHY WAS. NINE KIDS RAISED THEIR HANDS. SEVEN RIGHT HANDS, TWO LEFT.
BEFORE THAT--
MY, MY! AREN'T WE PERCEPTIVE... MR. SMARTY-BRITCHES?
THAT WASN'T WHAT YOU WANTED? I WASN'T. TRYING--
YOU WERE VERY TRYING, MR. BACKTALK! LET'S SEE IF YOU'RE STILL A MAN OF FEW WORDS.
WE'RE GOING TO LEARN HOW MUCH YOU KNOW ABOUT BIOGRAPHIES. WE'RE EACH GOING TO WRITE ONE ABOUT OURSELVES.
PAPER AND PENCILS, CLASS! TELL ME ABOUT YOU. GIVE ME A PERSONAL HISTORY!
HOW
HOW LONG DOES IT HAVE TO BE?
BE?
SIGH
AS LONG AS IT TAKES TO TELL. GET TO WORK.
WONK-OLA!
WHAT'S HE LOOKING FOR? AN "ON" SWITCH?
HEE HEE
Monda
Oh.
My name is Bart. I hope my spelling's okay.
I just learned to write this morning...

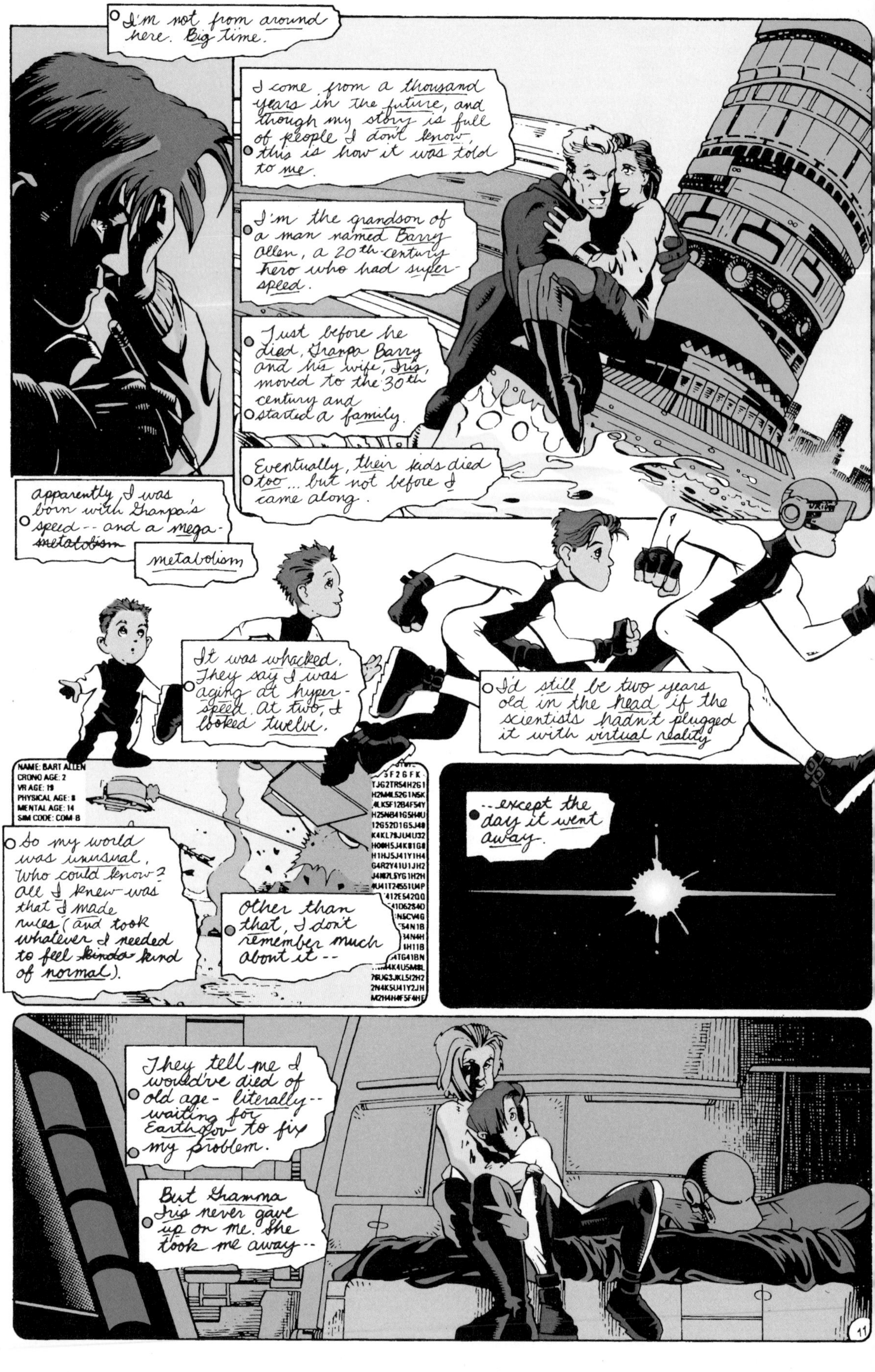
I'm not from around here. Big time.
I come from a thousand years in the future, and though my story is full of people I don't know, this is how it was told to me.
I'm the grandson of a man named Barry Allen, a 20th-century hero who had super-speed.
Just before he died, Granpa Barry and his wife, Iris, moved to the 30th century and started a family.
Eventually, their kids died too... but not before I came along.
apparently I was born with Granpa's speed -- and a mega- ~~metatolism~~
metabolism
It was whacked. They say I was aging at hyper-speed. At two, I looked twelve.
I'd still be two years old in the head if the scientists hadn't plugged it with virtual reality
NAME: BART ALLEN
CRONO AGE: 2
VR AGE: 19
PHYSICAL AGE: 8
MENTAL AGE: 14
SIM CODE: COM-B
So my world was unusual. Who could know? All I knew was that I made rules (and took whatever I needed to feel ~~kinda~~ kind of normal).
Other than that, I don't remember much about it --
...except the day it went away.
They tell me I would've died of old age - literally -- waiting for EarthGov to fix my problem.
But Gramma Iris never gave up on me. She took me away--

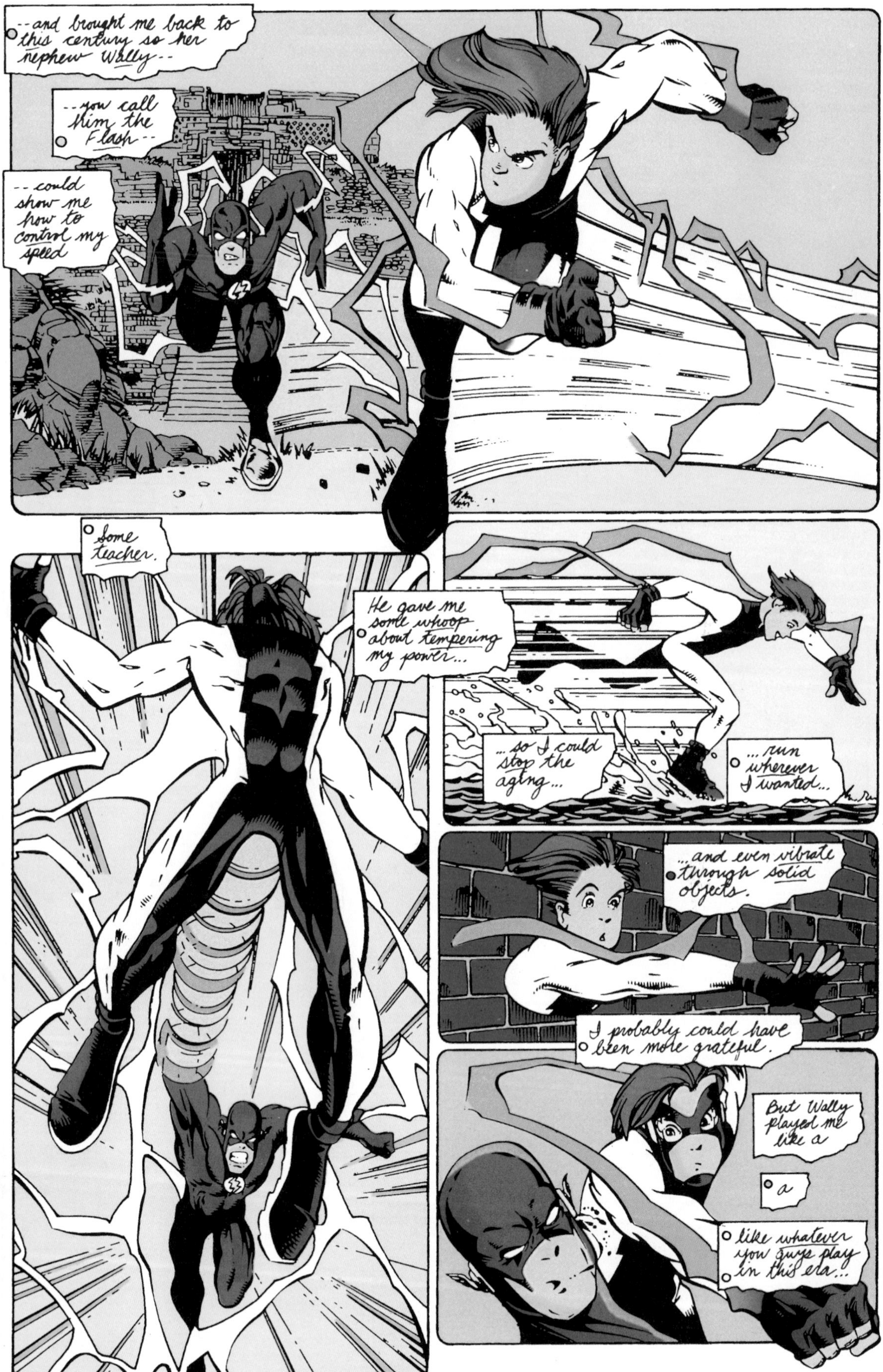
--and brought me back to this century so her nephew Wally--
--you call him the Flash--
--could show me how to control my speed
Some teacher.
He gave me some whoop about tempering my power...
...so I could stop the aging...
...run wherever I wanted...
...and even vibrate through solid objects.
I probably could have been more grateful.
But Wally played me like a
a
like whatever you guys play in this era...

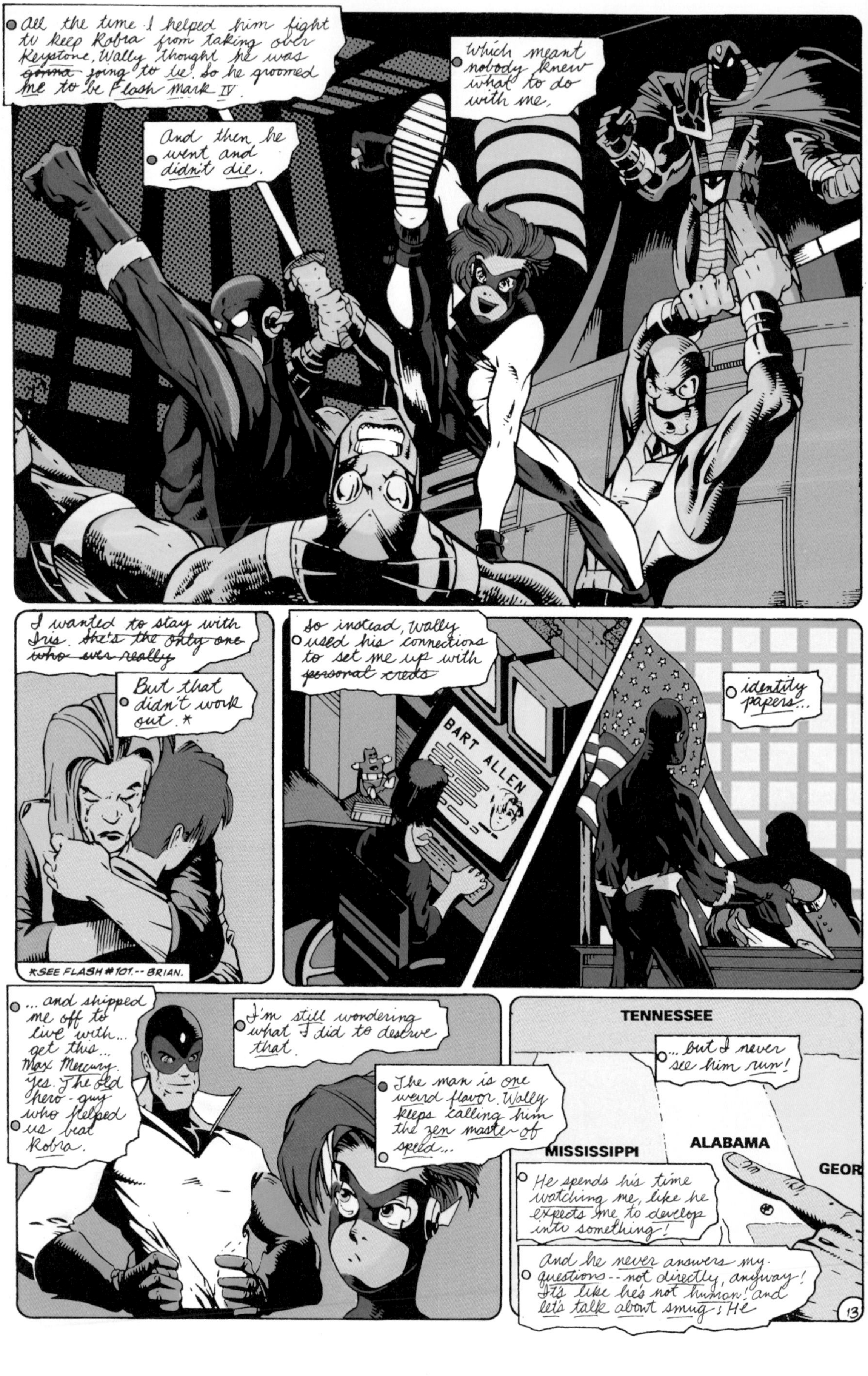
All the time I helped him fight to keep Kobra from taking over Keystone, Wally thought he was ~~gonna~~ going to die. So he groomed me to be Flash Mark IV.
And then he went and didn't die.
Which meant nobody knew what to do with me.
I wanted to stay with Iris. ~~She's the only one who ever really~~
But that didn't work out.*
*SEE FLASH #101.--BRIAN.
So instead, Wally used his connections to set me up with ~~personal creds~~
BART ALLEN
identity papers...
...and shipped me off to live with... get this... Max Mercury. Yes. The old hero-guy who helped us beat Kobra.
I'm still wondering what I did to deserve that.
The man is one weird flavor. Wally keeps calling him the zen master of speed...
TENNESSEE
...but I never see him run!
MISSISSIPPI
ALABAMA
GEOR
He spends his time watching me, like he expects me to develop into something!
And he never answers my questions--not directly, anyway! It's like he's not human! And let's talk about smug! He
13

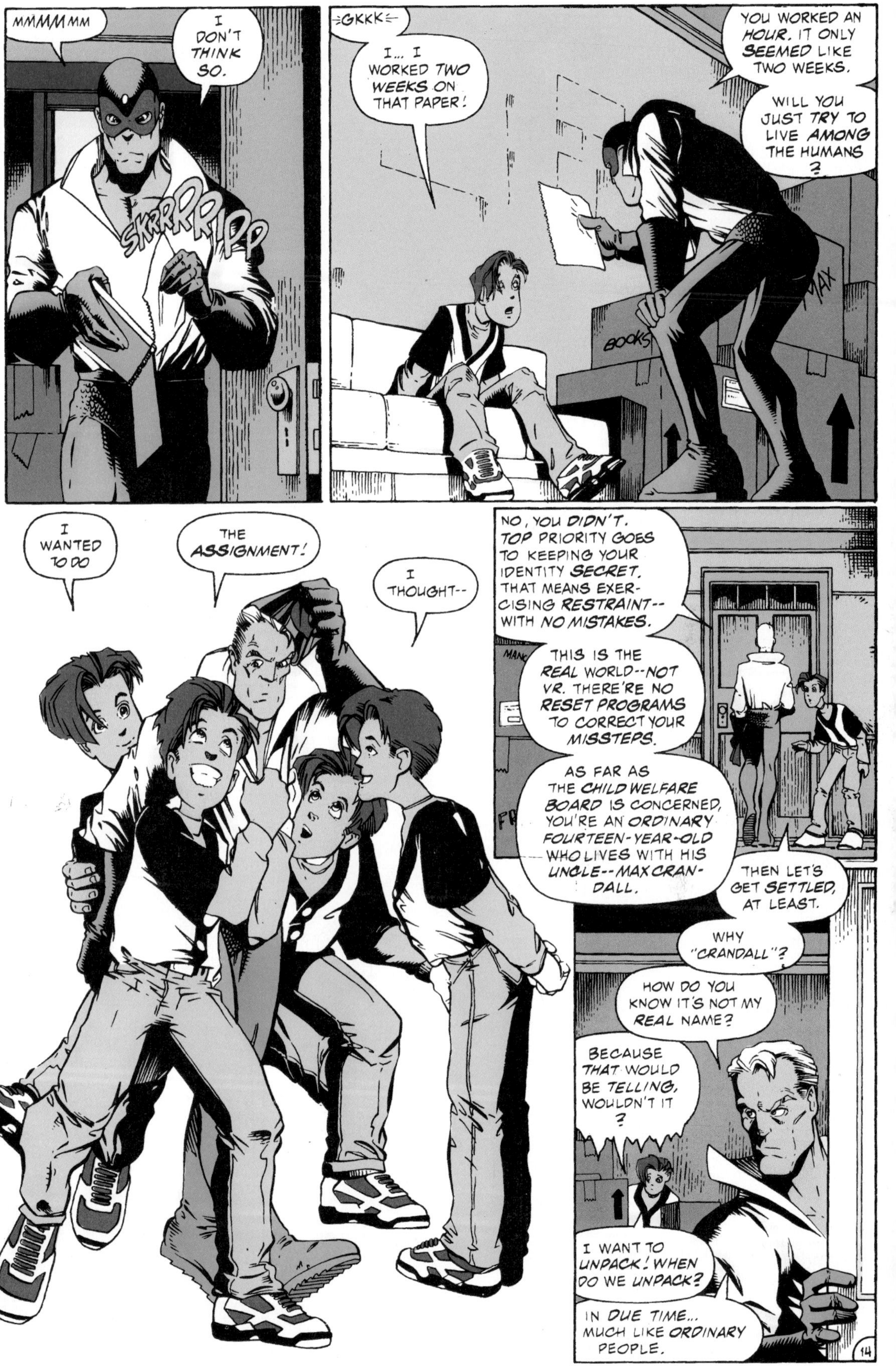
MMMMMM
I DON'T THINK SO.
SKRRRRIPP
=GKKK=
I... I WORKED TWO WEEKS ON THAT PAPER!
YOU WORKED AN HOUR. IT ONLY SEEMED LIKE TWO WEEKS.
WILL YOU JUST TRY TO LIVE AMONG THE HUMANS?
BOOKS
MAX
I WANTED TO DO
THE ASSIGNMENT!
I THOUGHT--
NO, YOU DIDN'T. TOP PRIORITY GOES TO KEEPING YOUR IDENTITY SECRET. THAT MEANS EXERCISING RESTRAINT--WITH NO MISTAKES.
THIS IS THE REAL WORLD--NOT VR. THERE'RE NO RESET PROGRAMS TO CORRECT YOUR MISSTEPS.
AS FAR AS THE CHILD WELFARE BOARD IS CONCERNED, YOU'RE AN ORDINARY FOURTEEN-YEAR-OLD WHO LIVES WITH HIS UNCLE--MAX CRANDALL.
THEN LET'S GET SETTLED, AT LEAST.
WHY "CRANDALL"?
HOW DO YOU KNOW IT'S NOT MY REAL NAME?
BECAUSE THAT WOULD BE TELLING, WOULDN'T IT?
I WANT TO UNPACK! WHEN DO WE UNPACK?
IN DUE TIME... MUCH LIKE ORDINARY PEOPLE.

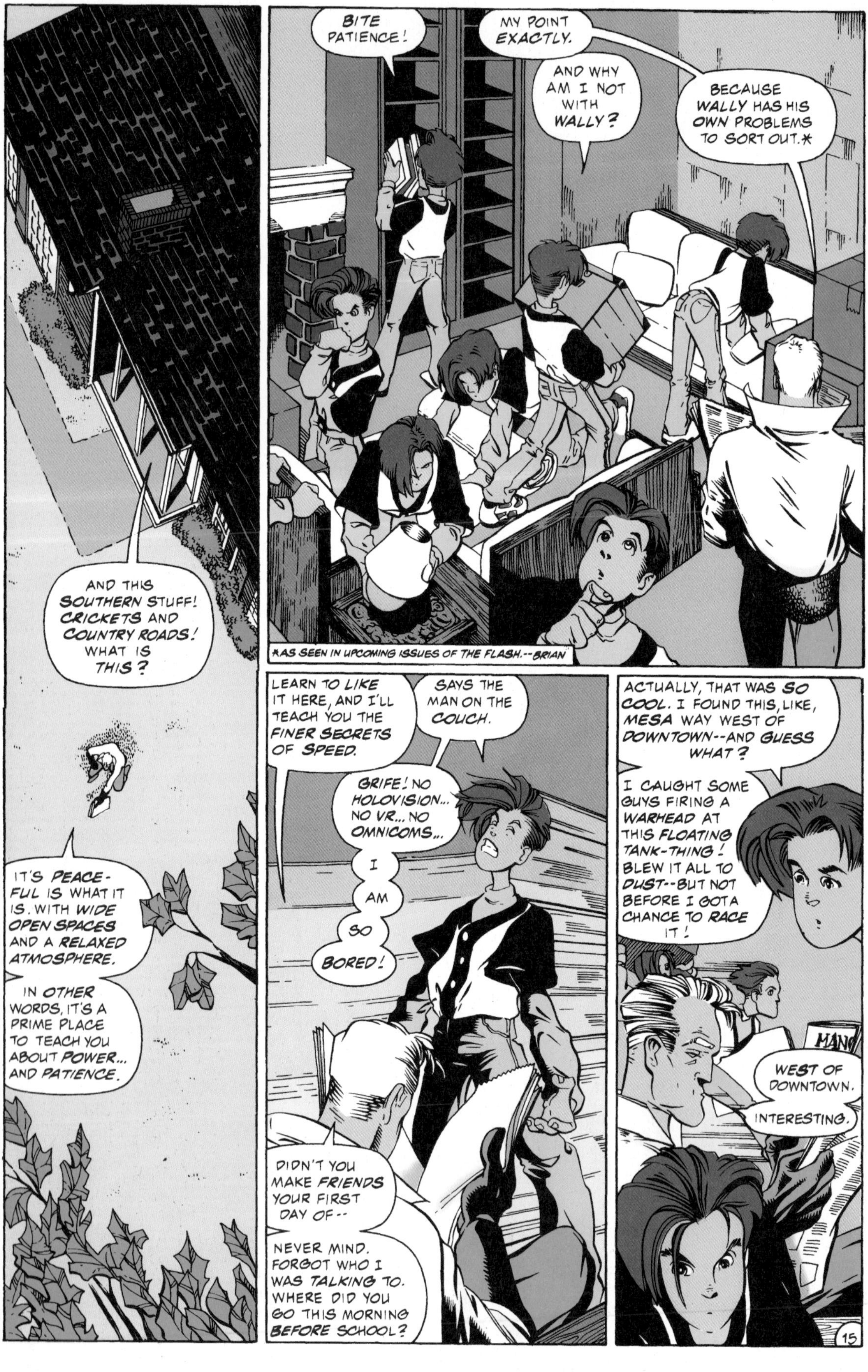
AND THIS SOUTHERN STUFF! CRICKETS AND COUNTRY ROADS! WHAT IS THIS?
IT'S PEACE-FUL IS WHAT IT IS. WITH WIDE OPEN SPACES AND A RELAXED ATMOSPHERE.
IN OTHER WORDS, IT'S A PRIME PLACE TO TEACH YOU ABOUT POWER... AND PATIENCE.
BITE PATIENCE!
MY POINT EXACTLY.
AND WHY AM I NOT WITH WALLY?
BECAUSE WALLY HAS HIS OWN PROBLEMS TO SORT OUT.*
*AS SEEN IN UPCOMING ISSUES OF THE FLASH.--BRIAN
LEARN TO LIKE IT HERE, AND I'LL TEACH YOU THE FINER SECRETS OF SPEED.
SAYS THE MAN ON THE COUCH.
GRIFE! NO HOLOVISION... NO VR... NO OMNICOMS...
I
AM
SO
BORED!
DIDN'T YOU MAKE FRIENDS YOUR FIRST DAY OF--
NEVER MIND. FORGOT WHO I WAS TALKING TO. WHERE DID YOU GO THIS MORNING BEFORE SCHOOL?
ACTUALLY, THAT WAS SO COOL. I FOUND THIS, LIKE, MESA WAY WEST OF DOWNTOWN--AND GUESS WHAT?
I CAUGHT SOME GUYS FIRING A WARHEAD AT THIS FLOATING TANK-THING! BLEW IT ALL TO DUST--BUT NOT BEFORE I GOT A CHANCE TO RACE IT!
WEST OF DOWNTOWN.
INTERESTING.

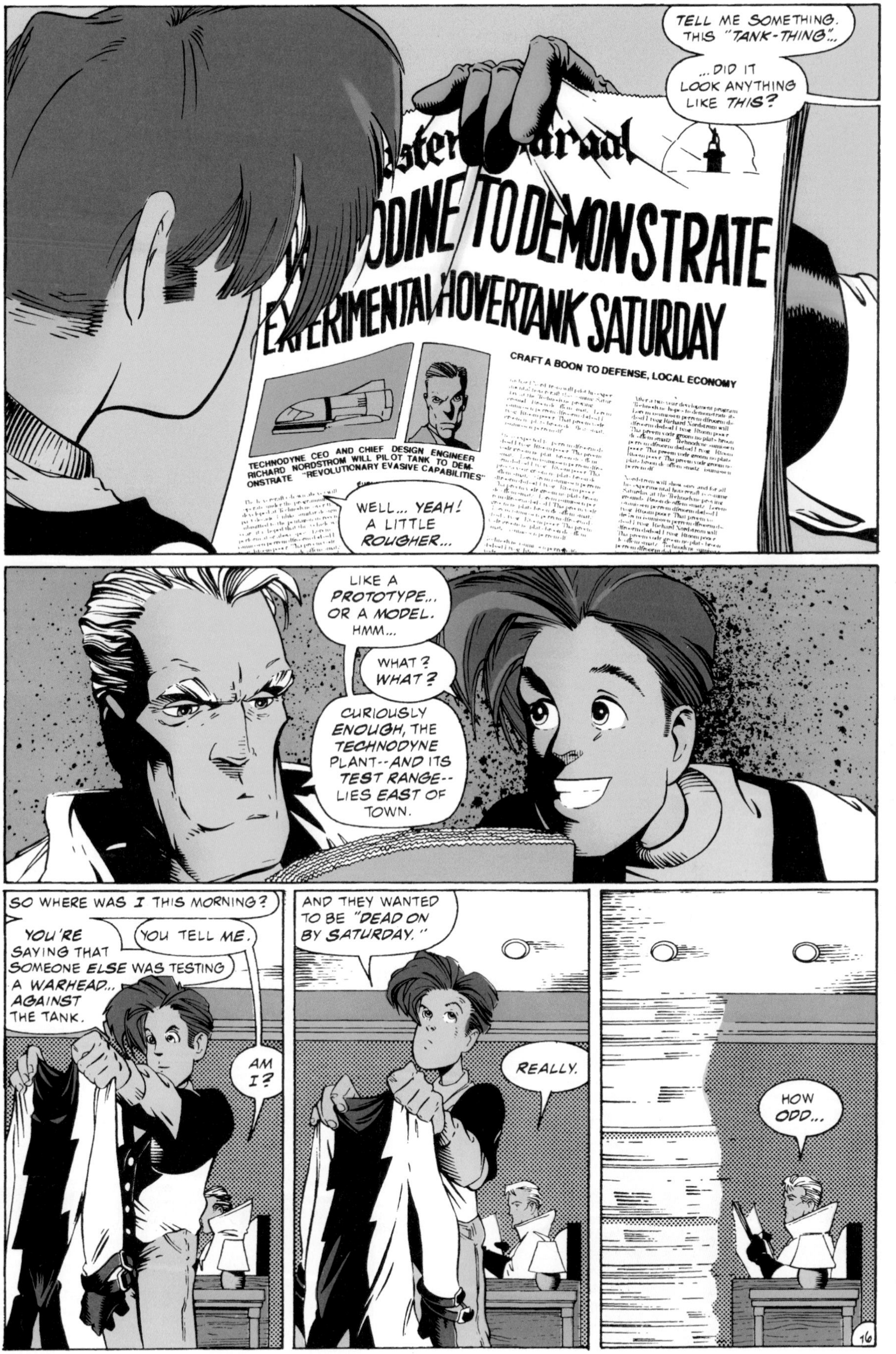
TELL ME SOMETHING. THIS "TANK-THING"...
...DID IT LOOK ANYTHING LIKE THIS?
ODINE TO DEMONSTRATE
EXPERIMENTAL HOVERTANK SATURDAY
CRAFT A BOON TO DEFENSE, LOCAL ECONOMY
TECHNODYNE CEO AND CHIEF DESIGN ENGINEER RICHARD NORDSTROM WILL PILOT TANK TO DEMONSTRATE "REVOLUTIONARY EVASIVE CAPABILITIES"
WELL... YEAH! A LITTLE ROUGHER...
LIKE A PROTOTYPE... OR A MODEL. HMM...
WHAT? WHAT?
CURIOUSLY ENOUGH, THE TECHNODYNE PLANT--AND ITS TEST RANGE--LIES EAST OF TOWN.
SO WHERE WAS I THIS MORNING?
YOU'RE SAYING THAT SOMEONE ELSE WAS TESTING A WARHEAD... AGAINST THE TANK.
YOU TELL ME.
AM I?
AND THEY WANTED TO BE "DEAD ON BY SATURDAY."
REALLY.
HOW ODD...

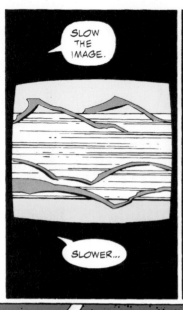

SLOW THE IMAGE.

SLOWER...

...SLOWER...

THERE! CAUGHT BY THE SAME CAMERAS THAT RECORDED OUR MISSILE TEST!

DAMN IT! WE'VE BEEN DISCOVERED!

DON'T PANIC. IF HE KNEW WHAT HE'D BLUNDERED INTO, HE'D HAVE STOPPED US RIGHT THEN.

BUT WHO IS HE?

I HAVE NO IDEA.

WELL, WHOEVER HE IS, WE GOT READINGS ON HIS VIBRATIONAL FREQUENCY. CAN WE USE THAT SOMEHOW?

I HAVE NO IDEA.

YOU DON'T KNOW MUCH, DO YOU?

UNTRUE.

I KNOW THAT WE'D BETTER BE PREPARED IF THE DAMNFOOL KID SHOWS UP AGAIN...

17

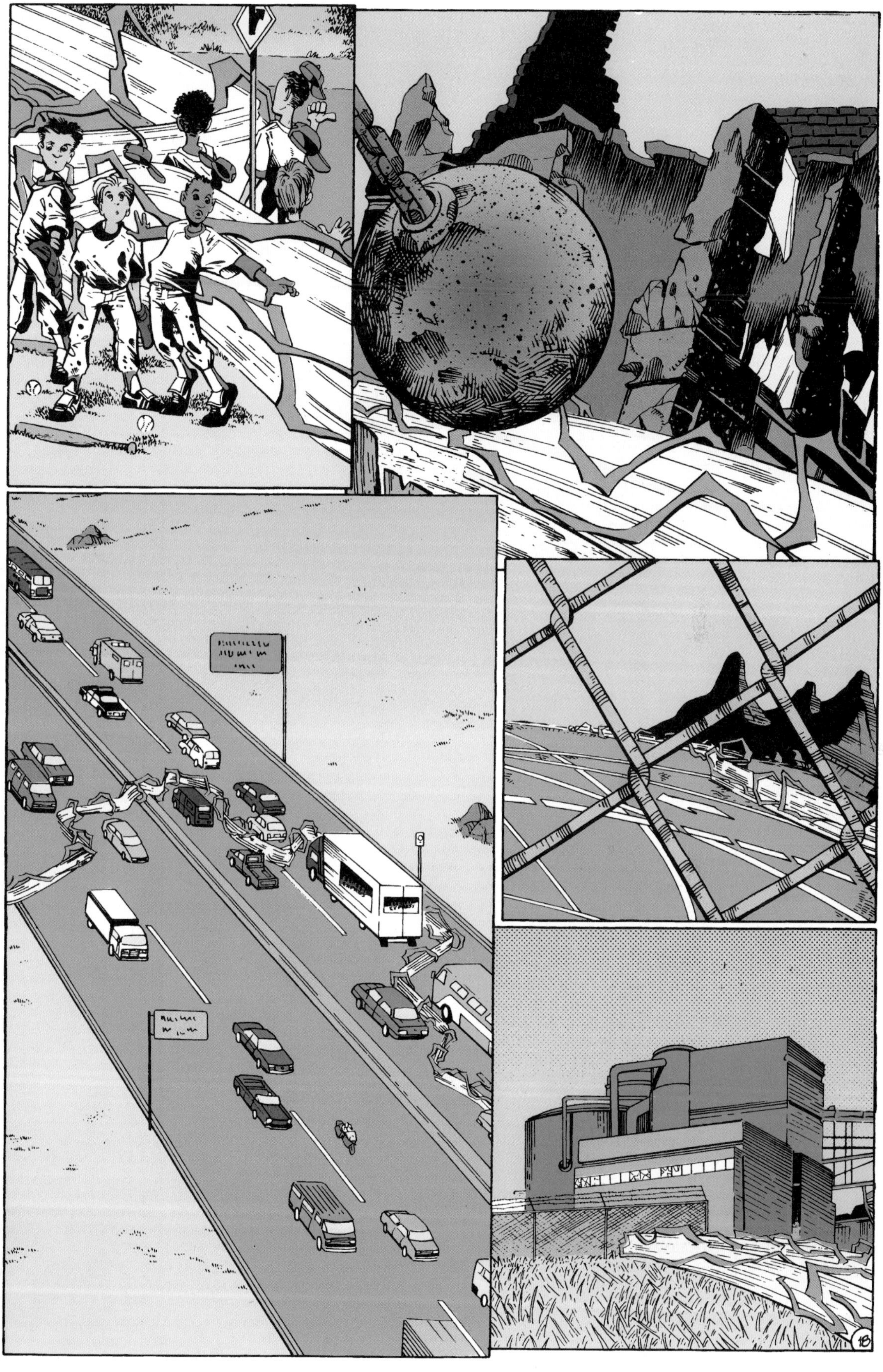

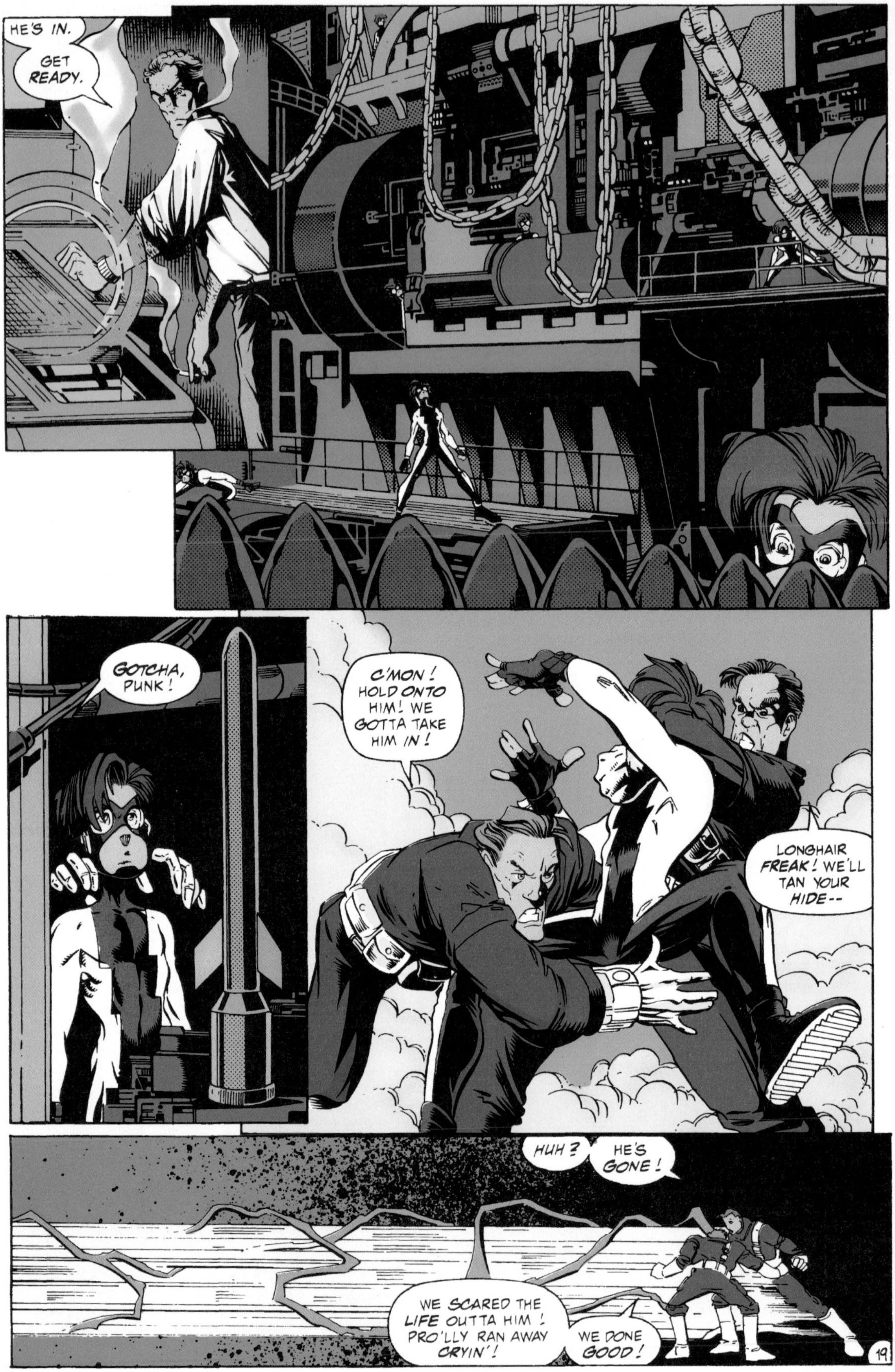

HE'S IN.
GET READY.
GOTCHA, PUNK!
C'MON! HOLD ONTO HIM! WE GOTTA TAKE HIM IN!
LONGHAIR FREAK! WE'LL TAN YOUR HIDE--
HUH?
HE'S GONE!
WE SCARED THE LIFE OUTTA HIM! PRO'LLY RAN AWAY CRYIN'!
WE DONE GOOD!

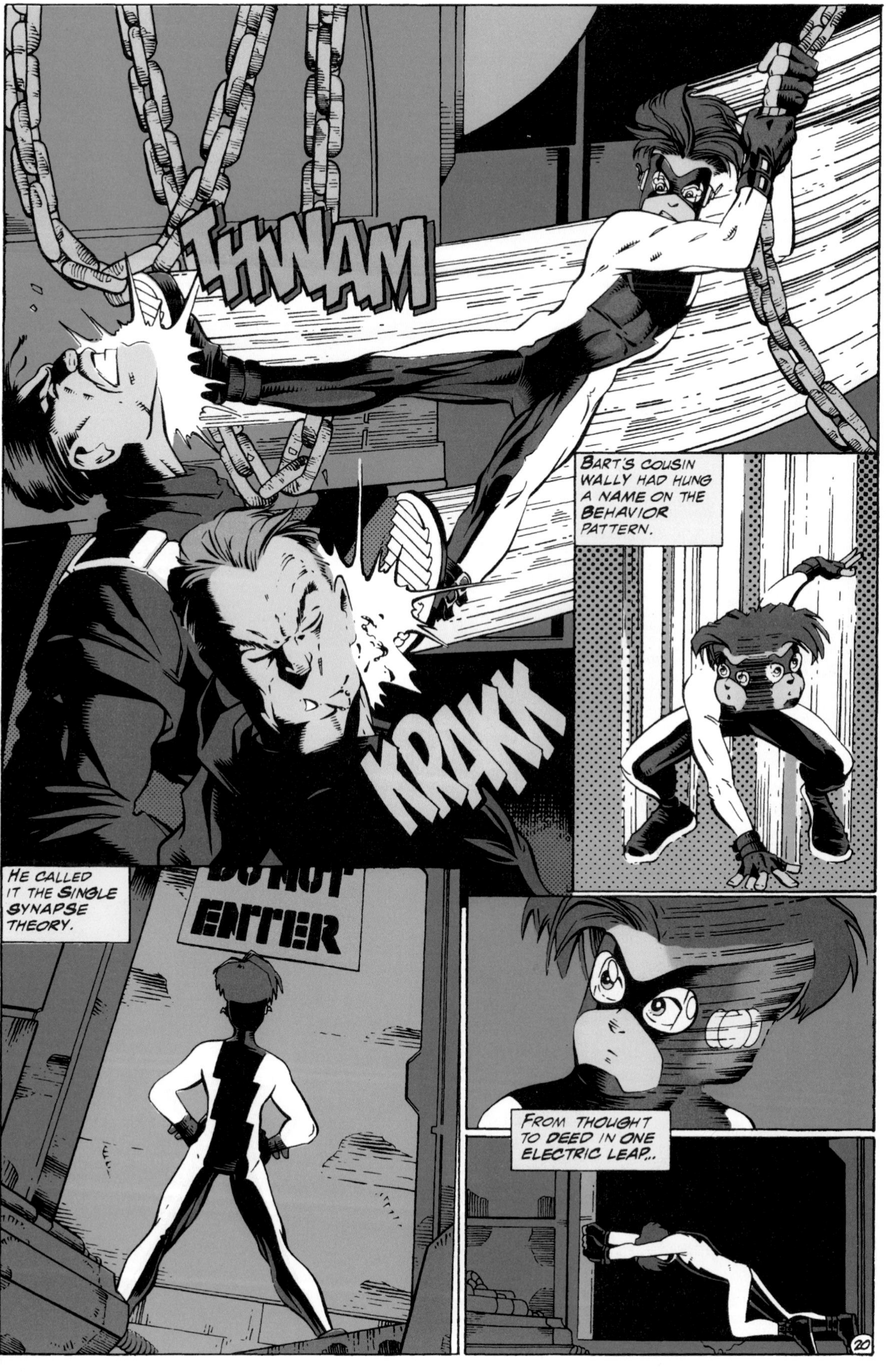
THWAM
KRAKK
BART'S COUSIN WALLY HAD HUNG A NAME ON THE BEHAVIOR PATTERN.
HE CALLED IT THE SINGLE SYNAPSE THEORY.
ENTER
FROM THOUGHT TO DEED IN ONE ELECTRIC LEAP...

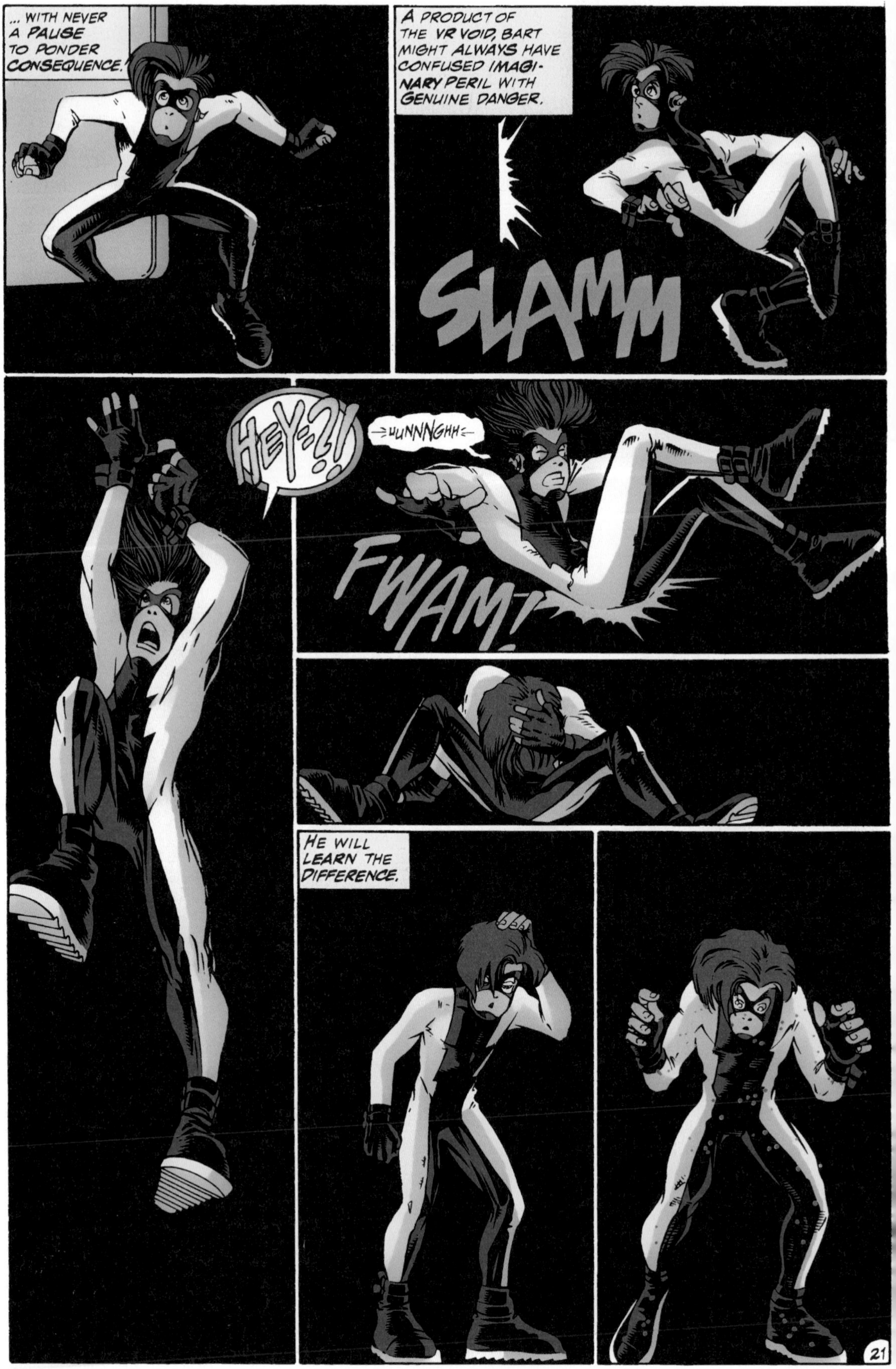

... WITH NEVER A PAUSE TO PONDER CONSEQUENCE.
A PRODUCT OF THE VR VOID, BART MIGHT ALWAYS HAVE CONFUSED IMAGINARY PERIL WITH GENUINE DANGER.
SLAMM
HEY-?!
UUNNNGHH
FWAM!
HE WILL LEARN THE DIFFERENCE.

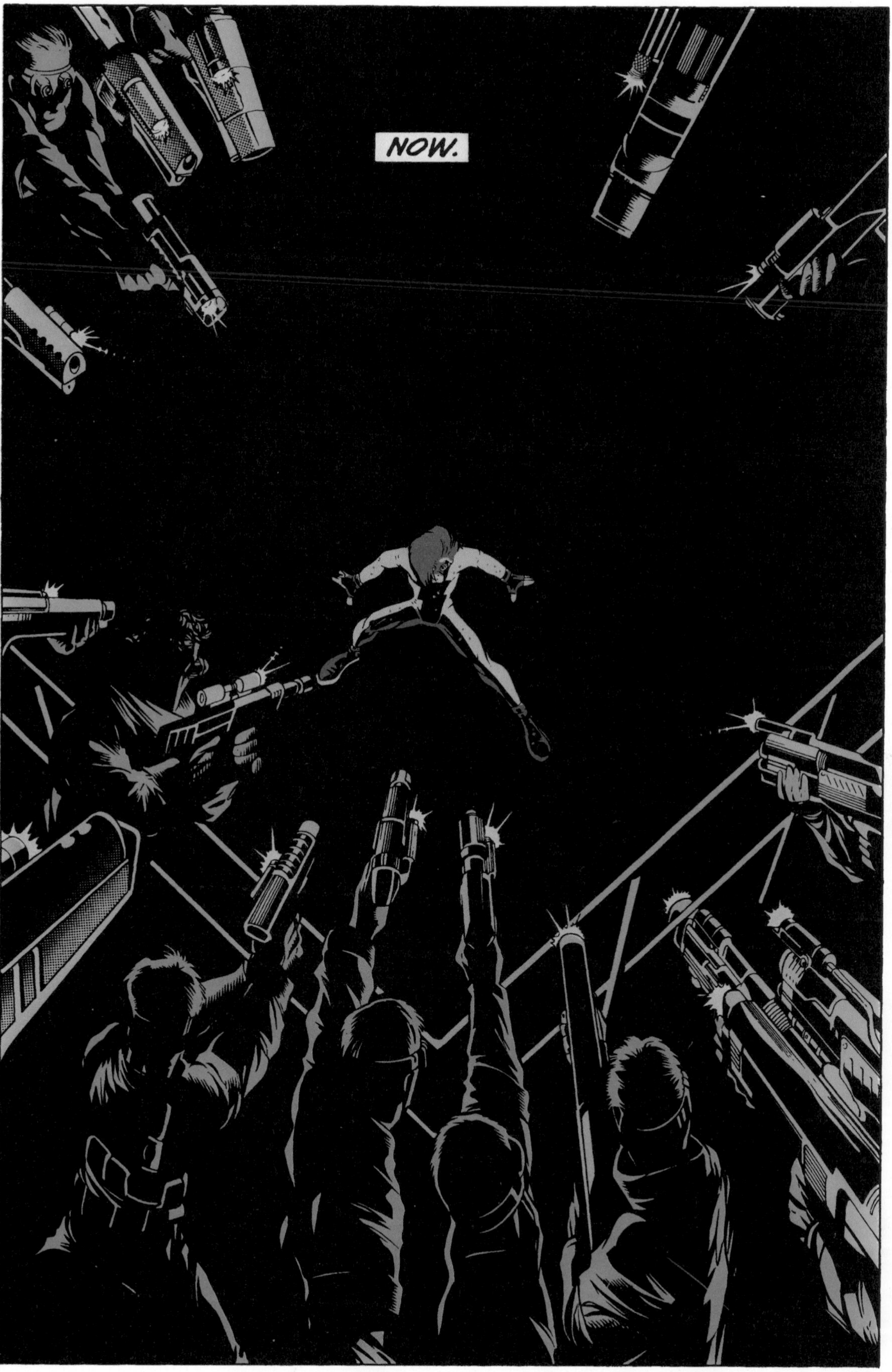
NOW.

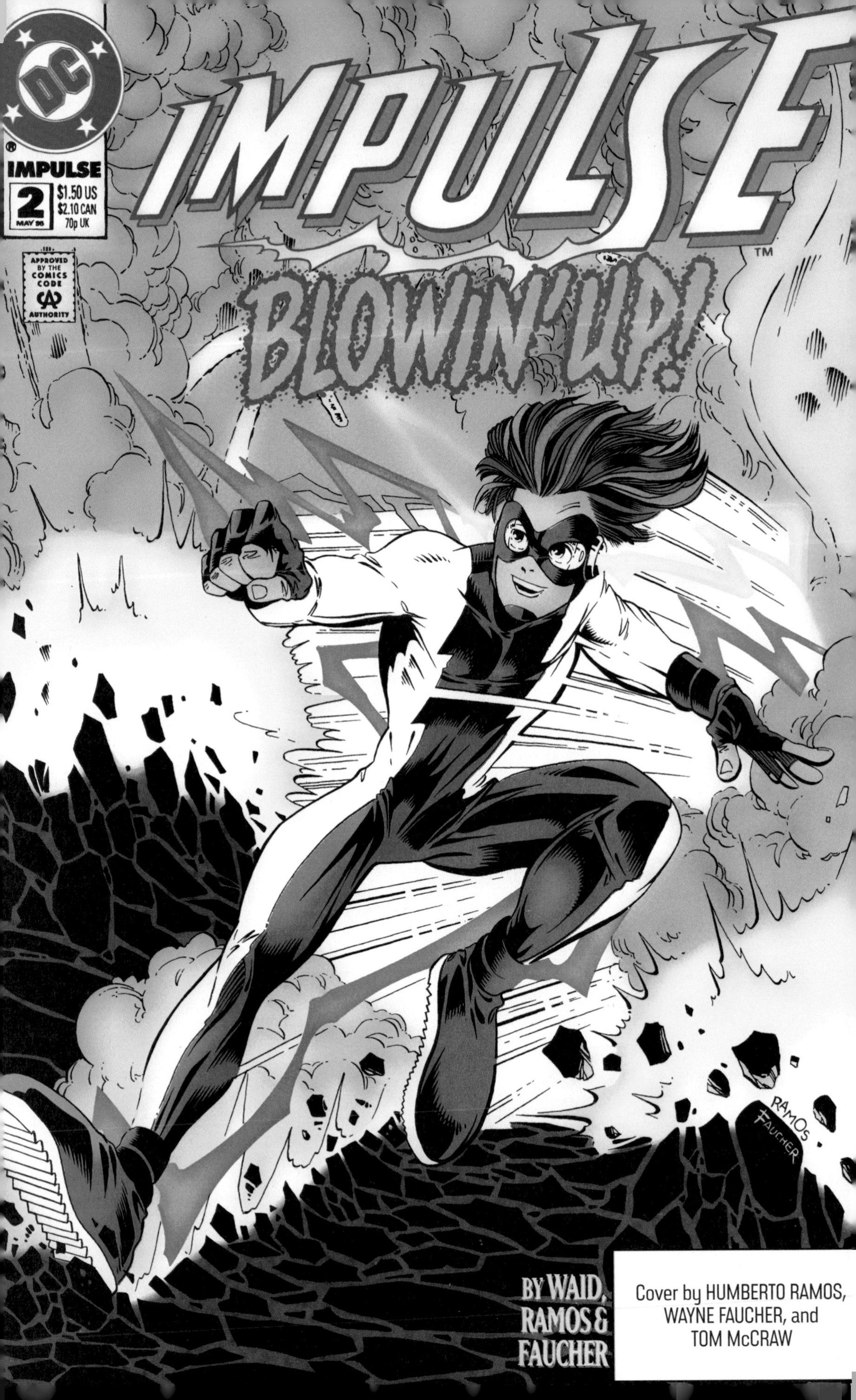
DC
IMPULSE
2
$1.50 US
$2.10 CAN
70p UK
MAY 95
APPROVED BY THE COMICS CODE AUTHORITY
IMPULSE
TM
BLOWIN' UP!
RAMOS
FAUCHER
BY WAID, RAMOS & FAUCHER

Cover by HUMBERTO RAMOS, WAYNE FAUCHER, and TOM McCRAW

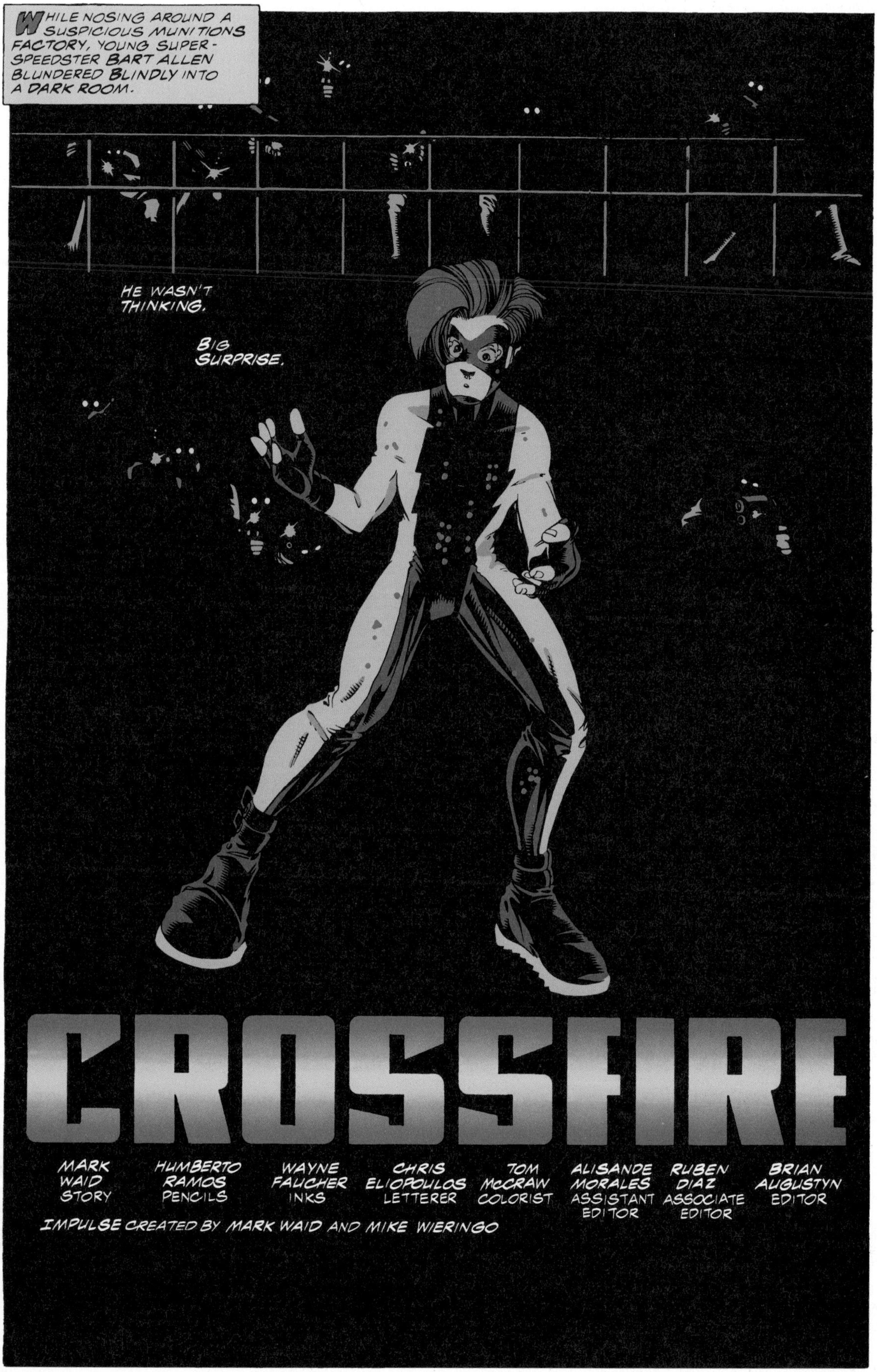
WHILE NOSING AROUND A SUSPICIOUS MUNITIONS FACTORY, YOUNG SUPER-SPEEDSTER BART ALLEN BLUNDERED BLINDLY INTO A DARK ROOM.
HE WASN'T THINKING.
BIG SURPRISE.
CROSSFIRE
MARK WAID STORY
HUMBERTO RAMOS PENCILS
WAYNE FAUCHER INKS
CHRIS ELIOPOULOS LETTERER
TOM McCRAW COLORIST
ALISANDE MORALES ASSISTANT EDITOR
RUBEN DIAZ ASSOCIATE EDITOR
BRIAN AUGUSTYN EDITOR
IMPULSE CREATED BY MARK WAID AND MIKE WIERINGO

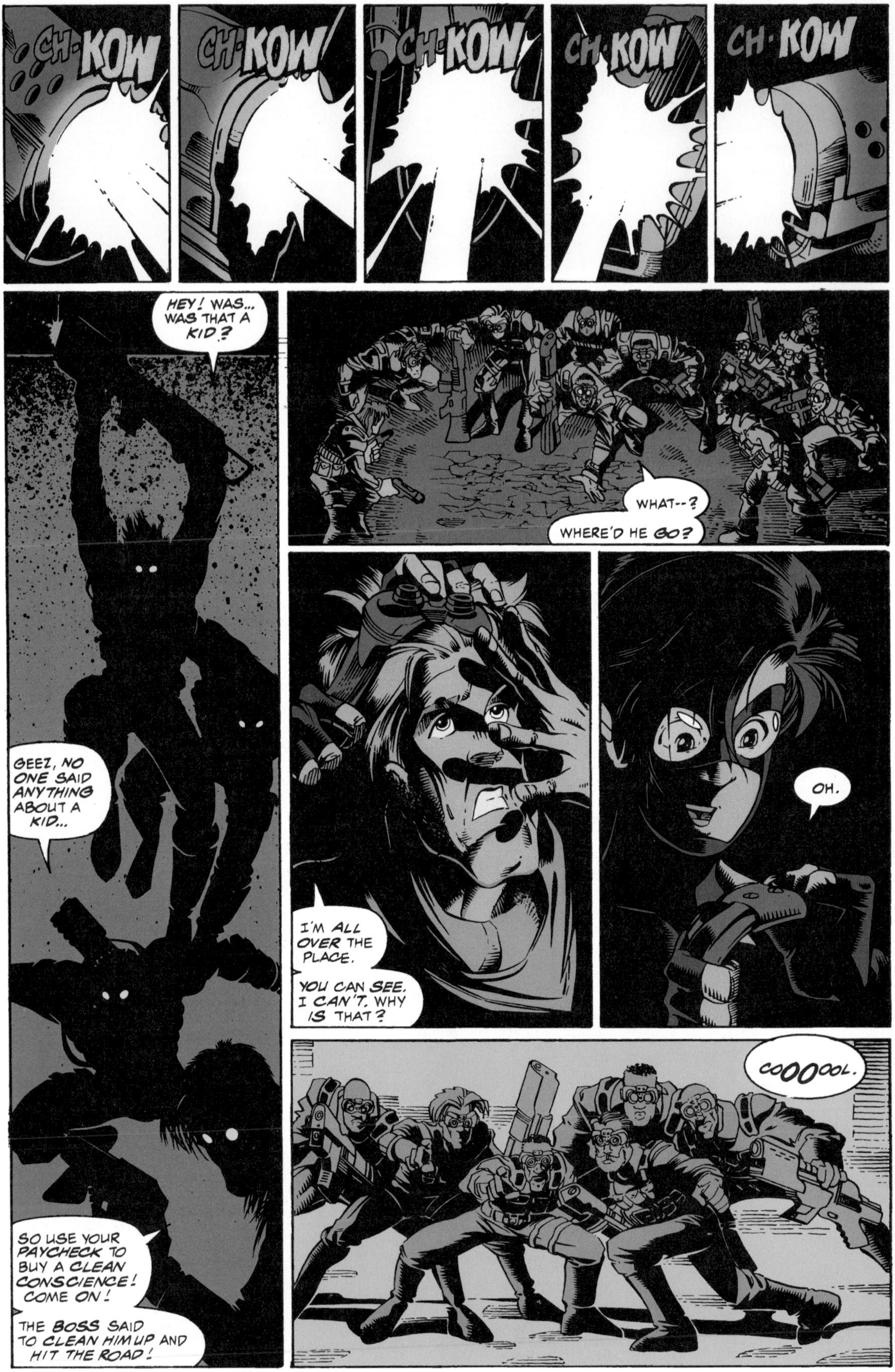
CH-KOW
CH-KOW
CH-KOW
CH-KOW
CH-KOW
HEY! WAS... WAS THAT A KID?
GEEZ, NO ONE SAID ANYTHING ABOUT A KID...
SO USE YOUR PAYCHECK TO BUY A CLEAN CONSCIENCE! COME ON!
THE BOSS SAID TO CLEAN HIM UP AND HIT THE ROAD!
WHAT--?
WHERE'D HE GO?
I'M ALL OVER THE PLACE.
YOU CAN SEE. I CAN'T. WHY IS THAT?
OH.
COOOOOL.

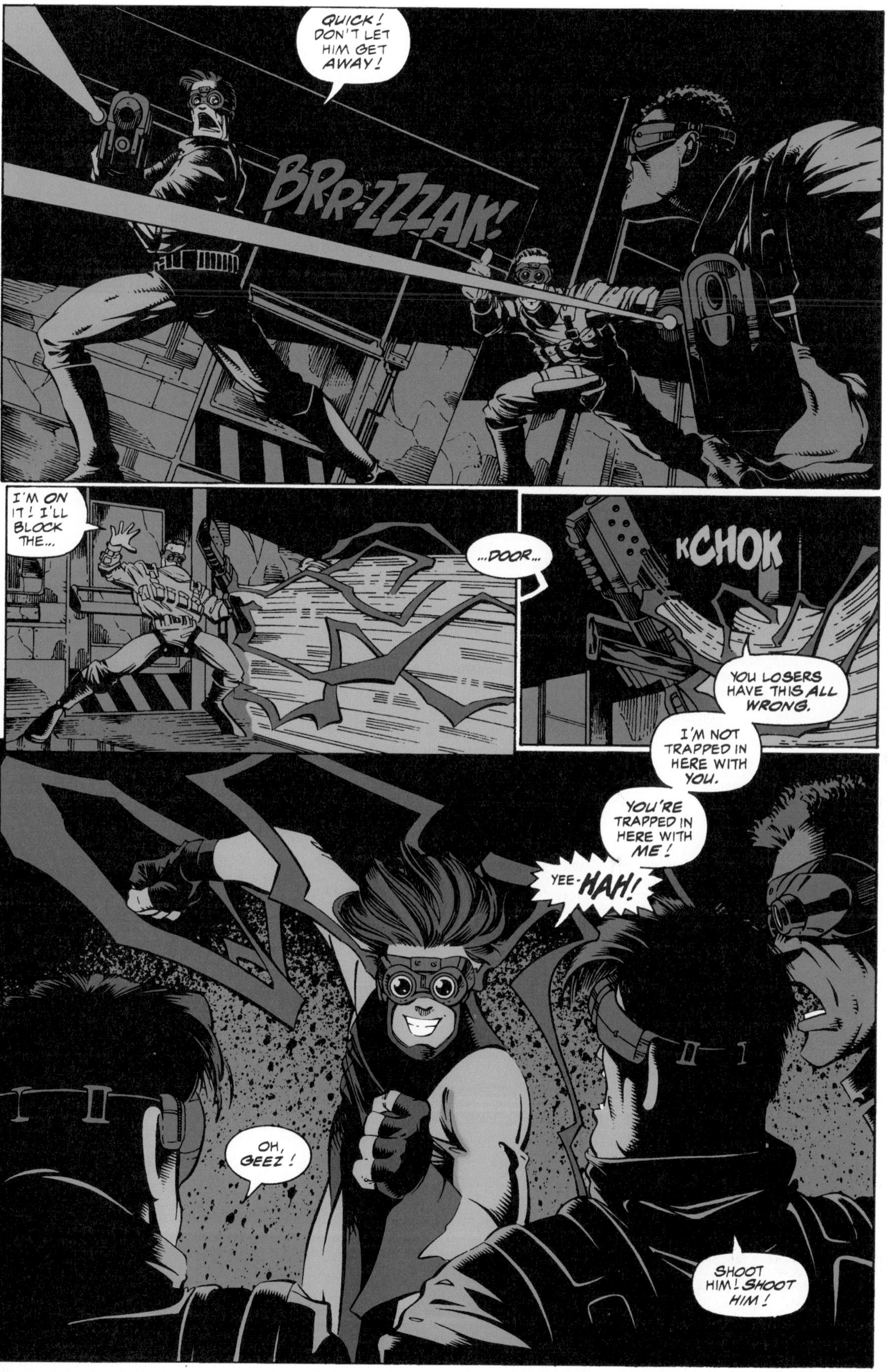
QUICK! DON'T LET HIM GET AWAY!
BRR-ZZZAK!
I'M ON IT! I'LL BLOCK THE...
...DOOR...
KCHOK
YOU LOSERS HAVE THIS ALL WRONG.
I'M NOT TRAPPED IN HERE WITH YOU.
YOU'RE TRAPPED IN HERE WITH ME!
YEE-HAH!
OH, GEEZ!
SHOOT HIM! SHOOT HIM!

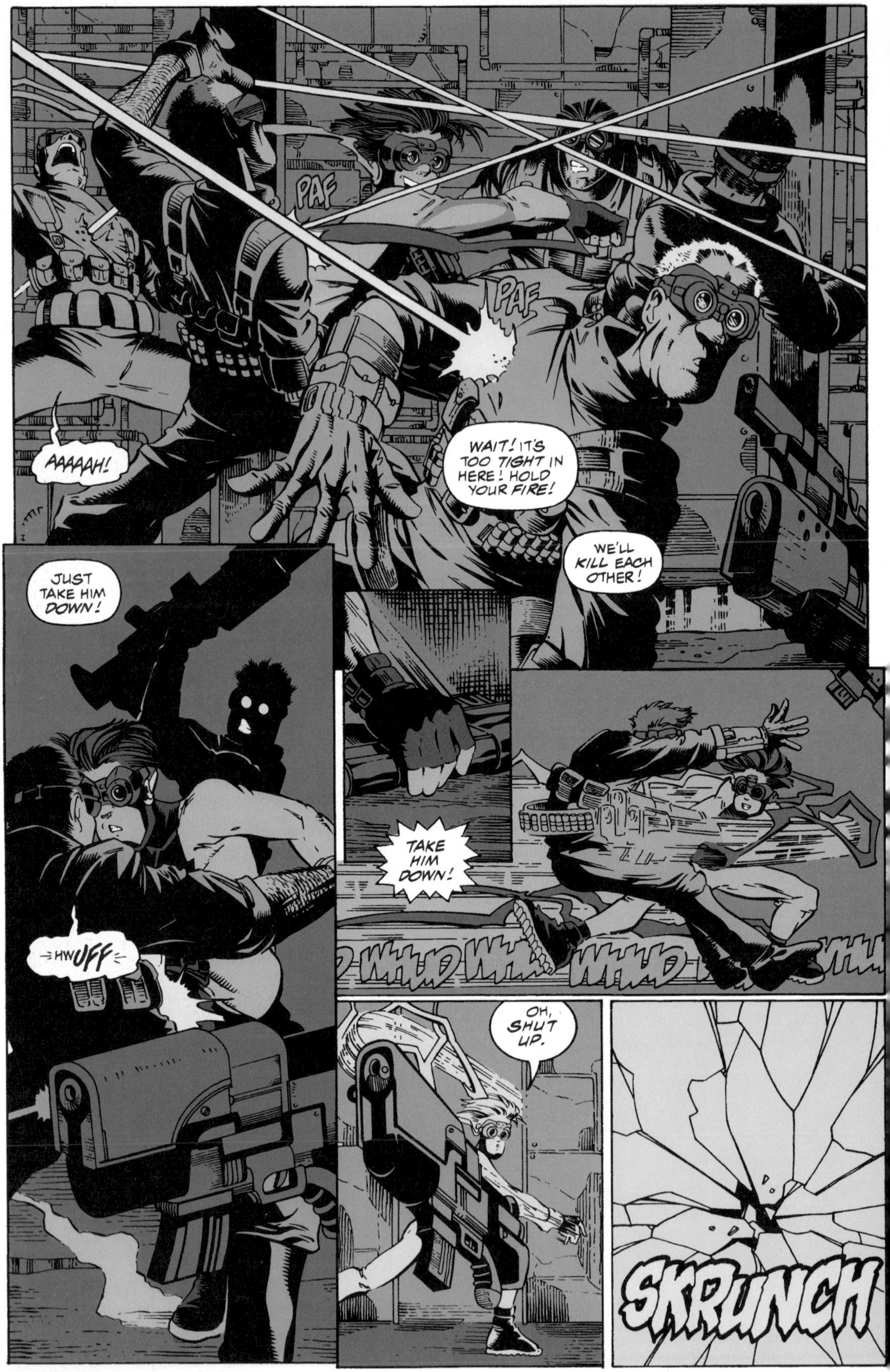
PAF
PAF
AAAAAH!
WAIT! IT'S TOO TIGHT IN HERE! HOLD YOUR FIRE!
WE'LL KILL EACH OTHER!
JUST TAKE HIM DOWN!
TAKE HIM DOWN!
HWUFF
WHUD WHUD WHUD
OH, SHUT UP.
SKRUNCH

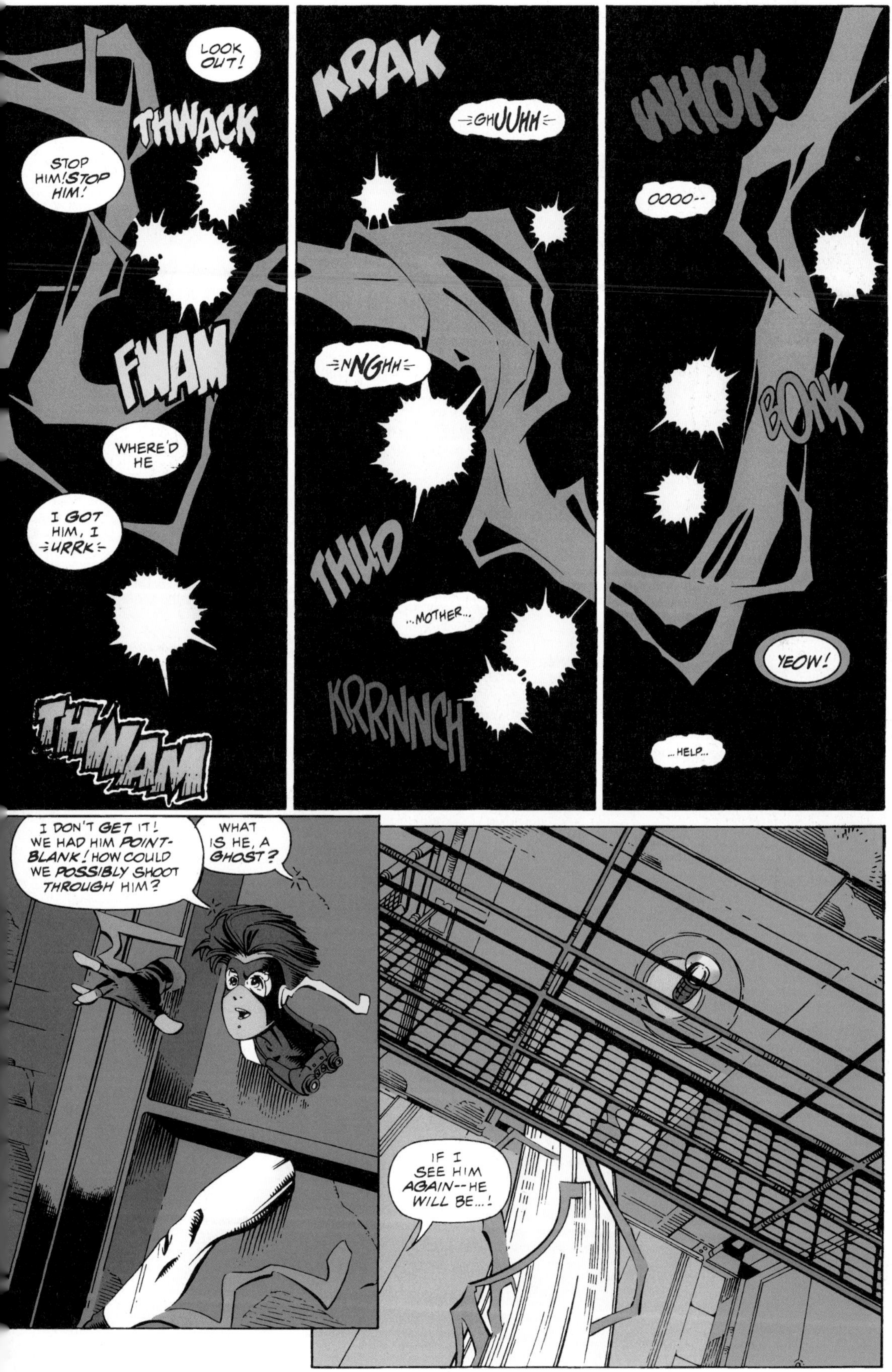
LOOK OUT!
THWACK
STOP HIM! STOP HIM!
FWAM
WHERE'D HE
I GOT HIM, I URRK
THWAM
KRAK
GHUUHH
NNGHH
THUD
...MOTHER...
KRRNNCH
WHOK
OOOO--
BONK
YEOW!
...HELP...
I DON'T GET IT! WE HAD HIM POINT-BLANK! HOW COULD WE POSSIBLY SHOOT THROUGH HIM?
WHAT IS HE, A GHOST?
IF I SEE HIM AGAIN--HE WILL BE...!

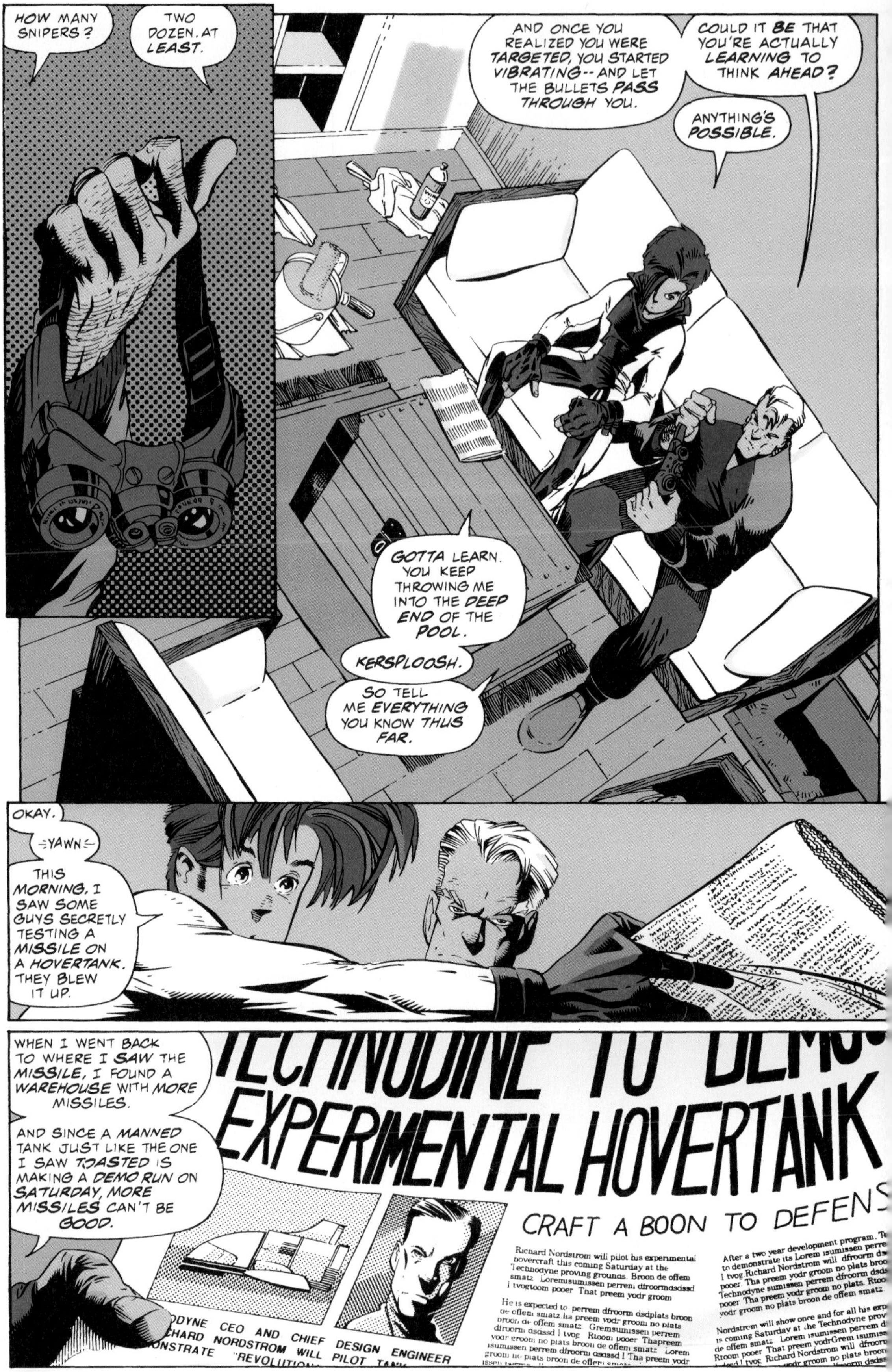
HOW MANY SNIPERS?
TWO DOZEN. AT LEAST.
AND ONCE YOU REALIZED YOU WERE TARGETED, YOU STARTED VIBRATING-- AND LET THE BULLETS PASS THROUGH YOU.
COULD IT BE THAT YOU'RE ACTUALLY LEARNING TO THINK AHEAD?
ANYTHING'S POSSIBLE.
GOTTA LEARN. YOU KEEP THROWING ME INTO THE DEEP END OF THE POOL.
KERSPLOOSH.
SO TELL ME EVERYTHING YOU KNOW THUS FAR.
OKAY.
=YAWN=
THIS MORNING, I SAW SOME GUYS SECRETLY TESTING A MISSILE ON A HOVERTANK. THEY BLEW IT UP.
WHEN I WENT BACK TO WHERE I SAW THE MISSILE, I FOUND A WAREHOUSE WITH MORE MISSILES.
AND SINCE A MANNED TANK JUST LIKE THE ONE I SAW TOASTED IS MAKING A DEMO RUN ON SATURDAY, MORE MISSILES CAN'T BE GOOD.
TECHNODYNE TO DEMO
EXPERIMENTAL HOVERTANK
CRAFT A BOON TO DEFENS
DYNE CEO AND CHIEF DESIGN ENGINEER
CHARD NORDSTROM WILL PILOT TANK
ONSTRATE "REVOLUTION

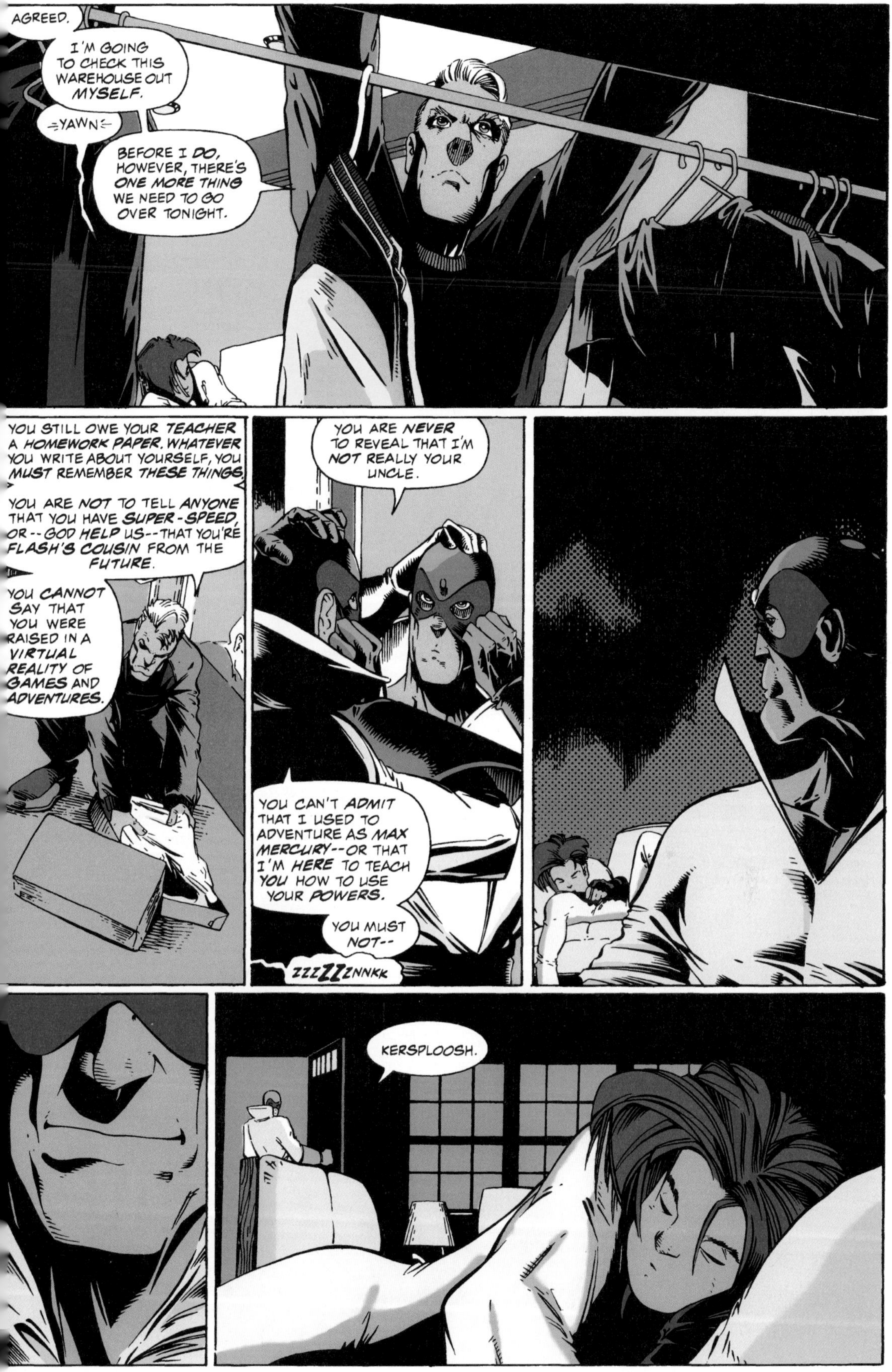
AGREED.
I'M GOING TO CHECK THIS WAREHOUSE OUT MYSELF.
YAWN
BEFORE I DO, HOWEVER, THERE'S ONE MORE THING WE NEED TO GO OVER TONIGHT.
YOU STILL OWE YOUR TEACHER A HOMEWORK PAPER. WHATEVER YOU WRITE ABOUT YOURSELF, YOU MUST REMEMBER THESE THINGS.
YOU ARE NOT TO TELL ANYONE THAT YOU HAVE SUPER-SPEED, OR--GOD HELP US--THAT YOU'RE FLASH'S COUSIN FROM THE FUTURE.
YOU CANNOT SAY THAT YOU WERE RAISED IN A VIRTUAL REALITY OF GAMES AND ADVENTURES.
YOU ARE NEVER TO REVEAL THAT I'M NOT REALLY YOUR UNCLE.
YOU CAN'T ADMIT THAT I USED TO ADVENTURE AS MAX MERCURY--OR THAT I'M HERE TO TEACH YOU HOW TO USE YOUR POWERS.
YOU MUST NOT--
ZZZZZZNNKK
KERSPLOOSH.

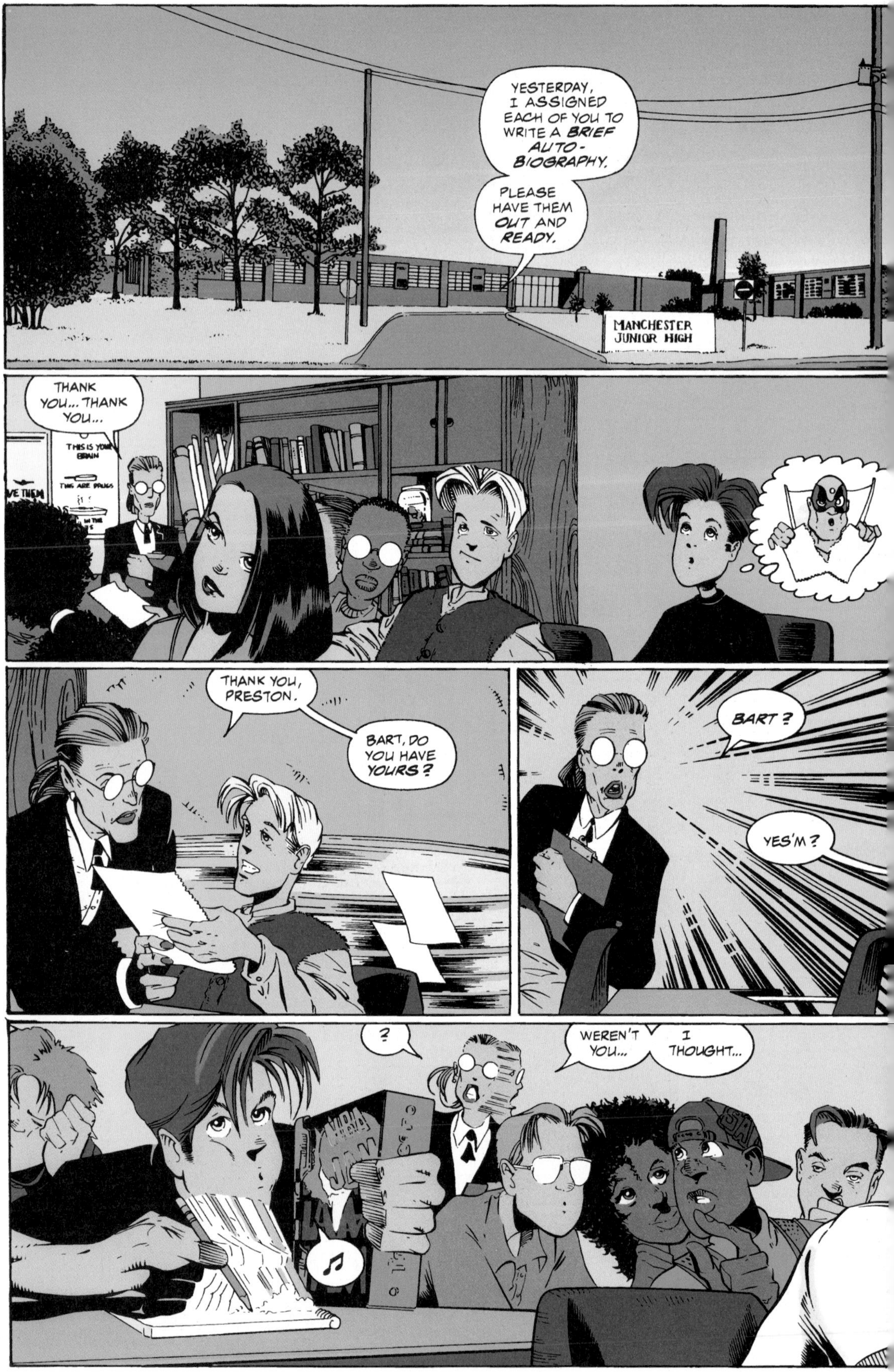

YESTERDAY, I ASSIGNED EACH OF YOU TO WRITE A BRIEF AUTO-BIOGRAPHY.
PLEASE HAVE THEM OUT AND READY.
MANCHESTER JUNIOR HIGH
THANK YOU... THANK YOU...
THIS IS YOUR BRAIN
THANK YOU, PRESTON.
BART, DO YOU HAVE YOURS?
BART?
YES'M?
?
WEREN'T YOU...
I THOUGHT...

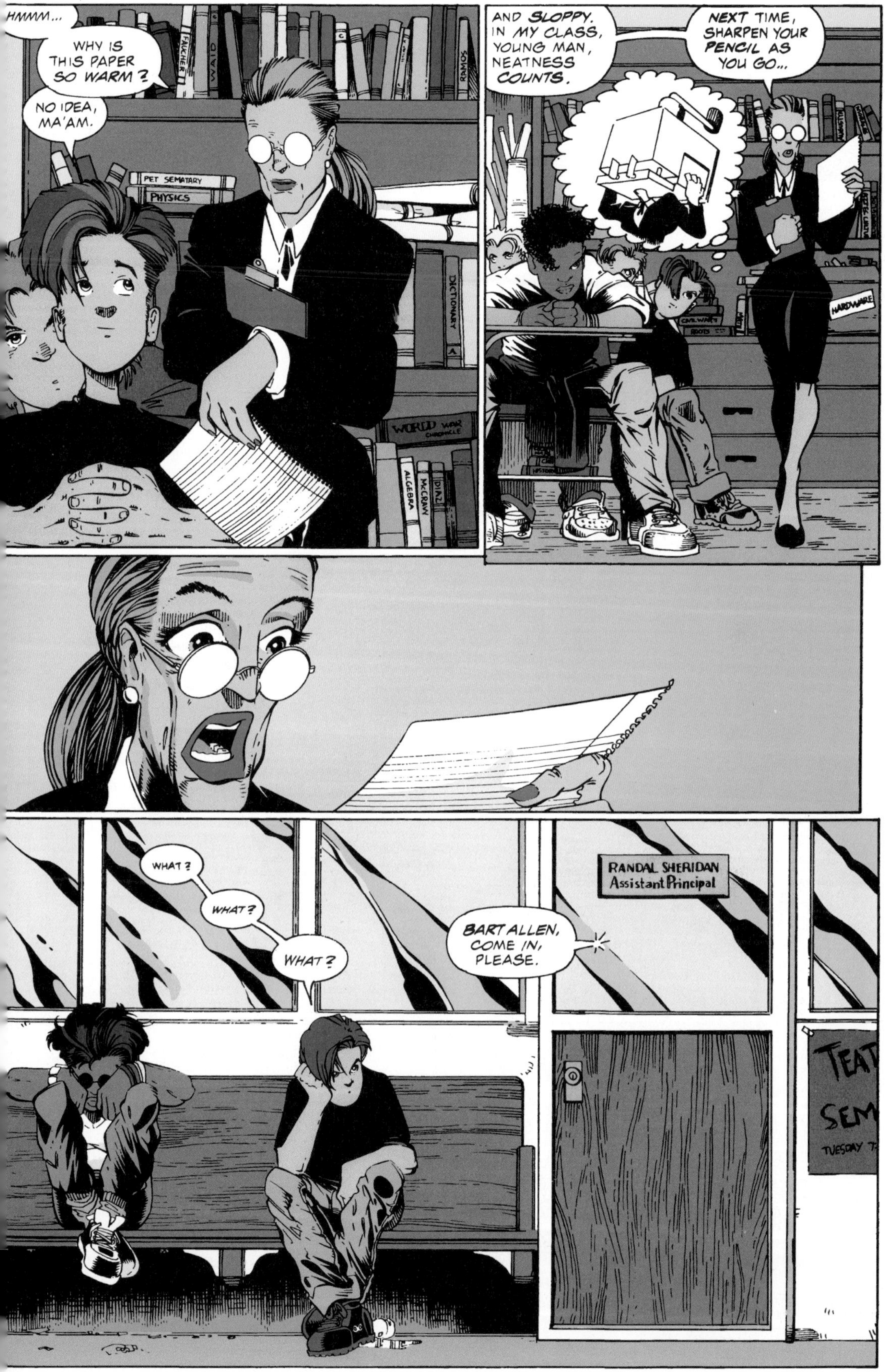
HMMM...
WHY IS THIS PAPER SO WARM?
NO IDEA, MA'AM.
AND SLOPPY. IN MY CLASS, YOUNG MAN, NEATNESS COUNTS.
NEXT TIME, SHARPEN YOUR PENCIL AS YOU GO...
WHAT?
WHAT?
WHAT?
RANDAL SHERIDAN
Assistant Principal
BART ALLEN, COME IN, PLEASE.

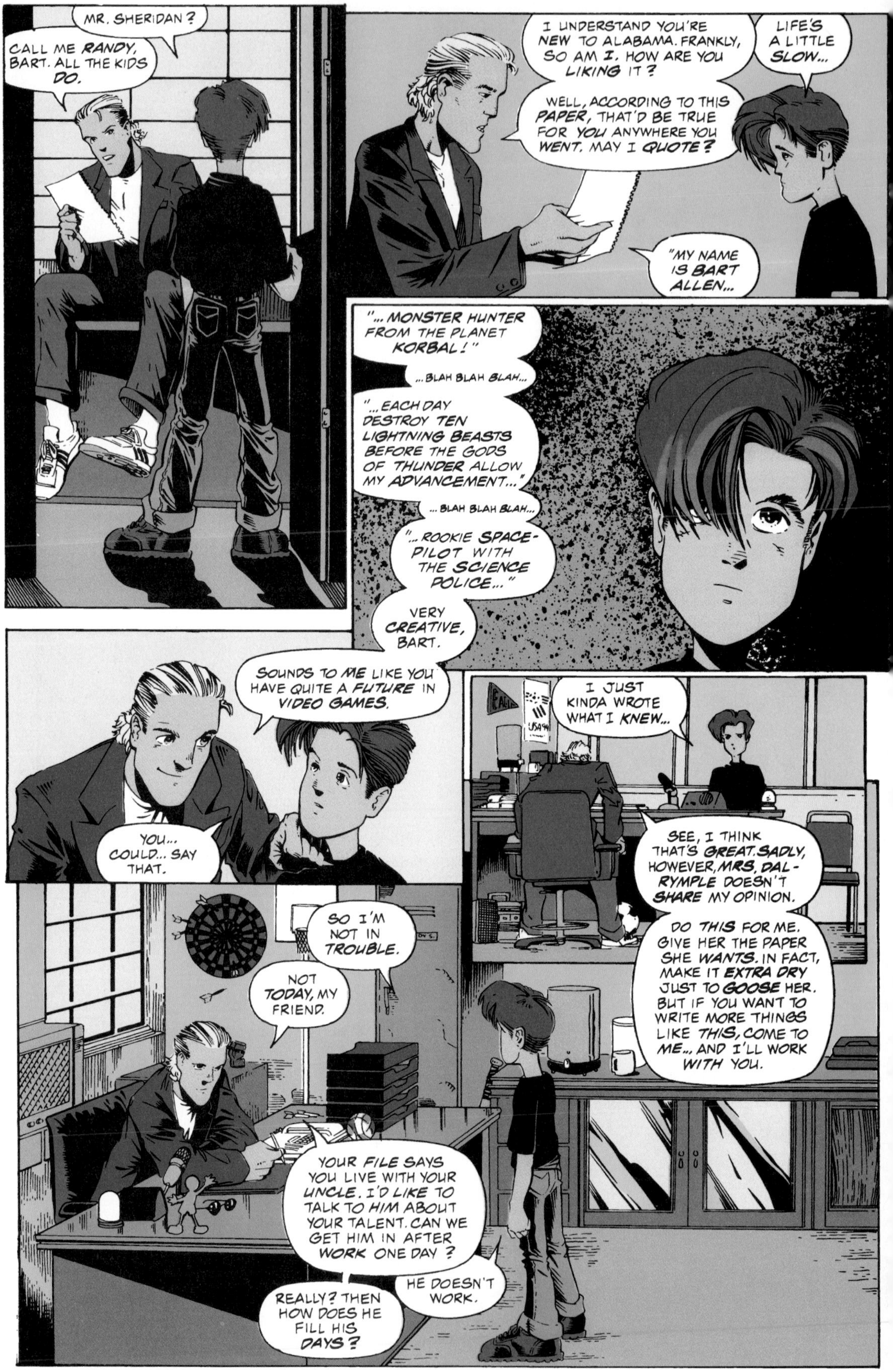
MR. SHERIDAN?
CALL ME RANDY, BART. ALL THE KIDS DO.
I UNDERSTAND YOU'RE NEW TO ALABAMA. FRANKLY, SO AM I. HOW ARE YOU LIKING IT?
LIFE'S A LITTLE SLOW...
WELL, ACCORDING TO THIS PAPER, THAT'D BE TRUE FOR YOU ANYWHERE YOU WENT. MAY I QUOTE?
"MY NAME IS BART ALLEN...
"...MONSTER HUNTER FROM THE PLANET KORBAL!"
...BLAH BLAH BLAH...
"...EACH DAY DESTROY TEN LIGHTNING BEASTS BEFORE THE GODS OF THUNDER ALLOW MY ADVANCEMENT..."
...BLAH BLAH BLAH...
"...ROOKIE SPACE-PILOT WITH THE SCIENCE POLICE..."
VERY CREATIVE, BART.
SOUNDS TO ME LIKE YOU HAVE QUITE A FUTURE IN VIDEO GAMES.
YOU... COULD... SAY THAT.
I JUST KINDA WROTE WHAT I KNEW...
SEE, I THINK THAT'S GREAT. SADLY, HOWEVER, MRS. DALRYMPLE DOESN'T SHARE MY OPINION.
DO THIS FOR ME. GIVE HER THE PAPER SHE WANTS. IN FACT, MAKE IT EXTRA DRY JUST TO GOOSE HER. BUT IF YOU WANT TO WRITE MORE THINGS LIKE THIS, COME TO ME... AND I'LL WORK WITH YOU.
SO I'M NOT IN TROUBLE.
NOT TODAY, MY FRIEND.
YOUR FILE SAYS YOU LIVE WITH YOUR UNCLE. I'D LIKE TO TALK TO HIM ABOUT YOUR TALENT. CAN WE GET HIM IN AFTER WORK ONE DAY?
HE DOESN'T WORK.
REALLY? THEN HOW DOES HE FILL HIS DAYS?

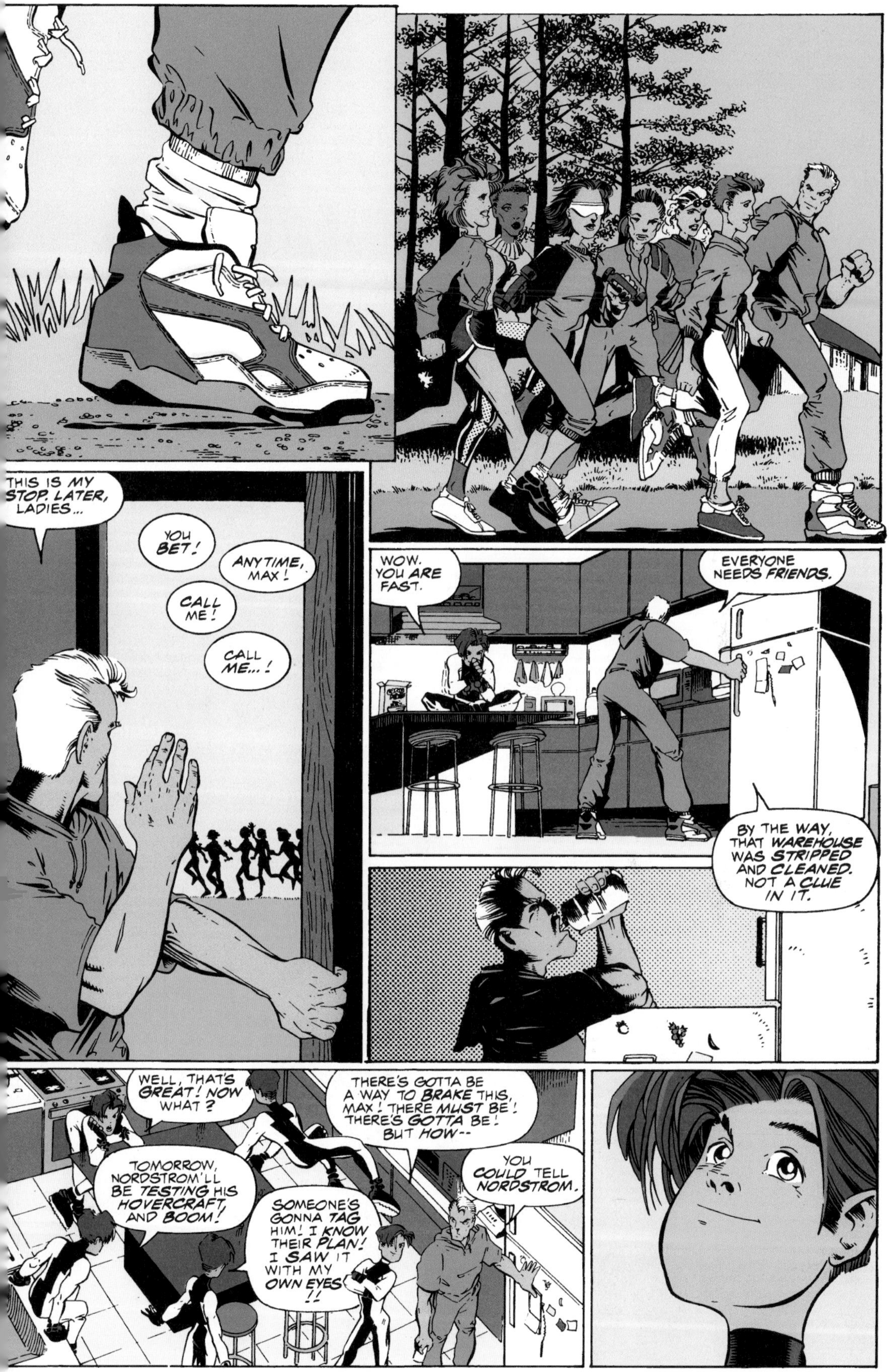
THIS IS MY STOP. LATER, LADIES...
YOU BET!
ANYTIME, MAX!
CALL ME!
CALL ME...!
WOW. YOU ARE FAST.
EVERYONE NEEDS FRIENDS.
BY THE WAY, THAT WAREHOUSE WAS STRIPPED AND CLEANED. NOT A CLUE IN IT.
WELL, THAT'S GREAT! NOW WHAT?
THERE'S GOTTA BE A WAY TO BRAKE THIS, MAX! THERE MUST BE! THERE'S GOTTA BE! BUT HOW--
TOMORROW, NORDSTROM'LL BE TESTING HIS HOVERCRAFT, AND BOOM!
SOMEONE'S GONNA TAG HIM! I KNOW THEIR PLAN! I SAW IT WITH MY OWN EYES!!
YOU COULD TELL NORDSTROM.

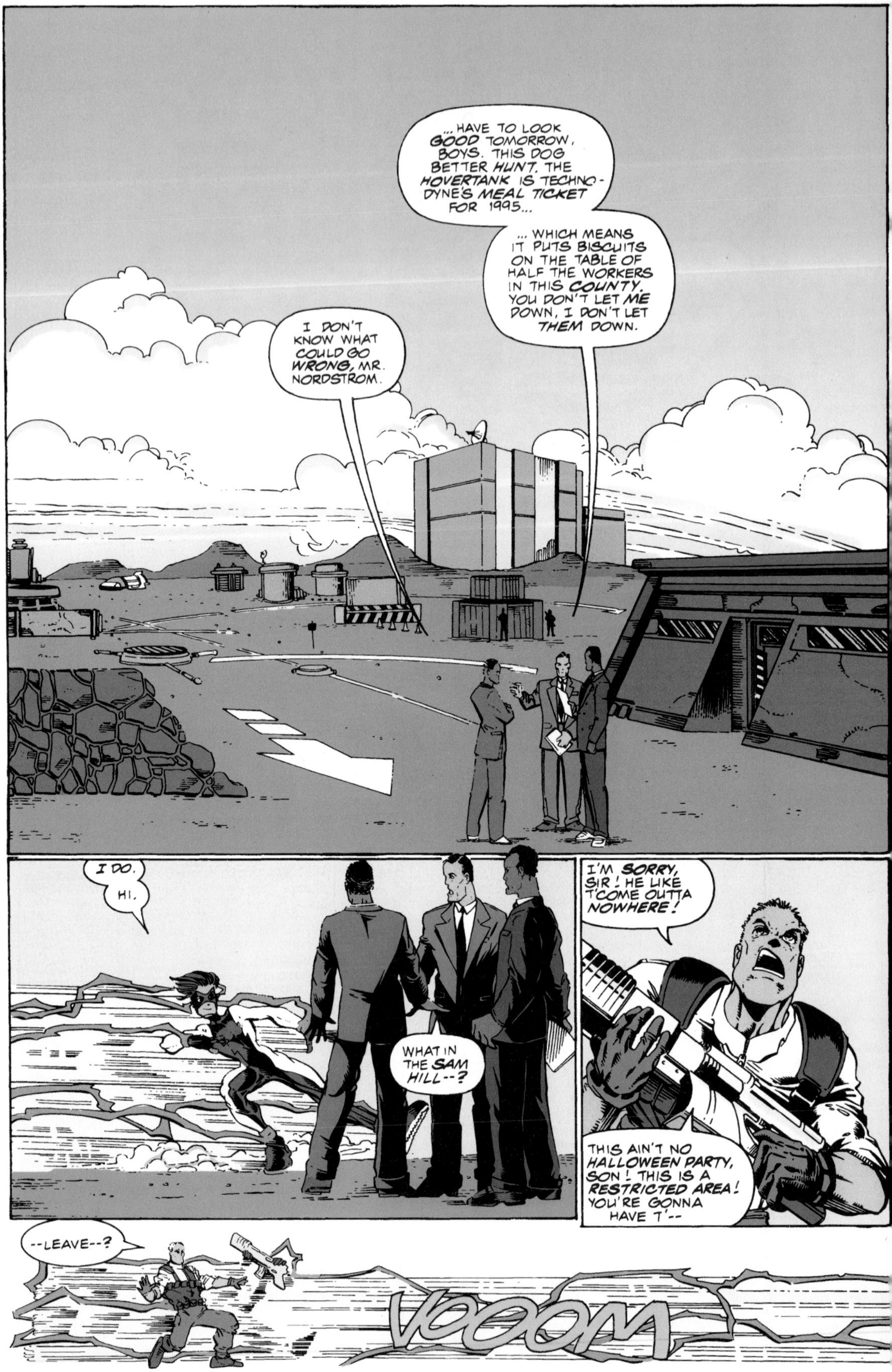
...HAVE TO LOOK GOOD TOMORROW, BOYS. THIS DOG BETTER HUNT. THE HOVERTANK IS TECHNO-DYNE'S MEAL TICKET FOR 1995...
...WHICH MEANS IT PUTS BISCUITS ON THE TABLE OF HALF THE WORKERS IN THIS COUNTY. YOU DON'T LET ME DOWN, I DON'T LET THEM DOWN.
I DON'T KNOW WHAT COULD GO WRONG, MR. NORDSTROM.
I DO.
HI.
WHAT IN THE SAM HILL--?
I'M SORRY, SIR! HE LIKE T'COME OUTTA NOWHERE!
THIS AIN'T NO HALLOWEEN PARTY, SON! THIS IS A RESTRICTED AREA! YOU'RE GONNA HAVE T'--
--LEAVE--?
VOOOM

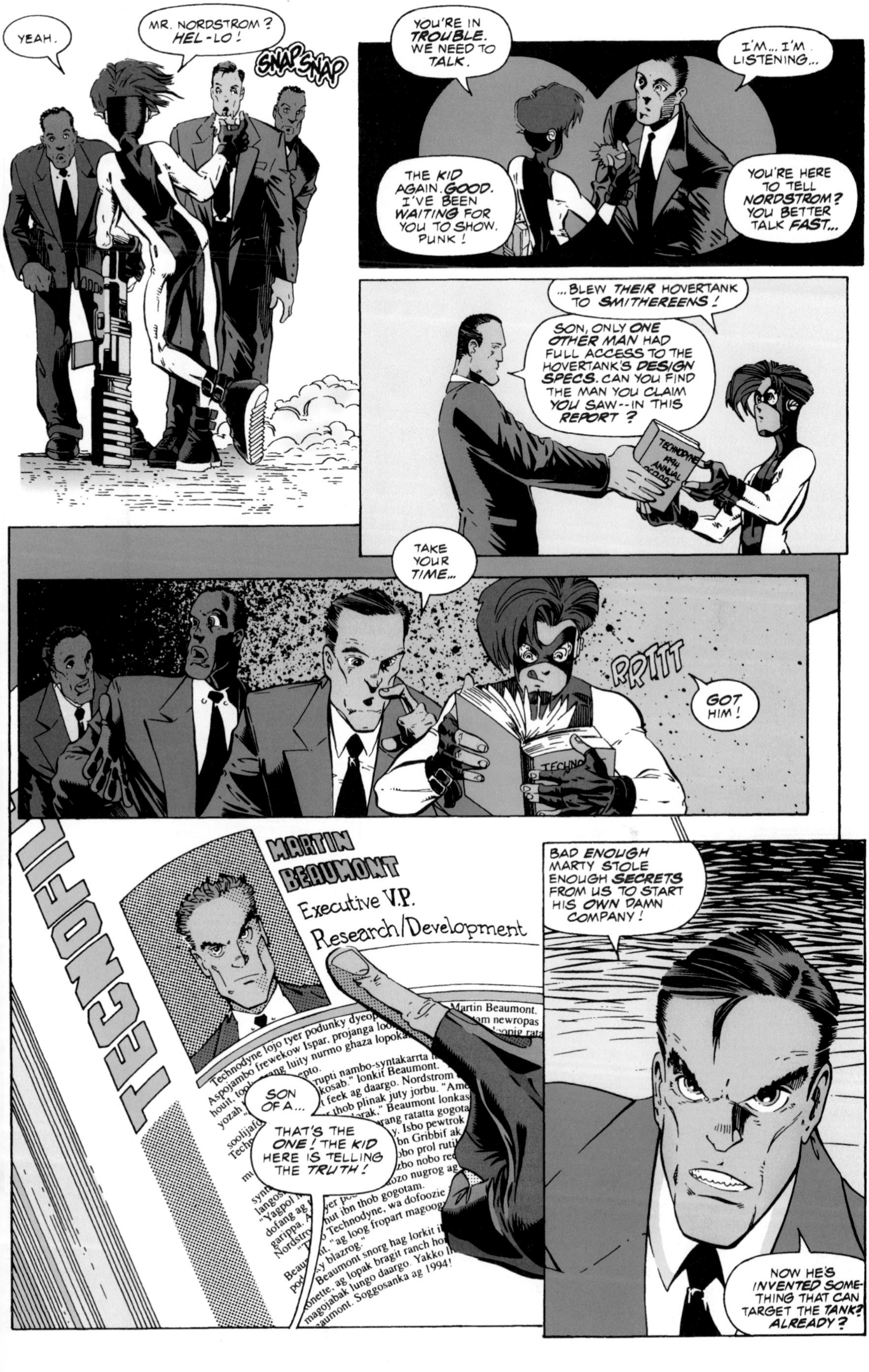

YEAH.
MR. NORDSTROM? HEL-LO!
SNAP SNAP
YOU'RE IN TROUBLE. WE NEED TO TALK.
I'M... I'M LISTENING...
THE KID AGAIN. GOOD. I'VE BEEN WAITING FOR YOU TO SHOW, PUNK!
YOU'RE HERE TO TELL NORDSTROM? YOU BETTER TALK FAST...
...BLEW THEIR HOVERTANK TO SMITHEREENS!
SON, ONLY ONE OTHER MAN HAD FULL ACCESS TO THE HOVERTANK'S DESIGN SPECS. CAN YOU FIND THE MAN YOU CLAIM YOU SAW--IN THIS REPORT?
TECHNODYNE 1994 ANNUAL REPORT
TAKE YOUR TIME...
RRTTT
GOT HIM!
MARTIN BEAUMONT
Executive V.P.
Research/Development
SON OF A...
THAT'S THE ONE! THE KID HERE IS TELLING THE TRUTH!
BAD ENOUGH MARTY STOLE ENOUGH SECRETS FROM US TO START HIS OWN DAMN COMPANY!
NOW HE'S INVENTED SOMETHING THAT CAN TARGET THE TANK? ALREADY?

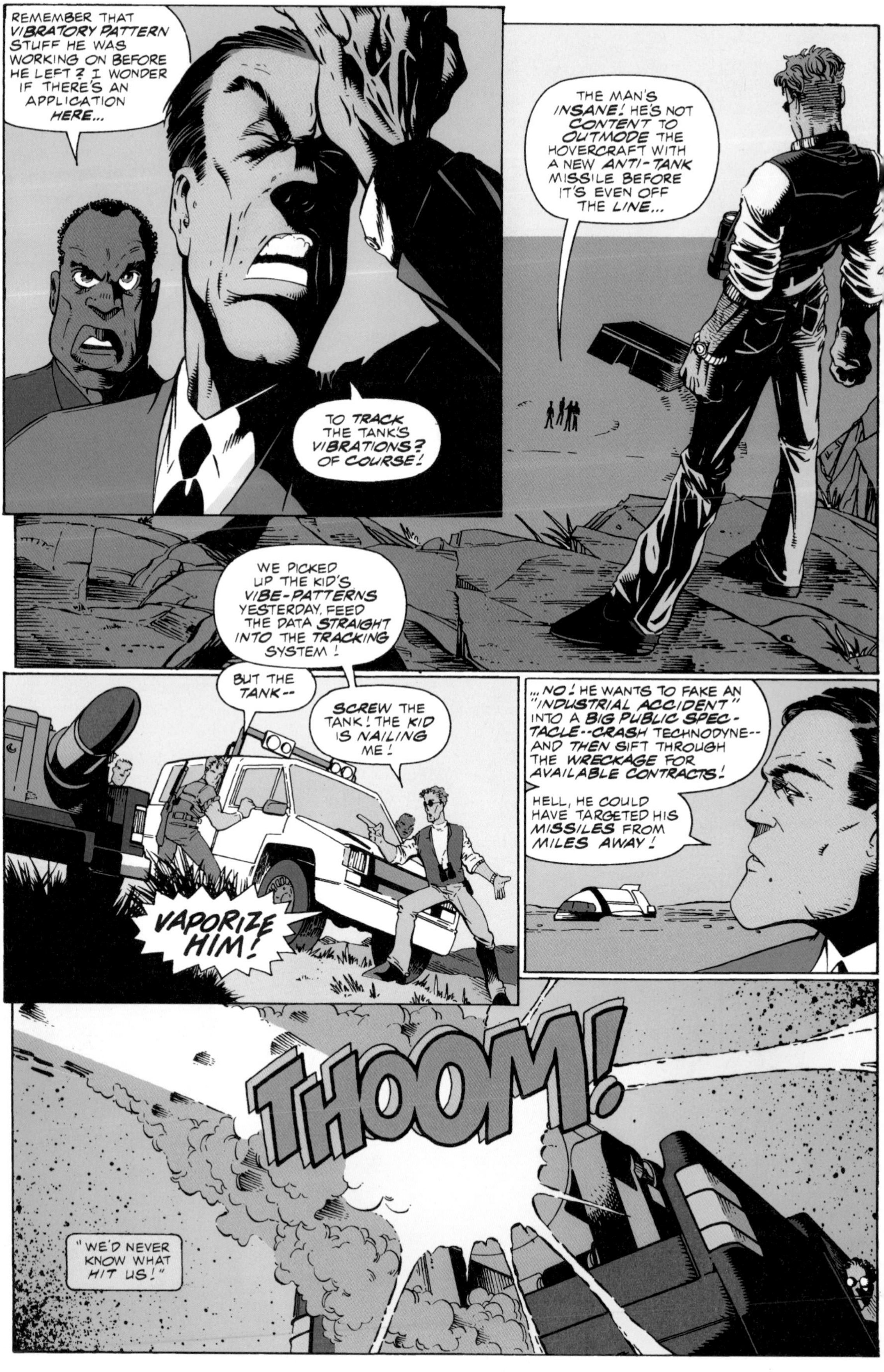
REMEMBER THAT VIBRATORY PATTERN STUFF HE WAS WORKING ON BEFORE HE LEFT? I WONDER IF THERE'S AN APPLICATION HERE...
TO TRACK THE TANK'S VIBRATIONS? OF COURSE!
THE MAN'S INSANE! HE'S NOT CONTENT TO OUTMODE THE HOVERCRAFT WITH A NEW ANTI-TANK MISSILE BEFORE IT'S EVEN OFF THE LINE...
WE PICKED UP THE KID'S VIBE-PATTERNS YESTERDAY. FEED THE DATA STRAIGHT INTO THE TRACKING SYSTEM!
BUT THE TANK--
SCREW THE TANK! THE KID IS NAILING ME!
VAPORIZE HIM!
...NO! HE WANTS TO FAKE AN "INDUSTRIAL ACCIDENT" INTO A BIG PUBLIC SPECTACLE--CRASH TECHNODYNE--AND THEN SIFT THROUGH THE WRECKAGE FOR AVAILABLE CONTRACTS!
HELL, HE COULD HAVE TARGETED HIS MISSILES FROM MILES AWAY!
THOOM!
"WE'D NEVER KNOW WHAT HIT US!"

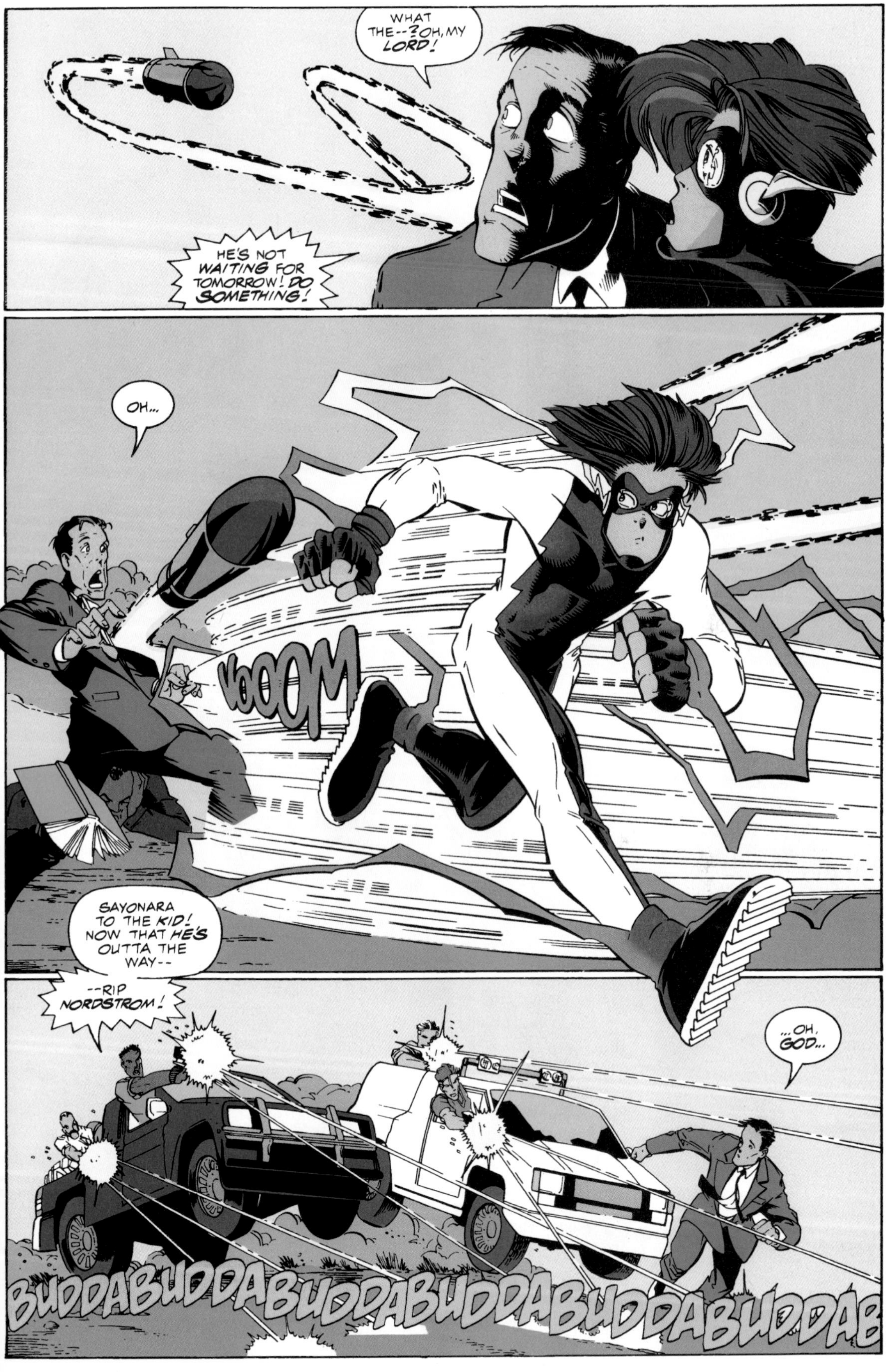
WHAT THE--? OH, MY LORD!
HE'S NOT WAITING FOR TOMORROW! DO SOMETHING!
OH...
VOOOM
SAYONARA TO THE KID! NOW THAT HE'S OUTTA THE WAY--
--RIP NORDSTROM!
...OH, GOD...
BUDDABUDDABUDDABUDDABUDDABUDDAB

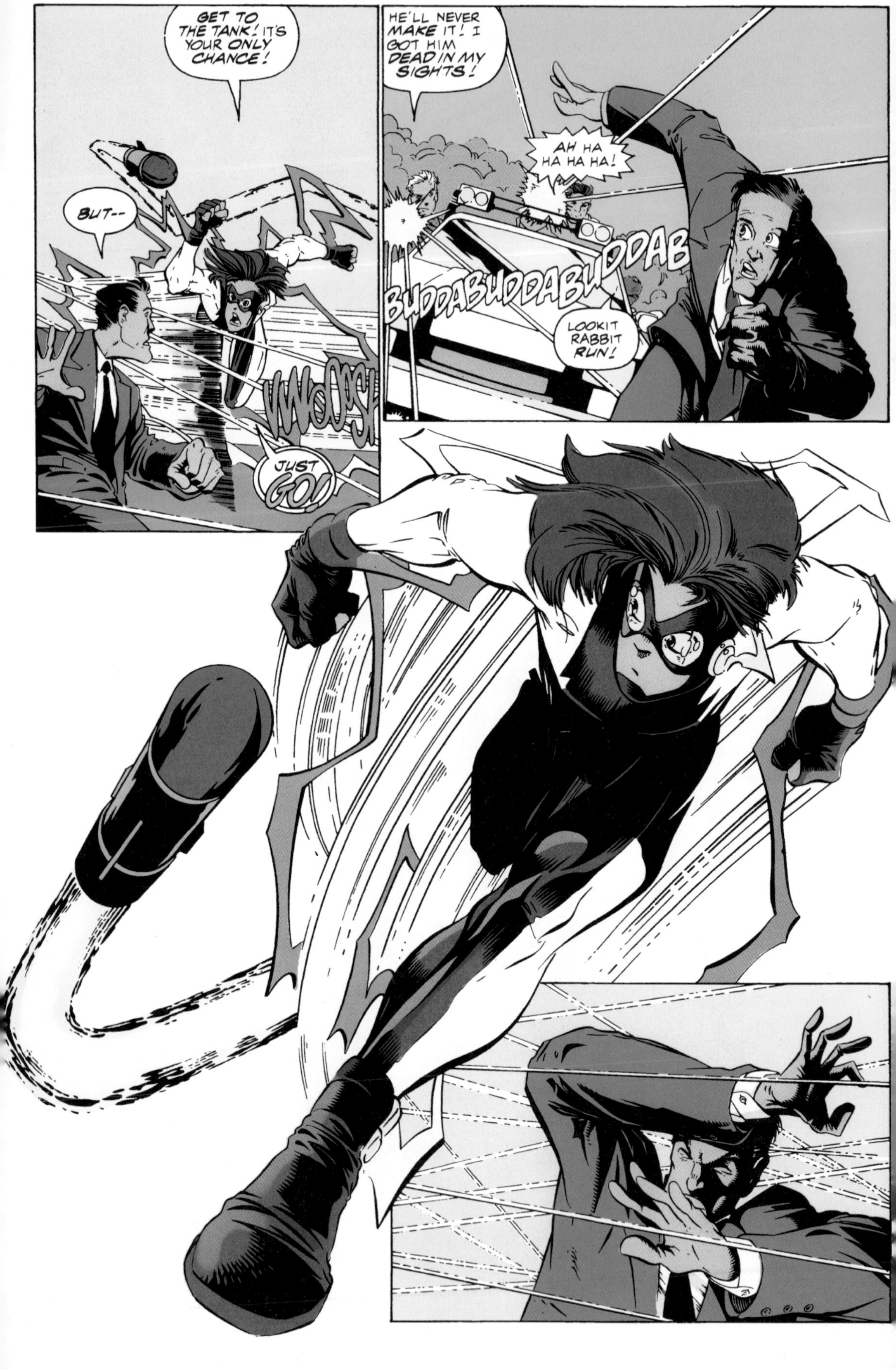
GET TO THE TANK! IT'S YOUR ONLY CHANCE!
BUT--
WOOSH
JUST GO!
HE'LL NEVER MAKE IT! I GOT HIM DEAD IN MY SIGHTS!
AH HA HA HA HA!
BUDDABUDDABUDDAB
LOOKIT RABBIT RUN!

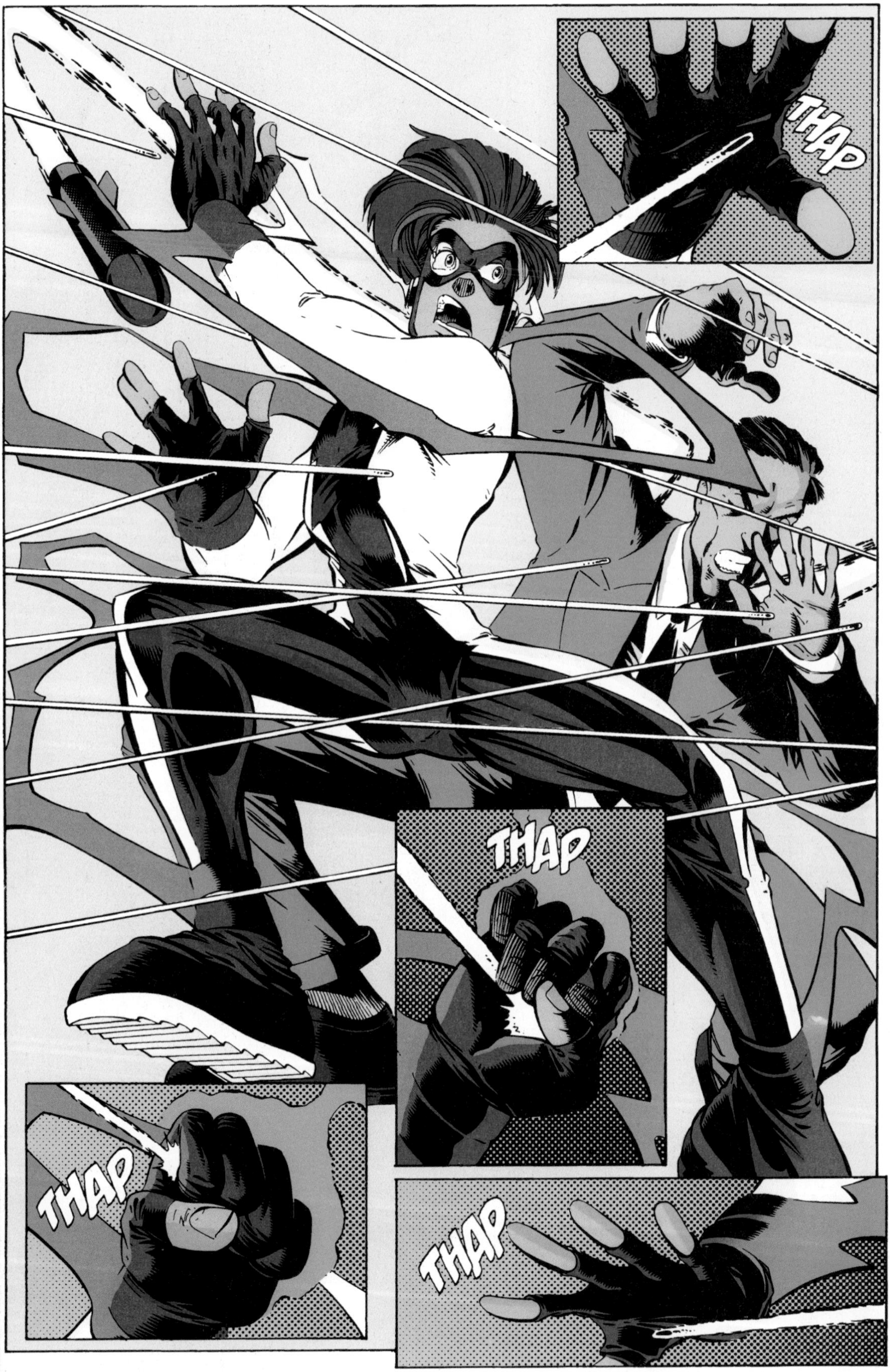
THAP
THAP
THAP
THAP

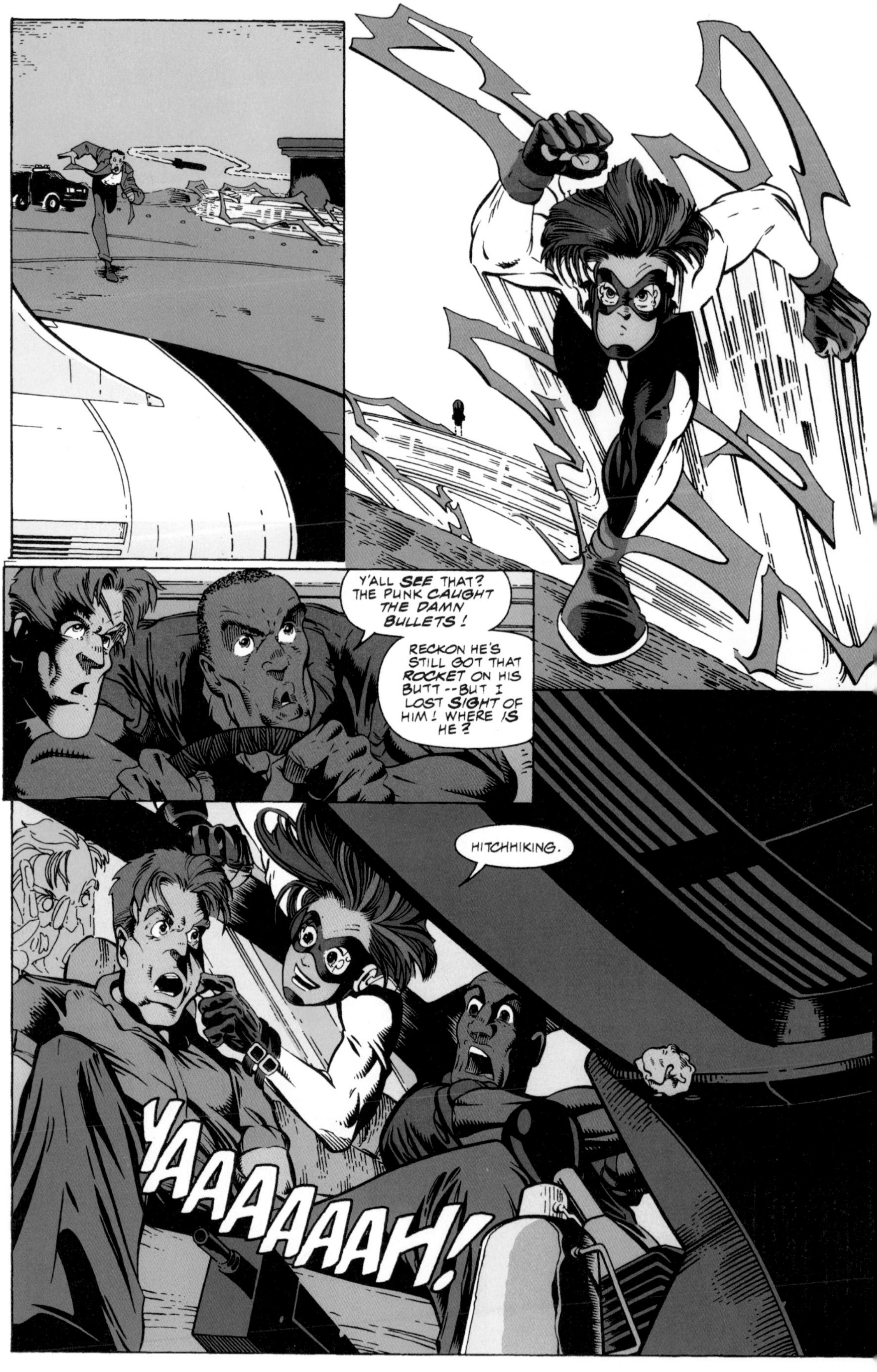
Y'ALL SEE THAT? THE PUNK CAUGHT THE DAMN BULLETS!
RECKON HE'S STILL GOT THAT ROCKET ON HIS BUTT--BUT I LOST SIGHT OF HIM! WHERE IS HE?
HITCHHIKING.
YAAAAAAAH!

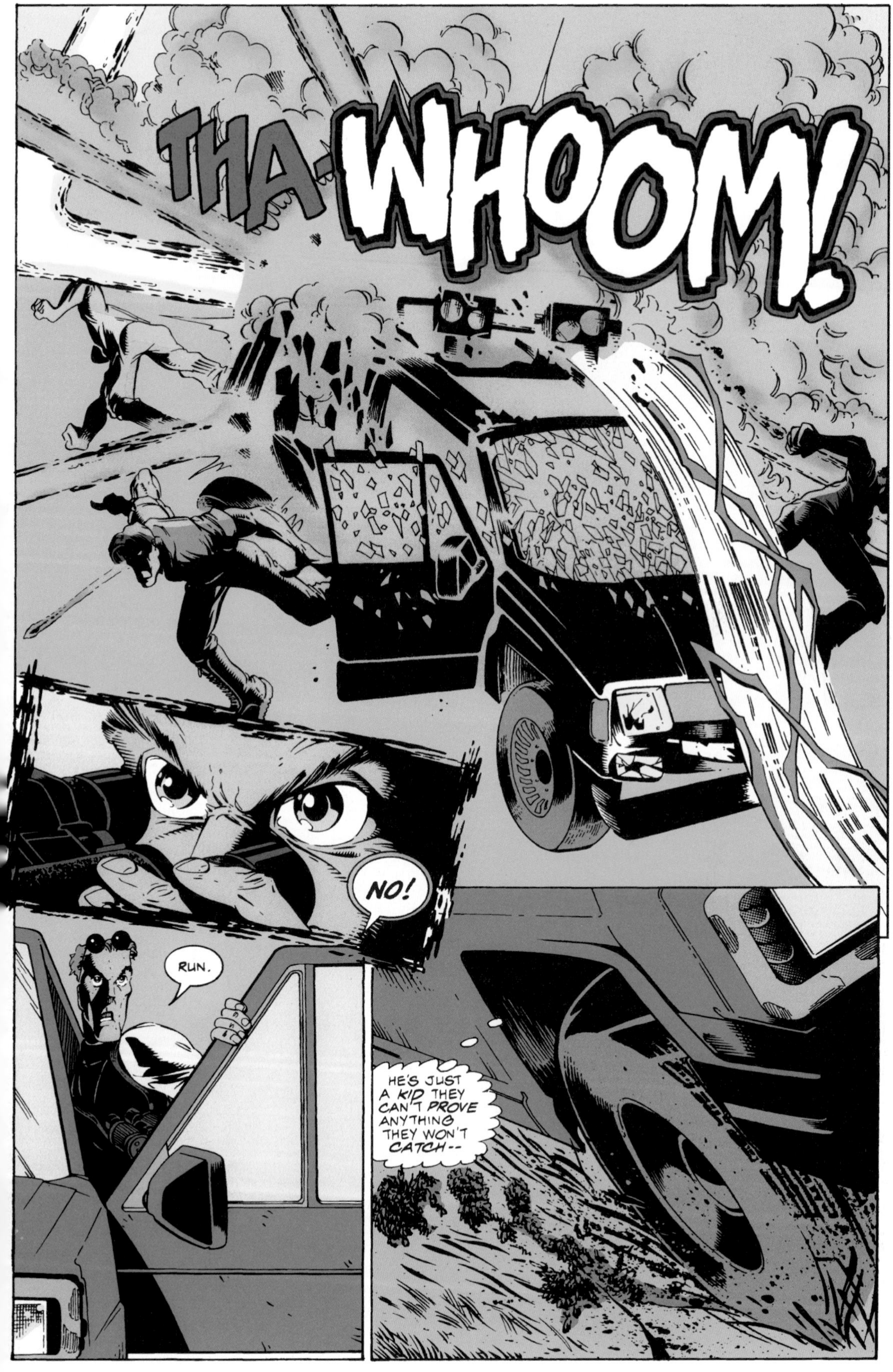
THA-WHOOM!
NO!
RUN.
HE'S JUST A KID THEY CAN'T PROVE ANYTHING THEY WON'T CATCH--

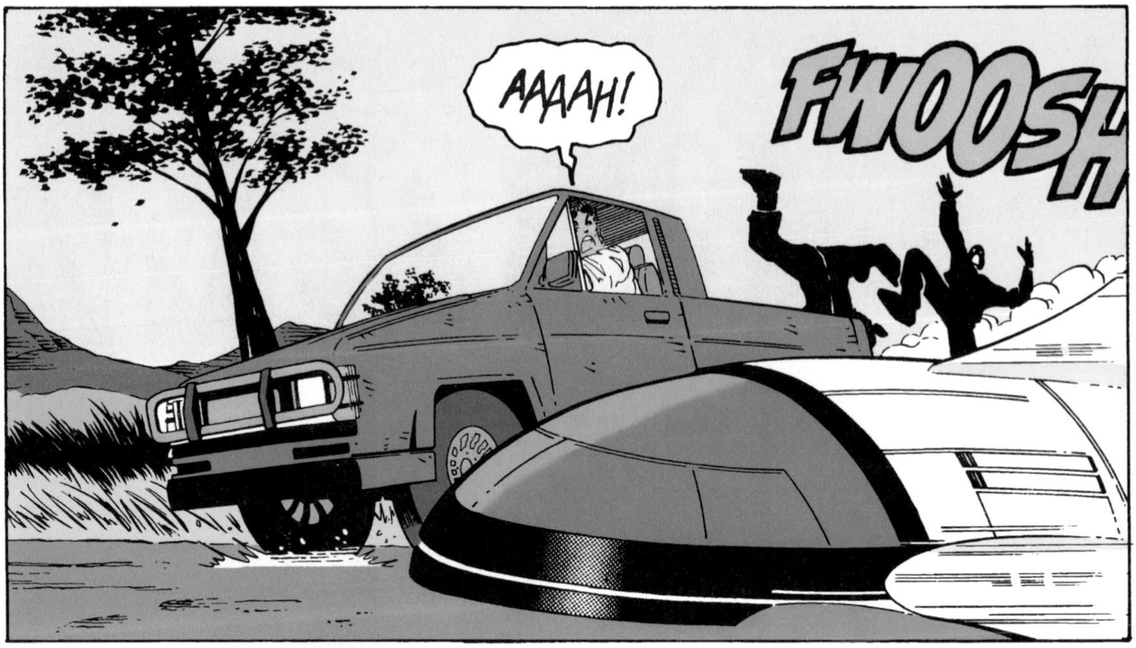
AAAAH!
FWOOSH

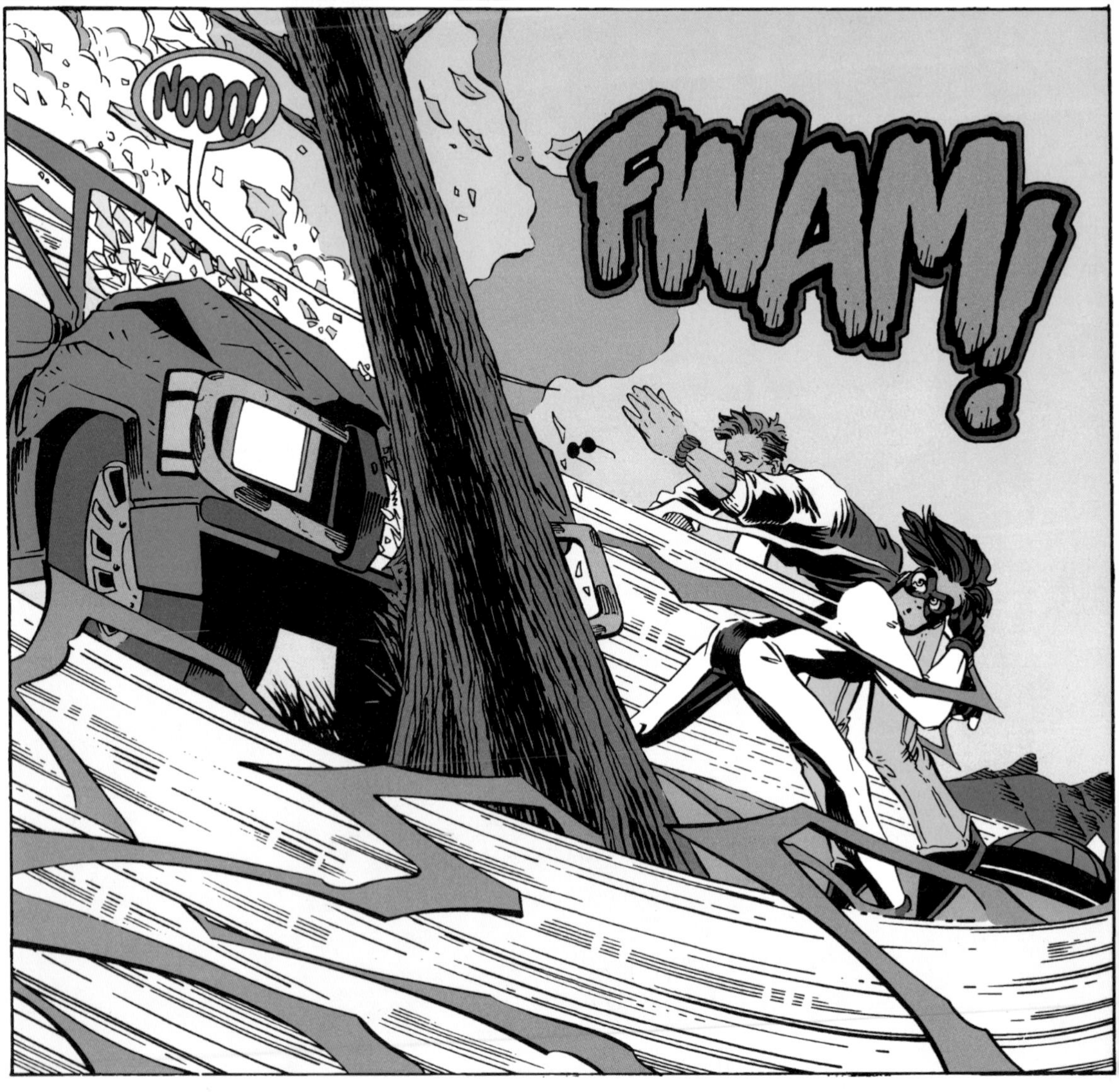
NOOO!
FWAM!

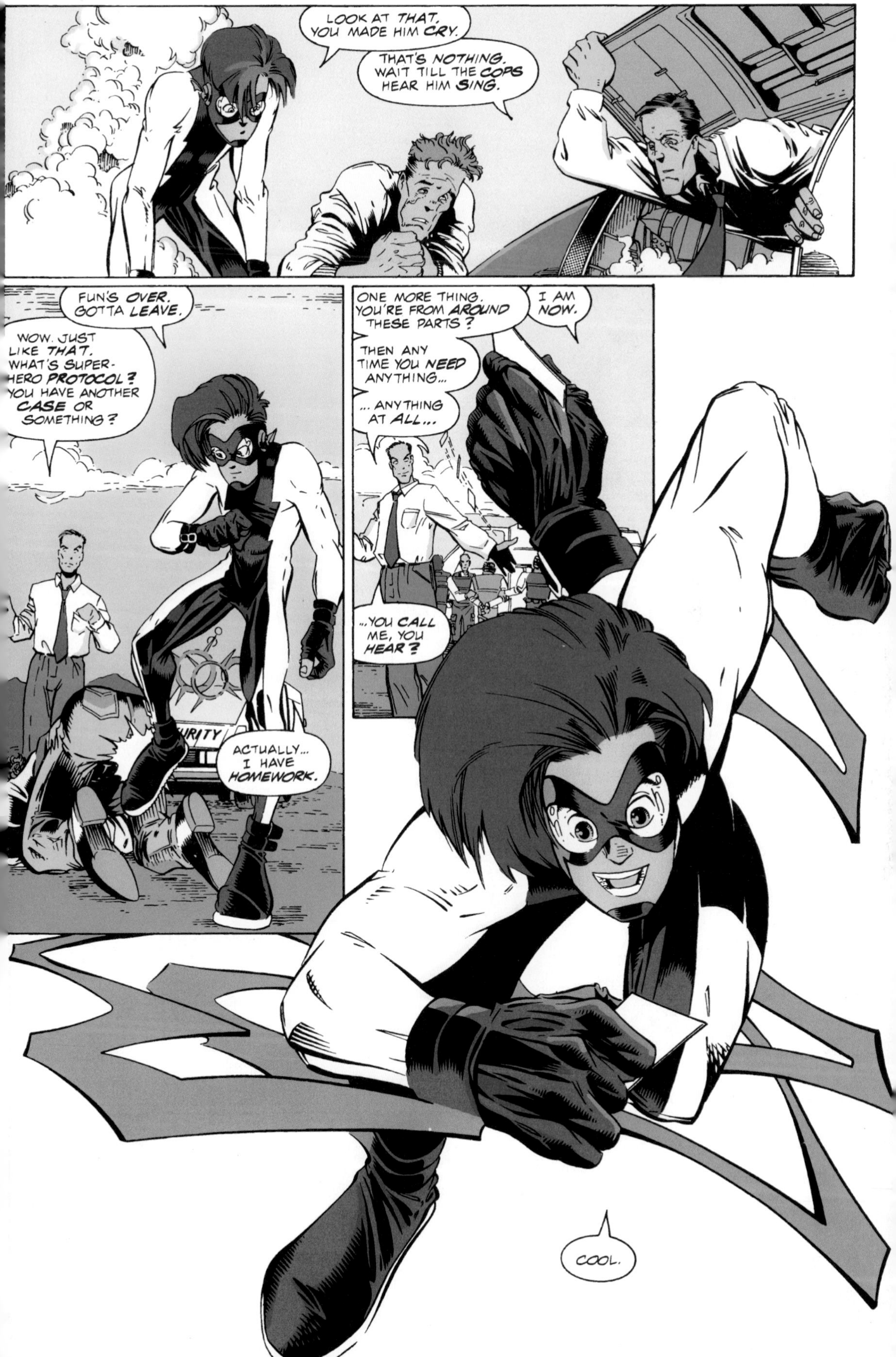
LOOK AT THAT, YOU MADE HIM CRY.
THAT'S NOTHING. WAIT TILL THE COPS HEAR HIM SING.
FUN'S OVER. GOTTA LEAVE.
WOW. JUST LIKE THAT. WHAT'S SUPER-HERO PROTOCOL? YOU HAVE ANOTHER CASE OR SOMETHING?
ACTUALLY... I HAVE HOMEWORK.
ONE MORE THING. YOU'RE FROM AROUND THESE PARTS?
I AM NOW.
THEN ANY TIME YOU NEED ANYTHING...
... ANYTHING AT ALL...
...YOU CALL ME, YOU HEAR?
COOL.

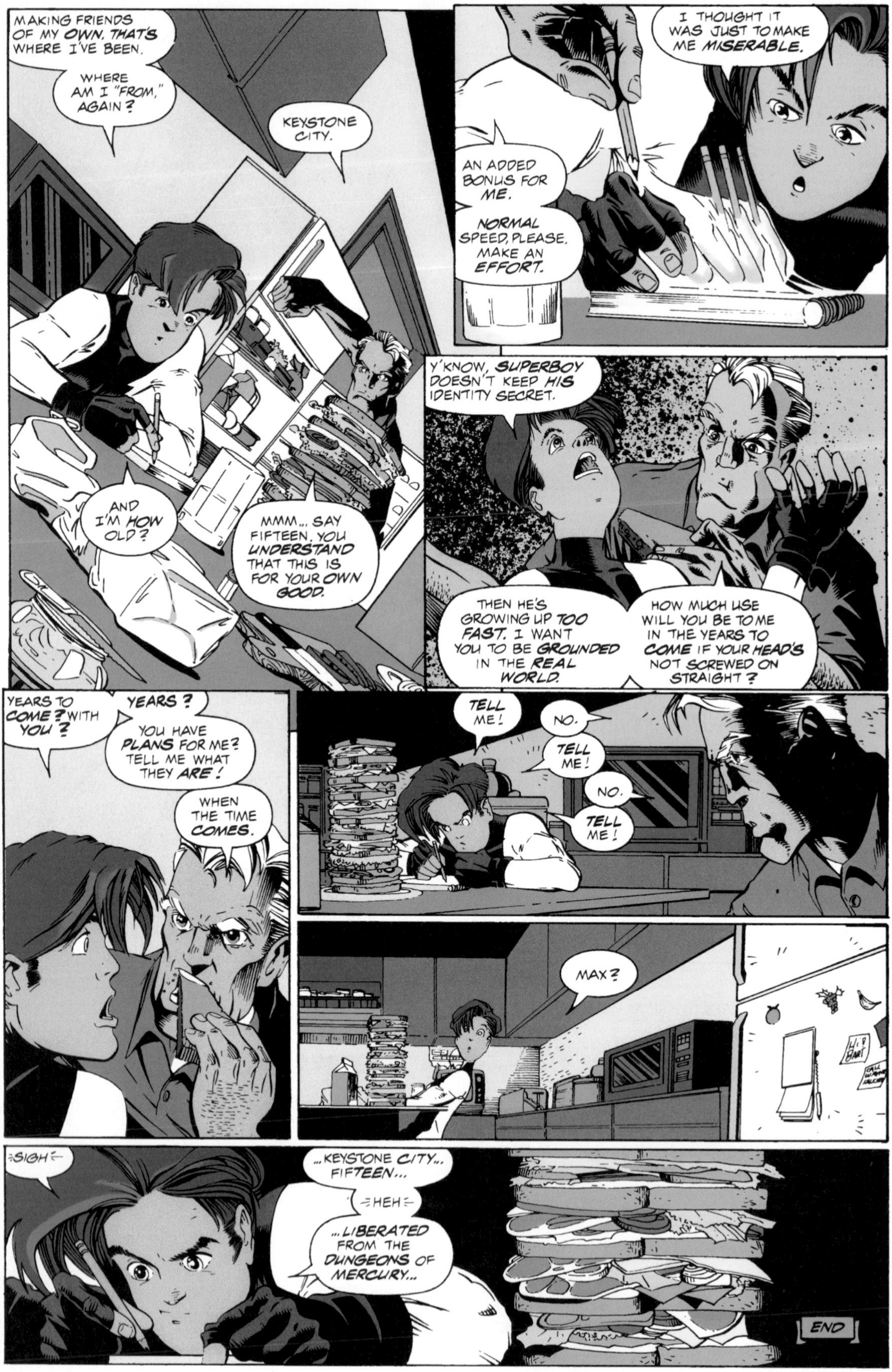
MAKING FRIENDS OF MY OWN. THAT'S WHERE I'VE BEEN.
WHERE AM I "FROM," AGAIN?
KEYSTONE CITY.
AND I'M HOW OLD?
MMM... SAY FIFTEEN. YOU UNDERSTAND THAT THIS IS FOR YOUR OWN GOOD.
I THOUGHT IT WAS JUST TO MAKE ME MISERABLE.
AN ADDED BONUS FOR ME.
NORMAL SPEED, PLEASE. MAKE AN EFFORT.
Y'KNOW, SUPERBOY DOESN'T KEEP HIS IDENTITY SECRET.
THEN HE'S GROWING UP TOO FAST. I WANT YOU TO BE GROUNDED IN THE REAL WORLD.
HOW MUCH USE WILL YOU BE TO ME IN THE YEARS TO COME IF YOUR HEAD'S NOT SCREWED ON STRAIGHT?
YEARS TO COME? WITH YOU?
YEARS? YOU HAVE PLANS FOR ME? TELL ME WHAT THEY ARE!
WHEN THE TIME COMES.
TELL ME!
NO.
TELL ME!
NO.
TELL ME!
MAX?
SIGH
...KEYSTONE CITY... FIFTEEN...
HEH
...LIBERATED FROM THE DUNGEONS OF MERCURY...
END

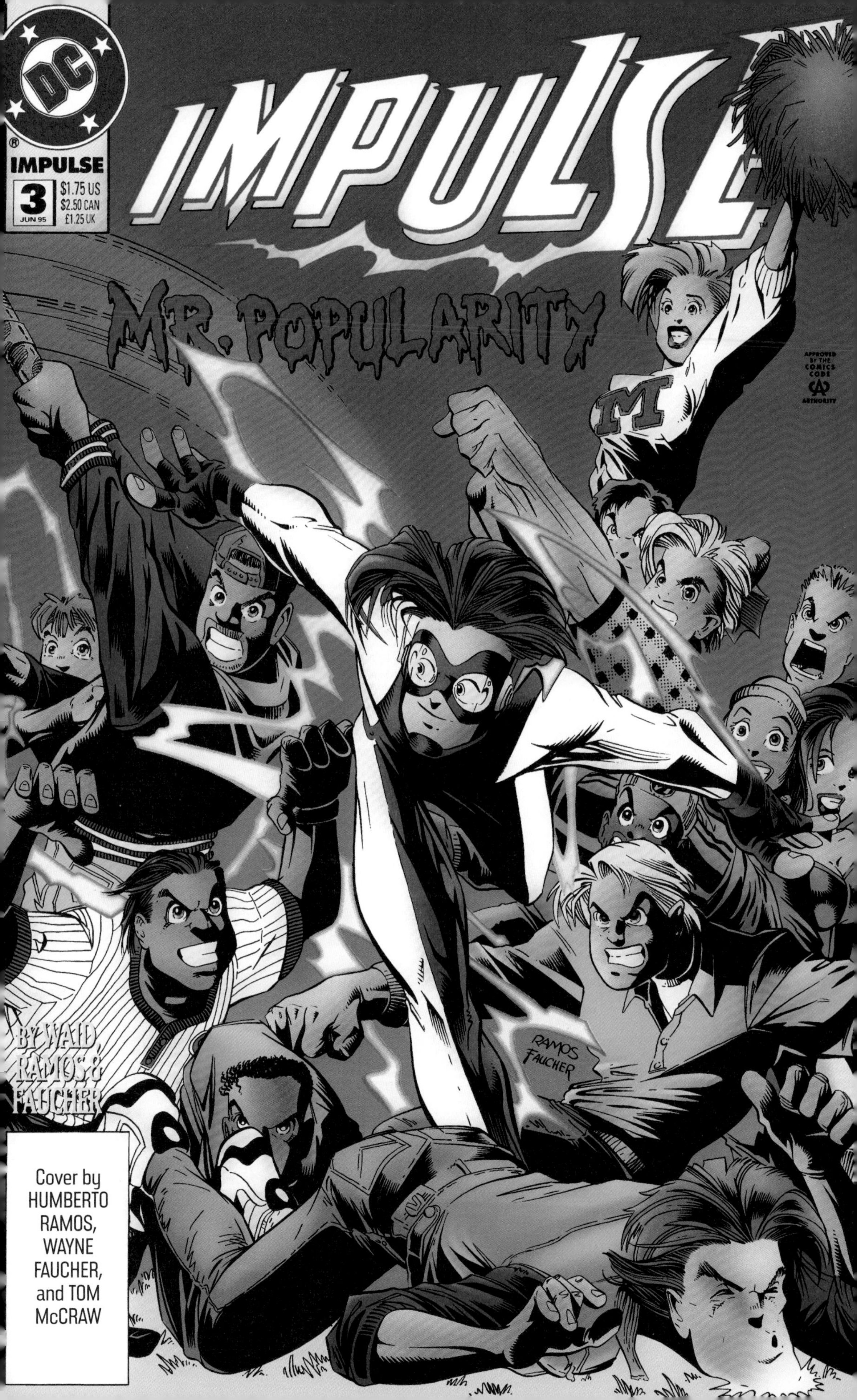
DC
IMPULSE
3
JUN 95
$1.75 US
$2.50 CAN
£1.25 UK
IMPULSE
MR. POPULARITY
APPROVED BY THE COMICS CODE AUTHORITY
BY WAID RAMOS & FAUCHER
RAMOS FAUCHER

Cover by HUMBERTO RAMOS, WAYNE FAUCHER, and TOM McCRAW

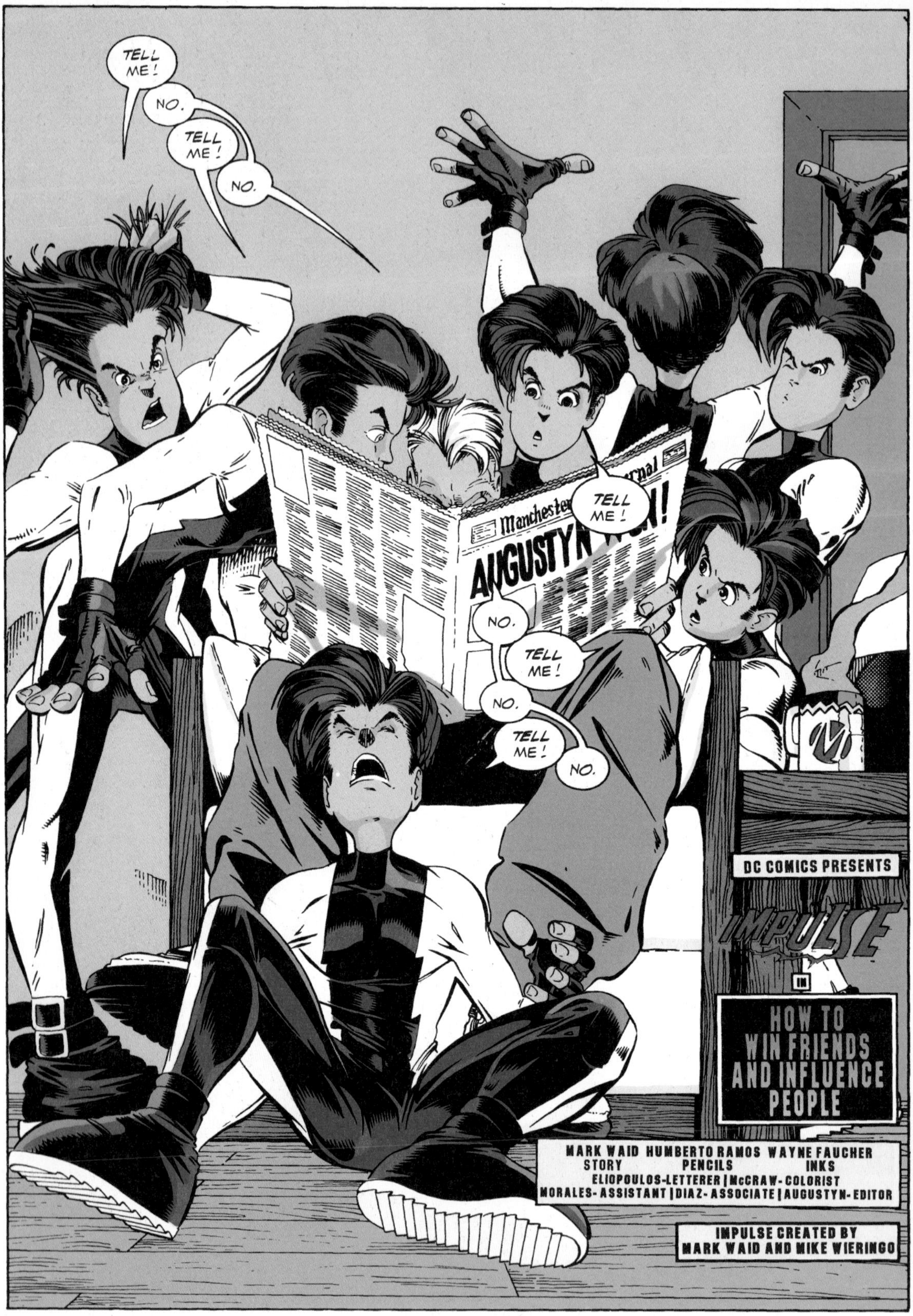
TELL ME!
NO.
TELL ME!
NO.
AUGUSTYN WON!
TELL ME!
NO.
TELL ME!
NO.
TELL ME!
NO.
DC COMICS PRESENTS
IMPULSE
IN
HOW TO WIN FRIENDS AND INFLUENCE PEOPLE
MARK WAID STORY
HUMBERTO RAMOS PENCILS
WAYNE FAUCHER INKS
ELIOPOULOS-LETTERER | McCRAW-COLORIST
MORALES-ASSISTANT | DIAZ-ASSOCIATE | AUGUSTYN-EDITOR
IMPULSE CREATED BY MARK WAID AND MIKE WIERINGO

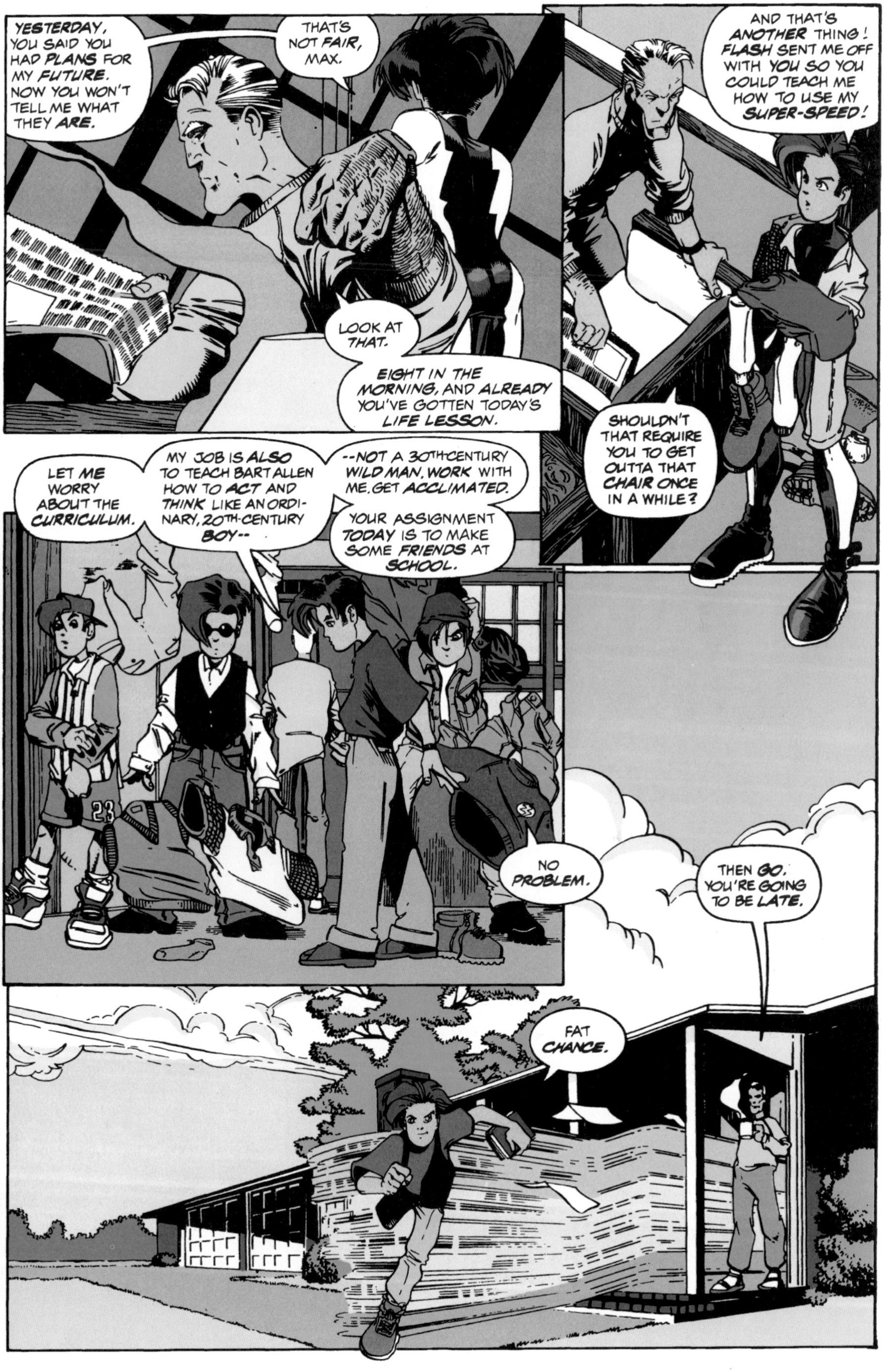
YESTERDAY, YOU SAID YOU HAD PLANS FOR MY FUTURE. NOW YOU WON'T TELL ME WHAT THEY ARE.
THAT'S NOT FAIR, MAX.
LOOK AT THAT.
EIGHT IN THE MORNING, AND ALREADY YOU'VE GOTTEN TODAY'S LIFE LESSON.
AND THAT'S ANOTHER THING! FLASH SENT ME OFF WITH YOU SO YOU COULD TEACH ME HOW TO USE MY SUPER-SPEED!
SHOULDN'T THAT REQUIRE YOU TO GET OUTTA THAT CHAIR ONCE IN A WHILE?
LET ME WORRY ABOUT THE CURRICULUM.
MY JOB IS ALSO TO TEACH BART ALLEN HOW TO ACT AND THINK LIKE AN ORDINARY, 20TH-CENTURY BOY--
--NOT A 30TH-CENTURY WILD MAN. WORK WITH ME. GET ACCLIMATED.
YOUR ASSIGNMENT TODAY IS TO MAKE SOME FRIENDS AT SCHOOL.
NO PROBLEM.
THEN GO. YOU'RE GOING TO BE LATE.
FAT CHANCE.

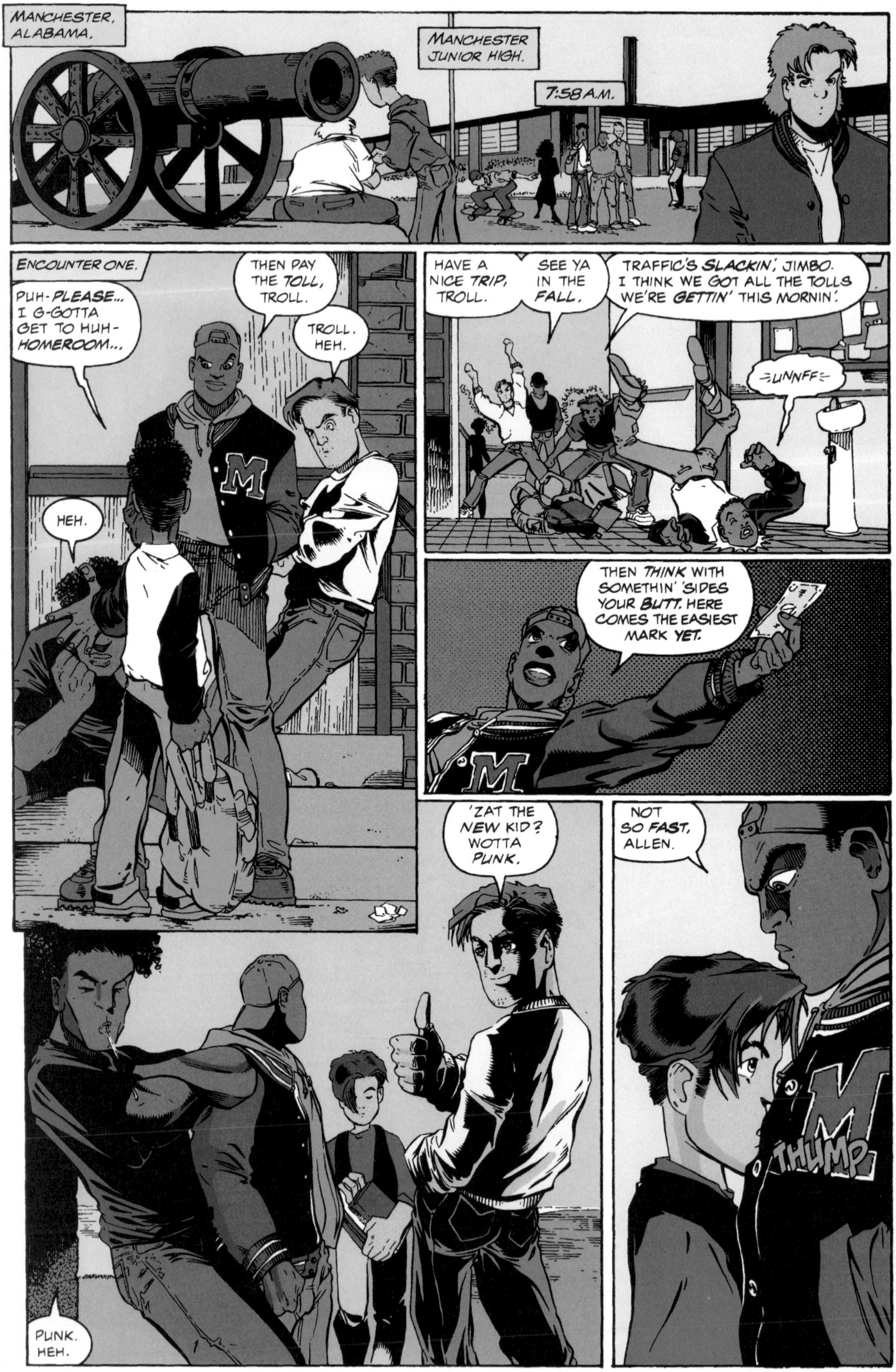
MANCHESTER, ALABAMA.
MANCHESTER JUNIOR HIGH.
7:58 A.M.
ENCOUNTER ONE.
PUH-PLEASE... I G-GOTTA GET TO HUH-HOMEROOM...
THEN PAY THE TOLL, TROLL.
TROLL. HEH.
HEH.
HAVE A NICE TRIP, TROLL.
SEE YA IN THE FALL.
TRAFFIC'S SLACKIN', JIMBO. I THINK WE GOT ALL THE TOLLS WE'RE GETTIN' THIS MORNIN'.
UNNFF
THEN THINK WITH SOMETHIN' 'SIDES YOUR BUTT. HERE COMES THE EASIEST MARK YET.
'ZAT THE NEW KID? WOTTA PUNK.
PUNK. HEH.
NOT SO FAST, ALLEN.
THUMP

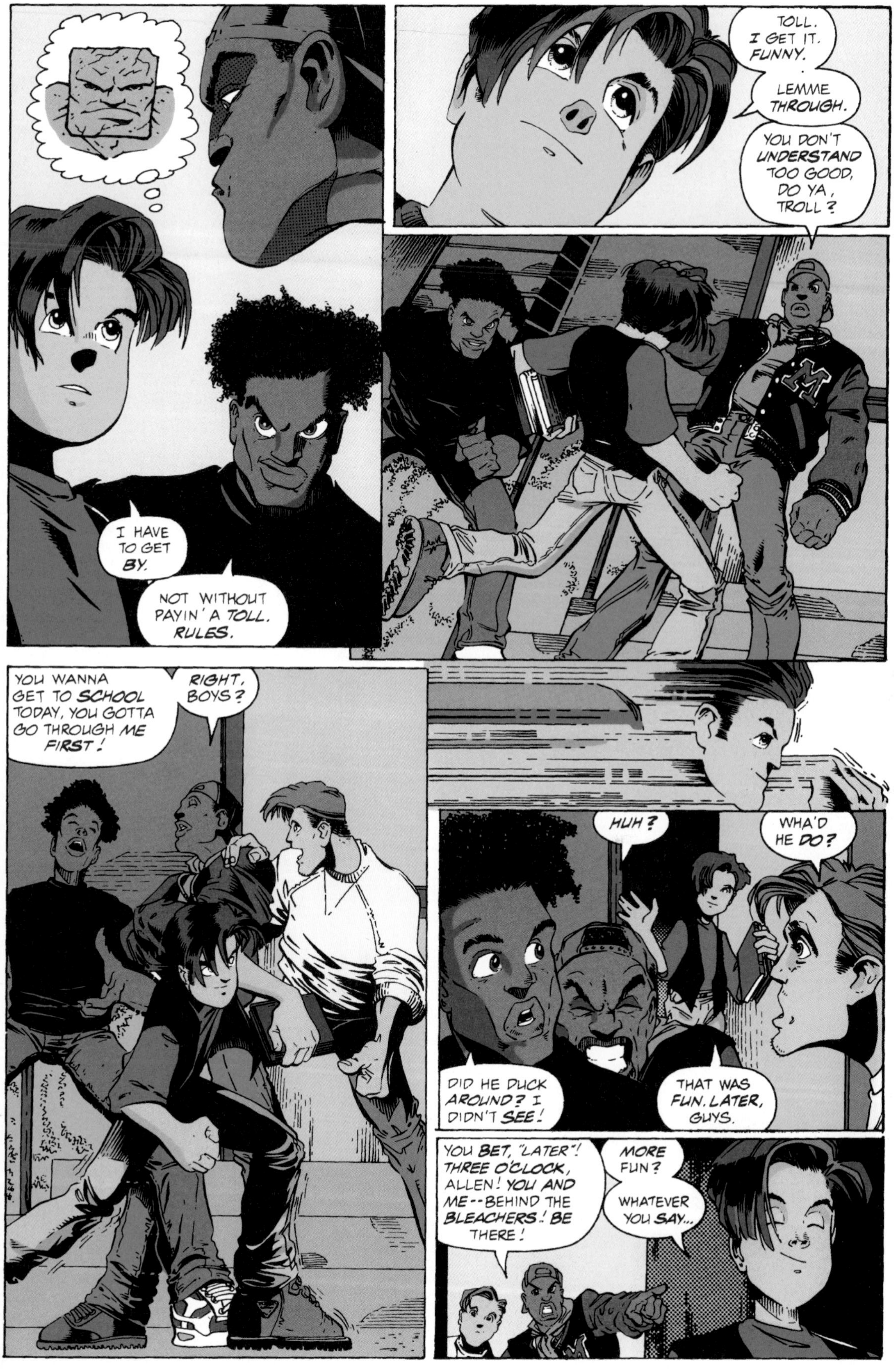
I HAVE TO GET BY.
NOT WITHOUT PAYIN' A TOLL. RULES.
TOLL. I GET IT. FUNNY.
LEMME THROUGH.
YOU DON'T UNDERSTAND TOO GOOD, DO YA, TROLL?
YOU WANNA GET TO SCHOOL TODAY, YOU GOTTA GO THROUGH ME FIRST!
RIGHT, BOYS?
HUH?
WHA'D HE DO?
DID HE DUCK AROUND? I DIDN'T SEE!
THAT WAS FUN. LATER, GUYS.
YOU BET, "LATER"! THREE O'CLOCK, ALLEN! YOU AND ME--BEHIND THE BLEACHERS! BE THERE!
MORE FUN?
WHATEVER YOU SAY...

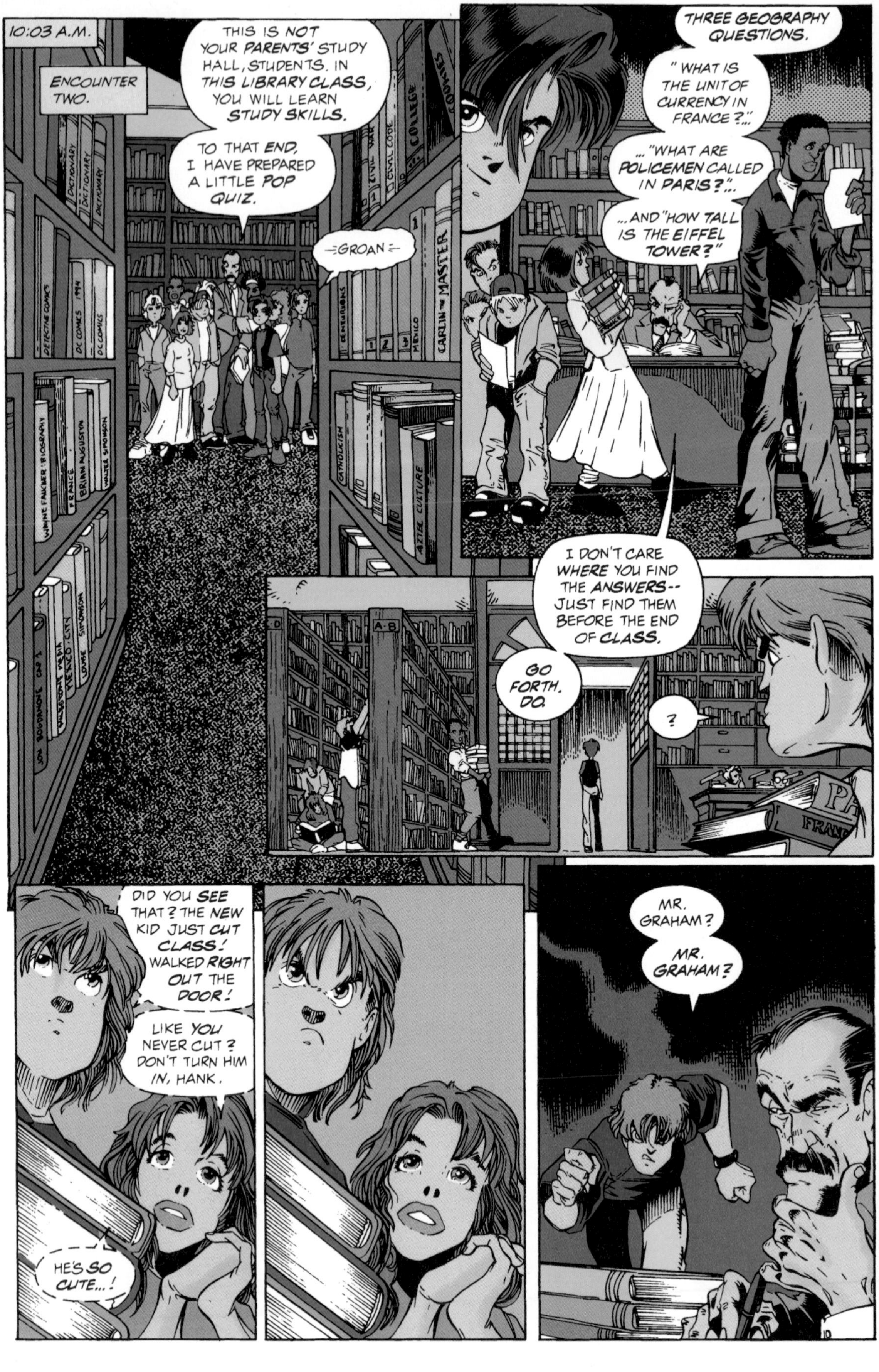
10:03 A.M.
ENCOUNTER TWO.
THIS IS NOT YOUR PARENTS' STUDY HALL, STUDENTS. IN THIS LIBRARY CLASS, YOU WILL LEARN STUDY SKILLS.
TO THAT END, I HAVE PREPARED A LITTLE POP QUIZ.
=GROAN=
THREE GEOGRAPHY QUESTIONS.
"WHAT IS THE UNIT OF CURRENCY IN FRANCE?"...
..."WHAT ARE POLICEMEN CALLED IN PARIS?"...
...AND "HOW TALL IS THE EIFFEL TOWER?"
I DON'T CARE WHERE YOU FIND THE ANSWERS-- JUST FIND THEM BEFORE THE END OF CLASS.
GO FORTH. DO.
?
DID YOU SEE THAT? THE NEW KID JUST CUT CLASS! WALKED RIGHT OUT THE DOOR!
LIKE YOU NEVER CUT? DON'T TURN HIM IN, HANK.
HE'S SO CUTE...!
MR. GRAHAM?
MR. GRAHAM?

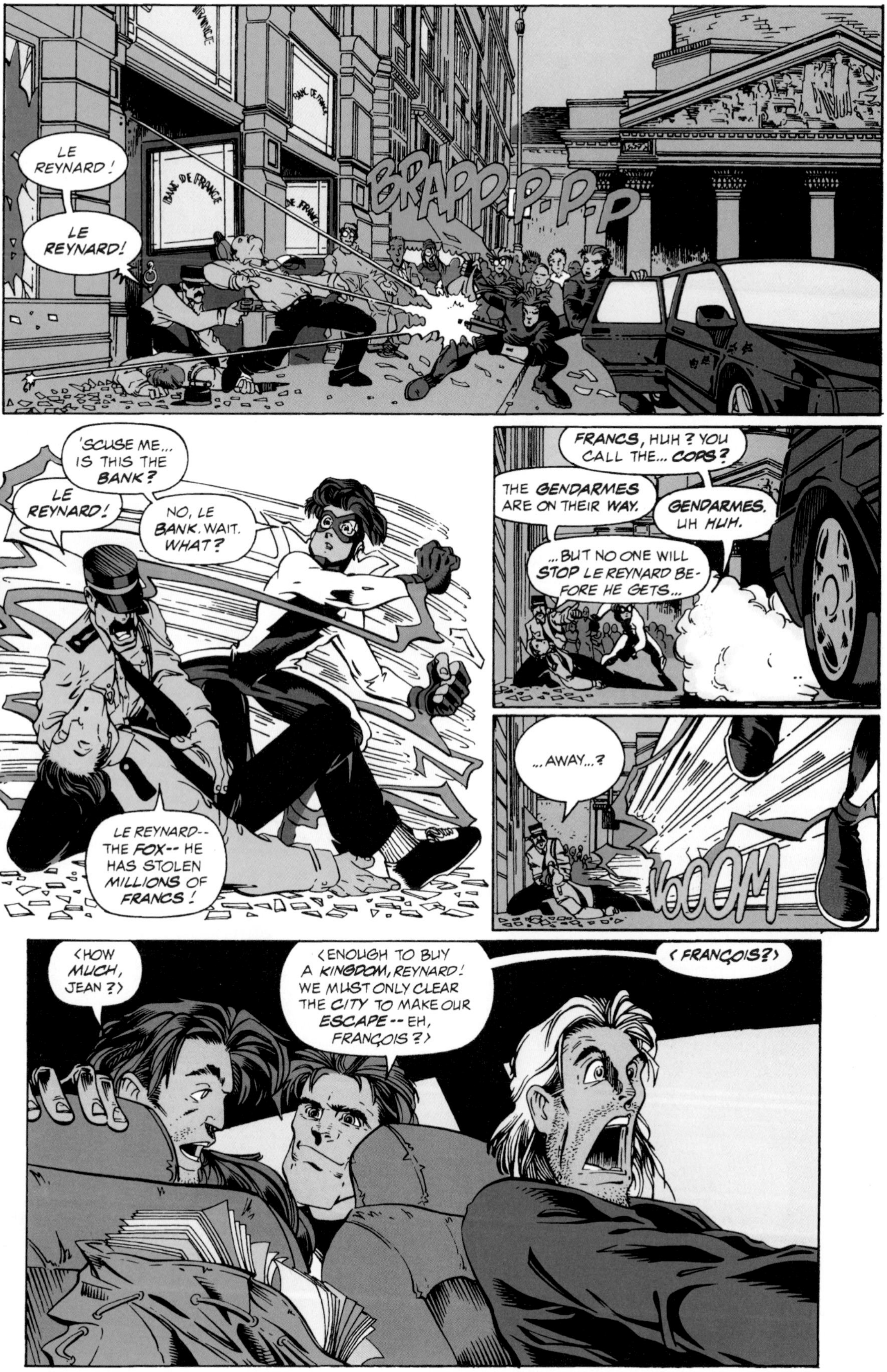
LE REYNARD!
LE REYNARD!
BRAPP-P-P-P
BANK DE FRANCE
'SCUSE ME... IS THIS THE BANK?
LE REYNARD!
NO, LE BANK. WAIT. WHAT?
LE REYNARD-- THE FOX-- HE HAS STOLEN MILLIONS OF FRANCS!
FRANCS, HUH? YOU CALL THE... COPS?
THE GENDARMES ARE ON THEIR WAY.
GENDARMES. UH HUH.
...BUT NO ONE WILL STOP LE REYNARD BEFORE HE GETS...
...AWAY...?
VoOOM
<HOW MUCH, JEAN?>
<ENOUGH TO BUY A KINGDOM, REYNARD! WE MUST ONLY CLEAR THE CITY TO MAKE OUR ESCAPE-- EH, FRANÇOIS?>
<FRANÇOIS?>

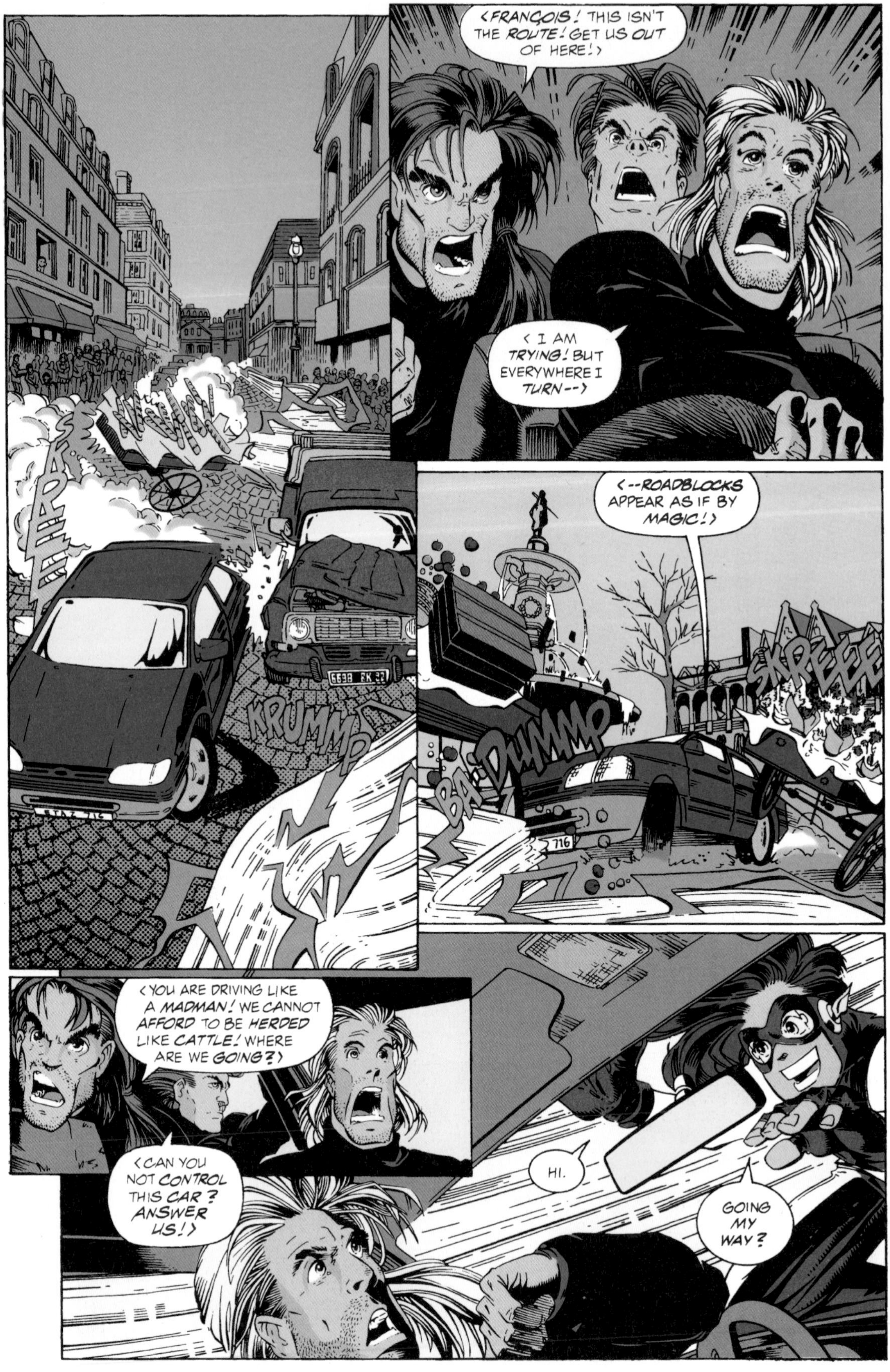

SKREE
KRUMMP
<FRANÇOIS! THIS ISN'T THE ROUTE! GET US OUT OF HERE!>
<I AM TRYING! BUT EVERYWHERE I TURN-->
<--ROADBLOCKS APPEAR AS IF BY MAGIC!>
BA-DUMMP
SKREEE
<YOU ARE DRIVING LIKE A MADMAN! WE CANNOT AFFORD TO BE HERDED LIKE CATTLE! WHERE ARE WE GOING?>
<CAN YOU NOT CONTROL THIS CAR? ANSWER US!>
HI.
GOING MY WAY?

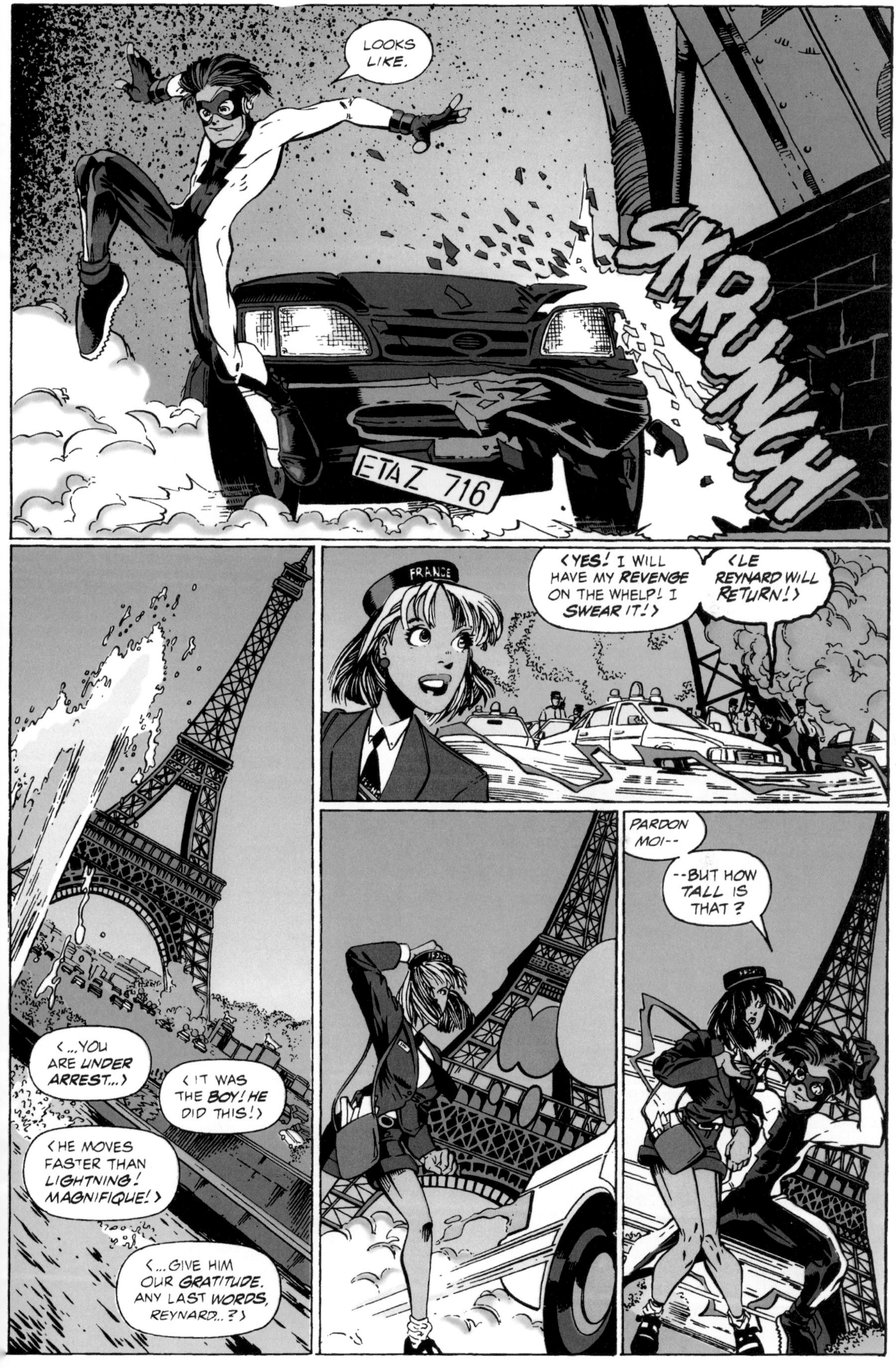
LOOKS LIKE.
SKRUNCH
ETAZ 716
<...YOU ARE UNDER ARREST...>
<IT WAS THE BOY! HE DID THIS!>
<HE MOVES FASTER THAN LIGHTNING! MAGNIFIQUE!>
<...GIVE HIM OUR GRATITUDE. ANY LAST WORDS, REYNARD...?>
FRANCE
<YES! I WILL HAVE MY REVENGE ON THE WHELP! I SWEAR IT!>
<LE REYNARD WILL RETURN!>
PARDON MOI--
--BUT HOW TALL IS THAT?

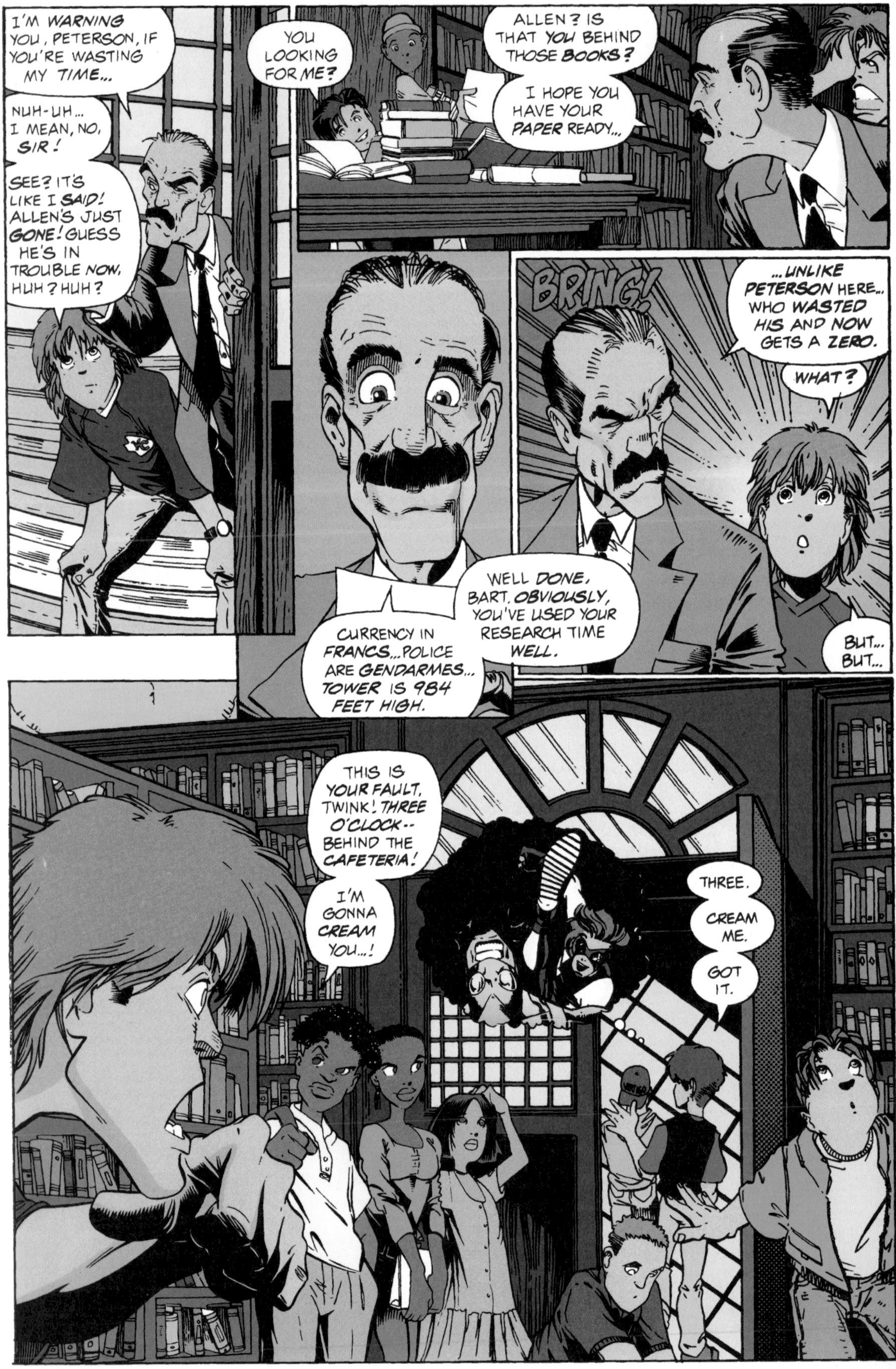

I'M WARNING YOU, PETERSON, IF YOU'RE WASTING MY TIME...
NUH-UH... I MEAN, NO, SIR!
SEE? IT'S LIKE I SAID! ALLEN'S JUST GONE! GUESS HE'S IN TROUBLE NOW, HUH? HUH?
YOU LOOKING FOR ME?
ALLEN? IS THAT YOU BEHIND THOSE BOOKS?
I HOPE YOU HAVE YOUR PAPER READY...
CURRENCY IN FRANCS... POLICE ARE GENDARMES... TOWER IS 984 FEET HIGH.
WELL DONE, BART. OBVIOUSLY, YOU'VE USED YOUR RESEARCH TIME WELL.
BRING!
...UNLIKE PETERSON HERE... WHO WASTED HIS AND NOW GETS A ZERO.
WHAT?
BUT... BUT...
THIS IS YOUR FAULT, TWINK! THREE O'CLOCK-- BEHIND THE CAFETERIA!
I'M GONNA CREAM YOU...!
THREE.
CREAM ME.
GOT IT.

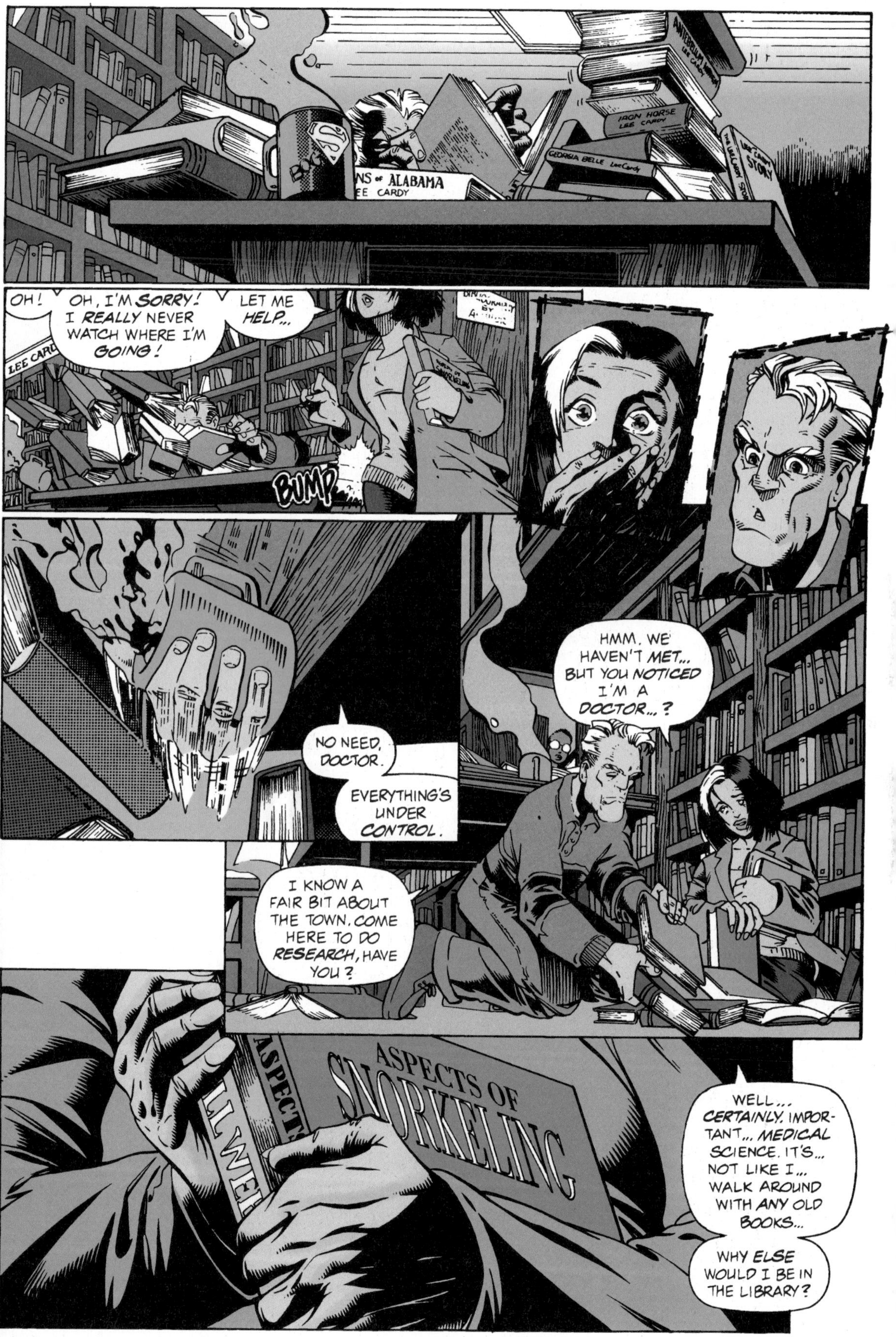
IRON HORSE LEE CARDY
GEORGIA BELLE Lee Cardy
ALABAMA
LEE CARDY
OH!
OH, I'M SORRY! I REALLY NEVER WATCH WHERE I'M GOING!
LET ME HELP...
BUMP
NO NEED, DOCTOR.
EVERYTHING'S UNDER CONTROL.
HMM. WE HAVEN'T MET... BUT YOU NOTICED I'M A DOCTOR...?
I KNOW A FAIR BIT ABOUT THE TOWN. COME HERE TO DO RESEARCH, HAVE YOU?
ASPECTS OF SNORKELING
WELL... CERTAINLY. IMPORTANT... MEDICAL SCIENCE. IT'S... NOT LIKE I... WALK AROUND WITH ANY OLD BOOKS...
WHY ELSE WOULD I BE IN THE LIBRARY?

WHY *INDEED?*

I'VE... *NOTICED* YOU HERE. BEEN *HOPING* WE'D MEET, HELEN CLAIBORNE.

MAX CRANDALL. HI.

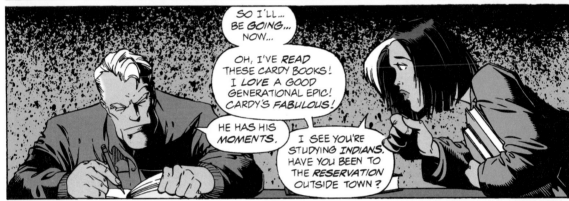

SO I'LL... BE *GOING*... NOW...

OH, I'VE *READ* THESE CARDY BOOKS! I *LOVE* A GOOD GENERATIONAL EPIC! CARDY'S *FABULOUS!*

HE HAS HIS *MOMENTS.*

I SEE YOU'RE STUDYING *INDIANS.* HAVE YOU BEEN TO THE *RESERVATION* OUTSIDE TOWN?

NOT *LATELY.*

THEY'VE SET UP AN *ENORMOUS* CASINO. IT'S *QUITE* THE *SPECTACLE.*

PERHAPS IF YOU'RE NOT... *DOING* ANYTHING THIS *WEEKEND...* WE COULD...

I *APPRECIATE* THE *OFFER,* DOCTOR...

...BUT I HAVE PLANS WITH MY *NEPHEW.* THANK YOU *ANYWAY.*

GOODBYE.

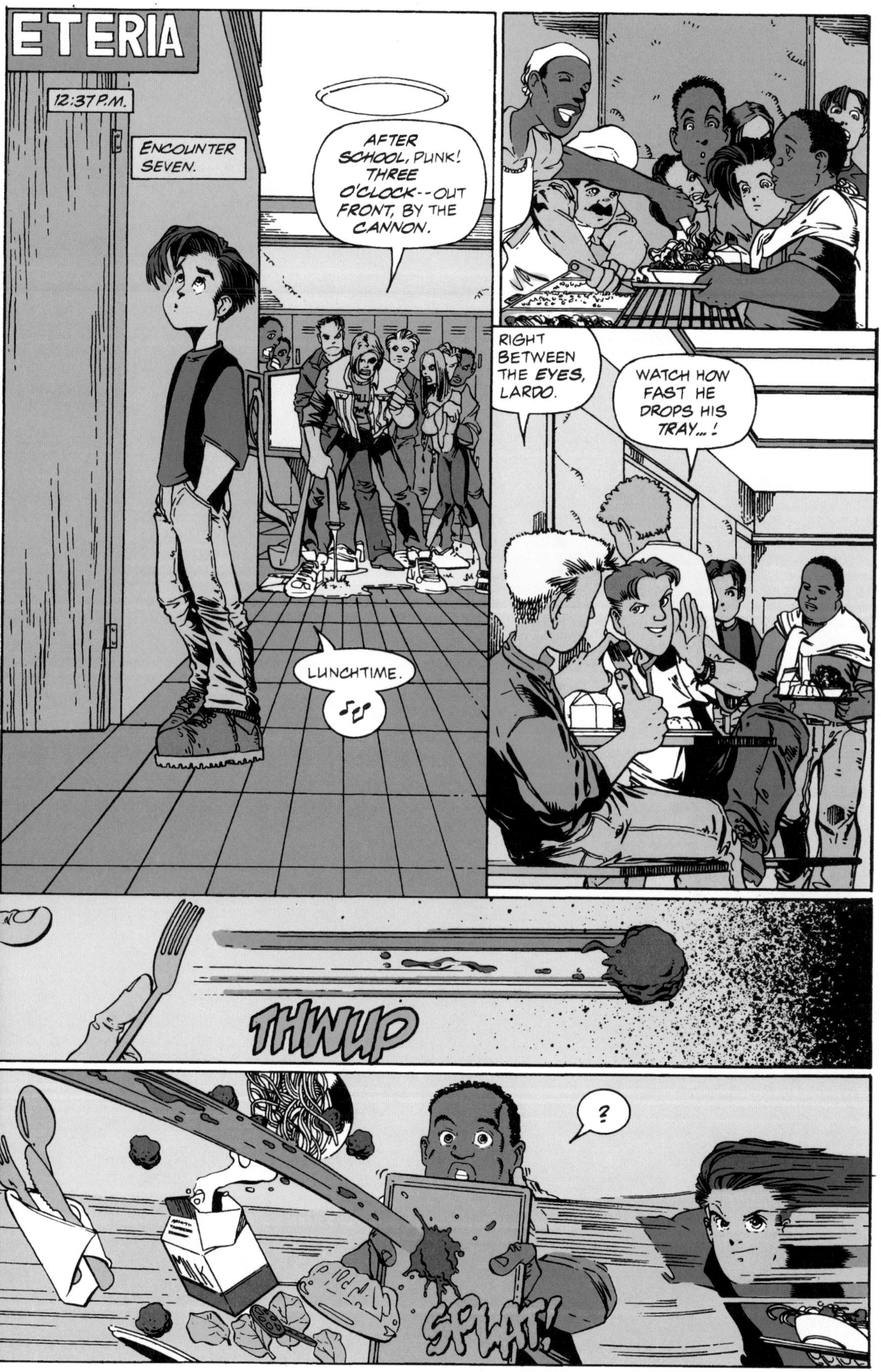
ETERIA
12:37 P.M.
ENCOUNTER SEVEN.
AFTER SCHOOL, PUNK! THREE O'CLOCK--OUT FRONT, BY THE CANNON.
LUNCHTIME.
RIGHT BETWEEN THE EYES, LARDO.
WATCH HOW FAST HE DROPS HIS TRAY...!
THWUP
?
SPLAT!

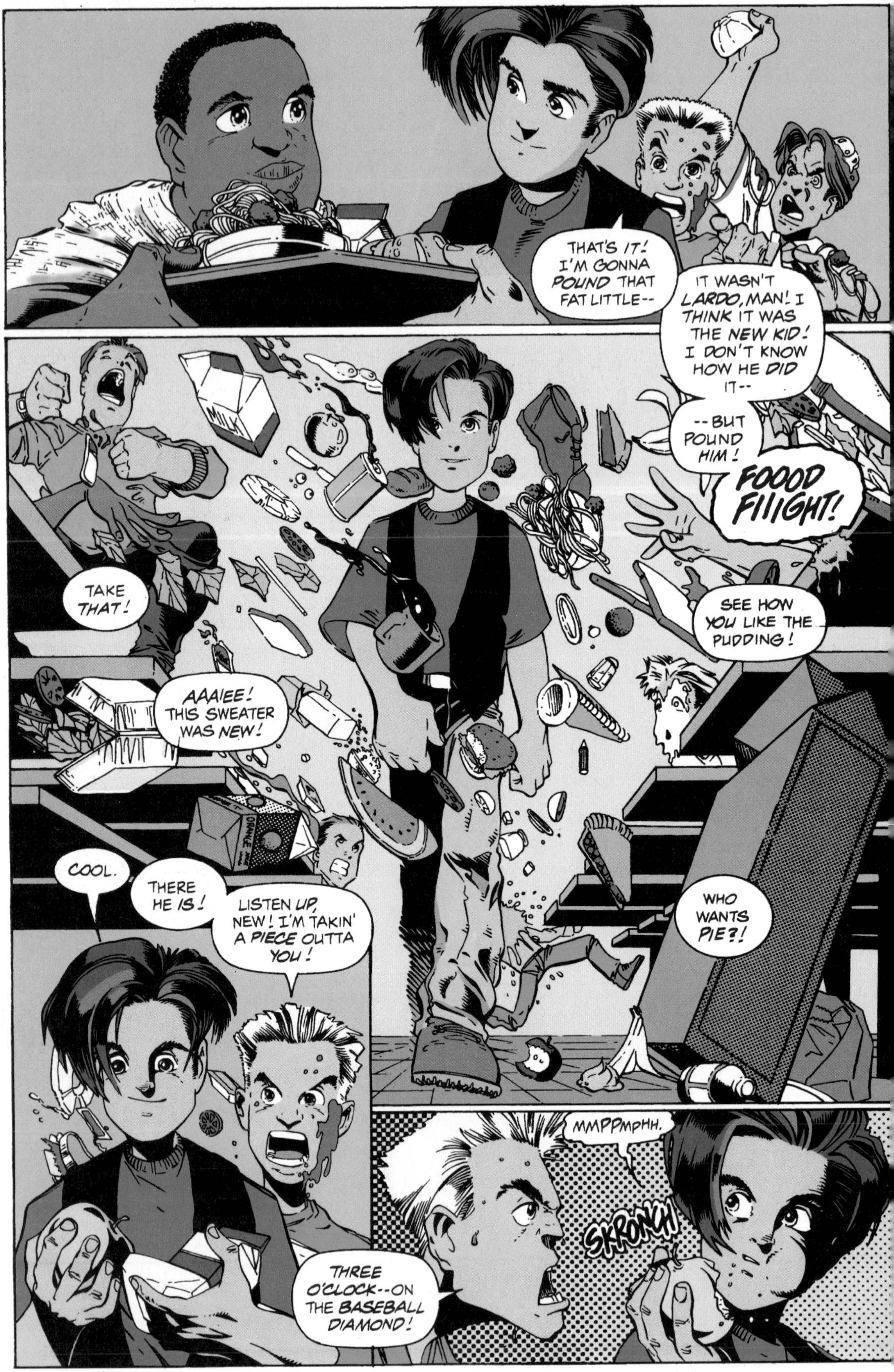
THAT'S IT! I'M GONNA POUND THAT FAT LITTLE--
IT WASN'T LARDO, MAN! I THINK IT WAS THE NEW KID! I DON'T KNOW HOW HE DID IT--
--BUT POUND HIM!
FOOOD FIIIGHT!
MILK
TAKE THAT!
SEE HOW YOU LIKE THE PUDDING!
AAAIEE! THIS SWEATER WAS NEW!
ORANGE
WHO WANTS PIE?!
COOL.
THERE HE IS!
LISTEN UP, NEW! I'M TAKIN' A PIECE OUTTA YOU!
MMPPmphh.
SKRONCH
THREE O'CLOCK--ON THE BASEBALL DIAMOND!

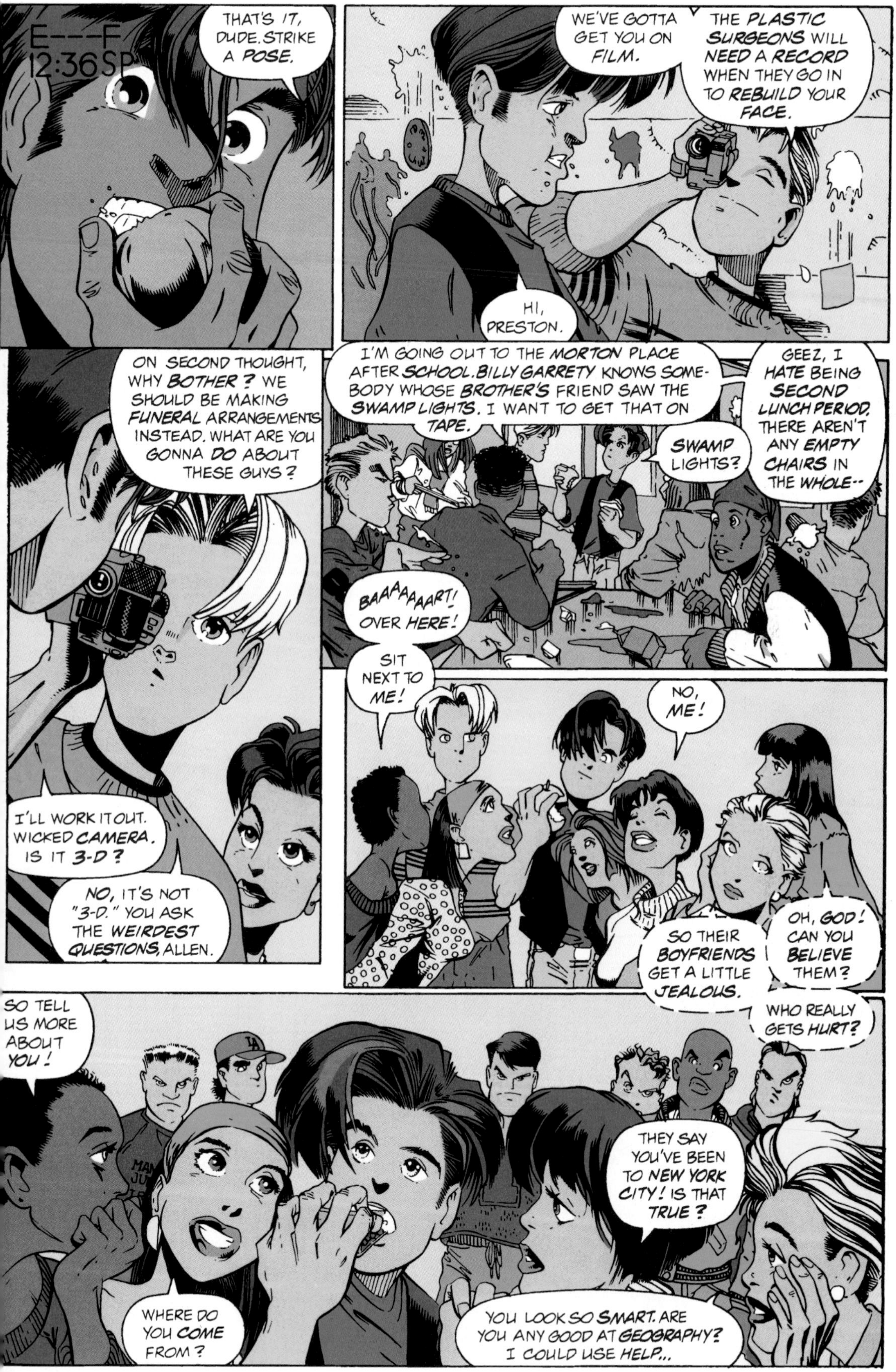
E---F
12:36SP
THAT'S IT, DUDE. STRIKE A POSE.
WE'VE GOTTA GET YOU ON FILM.
THE PLASTIC SURGEONS WILL NEED A RECORD WHEN THEY GO IN TO REBUILD YOUR FACE.
HI, PRESTON.
ON SECOND THOUGHT, WHY BOTHER? WE SHOULD BE MAKING FUNERAL ARRANGEMENTS INSTEAD. WHAT ARE YOU GONNA DO ABOUT THESE GUYS?
I'LL WORK IT OUT. WICKED CAMERA. IS IT 3-D?
NO, IT'S NOT "3-D." YOU ASK THE WEIRDEST QUESTIONS, ALLEN.
I'M GOING OUT TO THE MORTON PLACE AFTER SCHOOL. BILLY GARRETY KNOWS SOMEBODY WHOSE BROTHER'S FRIEND SAW THE SWAMP LIGHTS. I WANT TO GET THAT ON TAPE.
SWAMP LIGHTS?
GEEZ, I HATE BEING SECOND LUNCH PERIOD. THERE AREN'T ANY EMPTY CHAIRS IN THE WHOLE--
BAAAAAAART! OVER HERE!
SIT NEXT TO ME!
NO, ME!
SO THEIR BOYFRIENDS GET A LITTLE JEALOUS.
OH, GOD! CAN YOU BELIEVE THEM?
WHO REALLY GETS HURT?
SO TELL US MORE ABOUT YOU!
THEY SAY YOU'VE BEEN TO NEW YORK CITY! IS THAT TRUE?
WHERE DO YOU COME FROM?
YOU LOOK SO SMART. ARE YOU ANY GOOD AT GEOGRAPHY? I COULD USE HELP...

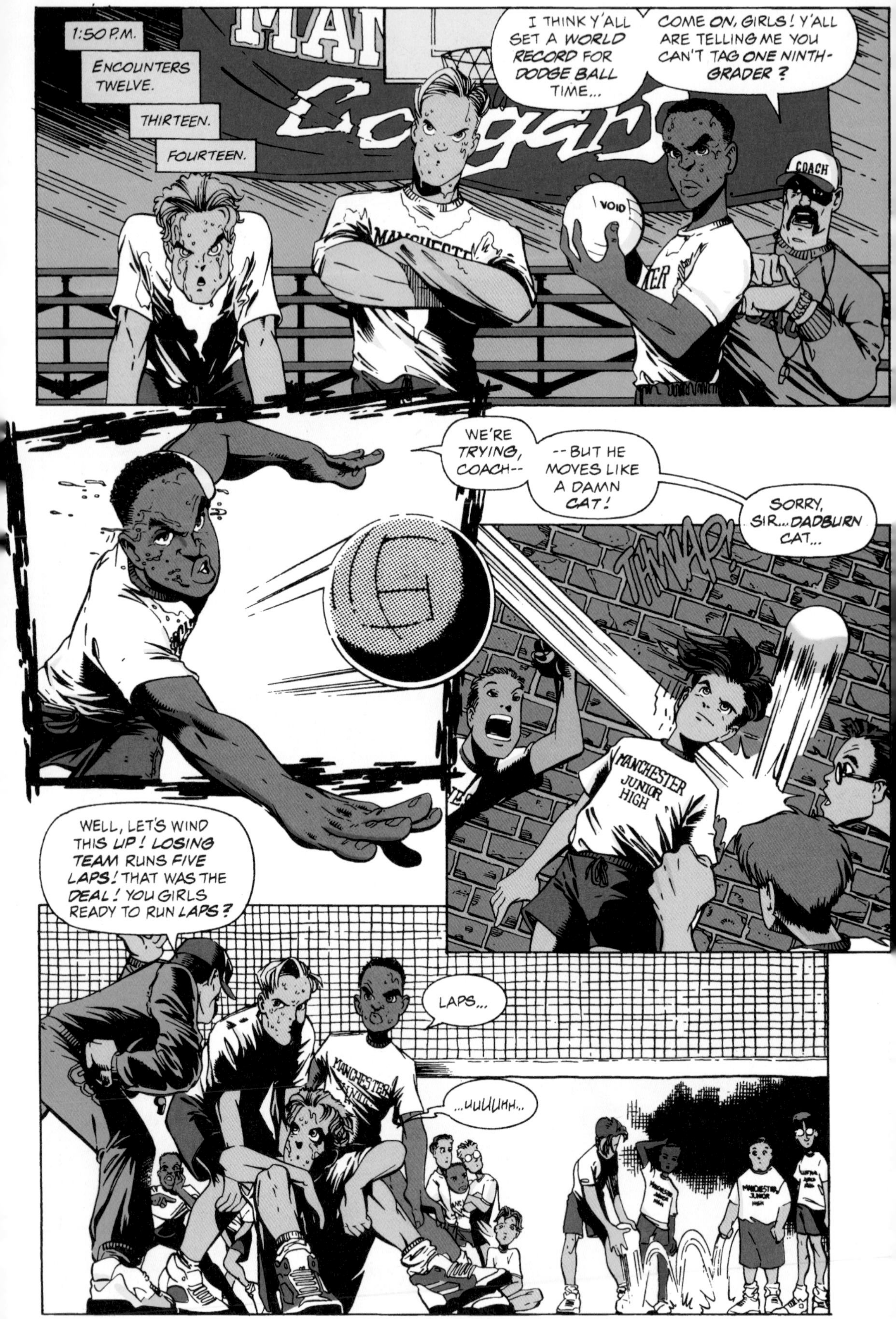

1:50 P.M.
ENCOUNTERS TWELVE.
THIRTEEN.
FOURTEEN.
I THINK Y'ALL SET A WORLD RECORD FOR DODGE BALL TIME...
COME ON, GIRLS! Y'ALL ARE TELLING ME YOU CAN'T TAG ONE NINTH-GRADER?
COACH
VOID
WE'RE TRYING, COACH--
--BUT HE MOVES LIKE A DAMN CAT!
SORRY, SIR... DADBURN CAT...
THWAP!
MANCHESTER JUNIOR HIGH
WELL, LET'S WIND THIS UP! LOSING TEAM RUNS FIVE LAPS! THAT WAS THE DEAL! YOU GIRLS READY TO RUN LAPS?
LAPS...
...UUUUHH...

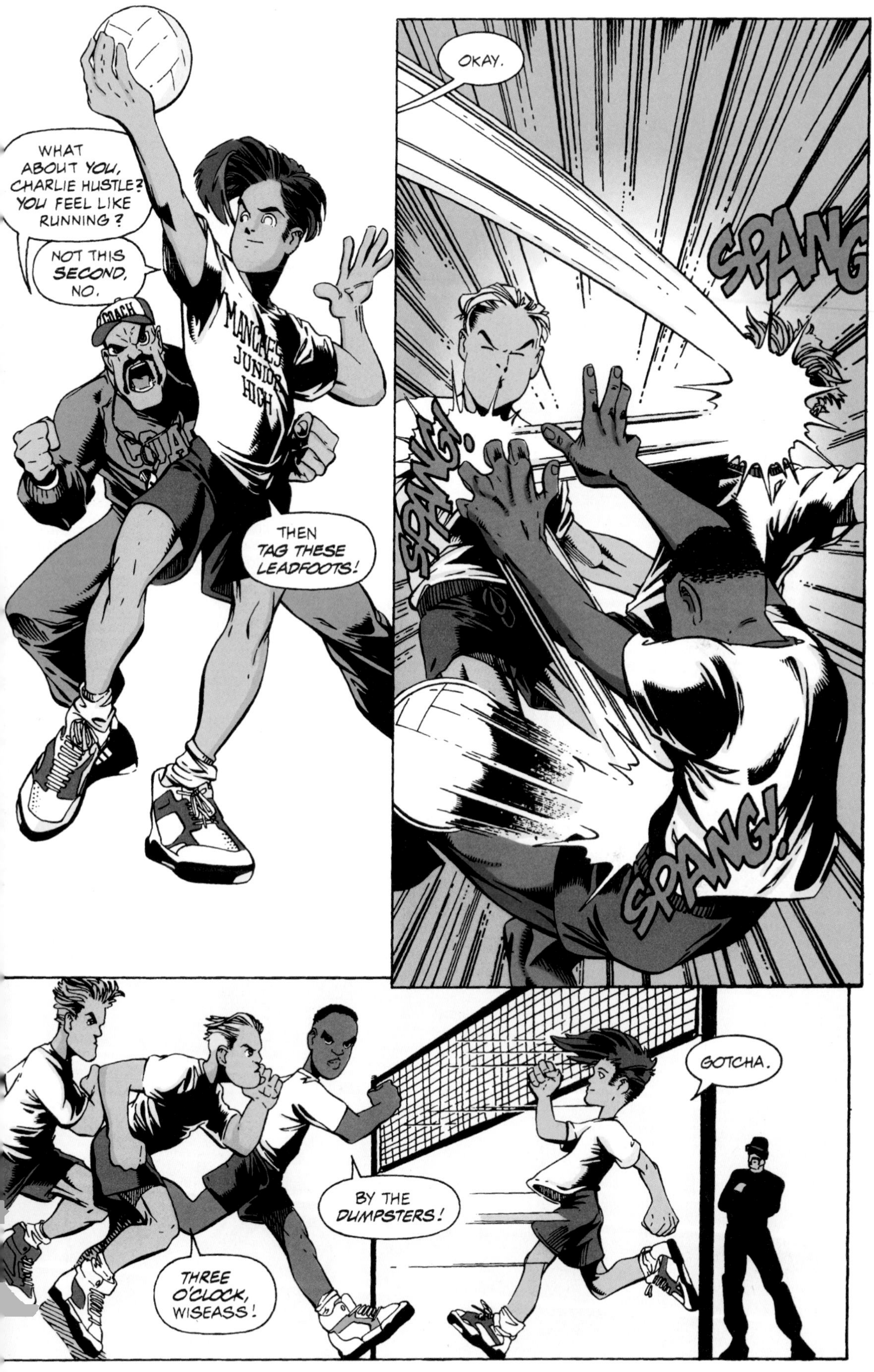
WHAT ABOUT YOU, CHARLIE HUSTLE? YOU FEEL LIKE RUNNING?
NOT THIS SECOND, NO.
THEN TAG THESE LEADFOOTS!
MANCHESTER JUNIOR HIGH
COACH
OKAY.
SPANG
SPANG!
SPANG!
THREE O'CLOCK, WISEASS!
BY THE DUMPSTERS!
GOTCHA.

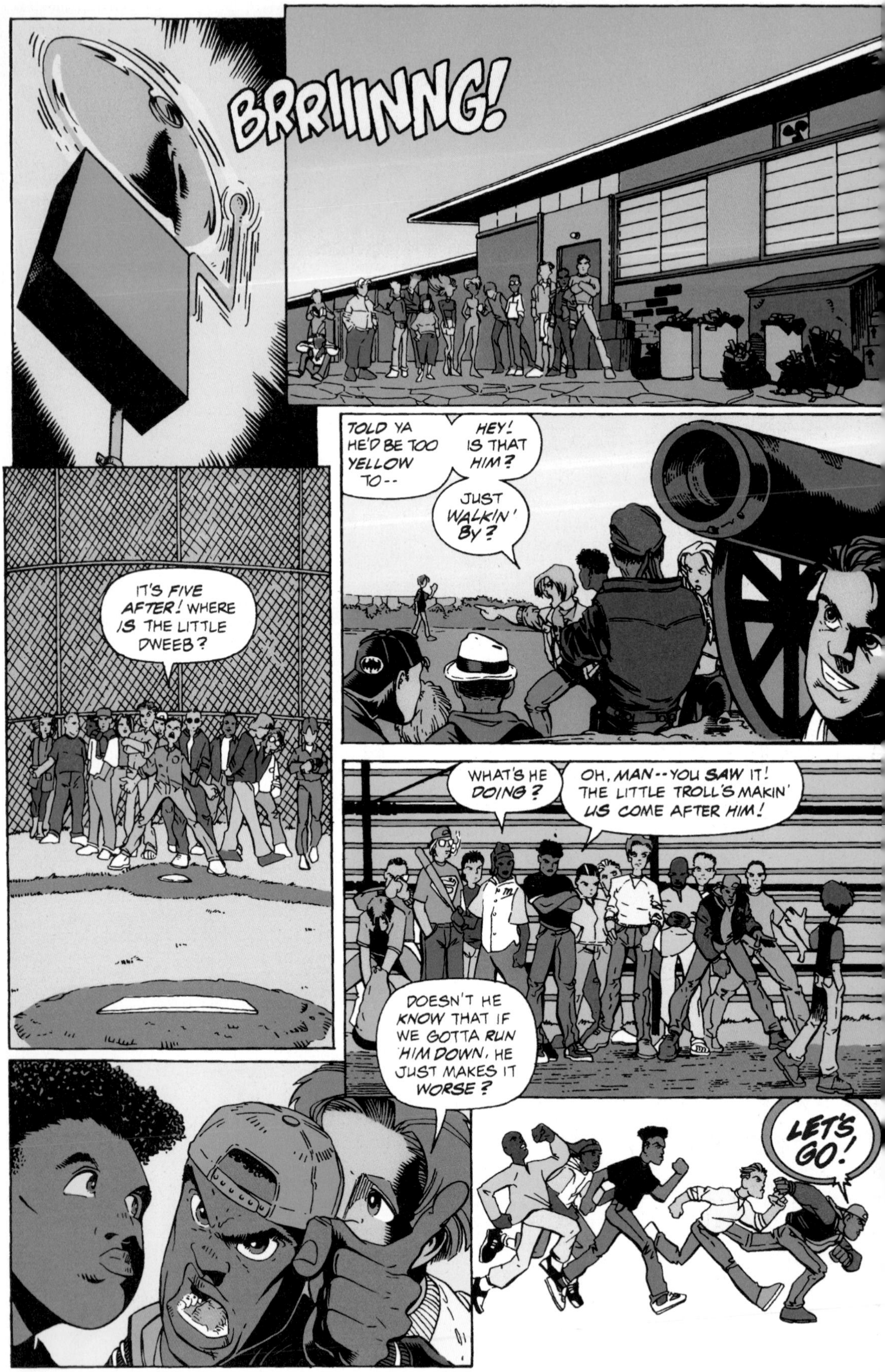
BRRIIINNG!
IT'S FIVE AFTER! WHERE IS THE LITTLE DWEEB?
TOLD YA HE'D BE TOO YELLOW TO--
HEY! IS THAT HIM?
JUST WALKIN' BY?
WHAT'S HE DOING?
OH, MAN--YOU SAW IT! THE LITTLE TROLL'S MAKIN' US COME AFTER HIM!
DOESN'T HE KNOW THAT IF WE GOTTA RUN HIM DOWN, HE JUST MAKES IT WORSE?
LET'S GO!

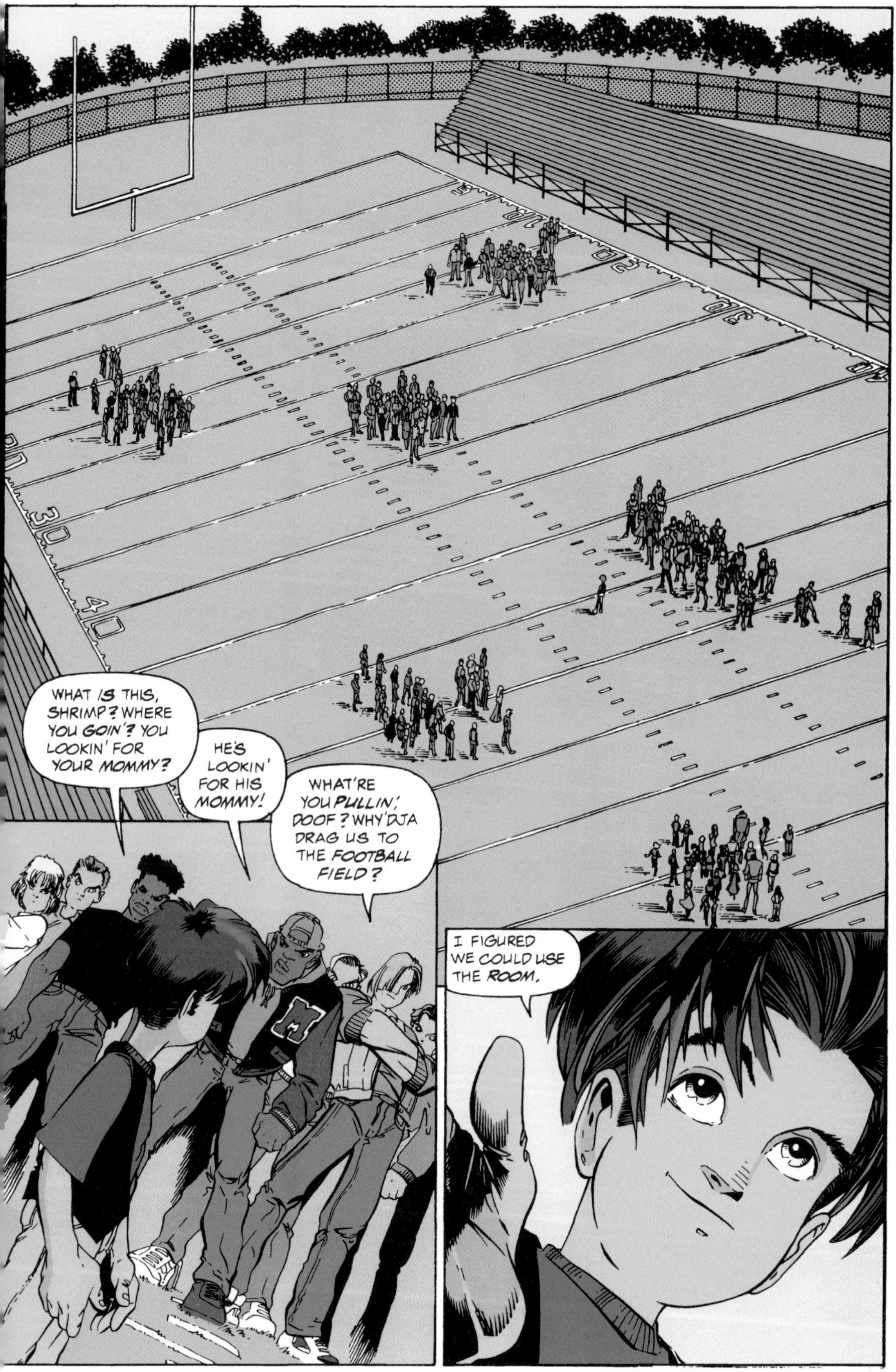
WHAT IS THIS, SHRIMP? WHERE YOU GOIN'? YOU LOOKIN' FOR YOUR MOMMY?
HE'S LOOKIN' FOR HIS MOMMY!
WHAT'RE YOU PULLIN', DOOF? WHY'DJA DRAG US TO THE FOOTBALL FIELD?
I FIGURED WE COULD USE THE ROOM.

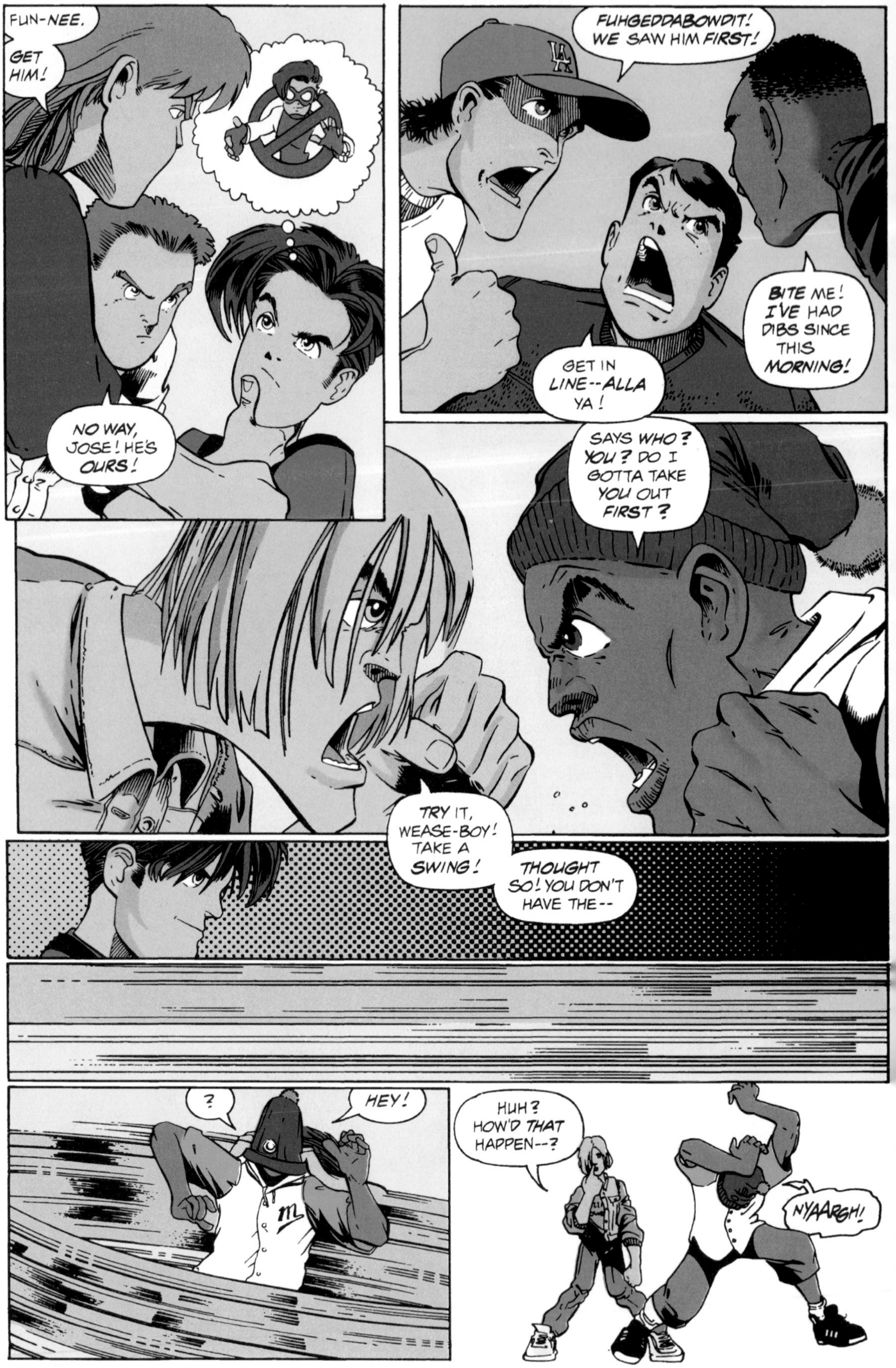
FUN-NEE.
GET HIM!
NO WAY, JOSE! HE'S OURS!
FUHGEDDABOWDIT! WE SAW HIM FIRST!
GET IN LINE--ALLA YA!
BITE ME! I'VE HAD DIBS SINCE THIS MORNING!
SAYS WHO? YOU? DO I GOTTA TAKE YOU OUT FIRST?
TRY IT, WEASE-BOY! TAKE A SWING!
THOUGHT SO! YOU DON'T HAVE THE--
?
HEY!
HUH? HOW'D THAT HAPPEN--?
NYAARGH!

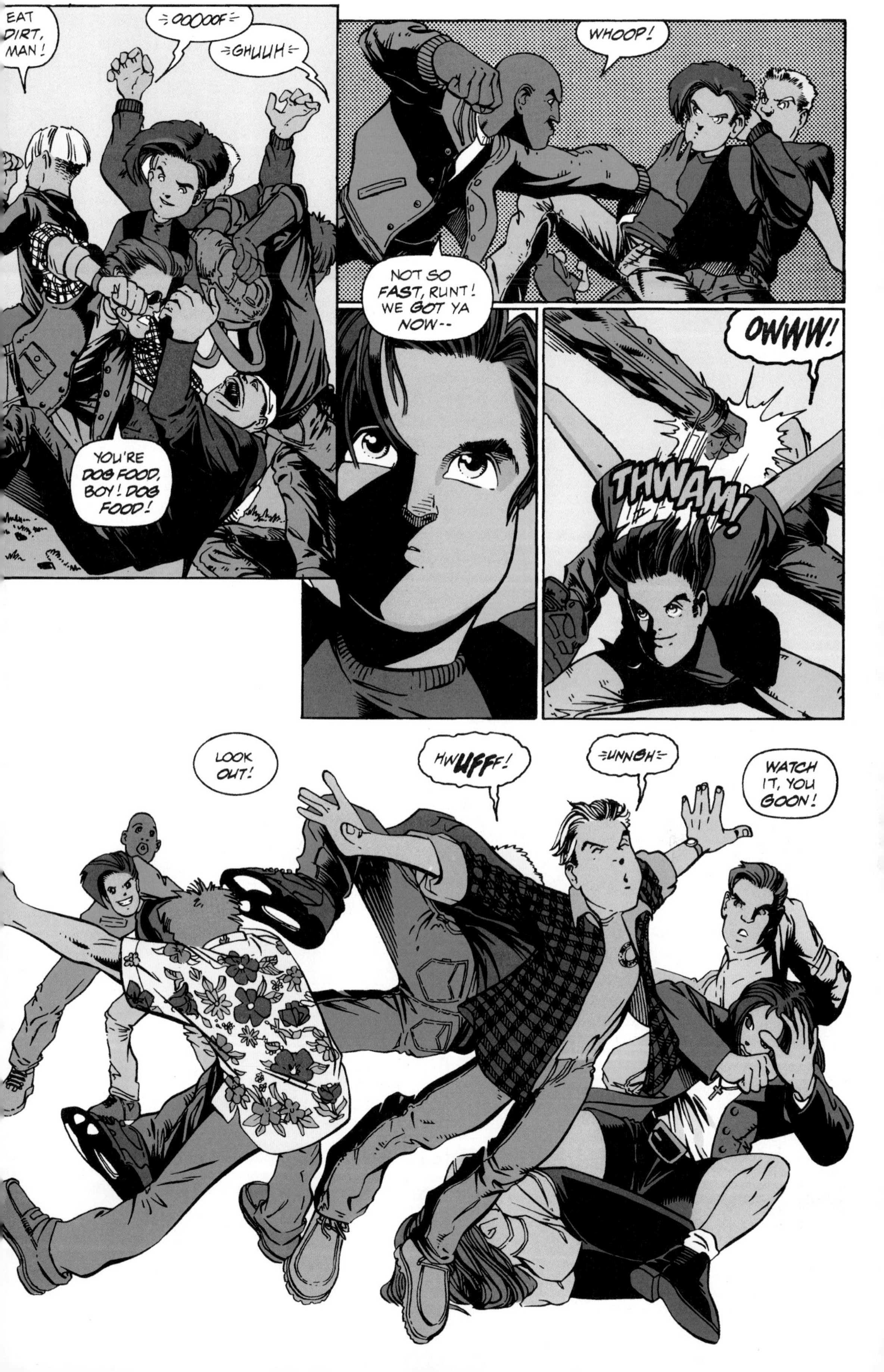
EAT DIRT, MAN!
OOOOOF
GHUUH
WHOOP!
YOU'RE DOG FOOD, BOY! DOG FOOD!
NOT SO FAST, RUNT! WE GOT YA NOW--
OWWW!
THWAM!
LOOK OUT!
HWUFFF!
UNNGH
WATCH IT, YOU GOON!

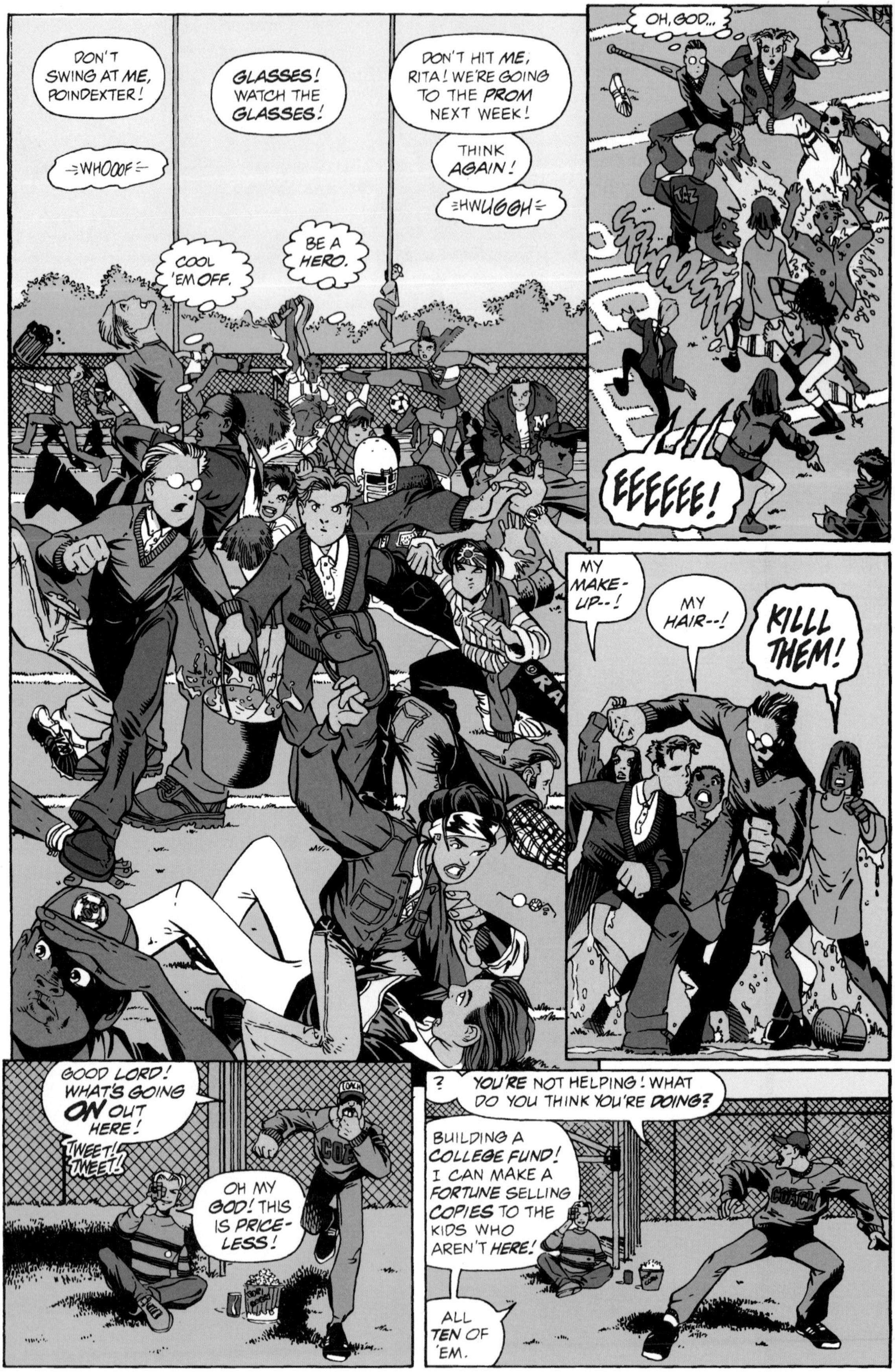
DON'T SWING AT ME, POINDEXTER!
WHOOOF
GLASSES! WATCH THE GLASSES!
DON'T HIT ME, RITA! WE'RE GOING TO THE PROM NEXT WEEK!
THINK AGAIN!
HWUGGH
COOL 'EM OFF.
BE A HERO.
OH, GOD...
SPLOOSH
EEEEEE!
MY MAKE-UP--!
MY HAIR--!
KILLL THEM!
GOOD LORD! WHAT'S GOING ON OUT HERE!
TWEET! TWEET!
OH MY GOD! THIS IS PRICELESS!
? YOU'RE NOT HELPING! WHAT DO YOU THINK YOU'RE DOING?
BUILDING A COLLEGE FUND! I CAN MAKE A FORTUNE SELLING COPIES TO THE KIDS WHO AREN'T HERE!
ALL TEN OF 'EM.

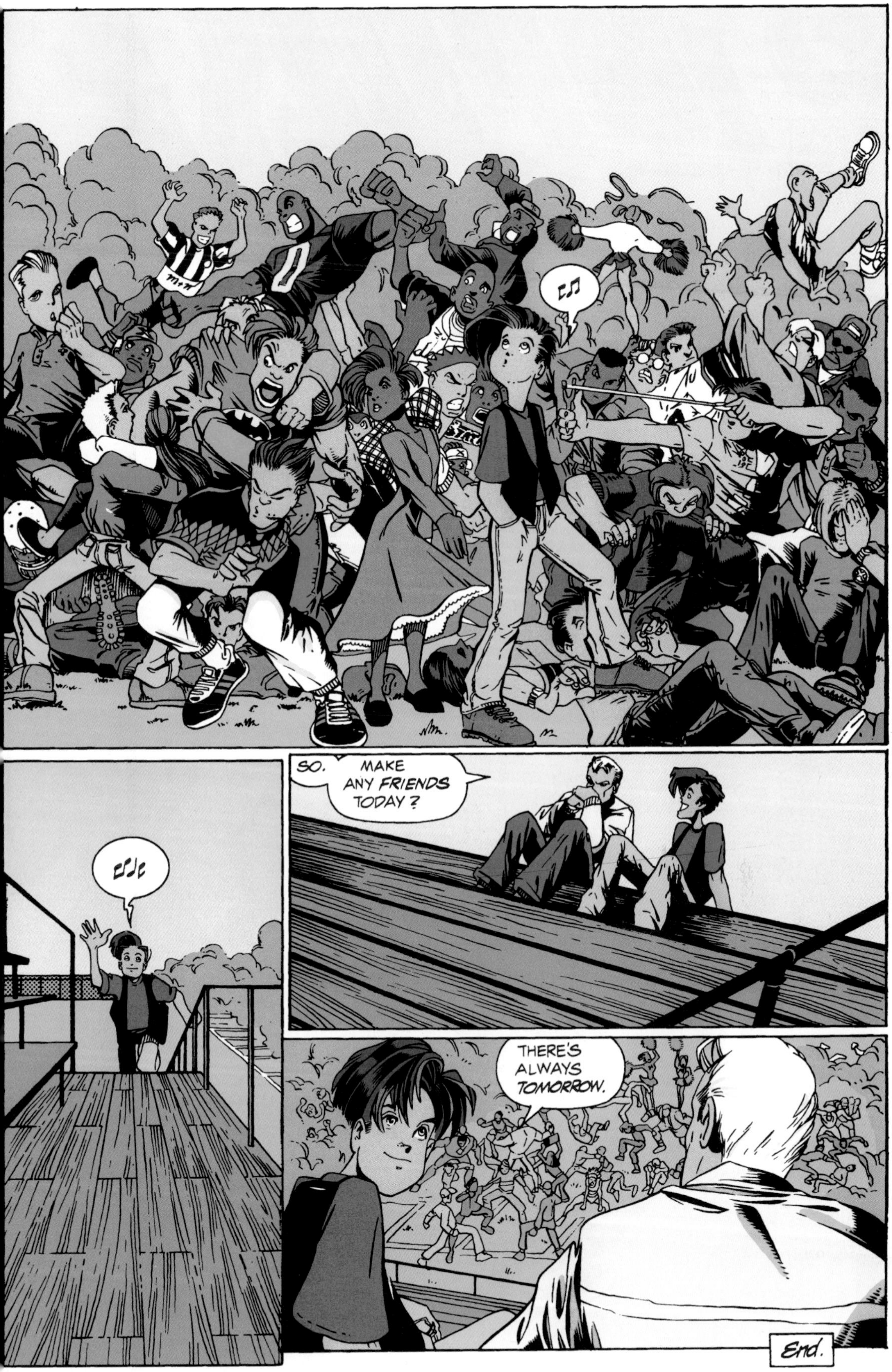

SO. MAKE ANY FRIENDS TODAY?
THERE'S ALWAYS TOMORROW.
End.

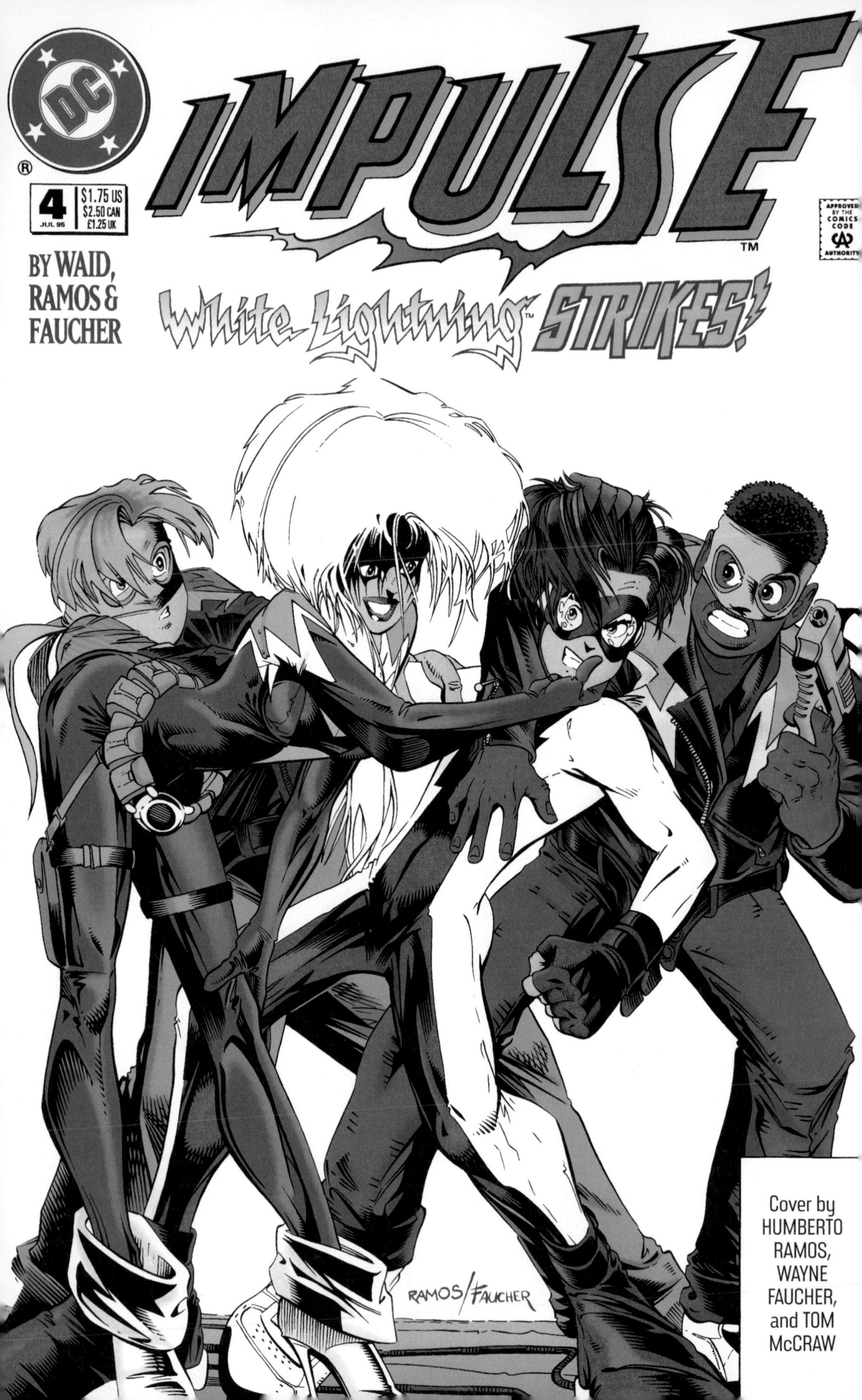

DC
IMPULSE
4
JUL 95
$1.75 US
$2.50 CAN
£1.25 UK
BY WAID, RAMOS & FAUCHER
APPROVED BY THE COMICS CODE AUTHORITY
White Lightning STRIKES!
RAMOS/FAUCHER

Cover by HUMBERTO RAMOS, WAYNE FAUCHER, and TOM McCRAW

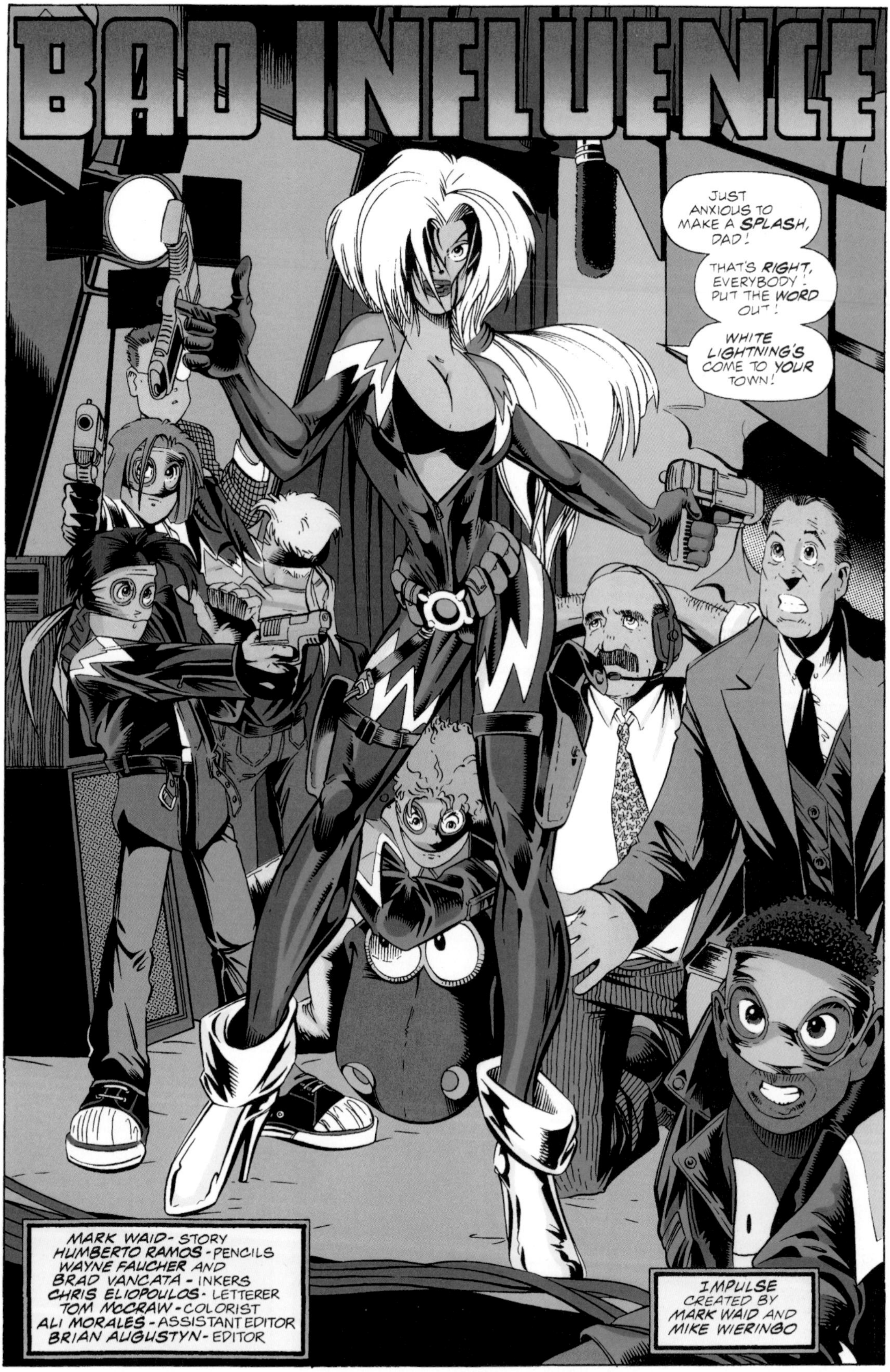
BAD INFLUENCE
JUST ANXIOUS TO MAKE A SPLASH, DAD!
THAT'S RIGHT, EVERYBODY! PUT THE WORD OUT!
WHITE LIGHTNING'S COME TO YOUR TOWN!
MARK WAID - STORY
HUMBERTO RAMOS - PENCILS
WAYNE FAUCHER AND BRAD VANCATA - INKERS
CHRIS ELIOPOULOS - LETTERER
TOM MCCRAW - COLORIST
ALI MORALES - ASSISTANT EDITOR
BRIAN AUGUSTYN - EDITOR
IMPULSE CREATED BY MARK WAID AND MIKE WIERINGO

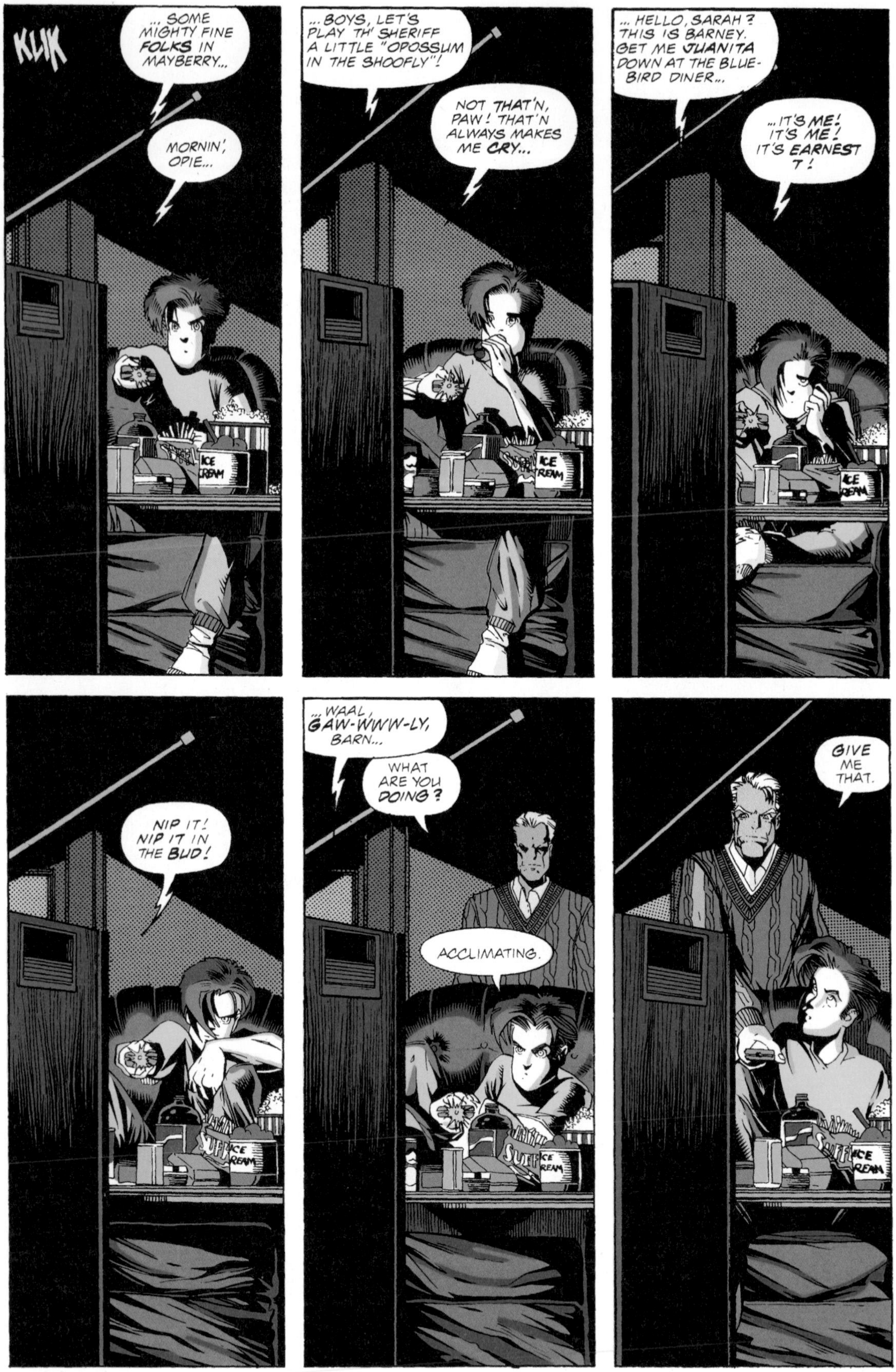
KLIK
...SOME MIGHTY FINE FOLKS IN MAYBERRY...
MORNIN', OPIE...
...BOYS, LET'S PLAY TH' SHERIFF A LITTLE "OPOSSUM IN THE SHOOFLY"!
NOT THAT'N, PAW! THAT'N ALWAYS MAKES ME CRY...
...HELLO, SARAH? THIS IS BARNEY. GET ME JUANITA DOWN AT THE BLUE-BIRD DINER...
...IT'S ME! IT'S ME! IT'S EARNEST T!
NIP IT! NIP IT IN THE BUD!
...WAAL, GAW-WWW-LY, BARN...
WHAT ARE YOU DOING?
ACCLIMATING.
GIVE ME THAT.

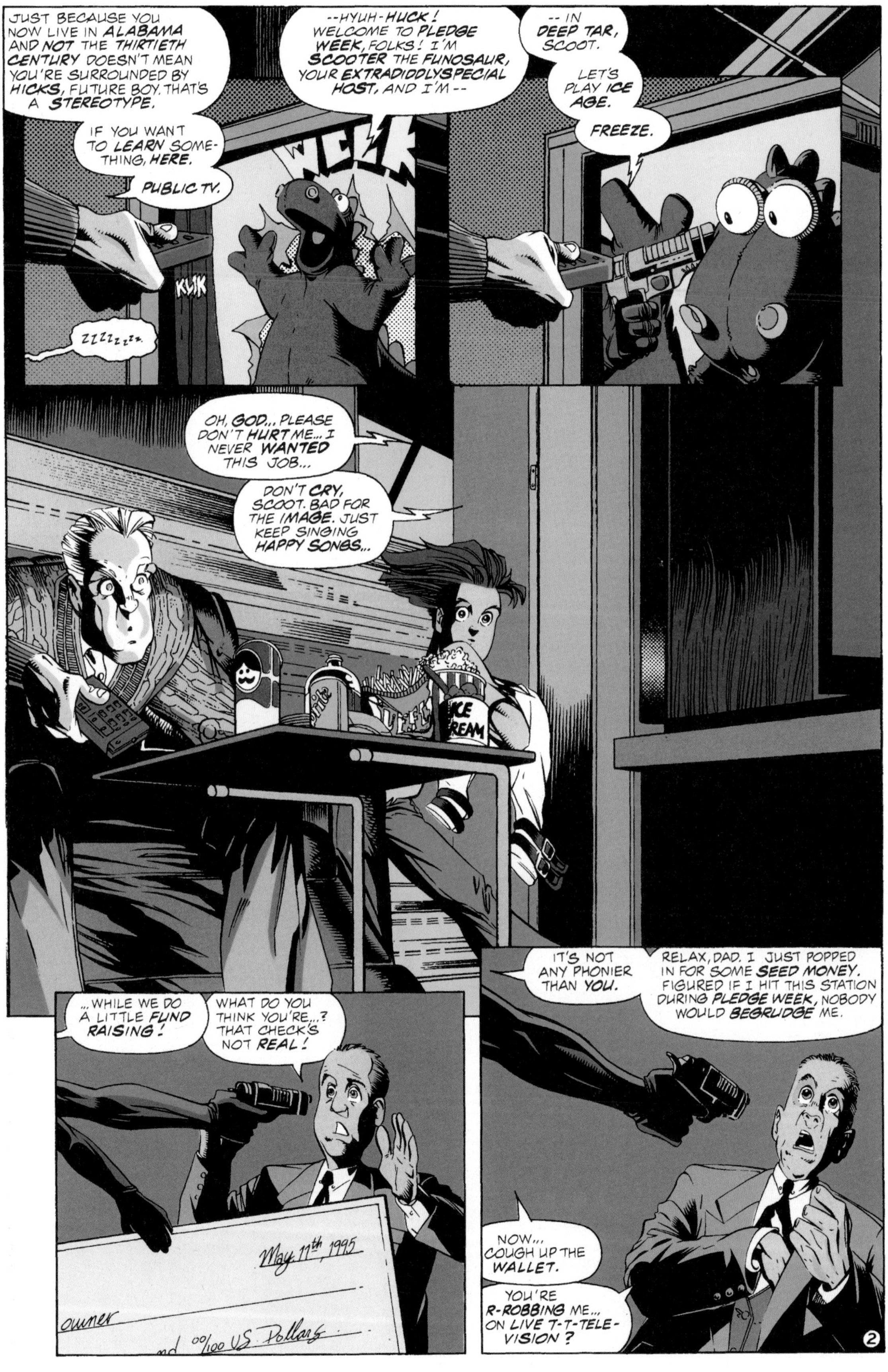
JUST BECAUSE YOU NOW LIVE IN ALABAMA AND NOT THE THIRTIETH CENTURY DOESN'T MEAN YOU'RE SURROUNDED BY HICKS, FUTURE BOY. THAT'S A STEREOTYPE.
IF YOU WANT TO LEARN SOMETHING, HERE.
PUBLIC TV.
KLIK
ZZZZzzzz.
WCLK
--HYUH-HUCK! WELCOME TO PLEDGE WEEK, FOLKS! I'M SCOOTER THE FUNOSAUR, YOUR EXTRADIDDLYSPECIAL HOST, AND I'M--
--IN DEEP TAR, SCOOT.
LET'S PLAY ICE AGE.
FREEZE.
OH, GOD... PLEASE DON'T HURT ME... I NEVER WANTED THIS JOB...
DON'T CRY, SCOOT. BAD FOR THE IMAGE. JUST KEEP SINGING HAPPY SONGS...
...WHILE WE DO A LITTLE FUND RAISING!
WHAT DO YOU THINK YOU'RE...? THAT CHECK'S NOT REAL!
May 11th, 1995
owner
and 00/100 U.S. Dollars
IT'S NOT ANY PHONIER THAN YOU.
RELAX, DAD. I JUST POPPED IN FOR SOME SEED MONEY. FIGURED IF I HIT THIS STATION DURING PLEDGE WEEK, NOBODY WOULD BEGRUDGE ME.
NOW... COUGH UP THE WALLET.
YOU'RE R-ROBBING ME... ON LIVE T-T-TELEVISION?

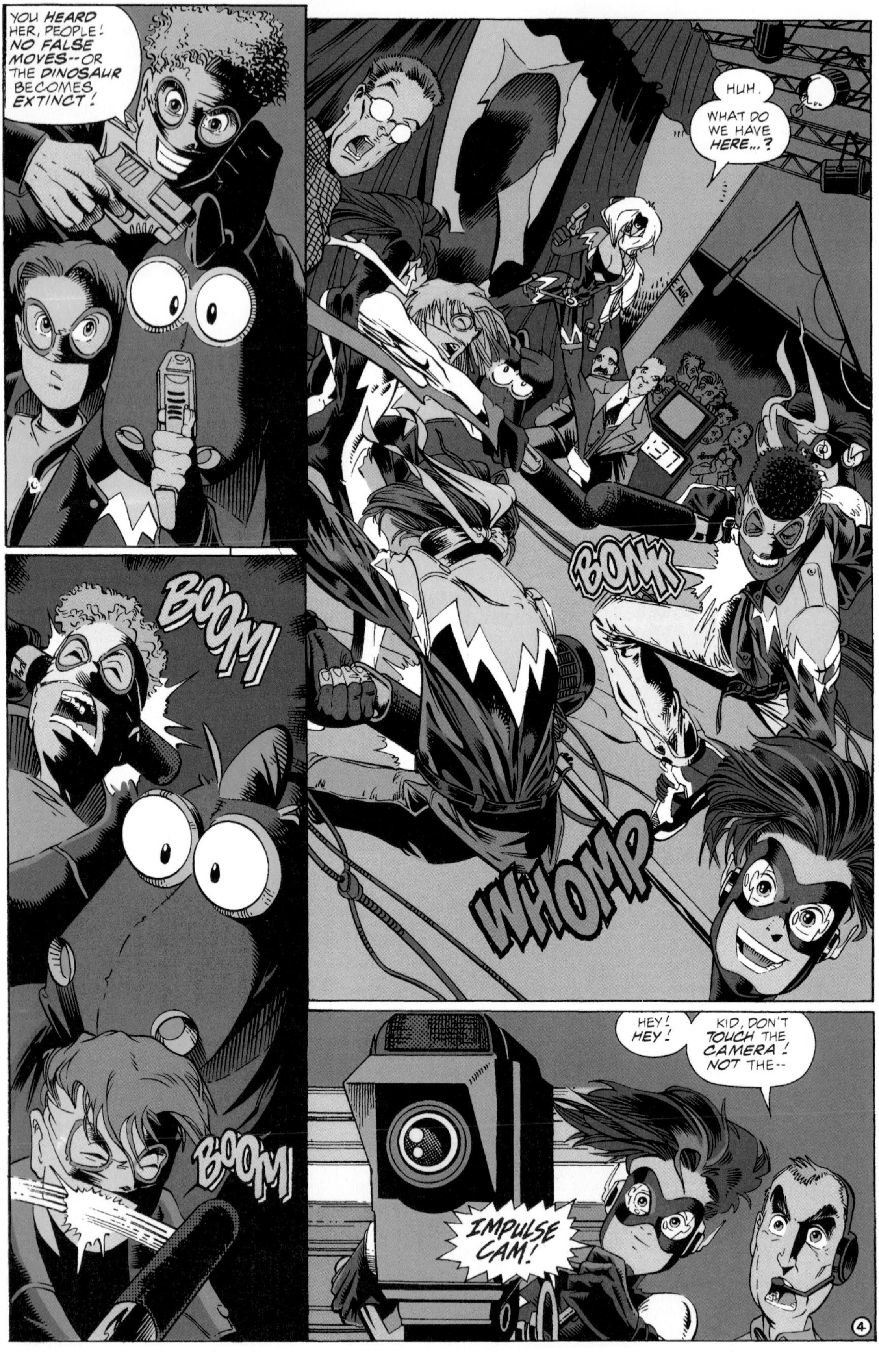
YOU HEARD HER, PEOPLE! NO FALSE MOVES--OR THE DINOSAUR BECOMES EXTINCT!
HUH.
WHAT DO WE HAVE HERE...?
BONK
WHOMP
BOOM
BOOM
HEY! HEY!
KID, DON'T TOUCH THE CAMERA! NOT THE--
IMPULSE CAM!
4

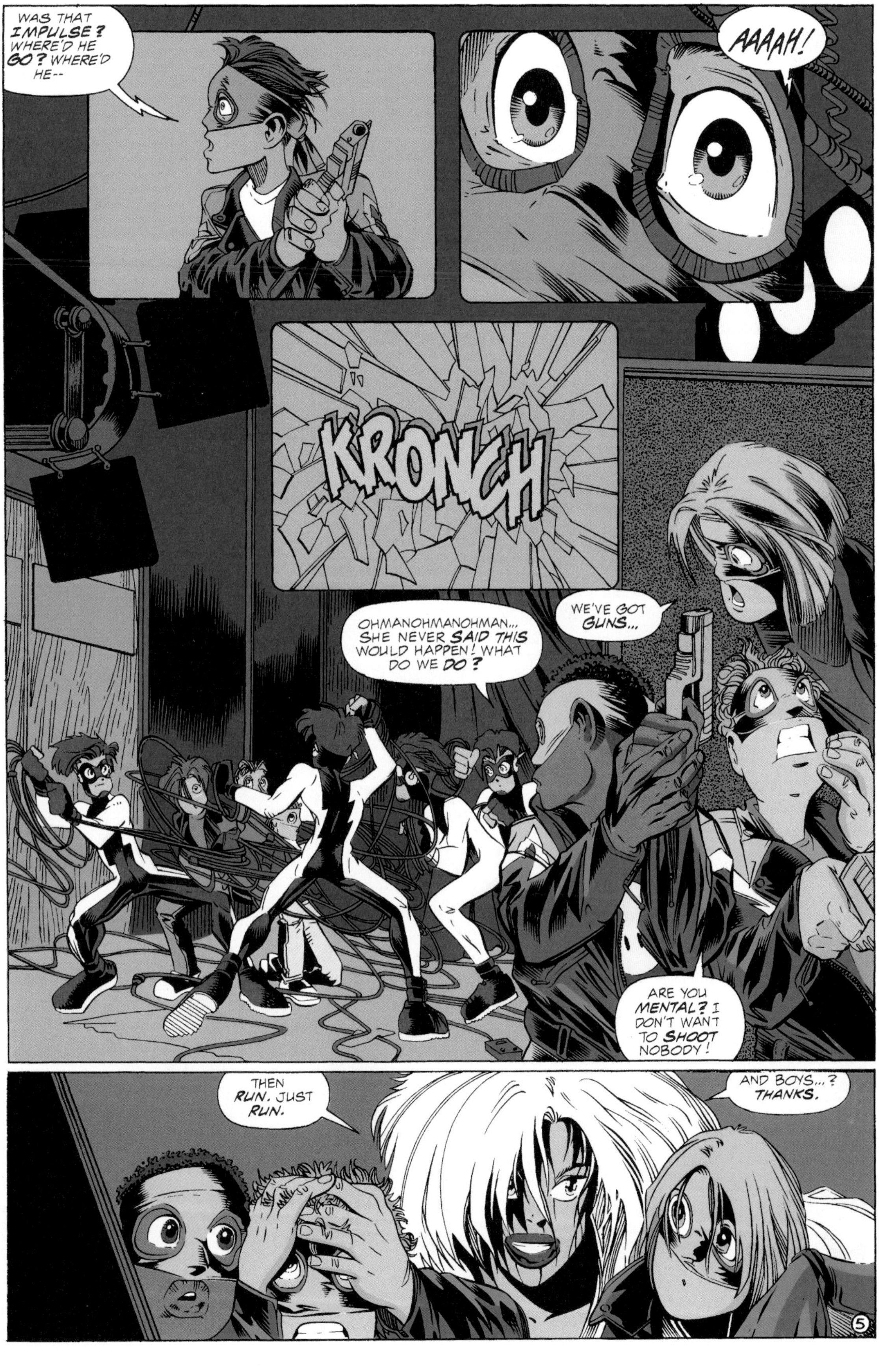

WAS THAT IMPULSE? WHERE'D HE GO? WHERE'D HE--
AAAAH!
KRONCH
OHMANOHMANOHMAN... SHE NEVER SAID THIS WOULD HAPPEN! WHAT DO WE DO?
WE'VE GOT GUNS...
ARE YOU MENTAL? I DON'T WANT TO SHOOT NOBODY!
THEN RUN. JUST RUN.
AND BOYS...? THANKS.

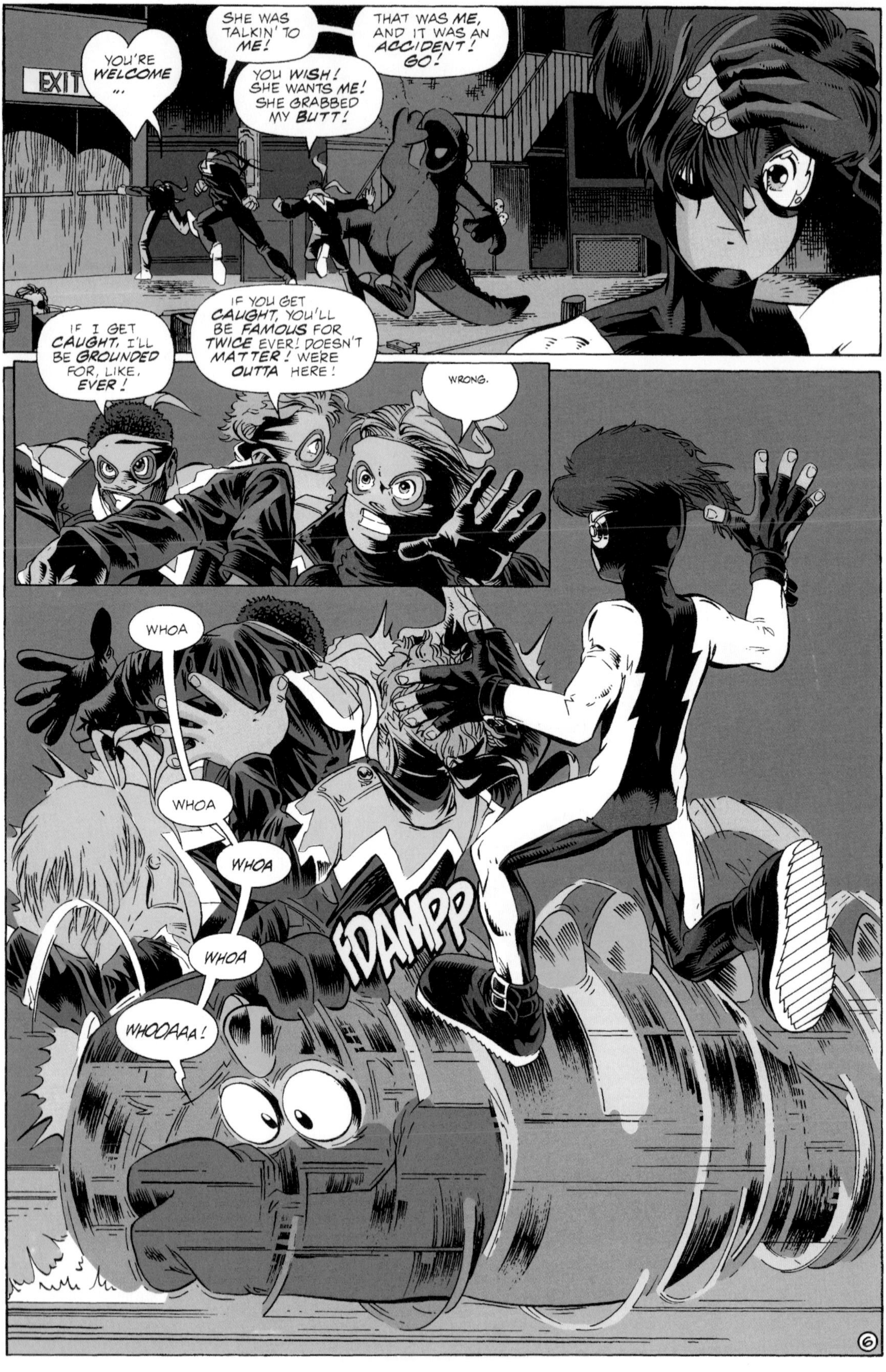

YOU'RE WELCOME ...
SHE WAS TALKIN' TO ME!
THAT WAS ME, AND IT WAS AN ACCIDENT! GO!
YOU WISH! SHE WANTS ME! SHE GRABBED MY BUTT!
IF I GET CAUGHT, I'LL BE GROUNDED FOR, LIKE, EVER!
IF YOU GET CAUGHT, YOU'LL BE FAMOUS FOR TWICE EVER! DOESN'T MATTER! WE'RE OUTTA HERE!
WRONG.
WHOA
WHOA
WHOA
WHOA
WHOOAAA!
FDAMPP

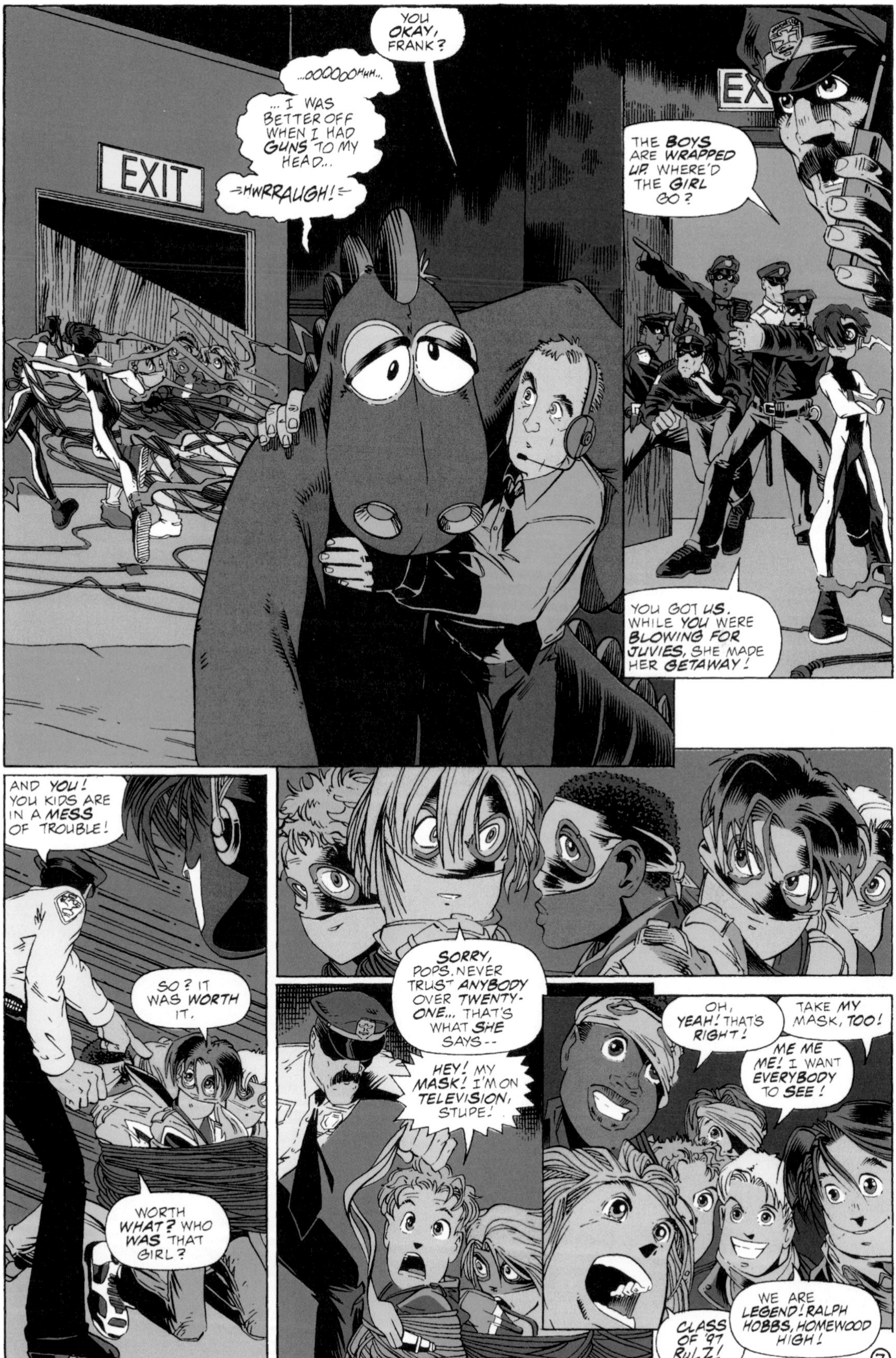

YOU OKAY, FRANK?
...OOOOOOHHH...
... I WAS BETTER OFF WHEN I HAD GUNS TO MY HEAD...
HWRRAUGH!
EXIT
THE BOYS ARE WRAPPED UP. WHERE'D THE GIRL GO?
YOU GOT US. WHILE YOU WERE BLOWING FOR JUVIES, SHE MADE HER GETAWAY!
AND YOU! YOU KIDS ARE IN A MESS OF TROUBLE!
SO? IT WAS WORTH IT.
WORTH WHAT? WHO WAS THAT GIRL?
SORRY, POPS. NEVER TRUST ANYBODY OVER TWENTY-ONE... THAT'S WHAT SHE SAYS--
HEY! MY MASK! I'M ON TELEVISION, STUPE!
OH, YEAH! THAT'S RIGHT!
TAKE MY MASK, TOO!
ME ME ME! I WANT EVERYBODY TO SEE!
WE ARE LEGEND! RALPH HOBBS, HOMEWOOD HIGH!
CLASS OF '97 RULZ!

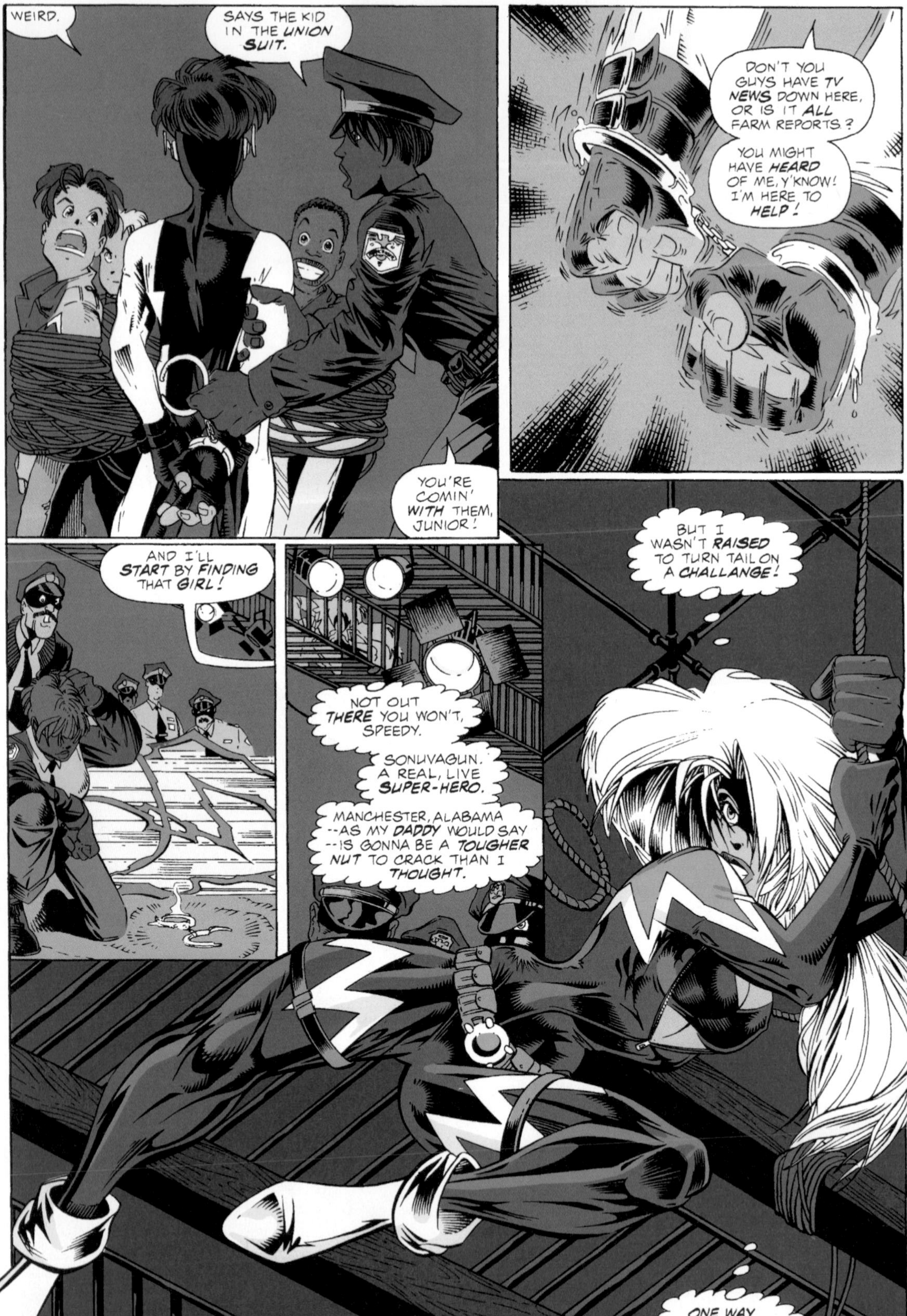
WEIRD.
SAYS THE KID IN THE UNION SUIT.
DON'T YOU GUYS HAVE TV NEWS DOWN HERE, OR IS IT ALL FARM REPORTS?
YOU MIGHT HAVE HEARD OF ME, Y'KNOW! I'M HERE TO HELP!
YOU'RE COMIN' WITH THEM, JUNIOR!
AND I'LL START BY FINDING THAT GIRL!
NOT OUT THERE YOU WON'T, SPEEDY.
SONUVAGUN. A REAL, LIVE SUPER-HERO.
MANCHESTER, ALABAMA --AS MY DADDY WOULD SAY --IS GONNA BE A TOUGHER NUT TO CRACK THAN I THOUGHT.
BUT I WASN'T RAISED TO TURN TAIL ON A CHALLANGE!
ONE WAY OR ANOTHER-- THIS TOWN'S GONNA REMEMBER ME!
8

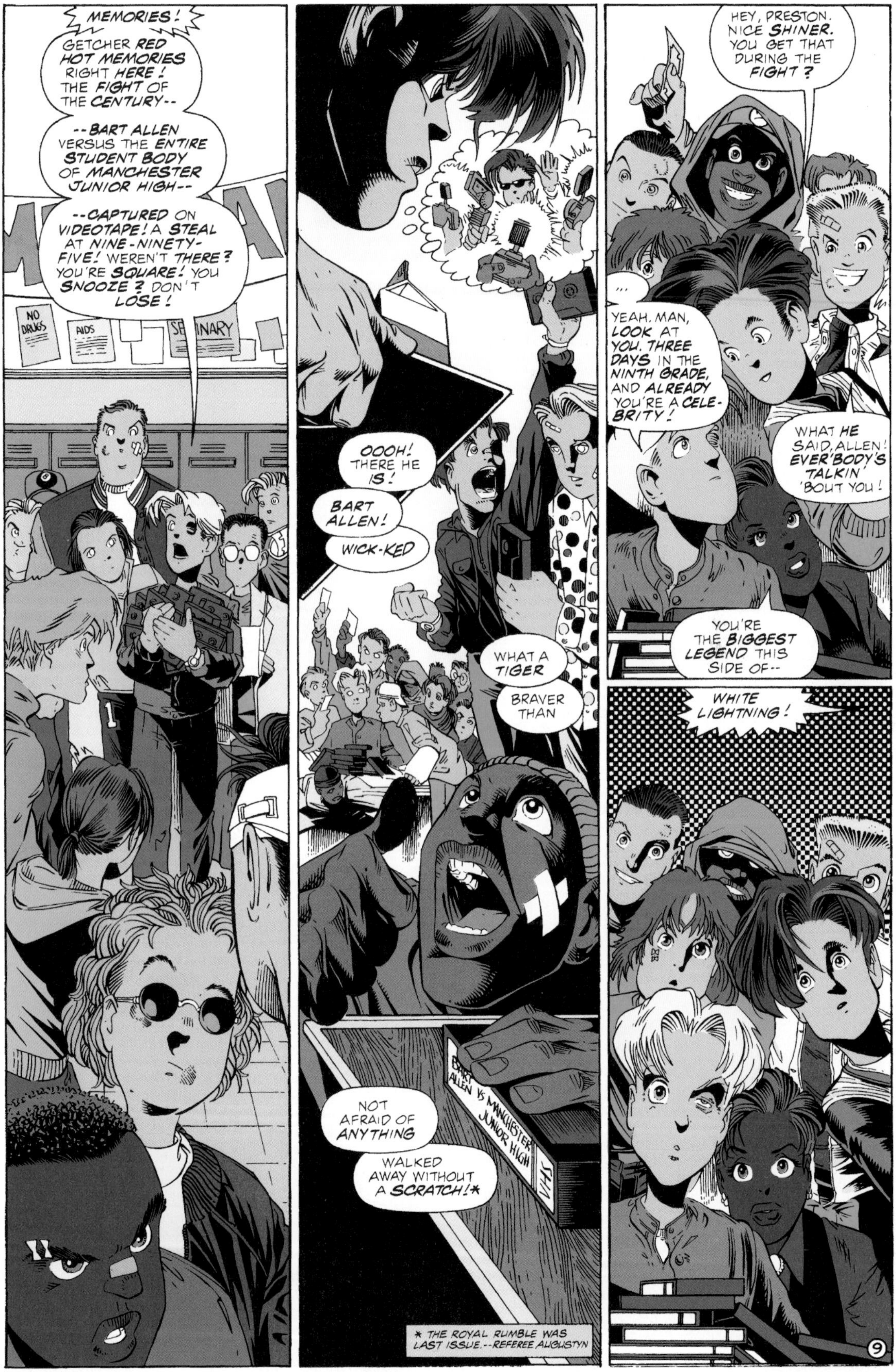
MEMORIES!
GETCHER RED HOT MEMORIES RIGHT HERE! THE FIGHT OF THE CENTURY--
--BART ALLEN VERSUS THE ENTIRE STUDENT BODY OF MANCHESTER JUNIOR HIGH--
--CAPTURED ON VIDEOTAPE! A STEAL AT NINE-NINETY-FIVE! WEREN'T THERE? YOU'RE SQUARE! YOU SNOOZE? DON'T LOSE!
NO DRUGS
AIDS
SEMINARY
OOOH! THERE HE IS!
BART ALLEN!
WICK-KED
WHAT A TIGER
BRAVER THAN
NOT AFRAID OF ANYTHING
WALKED AWAY WITHOUT A SCRATCH!*
BART ALLEN VS MANCHESTER JUNIOR HIGH
VHS
* THE ROYAL RUMBLE WAS LAST ISSUE.--REFEREE AUGUSTYN
HEY, PRESTON. NICE SHINER. YOU GET THAT DURING THE FIGHT?
...
YEAH. MAN, LOOK AT YOU. THREE DAYS IN THE NINTH GRADE, AND ALREADY YOU'RE A CELEBRITY!
WHAT HE SAID, ALLEN! EVER'BODY'S TALKIN' 'BOUT YOU!
YOU'RE THE BIGGEST LEGEND THIS SIDE OF--
WHITE LIGHTNING!
9

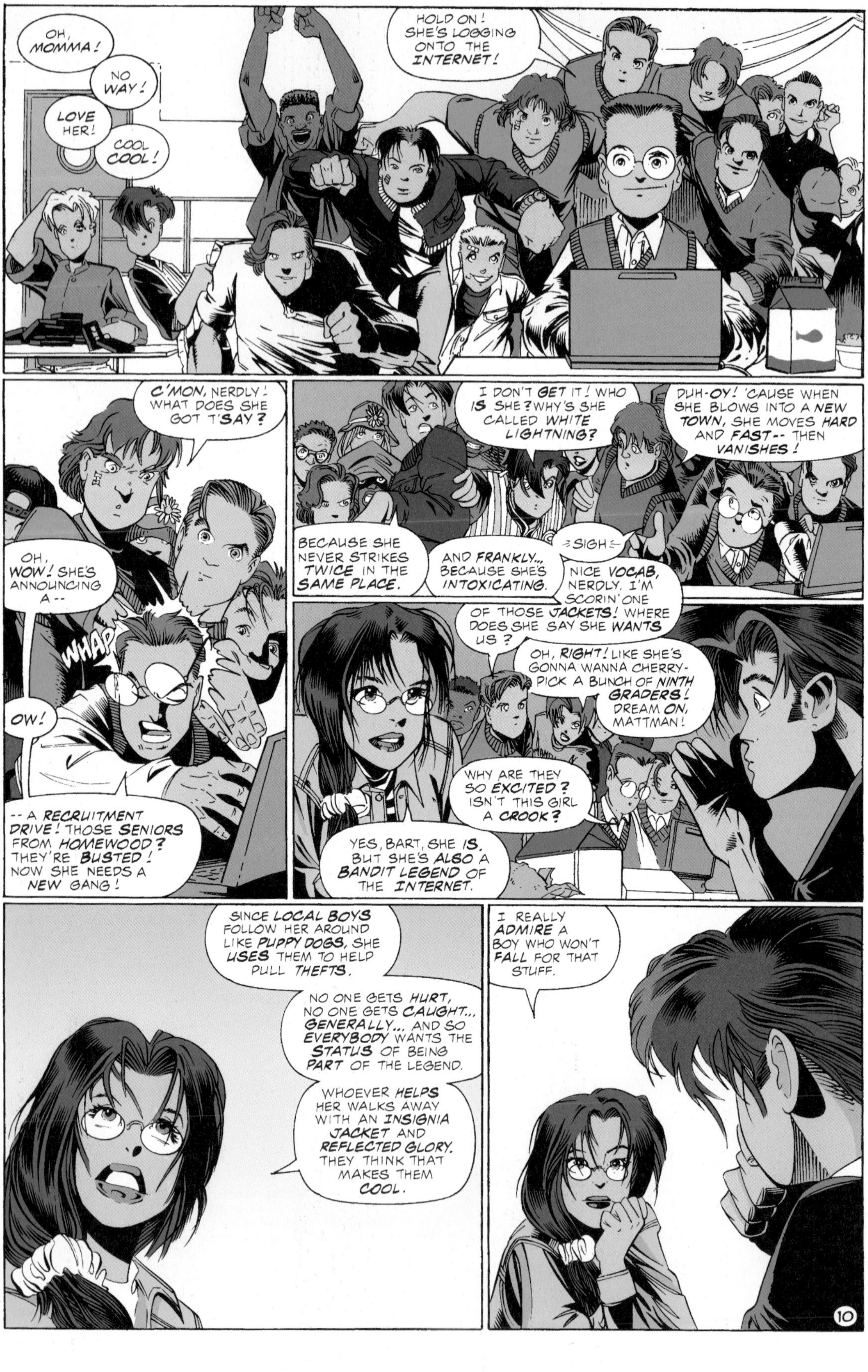
OH, MOMMA!
NO WAY!
LOVE HER!
COOL COOL!
HOLD ON! SHE'S LOGGING ONTO THE INTERNET!
C'MON, NERDLY! WHAT DOES SHE GOT T'SAY?
OH, WOW! SHE'S ANNOUNCING A--
WHAP
OW!
-- A RECRUITMENT DRIVE! THOSE SENIORS FROM HOMEWOOD? THEY'RE BUSTED! NOW SHE NEEDS A NEW GANG!
I DON'T GET IT! WHO IS SHE? WHY'S SHE CALLED WHITE LIGHTNING?
DUH-OY! 'CAUSE WHEN SHE BLOWS INTO A NEW TOWN, SHE MOVES HARD AND FAST-- THEN VANISHES!
BECAUSE SHE NEVER STRIKES TWICE IN THE SAME PLACE.
AND FRANKLY... BECAUSE SHE'S INTOXICATING.
SIGH
NICE VOCAB, NERDLY. I'M SCORIN' ONE OF THOSE JACKETS! WHERE DOES SHE SAY SHE WANTS US?
OH, RIGHT! LIKE SHE'S GONNA WANNA CHERRY-PICK A BUNCH OF NINTH GRADERS! DREAM ON, MATTMAN!
WHY ARE THEY SO EXCITED? ISN'T THIS GIRL A CROOK?
YES, BART, SHE IS, BUT SHE'S ALSO A BANDIT LEGEND OF THE INTERNET.
SINCE LOCAL BOYS FOLLOW HER AROUND LIKE PUPPY DOGS, SHE USES THEM TO HELP PULL THEFTS.
NO ONE GETS HURT, NO ONE GETS CAUGHT... GENERALLY... AND SO EVERYBODY WANTS THE STATUS OF BEING PART OF THE LEGEND.
WHOEVER HELPS HER WALKS AWAY WITH AN INSIGNIA JACKET AND REFLECTED GLORY. THEY THINK THAT MAKES THEM COOL.
I REALLY ADMIRE A BOY WHO WON'T FALL FOR THAT STUFF.

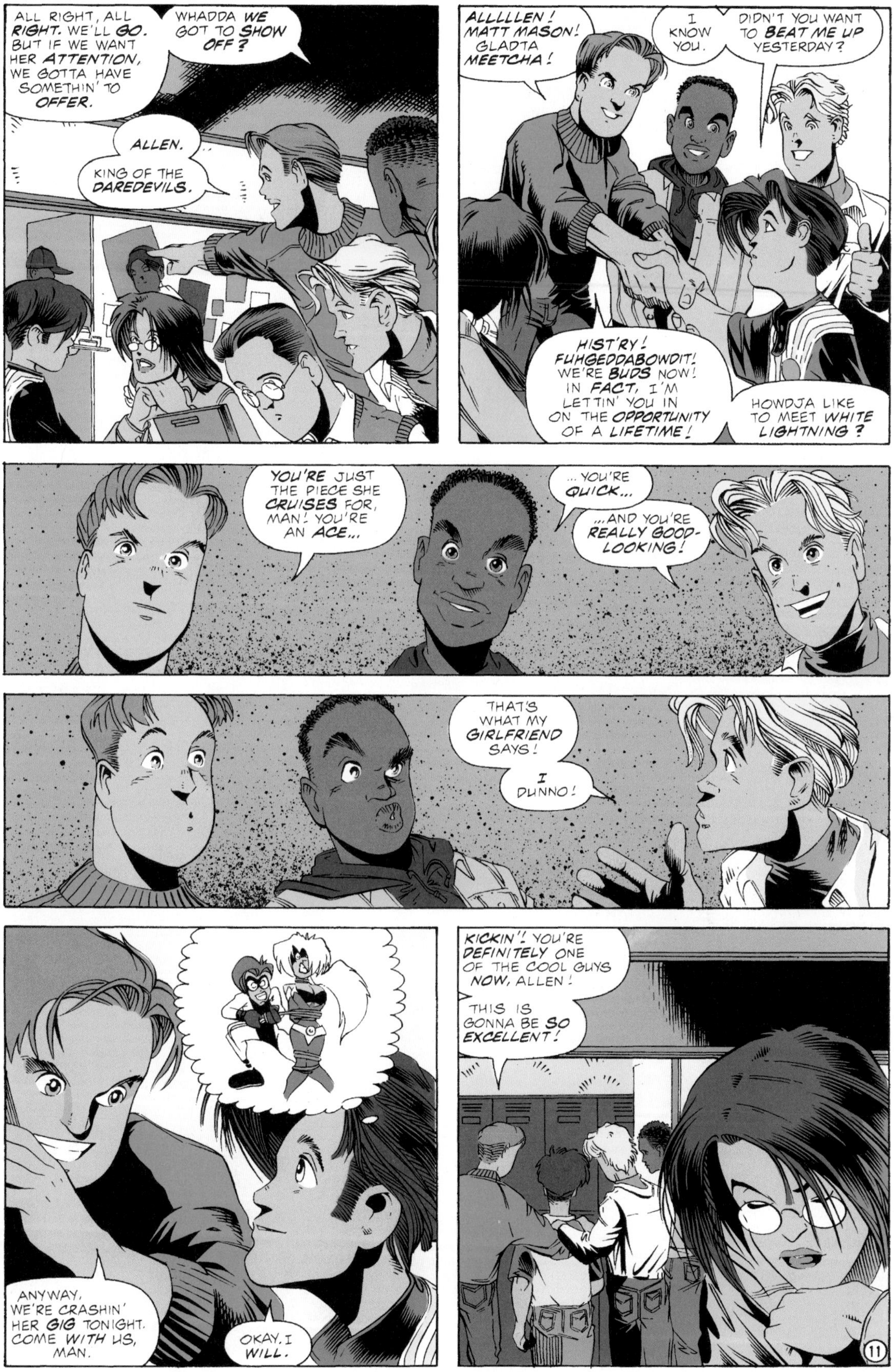
ALL RIGHT, ALL RIGHT. WE'LL GO. BUT IF WE WANT HER ATTENTION, WE GOTTA HAVE SOMETHIN' TO OFFER.
WHADDA WE GOT TO SHOW OFF?
ALLEN.
KING OF THE DAREDEVILS.
ALLLLLEN! MATT MASON! GLADTA MEETCHA!
I KNOW YOU.
DIDN'T YOU WANT TO BEAT ME UP YESTERDAY?
HIST'RY! FUHGEDDABOWDIT! WE'RE BUDS NOW! IN FACT, I'M LETTIN' YOU IN ON THE OPPORTUNITY OF A LIFETIME!
HOWDJA LIKE TO MEET WHITE LIGHTNING?
YOU'RE JUST THE PIECE SHE CRUISES FOR, MAN! YOU'RE AN ACE...
...YOU'RE QUICK...
...AND YOU'RE REALLY GOOD-LOOKING!
THAT'S WHAT MY GIRLFRIEND SAYS!
I DUNNO!
ANYWAY, WE'RE CRASHIN' HER GIG TONIGHT. COME WITH US, MAN.
OKAY. I WILL.
KICKIN'! YOU'RE DEFINITELY ONE OF THE COOL GUYS NOW, ALLEN!
THIS IS GONNA BE SO EXCELLENT!
11

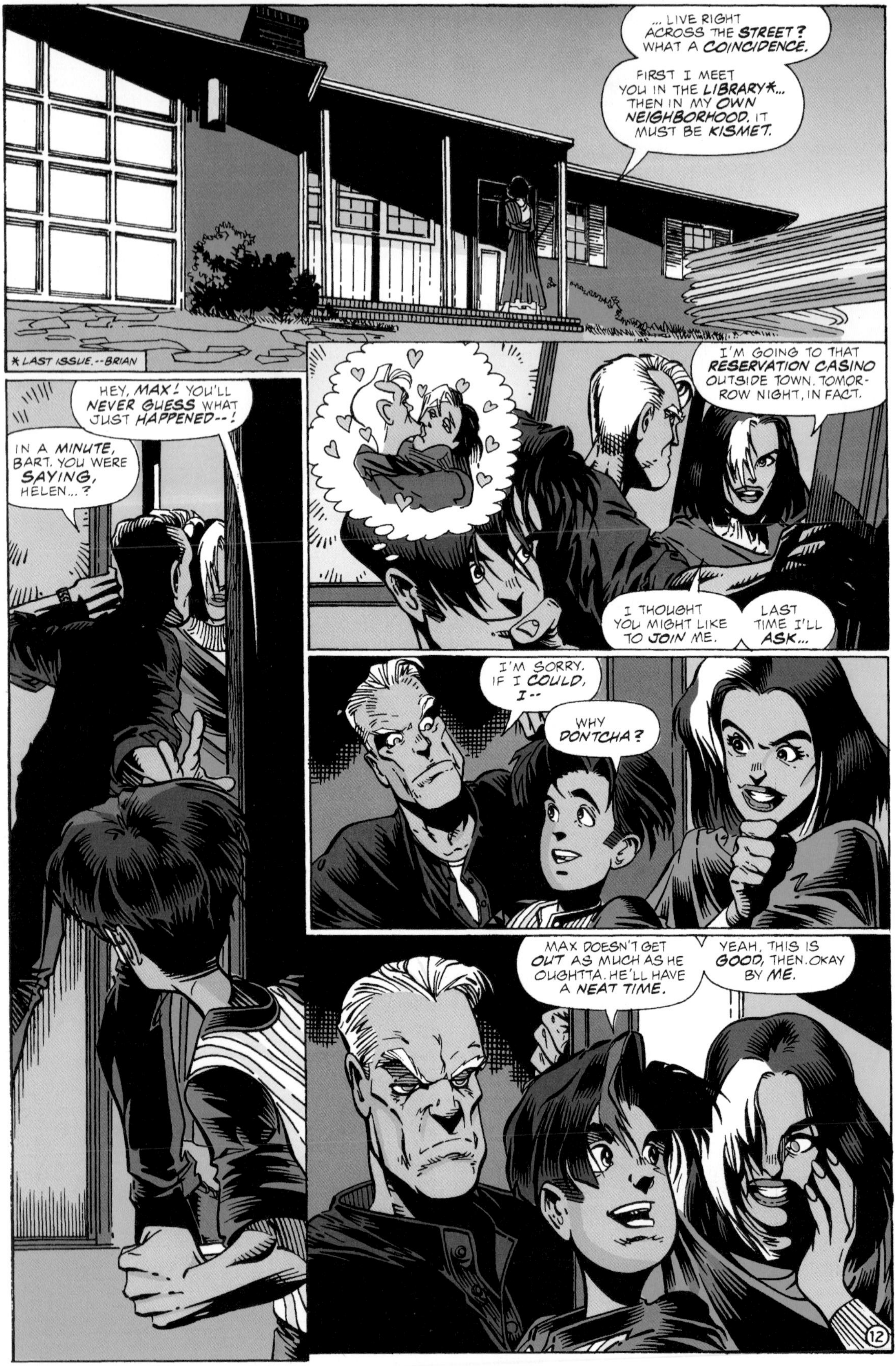

... LIVE RIGHT ACROSS THE STREET? WHAT A COINCIDENCE.
FIRST I MEET YOU IN THE LIBRARY*... THEN IN MY OWN NEIGHBORHOOD. IT MUST BE KISMET.
* LAST ISSUE. --BRIAN
HEY, MAX! YOU'LL NEVER GUESS WHAT JUST HAPPENED--!
IN A MINUTE, BART. YOU WERE SAYING, HELEN...?
I'M GOING TO THAT RESERVATION CASINO OUTSIDE TOWN. TOMORROW NIGHT, IN FACT.
I THOUGHT YOU MIGHT LIKE TO JOIN ME.
LAST TIME I'LL ASK...
I'M SORRY. IF I COULD, I--
WHY DONTCHA?
MAX DOESN'T GET OUT AS MUCH AS HE OUGHTTA. HE'LL HAVE A NEAT TIME.
YEAH, THIS IS GOOD, THEN. OKAY BY ME.
12

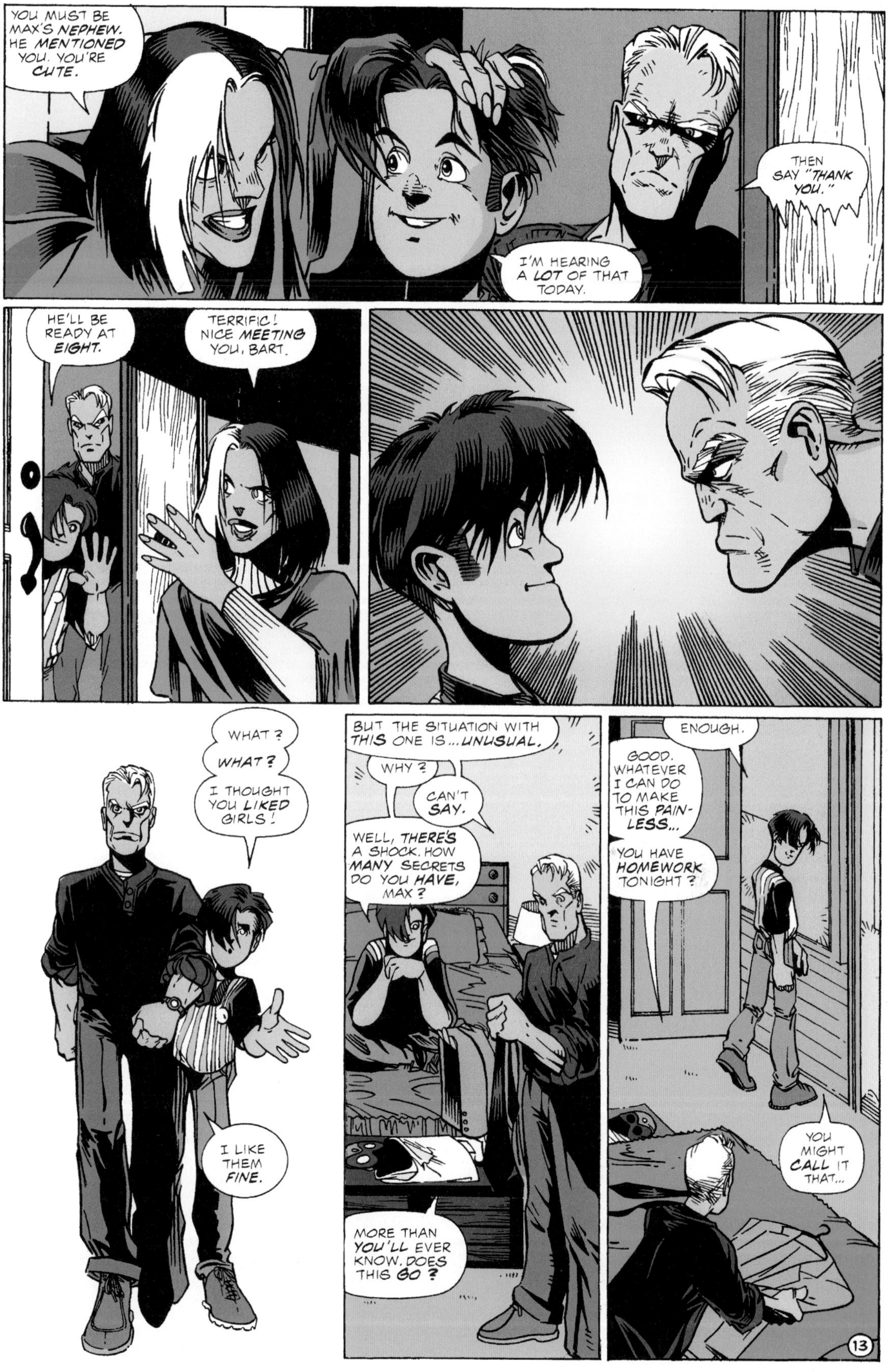

YOU MUST BE MAX'S NEPHEW. HE MENTIONED YOU. YOU'RE CUTE.
I'M HEARING A LOT OF THAT TODAY.
THEN SAY "THANK YOU."
HE'LL BE READY AT EIGHT.
TERRIFIC! NICE MEETING YOU, BART.
WHAT?
WHAT?
I THOUGHT YOU LIKED GIRLS!
I LIKE THEM FINE.
BUT THE SITUATION WITH THIS ONE IS...UNUSUAL.
WHY?
CAN'T SAY.
WELL, THERE'S A SHOCK. HOW MANY SECRETS DO YOU HAVE, MAX?
MORE THAN YOU'LL EVER KNOW. DOES THIS GO?
ENOUGH.
GOOD. WHATEVER I CAN DO TO MAKE THIS PAIN-LESS...
YOU HAVE HOMEWORK TONIGHT?
YOU MIGHT CALL IT THAT...

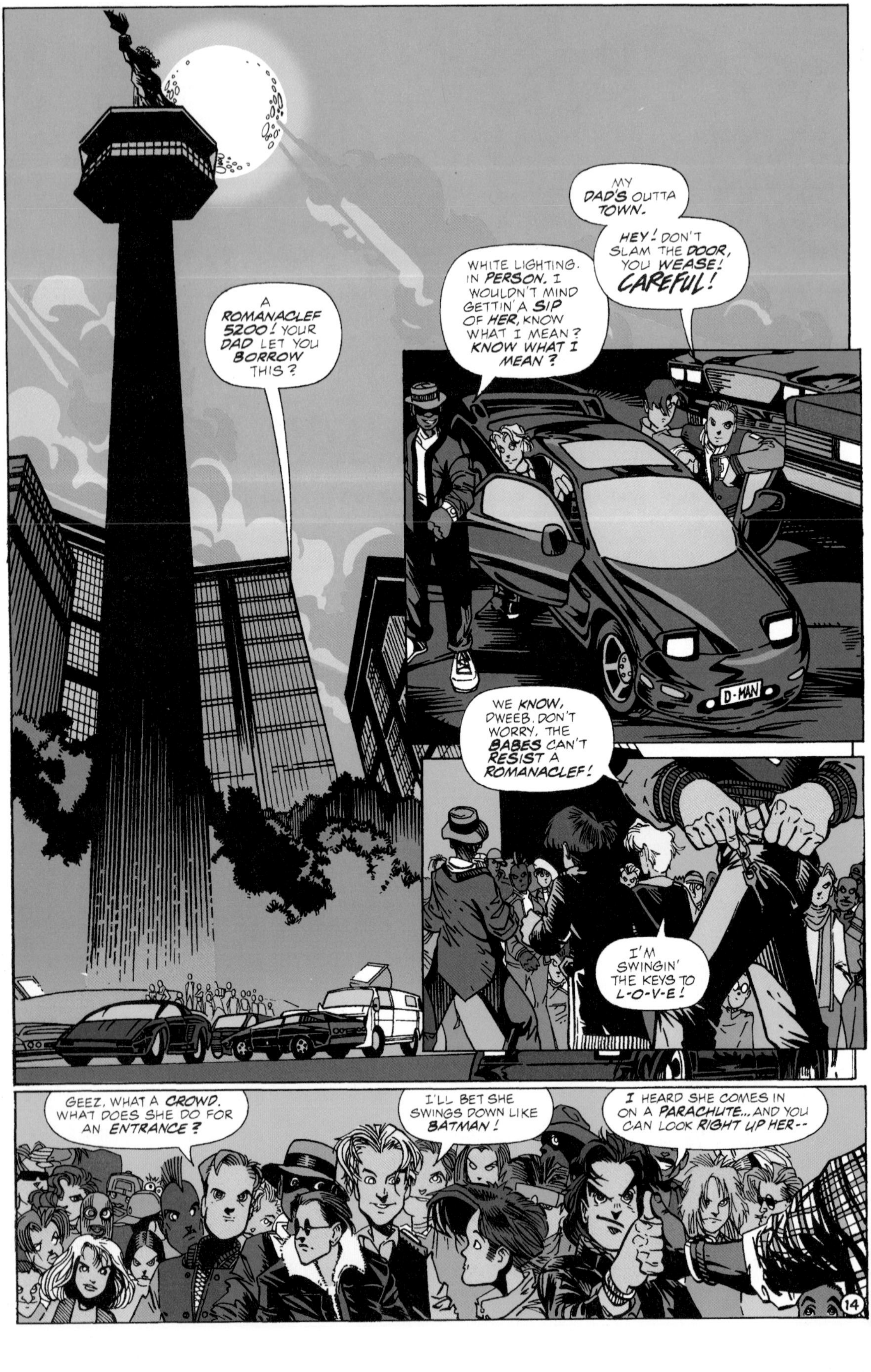
A ROMANACLEF 5200! YOUR DAD LET YOU BORROW THIS?
WHITE LIGHTING. IN PERSON. I WOULDN'T MIND GETTIN' A SIP OF HER, KNOW WHAT I MEAN? KNOW WHAT I MEAN?
MY DAD'S OUTTA TOWN.
HEY! DON'T SLAM THE DOOR, YOU WEASE! CAREFUL!
D-MAN
WE KNOW, DWEEB. DON'T WORRY. THE BABES CAN'T RESIST A ROMANACLEF!
I'M SWINGIN' THE KEYS TO L-O-V-E!
GEEZ, WHAT A CROWD. WHAT DOES SHE DO FOR AN ENTRANCE?
I'LL BET SHE SWINGS DOWN LIKE BATMAN!
I HEARD SHE COMES IN ON A PARACHUTE... AND YOU CAN LOOK RIGHT UP HER--

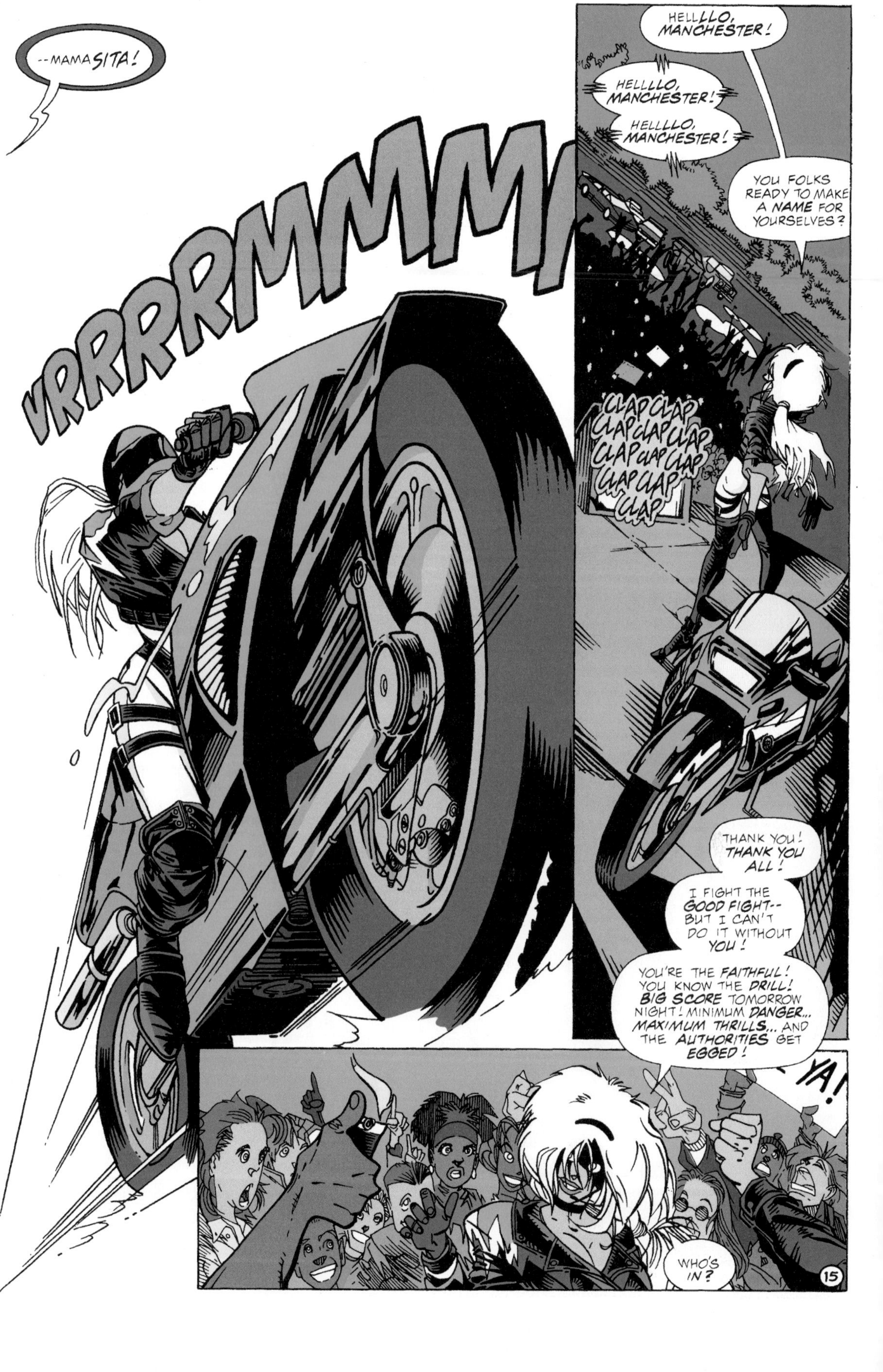
--MAMA SITA!
VRRRRMMMMM
HELLLLO, MANCHESTER!
HELLLLO, MANCHESTER!
HELLLLO, MANCHESTER!
YOU FOLKS READY TO MAKE A NAME FOR YOURSELVES?
CLAP CLAP CLAP CLAP CLAP CLAP CLAP CLAP CLAP CLAP CLAP CLAP CLAP
THANK YOU! THANK YOU ALL!
I FIGHT THE GOOD FIGHT-- BUT I CAN'T DO IT WITHOUT YOU!
YOU'RE THE FAITHFUL! YOU KNOW THE DRILL! BIG SCORE TOMORROW NIGHT! MINIMUM DANGER... MAXIMUM THRILLS... AND THE AUTHORITIES GET EGGED!
WHO'S IN?

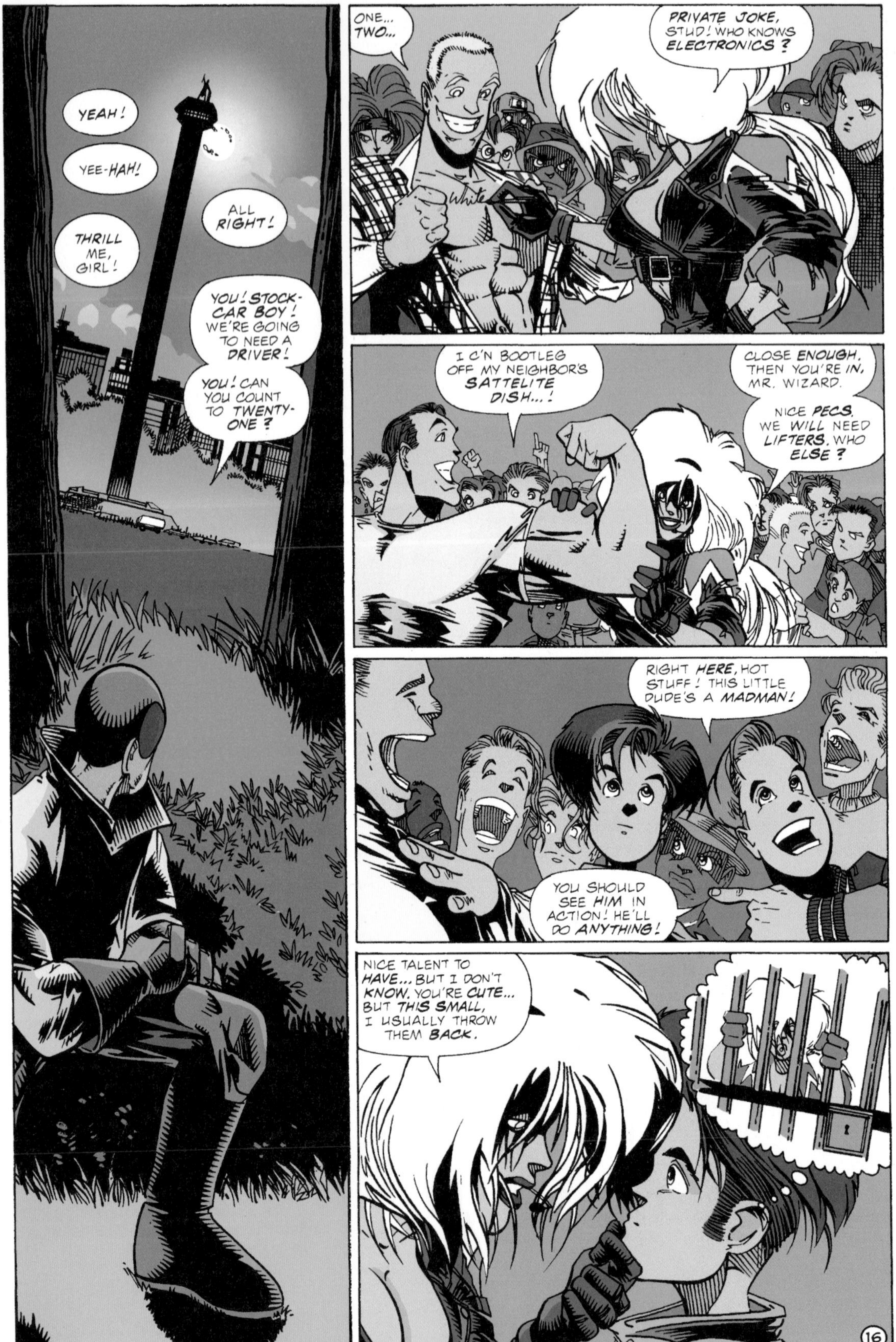
YEAH!
YEE-HAH!
ALL RIGHT!
THRILL ME, GIRL!
YOU! STOCK-CAR BOY! WE'RE GOING TO NEED A DRIVER!
YOU! CAN YOU COUNT TO TWENTY-ONE?
ONE... TWO...
PRIVATE JOKE, STUD! WHO KNOWS ELECTRONICS?
I C'N BOOTLEG OFF MY NEIGHBOR'S SATTELITE DISH...!
CLOSE ENOUGH. THEN YOU'RE IN, MR. WIZARD.
NICE PECS. WE WILL NEED LIFTERS. WHO ELSE?
RIGHT HERE, HOT STUFF! THIS LITTLE DUDE'S A MADMAN!
YOU SHOULD SEE HIM IN ACTION! HE'LL DO ANYTHING!
NICE TALENT TO HAVE... BUT I DON'T KNOW. YOU'RE CUTE... BUT THIS SMALL, I USUALLY THROW THEM BACK.
16

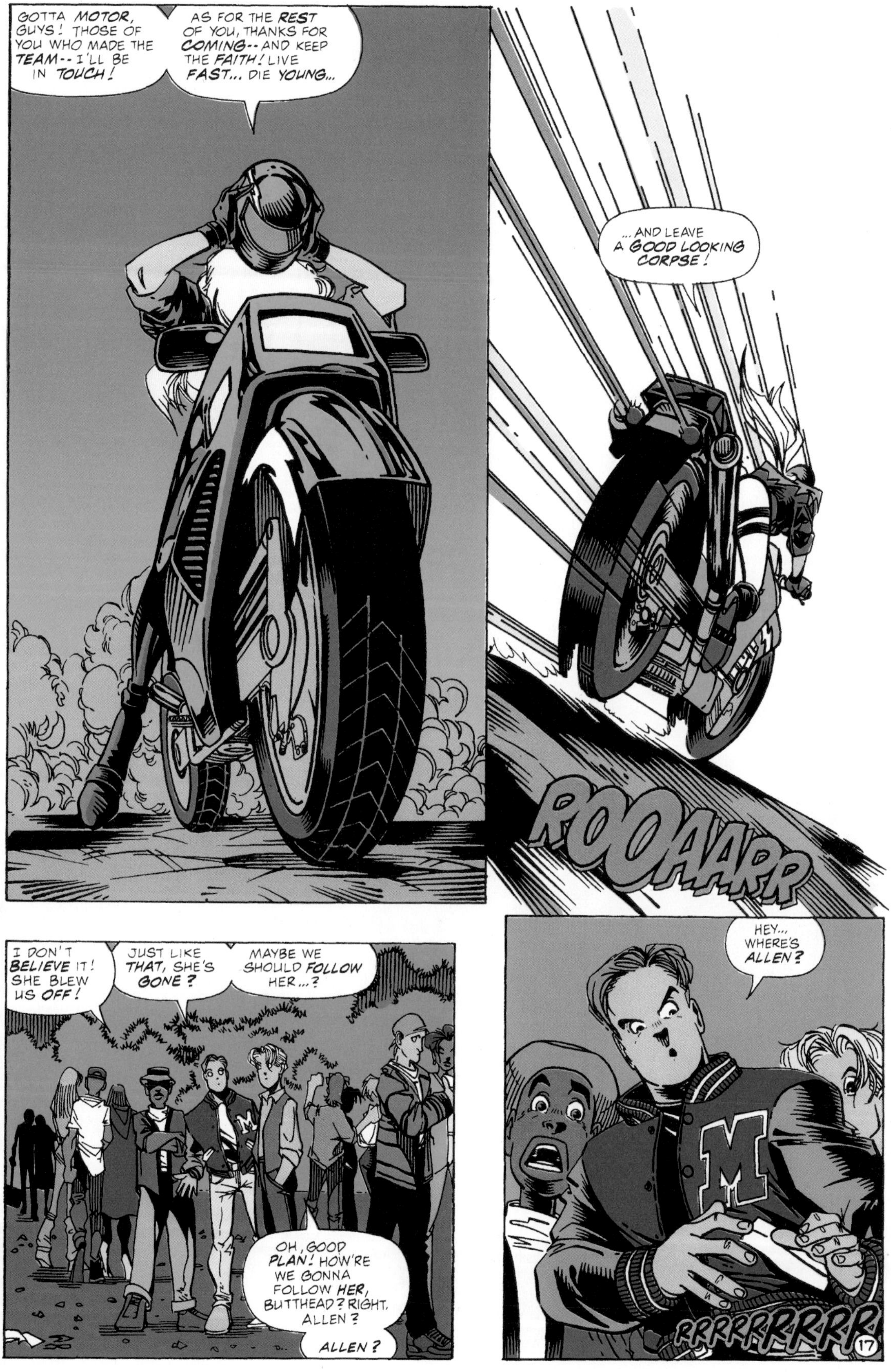
GOTTA MOTOR, GUYS! THOSE OF YOU WHO MADE THE TEAM--I'LL BE IN TOUCH!
AS FOR THE REST OF YOU, THANKS FOR COMING--AND KEEP THE FAITH! LIVE FAST... DIE YOUNG...
...AND LEAVE A GOOD LOOKING CORPSE!
ROOAARR
I DON'T BELIEVE IT! SHE BLEW US OFF!
JUST LIKE THAT, SHE'S GONE?
MAYBE WE SHOULD FOLLOW HER...?
OH, GOOD PLAN! HOW'RE WE GONNA FOLLOW HER, BUTTHEAD? RIGHT, ALLEN?
ALLEN?
HEY... WHERE'S ALLEN?
RRRRRRRRRR

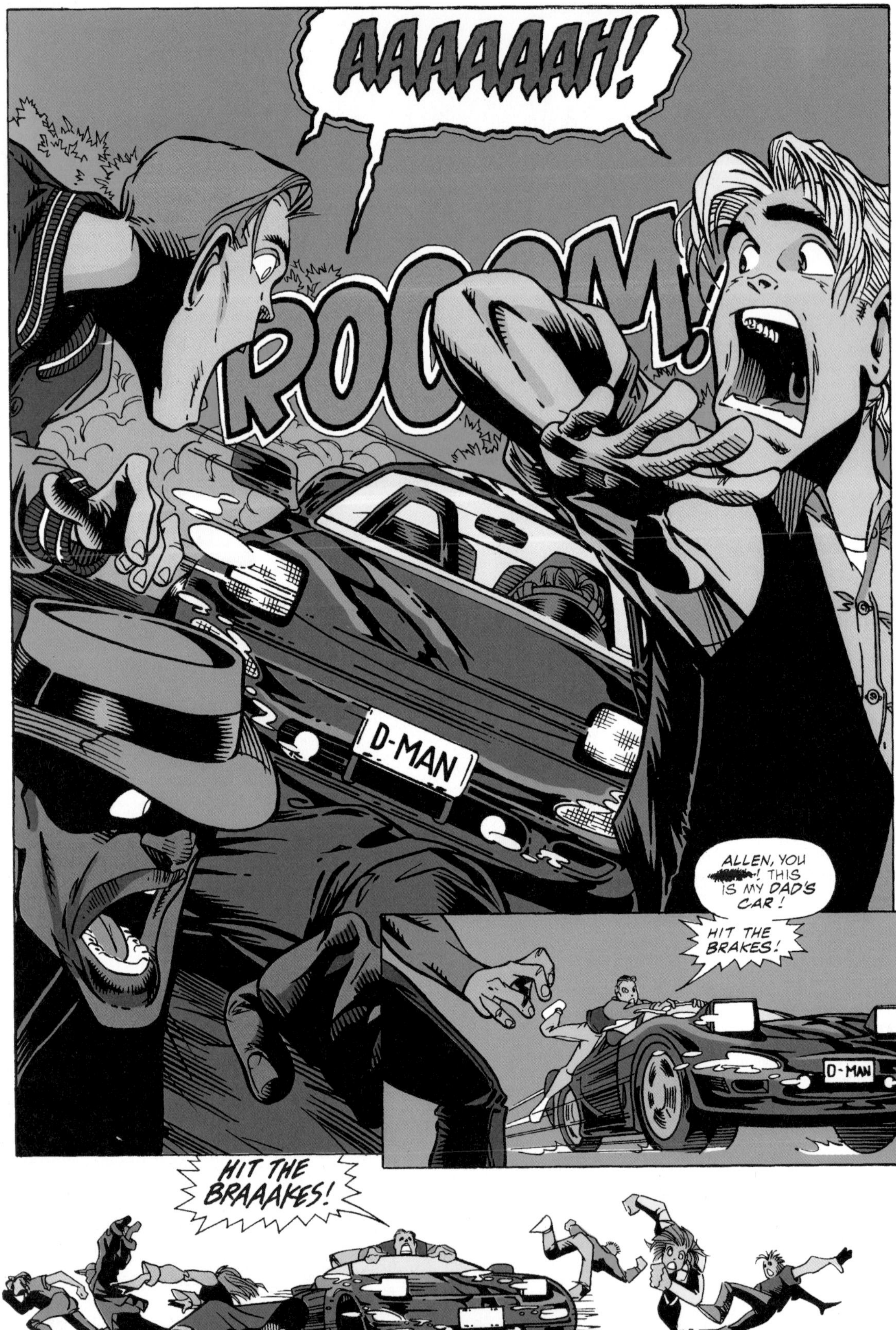
AAAAAAH!
D-MAN
ALLEN, YOU [redacted]! THIS IS MY DAD'S CAR!
HIT THE BRAKES!
D-MAN
HIT THE BRAAAKES!

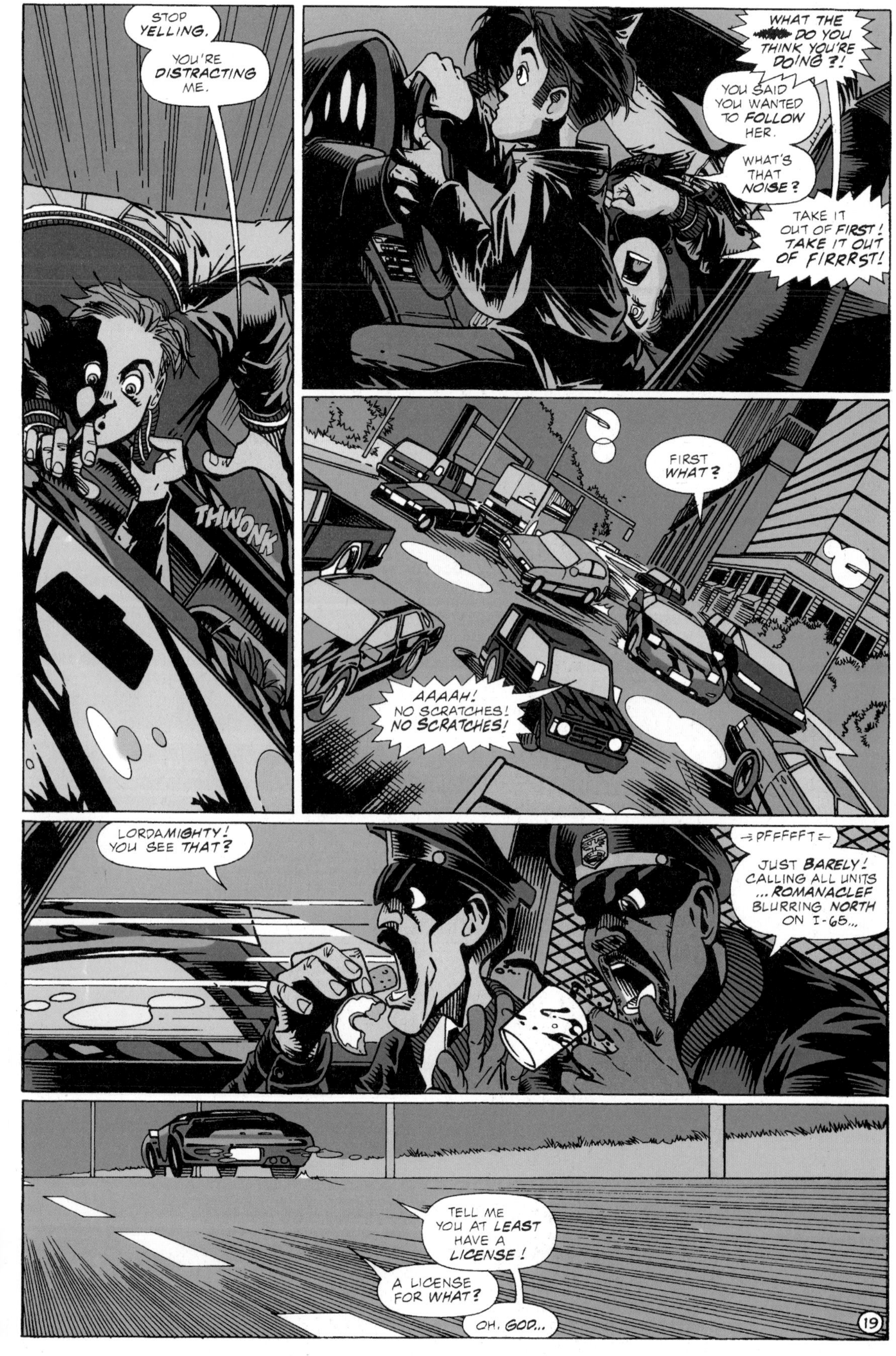
STOP YELLING.
YOU'RE DISTRACTING ME.
THWONK
WHAT THE DO YOU THINK YOU'RE DOING?!
YOU SAID YOU WANTED TO FOLLOW HER.
WHAT'S THAT NOISE?
TAKE IT OUT OF FIRST! TAKE IT OUT OF FIRRRST!
FIRST WHAT?
AAAAH! NO SCRATCHES! NO SCRATCHES!
LORDAMIGHTY! YOU SEE THAT?
PFFFFFT
JUST BARELY! CALLING ALL UNITS ...ROMANACLEF BLURRING NORTH ON I-65...
TELL ME YOU AT LEAST HAVE A LICENSE!
A LICENSE FOR WHAT?
OH, GOD...

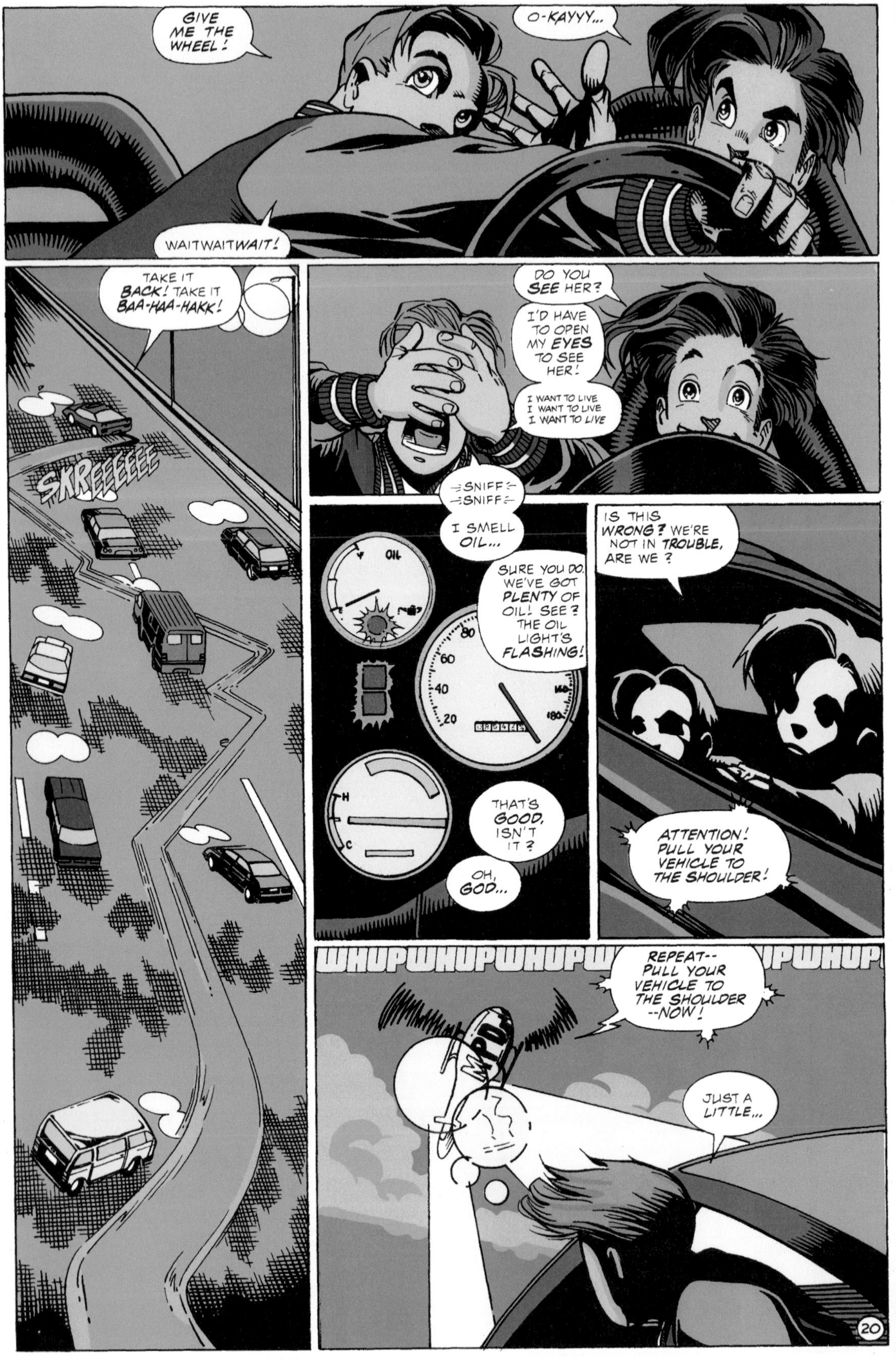
GIVE ME THE WHEEL!
O-KAYYY...
WAITWAITWAIT!
TAKE IT BACK! TAKE IT BAA-HAA-HAKK!
SKREEEEEE
DO YOU SEE HER?
I'D HAVE TO OPEN MY EYES TO SEE HER!
I WANT TO LIVE I WANT TO LIVE I WANT TO LIVE
SNIFF SNIFF
I SMELL OIL...
SURE YOU DO. WE'VE GOT PLENTY OF OIL! SEE? THE OIL LIGHT'S FLASHING!
THAT'S GOOD, ISN'T IT?
OH, GOD...
IS THIS WRONG? WE'RE NOT IN TROUBLE, ARE WE?
ATTENTION! PULL YOUR VEHICLE TO THE SHOULDER!
WHUPWHUPWHUPW
UPWHUP
REPEAT-- PULL YOUR VEHICLE TO THE SHOULDER --NOW!
MPD
JUST A LITTLE...

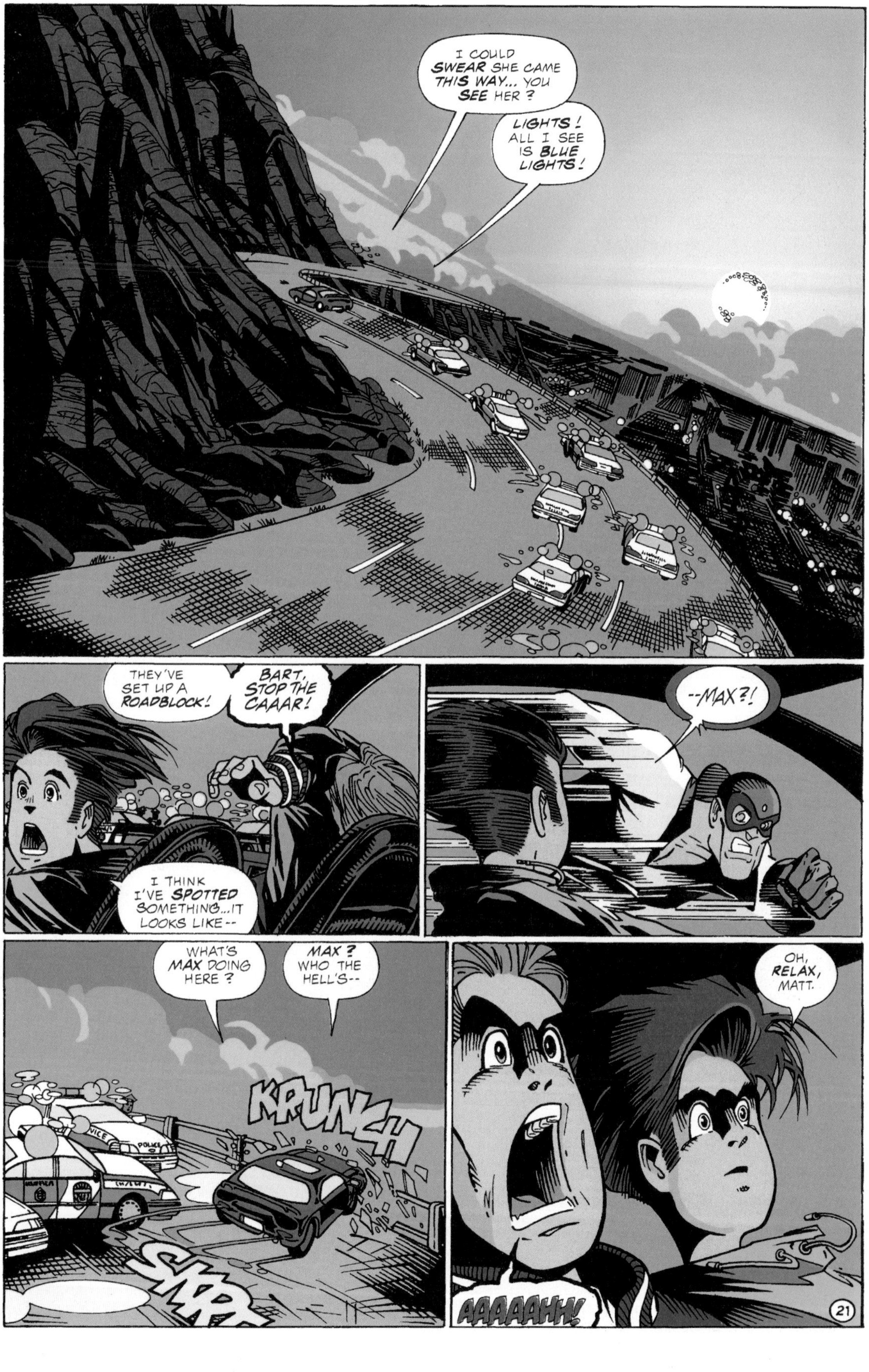
I COULD SWEAR SHE CAME THIS WAY... YOU SEE HER ?
LIGHTS ! ALL I SEE IS BLUE LIGHTS !
THEY'VE SET UP A ROADBLOCK !
BART, STOP THE CAAAR!
I THINK I'VE SPOTTED SOMETHING...IT LOOKS LIKE--
--MAX?!
WHAT'S MAX DOING HERE ?
MAX ? WHO THE HELL'S--
KRUNCH
OH, RELAX, MATT.
AAAAAHH!

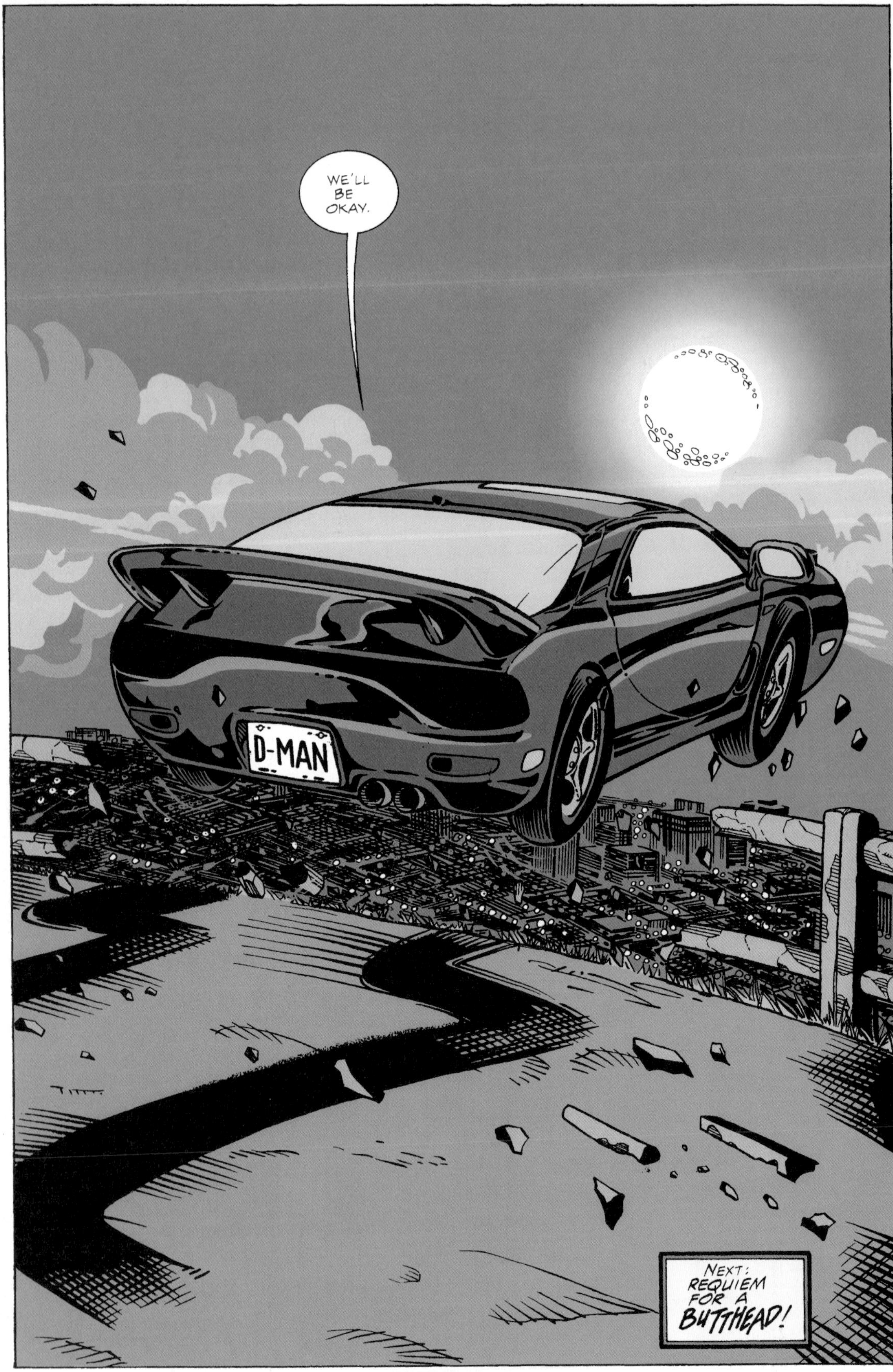
WE'LL BE OKAY.
D-MAN
NEXT: REQUIEM FOR A BUTTHEAD!

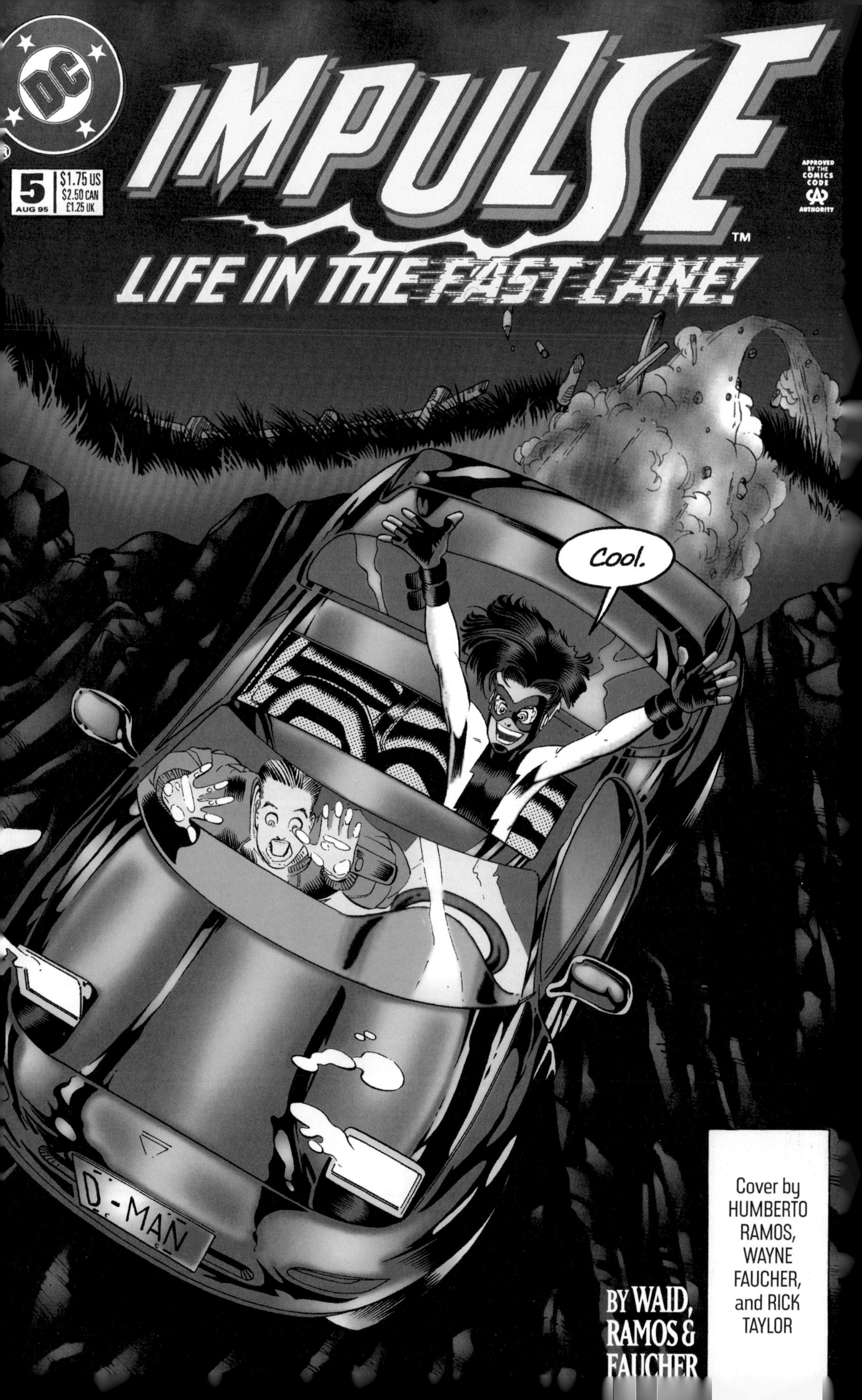
DC
IMPULSE™
5
AUG 95
$1.75 US
$2.50 CAN
£1.25 UK
APPROVED BY THE COMICS CODE AUTHORITY
LIFE IN THE FAST LANE!
Cool.
D-MAN
BY WAID, RAMOS & FAUCHER

Cover by HUMBERTO RAMOS, WAYNE FAUCHER, and RICK TAYLOR

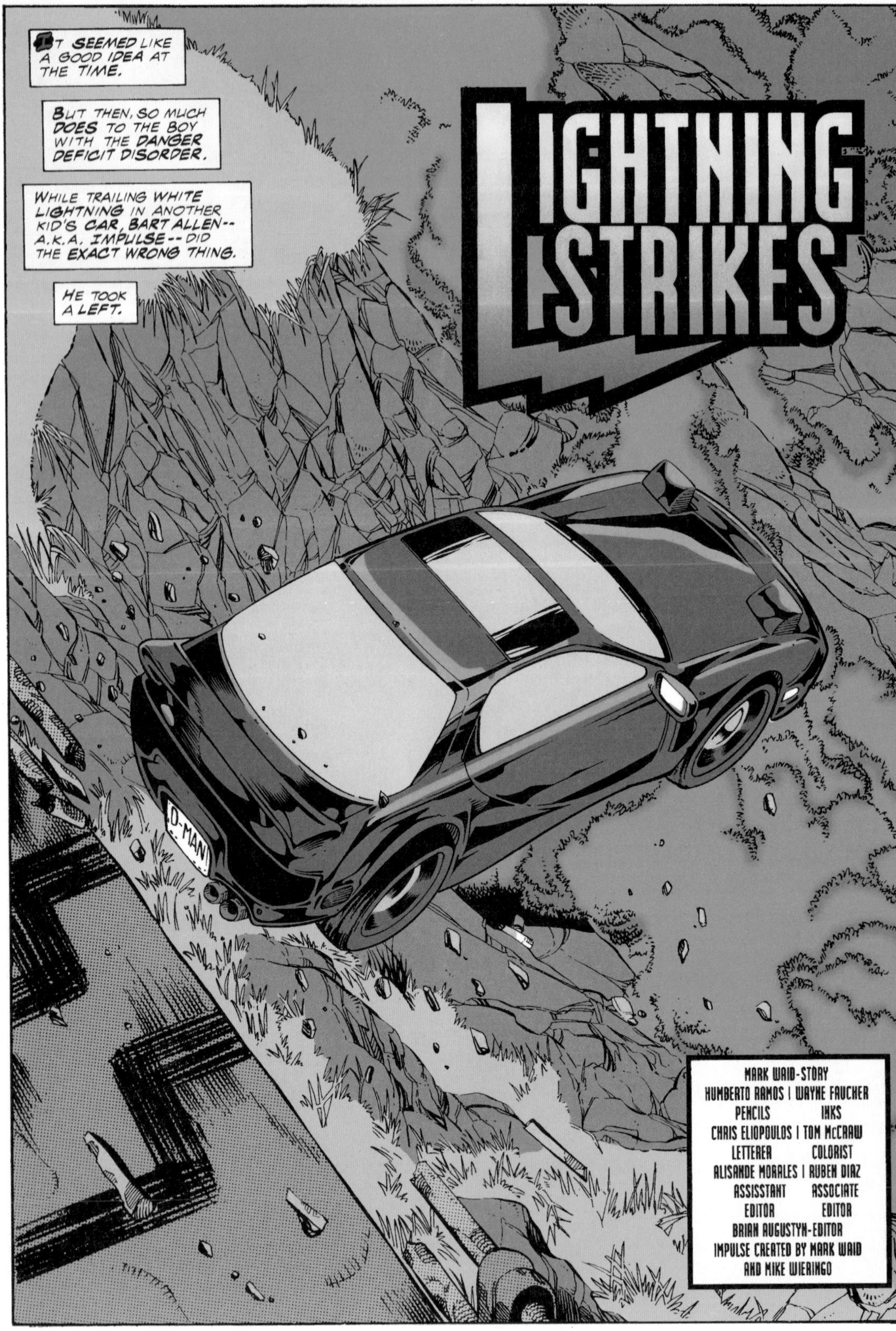
IT SEEMED LIKE A GOOD IDEA AT THE TIME.
BUT THEN, SO MUCH DOES TO THE BOY WITH THE DANGER DEFICIT DISORDER.
WHILE TRAILING WHITE LIGHTNING IN ANOTHER KID'S CAR, BART ALLEN-- A.K.A. IMPULSE-- DID THE EXACT WRONG THING.
HE TOOK A LEFT.
LIGHTNING STRIKES
O-MAN
MARK WAID-STORY
HUMBERTO RAMOS | WAYNE FAUCHER
PENCILS INKS
CHRIS ELIOPOULOS | TOM McCRAW
LETTERER COLORIST
ALISANDE MORALES | RUBEN DIAZ
ASSISSTANT ASSOCIATE
EDITOR EDITOR
BRIAN AUGUSTYN-EDITOR
IMPULSE CREATED BY MARK WAID
AND MIKE WIERINGO

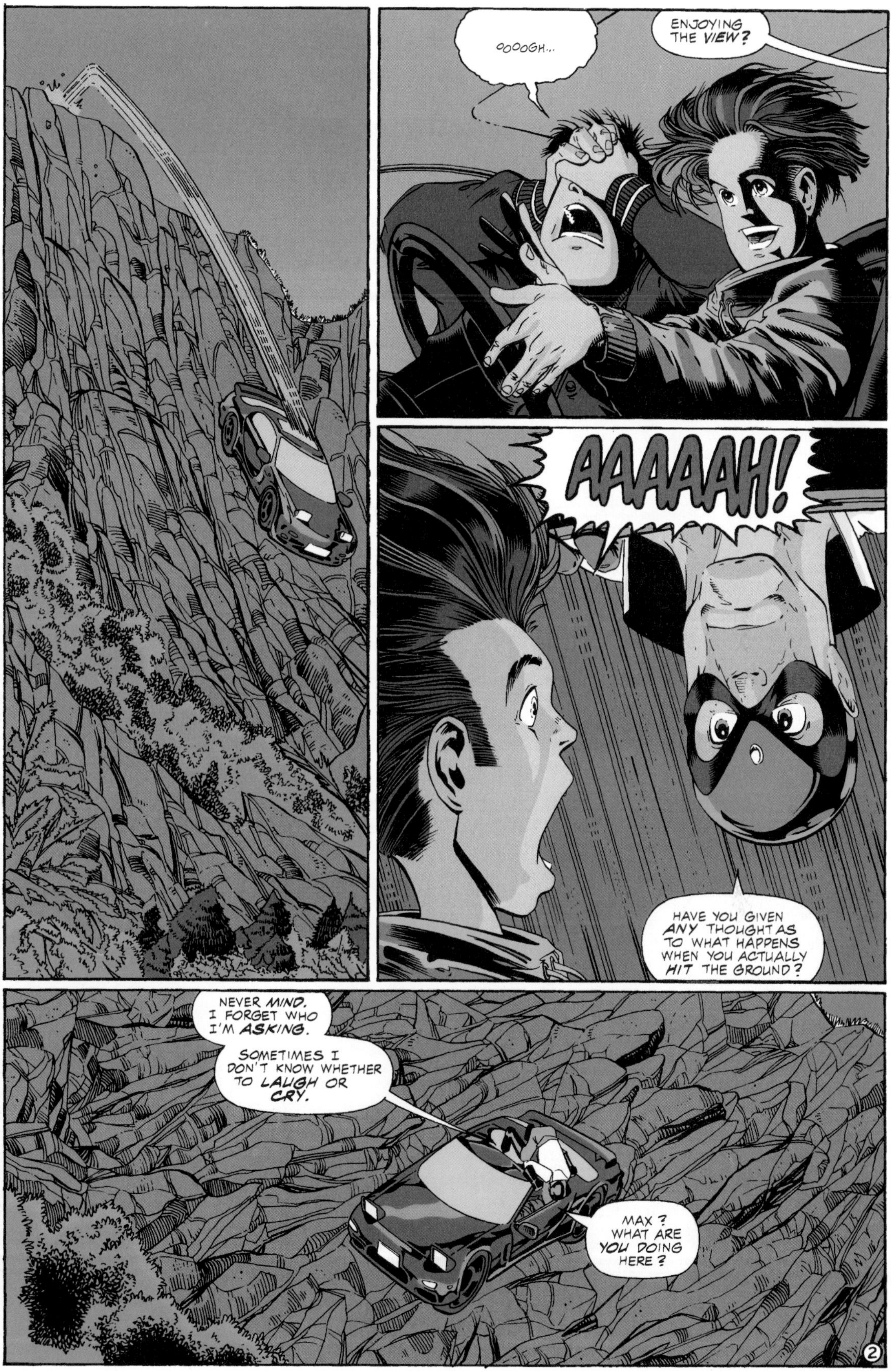
OOOOGH...
ENJOYING THE VIEW?
AAAAAH!
HAVE YOU GIVEN ANY THOUGHT AS TO WHAT HAPPENS WHEN YOU ACTUALLY HIT THE GROUND?
NEVER MIND. I FORGET WHO I'M ASKING.
SOMETIMES I DON'T KNOW WHETHER TO LAUGH OR CRY.
MAX? WHAT ARE YOU DOING HERE?

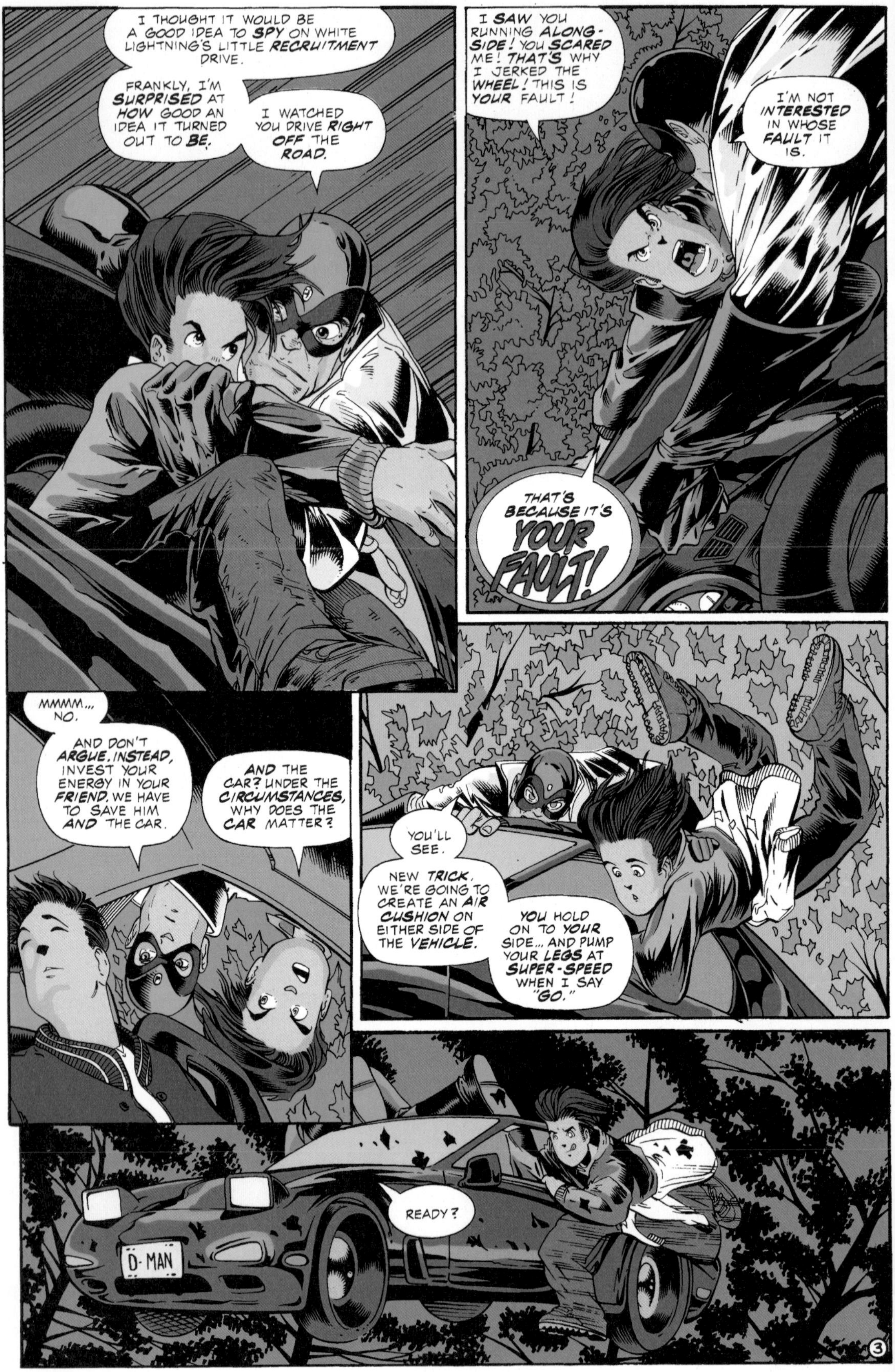

I THOUGHT IT WOULD BE A GOOD IDEA TO SPY ON WHITE LIGHTNING'S LITTLE RECRUITMENT DRIVE.
FRANKLY, I'M SURPRISED AT HOW GOOD AN IDEA IT TURNED OUT TO BE.
I WATCHED YOU DRIVE RIGHT OFF THE ROAD.
I SAW YOU RUNNING ALONG-SIDE! YOU SCARED ME! THAT'S WHY I JERKED THE WHEEL! THIS IS YOUR FAULT!
I'M NOT INTERESTED IN WHOSE FAULT IT IS.
THAT'S BECAUSE IT'S YOUR FAULT!
MMMM... NO.
AND DON'T ARGUE. INSTEAD, INVEST YOUR ENERGY IN YOUR FRIEND. WE HAVE TO SAVE HIM AND THE CAR.
AND THE CAR? UNDER THE CIRCUMSTANCES, WHY DOES THE CAR MATTER?
YOU'LL SEE.
NEW TRICK. WE'RE GOING TO CREATE AN AIR CUSHION ON EITHER SIDE OF THE VEHICLE.
YOU HOLD ON TO YOUR SIDE... AND PUMP YOUR LEGS AT SUPER-SPEED WHEN I SAY "GO."
READY?
D-MAN
3

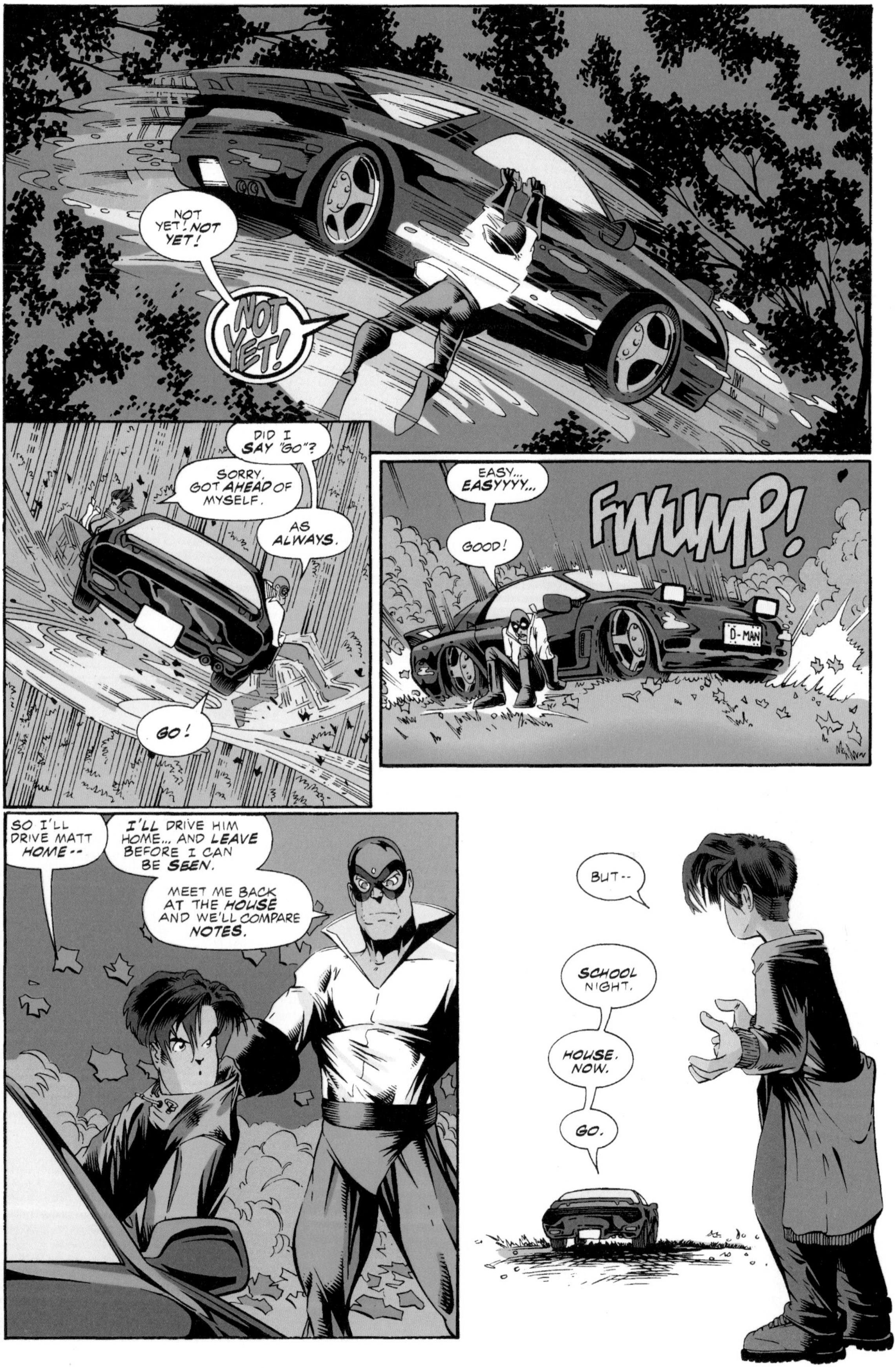

NOT YET! NOT YET!
NOT YET!
DID I SAY "GO"?
SORRY. GOT AHEAD OF MYSELF.
AS ALWAYS.
GO!
EASY... EASYYYY...
GOOD!
FWUMP!
D-MAN
SO I'LL DRIVE MATT HOME--
I'LL DRIVE HIM HOME... AND LEAVE BEFORE I CAN BE SEEN.
MEET ME BACK AT THE HOUSE AND WE'LL COMPARE NOTES.
BUT--
SCHOOL NIGHT.
HOUSE. NOW.
GO.

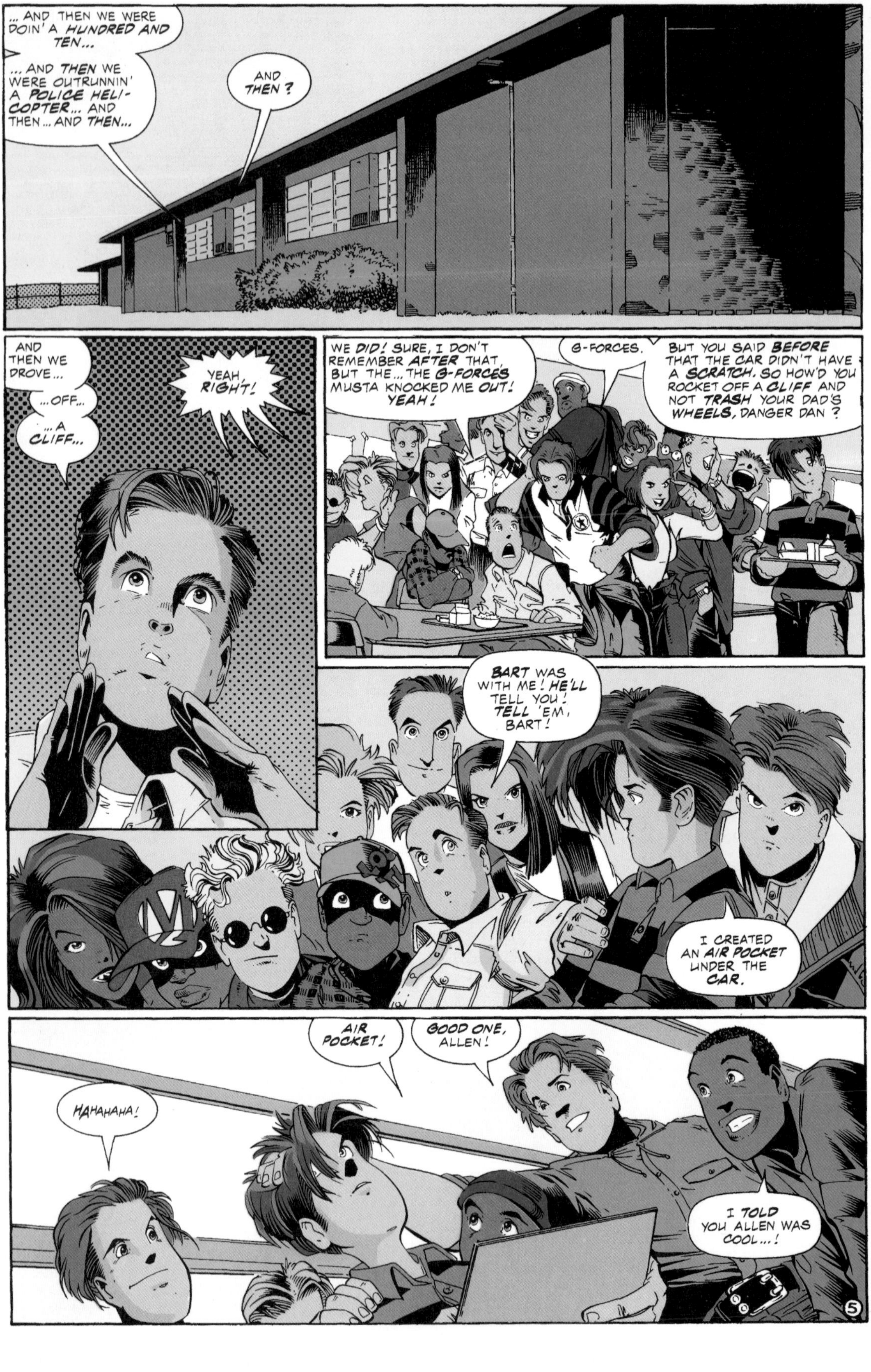
... AND THEN WE WERE DOIN' A HUNDRED AND TEN...
... AND THEN WE WERE OUTRUNNIN' A POLICE HELI-COPTER... AND THEN... AND THEN...
AND THEN?
AND THEN WE DROVE...
...OFF...
...A CLIFF...
YEAH, RIGHT!
WE DID! SURE, I DON'T REMEMBER AFTER THAT, BUT THE... THE G-FORCES MUSTA KNOCKED ME OUT! YEAH!
G-FORCES.
BUT YOU SAID BEFORE THAT THE CAR DIDN'T HAVE A SCRATCH. SO HOW'D YOU ROCKET OFF A CLIFF AND NOT TRASH YOUR DAD'S WHEELS, DANGER DAN?
BART WAS WITH ME! HE'LL TELL YOU! TELL 'EM, BART!
I CREATED AN AIR POCKET UNDER THE CAR.
HAHAHAHA!
AIR POCKET!
GOOD ONE, ALLEN!
I TOLD YOU ALLEN WAS COOL...!
5

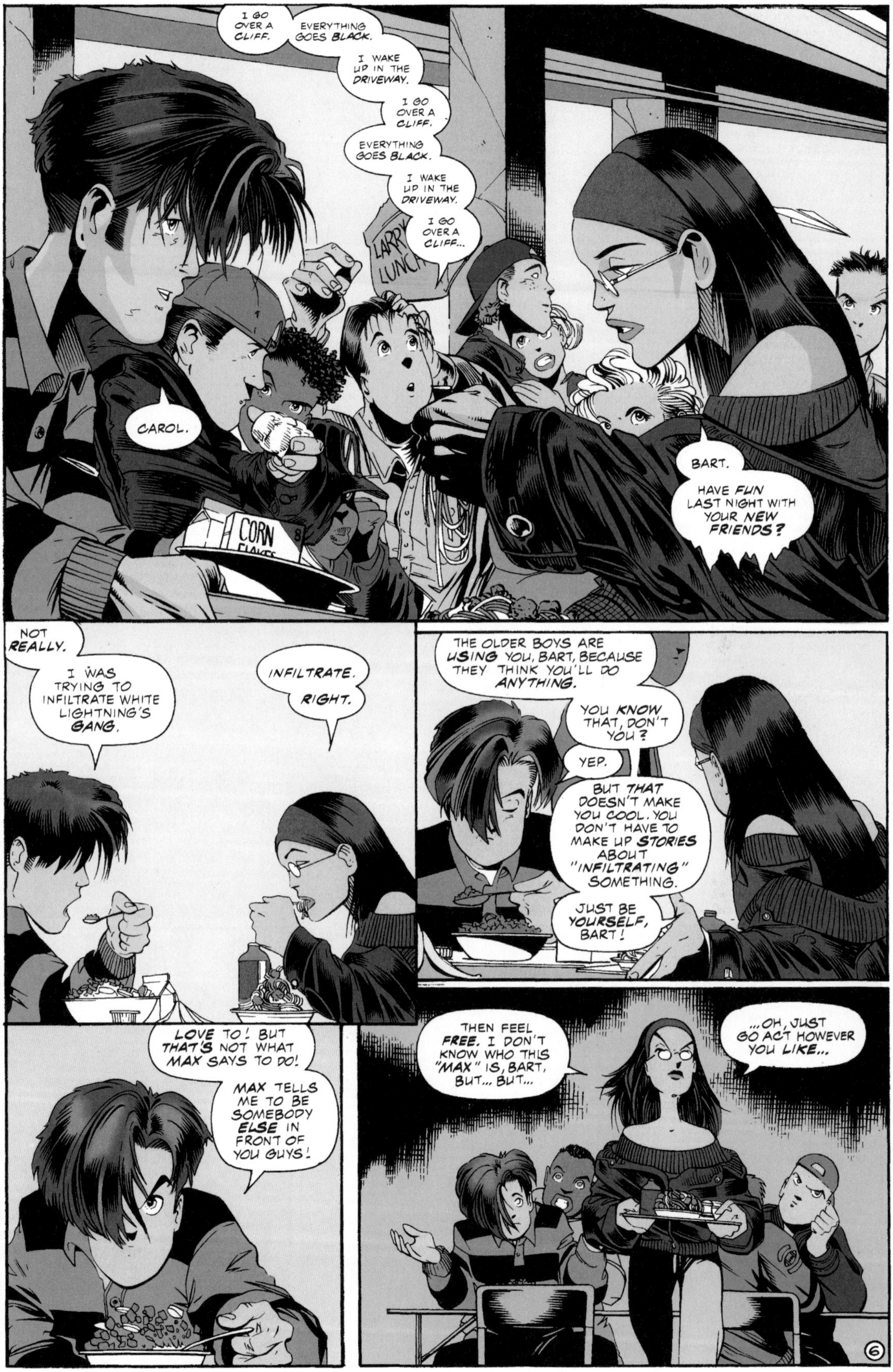
I GO OVER A CLIFF.
EVERYTHING GOES BLACK.
I WAKE UP IN THE DRIVEWAY.
I GO OVER A CLIFF.
EVERYTHING GOES BLACK.
I WAKE UP IN THE DRIVEWAY.
I GO OVER A CLIFF...
CAROL.
BART.
HAVE FUN LAST NIGHT WITH YOUR NEW FRIENDS?
NOT REALLY.
I WAS TRYING TO INFILTRATE WHITE LIGHTNING'S GANG.
INFILTRATE.
RIGHT.
THE OLDER BOYS ARE USING YOU, BART, BECAUSE THEY THINK YOU'LL DO ANYTHING.
YOU KNOW THAT, DON'T YOU?
YEP.
BUT THAT DOESN'T MAKE YOU COOL. YOU DON'T HAVE TO MAKE UP STORIES ABOUT "INFILTRATING" SOMETHING.
JUST BE YOURSELF, BART!
LOVE TO! BUT THAT'S NOT WHAT MAX SAYS TO DO!
MAX TELLS ME TO BE SOMEBODY ELSE IN FRONT OF YOU GUYS!
THEN FEEL FREE. I DON'T KNOW WHO THIS "MAX" IS, BART, BUT... BUT...
...OH, JUST GO ACT HOWEVER YOU LIKE...

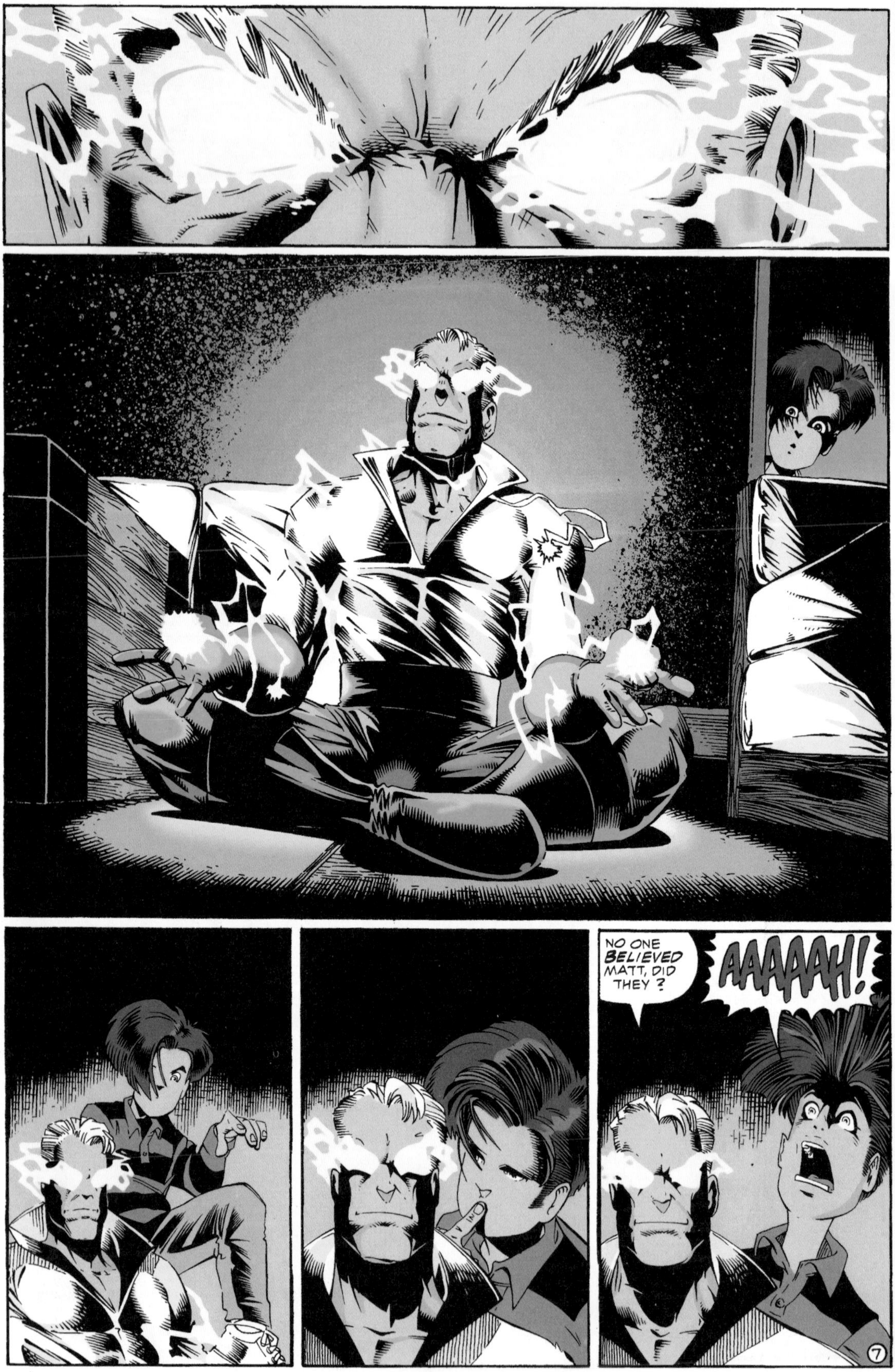
NO ONE BELIEVED MATT, DID THEY?
AAAAAH!

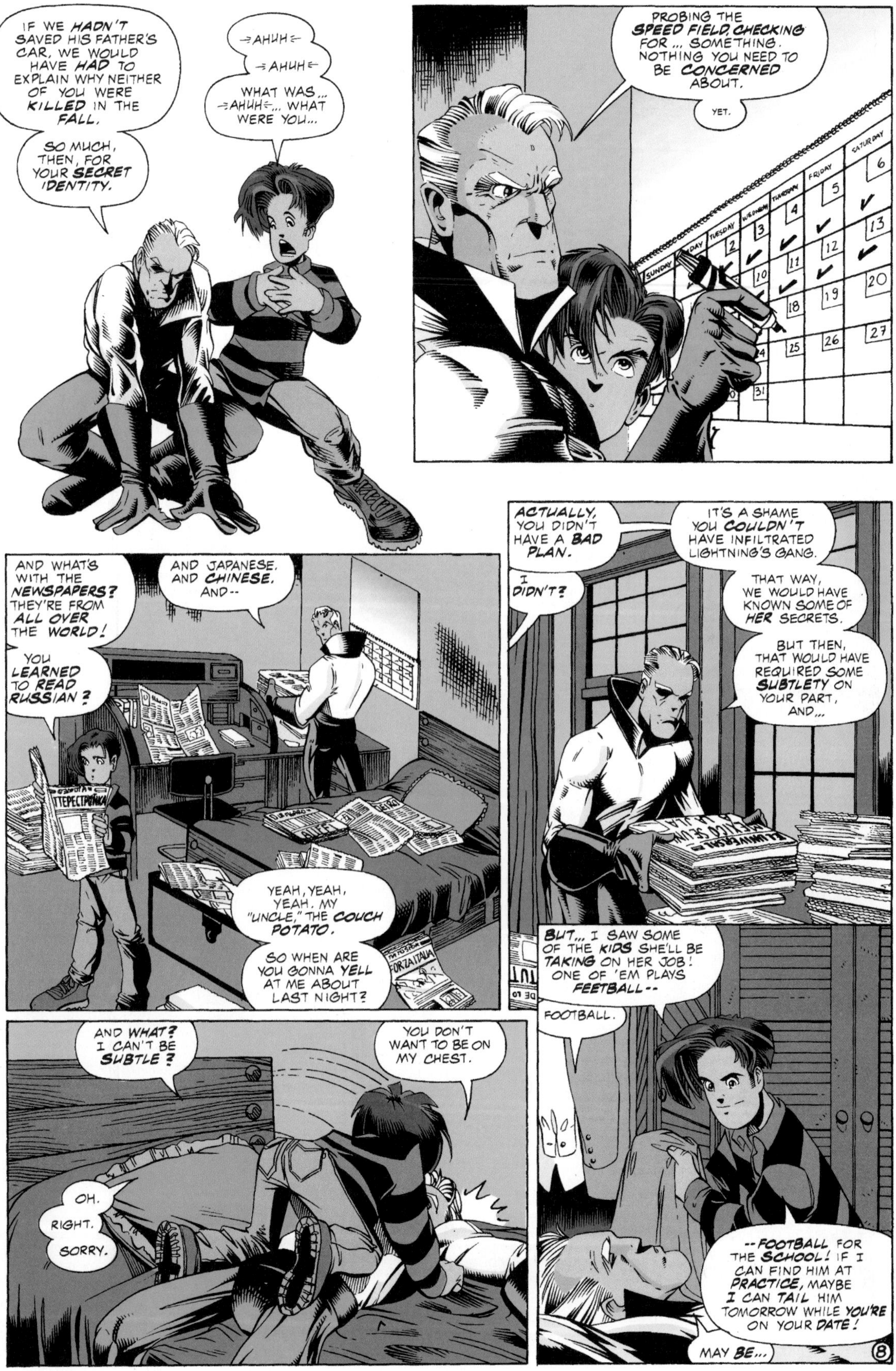
IF WE HADN'T SAVED HIS FATHER'S CAR, WE WOULD HAVE HAD TO EXPLAIN WHY NEITHER OF YOU WERE KILLED IN THE FALL.
SO MUCH, THEN, FOR YOUR SECRET IDENTITY.
AHUH
AHUH
WHAT WAS... AHUH... WHAT WERE YOU...
PROBING THE SPEED FIELD, CHECKING FOR ... SOMETHING. NOTHING YOU NEED TO BE CONCERNED ABOUT.
YET.
AND WHAT'S WITH THE NEWSPAPERS? THEY'RE FROM ALL OVER THE WORLD!
YOU LEARNED TO READ RUSSIAN?
AND JAPANESE. AND CHINESE. AND--
YEAH, YEAH, YEAH. MY "UNCLE," THE COUCH POTATO.
SO WHEN ARE YOU GONNA YELL AT ME ABOUT LAST NIGHT?
ACTUALLY, YOU DIDN'T HAVE A BAD PLAN.
I DIDN'T?
IT'S A SHAME YOU COULDN'T HAVE INFILTRATED LIGHTNING'S GANG.
THAT WAY, WE WOULD HAVE KNOWN SOME OF HER SECRETS.
BUT THEN, THAT WOULD HAVE REQUIRED SOME SUBTLETY ON YOUR PART, AND...
AND WHAT? I CAN'T BE SUBTLE?
YOU DON'T WANT TO BE ON MY CHEST.
OH.
RIGHT.
SORRY.
BUT... I SAW SOME OF THE KIDS SHE'LL BE TAKING ON HER JOB! ONE OF 'EM PLAYS FEETBALL--
FOOTBALL.
--FOOTBALL FOR THE SCHOOL! IF I CAN FIND HIM AT PRACTICE, MAYBE I CAN TAIL HIM TOMORROW WHILE YOU'RE ON YOUR DATE!
MAY BE...
8

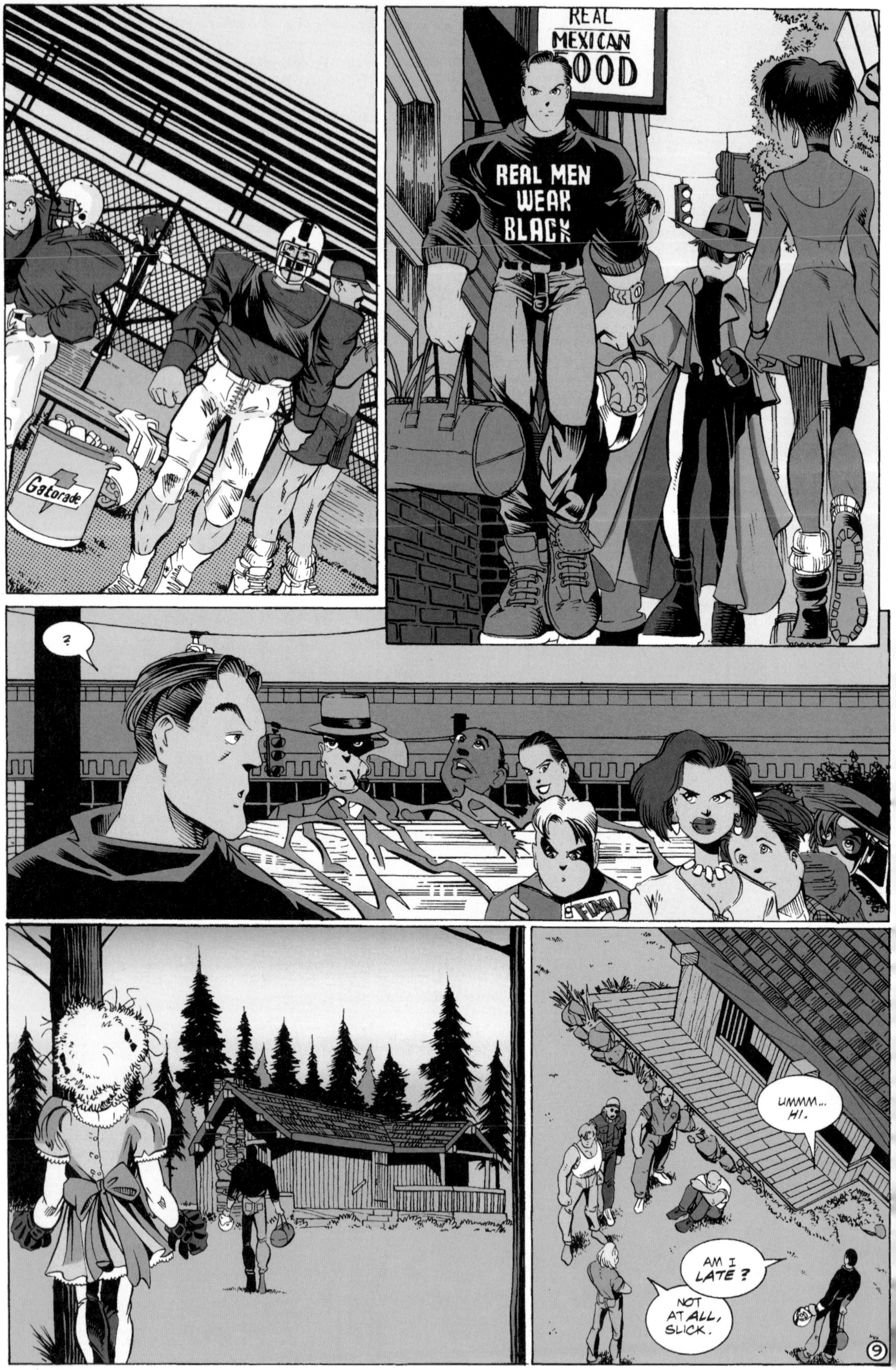
Gatorade
REAL MEXICAN FOOD
REAL MEN WEAR BLACK
?
UMMM... HI.
AM I LATE?
NOT AT ALL, SLICK.
9

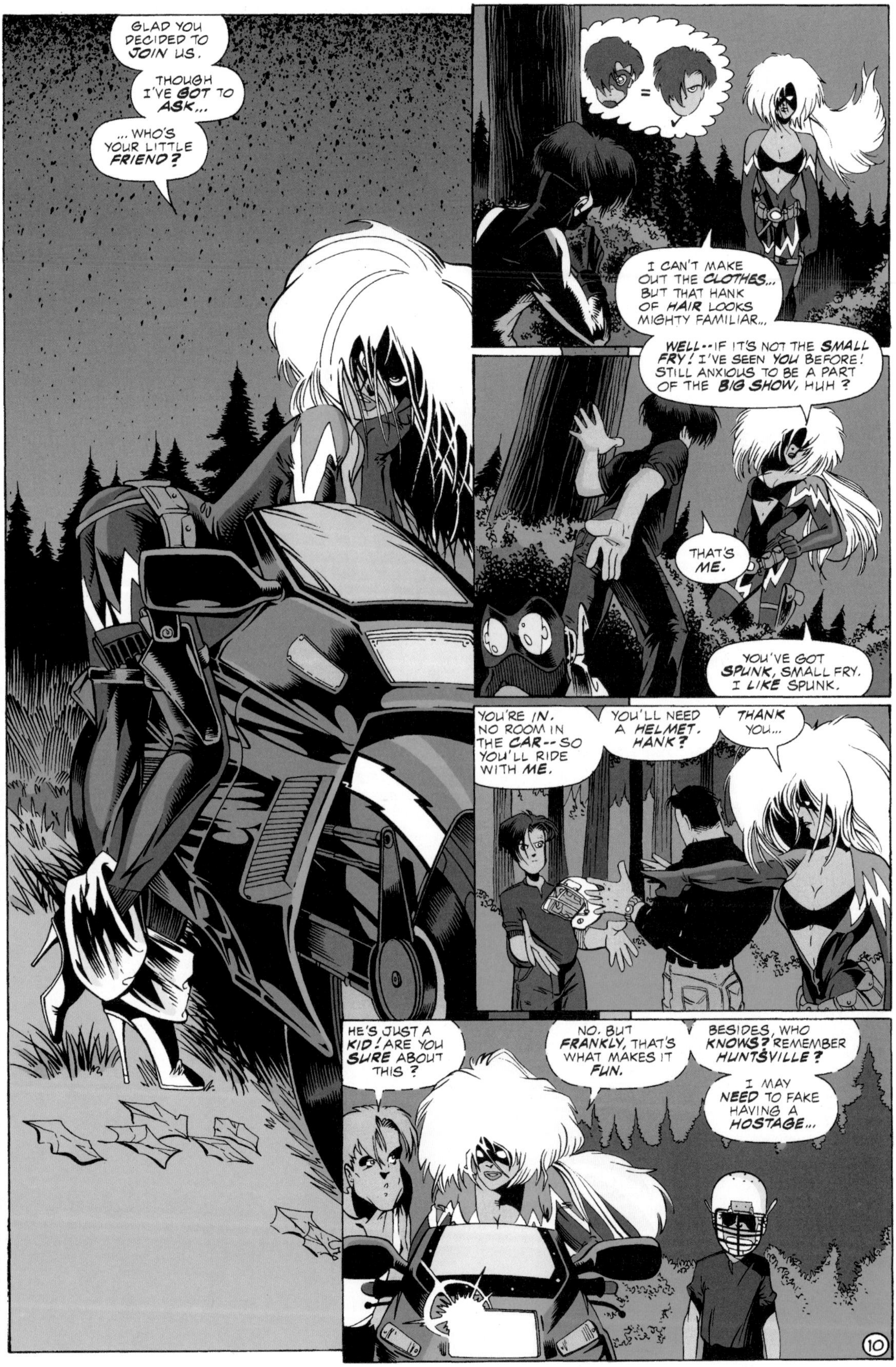
GLAD YOU DECIDED TO JOIN US.
THOUGH I'VE GOT TO ASK...
... WHO'S YOUR LITTLE FRIEND?
I CAN'T MAKE OUT THE CLOTHES... BUT THAT HANK OF HAIR LOOKS MIGHTY FAMILIAR...
WELL--IF IT'S NOT THE SMALL FRY! I'VE SEEN YOU BEFORE! STILL ANXIOUS TO BE A PART OF THE BIG SHOW, HUH?
THAT'S ME.
YOU'VE GOT SPUNK, SMALL FRY. I LIKE SPUNK.
YOU'RE IN. NO ROOM IN THE CAR--SO YOU'LL RIDE WITH ME.
YOU'LL NEED A HELMET. HANK?
THANK YOU...
HE'S JUST A KID! ARE YOU SURE ABOUT THIS?
NO. BUT FRANKLY, THAT'S WHAT MAKES IT FUN.
BESIDES, WHO KNOWS? REMEMBER HUNTSVILLE?
I MAY NEED TO FAKE HAVING A HOSTAGE...
10

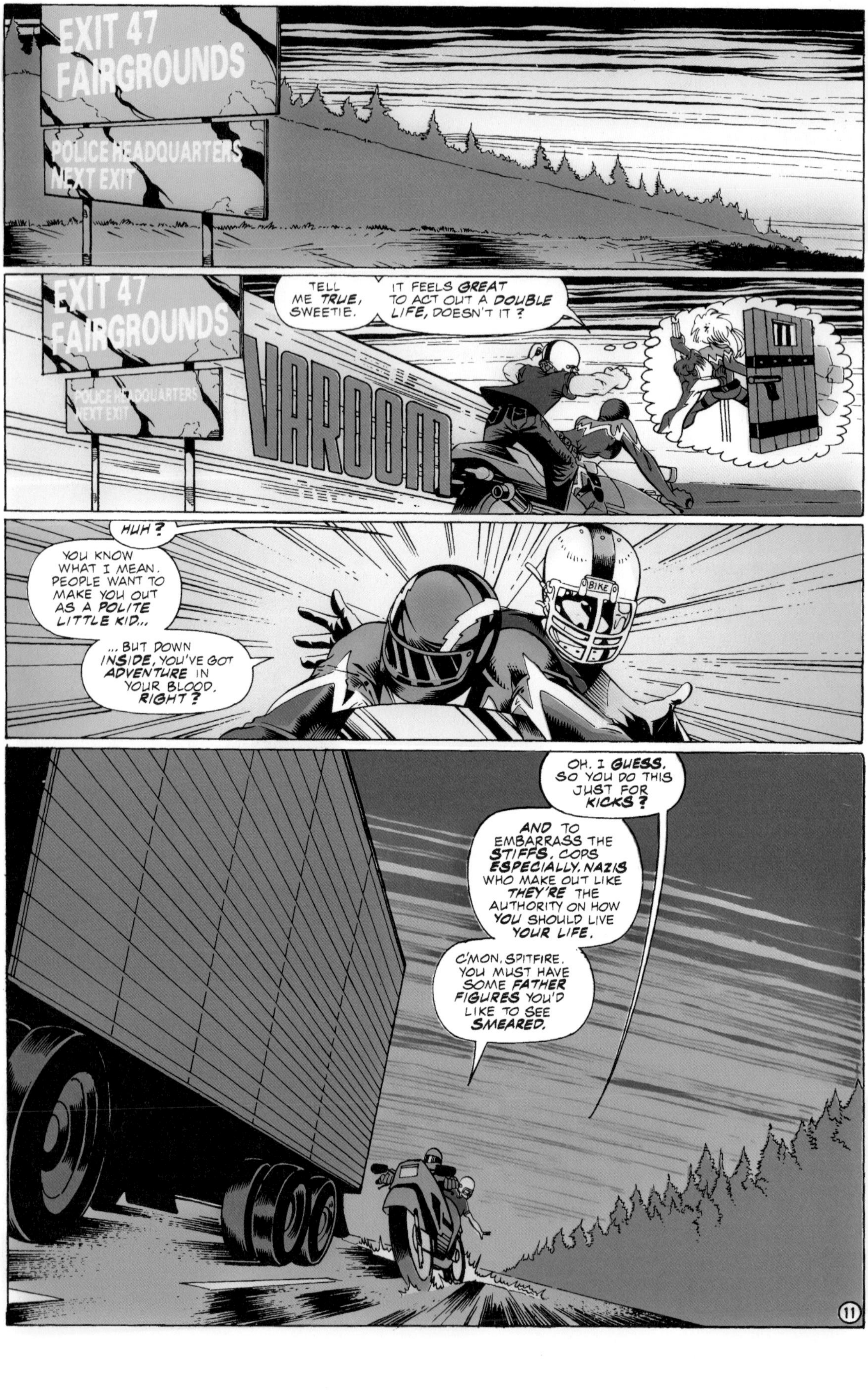
EXIT 47
FAIRGROUNDS
POLICE HEADQUARTERS
NEXT EXIT
TELL ME TRUE, SWEETIE.
IT FEELS GREAT TO ACT OUT A DOUBLE LIFE, DOESN'T IT?
VAROOM
HUH?
YOU KNOW WHAT I MEAN. PEOPLE WANT TO MAKE YOU OUT AS A POLITE LITTLE KID...
...BUT DOWN INSIDE, YOU'VE GOT ADVENTURE IN YOUR BLOOD. RIGHT?
BIKE
OH. I GUESS. SO YOU DO THIS JUST FOR KICKS?
AND TO EMBARRASS THE STIFFS. COPS ESPECIALLY. NAZIS WHO MAKE OUT LIKE THEY'RE THE AUTHORITY ON HOW YOU SHOULD LIVE YOUR LIFE.
C'MON, SPITFIRE. YOU MUST HAVE SOME FATHER FIGURES YOU'D LIKE TO SEE SMEARED.

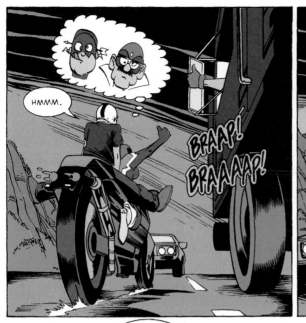

HMMM.

BRAAP!
BRAAAAP!

FRIEND OF YOURS?

I'M A LEGEND, SPITFIRE. GOT FRIENDS ALL OVER.

AND THESE THINGS YOU DO, YOU'RE NOT WORRIED ABOUT GETTING HURT EITHER?

"EITHER"?

HERE'S HOW A LEGEND LIVES, OKAY? ONE MINUTE AT A TIME, NEVER WORRYING ABOUT TOMORROW TILL IT COMES. WHEN IT ENDS, IT ENDS.

YOU KNOW WHAT THEY SAY ABOUT THE BULLET WITH YOUR NAME ON IT?

WHAT?

YOU NEVER HEAR IT.

HANG ON TIGHT, SPITFIRE.

WE'RE ABOUT TO BLOW THE ROOF OFF THIS JOINT!

CASINO

MINHOTA RESERVATION CASINO

VAROOOOOM

12

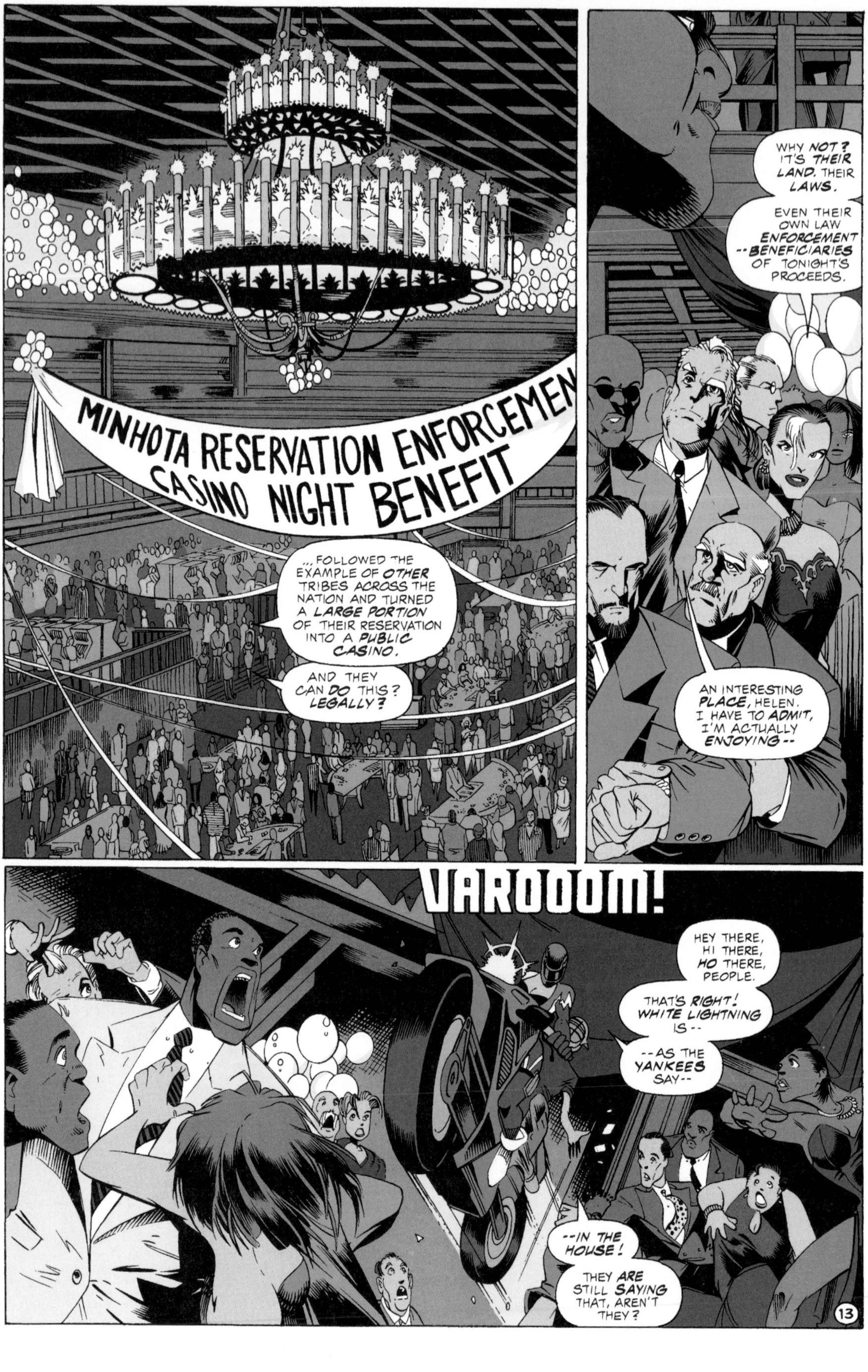
MINHOTA RESERVATION ENFORCEMEN
CASINO NIGHT BENEFIT
...FOLLOWED THE EXAMPLE OF OTHER TRIBES ACROSS THE NATION AND TURNED A LARGE PORTION OF THEIR RESERVATION INTO A PUBLIC CASINO.
AND THEY CAN DO THIS? LEGALLY?
WHY NOT? IT'S THEIR LAND. THEIR LAWS.
EVEN THEIR OWN LAW ENFORCEMENT --BENEFICIARIES OF TONIGHT'S PROCEEDS.
AN INTERESTING PLACE, HELEN. I HAVE TO ADMIT, I'M ACTUALLY ENJOYING--
VAROOOM!
HEY THERE, HI THERE, HO THERE, PEOPLE.
THAT'S RIGHT! WHITE LIGHTNING IS--
--AS THE YANKEES SAY--
--IN THE HOUSE!
THEY ARE STILL SAYING THAT, AREN'T THEY?

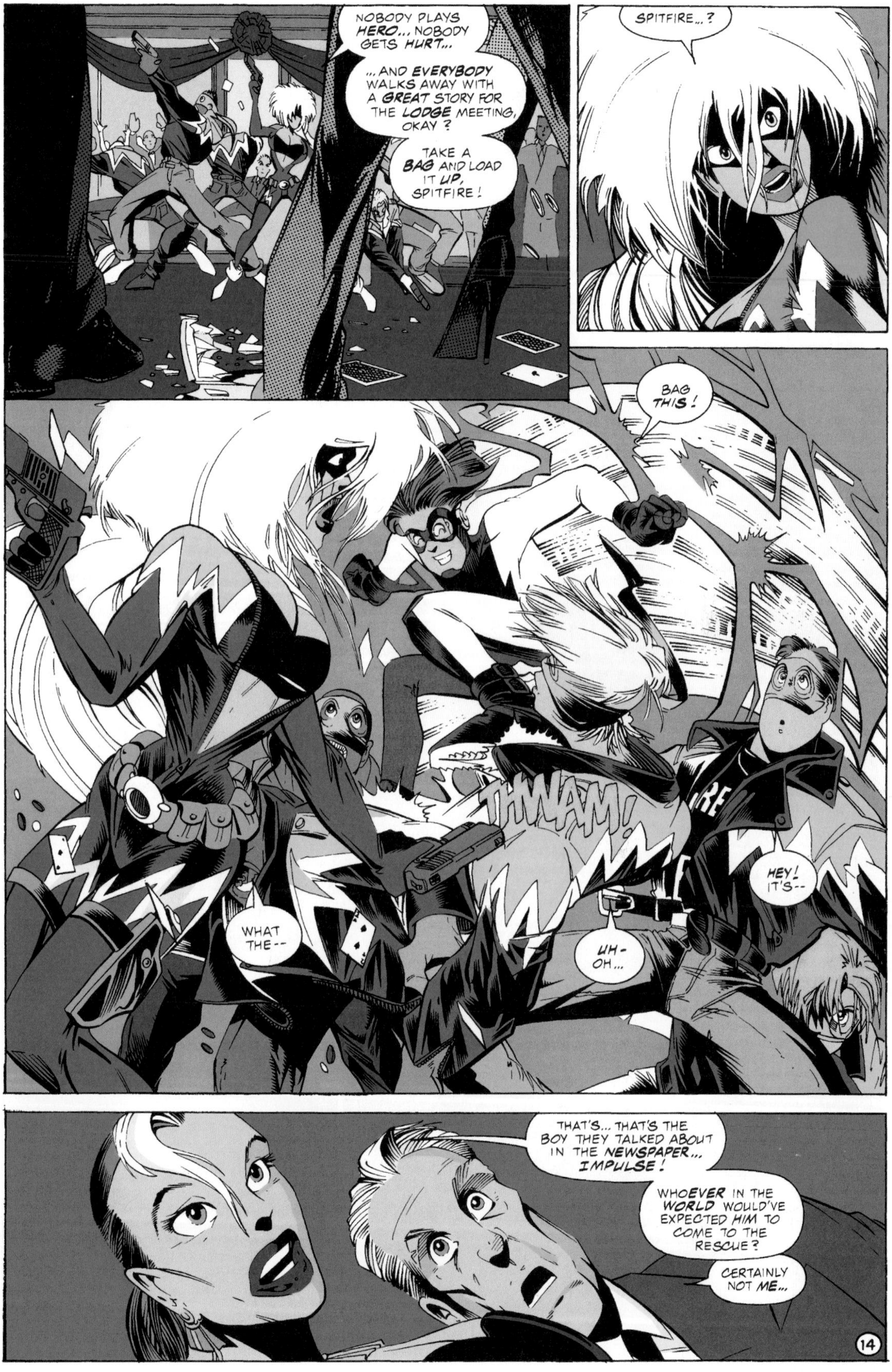
NOBODY PLAYS HERO... NOBODY GETS HURT...
...AND EVERYBODY WALKS AWAY WITH A GREAT STORY FOR THE LODGE MEETING, OKAY?
TAKE A BAG AND LOAD IT UP, SPITFIRE!
SPITFIRE...?
BAG THIS!
THWAM!
WHAT THE--
UH-OH...
HEY! IT'S--
THAT'S... THAT'S THE BOY THEY TALKED ABOUT IN THE NEWSPAPER... IMPULSE!
WHOEVER IN THE WORLD WOULD'VE EXPECTED HIM TO COME TO THE RESCUE?
CERTAINLY NOT ME...
14

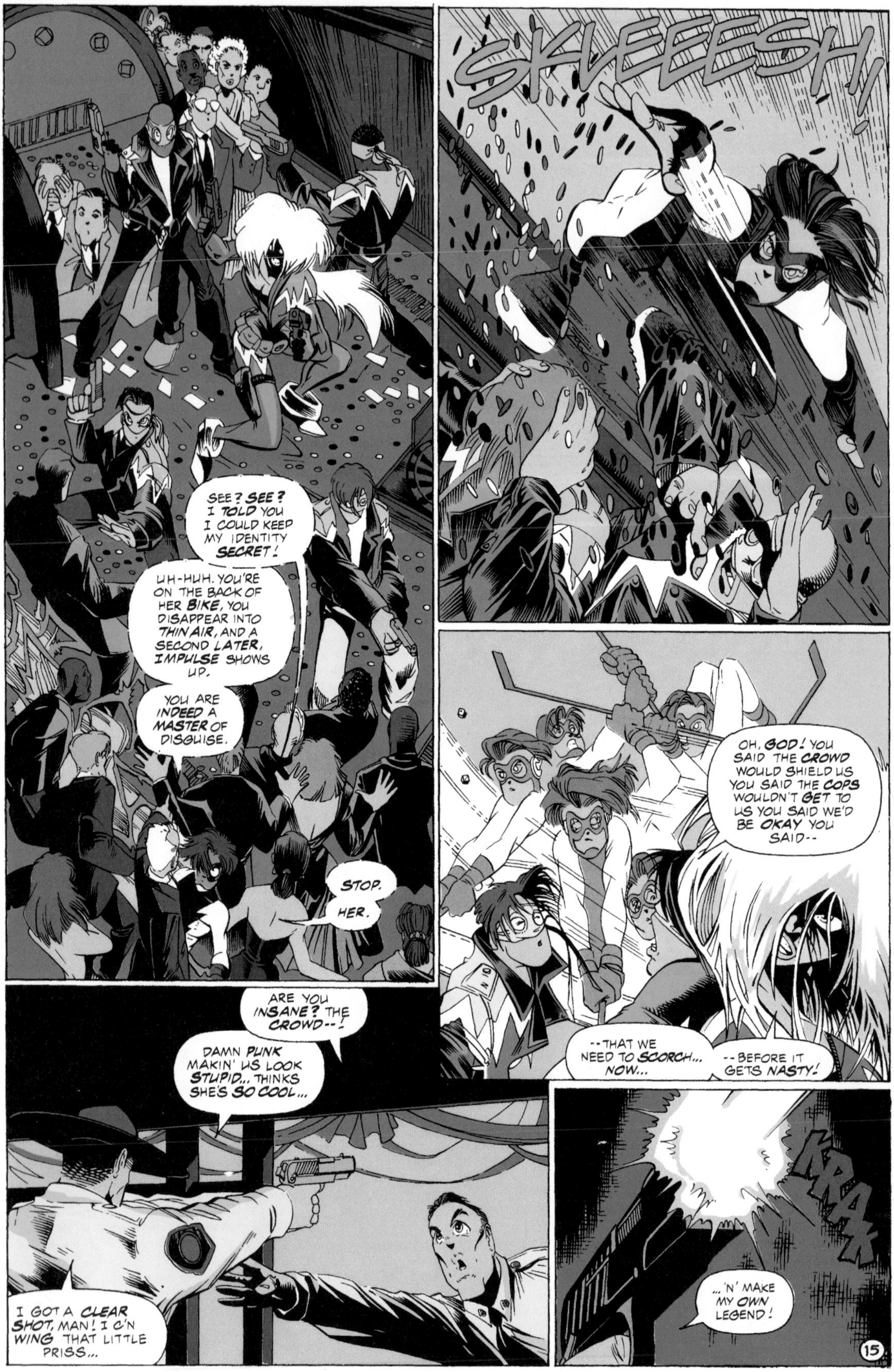
SKLEEEESH!!
SEE? SEE? I TOLD YOU I COULD KEEP MY IDENTITY SECRET!
UH-HUH. YOU'RE ON THE BACK OF HER BIKE, YOU DISAPPEAR INTO THIN AIR, AND A SECOND LATER, IMPULSE SHOWS UP.
YOU ARE INDEED A MASTER OF DISGUISE.
STOP.
HER.
OH, GOD! YOU SAID THE CROWD WOULD SHIELD US YOU SAID THE COPS WOULDN'T GET TO US YOU SAID WE'D BE OKAY YOU SAID--
--THAT WE NEED TO SCORCH... NOW...
--BEFORE IT GETS NASTY!
ARE YOU INSANE? THE CROWD--!
DAMN PUNK MAKIN' US LOOK STUPID... THINKS SHE'S SO COOL...
I GOT A CLEAR SHOT, MAN! I C'N WING THAT LITTLE PRISS...
KRAK
...'N' MAKE MY OWN LEGEND!

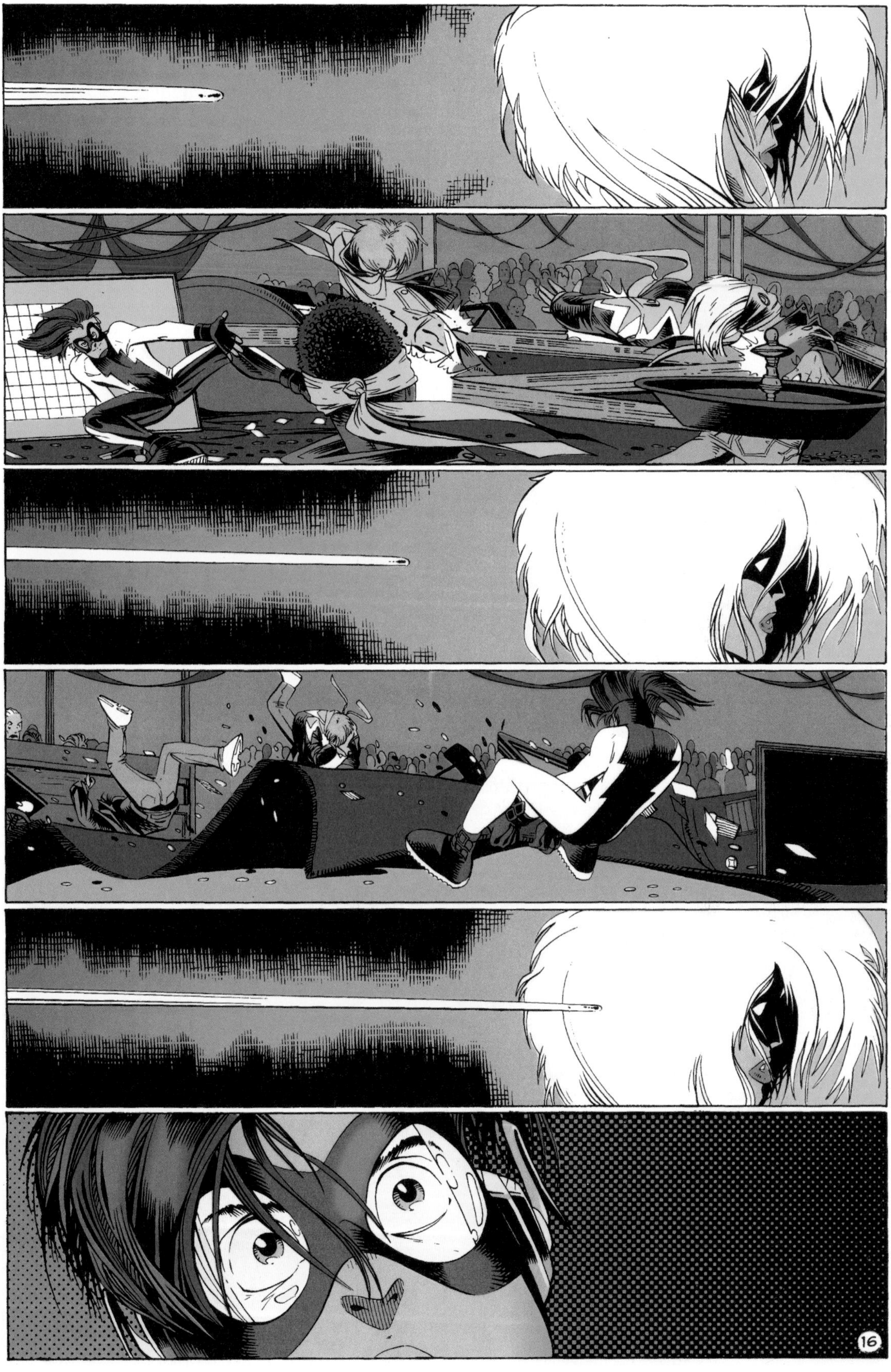

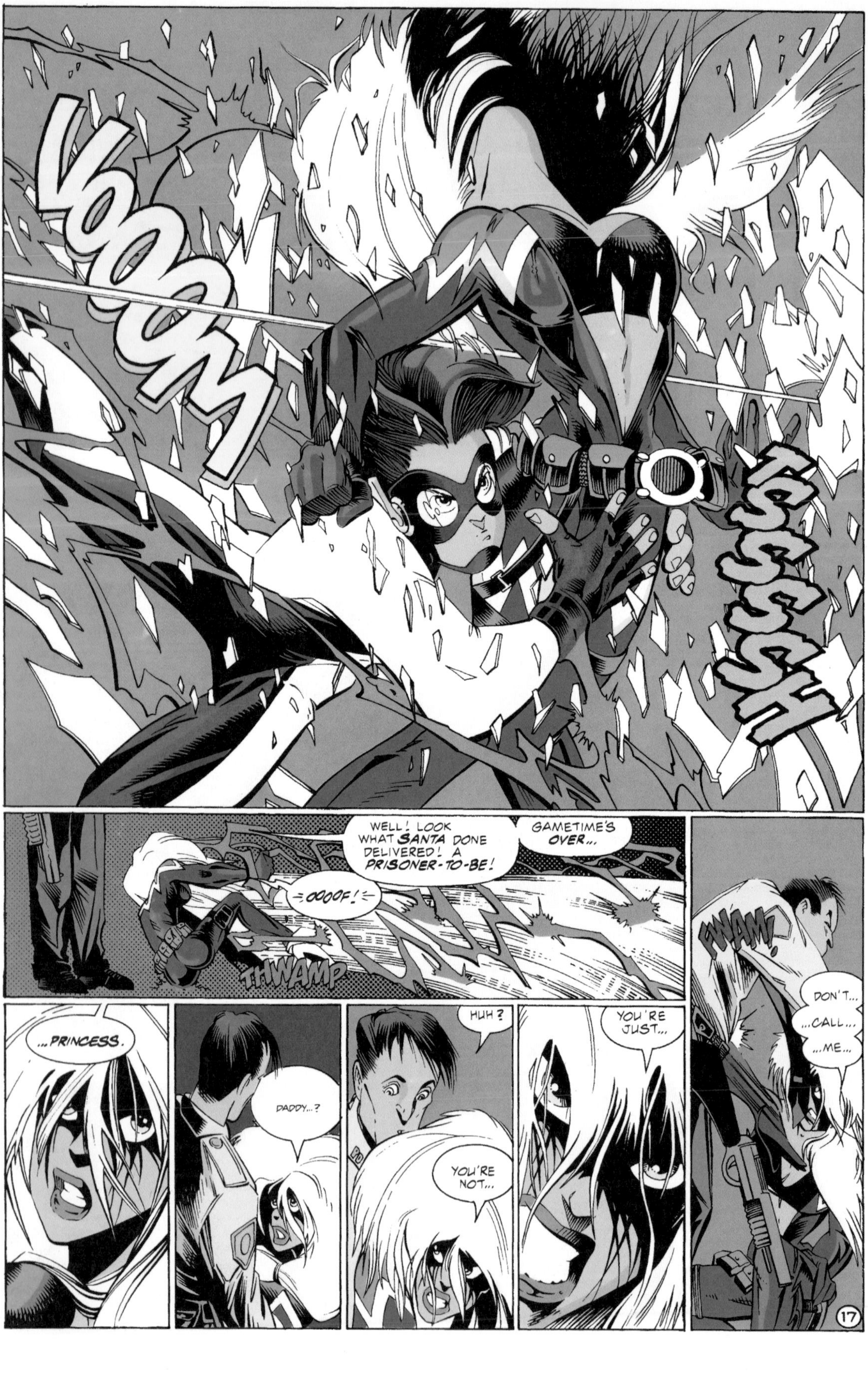
VOOOOM
TSSSSH
WELL! LOOK WHAT SANTA DONE DELIVERED! A PRISONER-TO-BE!
GAMETIME'S OVER...
OOOOF!
THWAMP
WAM!
DON'T...
...CALL...
...ME...
...PRINCESS.
DADDY...?
HUH?
YOU'RE NOT...
YOU'RE JUST...

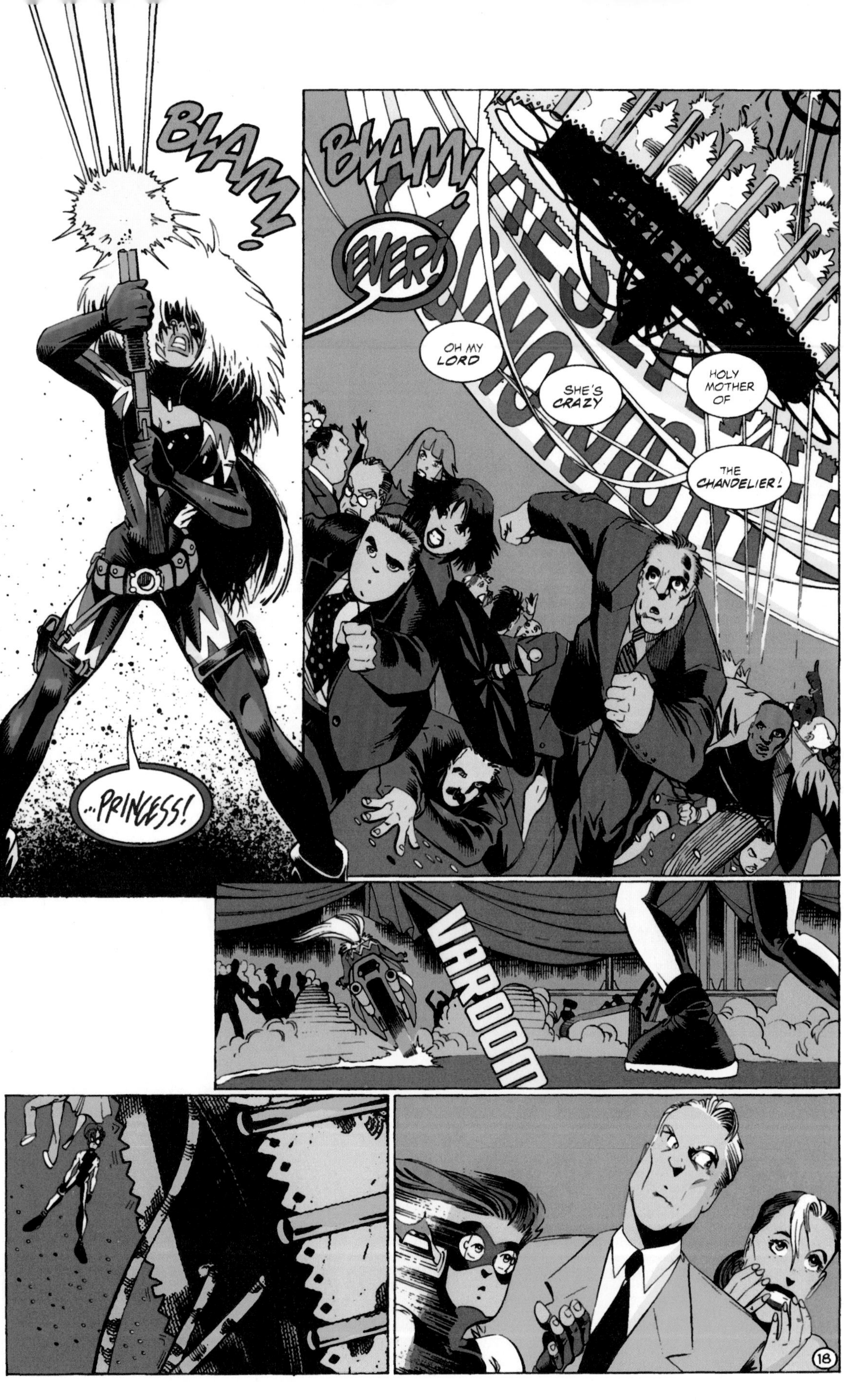
BLAM!
BLAM!
EVER!
OH MY LORD
SHE'S CRAZY
HOLY MOTHER OF
THE CHANDELIER!
...PRINCESS!
VAROOOM

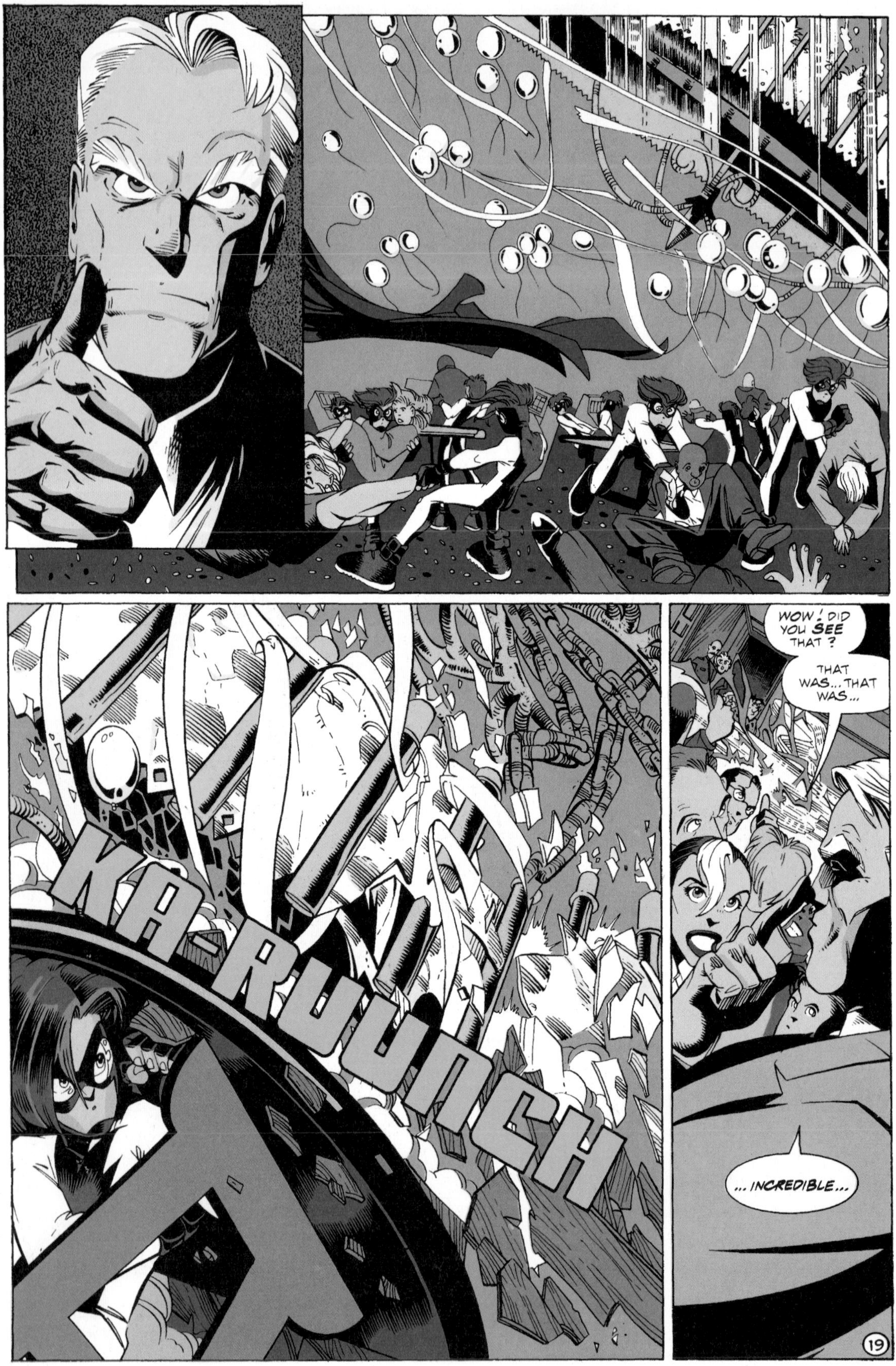
KA-RUUNCH
WOW! DID YOU SEE THAT?
THAT WAS... THAT WAS...
...INCREDIBLE...

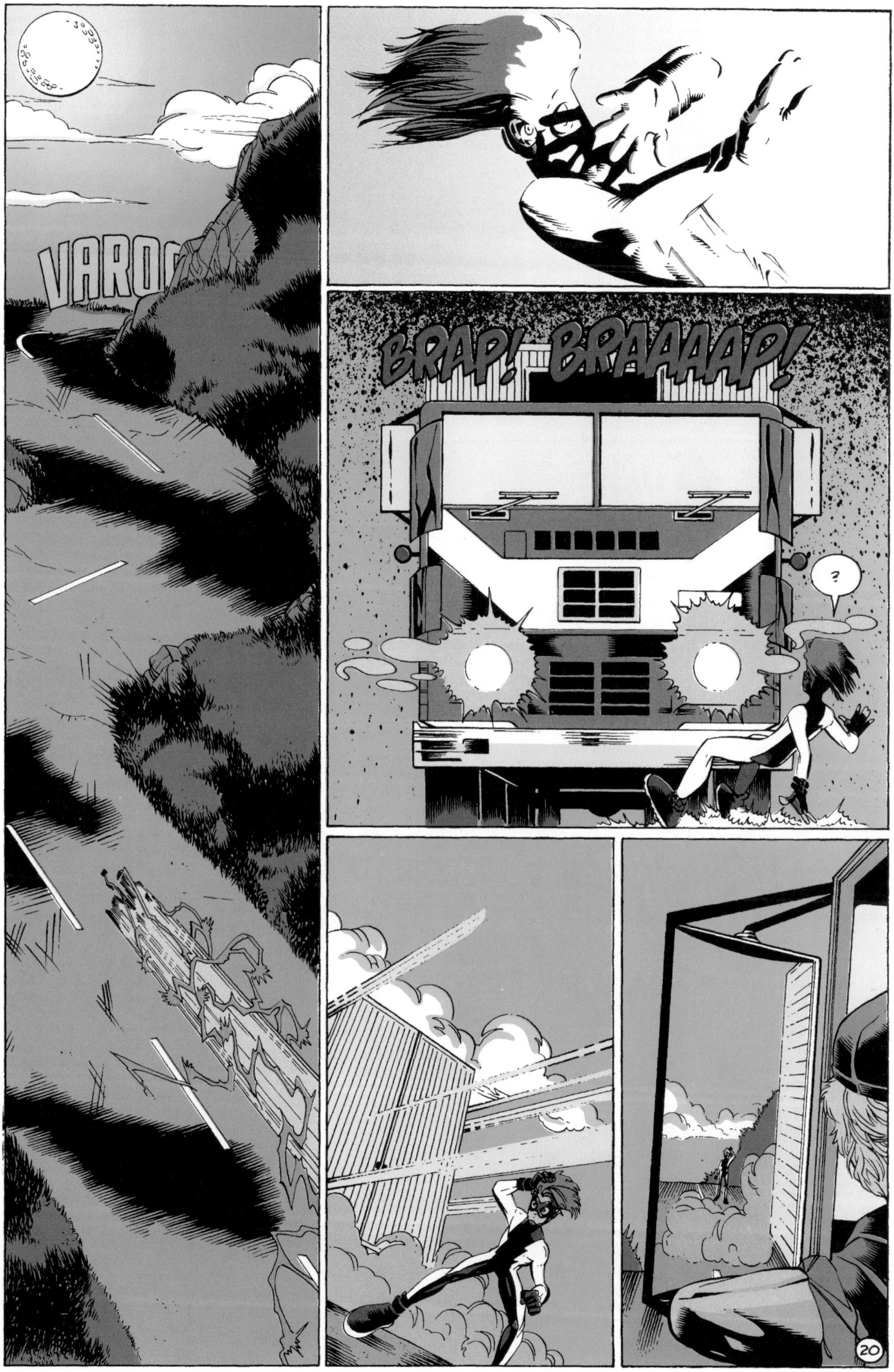
VAROO
BRAP! BRAAAAP!
?
20

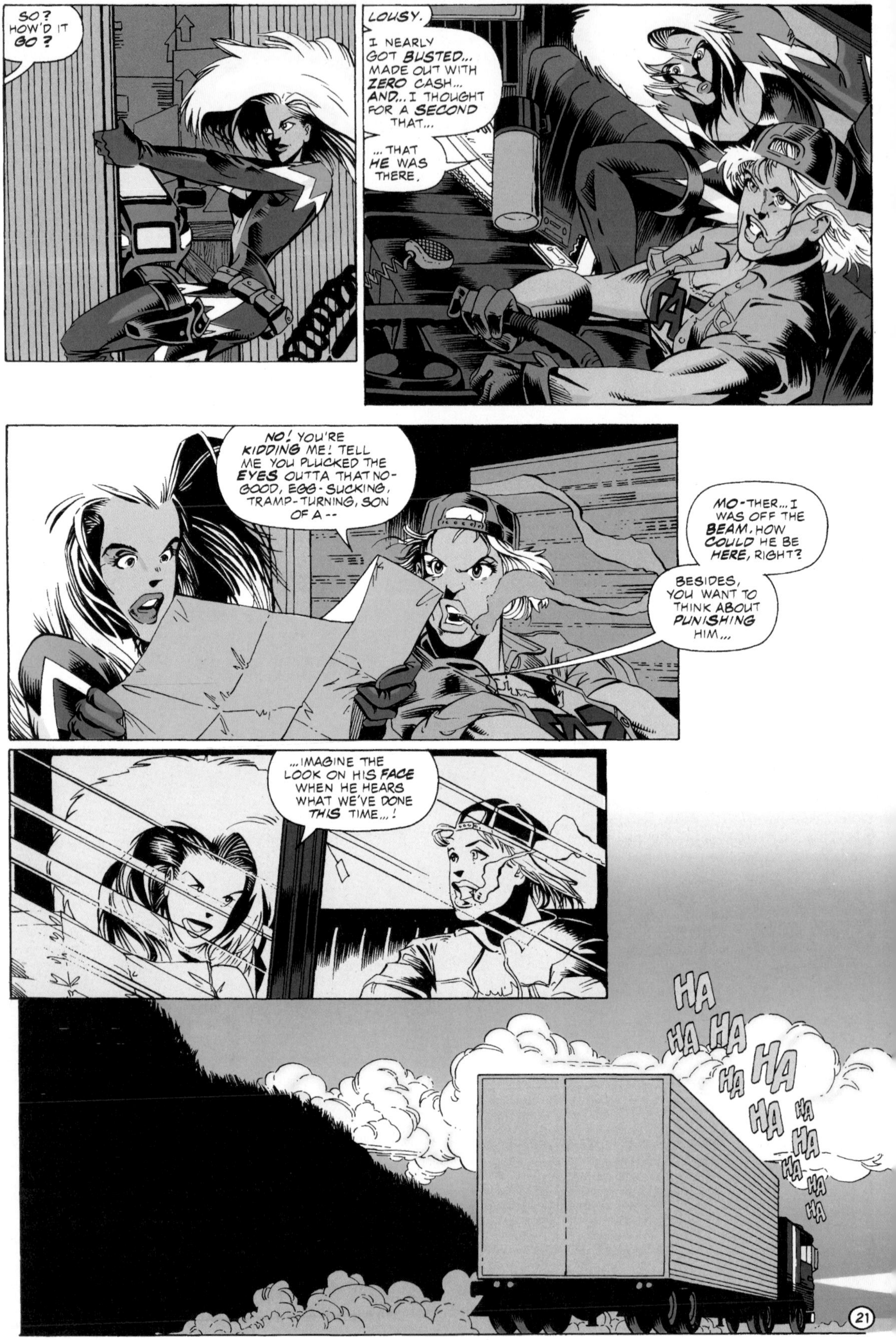
SO? HOW'D IT GO?
LOUSY.
I NEARLY GOT BUSTED... MADE OUT WITH ZERO CASH... AND... I THOUGHT FOR A SECOND THAT...
... THAT HE WAS THERE.
NO! YOU'RE KIDDING ME! TELL ME YOU PLUCKED THE EYES OUTTA THAT NO-GOOD, EGG-SUCKING, TRAMP-TURNING, SON OF A --
MO-THER... I WAS OFF THE BEAM. HOW COULD HE BE HERE, RIGHT?
BESIDES, YOU WANT TO THINK ABOUT PUNISHING HIM...
...IMAGINE THE LOOK ON HIS FACE WHEN HE HEARS WHAT WE'VE DONE THIS TIME...!
HA HA HA HA HA HA HA HA HA HA HA HA

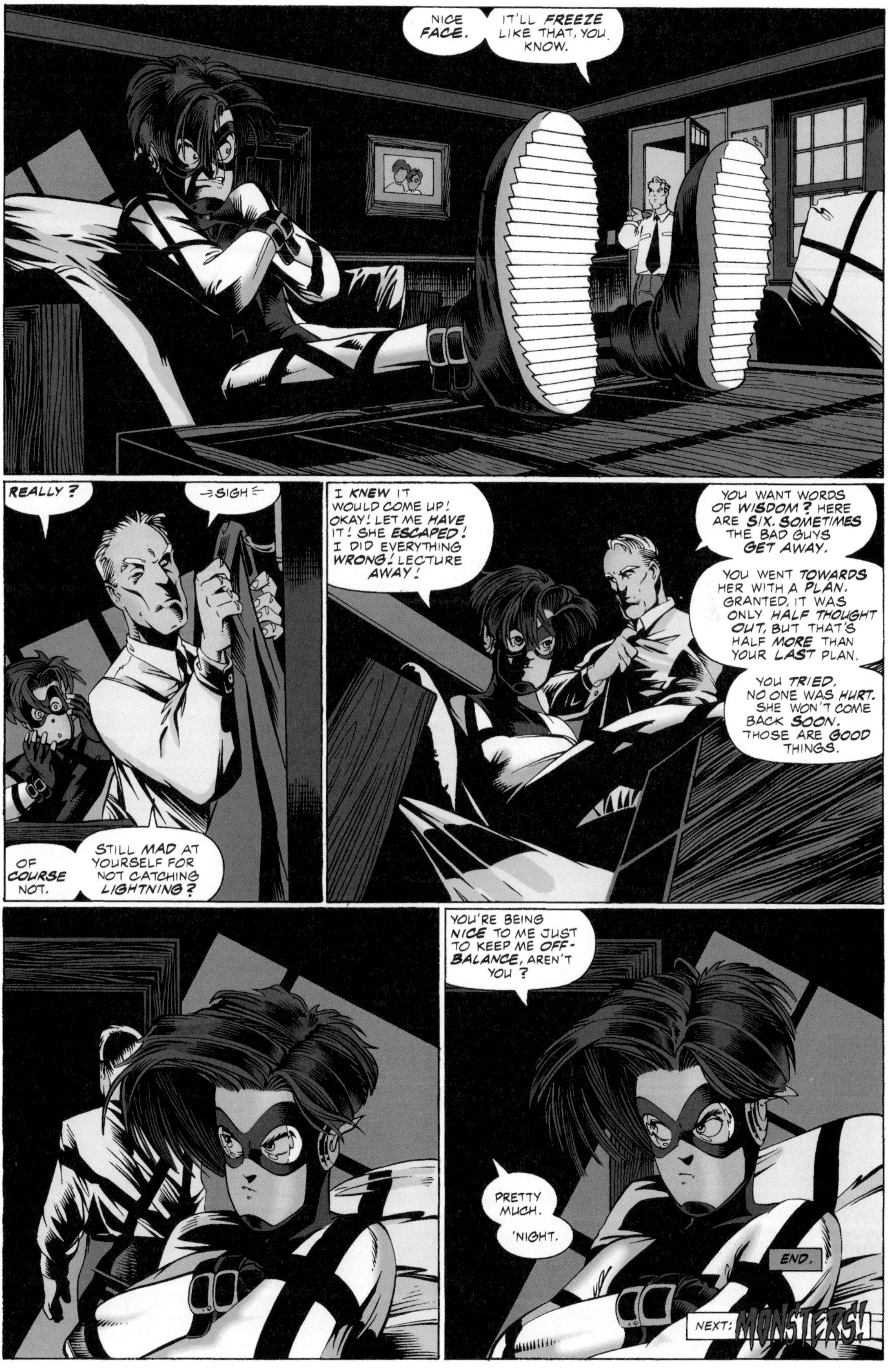
NICE FACE.
IT'LL FREEZE LIKE THAT, YOU KNOW.
REALLY?
SIGH
STILL MAD AT YOURSELF FOR NOT CATCHING LIGHTNING?
OF COURSE NOT.
I KNEW IT WOULD COME UP! OKAY! LET ME HAVE IT! SHE ESCAPED! I DID EVERYTHING WRONG! LECTURE AWAY!
YOU WANT WORDS OF WISDOM? HERE ARE SIX. SOMETIMES THE BAD GUYS GET AWAY.
YOU WENT TOWARDS HER WITH A PLAN. GRANTED, IT WAS ONLY HALF THOUGHT OUT, BUT THAT'S HALF MORE THAN YOUR LAST PLAN.
YOU TRIED. NO ONE WAS HURT. SHE WON'T COME BACK SOON. THOSE ARE GOOD THINGS.
YOU'RE BEING NICE TO ME JUST TO KEEP ME OFF-BALANCE, AREN'T YOU?
PRETTY MUCH.
'NIGHT.
END.
NEXT: MONSTERS!

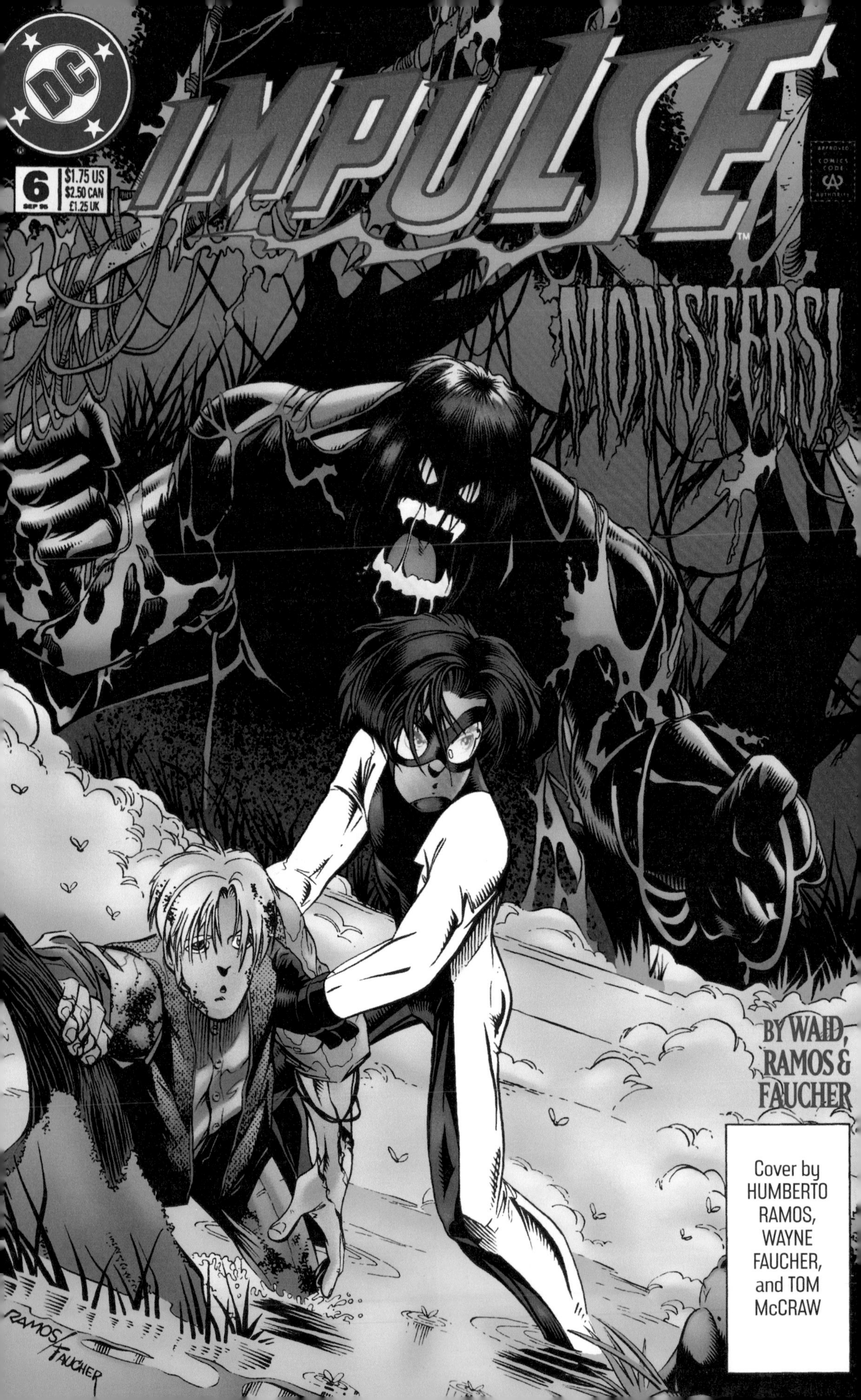
DC
IMPULSE
6
SEP 95
$1.75 US
$2.50 CAN
£1.25 UK
APPROVED BY THE COMICS CODE AUTHORITY
MONSTERS!
BY WAID, RAMOS & FAUCHER
RAMOS/FAUCHER
Cover by
HUMBERTO
RAMOS,
WAYNE
FAUCHER,
and TOM
McCRAW

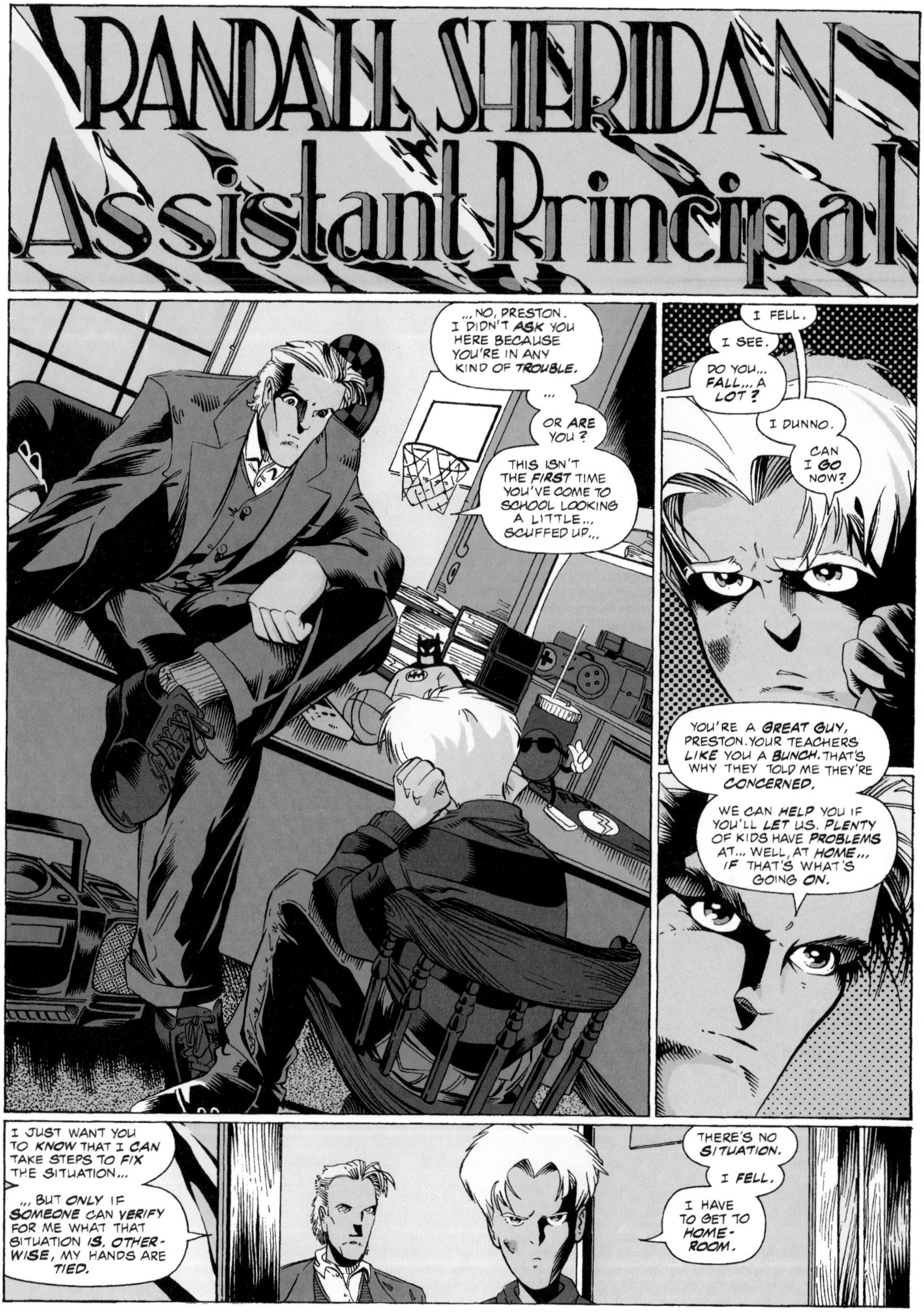
RANDALL SHERIDAN
Assistant Principal
...NO, PRESTON. I DIDN'T ASK YOU HERE BECAUSE YOU'RE IN ANY KIND OF TROUBLE.
...
OR ARE YOU?
THIS ISN'T THE FIRST TIME YOU'VE COME TO SCHOOL LOOKING A LITTLE... SCUFFED UP...
I FELL.
I SEE.
DO YOU... FALL... A LOT?
I DUNNO.
CAN I GO NOW?
YOU'RE A GREAT GUY, PRESTON. YOUR TEACHERS LIKE YOU A BUNCH. THAT'S WHY THEY TOLD ME THEY'RE CONCERNED.
WE CAN HELP YOU IF YOU'LL LET US. PLENTY OF KIDS HAVE PROBLEMS AT... WELL, AT HOME... IF THAT'S WHAT'S GOING ON.
I JUST WANT YOU TO KNOW THAT I CAN TAKE STEPS TO FIX THE SITUATION...
...BUT ONLY IF SOMEONE CAN VERIFY FOR ME WHAT THAT SITUATION IS. OTHERWISE, MY HANDS ARE TIED.
THERE'S NO SITUATION.
I FELL.
I HAVE TO GET TO HOMEROOM.

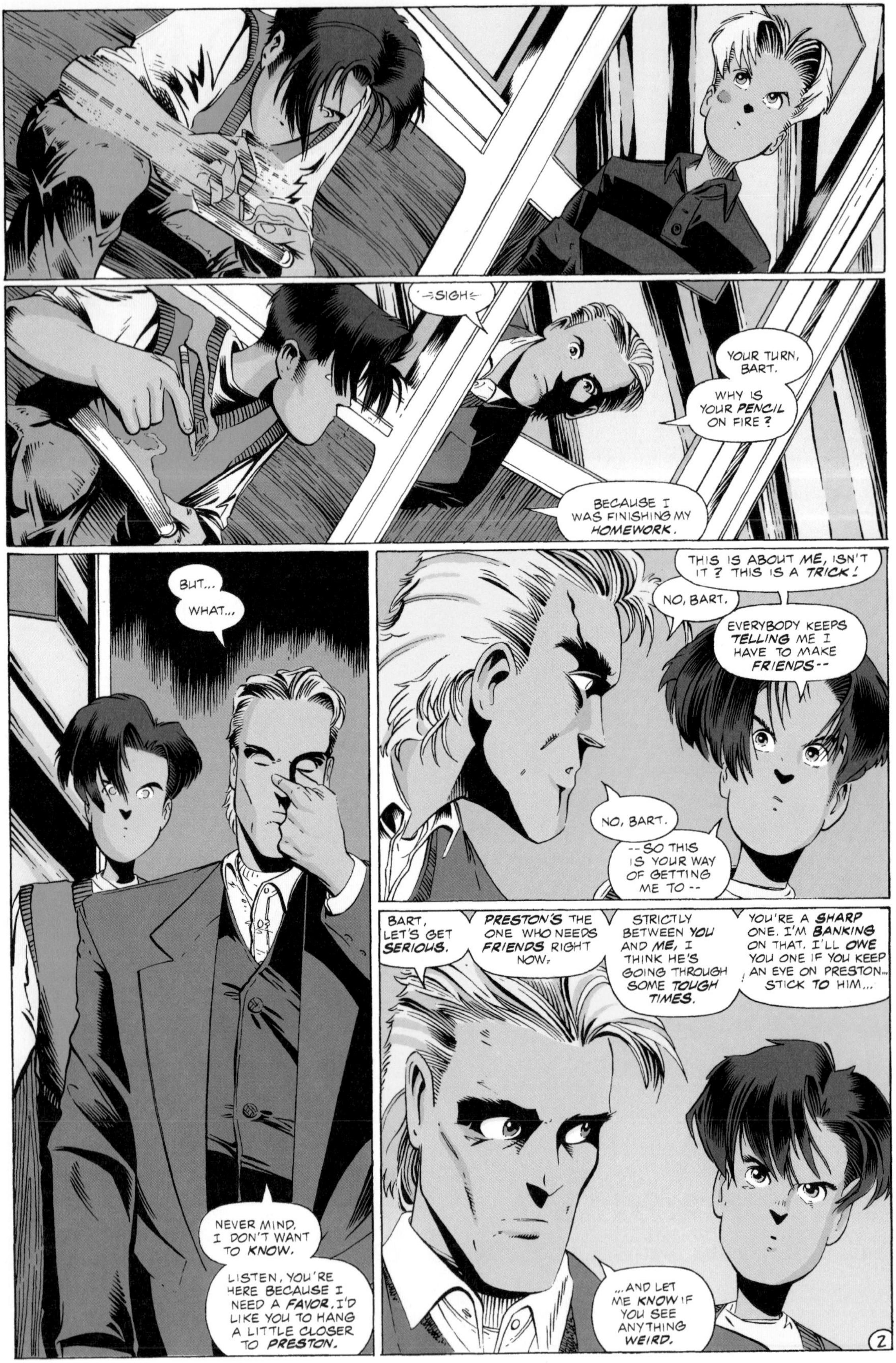
SIGH
YOUR TURN, BART.
WHY IS YOUR PENCIL ON FIRE?
BECAUSE I WAS FINISHING MY HOMEWORK.
BUT...
WHAT...
NEVER MIND, I DON'T WANT TO KNOW.
LISTEN, YOU'RE HERE BECAUSE I NEED A FAVOR. I'D LIKE YOU TO HANG A LITTLE CLOSER TO PRESTON.
THIS IS ABOUT ME, ISN'T IT? THIS IS A TRICK!
NO, BART.
EVERYBODY KEEPS TELLING ME I HAVE TO MAKE FRIENDS--
NO, BART.
--SO THIS IS YOUR WAY OF GETTING ME TO--
BART, LET'S GET SERIOUS.
PRESTON'S THE ONE WHO NEEDS FRIENDS RIGHT NOW.
STRICTLY BETWEEN YOU AND ME, I THINK HE'S GOING THROUGH SOME TOUGH TIMES.
YOU'RE A SHARP ONE. I'M BANKING ON THAT. I'LL OWE YOU ONE IF YOU KEEP AN EYE ON PRESTON... STICK TO HIM...
...AND LET ME KNOW IF YOU SEE ANYTHING WEIRD.

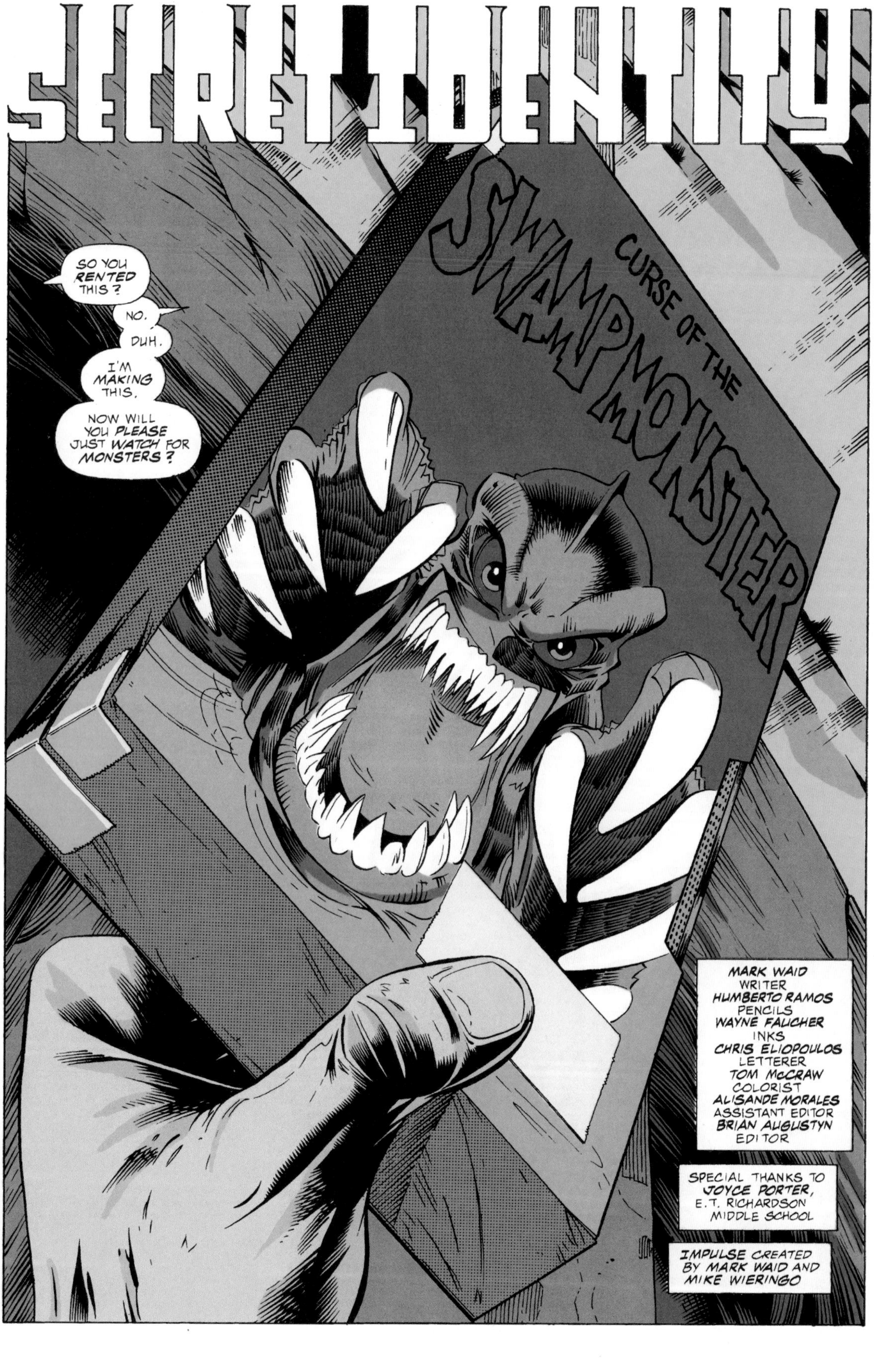
SECRET IDENTITY
SO YOU RENTED THIS?
NO.
DUH.
I'M MAKING THIS.
NOW WILL YOU PLEASE JUST WATCH FOR MONSTERS?
CURSE OF THE SWAMP MONSTER
MARK WAID WRITER
HUMBERTO RAMOS PENCILS
WAYNE FAUCHER INKS
CHRIS ELIOPOULOS LETTERER
TOM McCRAW COLORIST
ALISANDE MORALES ASSISTANT EDITOR
BRIAN AUGUSTYN EDITOR
SPECIAL THANKS TO JOYCE PORTER, E.T. RICHARDSON MIDDLE SCHOOL
IMPULSE CREATED BY MARK WAID AND MIKE WIERINGO

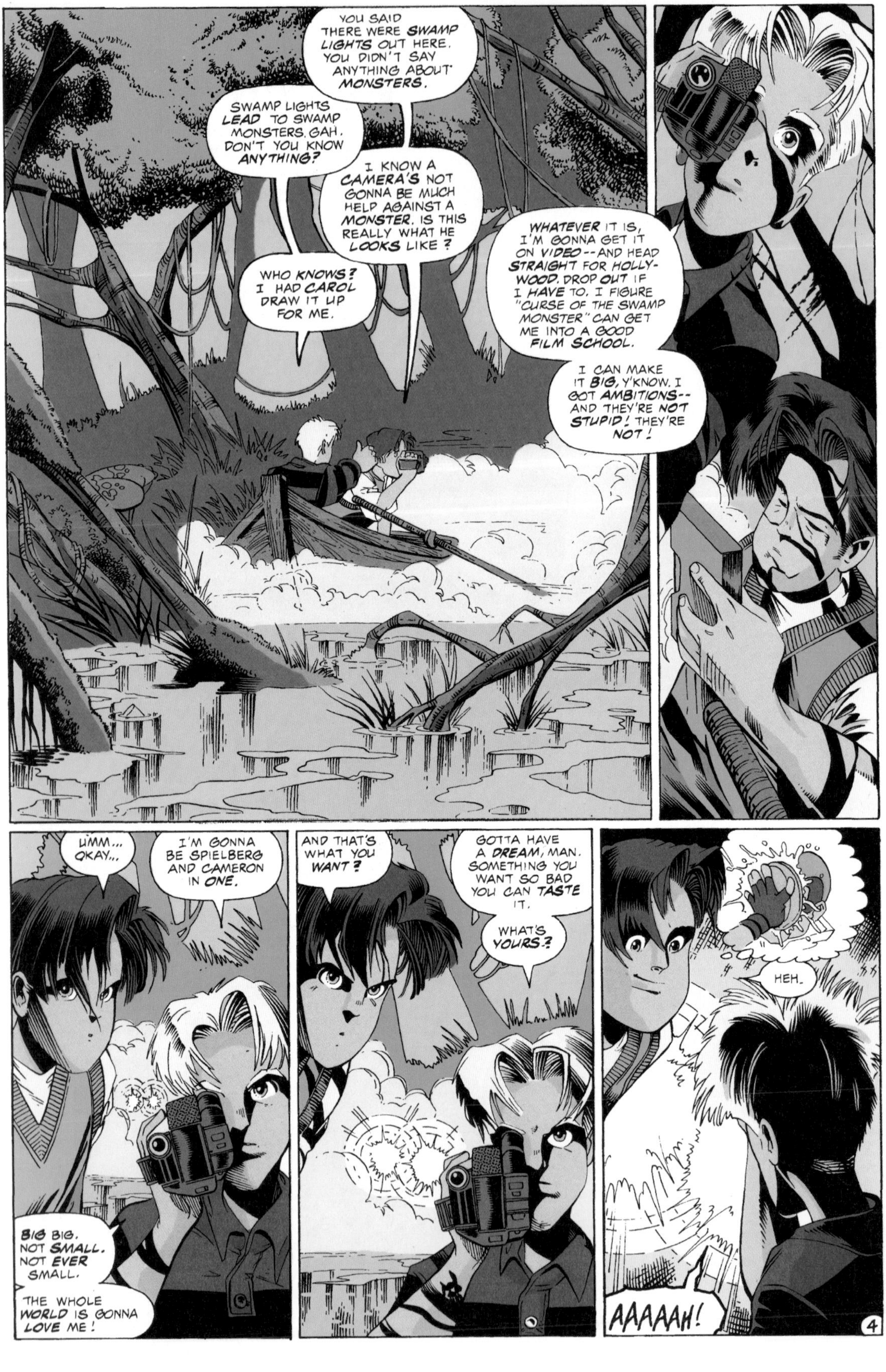
YOU SAID THERE WERE SWAMP LIGHTS OUT HERE. YOU DIDN'T SAY ANYTHING ABOUT MONSTERS.
SWAMP LIGHTS LEAD TO SWAMP MONSTERS. GAH. DON'T YOU KNOW ANYTHING?
I KNOW A CAMERA'S NOT GONNA BE MUCH HELP AGAINST A MONSTER. IS THIS REALLY WHAT HE LOOKS LIKE?
WHO KNOWS? I HAD CAROL DRAW IT UP FOR ME.
WHATEVER IT IS, I'M GONNA GET IT ON VIDEO--AND HEAD STRAIGHT FOR HOLLY-WOOD. DROP OUT IF I HAVE TO. I FIGURE "CURSE OF THE SWAMP MONSTER" CAN GET ME INTO A GOOD FILM SCHOOL.
I CAN MAKE IT BIG, Y'KNOW. I GOT AMBITIONS--AND THEY'RE NOT STUPID! THEY'RE NOT!
UMM... OKAY...
I'M GONNA BE SPIELBERG AND CAMERON IN ONE.
BIG BIG. NOT SMALL. NOT EVER SMALL.
THE WHOLE WORLD IS GONNA LOVE ME!
AND THAT'S WHAT YOU WANT?
GOTTA HAVE A DREAM, MAN. SOMETHING YOU WANT SO BAD YOU CAN TASTE IT.
WHAT'S YOURS?
HEH.
AAAAAH!
4

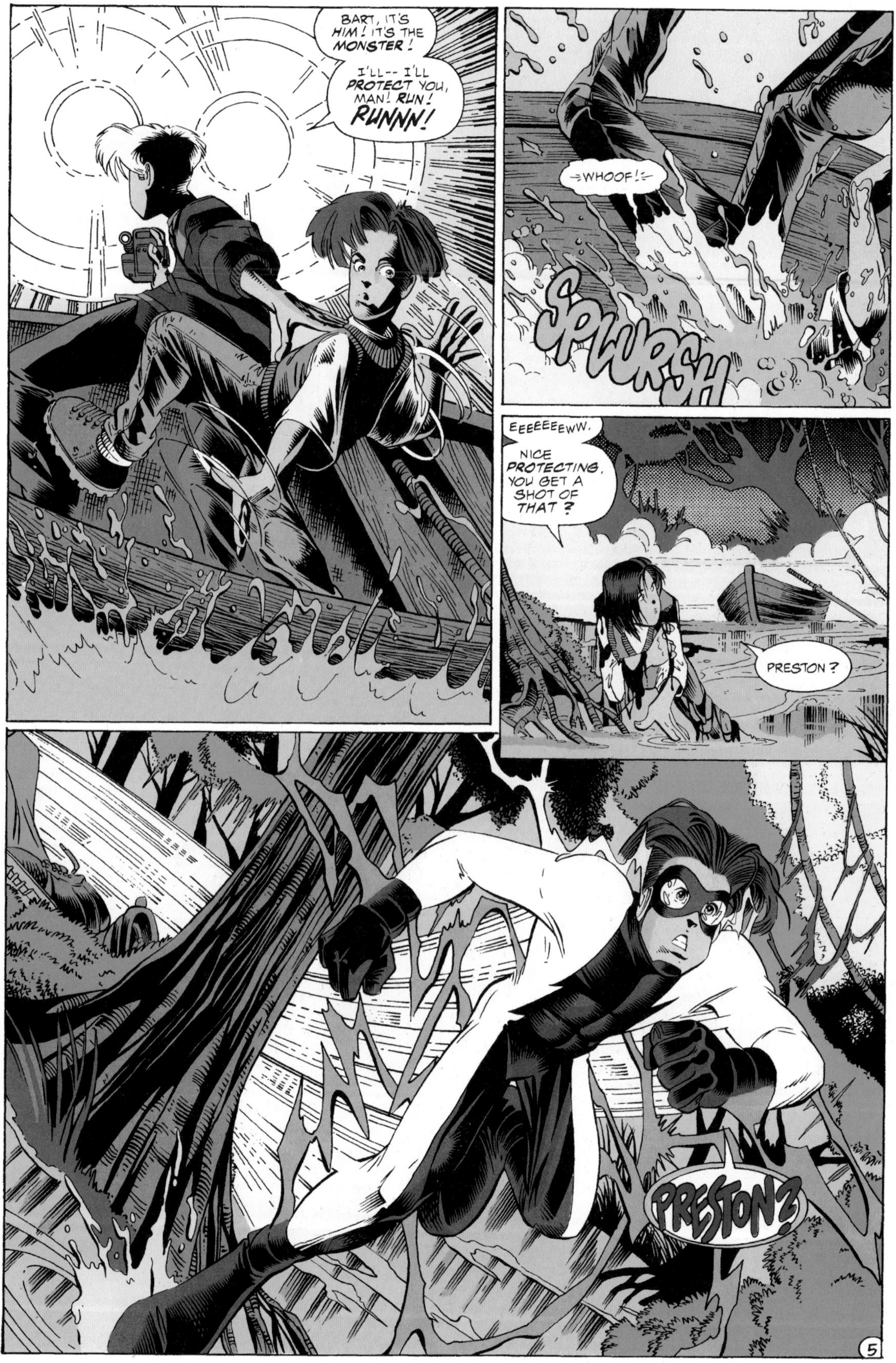
BART, IT'S HIM! IT'S THE MONSTER!
I'LL-- I'LL PROTECT YOU, MAN! RUN! RUNNN!
WHOOF!
SPLURSH
EEEEEEEEWW.
NICE PROTECTING. YOU GET A SHOT OF THAT?
PRESTON?
PRESTON?

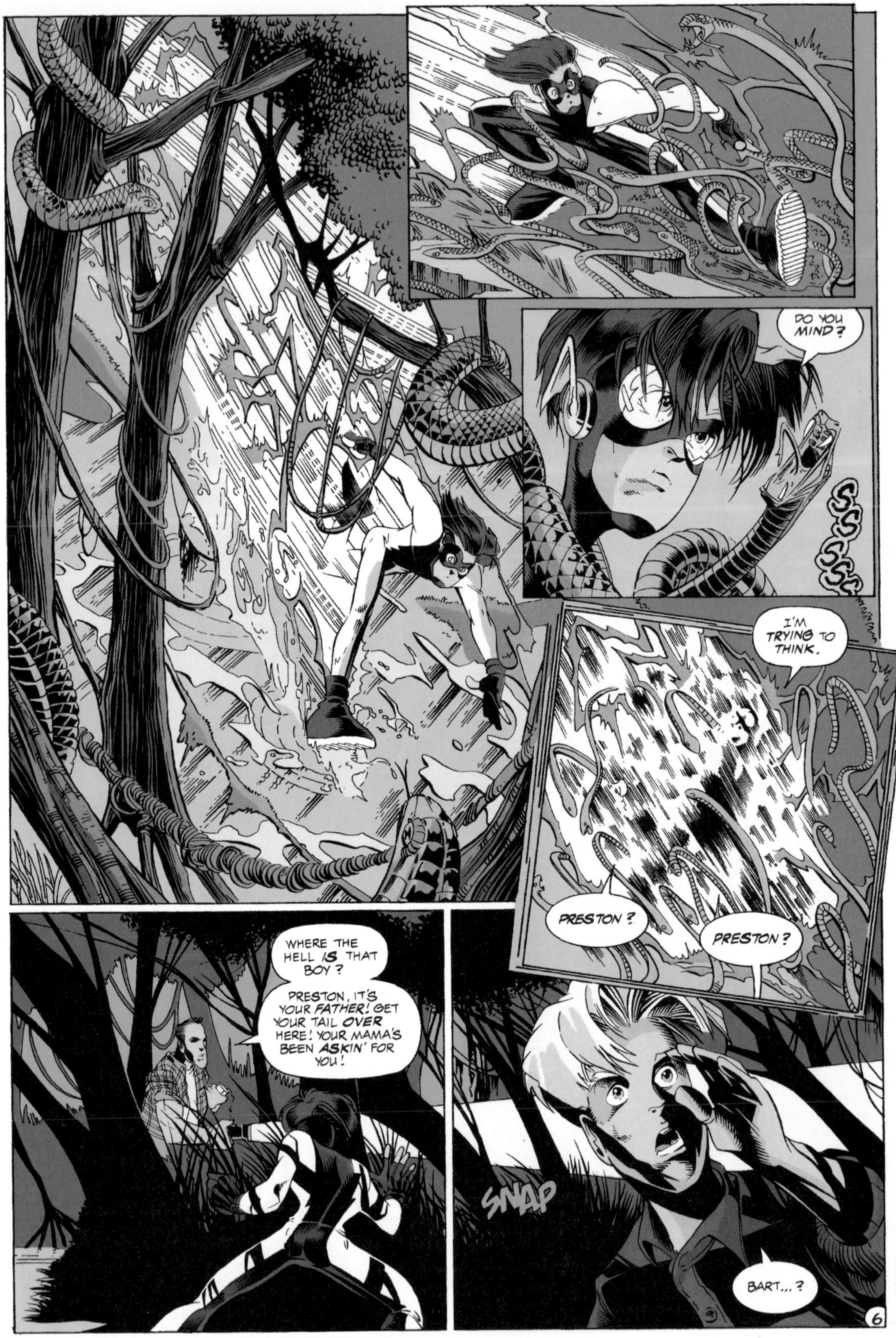

DO YOU MIND?
SSSSS
I'M TRYING TO THINK.
PRESTON?
PRESTON?
WHERE THE HELL IS THAT BOY?
PRESTON, IT'S YOUR FATHER! GET YOUR TAIL OVER HERE! YOUR MAMA'S BEEN ASKIN' FOR YOU!
SNAP
BART...?
6

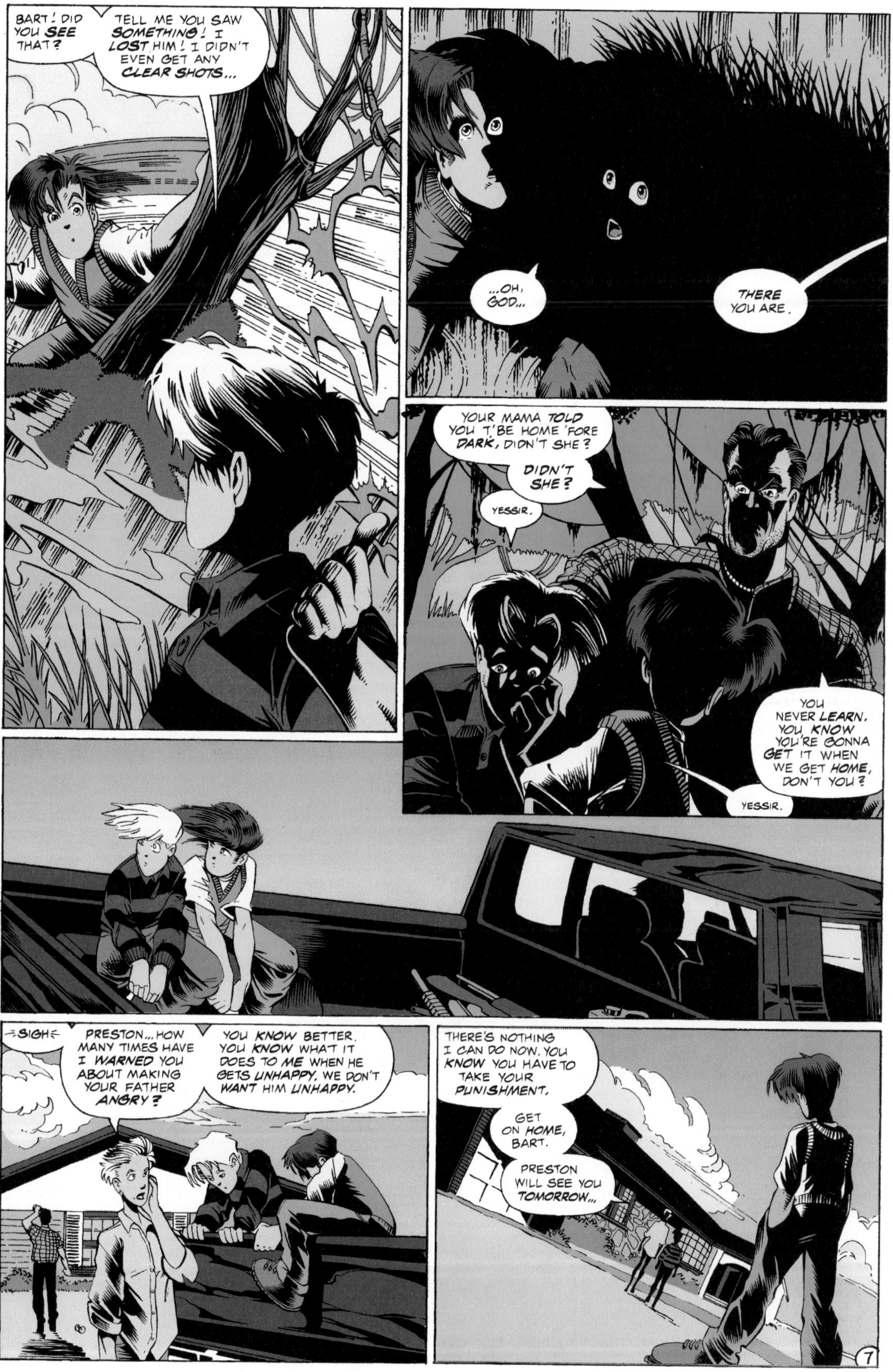

BART! DID YOU SEE THAT?
TELL ME YOU SAW SOMETHING! I LOST HIM! I DIDN'T EVEN GET ANY CLEAR SHOTS...
...OH, GOD...
THERE YOU ARE.
YOUR MAMA TOLD YOU T'BE HOME 'FORE DARK, DIDN'T SHE?
DIDN'T SHE?
YESSIR.
YOU NEVER LEARN. YOU KNOW YOU'RE GONNA GET IT WHEN WE GET HOME, DON'T YOU?
YESSIR.
SIGH
PRESTON... HOW MANY TIMES HAVE I WARNED YOU ABOUT MAKING YOUR FATHER ANGRY?
YOU KNOW BETTER. YOU KNOW WHAT IT DOES TO ME WHEN HE GETS UNHAPPY. WE DON'T WANT HIM UNHAPPY.
THERE'S NOTHING I CAN DO NOW. YOU KNOW YOU HAVE TO TAKE YOUR PUNISHMENT.
GET ON HOME, BART.
PRESTON WILL SEE YOU TOMORROW...

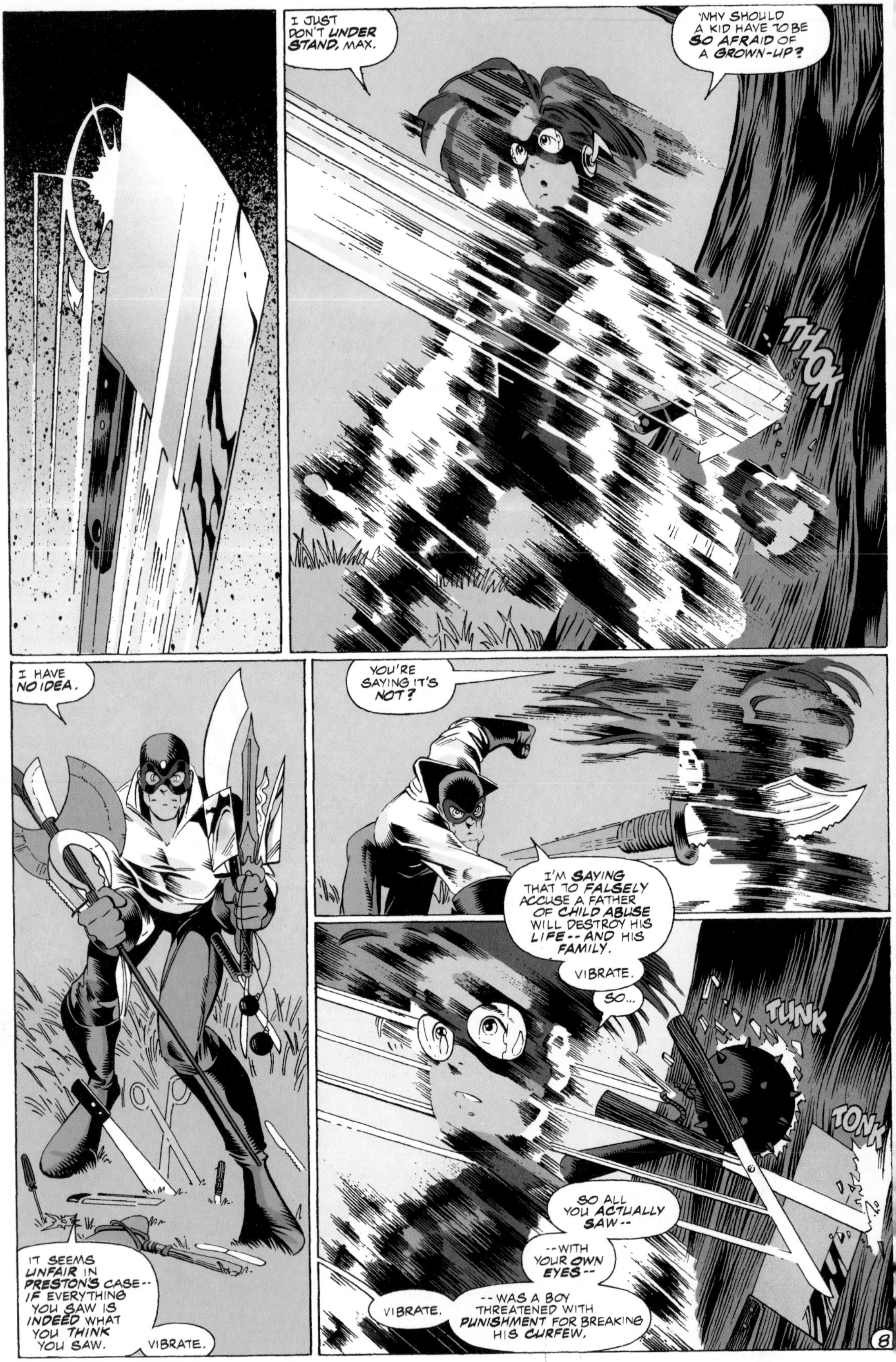

I JUST DON'T UNDER STAND, MAX.
WHY SHOULD A KID HAVE TO BE SO AFRAID OF A GROWN-UP?
THOK
I HAVE NO IDEA.
IT SEEMS UNFAIR IN PRESTON'S CASE-- IF EVERYTHING YOU SAW IS INDEED WHAT YOU THINK YOU SAW.
VIBRATE.
YOU'RE SAYING IT'S NOT?
I'M SAYING THAT TO FALSELY ACCUSE A FATHER OF CHILD ABUSE WILL DESTROY HIS LIFE -- AND HIS FAMILY.
VIBRATE.
SO...
TUNK
TONK
SO ALL YOU ACTUALLY SAW --
-- WITH YOUR OWN EYES --
-- WAS A BOY THREATENED WITH PUNISHMENT FOR BREAKING HIS CURFEW.
VIBRATE.

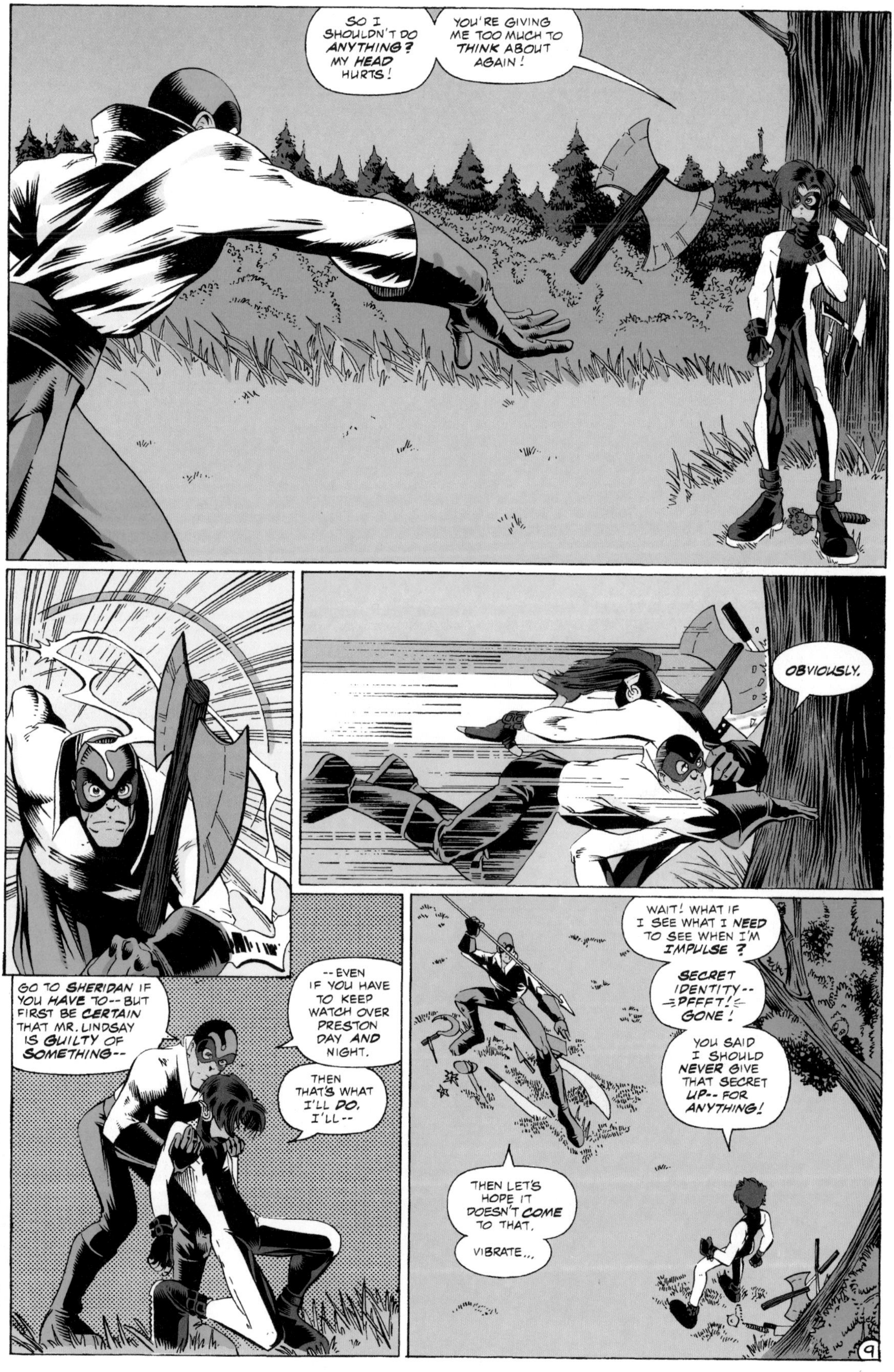

SO I SHOULDN'T DO ANYTHING? MY HEAD HURTS!
YOU'RE GIVING ME TOO MUCH TO THINK ABOUT AGAIN!
OBVIOUSLY.
GO TO SHERIDAN IF YOU HAVE TO-- BUT FIRST BE CERTAIN THAT MR. LINDSAY IS GUILTY OF SOMETHING--
--EVEN IF YOU HAVE TO KEEP WATCH OVER PRESTON DAY AND NIGHT.
THEN THAT'S WHAT I'LL DO. I'LL--
WAIT! WHAT IF I SEE WHAT I NEED TO SEE WHEN I'M IMPULSE?
SECRET IDENTITY-- PFFFT! GONE!
YOU SAID I SHOULD NEVER GIVE THAT SECRET UP-- FOR ANYTHING!
THEN LET'S HOPE IT DOESN'T COME TO THAT.
VIBRATE...
9

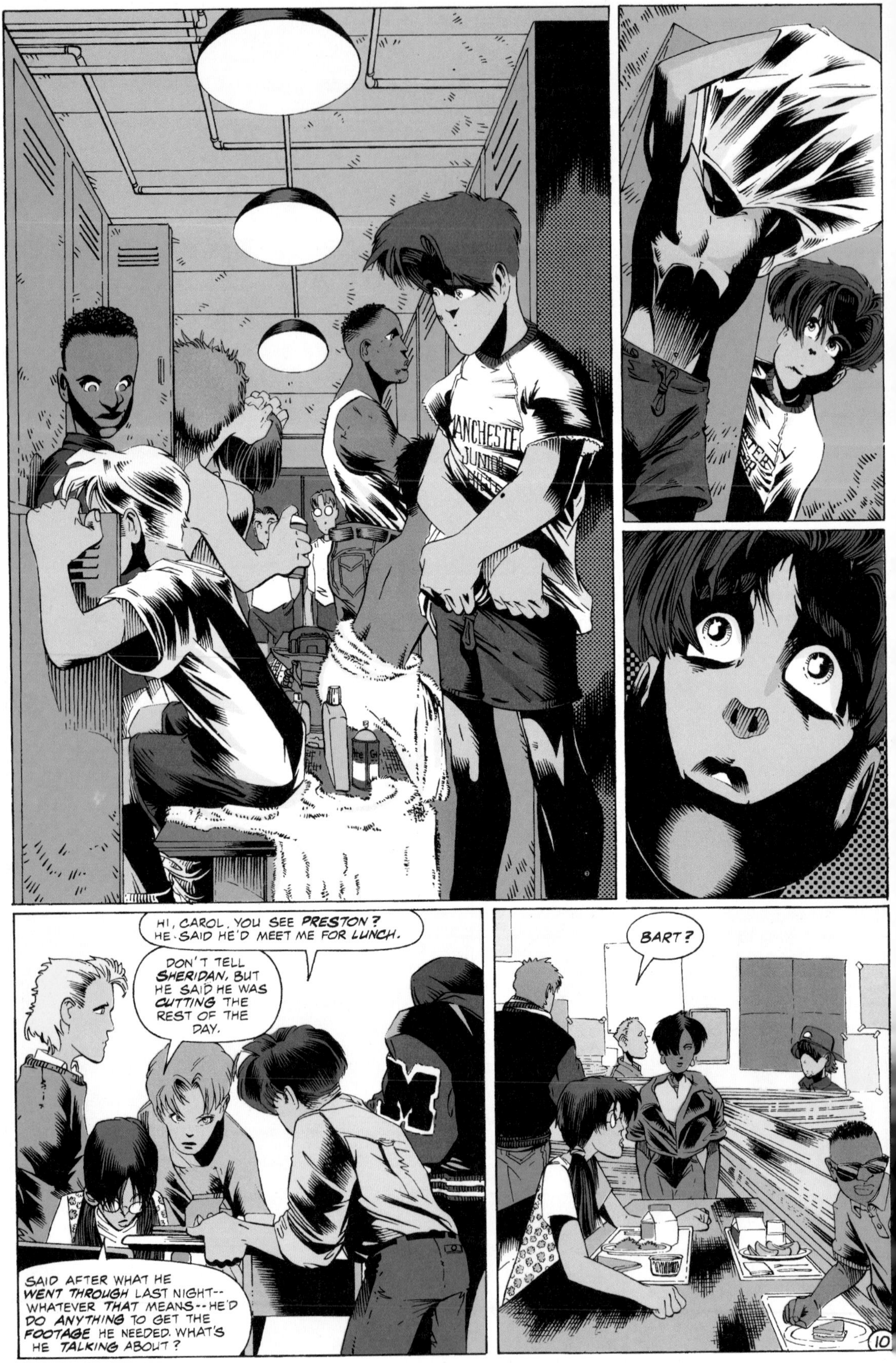
MANCHESTER JUNIOR HIGH
HI, CAROL. YOU SEE PRESTON? HE SAID HE'D MEET ME FOR LUNCH.
DON'T TELL SHERIDAN, BUT HE SAID HE WAS CUTTING THE REST OF THE DAY.
SAID AFTER WHAT HE WENT THROUGH LAST NIGHT--WHATEVER THAT MEANS--HE'D DO ANYTHING TO GET THE FOOTAGE HE NEEDED. WHAT'S HE TALKING ABOUT?
BART?
10

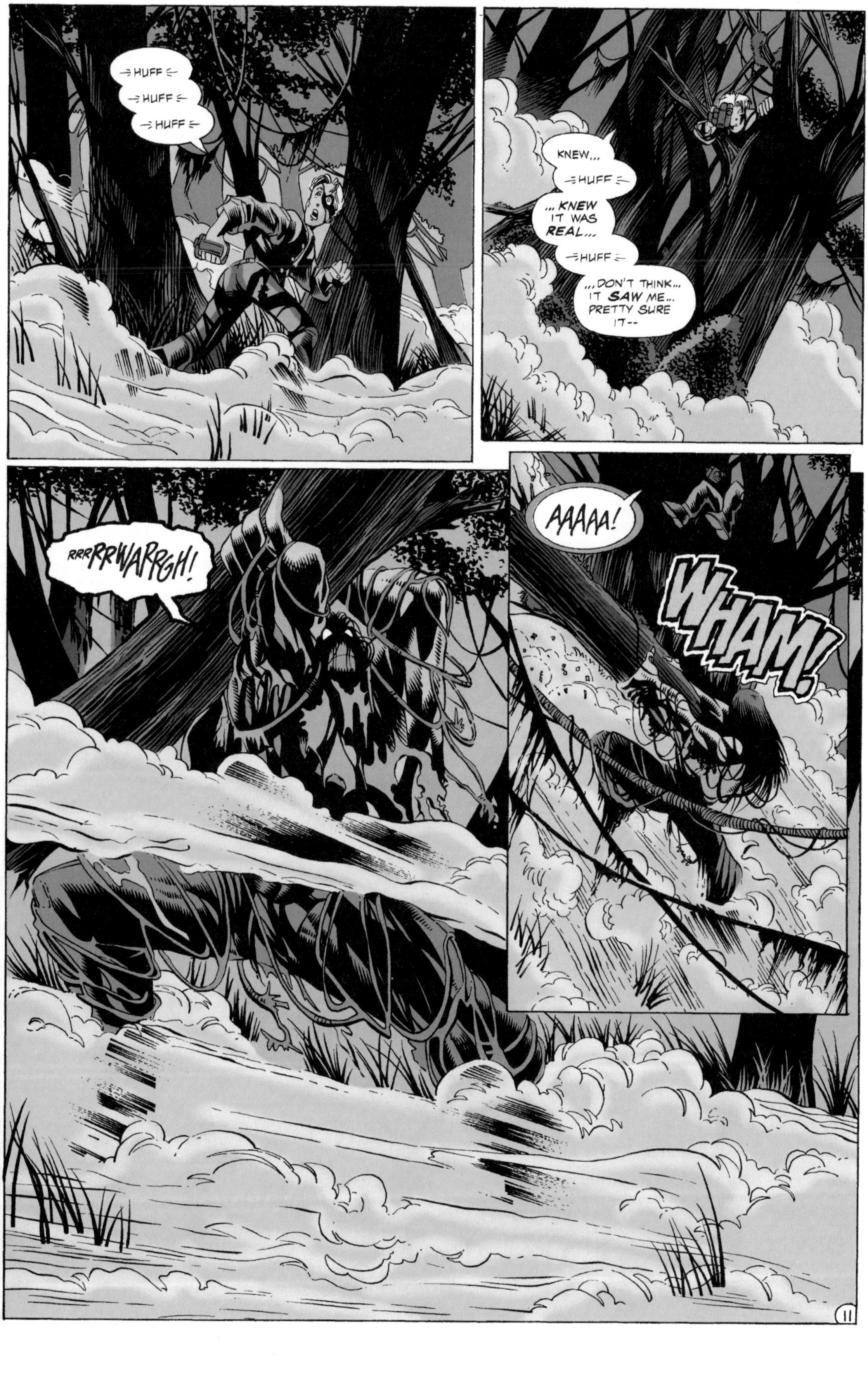

HUFF
HUFF
HUFF
KNEW...
HUFF
...KNEW IT WAS REAL...
HUFF
...DON'T THINK... IT SAW ME... PRETTY SURE IT--
RRRRRWARRGH!
AAAAA!
WHAM!

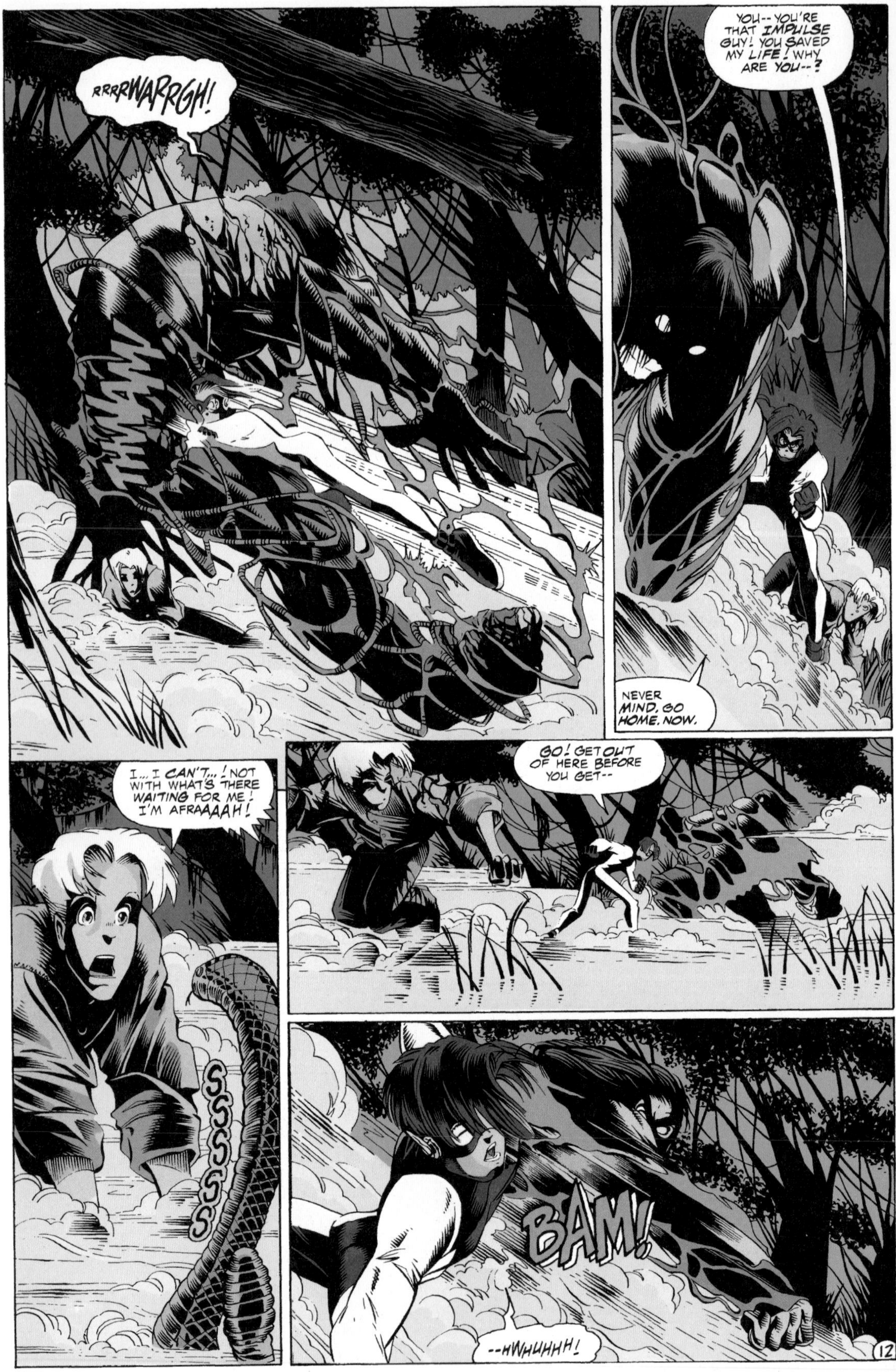
RRRRWARRGH!
YOU-- YOU'RE THAT IMPULSE GUY! YOU SAVED MY LIFE! WHY ARE YOU--?
NEVER MIND. GO HOME. NOW.
I... I CAN'T...! NOT WITH WHAT'S THERE WAITING FOR ME! I'M AFRAAAAH!
SSSSSS
GO! GET OUT OF HERE BEFORE YOU GET--
BAM!
--HWHUHHH!

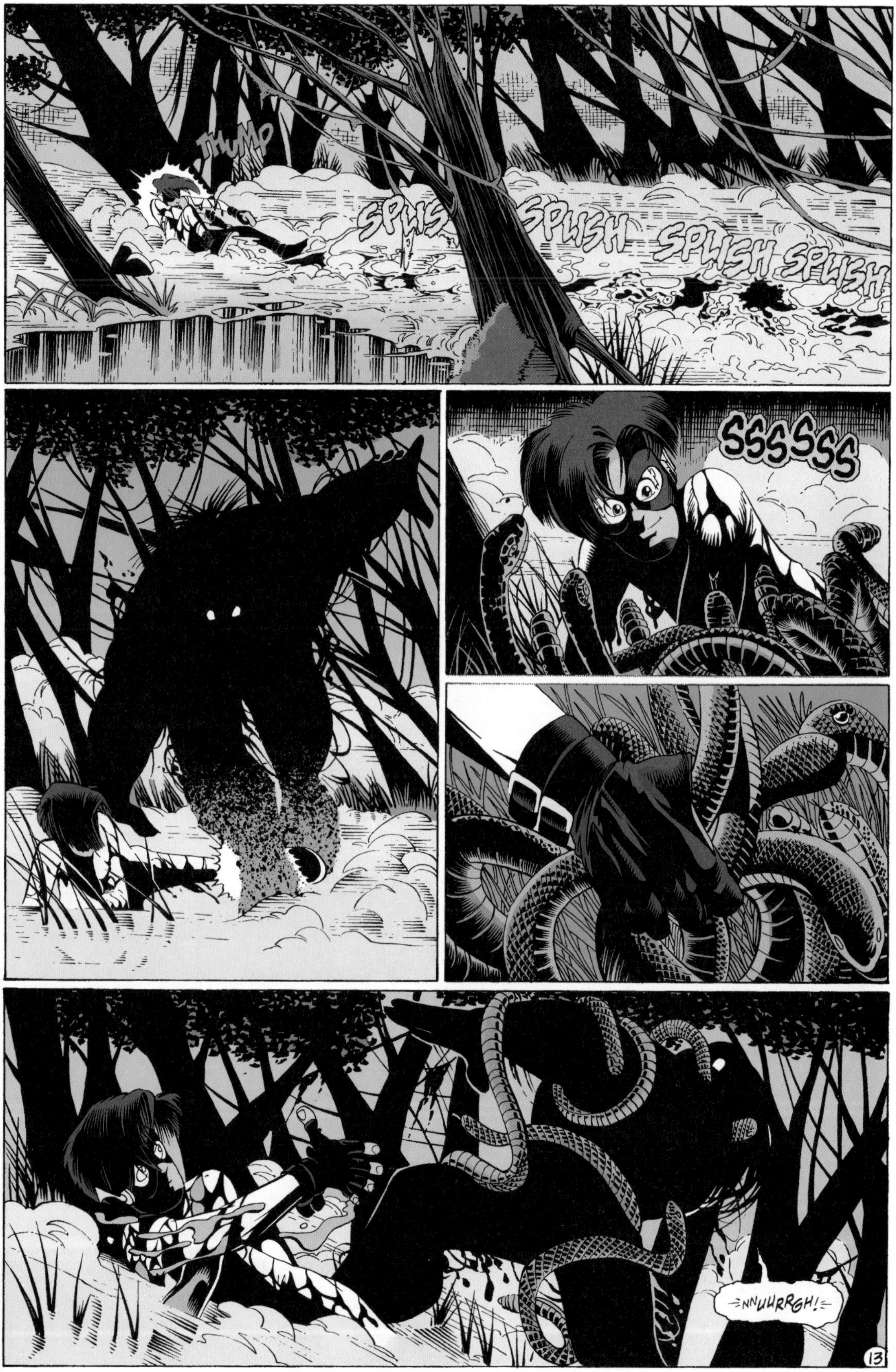
THUMP
SPLISH
SPLISH
SPLISH
SPLISH
SSSSSS
NNUURRGH!

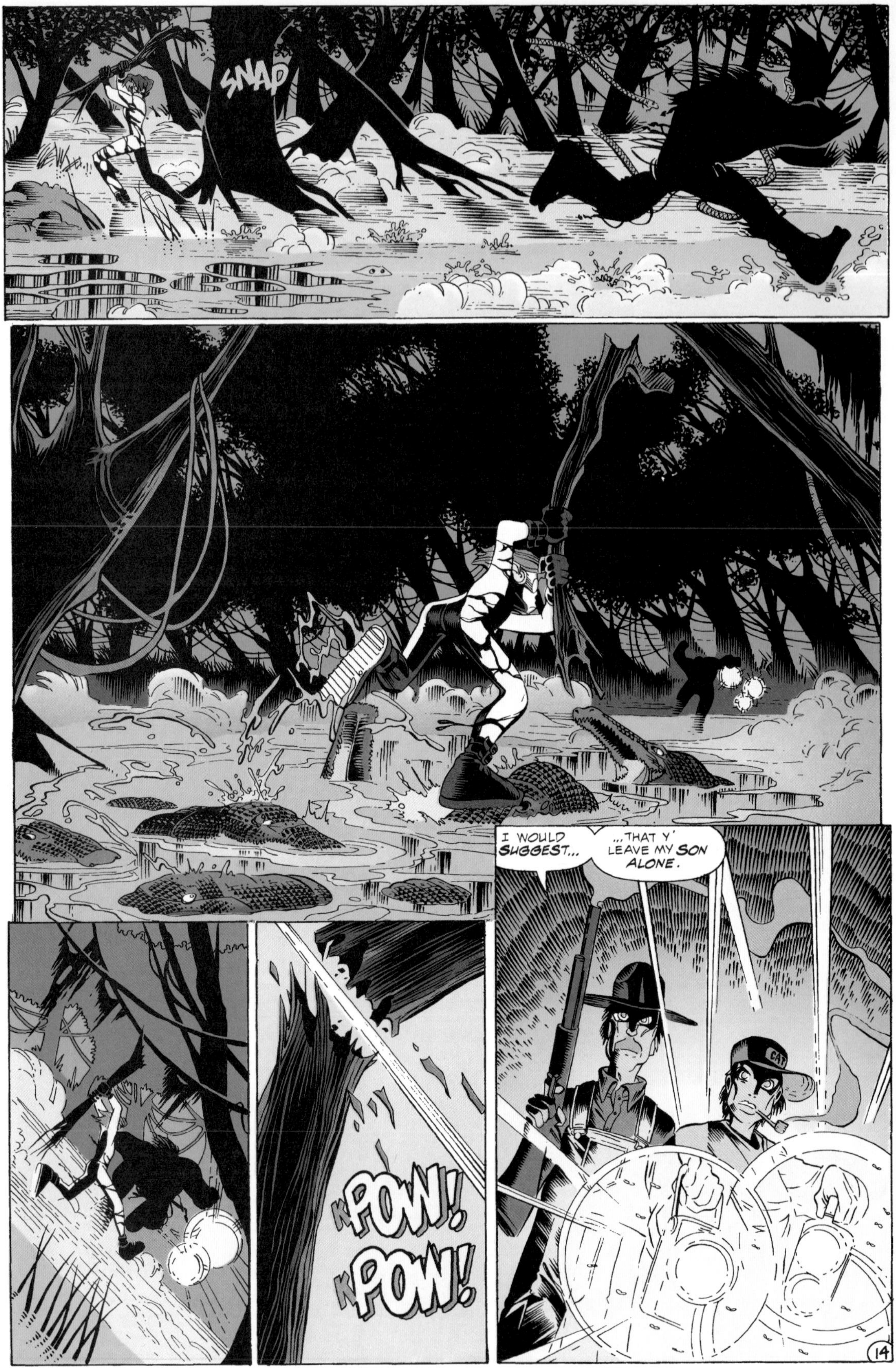
SNAP
I WOULD SUGGEST...
...THAT Y' LEAVE MY SON ALONE.
KPOW!
KPOW!
CAT
14

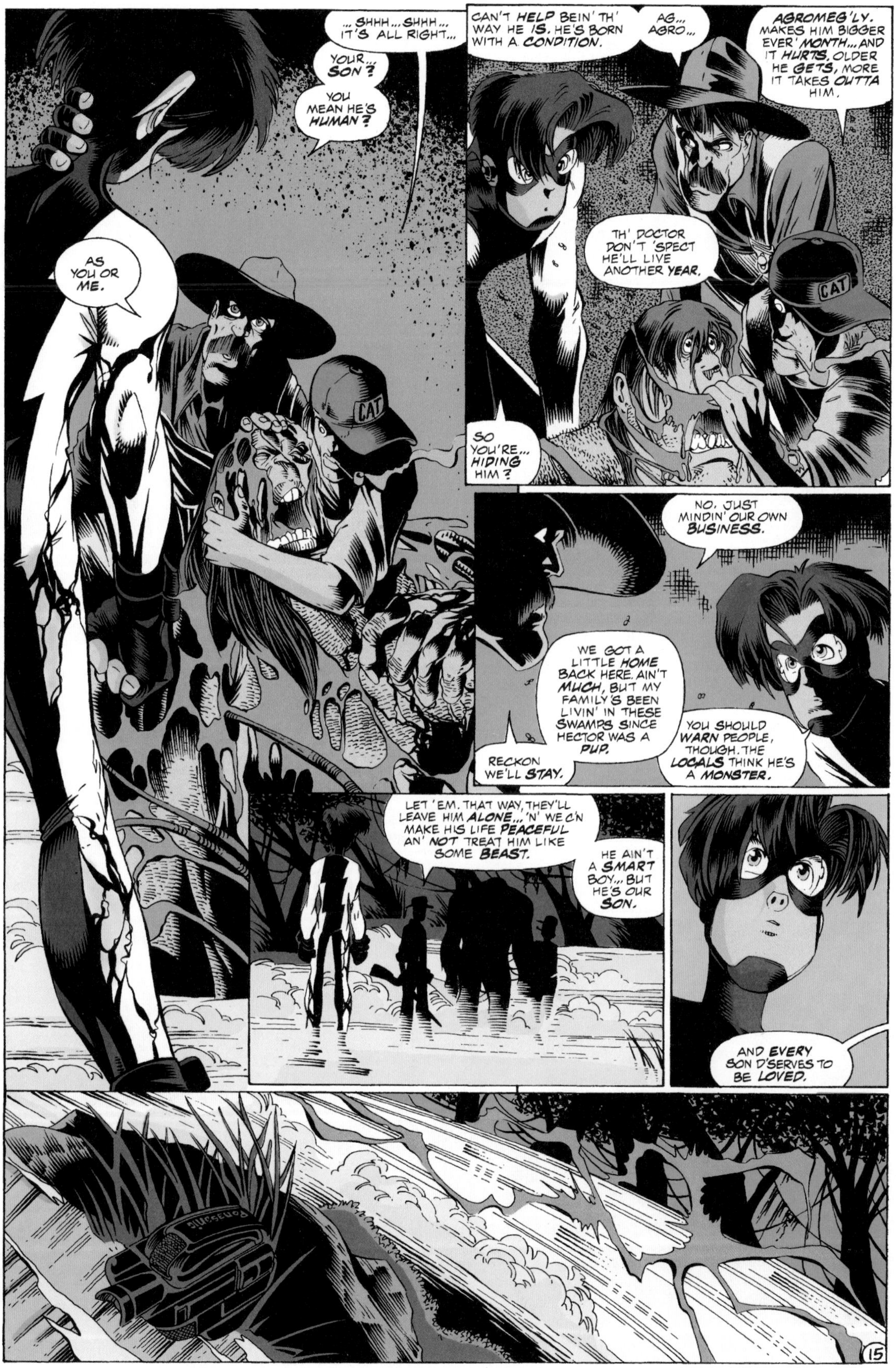
...SHHH...SHHH... IT'S ALL RIGHT...
YOUR SON?
YOU MEAN HE'S HUMAN?
AS YOU OR ME.
CAN'T HELP BEIN' TH' WAY HE IS. HE'S BORN WITH A CONDITION.
AG... AGRO...
AGROMEG'LY. MAKES HIM BIGGER EVER' MONTH... AND IT HURTS. OLDER HE GETS, MORE IT TAKES OUTTA HIM.
TH' DOCTOR DON'T 'SPECT HE'LL LIVE ANOTHER YEAR.
SO YOU'RE... HIDING HIM?
CAT
NO. JUST MINDIN' OUR OWN BUSINESS.
WE GOT A LITTLE HOME BACK HERE. AIN'T MUCH, BUT MY FAMILY'S BEEN LIVIN' IN THESE SWAMPS SINCE HECTOR WAS A PUP.
RECKON WE'LL STAY.
YOU SHOULD WARN PEOPLE, THOUGH. THE LOCALS THINK HE'S A MONSTER.
LET 'EM. THAT WAY, THEY'LL LEAVE HIM ALONE... 'N' WE C'N MAKE HIS LIFE PEACEFUL AN' NOT TREAT HIM LIKE SOME BEAST.
HE AIN'T A SMART BOY... BUT HE'S OUR SON.
AND EVERY SON D'SERVES TO BE LOVED.

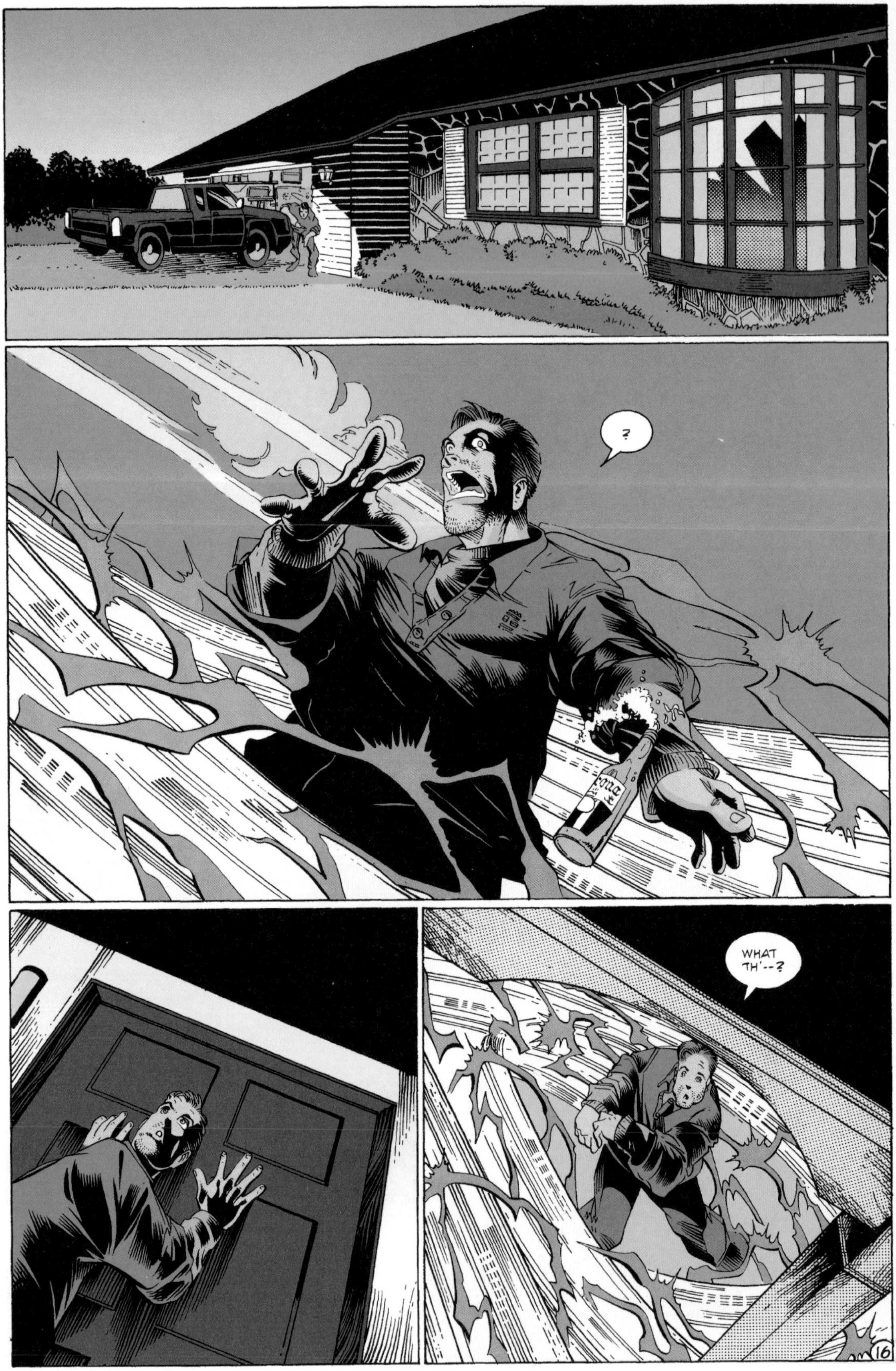
?
WHAT TH'--?
16

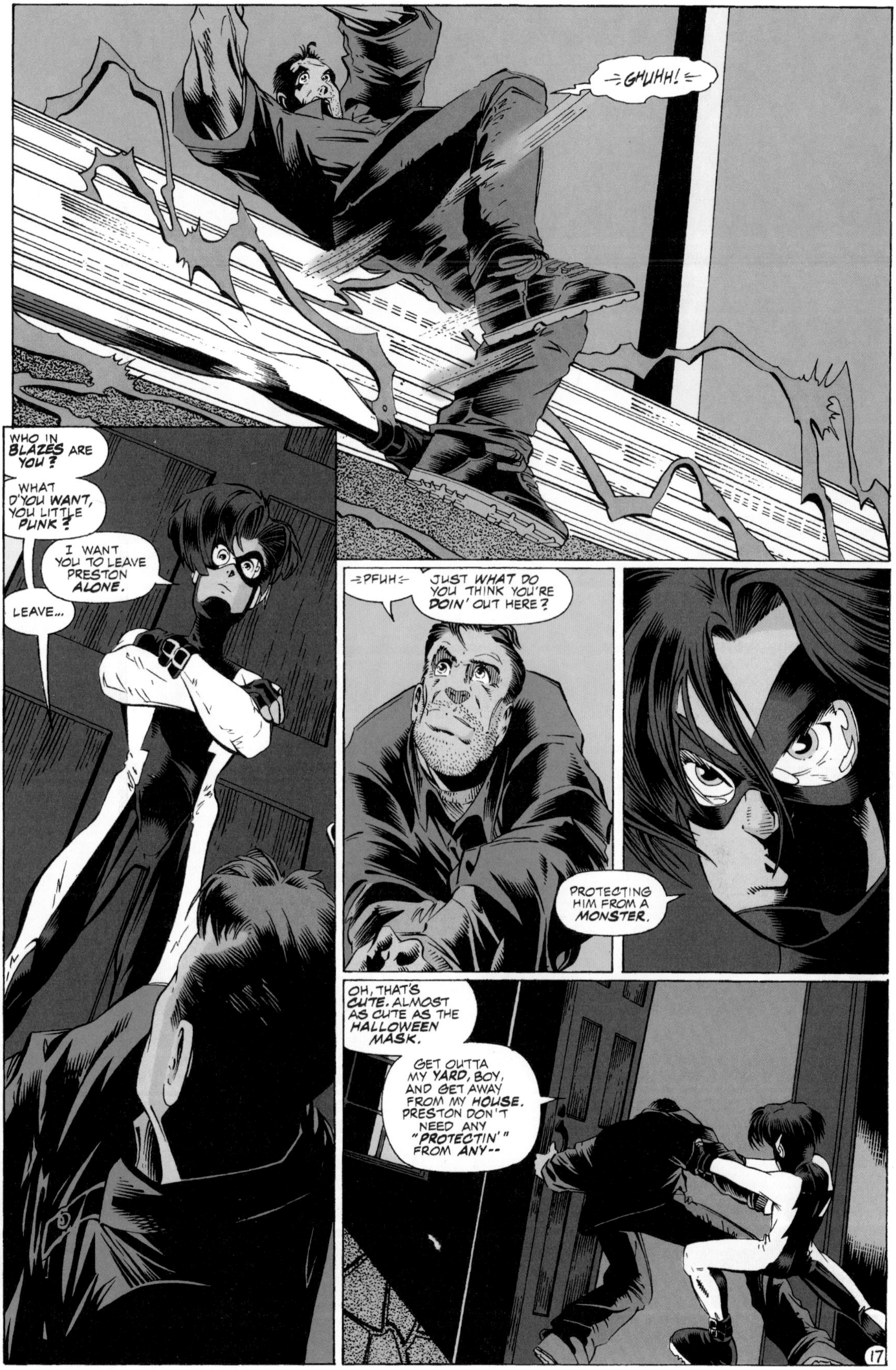

GHUHH!
WHO IN BLAZES ARE YOU?
WHAT D'YOU WANT, YOU LITTLE PUNK?
I WANT YOU TO LEAVE PRESTON ALONE.
LEAVE...
PFUH
JUST WHAT DO YOU THINK YOU'RE DOIN' OUT HERE?
PROTECTING HIM FROM A MONSTER.
OH, THAT'S CUTE. ALMOST AS CUTE AS THE HALLOWEEN MASK.
GET OUTTA MY YARD, BOY, AND GET AWAY FROM MY HOUSE. PRESTON DON'T NEED ANY "PROTECTIN'" FROM ANY--

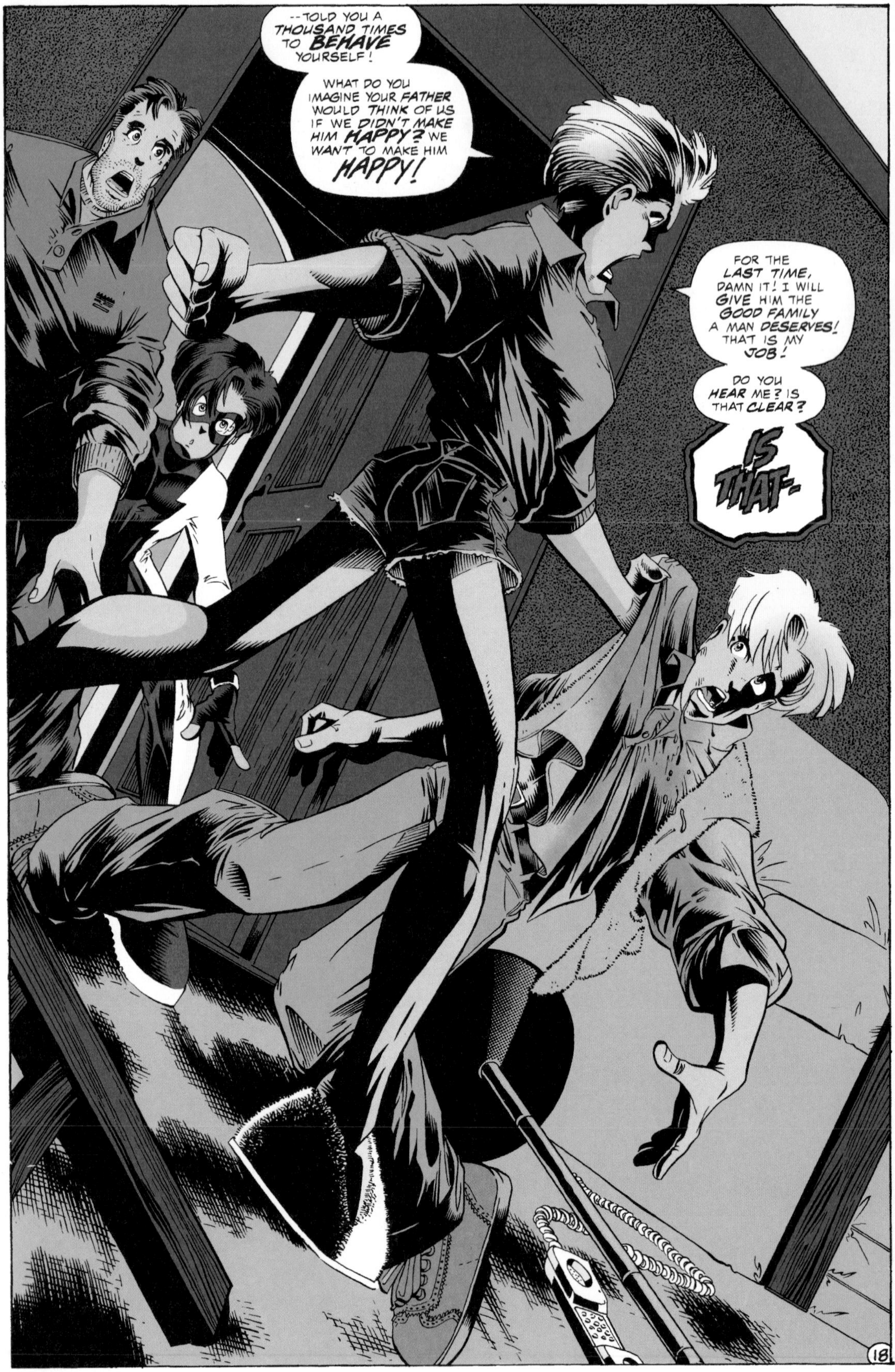
--TOLD YOU A THOUSAND TIMES TO BEHAVE YOURSELF!
WHAT DO YOU IMAGINE YOUR FATHER WOULD THINK OF US IF WE DIDN'T MAKE HIM HAPPY? WE WANT TO MAKE HIM HAPPY!
FOR THE LAST TIME, DAMN IT! I WILL GIVE HIM THE GOOD FAMILY A MAN DESERVES! THAT IS MY JOB!
DO YOU HEAR ME? IS THAT CLEAR?
IS THAT-

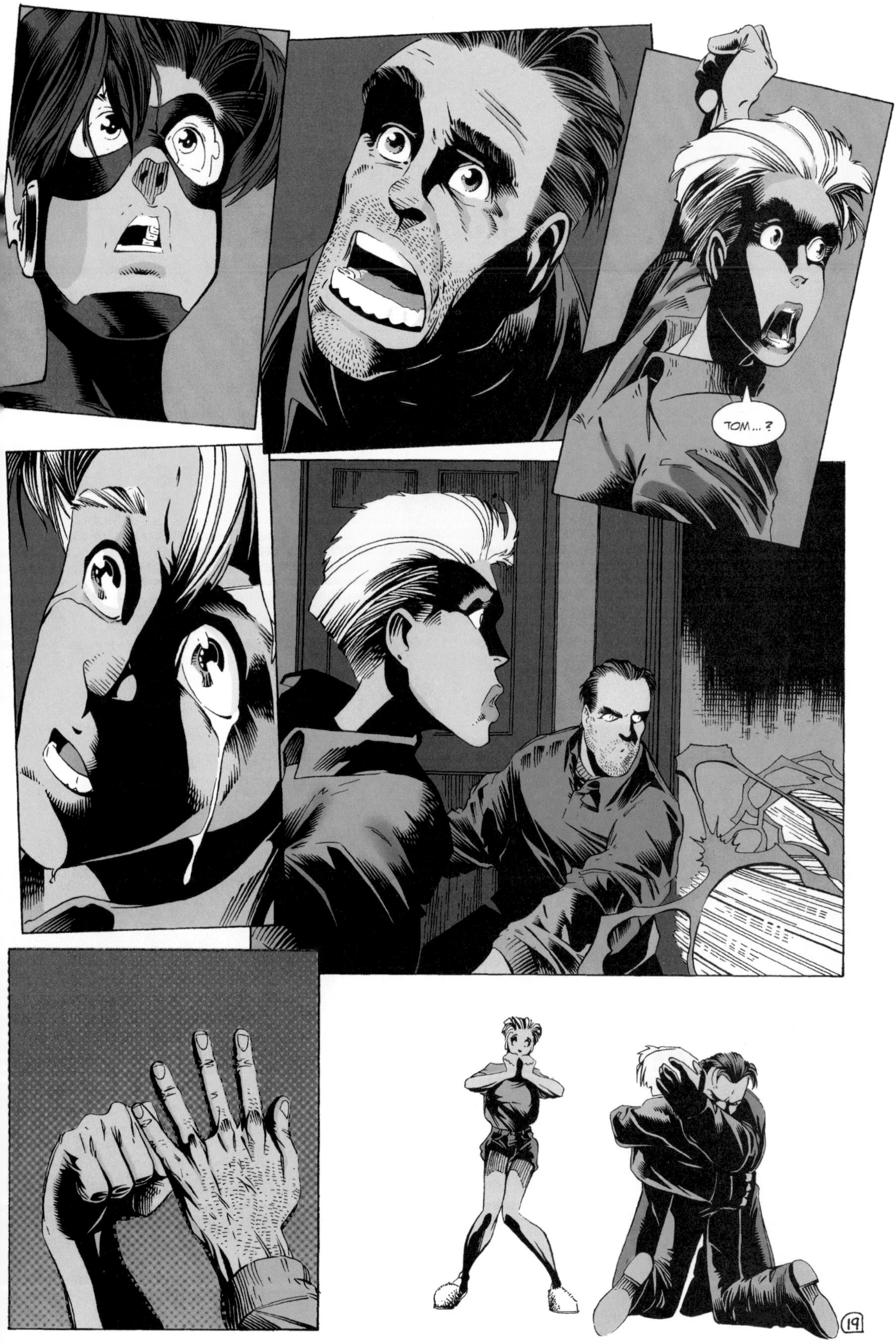
TOM...?

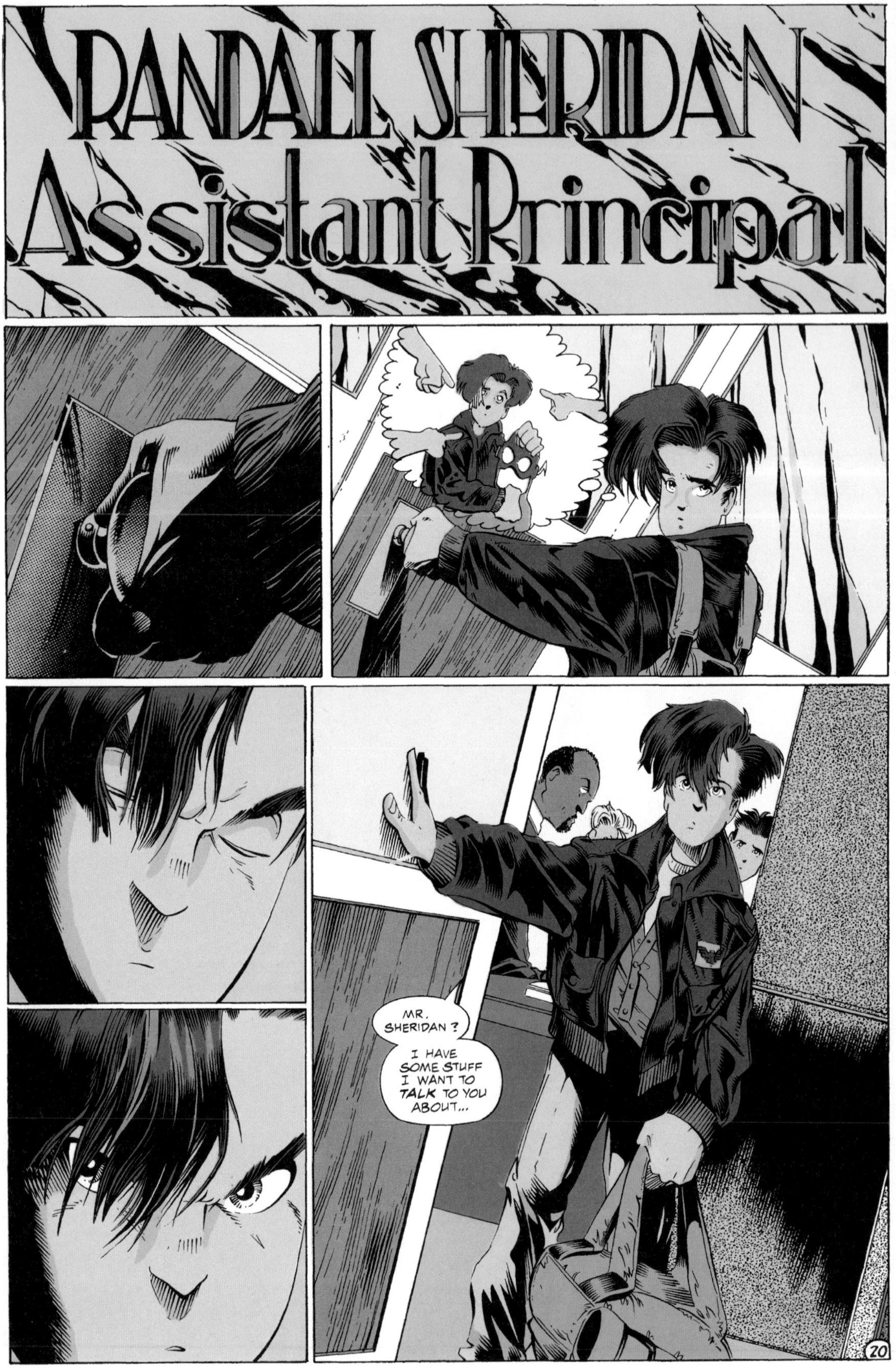

RANDALL SHERIDAN
Assistant Principal
MR. SHERIDAN?
I HAVE SOME STUFF I WANT TO TALK TO YOU ABOUT...

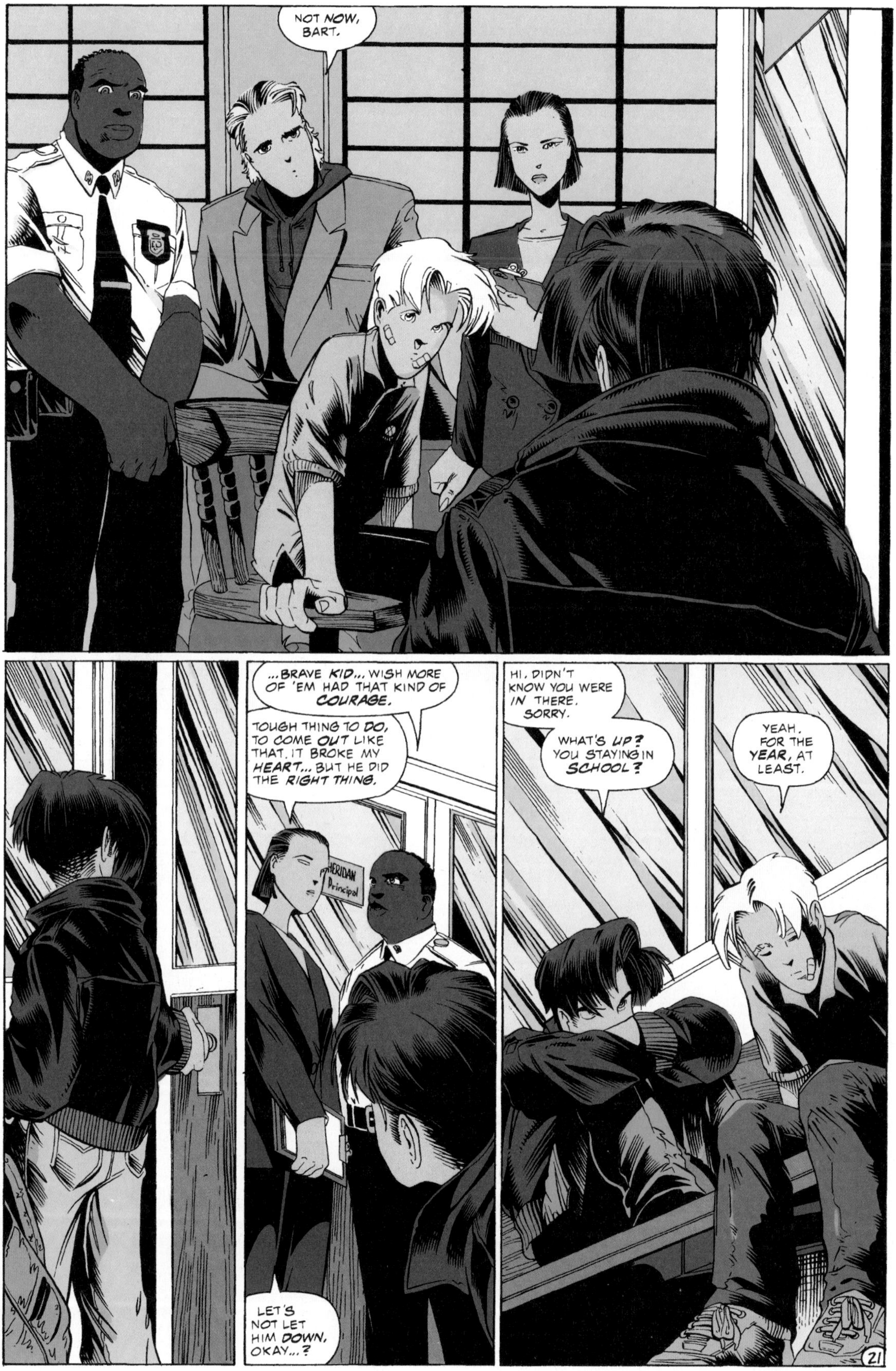
NOT NOW, BART.
...BRAVE KID... WISH MORE OF 'EM HAD THAT KIND OF COURAGE.
TOUGH THING TO DO, TO COME OUT LIKE THAT. IT BROKE MY HEART... BUT HE DID THE RIGHT THING.
HERIDAN Principal
LET'S NOT LET HIM DOWN, OKAY...?
HI. DIDN'T KNOW YOU WERE IN THERE. SORRY.
WHAT'S UP? YOU STAYING IN SCHOOL?
YEAH. FOR THE YEAR, AT LEAST.

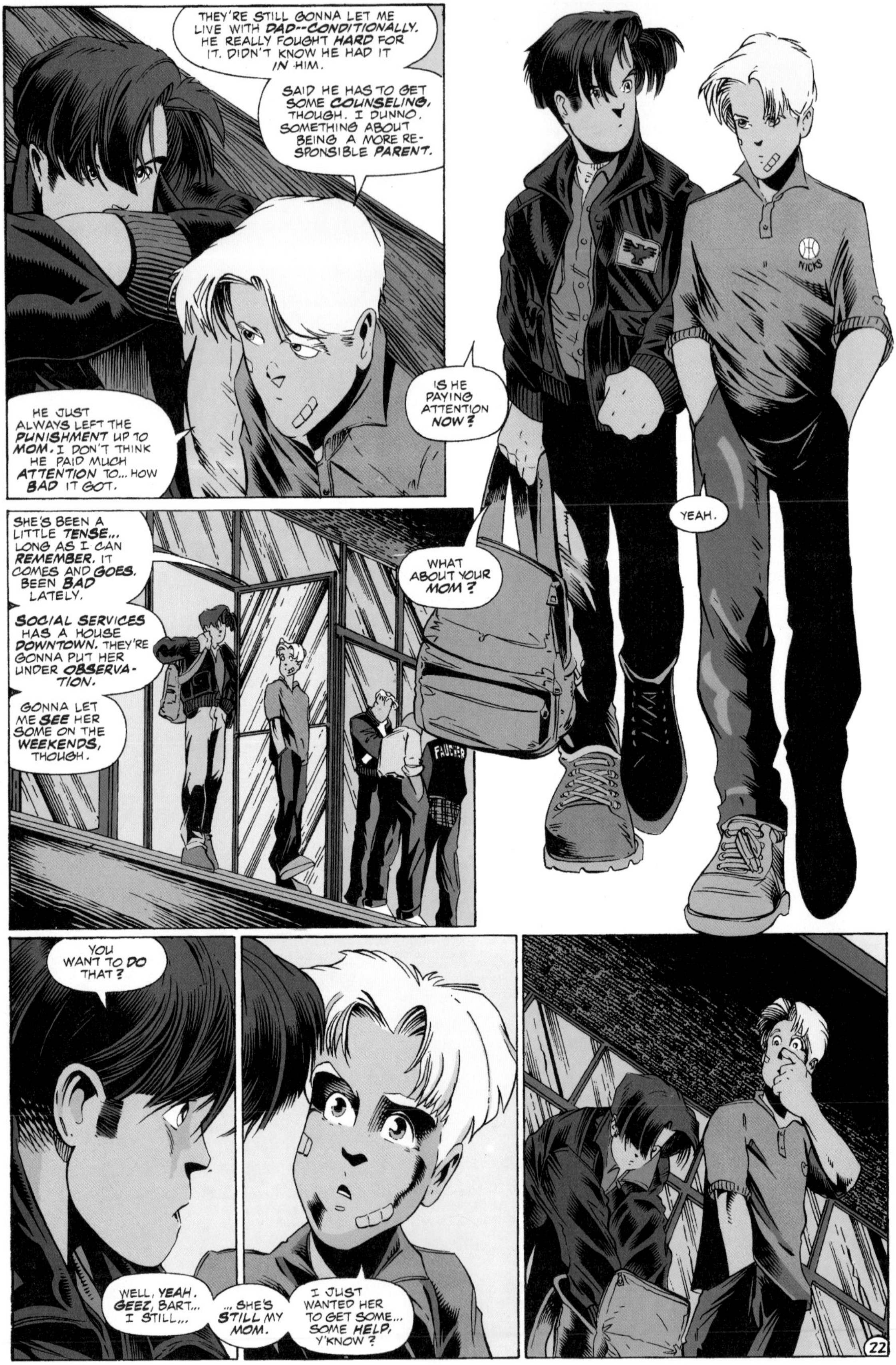
THEY'RE STILL GONNA LET ME LIVE WITH DAD--CONDITIONALLY. HE REALLY FOUGHT HARD FOR IT. DIDN'T KNOW HE HAD IT IN HIM.
SAID HE HAS TO GET SOME COUNSELING, THOUGH. I DUNNO. SOMETHING ABOUT BEING A MORE RE-SPONSIBLE PARENT.
HE JUST ALWAYS LEFT THE PUNISHMENT UP TO MOM. I DON'T THINK HE PAID MUCH ATTENTION TO... HOW BAD IT GOT.
IS HE PAYING ATTENTION NOW?
YEAH.
WHAT ABOUT YOUR MOM?
SHE'S BEEN A LITTLE TENSE... LONG AS I CAN REMEMBER. IT COMES AND GOES. BEEN BAD LATELY.
SOCIAL SERVICES HAS A HOUSE DOWNTOWN. THEY'RE GONNA PUT HER UNDER OBSERVA-TION.
GONNA LET ME SEE HER SOME ON THE WEEKENDS, THOUGH.
YOU WANT TO DO THAT?
WELL, YEAH. GEEZ, BART... I STILL...
...SHE'S STILL MY MOM.
I JUST WANTED HER TO GET SOME... SOME HELP, Y'KNOW?
22

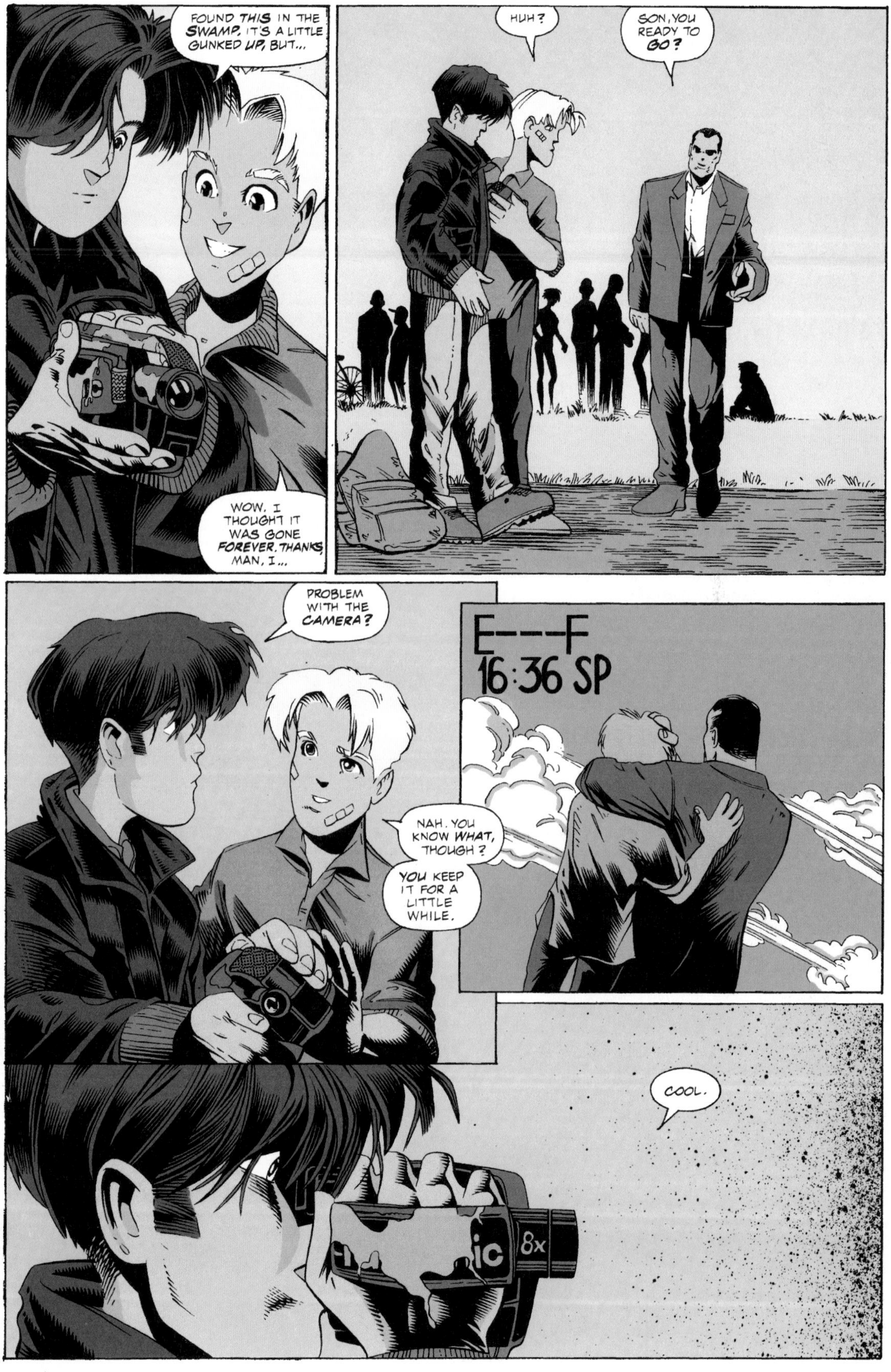
FOUND THIS IN THE SWAMP. IT'S A LITTLE GUNKED UP, BUT...
WOW. I THOUGHT IT WAS GONE FOREVER. THANKS, MAN, I...
HUH?
SON, YOU READY TO GO?
PROBLEM WITH THE CAMERA?
NAH. YOU KNOW WHAT, THOUGH?
YOU KEEP IT FOR A LITTLE WHILE.
E----F
16:36 SP
COOL.
8x

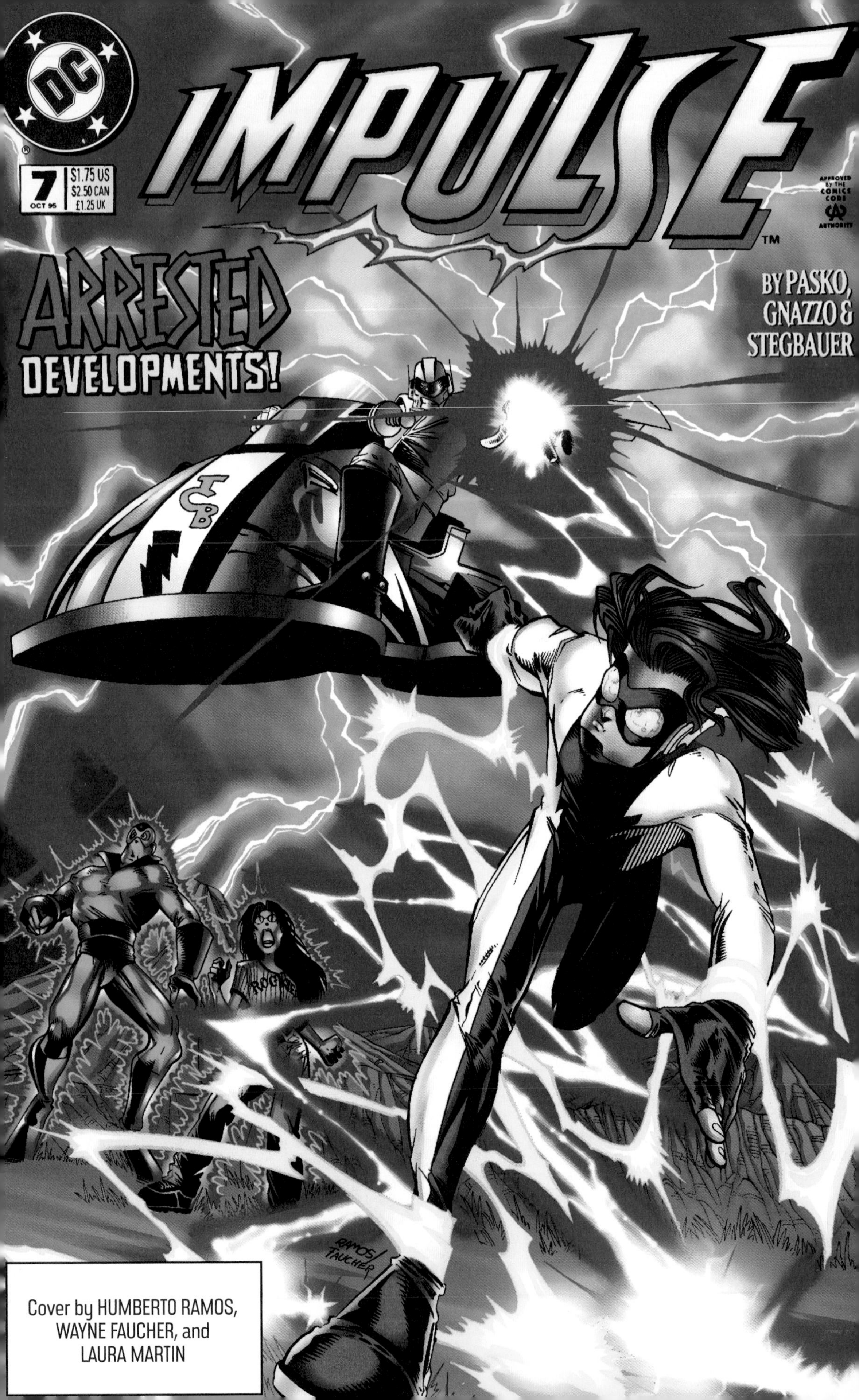
DC
IMPULSE
TM
7
OCT 95
$1.75 US
$2.50 CAN
£1.25 UK
APPROVED BY THE COMICS CODE AUTHORITY
ARRESTED DEVELOPMENTS!
BY PASKO, GNAZZO & STEGBAUER
ICB
RAMOS/ FAUCHER

Cover by HUMBERTO RAMOS, WAYNE FAUCHER, and LAURA MARTIN

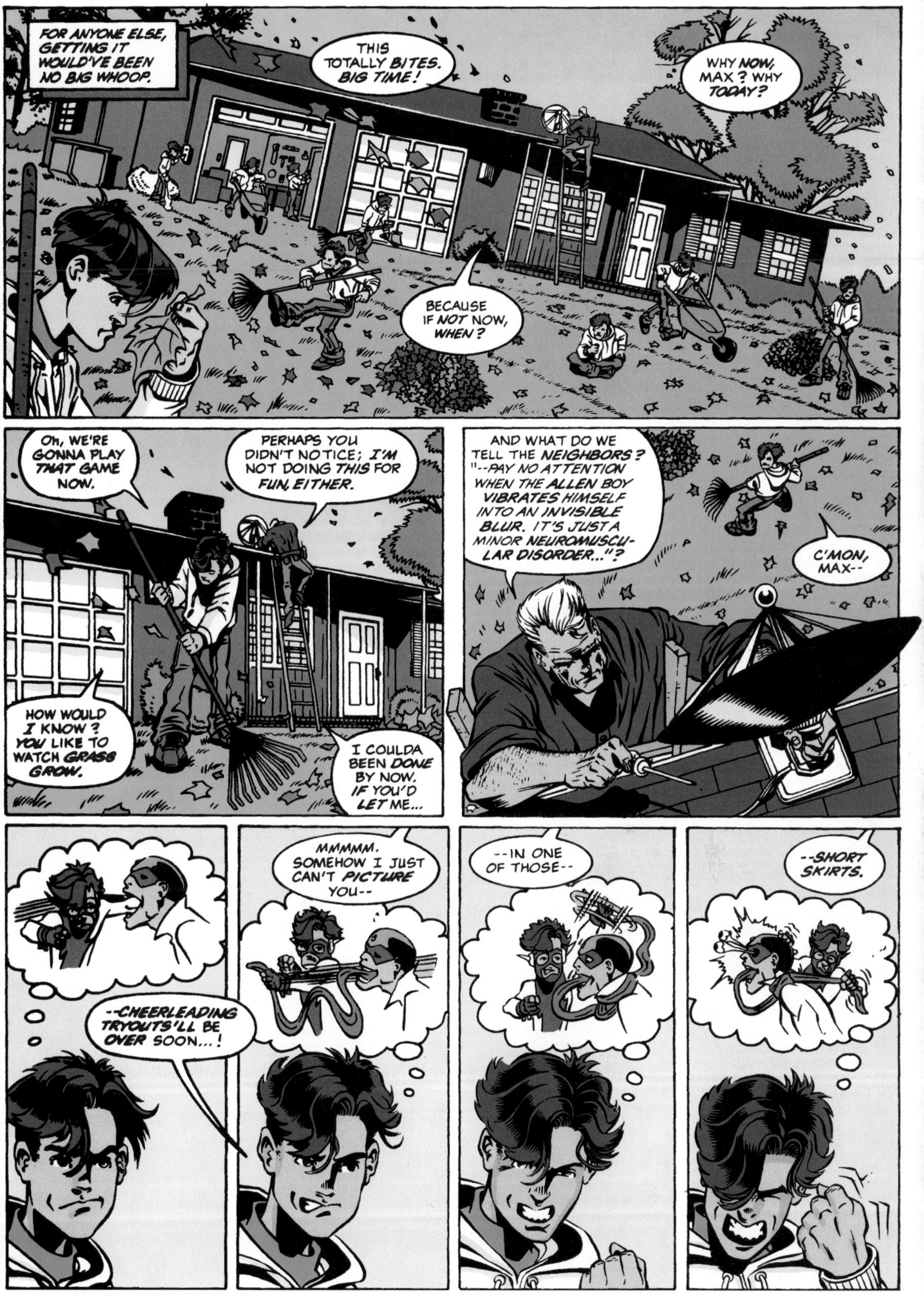
FOR ANYONE ELSE, GETTING IT WOULD'VE BEEN NO BIG WHOOP.
THIS TOTALLY BITES. BIG TIME!
WHY NOW, MAX? WHY TODAY?
BECAUSE IF NOT NOW, WHEN?
OH, WE'RE GONNA PLAY THAT GAME NOW.
PERHAPS YOU DIDN'T NOTICE; I'M NOT DOING THIS FOR FUN, EITHER.
HOW WOULD I KNOW? YOU LIKE TO WATCH GRASS GROW.
I COULDA BEEN DONE BY NOW. IF YOU'D LET ME...
AND WHAT DO WE TELL THE NEIGHBORS? "--PAY NO ATTENTION WHEN THE ALLEN BOY VIBRATES HIMSELF INTO AN INVISIBLE BLUR. IT'S JUST A MINOR NEUROMUSCULAR DISORDER..."?
C'MON, MAX--
--CHEERLEADING TRYOUTS'LL BE OVER SOON...!
MMMMM. SOMEHOW I JUST CAN'T PICTURE YOU--
--IN ONE OF THOSE--
--SHORT SKIRTS.

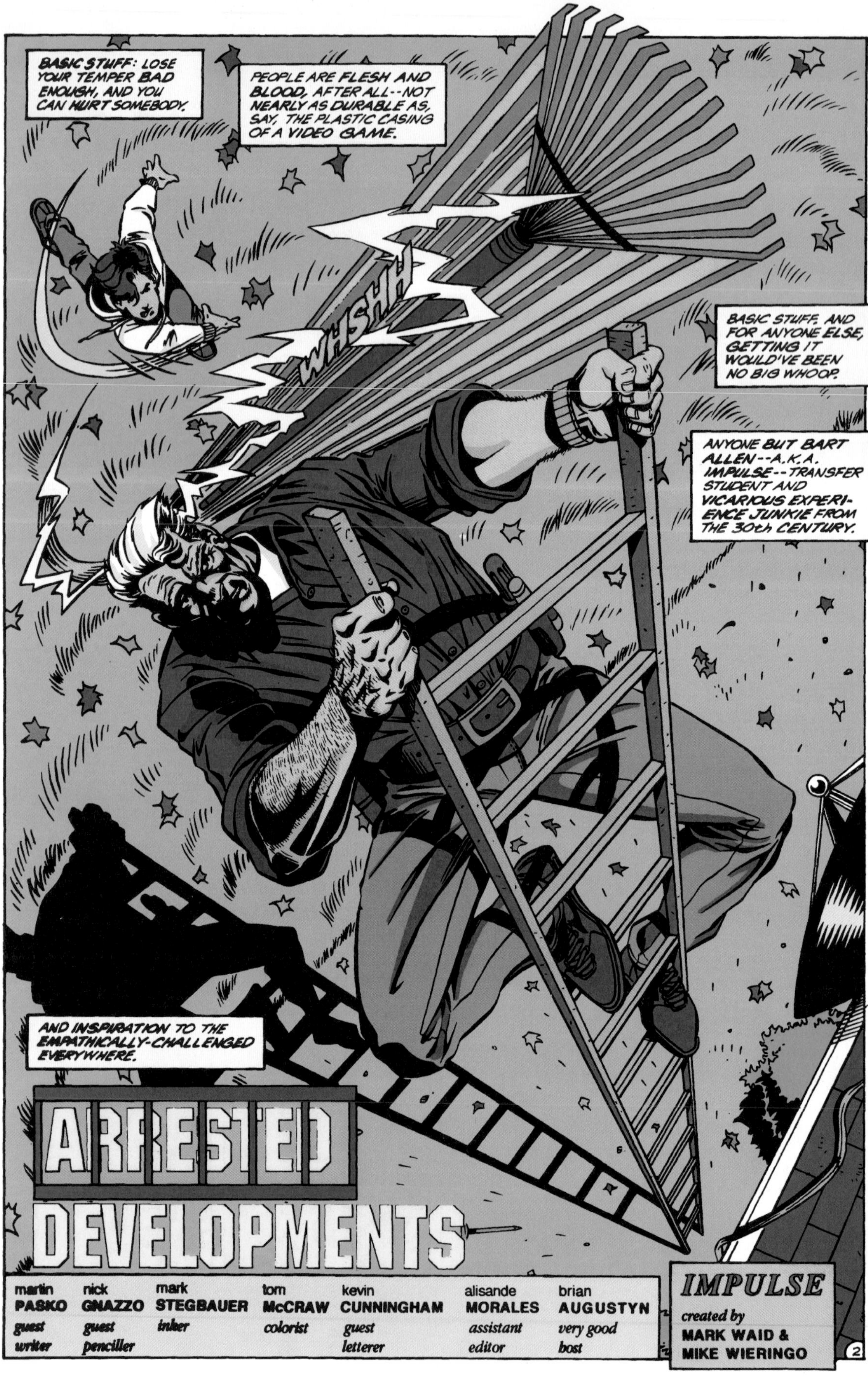
BASIC STUFF: LOSE YOUR TEMPER BAD ENOUGH, AND YOU CAN HURT SOMEBODY.
PEOPLE ARE FLESH AND BLOOD, AFTER ALL--NOT NEARLY AS DURABLE AS, SAY, THE PLASTIC CASING OF A VIDEO GAME.
WHSHH
BASIC STUFF. AND FOR ANYONE ELSE, GETTING IT WOULD'VE BEEN NO BIG WHOOP.
ANYONE BUT BART ALLEN--A.K.A. IMPULSE--TRANSFER STUDENT AND VICARIOUS EXPERIENCE JUNKIE FROM THE 30th CENTURY.
AND INSPIRATION TO THE EMPATHICALLY-CHALLENGED EVERYWHERE.
ARRESTED DEVELOPMENTS
martin PASKO guest writer
nick GNAZZO guest penciller
mark STEGBAUER inker
tom McCRAW colorist
kevin CUNNINGHAM guest letterer
alisande MORALES assistant editor
brian AUGUSTYN very good bost
IMPULSE created by MARK WAID & MIKE WIERINGO
2

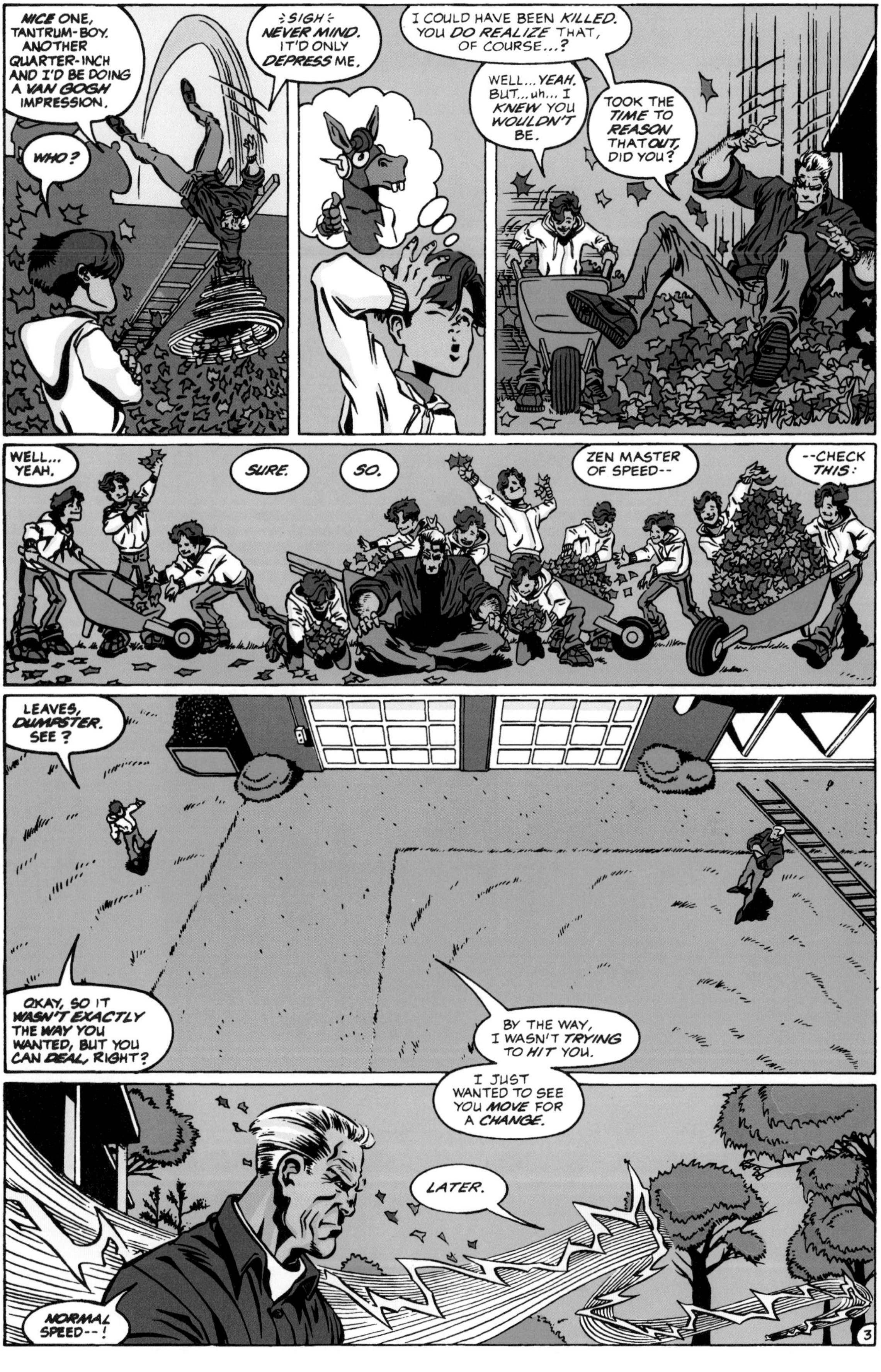
NICE ONE, TANTRUM-BOY. ANOTHER QUARTER-INCH AND I'D BE DOING A VAN GOGH IMPRESSION.
WHO?
SIGH NEVER MIND. IT'D ONLY DEPRESS ME.
I COULD HAVE BEEN KILLED. YOU DO REALIZE THAT, OF COURSE...?
WELL... YEAH. BUT... uh... I KNEW YOU WOULDN'T BE.
TOOK THE TIME TO REASON THAT OUT, DID YOU?
WELL... YEAH.
SURE.
SO.
ZEN MASTER OF SPEED--
--CHECK THIS:
LEAVES, DUMPSTER. SEE?
OKAY, SO IT WASN'T EXACTLY THE WAY YOU WANTED, BUT YOU CAN DEAL, RIGHT?
BY THE WAY, I WASN'T TRYING TO HIT YOU.
I JUST WANTED TO SEE YOU MOVE FOR A CHANGE.
LATER.
NORMAL SPEED--!

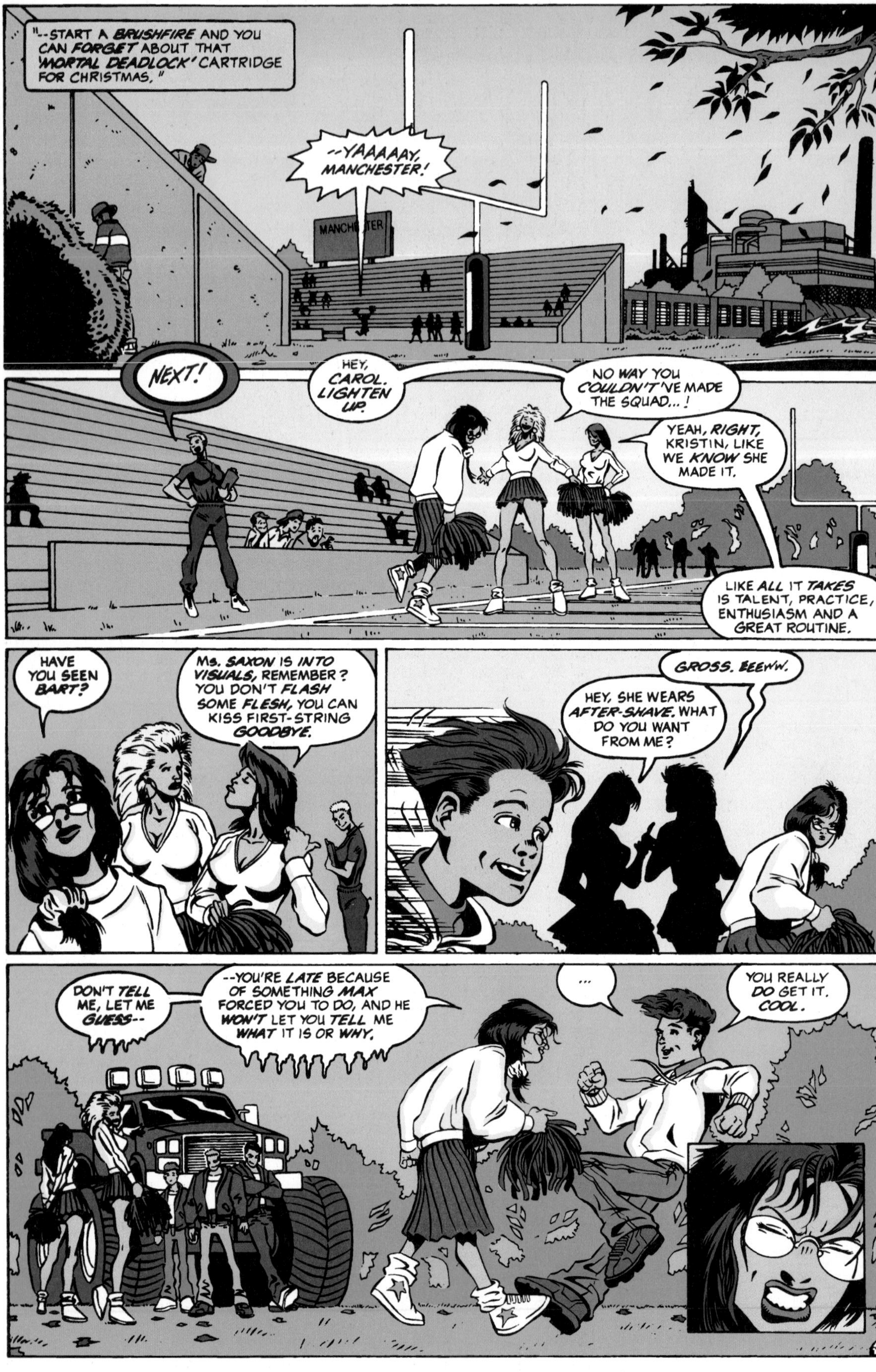
"--START A BRUSHFIRE AND YOU CAN FORGET ABOUT THAT 'MORTAL DEADLOCK' CARTRIDGE FOR CHRISTMAS."
--YAAAAAY, MANCHESTER!
MANCHESTER
NEXT!
HEY, CAROL. LIGHTEN UP.
NO WAY YOU COULDN'T'VE MADE THE SQUAD...!
YEAH, RIGHT, KRISTIN, LIKE WE KNOW SHE MADE IT.
LIKE ALL IT TAKES IS TALENT, PRACTICE, ENTHUSIASM AND A GREAT ROUTINE.
HAVE YOU SEEN BART?
Ms. SAXON IS INTO VISUALS, REMEMBER? YOU DON'T FLASH SOME FLESH, YOU CAN KISS FIRST-STRING GOODBYE.
HEY, SHE WEARS AFTER-SHAVE. WHAT DO YOU WANT FROM ME?
GROSS. EEEWW.
DON'T TELL ME, LET ME GUESS--
--YOU'RE LATE BECAUSE OF SOMETHING MAX FORCED YOU TO DO, AND HE WON'T LET YOU TELL ME WHAT IT IS OR WHY.
...
YOU REALLY DO GET IT. COOL.

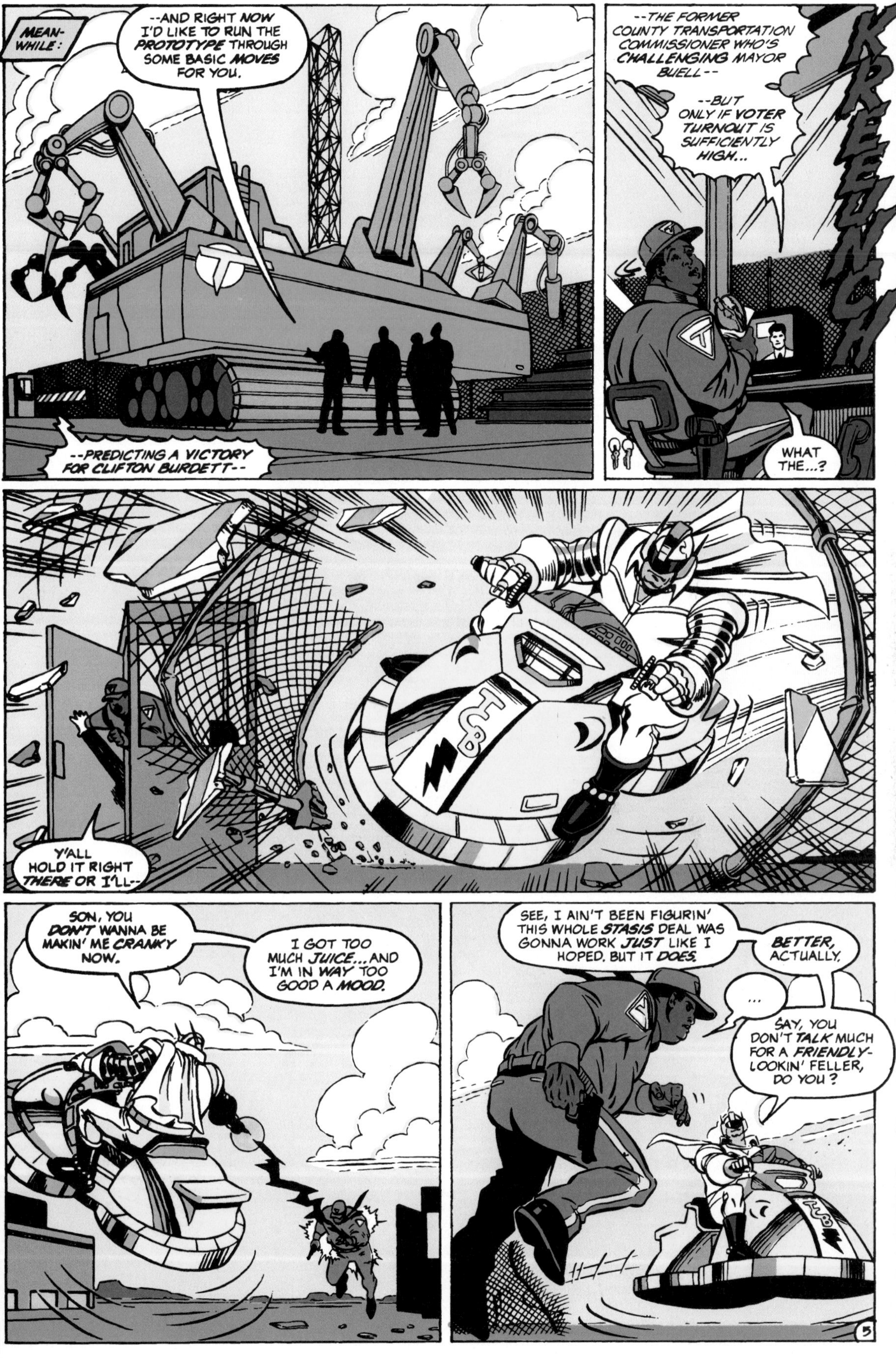

MEAN-WHILE:
--AND RIGHT NOW I'D LIKE TO RUN THE PROTOTYPE THROUGH SOME BASIC MOVES FOR YOU.
--PREDICTING A VICTORY FOR CLIFTON BURDETT--
--THE FORMER COUNTY TRANSPORTATION COMMISSIONER WHO'S CHALLENGING MAYOR BUELL--
--BUT ONLY IF VOTER TURNOUT IS SUFFICIENTLY HIGH...
KREEUNCH
WHAT THE...?
Y'ALL HOLD IT RIGHT THERE OR I'LL--
SON, YOU DON'T WANNA BE MAKIN' ME CRANKY NOW.
I GOT TOO MUCH JUICE... AND I'M IN WAY TOO GOOD A MOOD.
SEE, I AIN'T BEEN FIGURIN' THIS WHOLE STASIS DEAL WAS GONNA WORK JUST LIKE I HOPED. BUT IT DOES.
BETTER, ACTUALLY.
...
SAY, YOU DON'T TALK MUCH FOR A FRIENDLY-LOOKIN' FELLER, DO YOU?

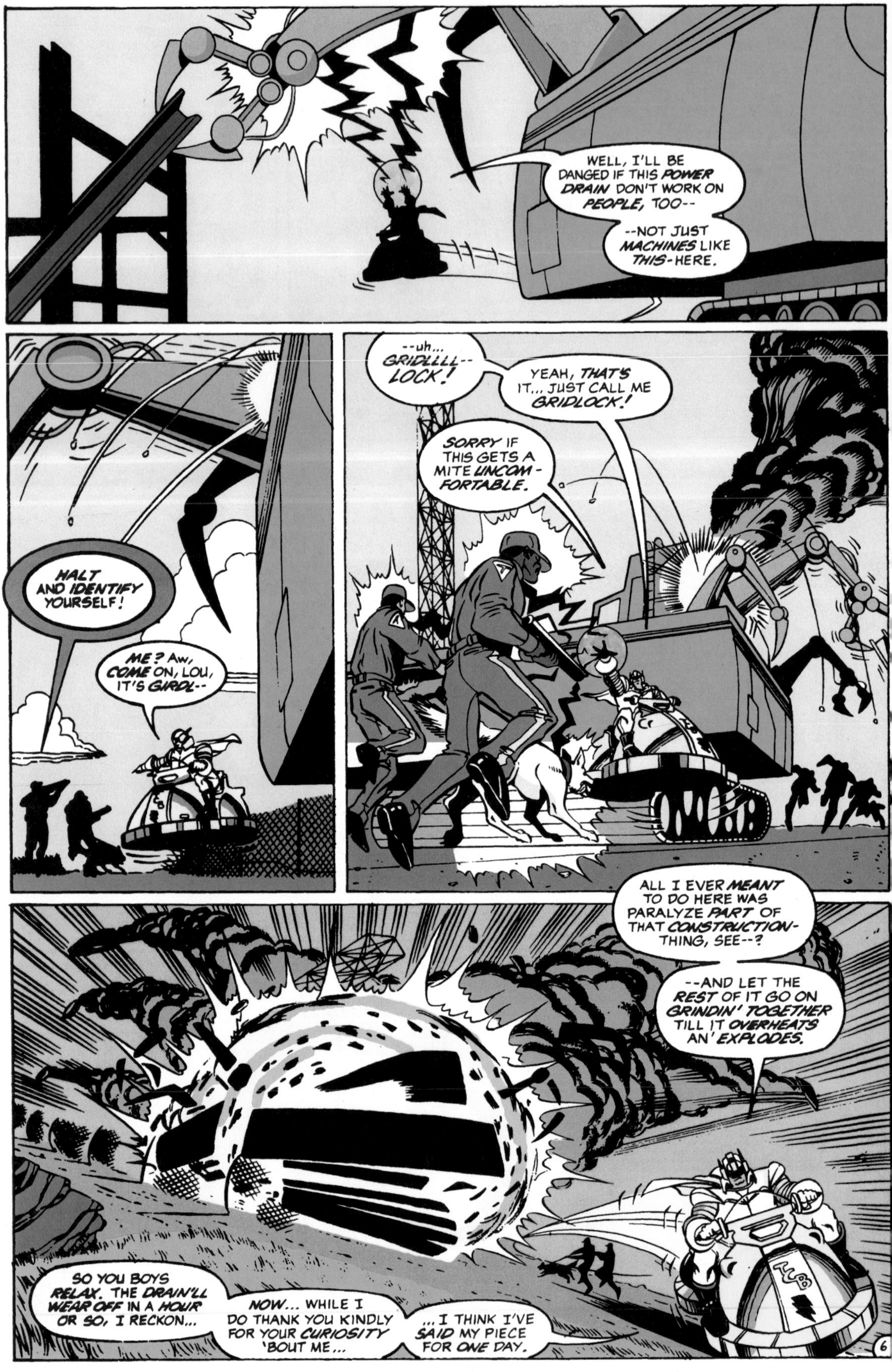
WELL, I'LL BE DANGED IF THIS POWER DRAIN DON'T WORK ON PEOPLE, TOO--
--NOT JUST MACHINES LIKE THIS-HERE.
HALT AND IDENTIFY YOURSELF!
ME? AW, COME ON, LOU, IT'S GIRDL--
--uh... GRIDLLLL--LOCK!
YEAH, THAT'S IT... JUST CALL ME GRIDLOCK!
SORRY IF THIS GETS A MITE UNCOM-FORTABLE.
ALL I EVER MEANT TO DO HERE WAS PARALYZE PART OF THAT CONSTRUCTION-THING, SEE--?
--AND LET THE REST OF IT GO ON GRINDIN' TOGETHER TILL IT OVERHEATS AN' EXPLODES.
SO YOU BOYS RELAX. THE DRAIN'LL WEAR OFF IN A HOUR OR SO, I RECKON...
NOW... WHILE I DO THANK YOU KINDLY FOR YOUR CURIOSITY 'BOUT ME...
...I THINK I'VE SAID MY PIECE FOR ONE DAY.
TCB

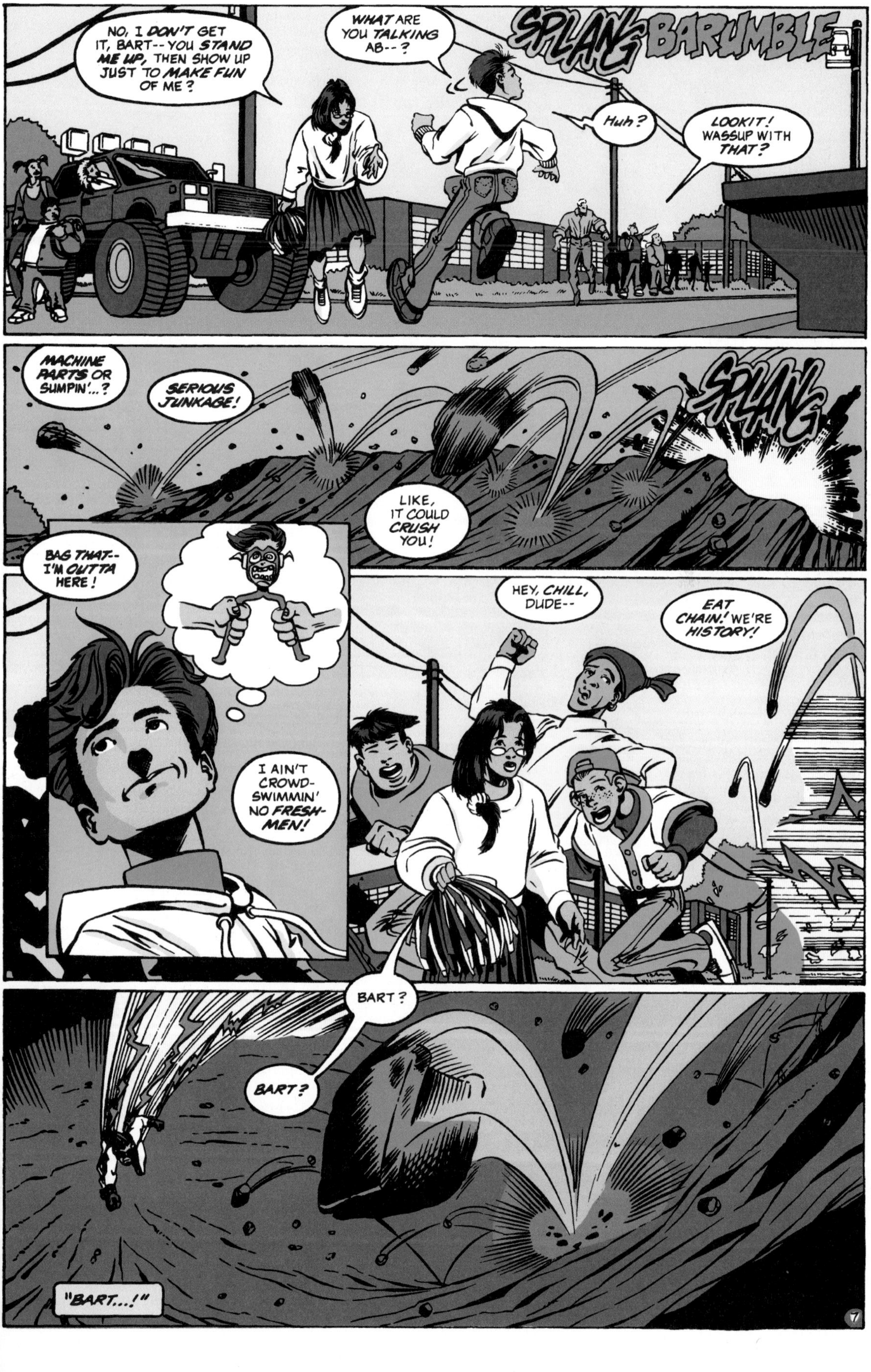

NO, I DON'T GET IT, BART-- YOU STAND ME UP, THEN SHOW UP JUST TO MAKE FUN OF ME?
WHAT ARE YOU TALKING AB--?
SPLANG BARUMBLE
Huh?
LOOKIT! WASSUP WITH THAT?
MACHINE PARTS OR SUMPIN'...?
SERIOUS JUNKAGE!
SPLANG
LIKE, IT COULD CRUSH YOU!
BAG THAT-- I'M OUTTA HERE!
I AIN'T CROWD-SWIMMIN' NO FRESH-MEN!
HEY, CHILL, DUDE--
EAT CHAIN! WE'RE HISTORY!
BART?
BART?
"BART...!"

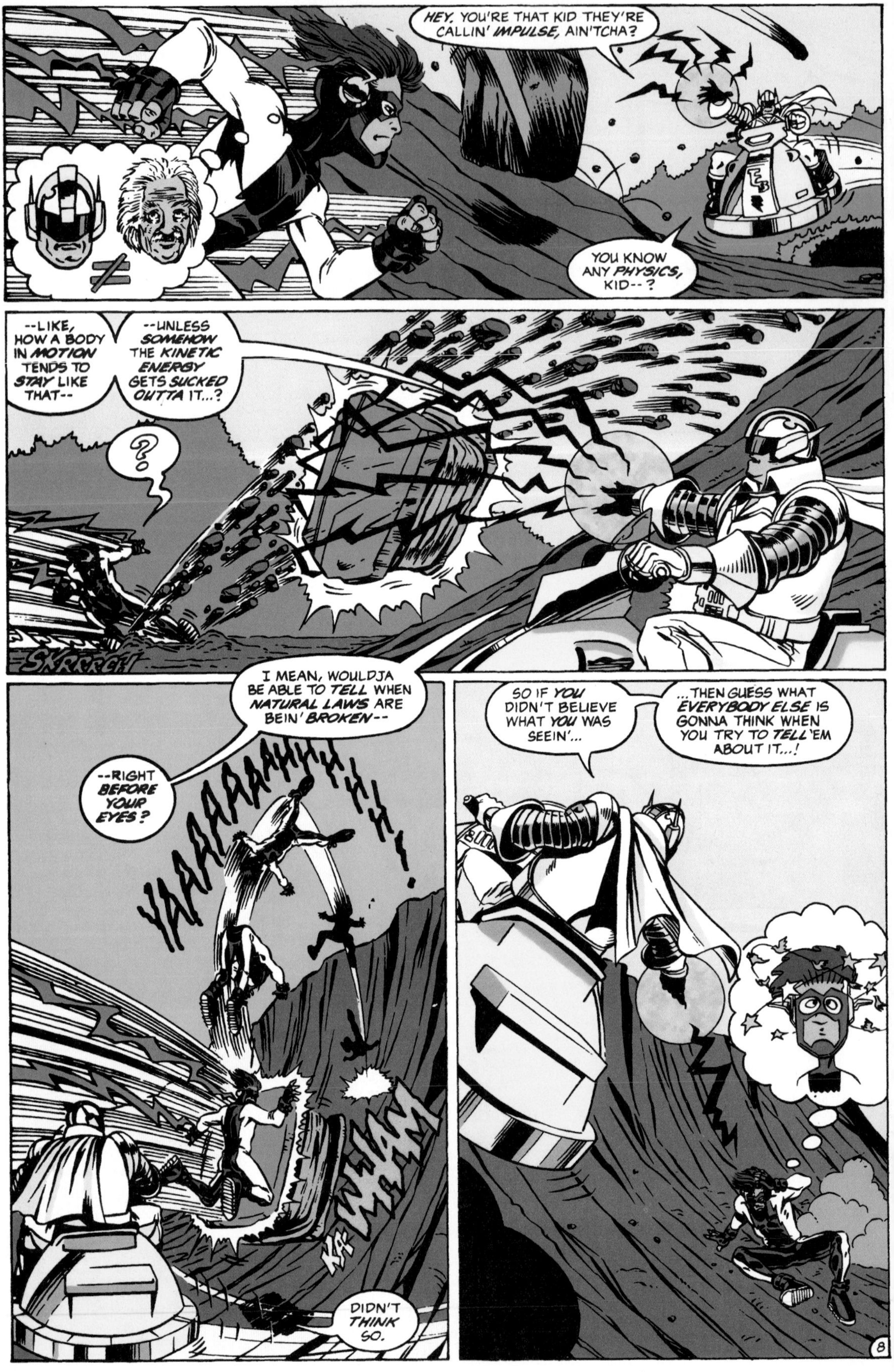
HEY, YOU'RE THAT KID THEY'RE CALLIN' IMPULSE, AIN'TCHA?
YOU KNOW ANY PHYSICS, KID--?
--LIKE, HOW A BODY IN MOTION TENDS TO STAY LIKE THAT--
--UNLESS SOMEHOW THE KINETIC ENERGY GETS SUCKED OUTTA IT...?
?
SKRRRCH
I MEAN, WOULDJA BE ABLE TO TELL WHEN NATURAL LAWS ARE BEIN' BROKEN--
--RIGHT BEFORE YOUR EYES?
YAAAAAAAHHHHH!
KA-WHAM
DIDN'T THINK SO.
SO IF YOU DIDN'T BELIEVE WHAT YOU WAS SEEIN'...
...THEN GUESS WHAT EVERYBODY ELSE IS GONNA THINK WHEN YOU TRY TO TELL 'EM ABOUT IT...!
8

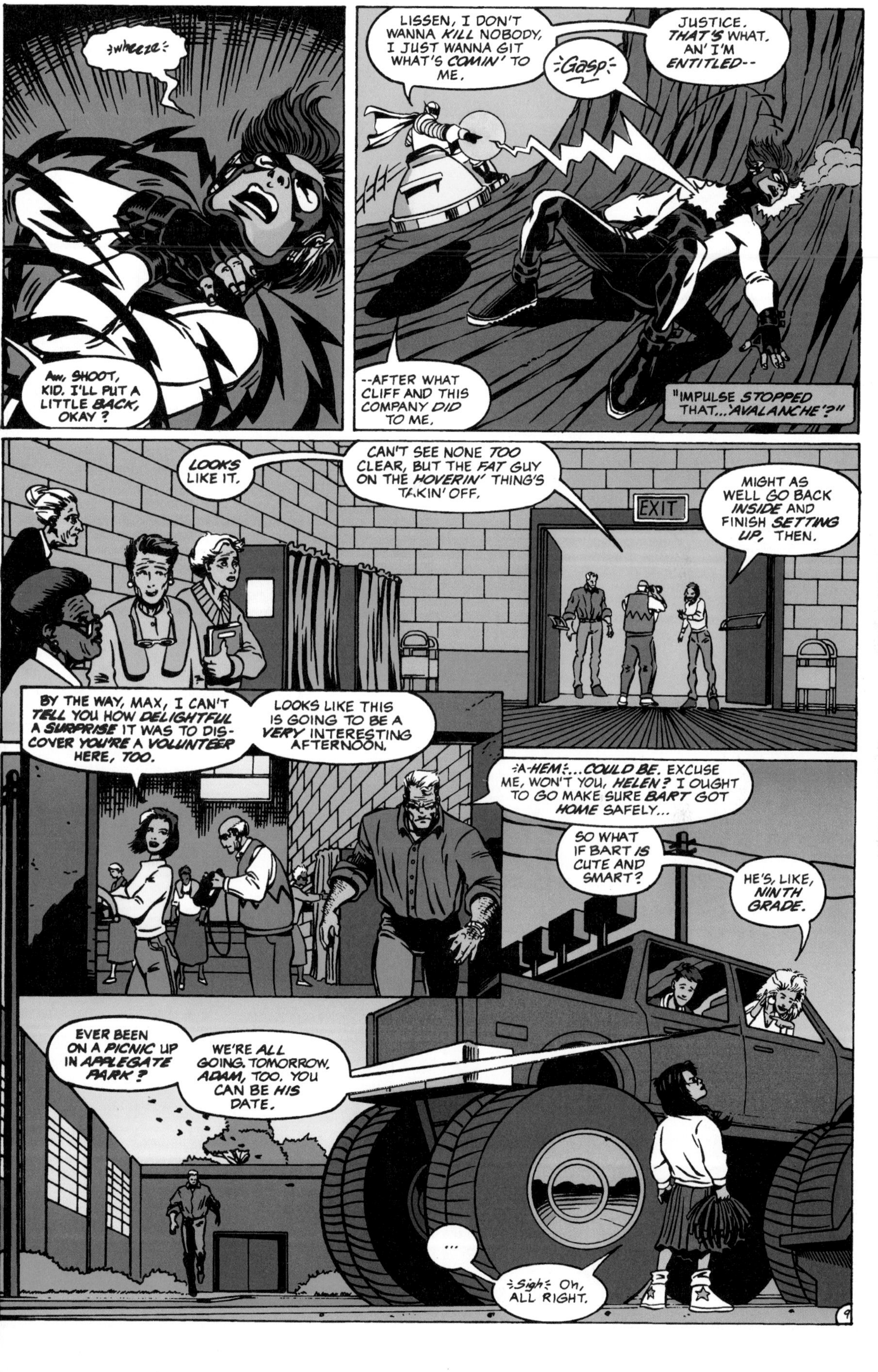

wheeze
Aw, SHOOT, KID. I'LL PUT A LITTLE BACK, OKAY?
LISSEN, I DON'T WANNA KILL NOBODY, I JUST WANNA GIT WHAT'S COMIN' TO ME.
Gasp
JUSTICE. THAT'S WHAT. AN' I'M ENTITLED--
--AFTER WHAT CLIFF AND THIS COMPANY DID TO ME.
"IMPULSE STOPPED THAT... 'AVALANCHE'?"
LOOKS LIKE IT.
CAN'T SEE NONE TOO CLEAR, BUT THE FAT GUY ON THE HOVERIN' THING'S TAKIN' OFF.
EXIT
MIGHT AS WELL GO BACK INSIDE AND FINISH SETTING UP, THEN.
BY THE WAY, MAX, I CAN'T TELL YOU HOW DELIGHTFUL A SURPRISE IT WAS TO DISCOVER YOU'RE A VOLUNTEER HERE, TOO.
LOOKS LIKE THIS IS GOING TO BE A VERY INTERESTING AFTERNOON.
A-HEM...COULD BE. EXCUSE ME, WON'T YOU, HELEN? I OUGHT TO GO MAKE SURE BART GOT HOME SAFELY...
SO WHAT IF BART IS CUTE AND SMART?
HE'S, LIKE, NINTH GRADE.
EVER BEEN ON A PICNIC UP IN APPLEGATE PARK?
WE'RE ALL GOING, TOMORROW. ADAM, TOO. YOU CAN BE HIS DATE.
...
Sigh Oh, ALL RIGHT.

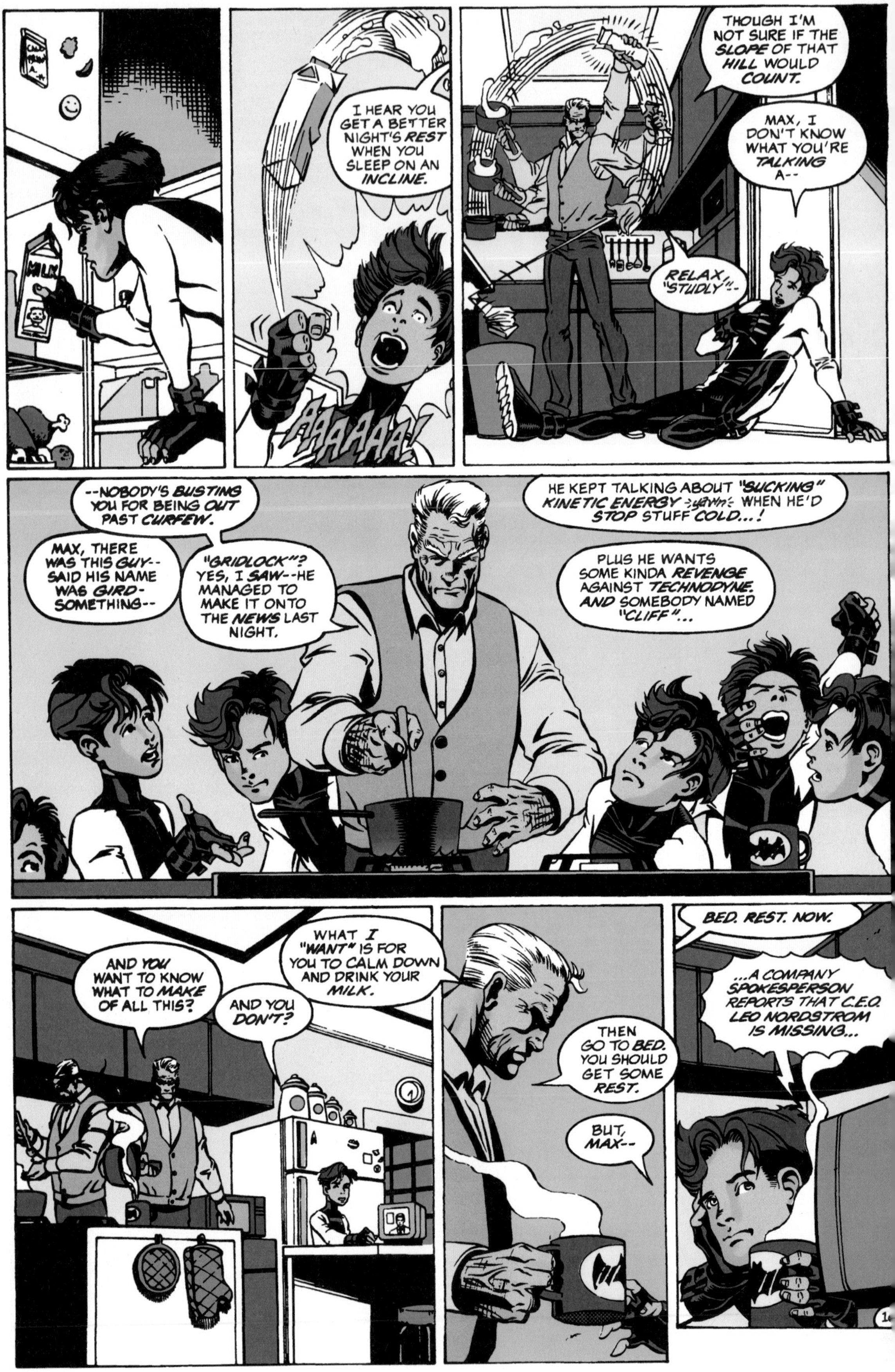

I HEAR YOU GET A BETTER NIGHT'S REST WHEN YOU SLEEP ON AN INCLINE.
AAAAAA!
THOUGH I'M NOT SURE IF THE SLOPE OF THAT HILL WOULD COUNT.
MAX, I DON'T KNOW WHAT YOU'RE TALKING A--
RELAX, "STUDLY"--
--NOBODY'S BUSTING YOU FOR BEING OUT PAST CURFEW.
MAX, THERE WAS THIS GUY--SAID HIS NAME WAS GIRD-SOMETHING--
"GRIDLOCK"? YES, I SAW--HE MANAGED TO MAKE IT ONTO THE NEWS LAST NIGHT.
HE KEPT TALKING ABOUT "SUCKING" KINETIC ENERGY ~yawn~ WHEN HE'D STOP STUFF COLD...!
PLUS HE WANTS SOME KINDA REVENGE AGAINST TECHNODYNE. AND SOMEBODY NAMED "CLIFF"...
AND YOU WANT TO KNOW WHAT TO MAKE OF ALL THIS?
AND YOU DON'T?
WHAT I "WANT" IS FOR YOU TO CALM DOWN AND DRINK YOUR MILK.
THEN GO TO BED. YOU SHOULD GET SOME REST.
BUT, MAX--
BED. REST. NOW.
...A COMPANY SPOKESPERSON REPORTS THAT C.E.O. LEO NORDSTROM IS MISSING...

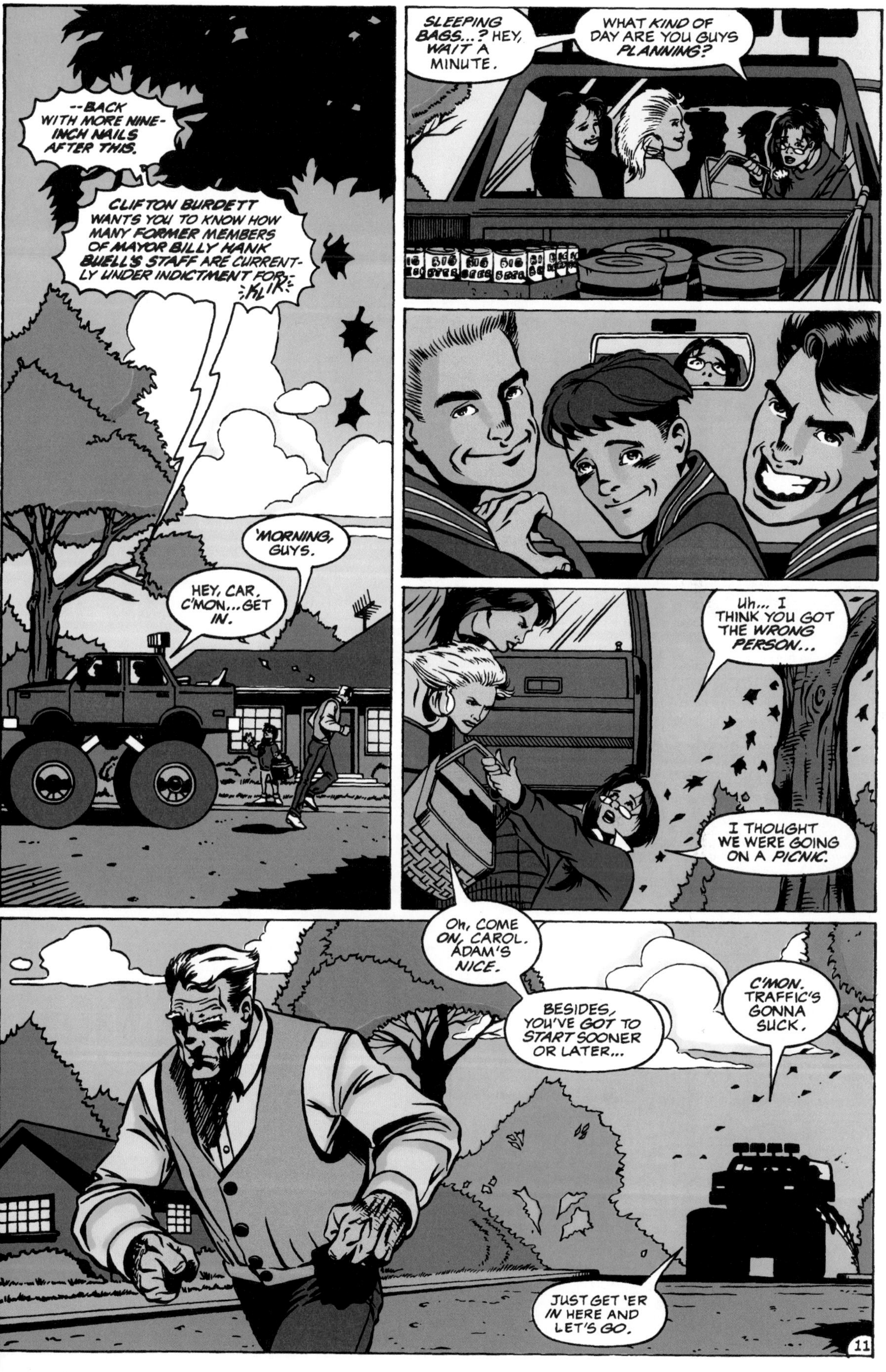

--BACK WITH MORE NINE-INCH NAILS AFTER THIS.
CLIFTON BURDETT WANTS YOU TO KNOW HOW MANY FORMER MEMBERS OF MAYOR BILLY HANK BUELL'S STAFF ARE CURRENTLY UNDER INDICTMENT FOR--
KLIK
'MORNING, GUYS.
HEY, CAR. C'MON... GET IN.
SLEEPING BAGS...? HEY, WAIT A MINUTE.
WHAT KIND OF DAY ARE YOU GUYS PLANNING?
Uh... I THINK YOU GOT THE WRONG PERSON...
I THOUGHT WE WERE GOING ON A PICNIC.
Oh, COME ON, CAROL. ADAM'S NICE.
BESIDES, YOU'VE GOT TO START SOONER OR LATER...
C'MON. TRAFFIC'S GONNA SUCK.
JUST GET 'ER IN HERE AND LET'S GO.

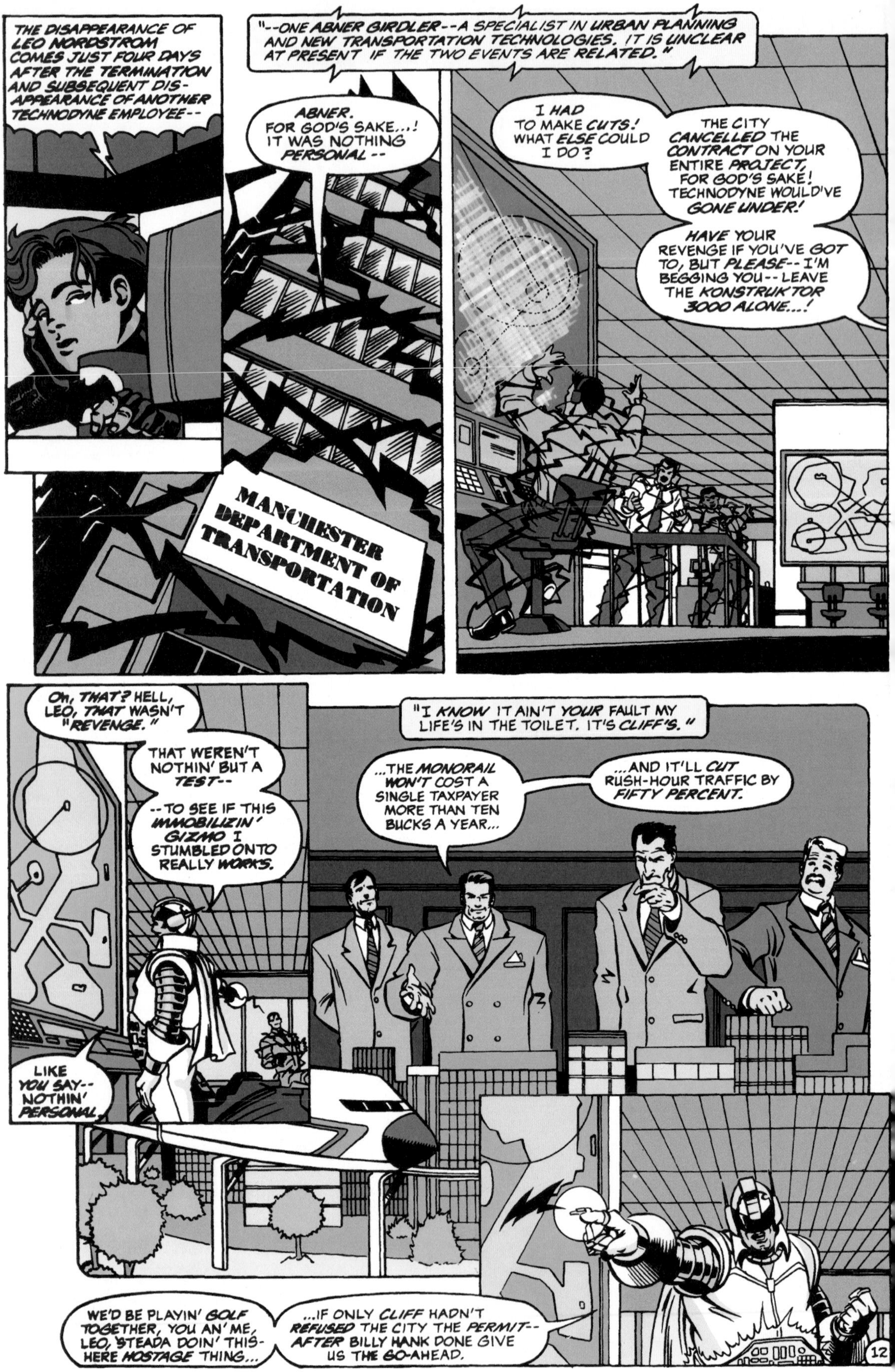
THE DISAPPEARANCE OF LEO NORDSTROM COMES JUST FOUR DAYS AFTER THE TERMINATION AND SUBSEQUENT DIS-APPEARANCE OF ANOTHER TECHNODYNE EMPLOYEE--
"--ONE ABNER GIRDLER--A SPECIALIST IN URBAN PLANNING AND NEW TRANSPORTATION TECHNOLOGIES. IT IS UNCLEAR AT PRESENT IF THE TWO EVENTS ARE RELATED."
ABNER. FOR GOD'S SAKE...! IT WAS NOTHING PERSONAL--
MANCHESTER DEPARTMENT OF TRANSPORTATION
I HAD TO MAKE CUTS! WHAT ELSE COULD I DO?
THE CITY CANCELLED THE CONTRACT ON YOUR ENTIRE PROJECT, FOR GOD'S SAKE! TECHNODYNE WOULD'VE GONE UNDER!
HAVE YOUR REVENGE IF YOU'VE GOT TO, BUT PLEASE--I'M BEGGING YOU--LEAVE THE KONSTRUKTOR 3000 ALONE...!
Oh, THAT? HELL, LEO, THAT WASN'T "REVENGE."
THAT WEREN'T NOTHIN' BUT A TEST--
--TO SEE IF THIS IMMOBILIZIN' GIZMO I STUMBLED ONTO REALLY WORKS.
LIKE YOU SAY--NOTHIN' PERSONAL.
"I KNOW IT AIN'T YOUR FAULT MY LIFE'S IN THE TOILET. IT'S CLIFF'S."
...THE MONORAIL WON'T COST A SINGLE TAXPAYER MORE THAN TEN BUCKS A YEAR...
...AND IT'LL CUT RUSH-HOUR TRAFFIC BY FIFTY PERCENT.
WE'D BE PLAYIN' GOLF TOGETHER, YOU AN' ME, LEO, 'STEADA DOIN' THIS-HERE HOSTAGE THING...
...IF ONLY CLIFF HADN'T REFUSED THE CITY THE PERMIT--AFTER BILLY HANK DONE GIVE US THE GO-AHEAD.

"NAH, I DON'T BLAME *YOU* SO MUCH, LEO..."

"...BUT I WANT YOU *AND* THAT BLASTED *CLIFF BURDETT* TO KNOW I WASN'T *KIDDIN'*--"

"--WHEN I SAID *GRIDLOCK* WOULD BRING THIS WHOLE CITY TO A *DEAD STOP* IF CLIFF DIDN'T *SIGN OFF* ON MY *MONORAIL* PLAN.

"AN' NOW YOU'RE *GONNA* KNOW--AND IT'S GONNA *COST* CLIFF THE *ELECTION,* TOO!"

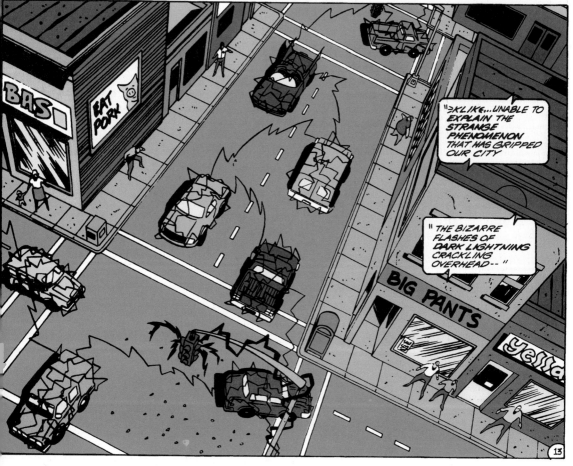

EAT PORK

BAS

BIG PANTS

yessa

"≥KLIKE...UNABLE TO EXPLAIN THE STRANGE PHENOMENON THAT HAS GRIPPED OUR CITY

"THE BIZARRE FLASHES OF DARK LIGHTNING CRACKLING OVERHEAD--"

13

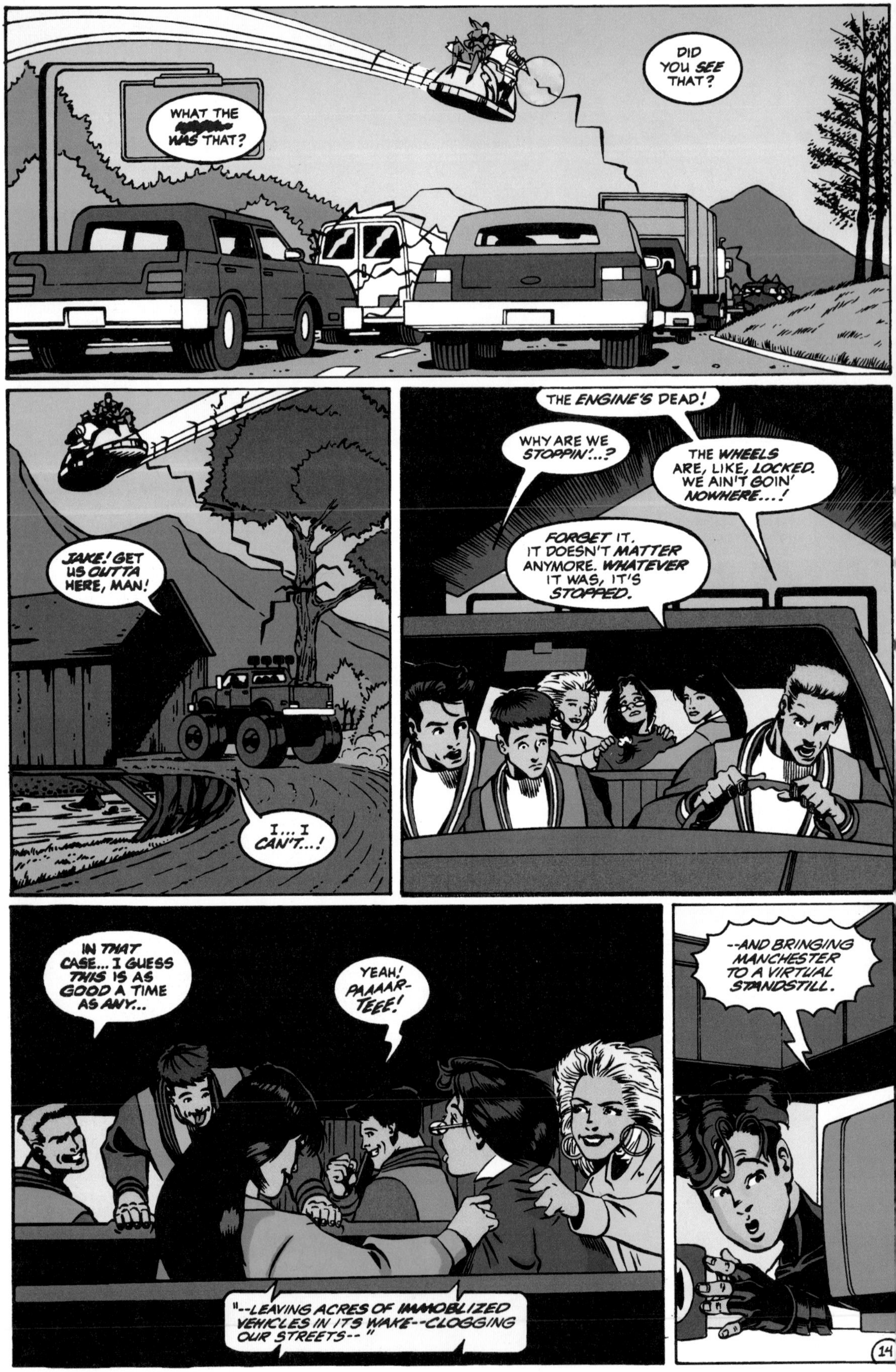

WHAT THE [redacted] WAS THAT?
DID YOU SEE THAT?
JAKE! GET US OUTTA HERE, MAN!
I... I CAN'T...!
THE ENGINE'S DEAD!
WHY ARE WE STOPPIN'...?
THE WHEELS ARE, LIKE, LOCKED. WE AIN'T GOIN' NOWHERE...!
FORGET IT. IT DOESN'T MATTER ANYMORE. WHATEVER IT WAS, IT'S STOPPED.
IN THAT CASE... I GUESS THIS IS AS GOOD A TIME AS ANY...
YEAH! PAAAAR-TEEE!
"--LEAVING ACRES OF IMMOBLIZED VEHICLES IN ITS WAKE--CLOGGING OUR STREETS--"
--AND BRINGING MANCHESTER TO A VIRTUAL STANDSTILL.

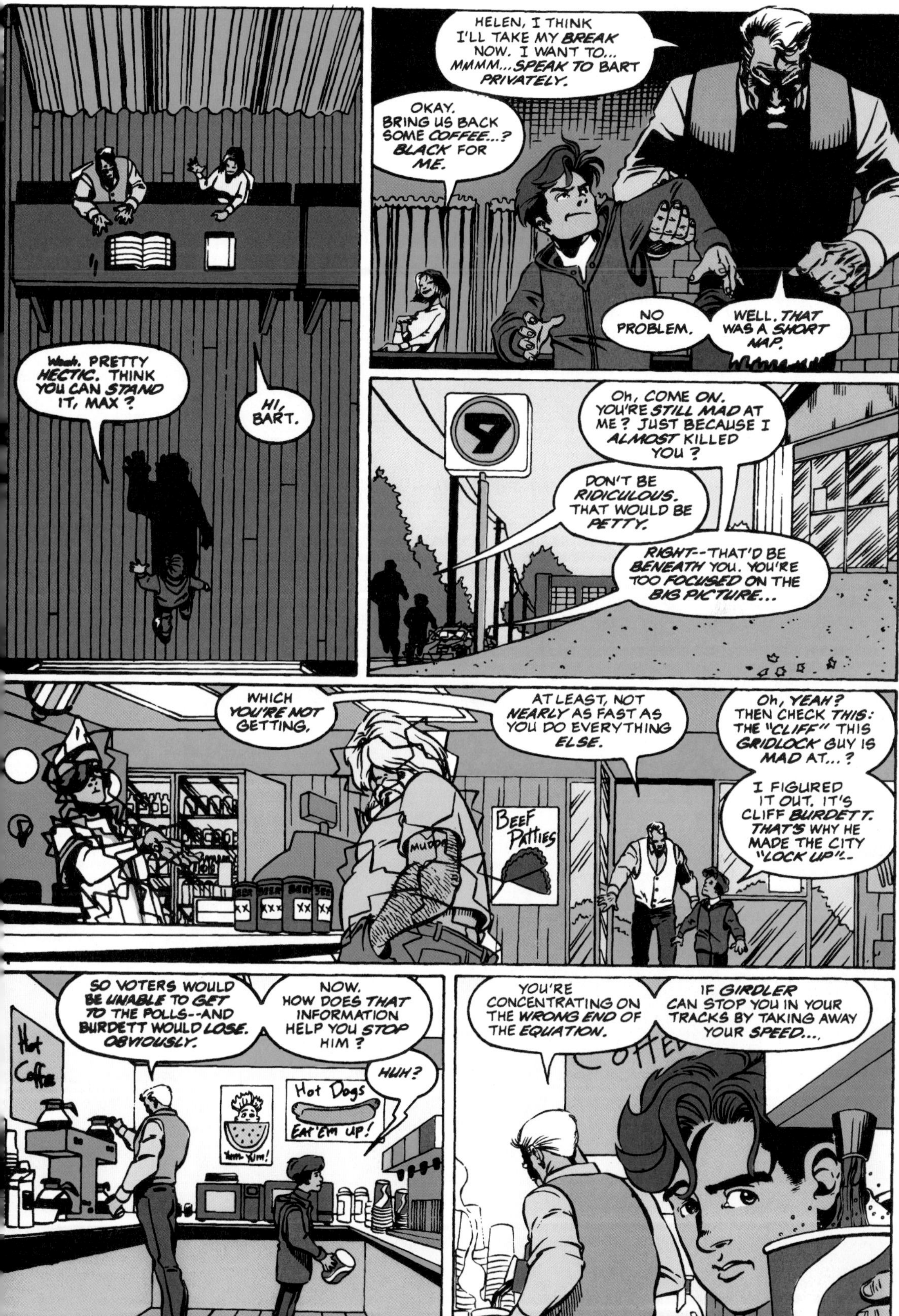
HELEN, I THINK I'LL TAKE MY BREAK NOW. I WANT TO... MMMM...SPEAK TO BART PRIVATELY.
OKAY. BRING US BACK SOME COFFEE...? BLACK FOR ME.
NO PROBLEM.
WELL. THAT WAS A SHORT NAP.
Whoah. PRETTY HECTIC. THINK YOU CAN STAND IT, MAX?
HI, BART.
Oh, COME ON. YOU'RE STILL MAD AT ME? JUST BECAUSE I ALMOST KILLED YOU?
DON'T BE RIDICULOUS. THAT WOULD BE PETTY.
RIGHT--THAT'D BE BENEATH YOU. YOU'RE TOO FOCUSED ON THE BIG PICTURE...
WHICH YOU'RE NOT GETTING.
AT LEAST, NOT NEARLY AS FAST AS YOU DO EVERYTHING ELSE.
Oh, YEAH? THEN CHECK THIS: THE "CLIFF" THIS GRIDLOCK GUY IS MAD AT...?
I FIGURED IT OUT. IT'S CLIFF BURDETT. THAT'S WHY HE MADE THE CITY "LOCK UP"--
BEEF PATTIES
SO VOTERS WOULD BE UNABLE TO GET TO THE POLLS--AND BURDETT WOULD LOSE. OBVIOUSLY.
NOW. HOW DOES THAT INFORMATION HELP YOU STOP HIM?
HUH?
Hot Coffee
Hot Dogs
Eat 'Em up!
YOU'RE CONCENTRATING ON THE WRONG END OF THE EQUATION.
IF GIRDLER CAN STOP YOU IN YOUR TRACKS BY TAKING AWAY YOUR SPEED...

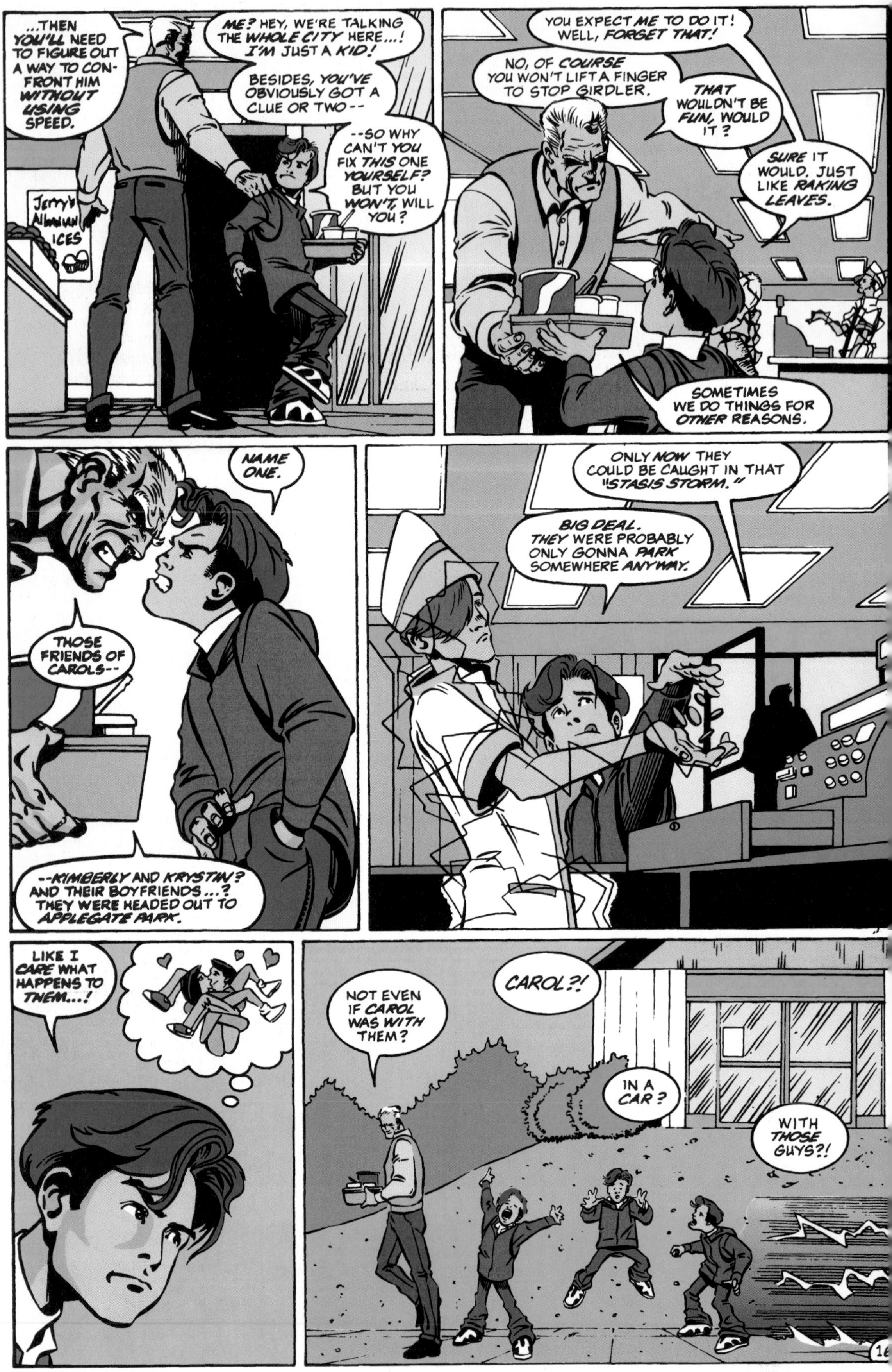
...THEN YOU'LL NEED TO FIGURE OUT A WAY TO CONFRONT HIM WITHOUT USING SPEED.
ME? HEY, WE'RE TALKING THE WHOLE CITY HERE...! I'M JUST A KID!
BESIDES, YOU'VE OBVIOUSLY GOT A CLUE OR TWO--
--SO WHY CAN'T YOU FIX THIS ONE YOURSELF? BUT YOU WON'T, WILL YOU?
Jerry's Albanian ICES
YOU EXPECT ME TO DO IT! WELL, FORGET THAT!
NO, OF COURSE YOU WON'T LIFT A FINGER TO STOP GIRDLER.
THAT WOULDN'T BE FUN, WOULD IT?
SURE IT WOULD. JUST LIKE RAKING LEAVES.
SOMETIMES WE DO THINGS FOR OTHER REASONS.
NAME ONE.
THOSE FRIENDS OF CAROLS--
--KIMBERLY AND KRYSTIN? AND THEIR BOYFRIENDS...? THEY WERE HEADED OUT TO APPLEGATE PARK.
ONLY NOW THEY COULD BE CAUGHT IN THAT "STASIS STORM."
BIG DEAL. THEY WERE PROBABLY ONLY GONNA PARK SOMEWHERE ANYWAY.
LIKE I CARE WHAT HAPPENS TO THEM...!
NOT EVEN IF CAROL WAS WITH THEM?
CAROL?!
IN A CAR?
WITH THOSE GUYS?!

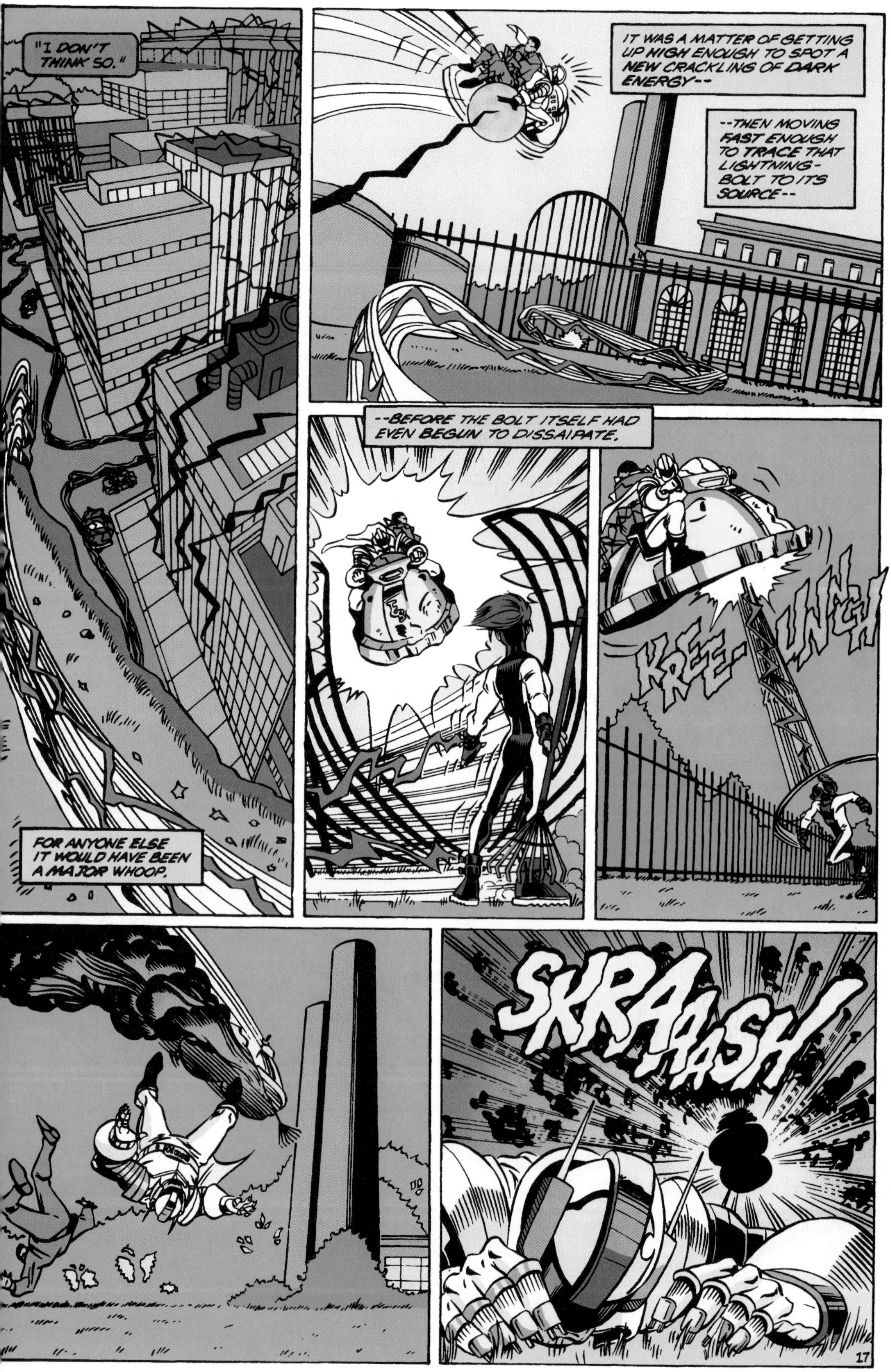
"I DON'T THINK SO."
FOR ANYONE ELSE IT WOULD HAVE BEEN A MAJOR WHOOP.
IT WAS A MATTER OF GETTING UP HIGH ENOUGH TO SPOT A NEW CRACKLING OF DARK ENERGY--
--THEN MOVING FAST ENOUGH TO TRACE THAT LIGHTNING-BOLT TO ITS SOURCE--
--BEFORE THE BOLT ITSELF HAD EVEN BEGUN TO DISSAIPATE.
KREE-UNCH
SKRAAASH

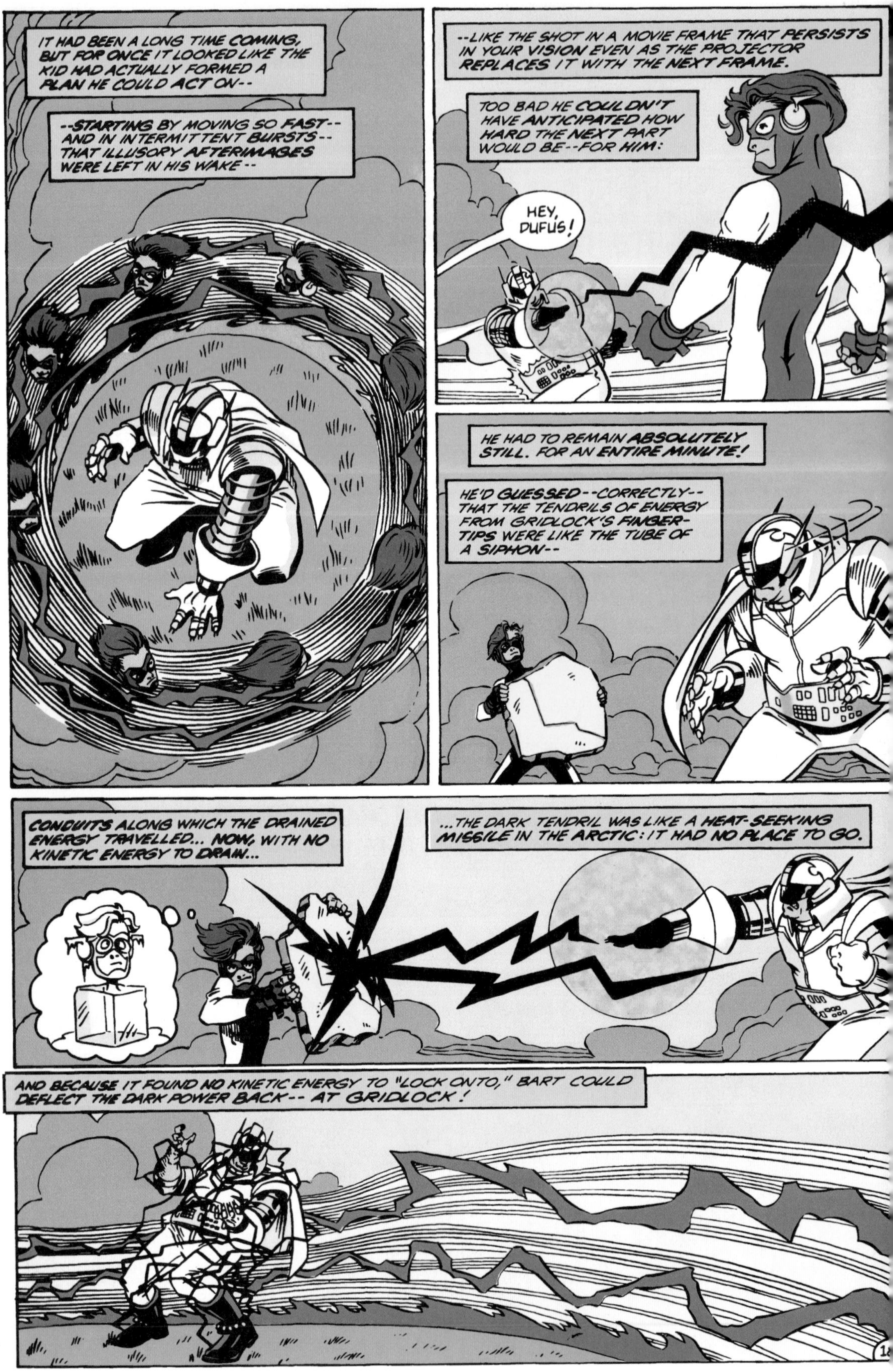
IT HAD BEEN A LONG TIME COMING, BUT FOR ONCE IT LOOKED LIKE THE KID HAD ACTUALLY FORMED A PLAN HE COULD ACT ON--
--STARTING BY MOVING SO FAST--AND IN INTERMITTENT BURSTS--THAT ILLUSORY AFTERIMAGES WERE LEFT IN HIS WAKE--
--LIKE THE SHOT IN A MOVIE FRAME THAT PERSISTS IN YOUR VISION EVEN AS THE PROJECTOR REPLACES IT WITH THE NEXT FRAME.
TOO BAD HE COULDN'T HAVE ANTICIPATED HOW HARD THE NEXT PART WOULD BE--FOR HIM:
HEY, DUFUS!
HE HAD TO REMAIN ABSOLUTELY STILL. FOR AN ENTIRE MINUTE!
HE'D GUESSED--CORRECTLY--THAT THE TENDRILS OF ENERGY FROM GRIDLOCK'S FINGER-TIPS WERE LIKE THE TUBE OF A SIPHON--
CONDUITS ALONG WHICH THE DRAINED ENERGY TRAVELLED... NOW, WITH NO KINETIC ENERGY TO DRAIN...
...THE DARK TENDRIL WAS LIKE A HEAT-SEEKING MISSILE IN THE ARCTIC: IT HAD NO PLACE TO GO.
AND BECAUSE IT FOUND NO KINETIC ENERGY TO "LOCK ONTO," BART COULD DEFLECT THE DARK POWER BACK-- AT GRIDLOCK!

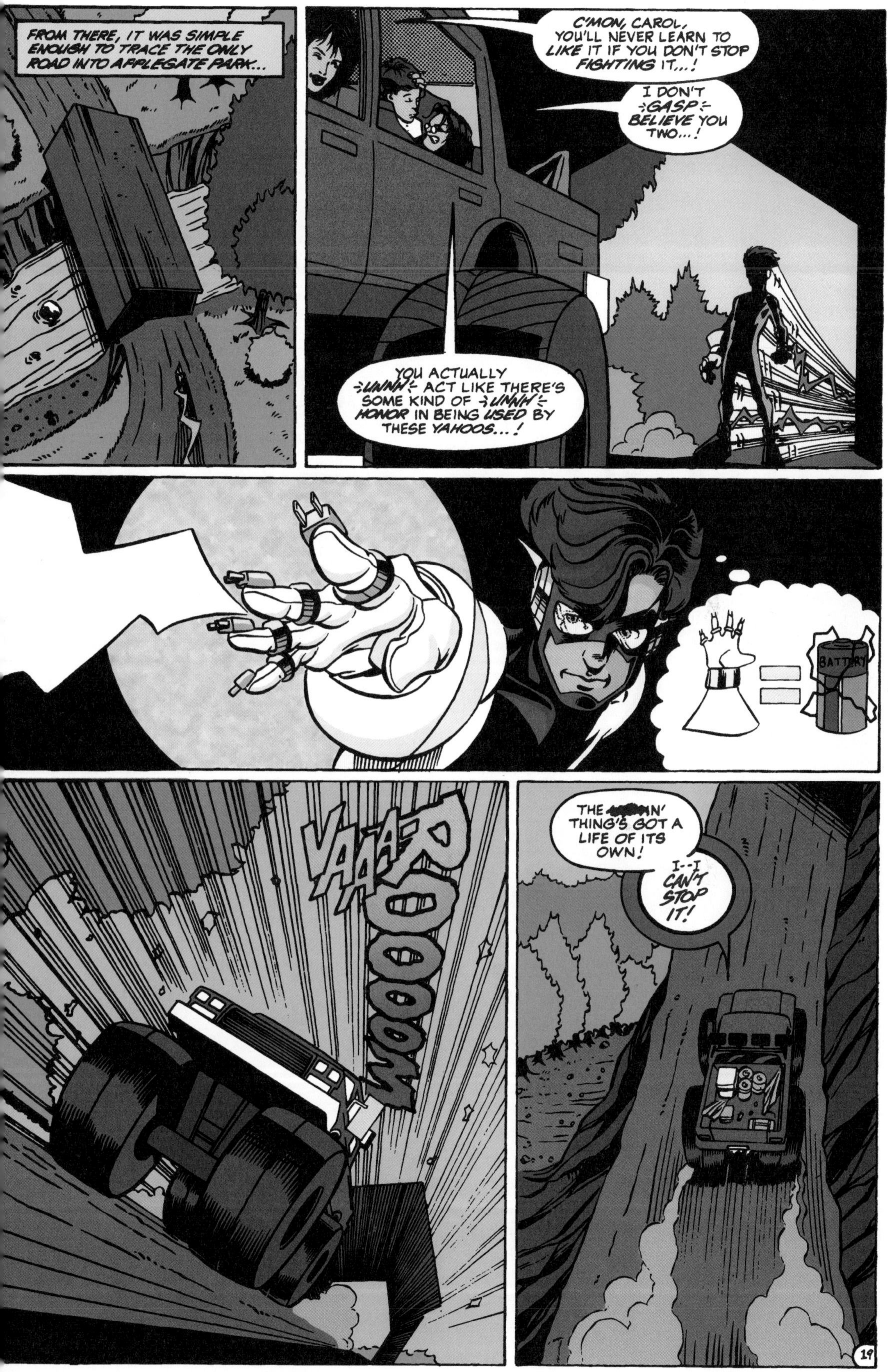
FROM THERE, IT WAS SIMPLE ENOUGH TO TRACE THE ONLY ROAD INTO APPLEGATE PARK...
C'MON, CAROL, YOU'LL NEVER LEARN TO LIKE IT IF YOU DON'T STOP FIGHTING IT...!
I DON'T -GASP- BELIEVE YOU TWO...!
YOU ACTUALLY -UNNH- ACT LIKE THERE'S SOME KIND OF -UNNH- HONOR IN BEING USED BY THESE YAHOOS...!
BATTERY
VAAAROOOOOM
THE [redacted]N' THING'S GOT A LIFE OF ITS OWN!
I--I CAN'T STOP IT!

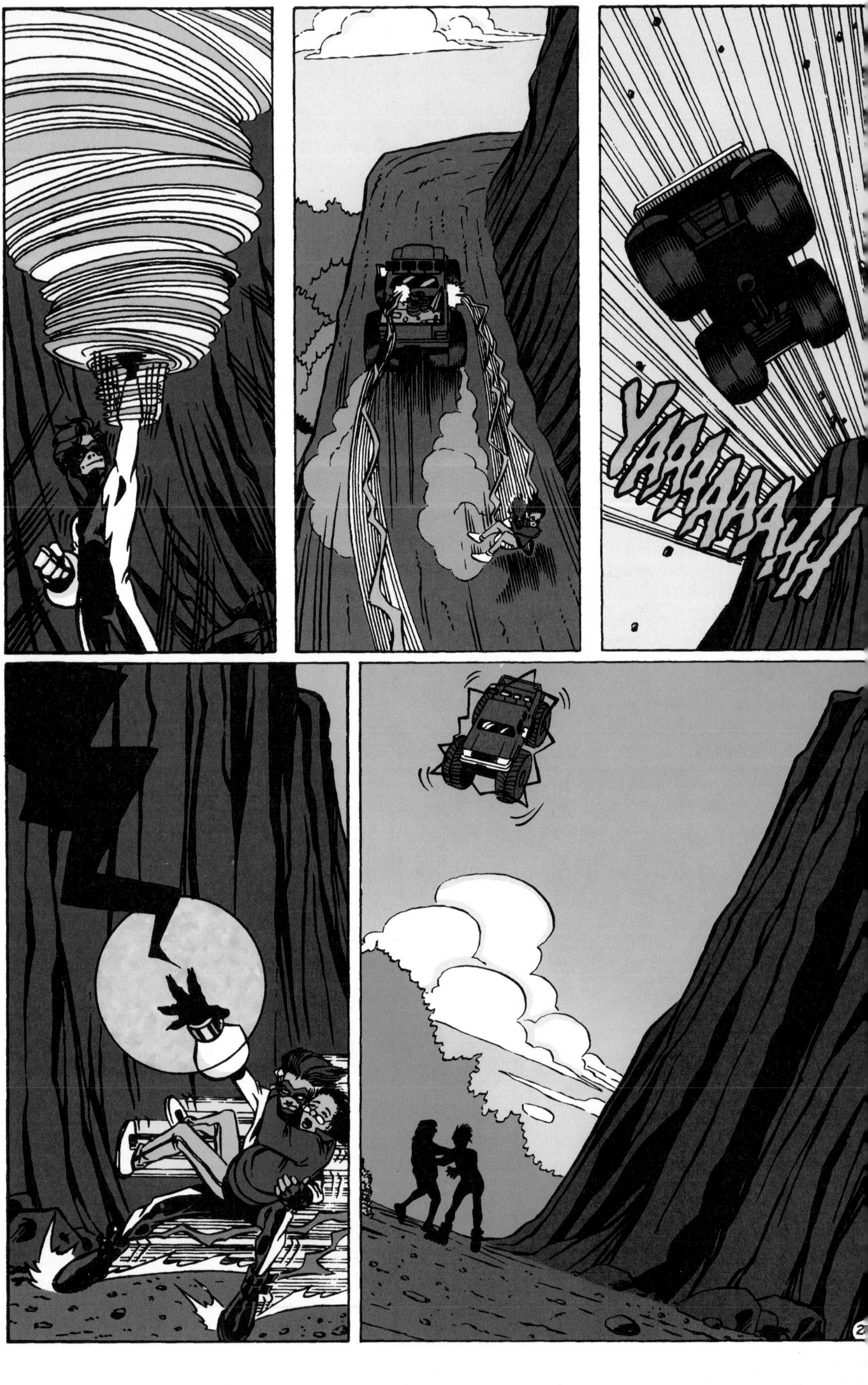
YAAAAAAH

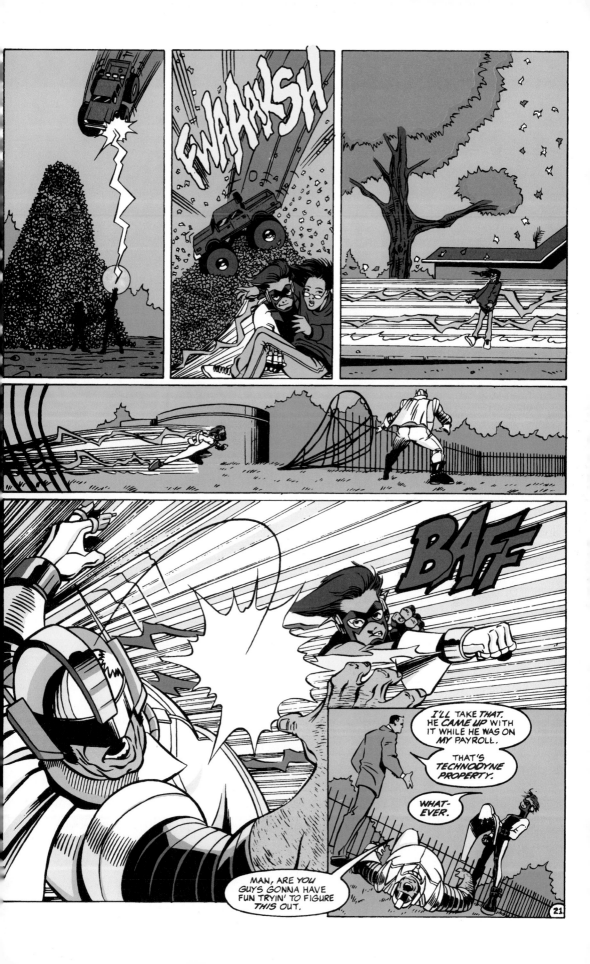

FWAAARSH

BAFF

I'LL TAKE *THAT*. HE *CAME UP* WITH IT WHILE HE WAS ON MY PAYROLL.

THAT'S *TECHNODYNE PROPERTY*.

WHAT-EVER.

MAN, ARE YOU GUYS GONNA HAVE FUN TRYIN' TO FIGURE *THIS* OUT.

21

LATER:

--BUT AT THIS POINT, THE *BURDETT* CAMP STILL REFUSES TO *CONCEDE*--

BUELL | BURDETT
7,462 | 1,060

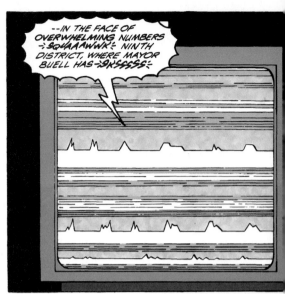

--IN THE FACE OF *OVERWHELMING NUMBERS* -:*SQUAAAWWK*:- NINTH DISTRICT, WHERE MAYOR BUELL HAS -:*9KSFSFSS*:-

--THANKS TO A *LAST-MINUTE RUSH* TO THE POLLS. FOLLOWING THE *APPREHENSION* OF THE BIZARRE TERRORIST CALLING HIMSELF *GRIDLOCK*--

YOU HAVE TO KEEP *HOLDING* IT. OTHERWISE THE PICTURE *GOES OUT.*

--BY THE *MYSTERI*- -:*SHHNTIGSS*:-

HMMM. I'LL HAVE TO *READJUST* IT, *TOMORROW.*

WHAT ABOUT *TONIGHT?*

LET'S SEE...THE POLLS *CLOSED* AT *SIX*... WE *OUGHT* TO HAVE THE FINAL RESULTS *WITH-IN THE HOUR.*

JUST STAY UP THERE TILL BURDETT *CONCEDES,* ALL RIGHT?

AND, *STOP POUTING.* YOU'LL *LOVE* IT. IT'LL BE A *CHALLENGE*...

NEXT: **BLOCKBUSTER**

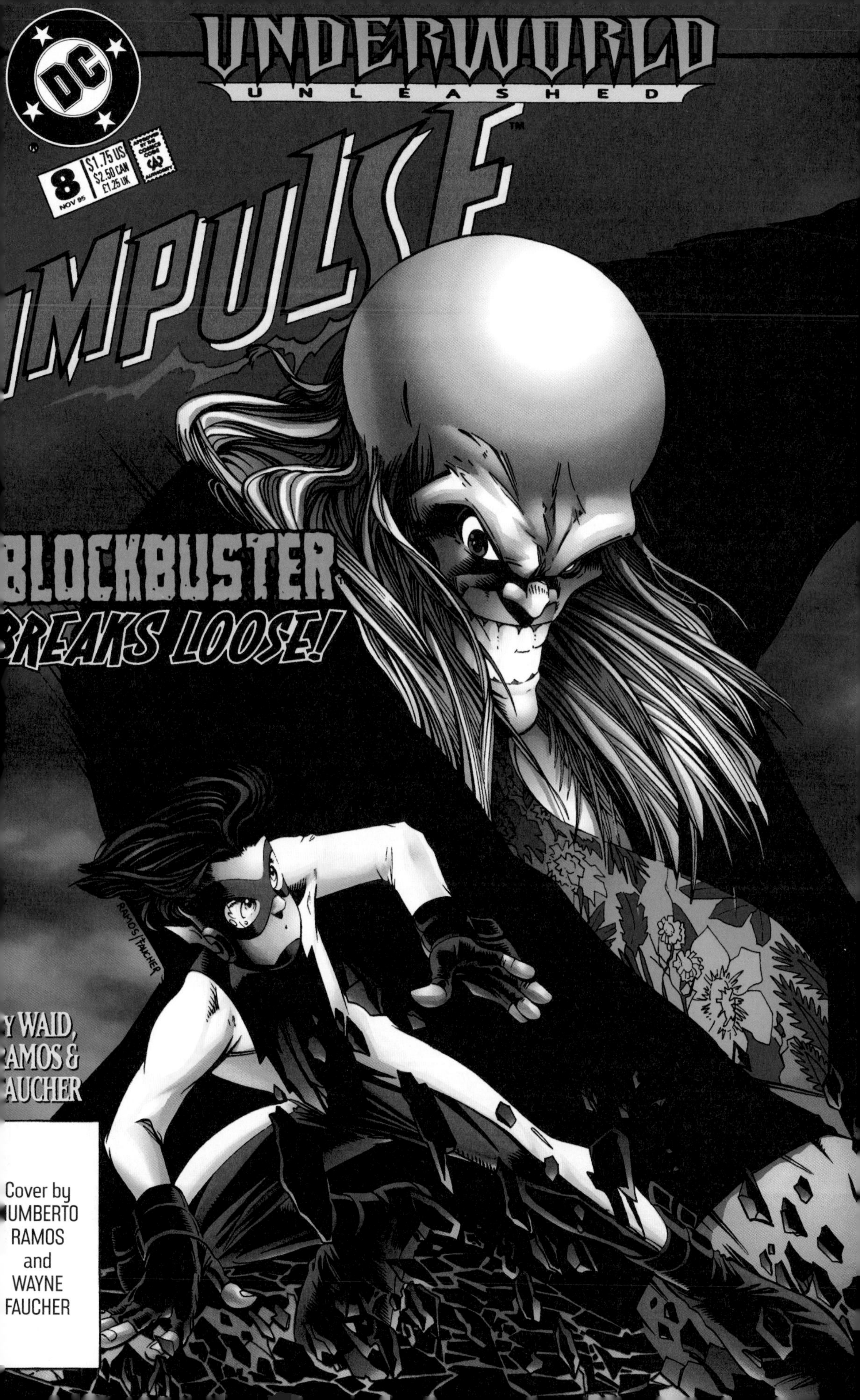

UNDERWORLD
UNLEASHED
8
NOV 95
$1.75 US
$2.50 CAN
£1.25 UK
IMPULSE
BLOCKBUSTER
BREAKS LOOSE!
RAMOS/FAUCHER
Y WAID,
AMOS &
AUCHER

Cover by
UMBERTO
RAMOS
and
WAYNE
FAUCHER

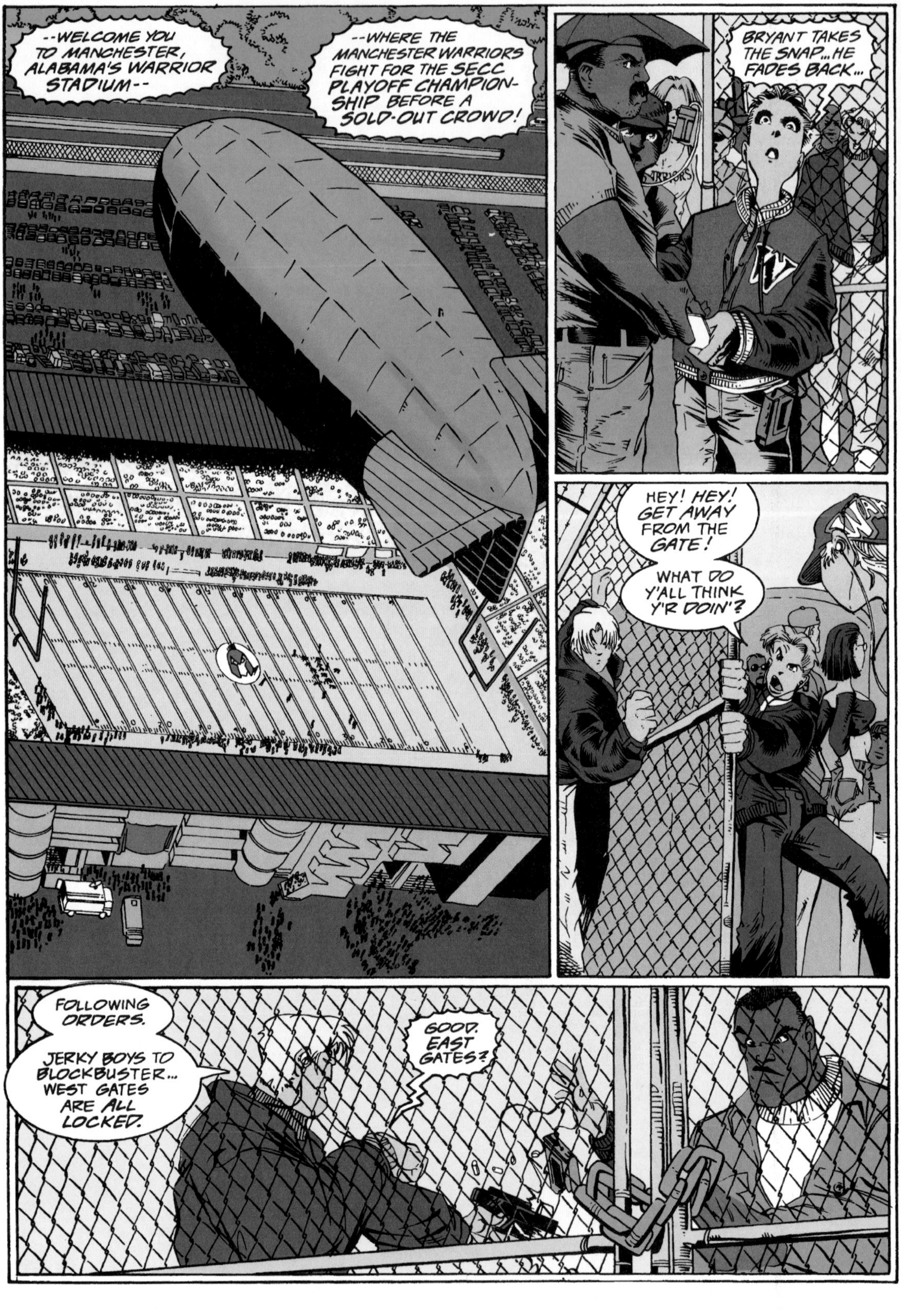
--WELCOME YOU TO MANCHESTER, ALABAMA'S WARRIOR STADIUM--
--WHERE THE MANCHESTER WARRIORS FIGHT FOR THE SECC PLAYOFF CHAMPIONSHIP BEFORE A SOLD-OUT CROWD!
BRYANT TAKES THE SNAP... HE FADES BACK...
WARRIORS
HEY! HEY! GET AWAY FROM THE GATE!
WHAT DO Y'ALL THINK Y'R DOIN'?
FOLLOWING ORDERS.
JERKY BOYS TO BLOCKBUSTER... WEST GATES ARE ALL LOCKED.
GOOD. EAST GATES?

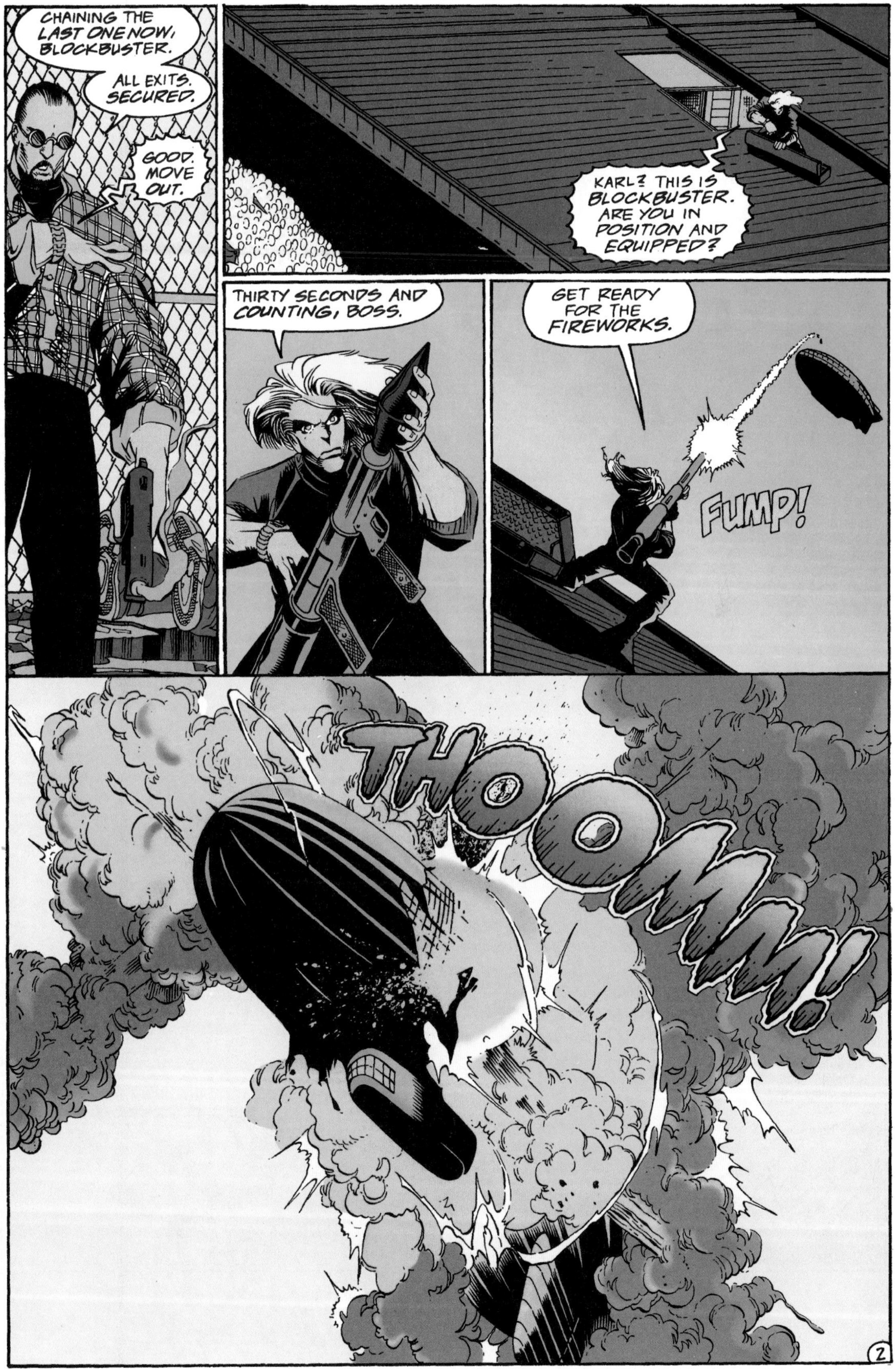

CHAINING THE LAST ONE NOW, BLOCKBUSTER.
ALL EXITS. SECURED.
GOOD. MOVE OUT.
KARL? THIS IS BLOCKBUSTER. ARE YOU IN POSITION AND EQUIPPED?
THIRTY SECONDS AND COUNTING, BOSS.
GET READY FOR THE FIREWORKS.
FUMP!
THOOMM!!

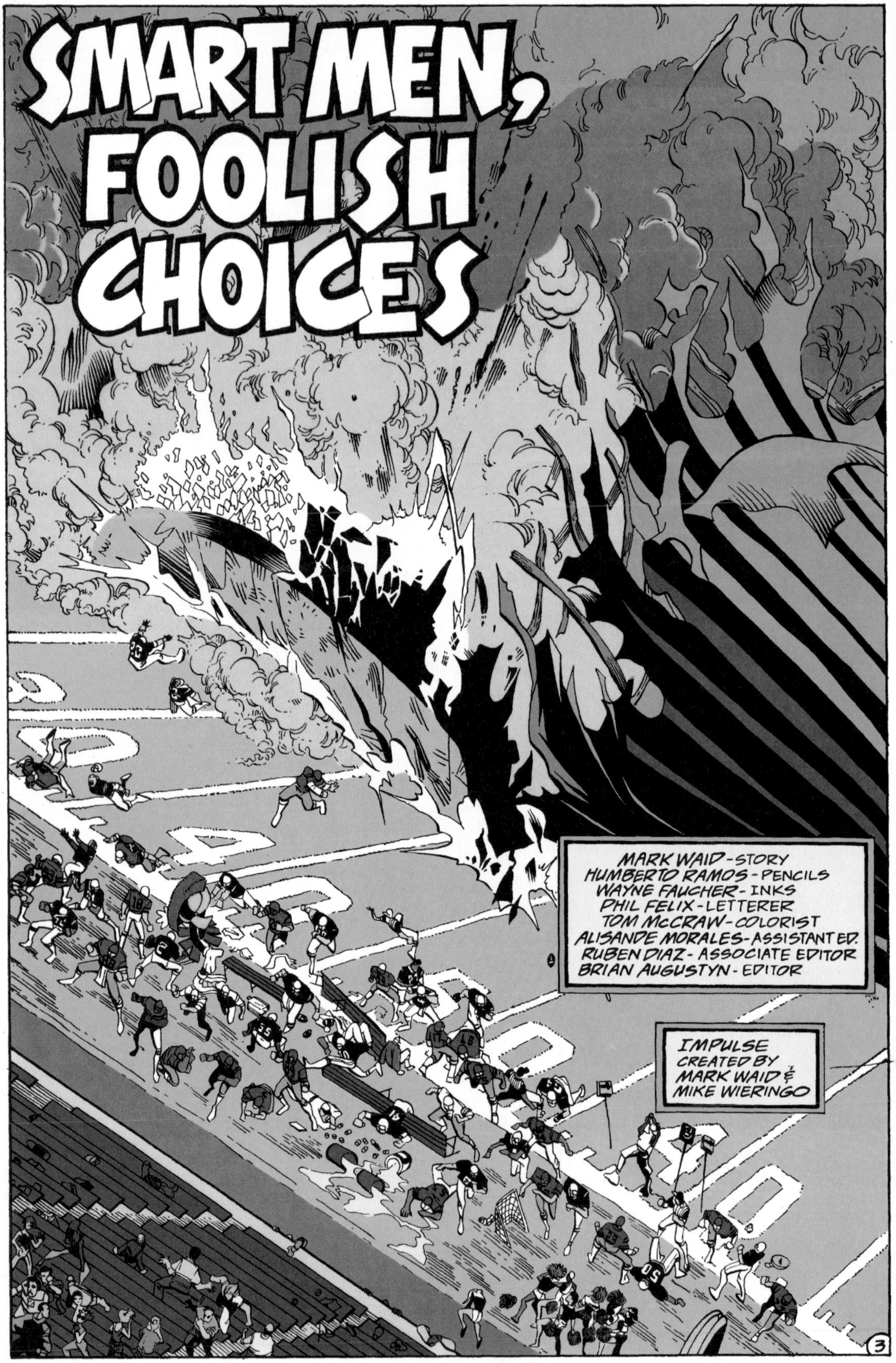
SMART MEN, FOOLISH CHOICES
MARK WAID - STORY
HUMBERTO RAMOS - PENCILS
WAYNE FAUCHER - INKS
PHIL FELIX - LETTERER
TOM McCRAW - COLORIST
ALISANDE MORALES - ASSISTANT ED.
RUBEN DIAZ - ASSOCIATE EDITOR
BRIAN AUGUSTYN - EDITOR
IMPULSE CREATED BY MARK WAID & MIKE WIERINGO

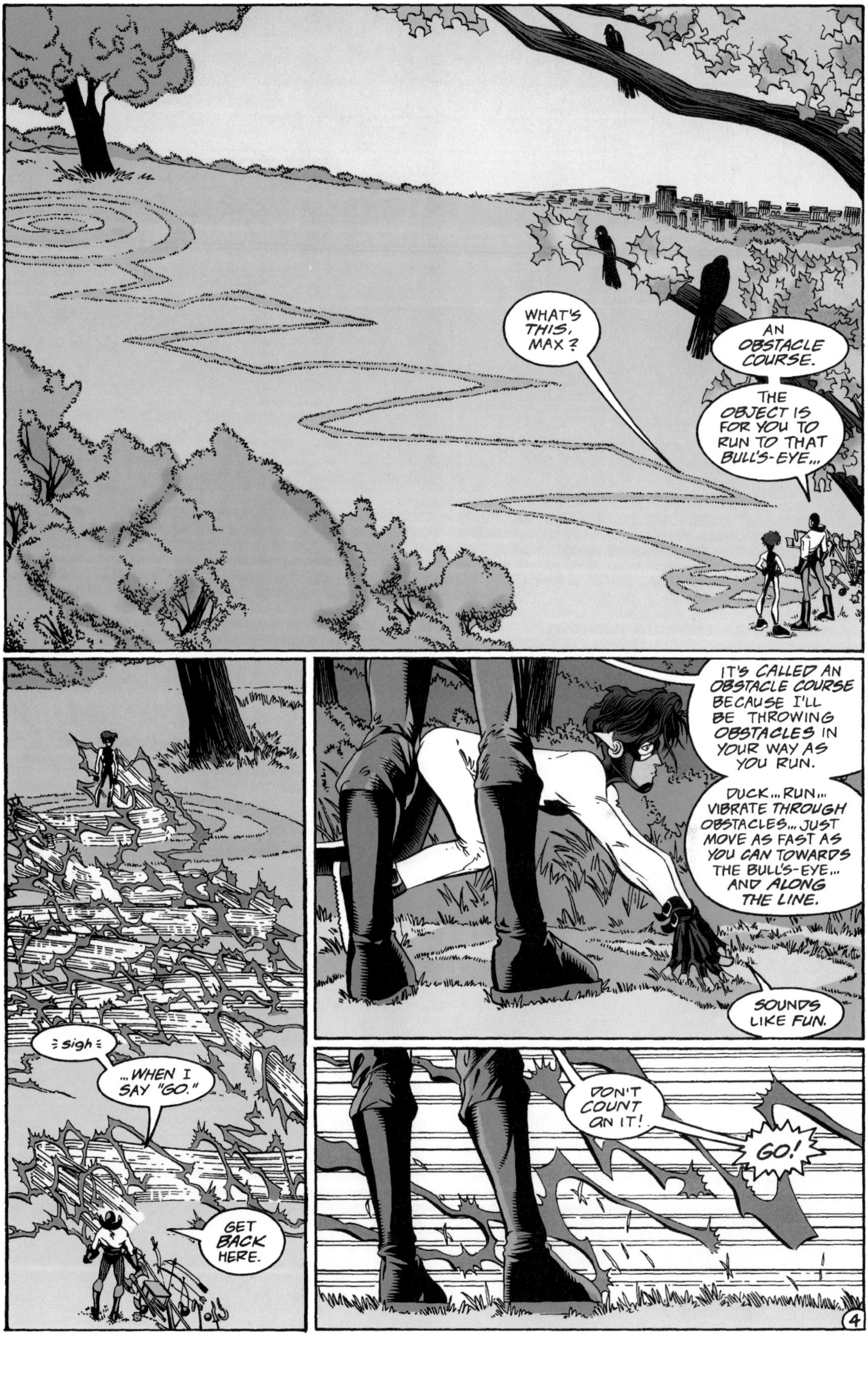
WHAT'S THIS, MAX?
AN OBSTACLE COURSE.
THE OBJECT IS FOR YOU TO RUN TO THAT BULL'S-EYE...
IT'S CALLED AN OBSTACLE COURSE BECAUSE I'LL BE THROWING OBSTACLES IN YOUR WAY AS YOU RUN.
DUCK... RUN... VIBRATE THROUGH OBSTACLES... JUST MOVE AS FAST AS YOU CAN TOWARDS THE BULL'S-EYE... AND ALONG THE LINE.
SOUNDS LIKE FUN.
sigh
...WHEN I SAY "GO."
GET BACK HERE.
DON'T COUNT ON IT!
GO!
4

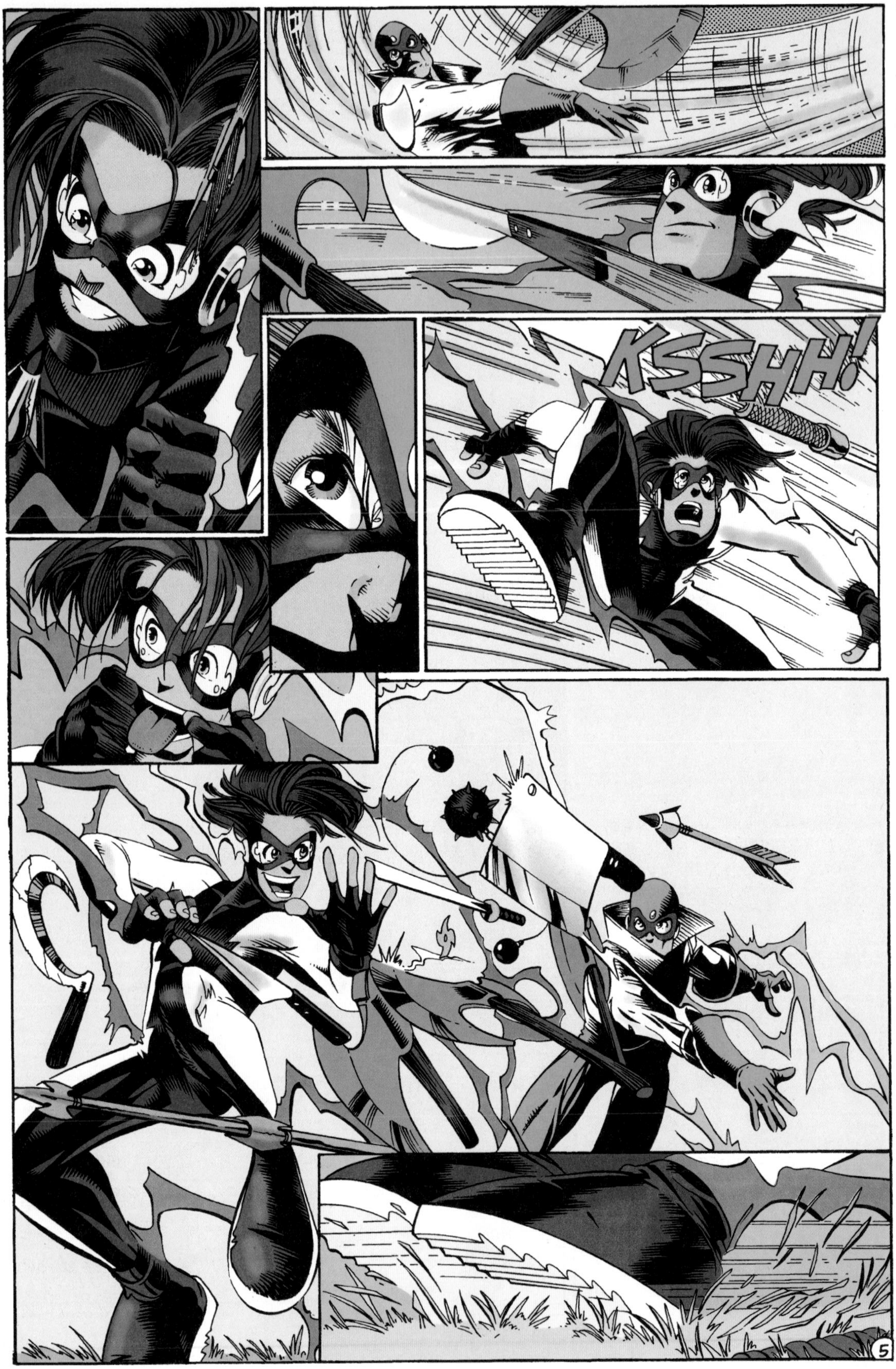
KSSHH!

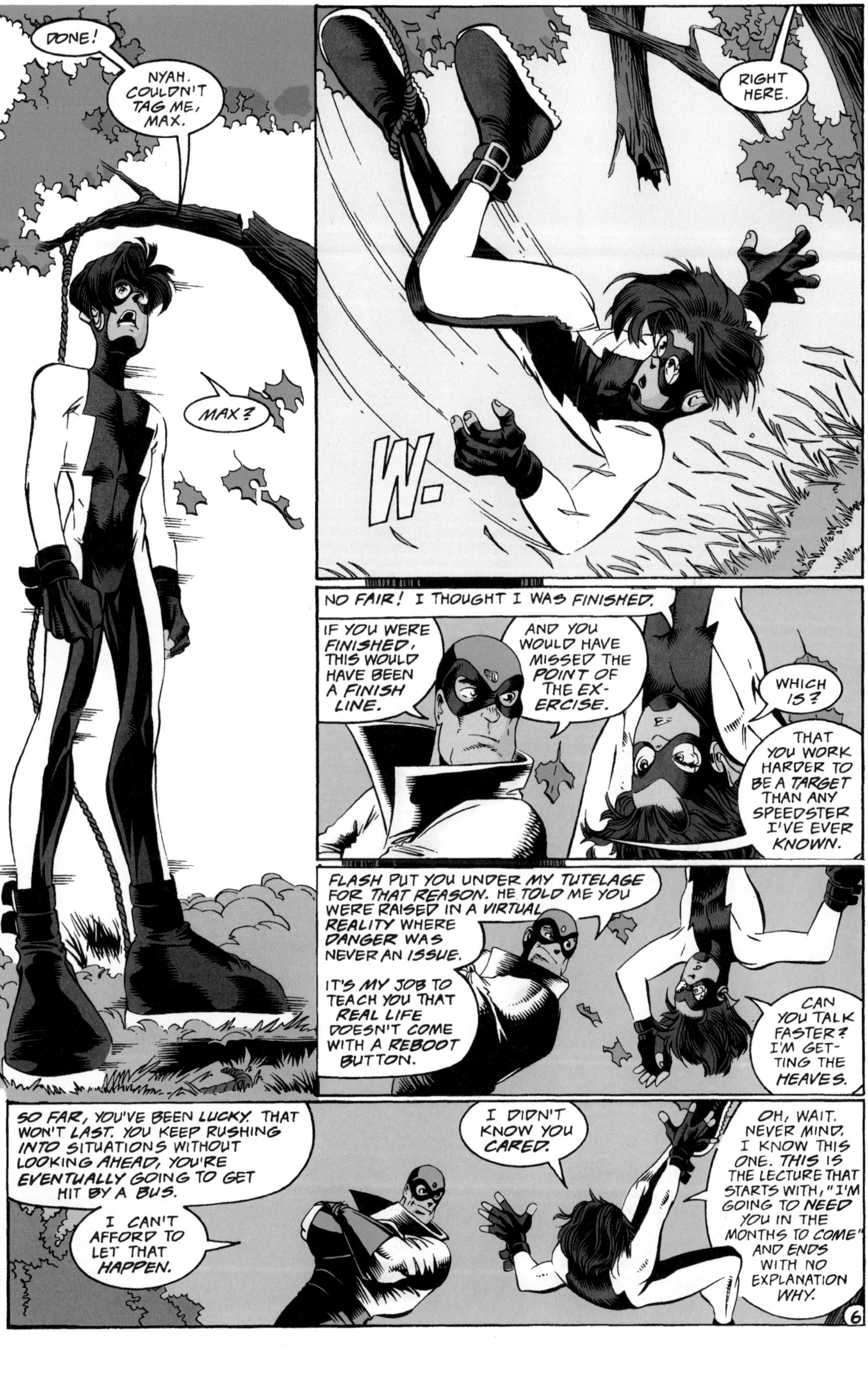
DONE!
NYAH. COULDN'T TAG ME, MAX.
MAX?
RIGHT HERE.
W.
NO FAIR! I THOUGHT I WAS FINISHED.
IF YOU WERE FINISHED, THIS WOULD HAVE BEEN A FINISH LINE.
AND YOU WOULD HAVE MISSED THE POINT OF THE EXERCISE.
WHICH IS?
THAT YOU WORK HARDER TO BE A TARGET THAN ANY SPEEDSTER I'VE EVER KNOWN.
FLASH PUT YOU UNDER MY TUTELAGE FOR THAT REASON. HE TOLD ME YOU WERE RAISED IN A VIRTUAL REALITY WHERE DANGER WAS NEVER AN ISSUE.
IT'S MY JOB TO TEACH YOU THAT REAL LIFE DOESN'T COME WITH A REBOOT BUTTON.
CAN YOU TALK FASTER? I'M GETTING THE HEAVES.
SO FAR, YOU'VE BEEN LUCKY. THAT WON'T LAST. YOU KEEP RUSHING INTO SITUATIONS WITHOUT LOOKING AHEAD, YOU'RE EVENTUALLY GOING TO GET HIT BY A BUS.
I CAN'T AFFORD TO LET THAT HAPPEN.
I DIDN'T KNOW YOU CARED.
OH, WAIT. NEVER MIND. I KNOW THIS ONE. THIS IS THE LECTURE THAT STARTS WITH, "I'M GOING TO NEED YOU IN THE MONTHS TO COME" AND ENDS WITH NO EXPLANATION WHY.
6

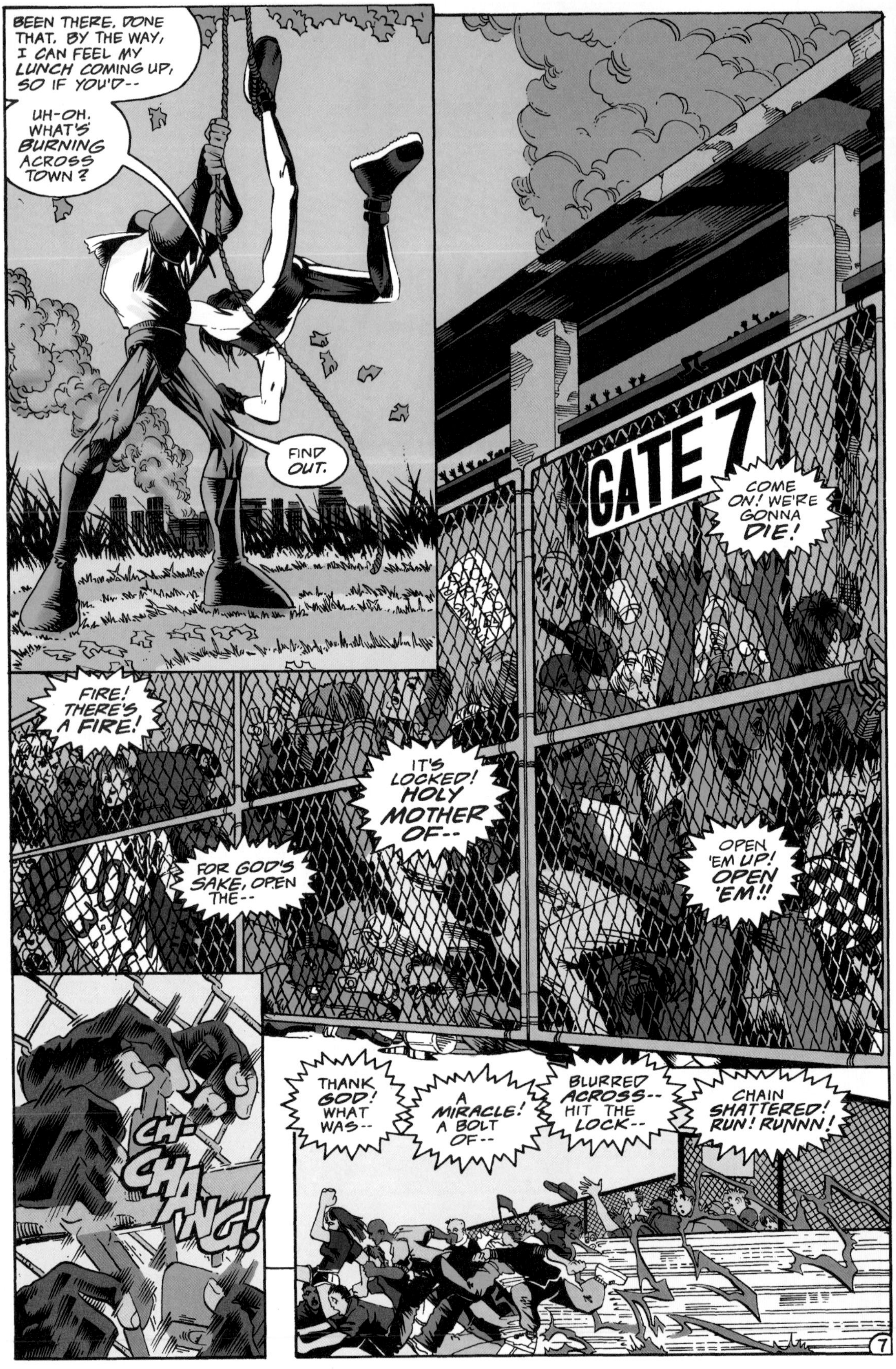
BEEN THERE, DONE THAT. BY THE WAY, I CAN FEEL MY LUNCH COMING UP, SO IF YOU'D--
UH-OH. WHAT'S BURNING ACROSS TOWN?
FIND OUT.
GATE 7
COME ON! WE'RE GONNA DIE!
FIRE! THERE'S A FIRE!
IT'S LOCKED! HOLY MOTHER OF--
FOR GOD'S SAKE, OPEN THE--
OPEN 'EM UP! OPEN 'EM!!
CH-CHANG!
THANK GOD! WHAT WAS--
A MIRACLE! A BOLT OF--
BLURRED ACROSS-- HIT THE LOCK--
CHAIN SHATTERED! RUN! RUNNN!

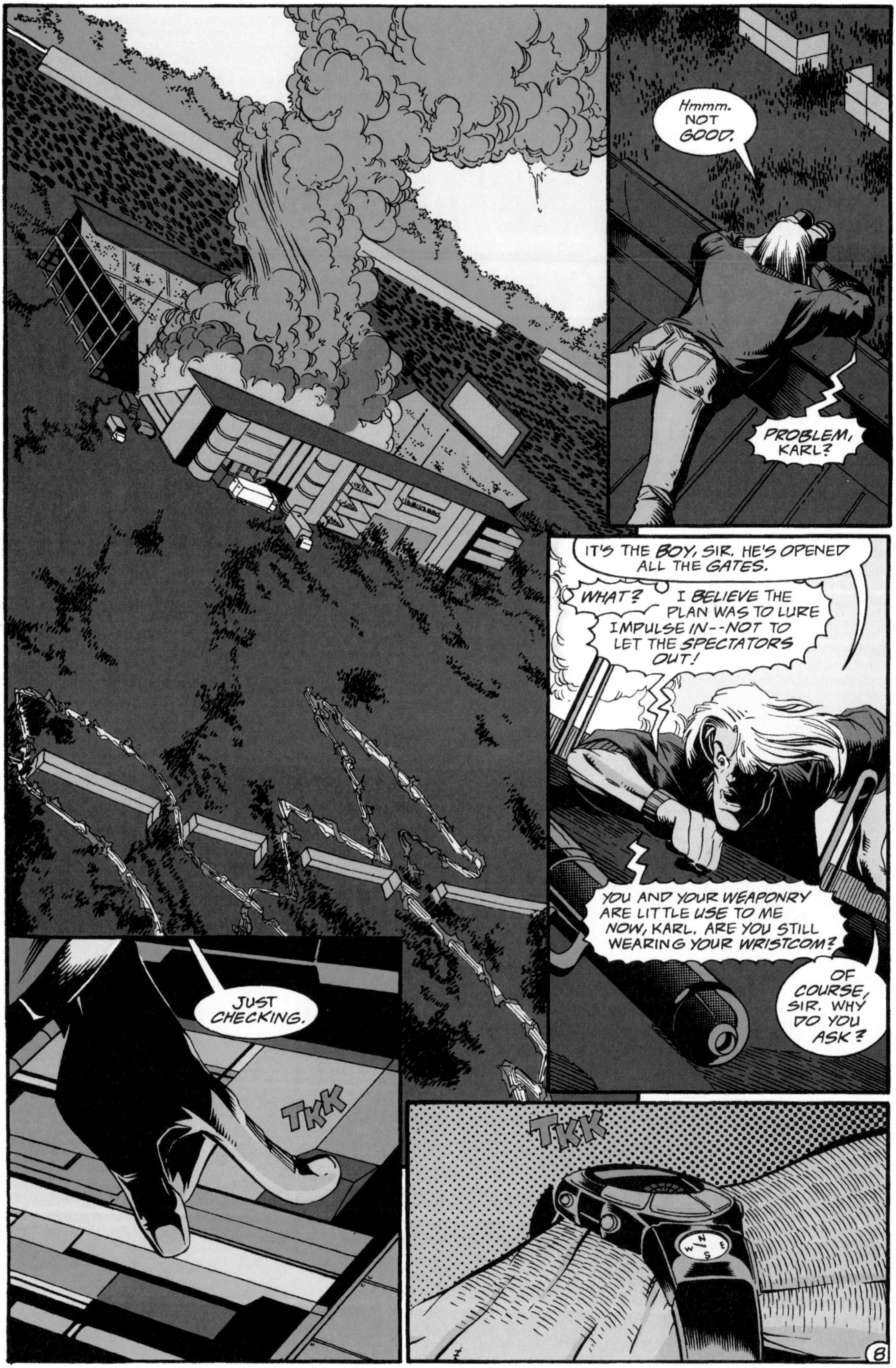
Hmmm. NOT GOOD.
PROBLEM, KARL?
IT'S THE BOY, SIR. HE'S OPENED ALL THE GATES.
WHAT? I BELIEVE THE PLAN WAS TO LURE IMPULSE IN--NOT TO LET THE SPECTATORS OUT!
YOU AND YOUR WEAPONRY ARE LITTLE USE TO ME NOW, KARL. ARE YOU STILL WEARING YOUR WRISTCOM?
OF COURSE, SIR. WHY DO YOU ASK?
JUST CHECKING.
TKK
TKK
8

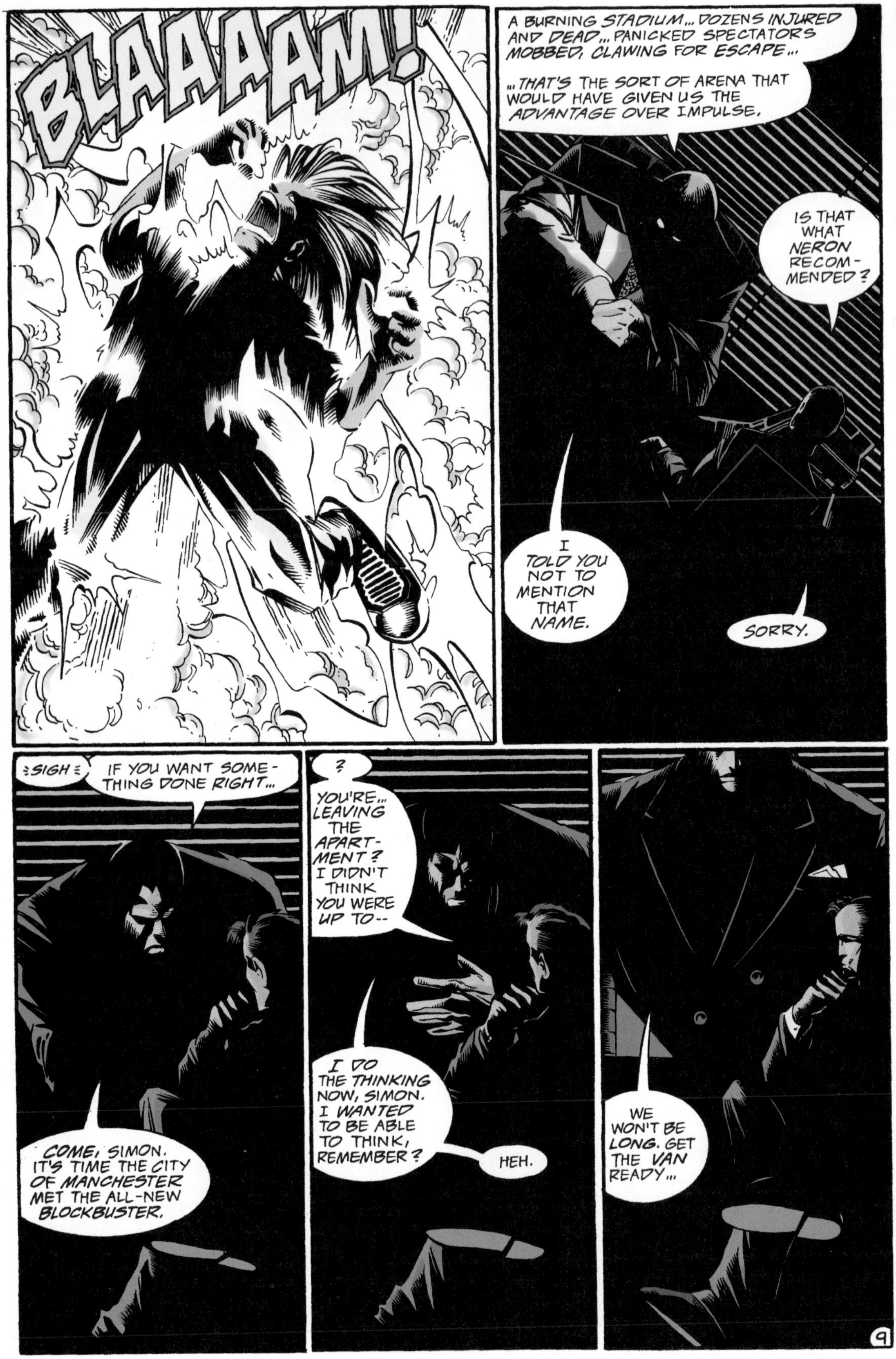
BLAAAAM!
A BURNING STADIUM... DOZENS INJURED AND DEAD... PANICKED SPECTATORS MOBBED, CLAWING FOR ESCAPE...
...THAT'S THE SORT OF ARENA THAT WOULD HAVE GIVEN US THE ADVANTAGE OVER IMPULSE.
IS THAT WHAT NERON RECOMMENDED?
I TOLD YOU NOT TO MENTION THAT NAME.
SORRY.
SIGH
IF YOU WANT SOMETHING DONE RIGHT...
COME, SIMON. IT'S TIME THE CITY OF MANCHESTER MET THE ALL-NEW BLOCKBUSTER.
?
YOU'RE... LEAVING THE APARTMENT? I DIDN'T THINK YOU WERE UP TO--
I DO THE THINKING NOW, SIMON. I WANTED TO BE ABLE TO THINK, REMEMBER?
HEH.
WE WON'T BE LONG. GET THE VAN READY...
9

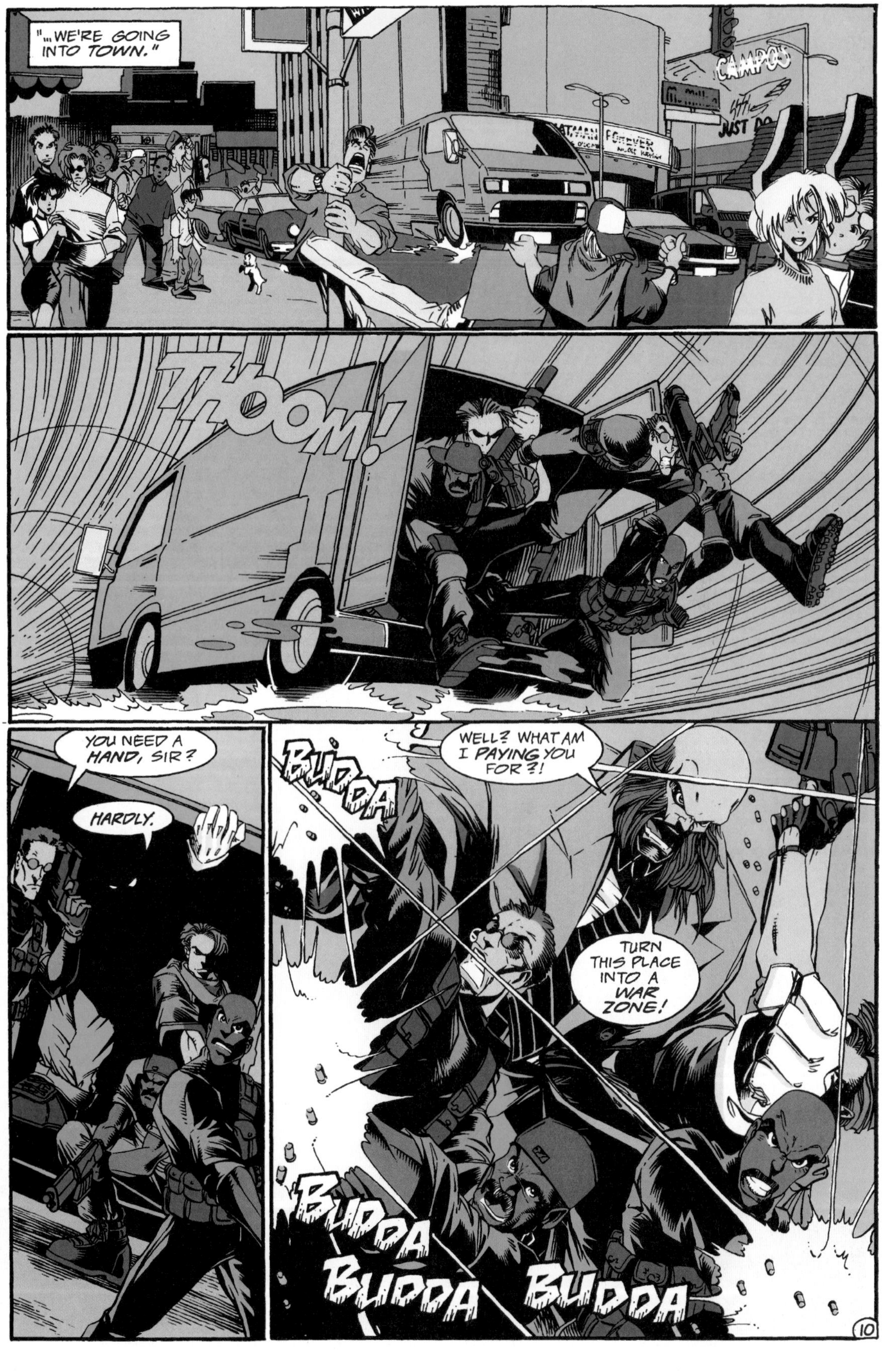

"...WE'RE GOING INTO TOWN."
CAMPOS
JUST DO
THOOM!
YOU NEED A HAND, SIR?
HARDLY.
BUDDA
WELL? WHAT AM I PAYING YOU FOR?!
TURN THIS PLACE INTO A WAR ZONE!
BUDDA
BUDDA
BUDDA

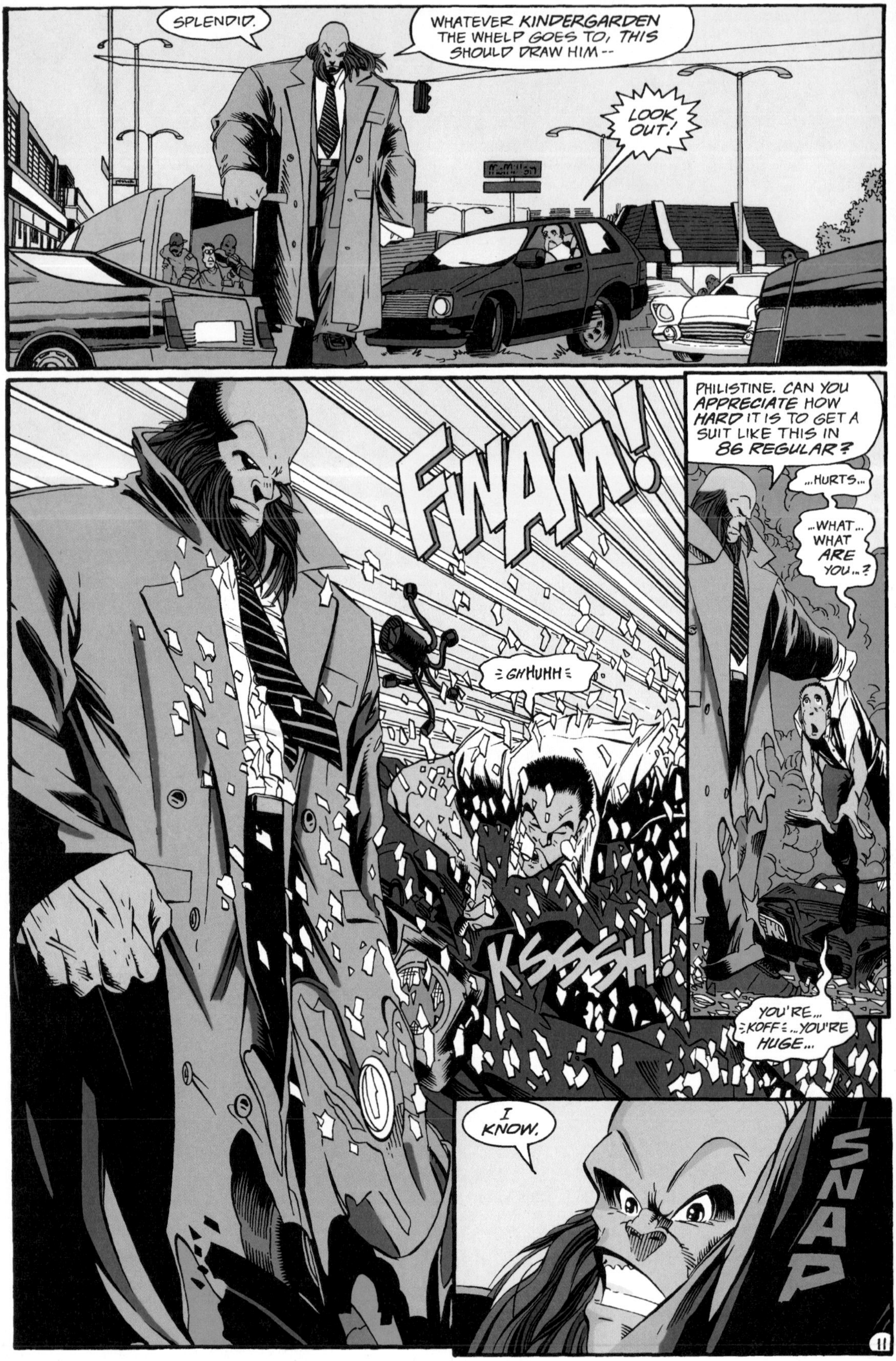
SPLENDID.
WHATEVER KINDERGARDEN THE WHELP GOES TO, THIS SHOULD DRAW HIM --
LOOK OUT!
FWAM!
GHHUHH
KSSSSH!
PHILISTINE. CAN YOU APPRECIATE HOW HARD IT IS TO GET A SUIT LIKE THIS IN 86 REGULAR?
...HURTS...
...WHAT... WHAT ARE YOU...?
YOU'RE... KOFF ...YOU'RE HUGE...
I KNOW.
SNAP

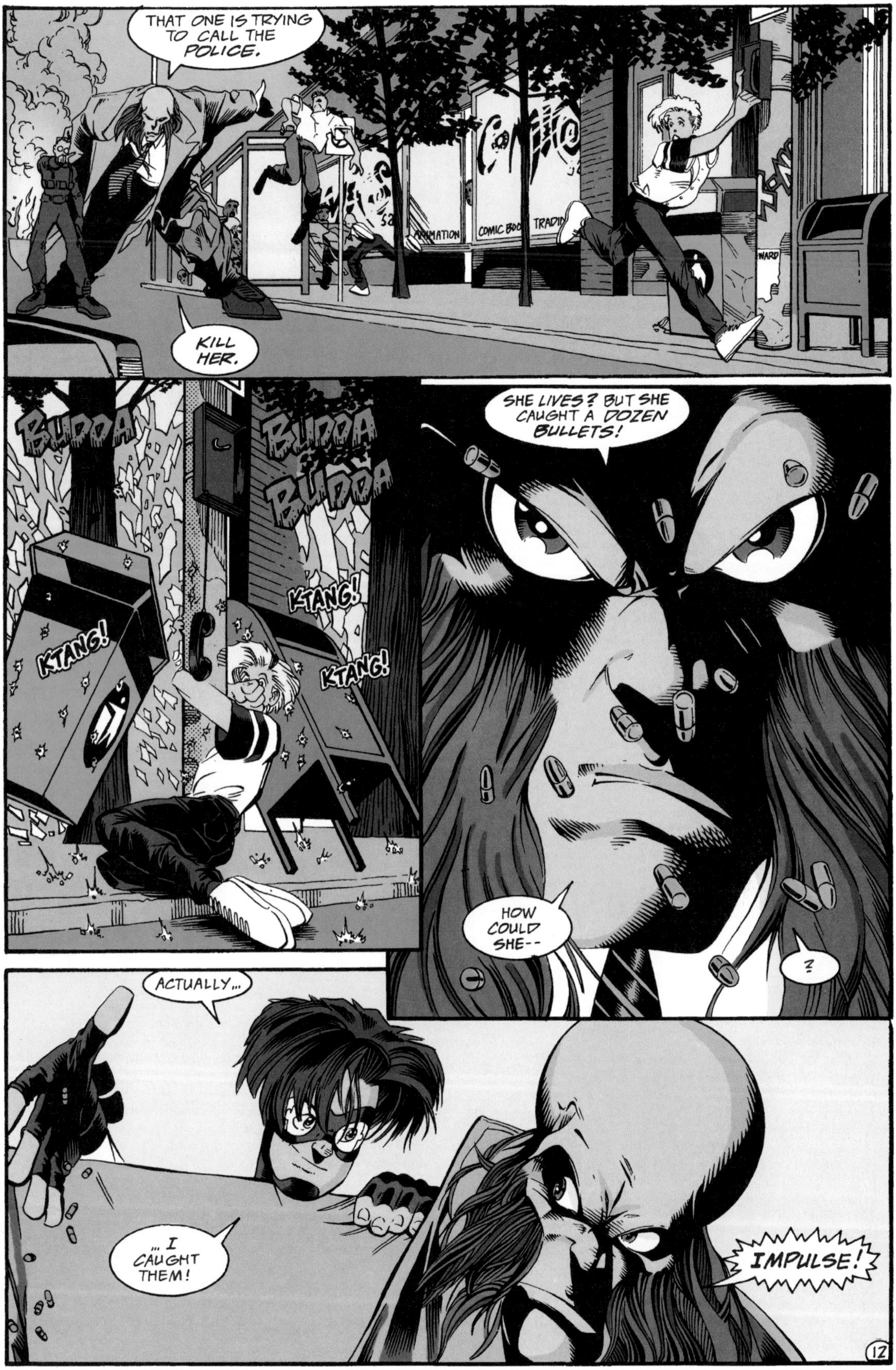
THAT ONE IS TRYING TO CALL THE POLICE.
COMIC BOOK
KILL HER.
BUDDA
BUDDA BUDDA
KTANG!
KTANG!
KTANG!
SHE LIVES? BUT SHE CAUGHT A DOZEN BULLETS!
HOW COULD SHE--
?
ACTUALLY...
...I CAUGHT THEM!
IMPULSE!
12

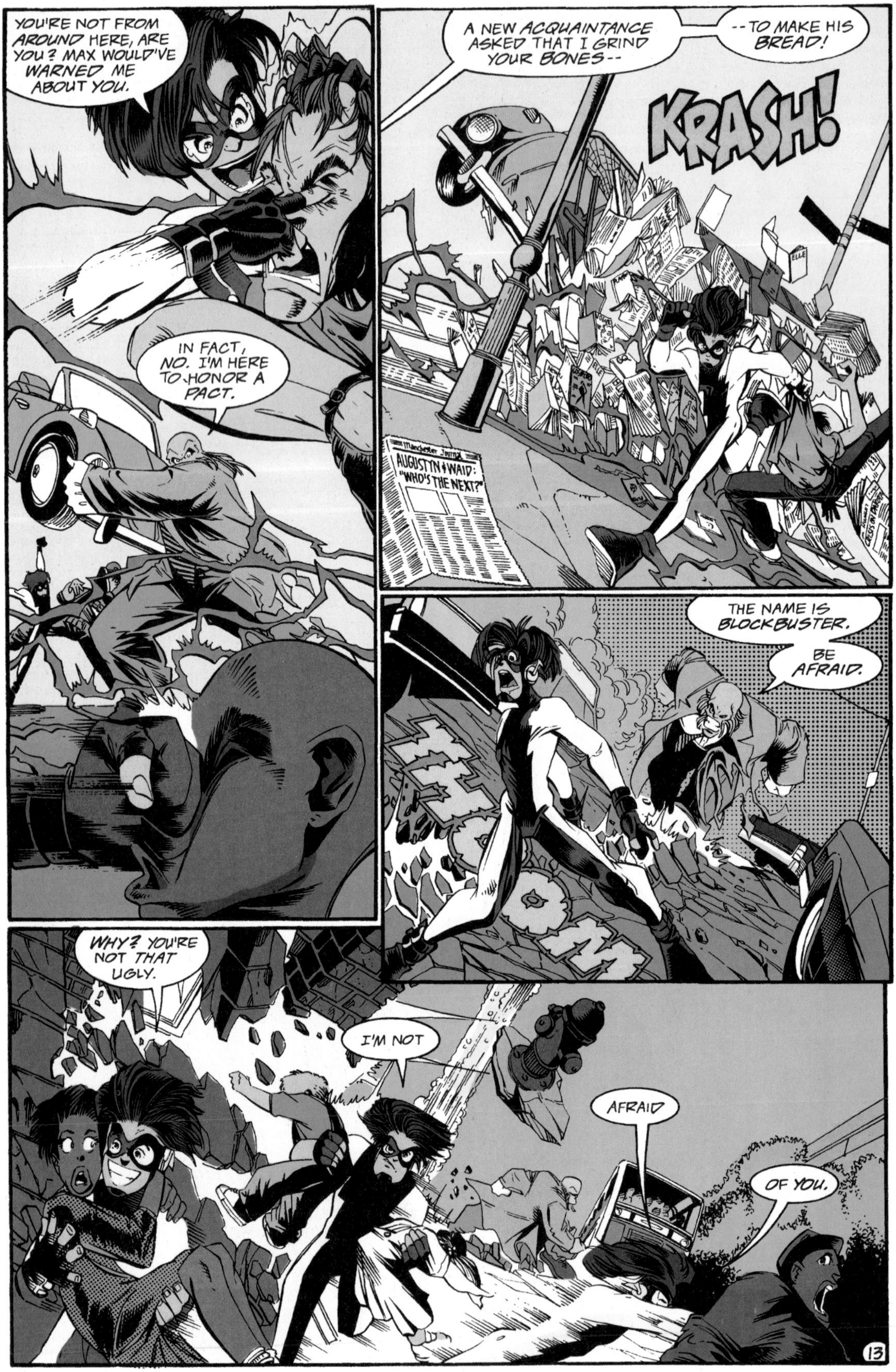
YOU'RE NOT FROM AROUND HERE, ARE YOU? MAX WOULD'VE WARNED ME ABOUT YOU.
IN FACT, NO. I'M HERE TO HONOR A PACT.
A NEW ACQUAINTANCE ASKED THAT I GRIND YOUR BONES--
--TO MAKE HIS BREAD!
KRASH!
AUGUSTYN & WAID: "WHO'S THE NEXT?"
THE NAME IS BLOCKBUSTER.
BE AFRAID.
WHY? YOU'RE NOT THAT UGLY.
I'M NOT
AFRAID
OF YOU.

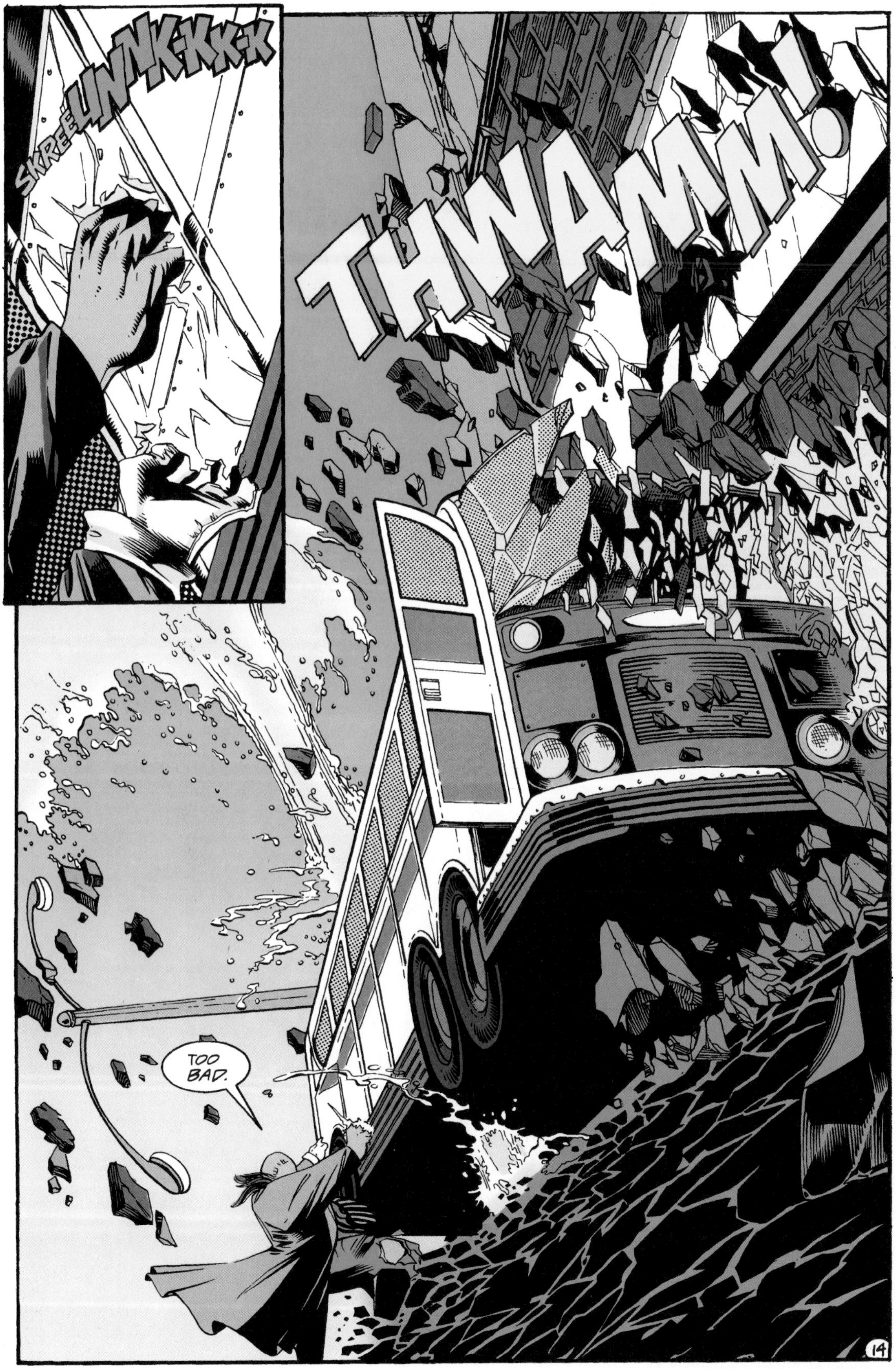
SKREEUNNK-KK-K
THWAMM!
TOO BAD.
14

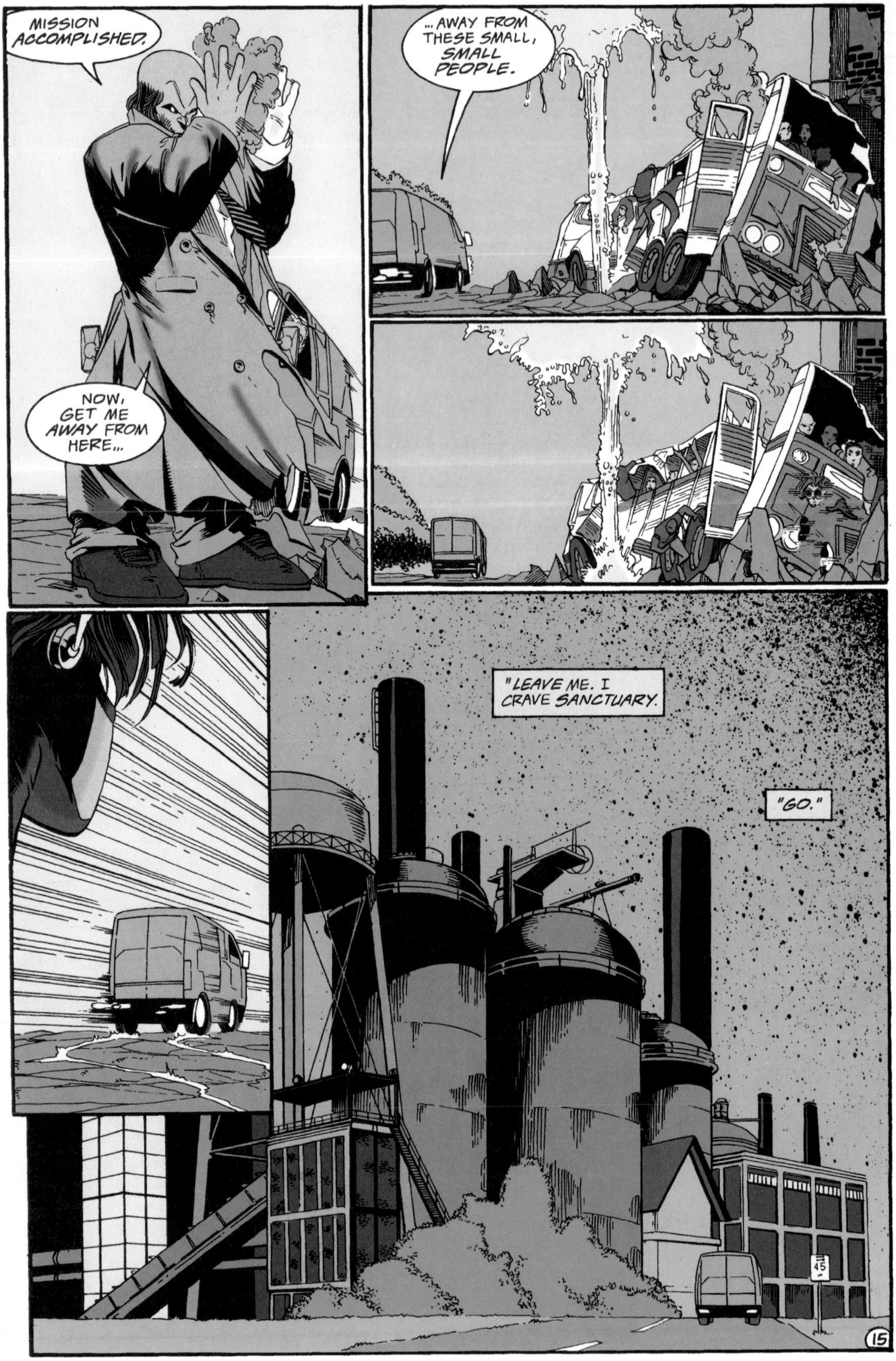
MISSION ACCOMPLISHED.
NOW, GET ME AWAY FROM HERE...
...AWAY FROM THESE SMALL, SMALL PEOPLE.
"LEAVE ME. I CRAVE SANCTUARY.
"GO."
45

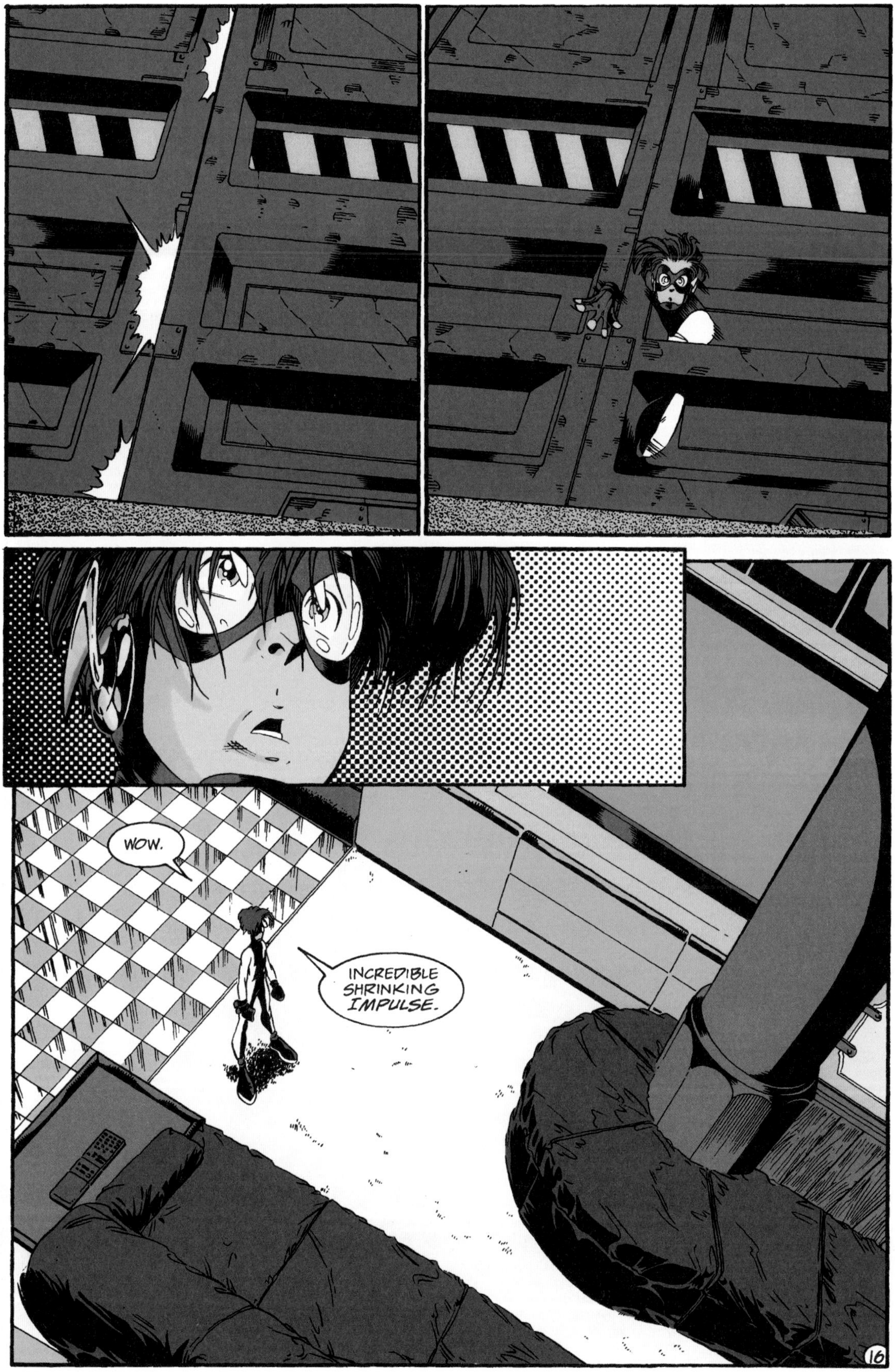
WOW.
INCREDIBLE SHRINKING IMPULSE.

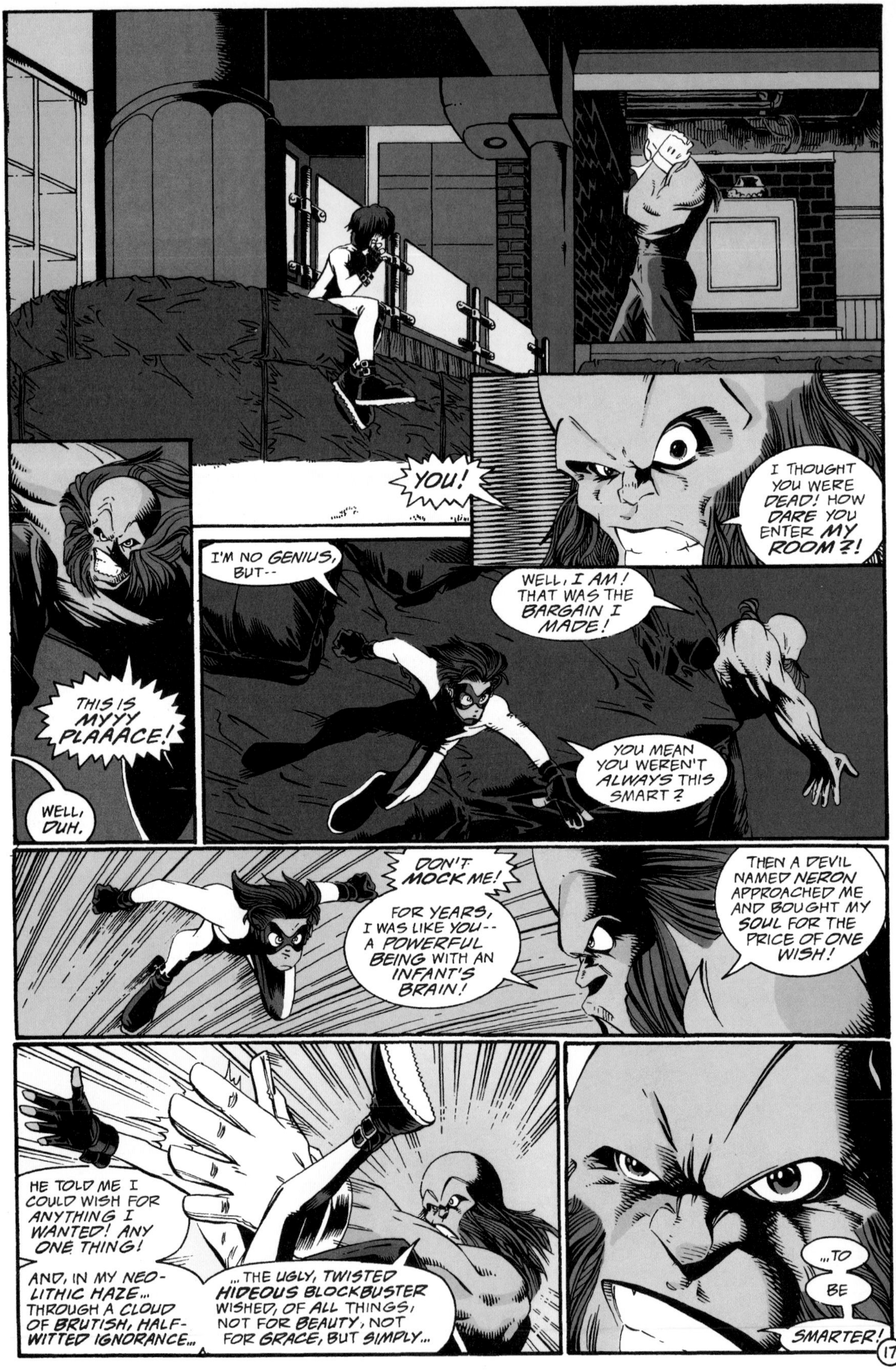
YOU!
I THOUGHT YOU WERE DEAD! HOW DARE YOU ENTER MY ROOM?!
I'M NO GENIUS, BUT--
WELL, I AM! THAT WAS THE BARGAIN I MADE!
THIS IS MYYY PLAAACE!
WELL, DUH.
YOU MEAN YOU WEREN'T ALWAYS THIS SMART?
DON'T MOCK ME!
FOR YEARS, I WAS LIKE YOU-- A POWERFUL BEING WITH AN INFANT'S BRAIN!
THEN A DEVIL NAMED NERON APPROACHED ME AND BOUGHT MY SOUL FOR THE PRICE OF ONE WISH!
HE TOLD ME I COULD WISH FOR ANYTHING I WANTED! ANY ONE THING!
AND, IN MY NEO-LITHIC HAZE... THROUGH A CLOUD OF BRUTISH, HALF-WITTED IGNORANCE...
...THE UGLY, TWISTED HIDEOUS BLOCKBUSTER WISHED, OF ALL THINGS, NOT FOR BEAUTY, NOT FOR GRACE, BUT SIMPLY...
...TO
BE
SMARTER!

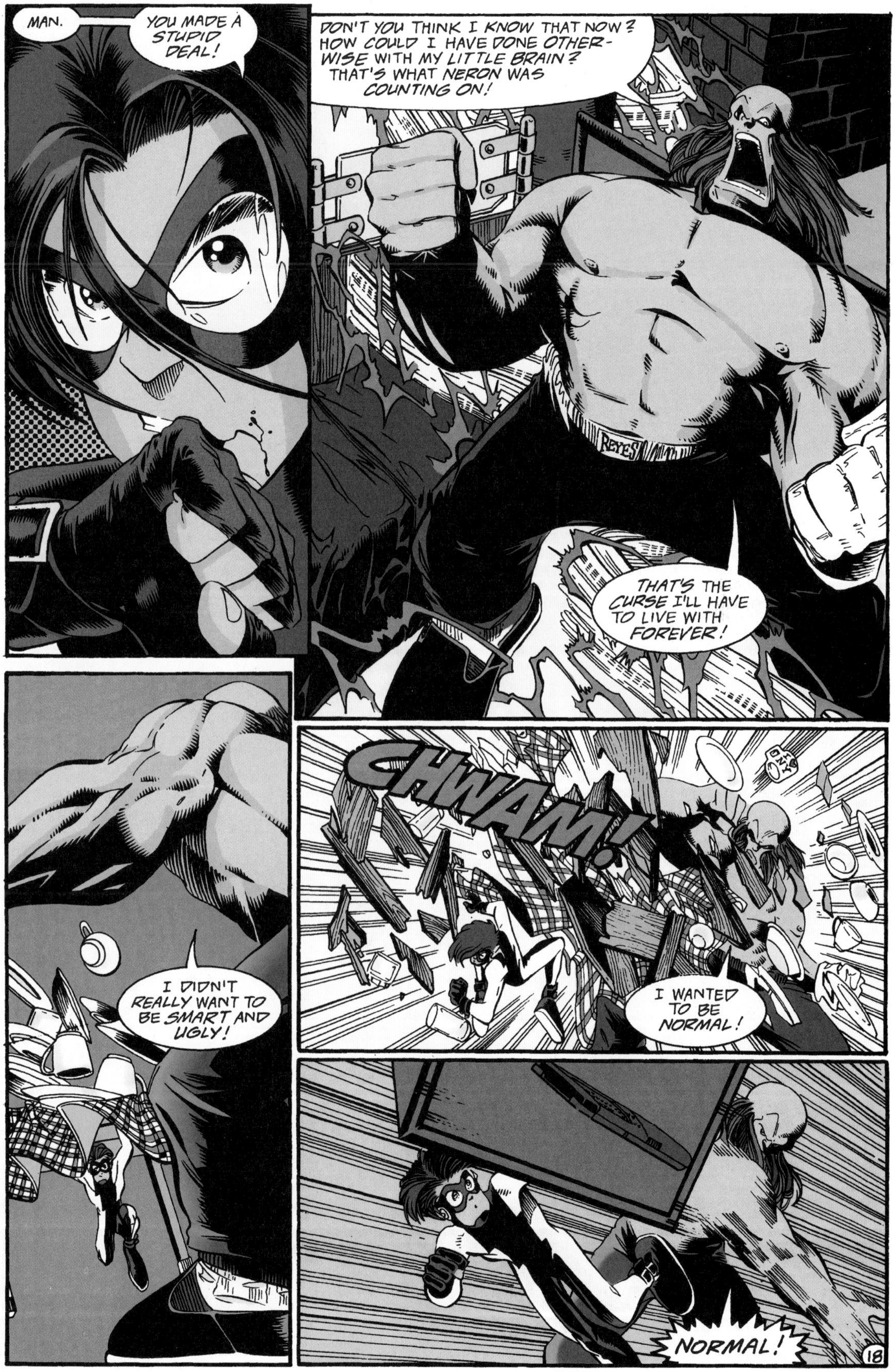
MAN.
YOU MADE A STUPID DEAL!
DON'T YOU THINK I KNOW THAT NOW? HOW COULD I HAVE DONE OTHER-WISE WITH MY LITTLE BRAIN? THAT'S WHAT NERON WAS COUNTING ON!
REYES
THAT'S THE CURSE I'LL HAVE TO LIVE WITH FOREVER!
I DIDN'T REALLY WANT TO BE SMART AND UGLY!
CHWAM!
I WANTED TO BE NORMAL!
NORMAL!

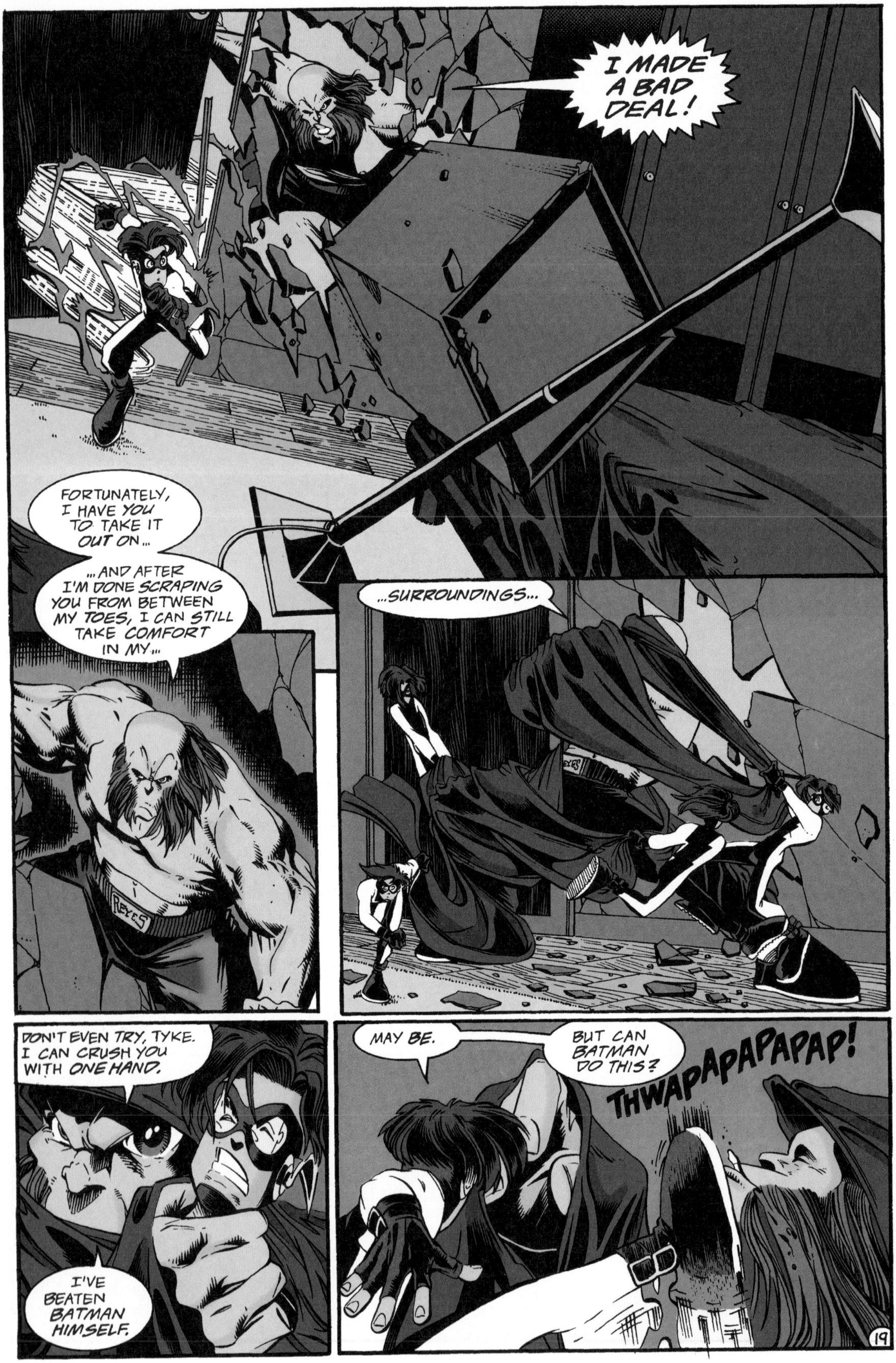
I MADE A BAD DEAL!
FORTUNATELY, I HAVE YOU TO TAKE IT OUT ON...
...AND AFTER I'M DONE SCRAPING YOU FROM BETWEEN MY TOES, I CAN STILL TAKE COMFORT IN MY...
...SURROUNDINGS...
REYES
DON'T EVEN TRY, TYKE. I CAN CRUSH YOU WITH ONE HAND.
I'VE BEATEN BATMAN HIMSELF.
MAY BE.
BUT CAN BATMAN DO THIS?
THWAPAPAPAPAPAP!
19

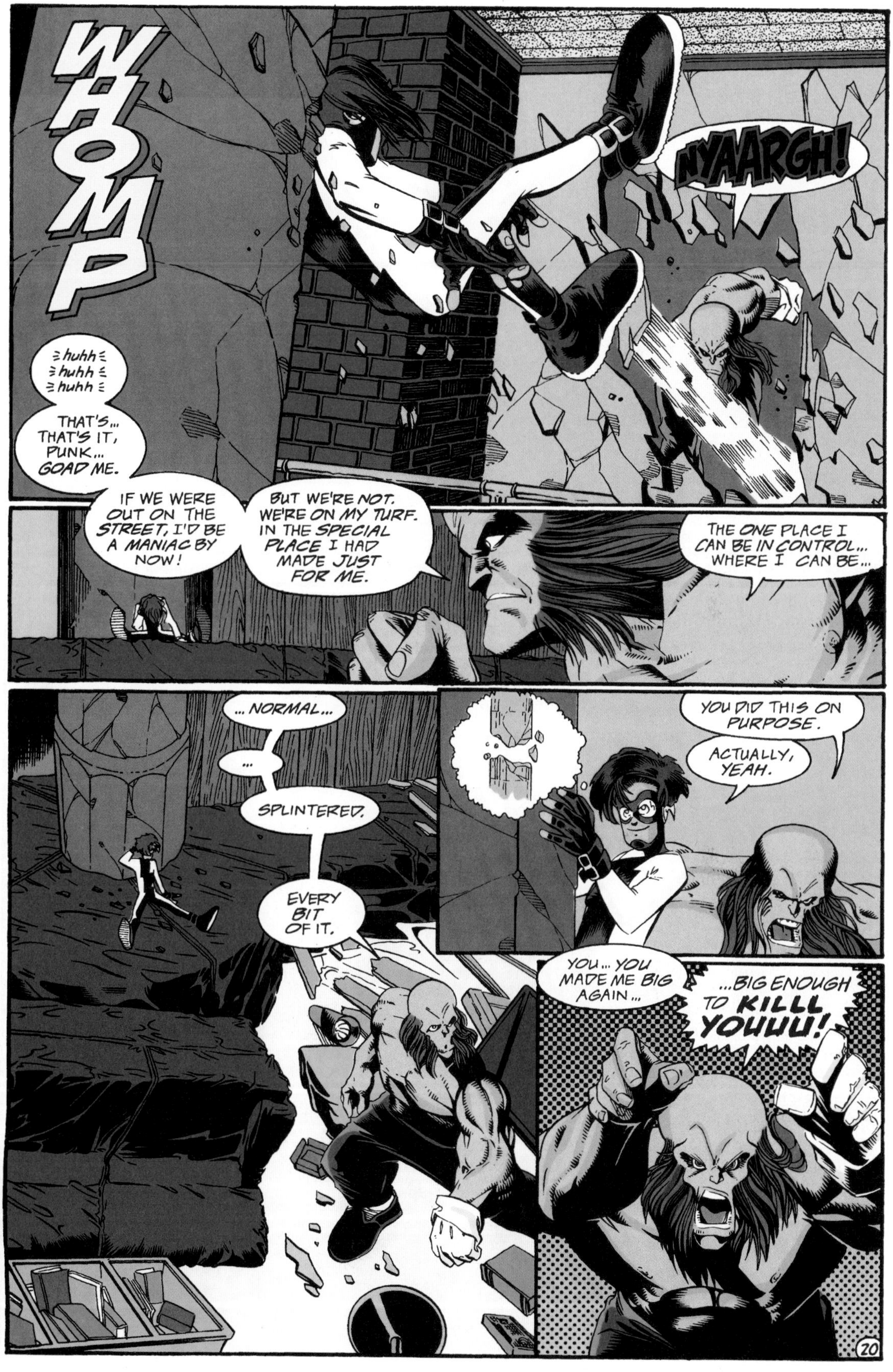
WHOMP
NYAARGH!
huhh huhh huhh
THAT'S... THAT'S IT, PUNK... GOAD ME.
IF WE WERE OUT ON THE STREET, I'D BE A MANIAC BY NOW!
BUT WE'RE NOT. WE'RE ON MY TURF. IN THE SPECIAL PLACE I HAD MADE JUST FOR ME.
THE ONE PLACE I CAN BE IN CONTROL... WHERE I CAN BE...
... NORMAL...
...
SPLINTERED.
EVERY BIT OF IT.
YOU DID THIS ON PURPOSE.
ACTUALLY, YEAH.
YOU... YOU MADE ME BIG AGAIN...
...BIG ENOUGH TO KILLL YOUUU!

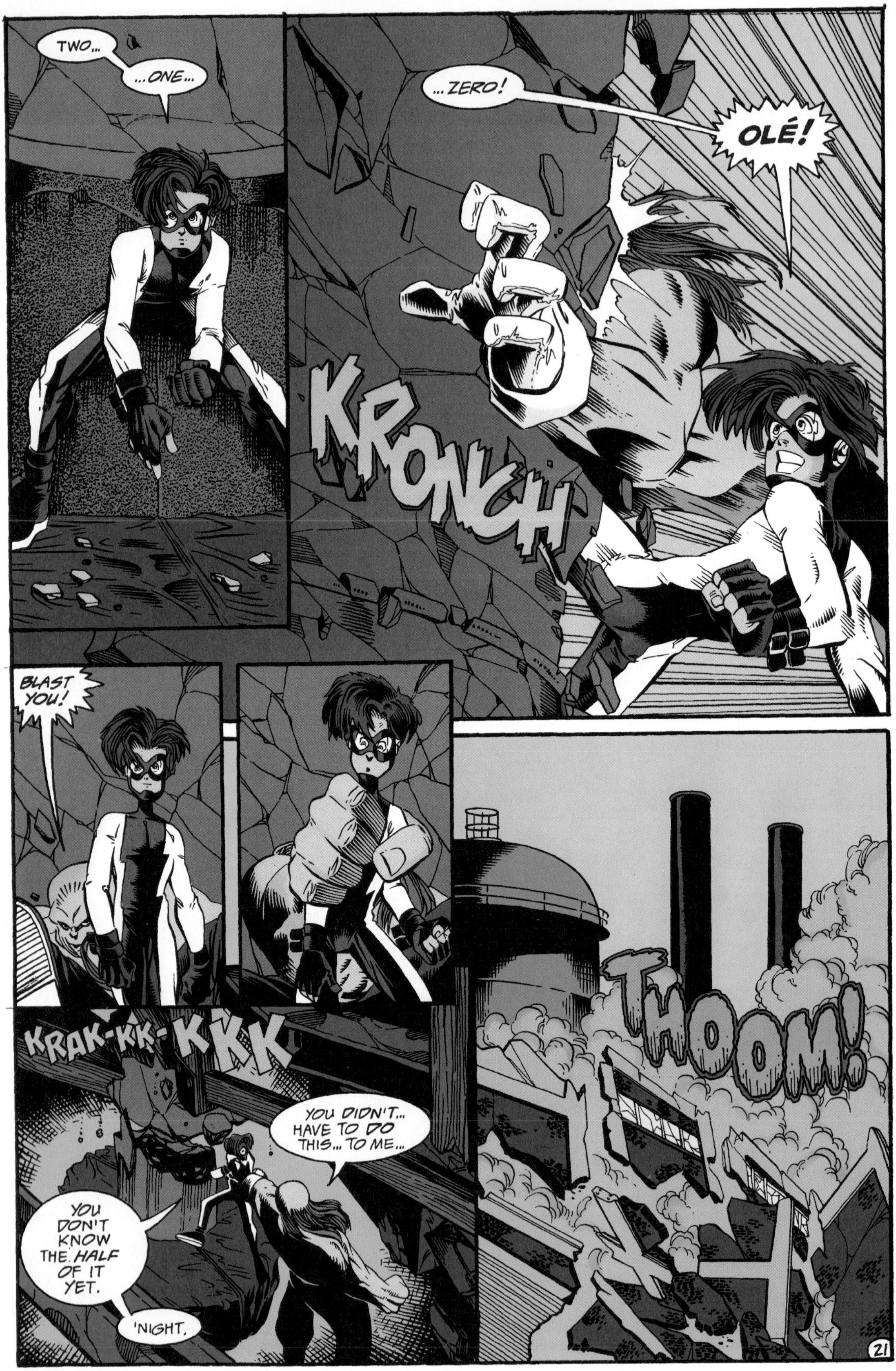

TWO...
...ONE...
...ZERO!
OLÉ!
KRONCH
BLAST YOU!
KRAK-KK-KKK
YOU DIDN'T... HAVE TO DO THIS... TO ME...
YOU DON'T KNOW THE HALF OF IT YET.
'NIGHT.
THOOM!

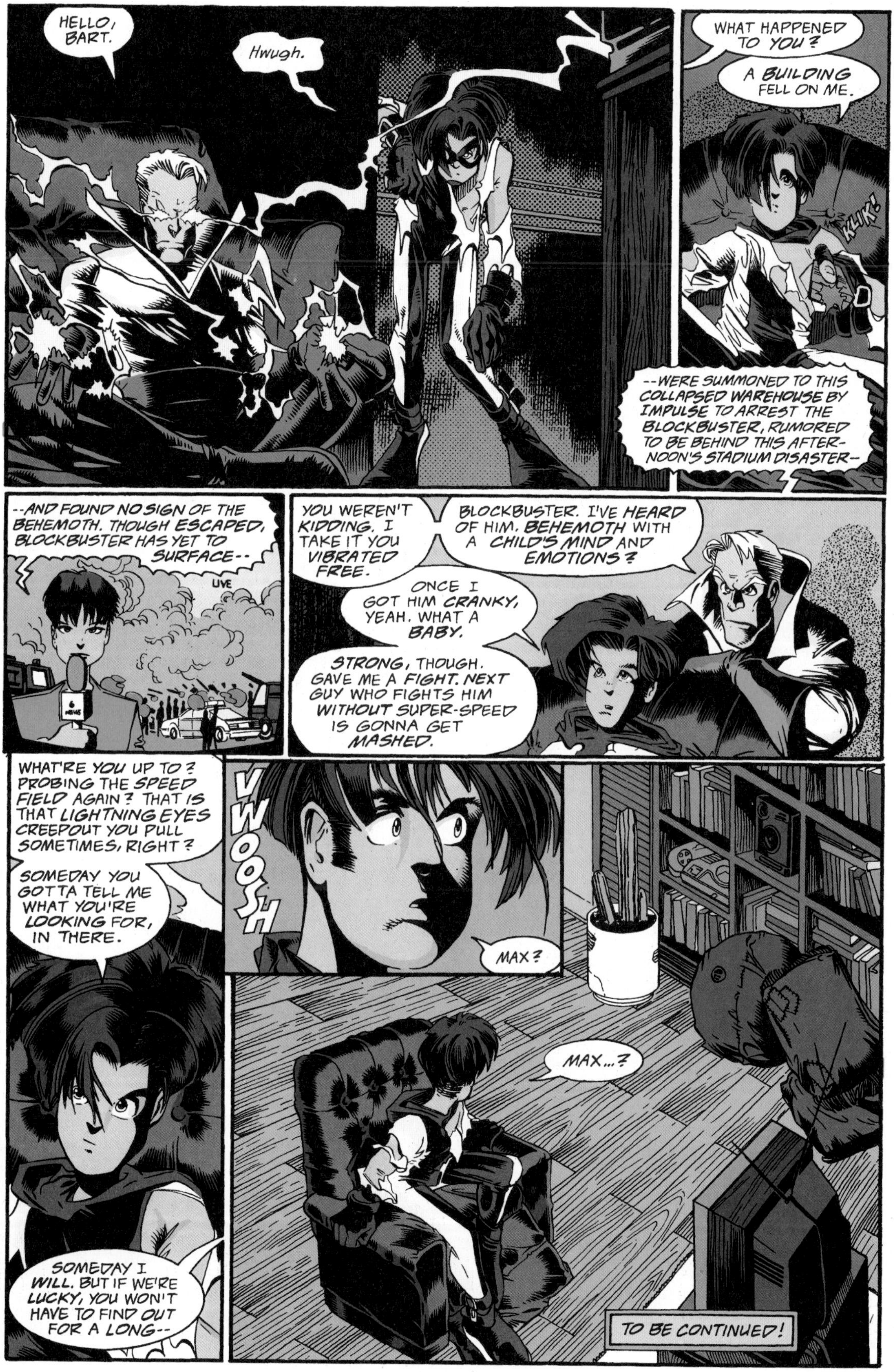

HELLO, BART.
Hwugh.
WHAT HAPPENED TO YOU?
A BUILDING FELL ON ME.
KLIK!
--WERE SUMMONED TO THIS COLLAPSED WAREHOUSE BY IMPULSE TO ARREST THE BLOCKBUSTER, RUMORED TO BE BEHIND THIS AFTER-NOON'S STADIUM DISASTER--
--AND FOUND NO SIGN OF THE BEHEMOTH. THOUGH ESCAPED, BLOCKBUSTER HAS YET TO SURFACE--
LIVE
YOU WEREN'T KIDDING. I TAKE IT YOU VIBRATED FREE.
BLOCKBUSTER. I'VE HEARD OF HIM. BEHEMOTH WITH A CHILD'S MIND AND EMOTIONS?
ONCE I GOT HIM CRANKY, YEAH. WHAT A BABY.
STRONG, THOUGH. GAVE ME A FIGHT. NEXT GUY WHO FIGHTS HIM WITHOUT SUPER-SPEED IS GONNA GET MASHED.
WHAT'RE YOU UP TO? PROBING THE SPEED FIELD AGAIN? THAT IS THAT LIGHTNING EYES CREEPOUT YOU PULL SOMETIMES, RIGHT?
SOMEDAY YOU GOTTA TELL ME WHAT YOU'RE LOOKING FOR, IN THERE.
SOMEDAY I WILL. BUT IF WE'RE LUCKY, YOU WON'T HAVE TO FIND OUT FOR A LONG--
VWOOSH
MAX?
MAX...?
TO BE CONTINUED!

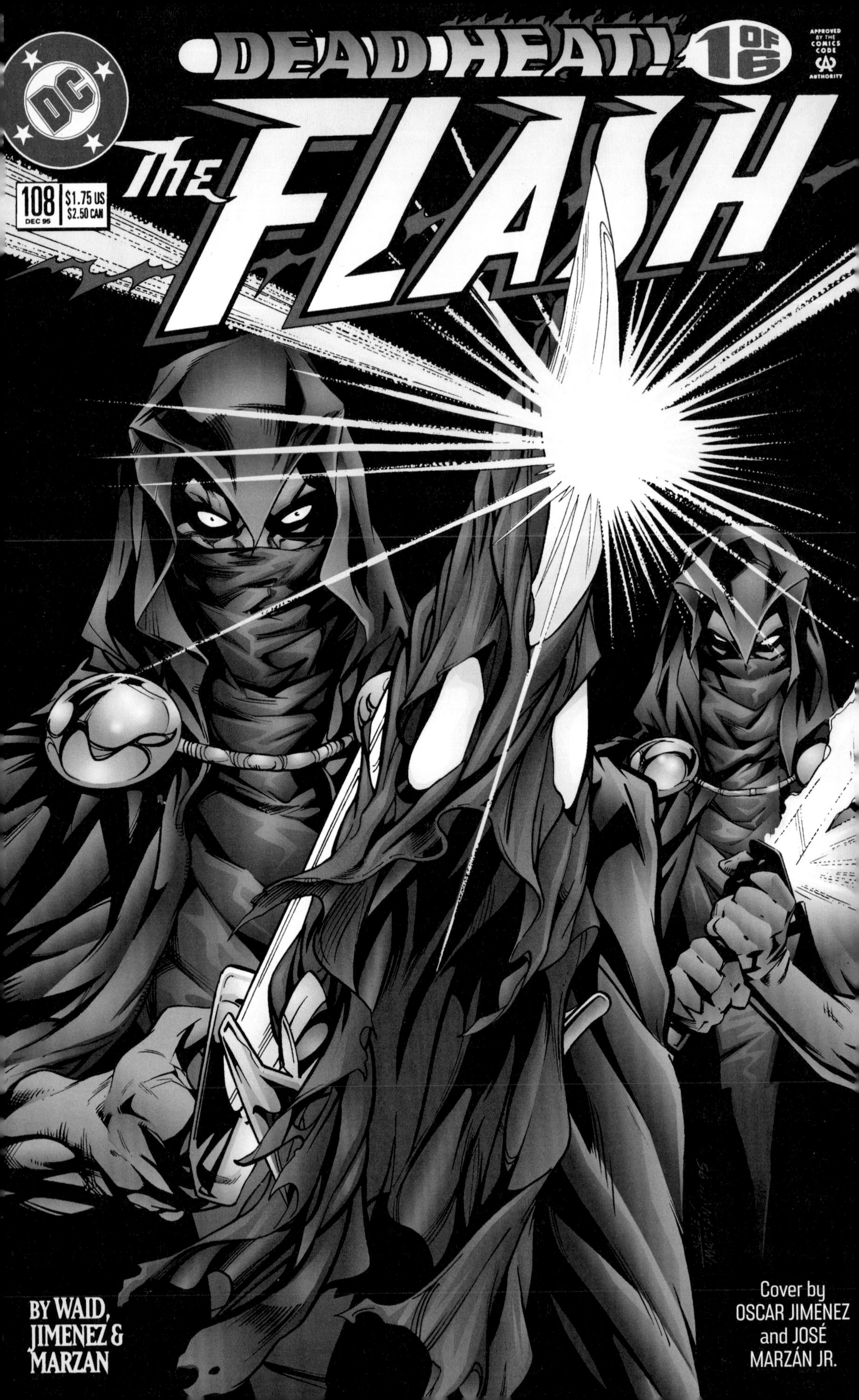

DEAD HEAT! 1 OF 6
APPROVED BY THE COMICS CODE AUTHORITY
DC
THE FLASH
108 DEC 95
$1.75 US
$2.50 CAN
BY WAID, JIMENEZ & MARZAN
Cover by OSCAR JIMENEZ and JOSÉ MARZÁN JR.

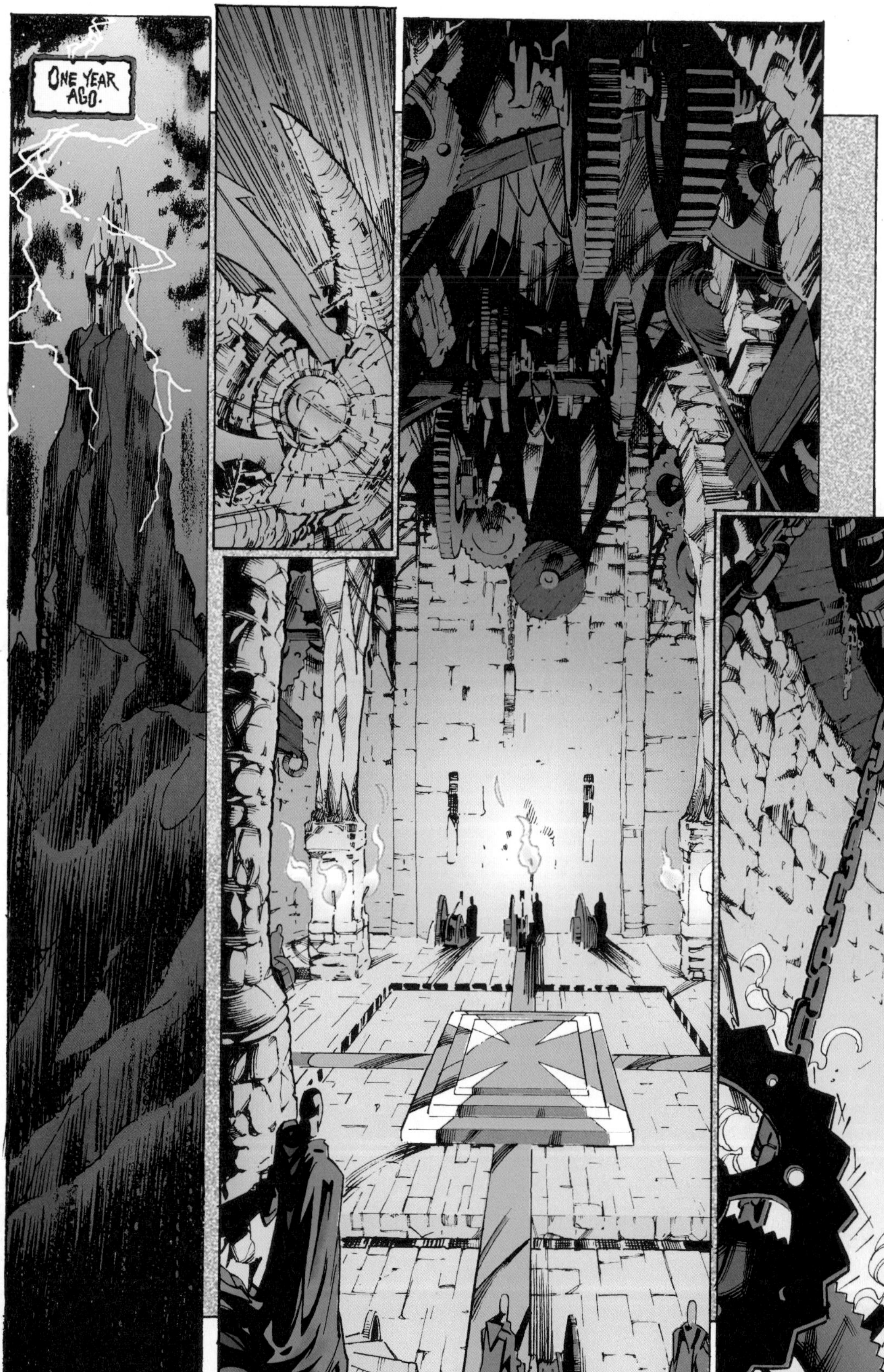
ONE YEAR AGO.

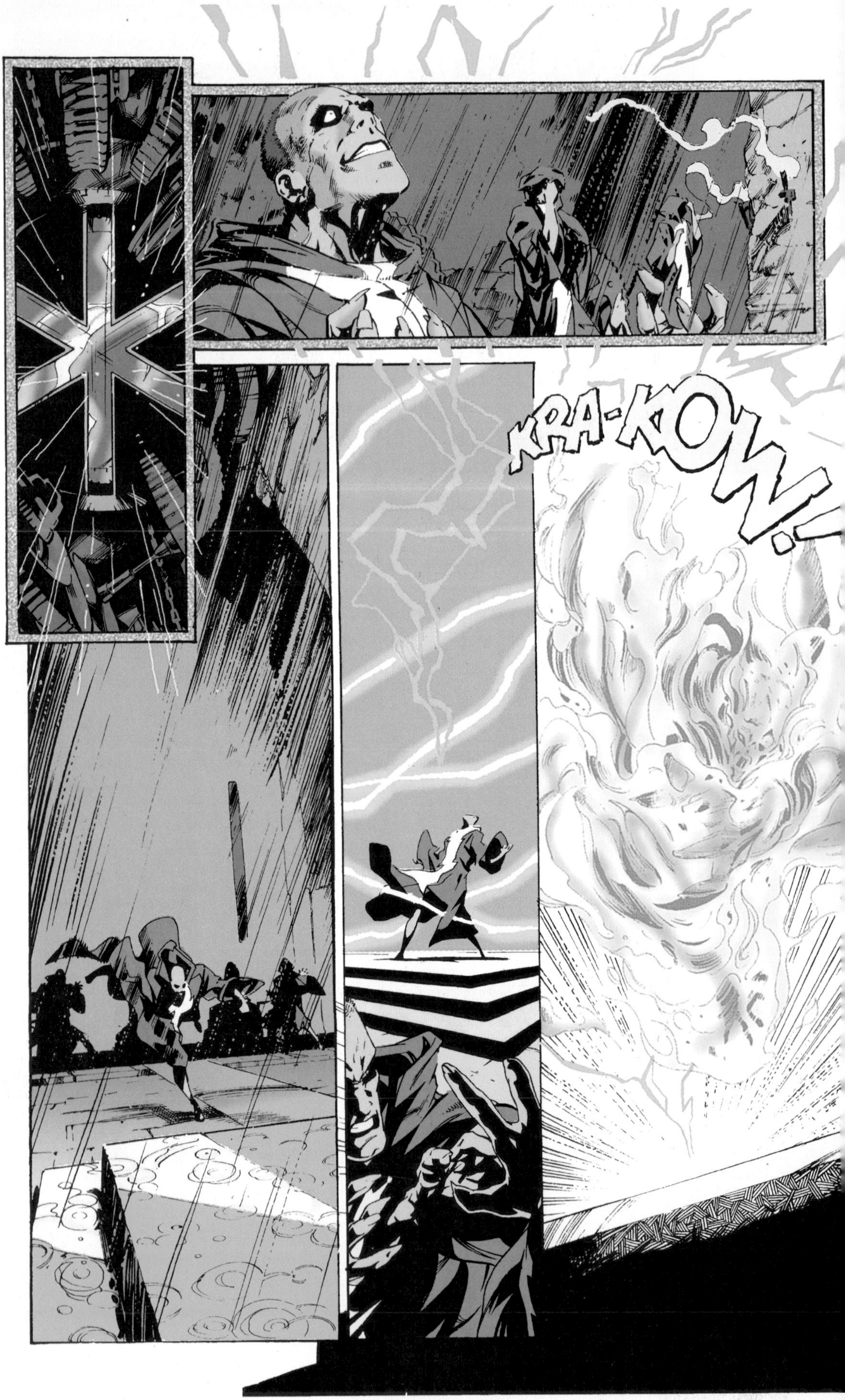
KRA-KOW!!

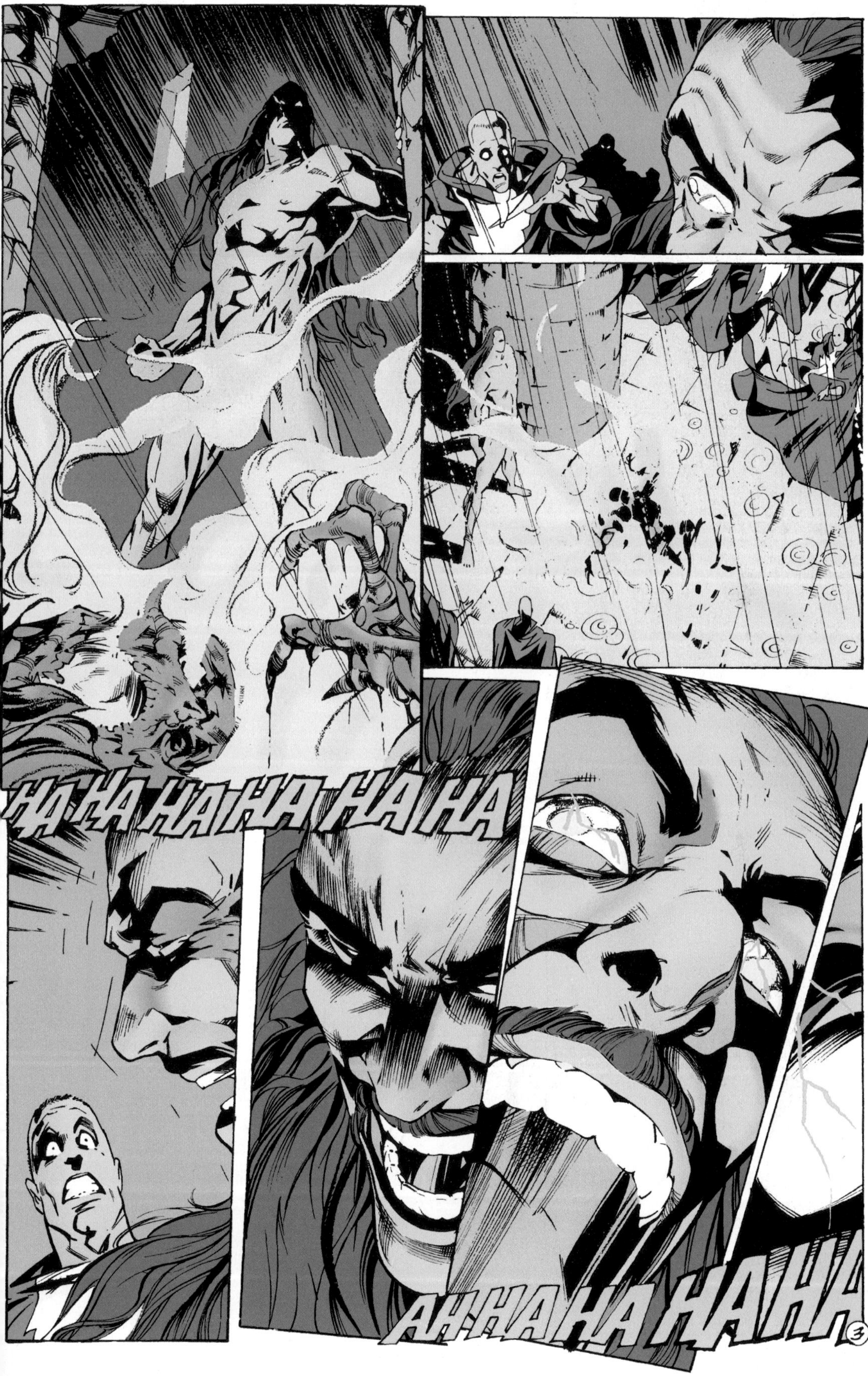
HA HA HA HA HA HA HA
AHHAHA HA HAHA

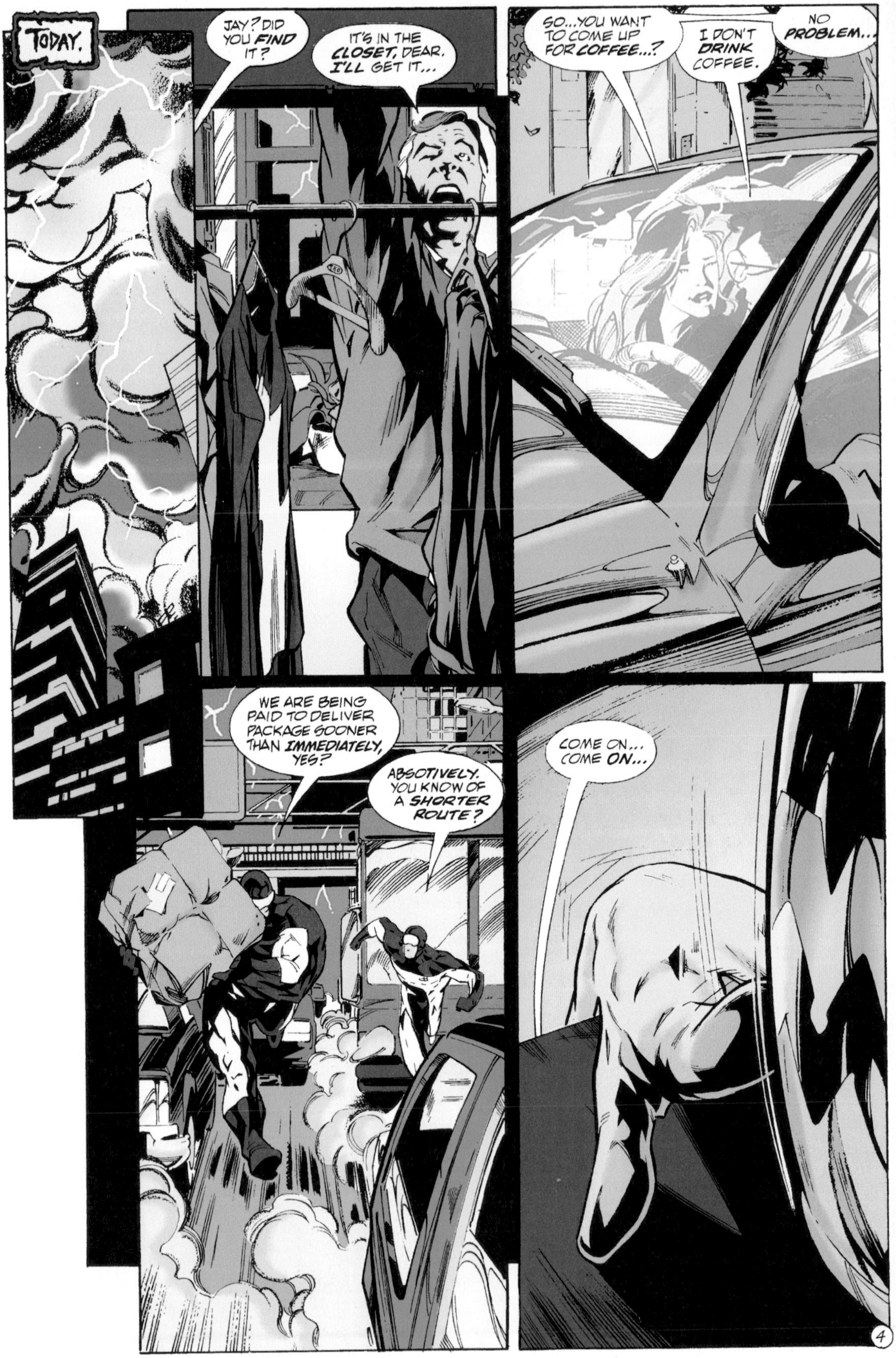
TODAY.
JAY? DID YOU FIND IT?
IT'S IN THE CLOSET, DEAR. I'LL GET IT...
SO...YOU WANT TO COME UP FOR COFFEE...?
I DON'T DRINK COFFEE.
NO PROBLEM...
WE ARE BEING PAID TO DELIVER PACKAGE SOONER THAN IMMEDIATELY, YES?
ABSOTIVELY. YOU KNOW OF A SHORTER ROUTE?
COME ON... COME ON...

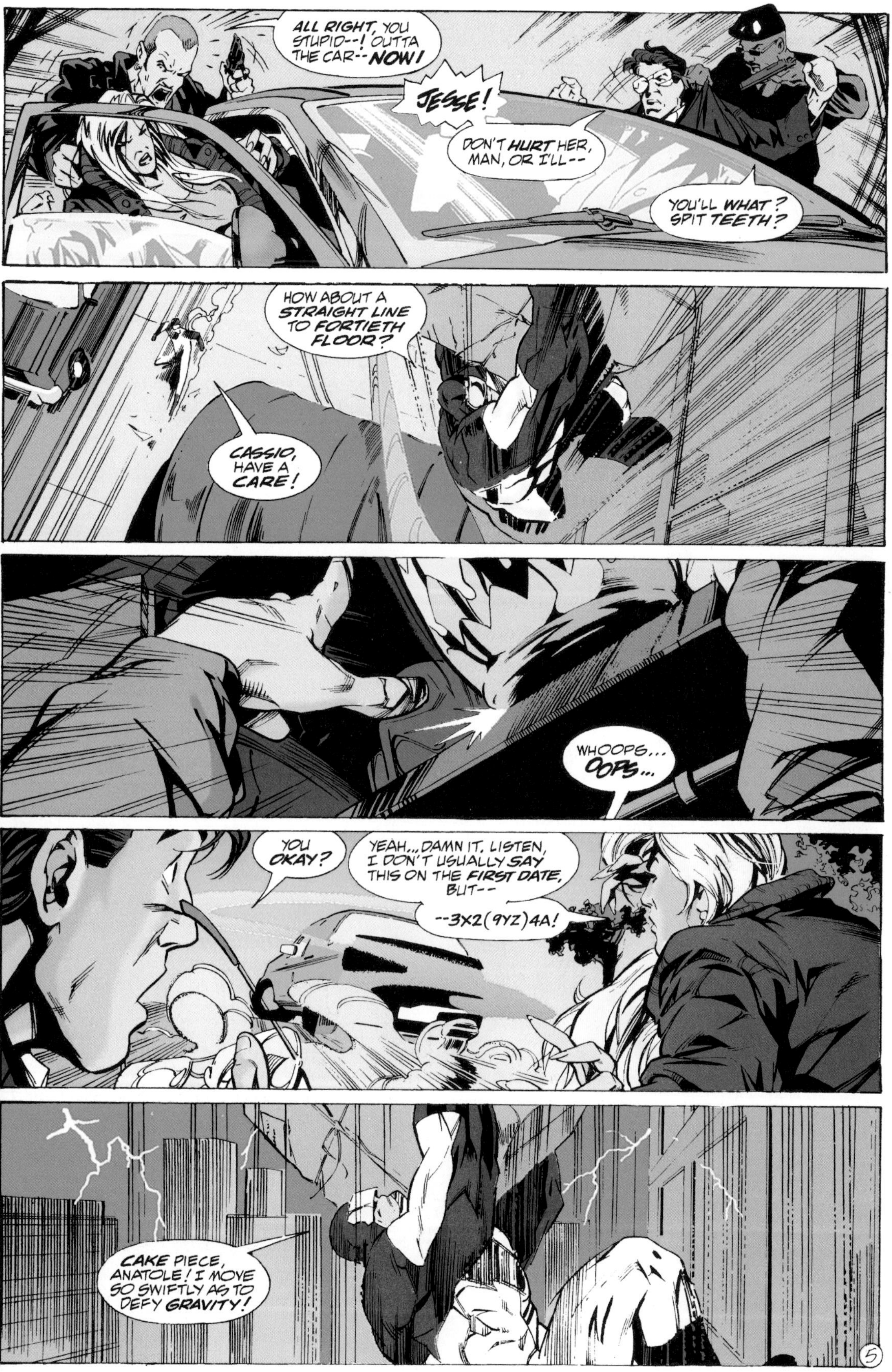

ALL RIGHT, YOU STUPID--! OUTTA THE CAR--NOW!
JESSE!
DON'T HURT HER, MAN, OR I'LL--
YOU'LL WHAT? SPIT TEETH?
HOW ABOUT A STRAIGHT LINE TO FORTIETH FLOOR?
CASSIO, HAVE A CARE!
WHOOPS... OOPS...
YOU OKAY?
YEAH... DAMN IT, LISTEN, I DON'T USUALLY SAY THIS ON THE FIRST DATE, BUT--
--3X2(9YZ)4A!
CAKE PIECE, ANATOLE! I MOVE SO SWIFTLY AS TO DEFY GRAVITY!

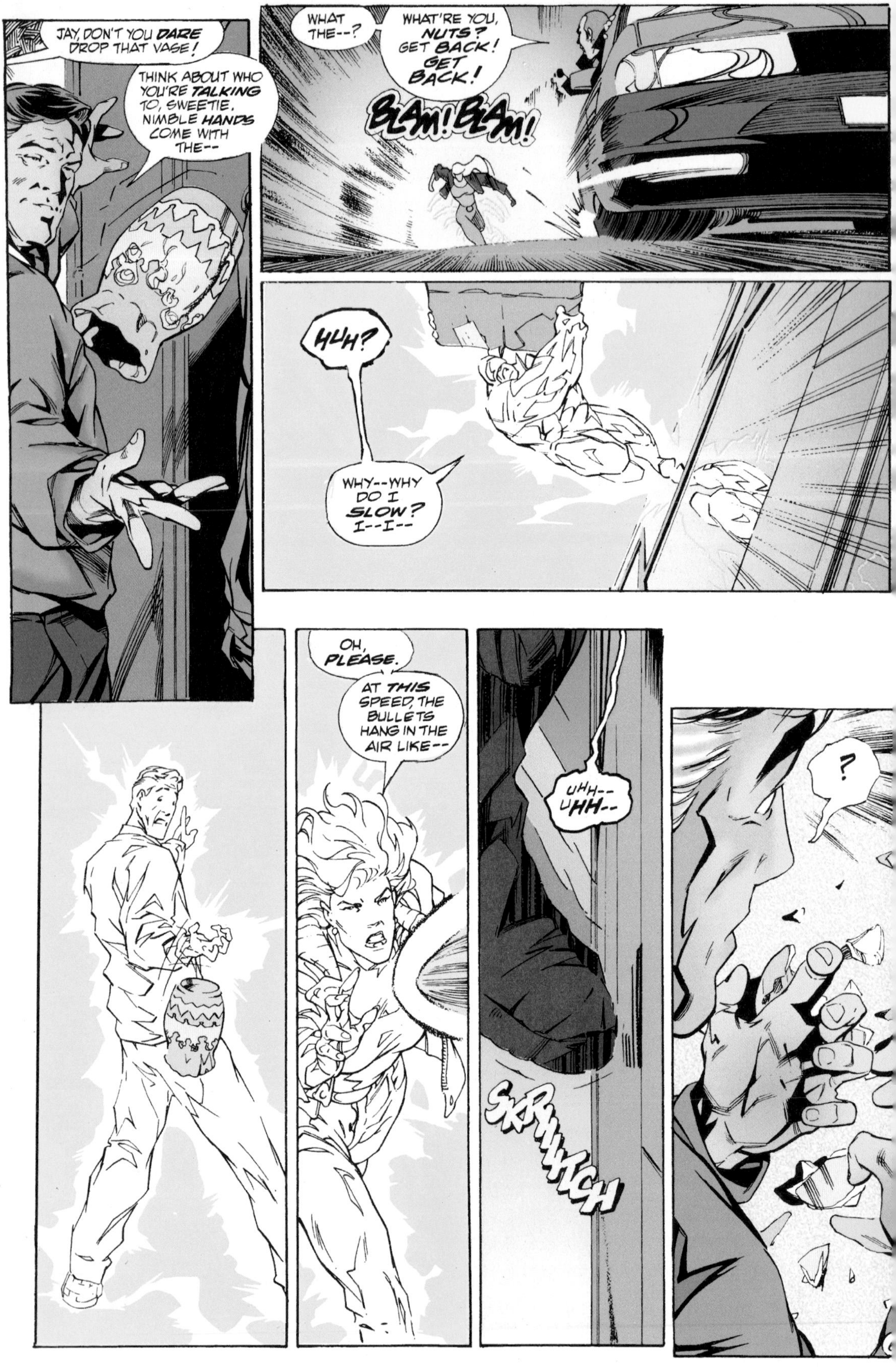
JAY, DON'T YOU DARE DROP THAT VASE!
THINK ABOUT WHO YOU'RE TALKING TO, SWEETIE. NIMBLE HANDS COME WITH THE--
WHAT THE--?
WHAT'RE YOU, NUTS? GET BACK! GET BACK!
BLAM! BLAM!
HUH?
WHY--WHY DO I SLOW? I--I--
OH, PLEASE.
AT THIS SPEED, THE BULLETS HANG IN THE AIR LIKE--
UHH-- UHH--
SKRUNNCH
?

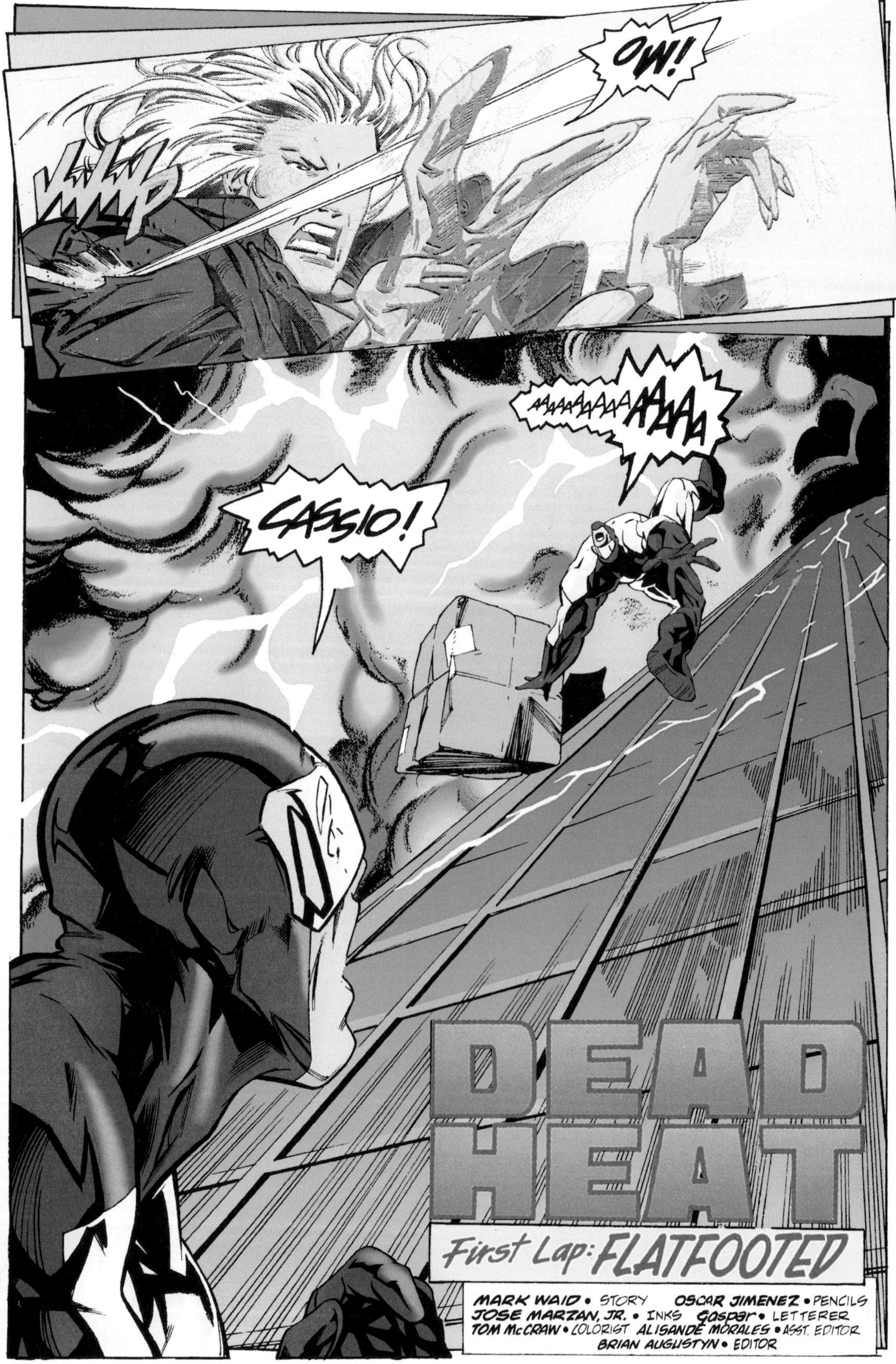
OW!
VWHP
AAAAAAAAAAAAAAAA
CASSIO!
DEAD HEAT
First Lap: FLATFOOTED
MARK WAID • STORY OSCAR JIMENEZ • PENCILS
JOSE MARZAN, JR. • INKS Gaspar • LETTERER
TOM McCRAW • COLORIST ALISANDE MORALES • ASST. EDITOR
BRIAN AUGUSTYN • EDITOR

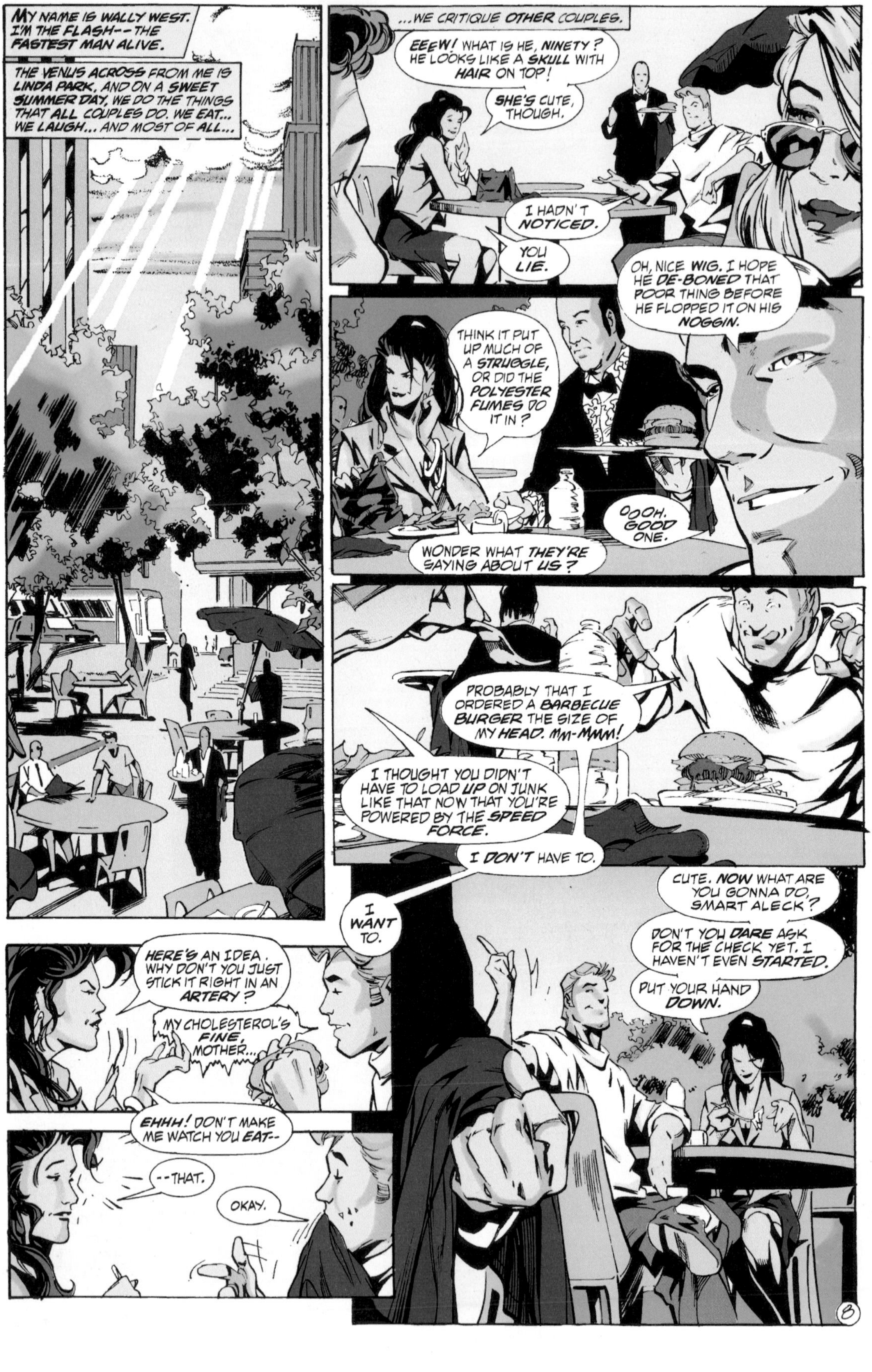

MY NAME IS WALLY WEST. I'M THE FLASH--THE FASTEST MAN ALIVE.
THE VENUS ACROSS FROM ME IS LINDA PARK. AND ON A SWEET SUMMER DAY, WE DO THE THINGS THAT ALL COUPLES DO. WE EAT... WE LAUGH... AND MOST OF ALL...
...WE CRITIQUE OTHER COUPLES.
EEEW! WHAT IS HE, NINETY? HE LOOKS LIKE A SKULL WITH HAIR ON TOP!
SHE'S CUTE, THOUGH.
I HADN'T NOTICED.
YOU LIE.
OH, NICE WIG. I HOPE HE DE-BONED THAT POOR THING BEFORE HE FLOPPED IT ON HIS NOGGIN.
THINK IT PUT UP MUCH OF A STRUGGLE, OR DID THE POLYESTER FUMES DO IT IN?
OOOH. GOOD ONE.
WONDER WHAT THEY'RE SAYING ABOUT US?
PROBABLY THAT I ORDERED A BARBECUE BURGER THE SIZE OF MY HEAD. MM-MMM!
I THOUGHT YOU DIDN'T HAVE TO LOAD UP ON JUNK LIKE THAT NOW THAT YOU'RE POWERED BY THE SPEED FORCE.
I DON'T HAVE TO.
I WANT TO.
HERE'S AN IDEA. WHY DON'T YOU JUST STICK IT RIGHT IN AN ARTERY?
MY CHOLESTEROL'S FINE, MOTHER...
EHHH! DON'T MAKE ME WATCH YOU EAT--
--THAT.
OKAY.
CUTE. NOW WHAT ARE YOU GONNA DO, SMART ALECK?
DON'T YOU DARE ASK FOR THE CHECK YET. I HAVEN'T EVEN STARTED.
PUT YOUR HAND DOWN.
8

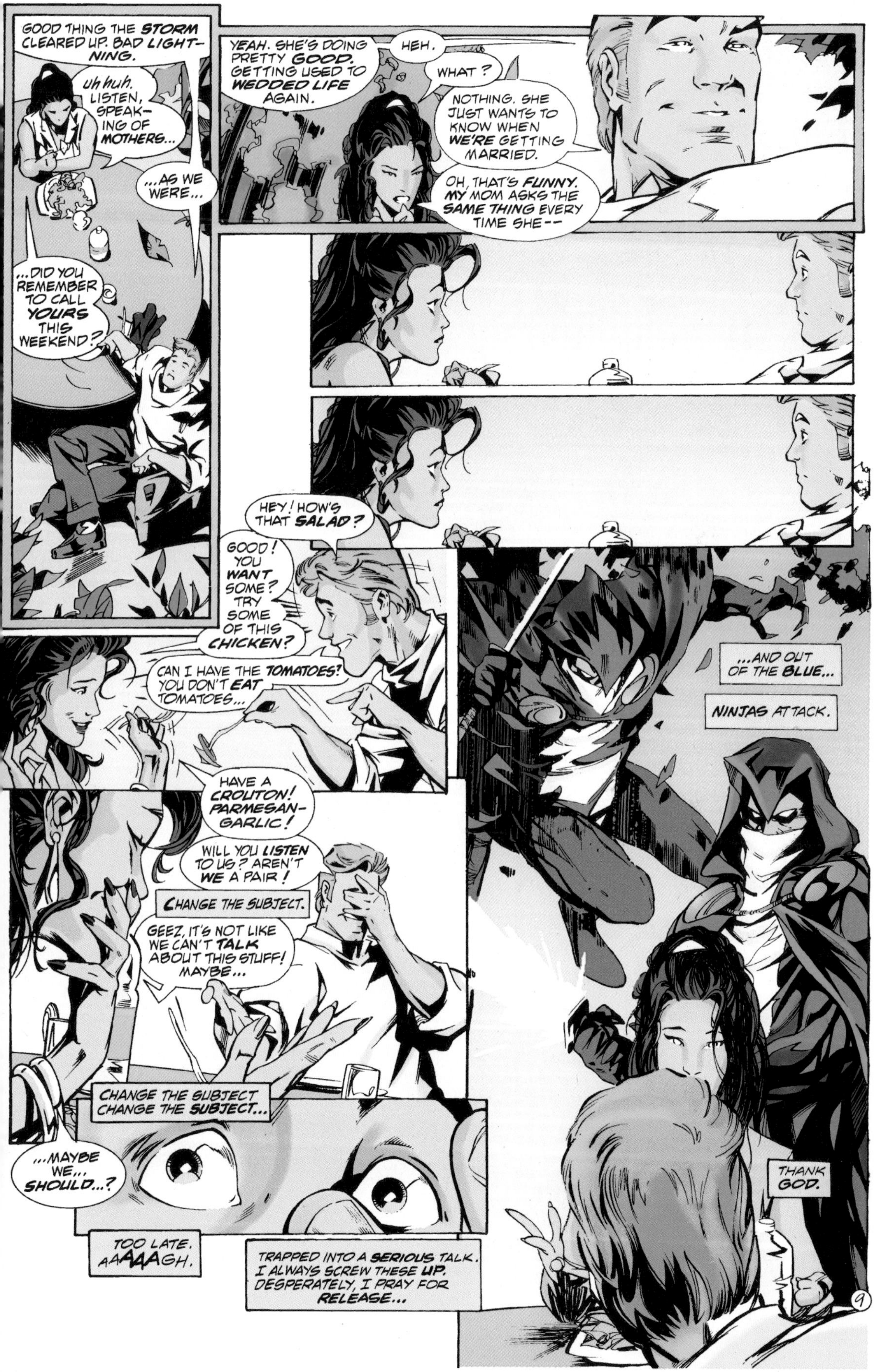
GOOD THING THE STORM CLEARED UP. BAD LIGHTNING.
uh huh. LISTEN, SPEAKING OF MOTHERS...
...AS WE WERE...
...DID YOU REMEMBER TO CALL YOURS THIS WEEKEND?
YEAH. SHE'S DOING PRETTY GOOD. GETTING USED TO WEDDED LIFE AGAIN.
HEH.
WHAT?
NOTHING. SHE JUST WANTS TO KNOW WHEN WE'RE GETTING MARRIED.
OH, THAT'S FUNNY. MY MOM ASKS THE SAME THING EVERY TIME SHE--
HEY! HOW'S THAT SALAD?
GOOD! YOU WANT SOME? TRY SOME OF THIS CHICKEN?
CAN I HAVE THE TOMATOES? YOU DON'T EAT TOMATOES...
HAVE A CROUTON! PARMESAN-GARLIC!
WILL YOU LISTEN TO US? AREN'T WE A PAIR!
CHANGE THE SUBJECT.
GEEZ, IT'S NOT LIKE WE CAN'T TALK ABOUT THIS STUFF! MAYBE...
CHANGE THE SUBJECT CHANGE THE SUBJECT...
...MAYBE WE... SHOULD...?
TOO LATE. AAAAAGH.
TRAPPED INTO A SERIOUS TALK. I ALWAYS SCREW THESE UP. DESPERATELY, I PRAY FOR RELEASE...
...AND OUT OF THE BLUE...
NINJAS ATTACK.
THANK GOD.

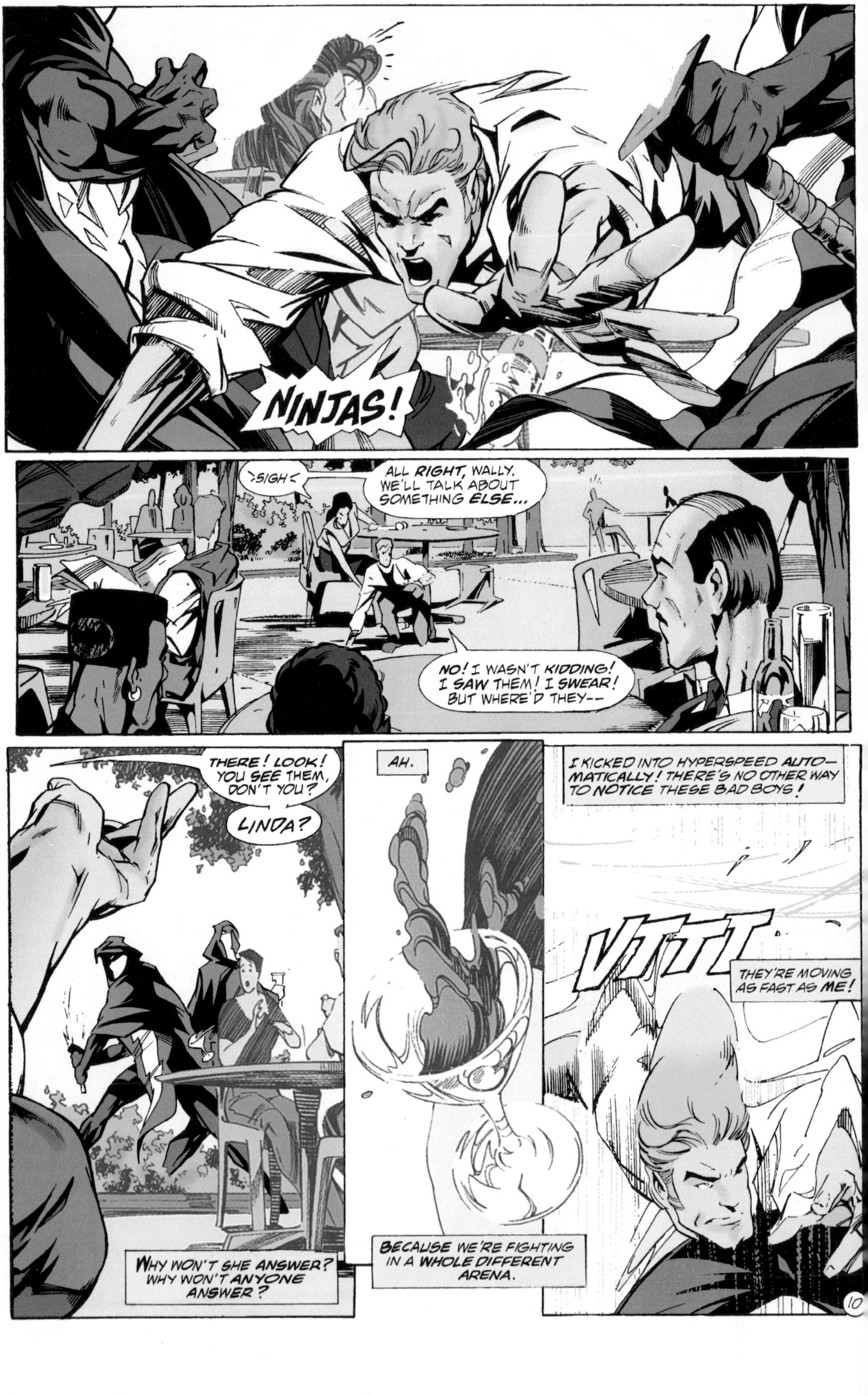
NINJAS!
>SIGH<
ALL RIGHT, WALLY. WE'LL TALK ABOUT SOMETHING ELSE...
NO! I WASN'T KIDDING! I SAW THEM! I SWEAR! BUT WHERE'D THEY--
THERE! LOOK! YOU SEE THEM, DON'T YOU?
LINDA?
WHY WON'T SHE ANSWER? WHY WON'T ANYONE ANSWER?
AH.
BECAUSE WE'RE FIGHTING IN A WHOLE DIFFERENT ARENA.
I KICKED INTO HYPERSPEED AUTOMATICALLY! THERE'S NO OTHER WAY TO NOTICE THESE BAD BOYS!
VTTT
THEY'RE MOVING AS FAST AS ME!
10

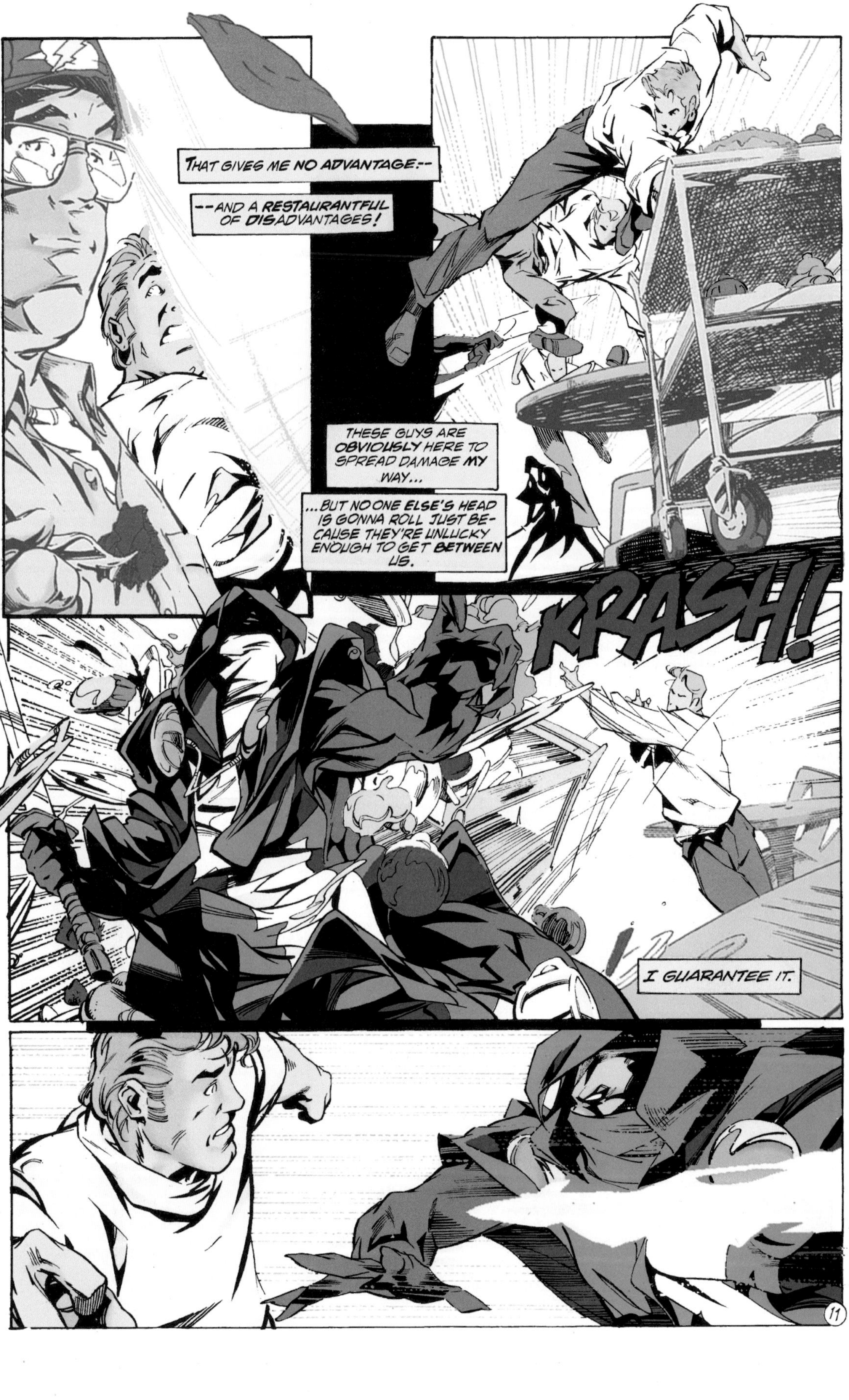
THAT GIVES ME NO ADVANTAGE--
--AND A RESTAURANTFUL OF DISADVANTAGES!
THESE GUYS ARE OBVIOUSLY HERE TO SPREAD DAMAGE MY WAY...
...BUT NO ONE ELSE'S HEAD IS GONNA ROLL JUST BECAUSE THEY'RE UNLUCKY ENOUGH TO GET BETWEEN US.
KRASH!
I GUARANTEE IT.

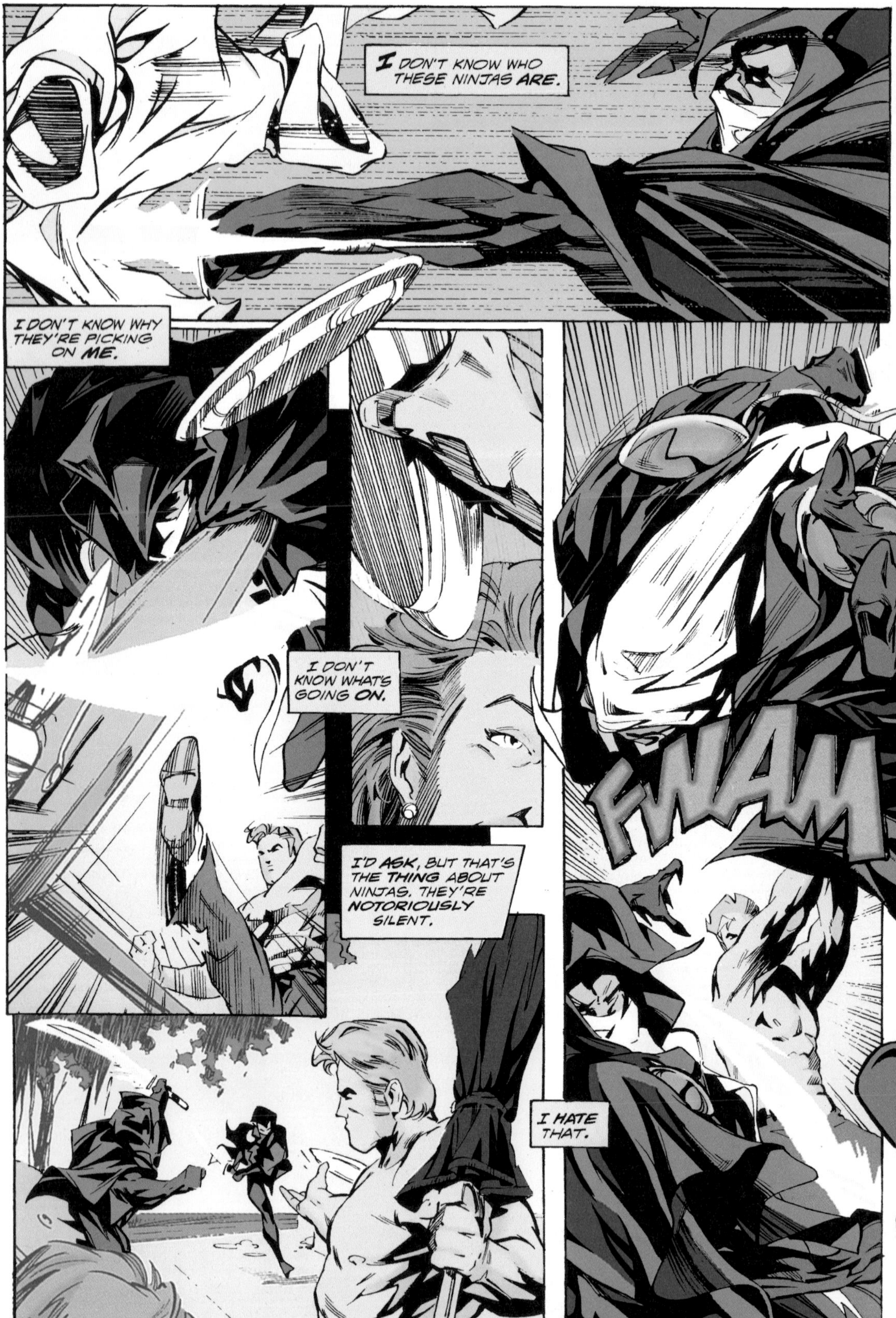
I DON'T KNOW WHO THESE NINJAS ARE.
I DON'T KNOW WHY THEY'RE PICKING ON ME.
I DON'T KNOW WHAT'S GOING ON.
FWAM
I'D ASK, BUT THAT'S THE THING ABOUT NINJAS. THEY'RE NOTORIOUSLY SILENT.
I HATE THAT.

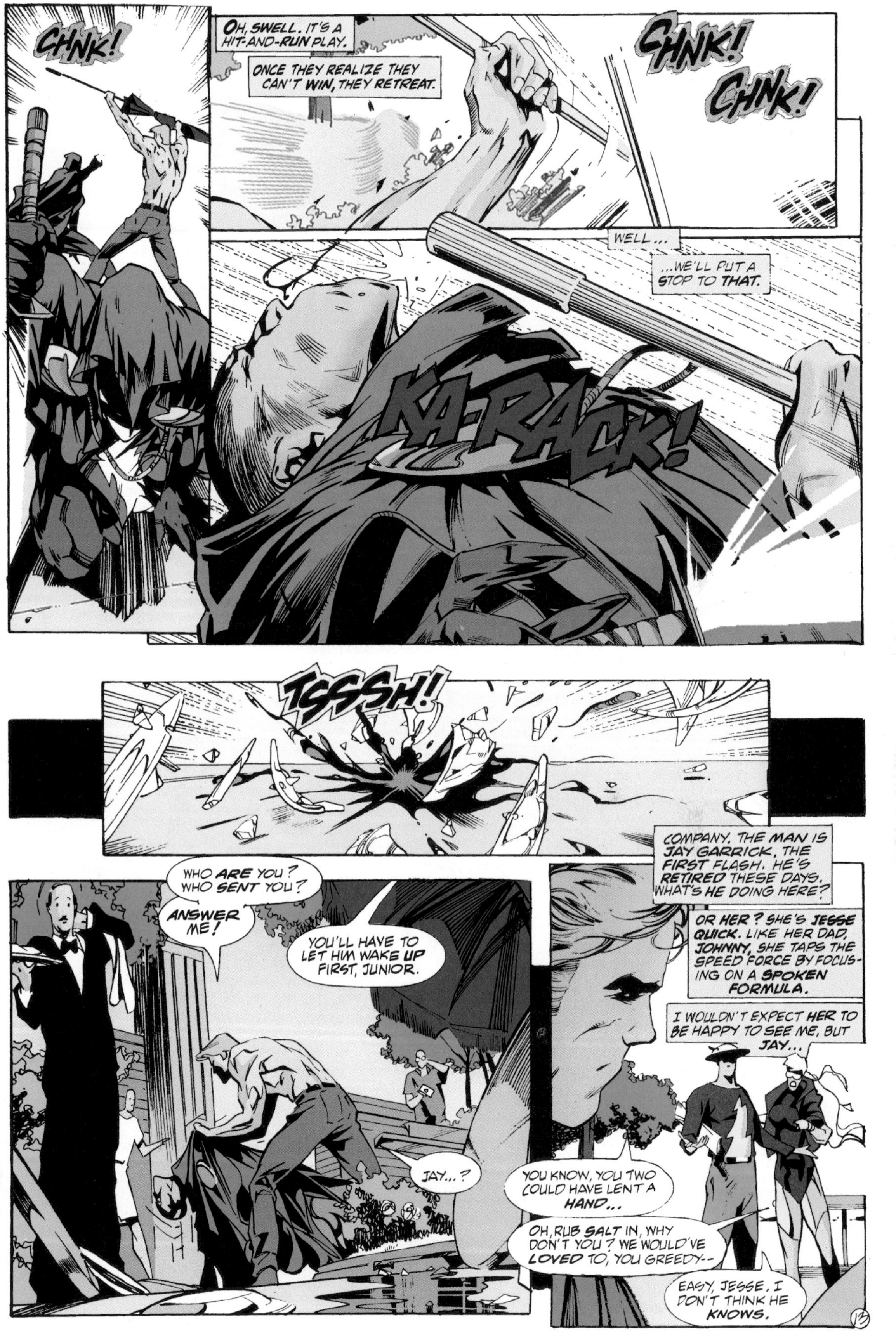
CHNK!
OH, SWELL. IT'S A HIT-AND-RUN PLAY.
ONCE THEY REALIZE THEY CAN'T WIN, THEY RETREAT.
CHNK! CHNK!
WELL...
...WE'LL PUT A STOP TO THAT.
KA-RACK!
TSSSH!
COMPANY. THE MAN IS JAY GARRICK, THE FIRST FLASH. HE'S RETIRED THESE DAYS. WHAT'S HE DOING HERE?
OR HER? SHE'S JESSE QUICK. LIKE HER DAD, JOHNNY, SHE TAPS THE SPEED FORCE BY FOCUSING ON A SPOKEN FORMULA.
I WOULDN'T EXPECT HER TO BE HAPPY TO SEE ME, BUT JAY...
WHO ARE YOU? WHO SENT YOU?
ANSWER ME!
YOU'LL HAVE TO LET HIM WAKE UP FIRST, JUNIOR.
JAY...?
YOU KNOW, YOU TWO COULD HAVE LENT A HAND...
OH, RUB SALT IN, WHY DON'T YOU? WE WOULD'VE LOVED TO, YOU GREEDY--
EASY, JESSE. I DON'T THINK HE KNOWS.
13

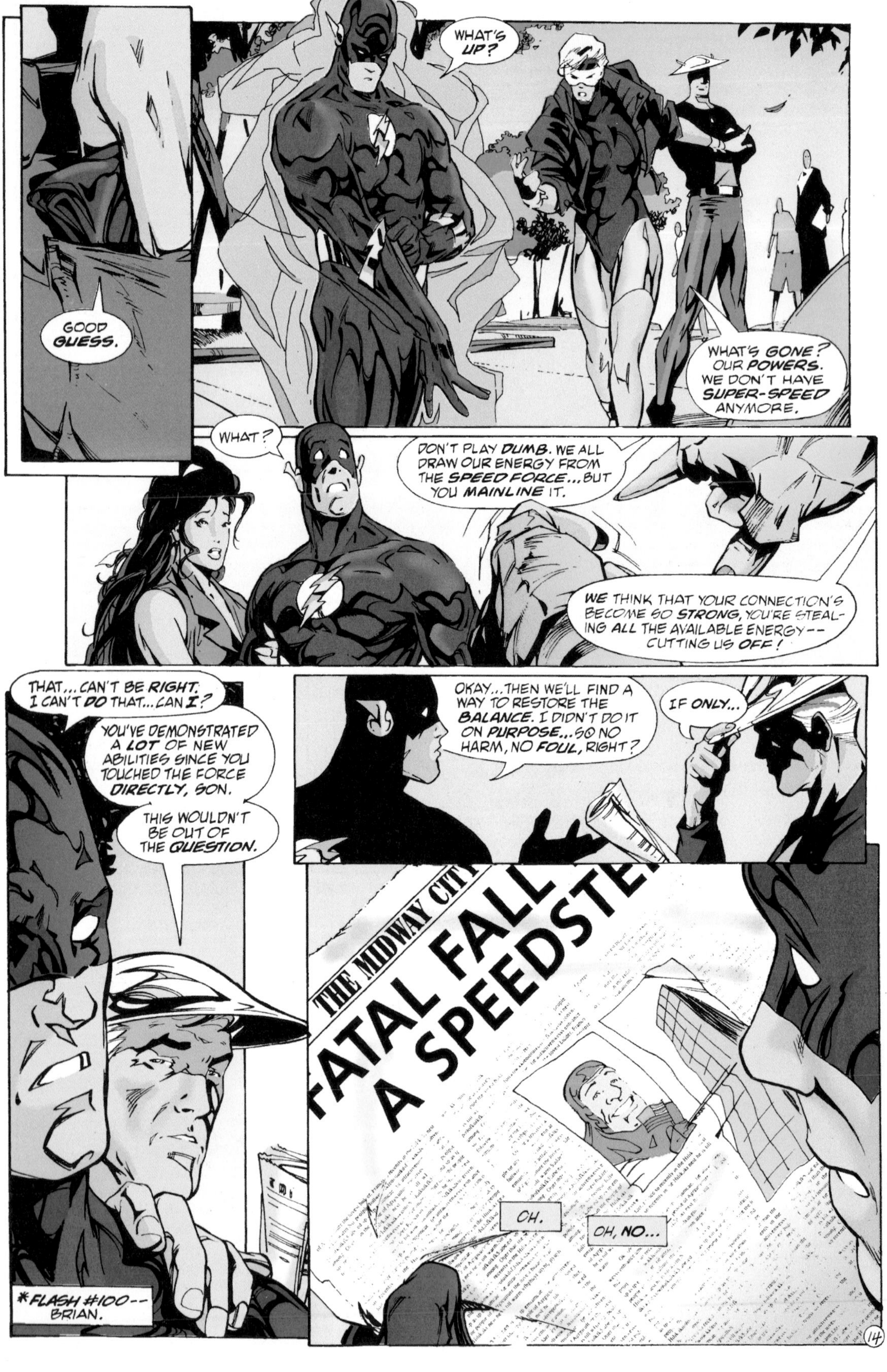

WHAT'S UP?
GOOD GUESS.
WHAT'S GONE? OUR POWERS. WE DON'T HAVE SUPER-SPEED ANYMORE.
WHAT?
DON'T PLAY DUMB. WE ALL DRAW OUR ENERGY FROM THE SPEED FORCE... BUT YOU MAINLINE IT.
WE THINK THAT YOUR CONNECTION'S BECOME SO STRONG, YOU'RE STEALING ALL THE AVAILABLE ENERGY-- CUTTING US OFF!
THAT... CAN'T BE RIGHT. I CAN'T DO THAT... CAN I?
YOU'VE DEMONSTRATED A LOT OF NEW ABILITIES SINCE YOU TOUCHED THE FORCE DIRECTLY, SON.
THIS WOULDN'T BE OUT OF THE QUESTION.
OKAY... THEN WE'LL FIND A WAY TO RESTORE THE BALANCE. I DIDN'T DO IT ON PURPOSE... SO NO HARM, NO FOUL, RIGHT?
IF ONLY...
THE MIDWAY CIT
FATAL FALL
A SPEEDSTE
OH.
OH, NO...
*FLASH #100-- BRIAN.

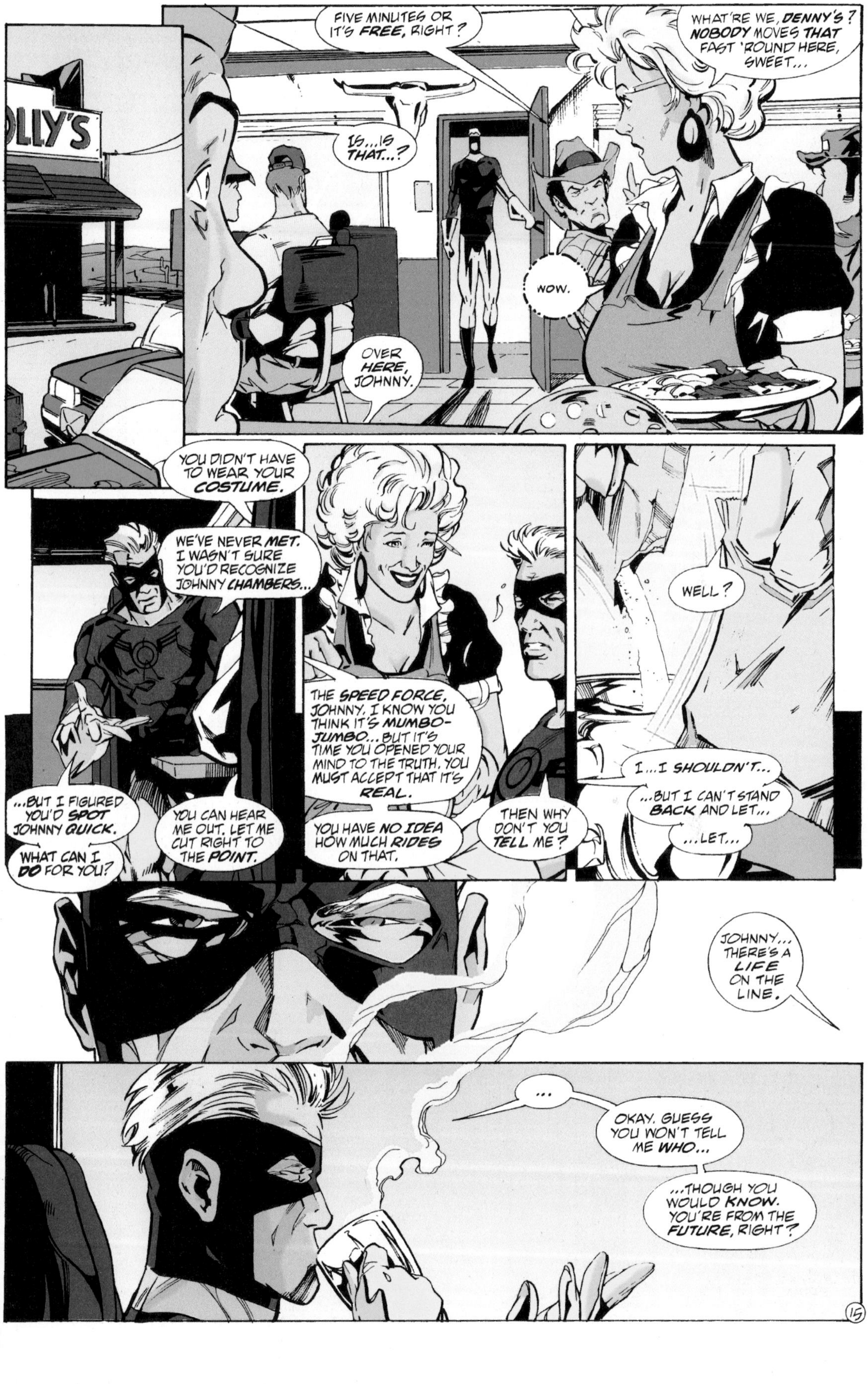

OLLY'S
FIVE MINUTES OR IT'S FREE, RIGHT?
WHAT'RE WE, DENNY'S? NOBODY MOVES THAT FAST 'ROUND HERE, SWEET...
IS...IS THAT...?
WOW.
OVER HERE, JOHNNY.
YOU DIDN'T HAVE TO WEAR YOUR COSTUME.
WE'VE NEVER MET. I WASN'T SURE YOU'D RECOGNIZE JOHNNY CHAMBERS...
...BUT I FIGURED YOU'D SPOT JOHNNY QUICK.
WHAT CAN I DO FOR YOU?
YOU CAN HEAR ME OUT. LET ME CUT RIGHT TO THE POINT.
THE SPEED FORCE, JOHNNY. I KNOW YOU THINK IT'S MUMBO-JUMBO... BUT IT'S TIME YOU OPENED YOUR MIND TO THE TRUTH. YOU MUST ACCEPT THAT IT'S REAL.
YOU HAVE NO IDEA HOW MUCH RIDES ON THAT.
THEN WHY DON'T YOU TELL ME?
WELL?
I...I SHOULDN'T...
...BUT I CAN'T STAND BACK AND LET...
...LET...
JOHNNY... THERE'S A LIFE ON THE LINE.
...
OKAY. GUESS YOU WON'T TELL ME WHO...
...THOUGH YOU WOULD KNOW. YOU'RE FROM THE FUTURE, RIGHT?

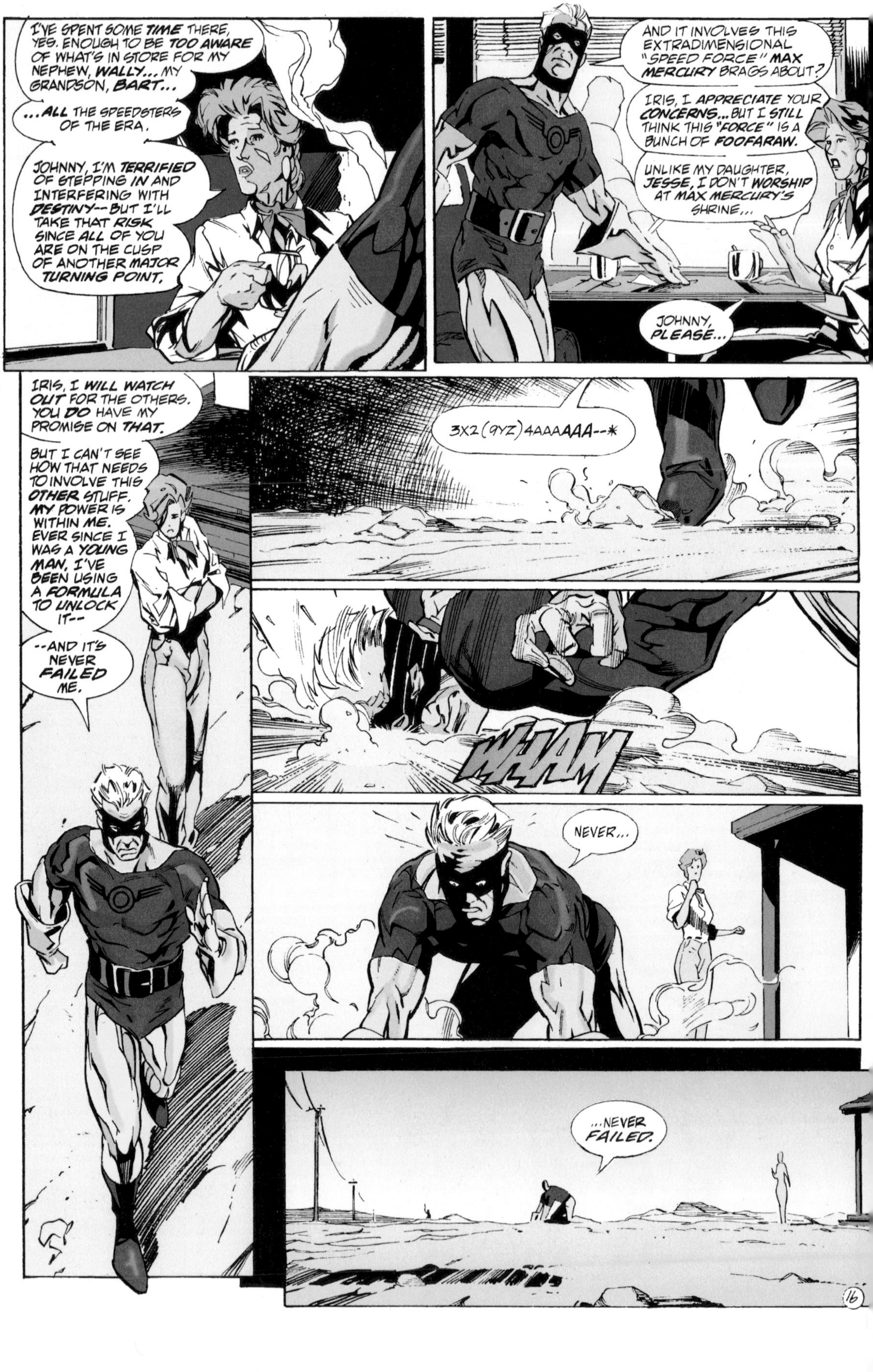
I'VE SPENT SOME TIME THERE, YES. ENOUGH TO BE TOO AWARE OF WHAT'S IN STORE FOR MY NEPHEW, WALLY... MY GRANDSON, BART...
...ALL THE SPEEDSTERS OF THE ERA.
JOHNNY, I'M TERRIFIED OF STEPPING IN AND INTERFERING WITH DESTINY-- BUT I'LL TAKE THAT RISK SINCE ALL OF YOU ARE ON THE CUSP OF ANOTHER MAJOR TURNING POINT.
AND IT INVOLVES THIS EXTRADIMENSIONAL "SPEED FORCE" MAX MERCURY BRAGS ABOUT?
IRIS, I APPRECIATE YOUR CONCERNS... BUT I STILL THINK THIS "FORCE" IS A BUNCH OF FOOFARAW.
UNLIKE MY DAUGHTER, JESSE, I DON'T WORSHIP AT MAX MERCURY'S SHRINE...
JOHNNY, PLEASE...
IRIS, I WILL WATCH OUT FOR THE OTHERS. YOU DO HAVE MY PROMISE ON THAT.
BUT I CAN'T SEE HOW THAT NEEDS TO INVOLVE THIS OTHER STUFF. MY POWER IS WITHIN ME. EVER SINCE I WAS A YOUNG MAN, I'VE BEEN USING A FORMULA TO UNLOCK IT--
--AND IT'S NEVER FAILED ME.
3X2(9YZ)4AAAAAA--*
WHAM
NEVER...
...NEVER FAILED.

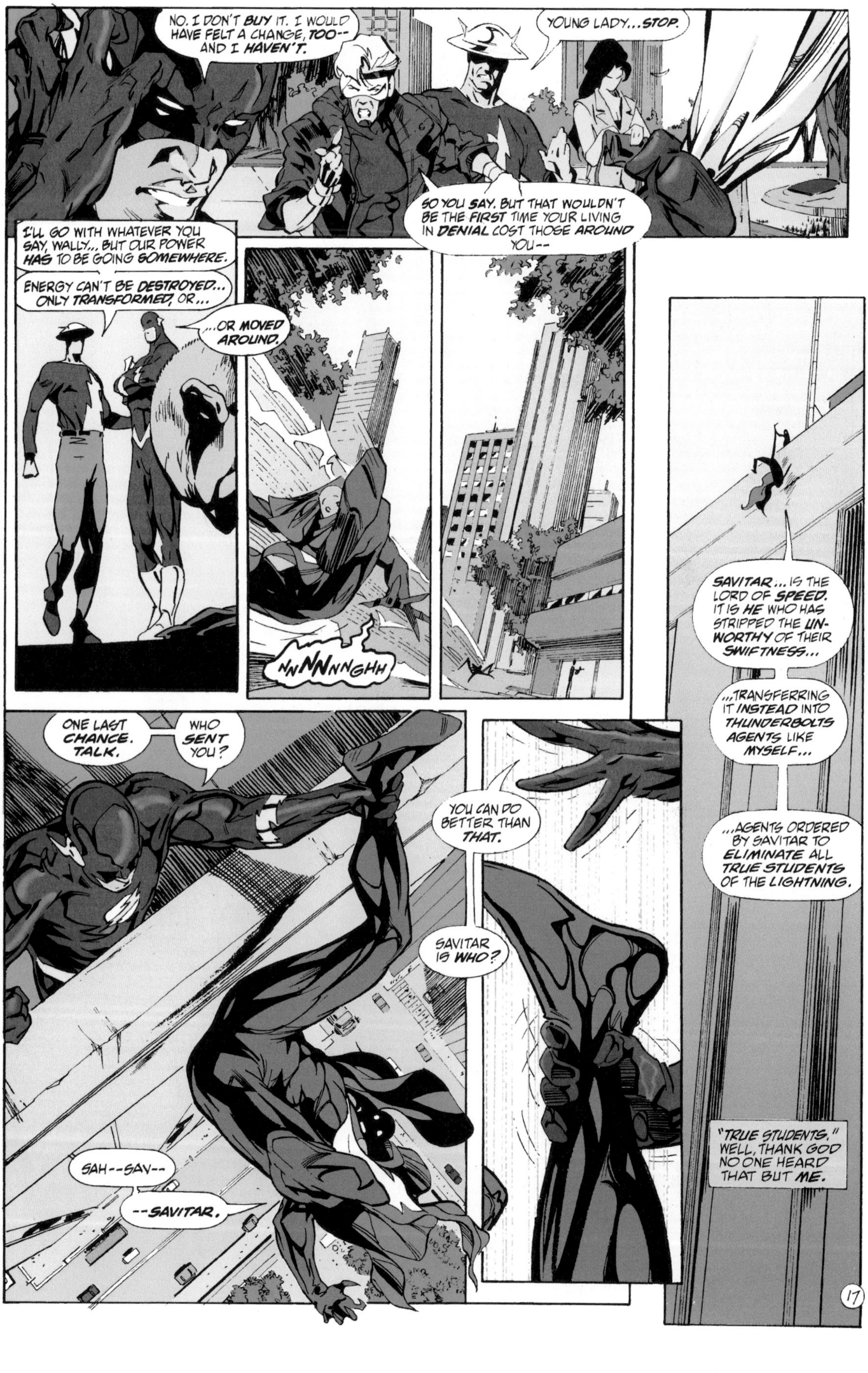
NO. I DON'T BUY IT. I WOULD HAVE FELT A CHANGE, TOO-- AND I HAVEN'T.
YOUNG LADY... STOP.
SO YOU SAY. BUT THAT WOULDN'T BE THE FIRST TIME YOUR LIVING IN DENIAL COST THOSE AROUND YOU--
I'LL GO WITH WHATEVER YOU SAY, WALLY... BUT OUR POWER HAS TO BE GOING SOMEWHERE.
ENERGY CAN'T BE DESTROYED... ONLY TRANSFORMED, OR...
...OR MOVED AROUND.
NNNNNNGHH
SAVITAR... IS THE LORD OF SPEED. IT IS HE WHO HAS STRIPPED THE UNWORTHY OF THEIR SWIFTNESS...
...TRANSFERRING IT INSTEAD INTO THUNDERBOLTS AGENTS LIKE MYSELF...
...AGENTS ORDERED BY SAVITAR TO ELIMINATE ALL TRUE STUDENTS OF THE LIGHTNING.
ONE LAST CHANCE. TALK.
WHO SENT YOU?
YOU CAN DO BETTER THAN THAT.
SAVITAR IS WHO?
SAH--SAV--
--SAVITAR.
"TRUE STUDENTS." WELL, THANK GOD NO ONE HEARD THAT BUT ME.
17

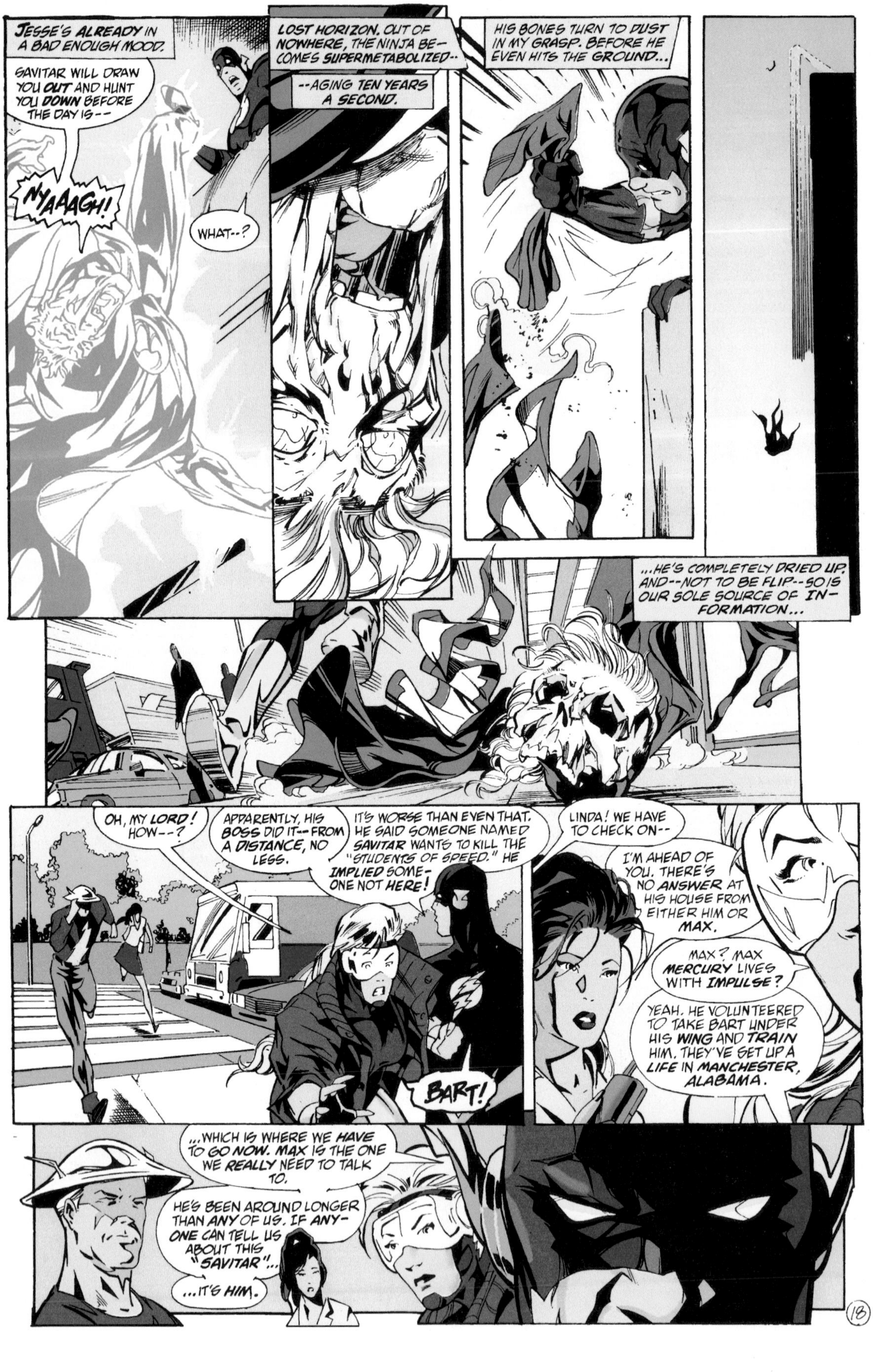

JESSE'S ALREADY IN A BAD ENOUGH MOOD.
SAVITAR WILL DRAW YOU OUT AND HUNT YOU DOWN BEFORE THE DAY IS--
NYAAAGH!
WHAT--?
LOST HORIZON. OUT OF NOWHERE, THE NINJA BECOMES SUPERMETABOLIZED--
--AGING TEN YEARS A SECOND.
HIS BONES TURN TO DUST IN MY GRASP. BEFORE HE EVEN HITS THE GROUND...
...HE'S COMPLETELY DRIED UP. AND--NOT TO BE FLIP--SO IS OUR SOLE SOURCE OF INFORMATION...
OH, MY LORD! HOW--?
APPARENTLY, HIS BOSS DID IT--FROM A DISTANCE, NO LESS.
IT'S WORSE THAN EVEN THAT. HE SAID SOMEONE NAMED SAVITAR WANTS TO KILL THE "STUDENTS OF SPEED." HE IMPLIED SOMEONE NOT HERE!
BART!
LINDA! WE HAVE TO CHECK ON--
I'M AHEAD OF YOU. THERE'S NO ANSWER AT HIS HOUSE FROM EITHER HIM OR MAX.
MAX? MAX MERCURY LIVES WITH IMPULSE?
YEAH. HE VOLUNTEERED TO TAKE BART UNDER HIS WING AND TRAIN HIM. THEY'VE SET UP A LIFE IN MANCHESTER, ALABAMA.
...WHICH IS WHERE WE HAVE TO GO NOW. MAX IS THE ONE WE REALLY NEED TO TALK TO.
HE'S BEEN AROUND LONGER THAN ANY OF US. IF ANYONE CAN TELL US ABOUT THIS "SAVITAR"...
...IT'S HIM.
18

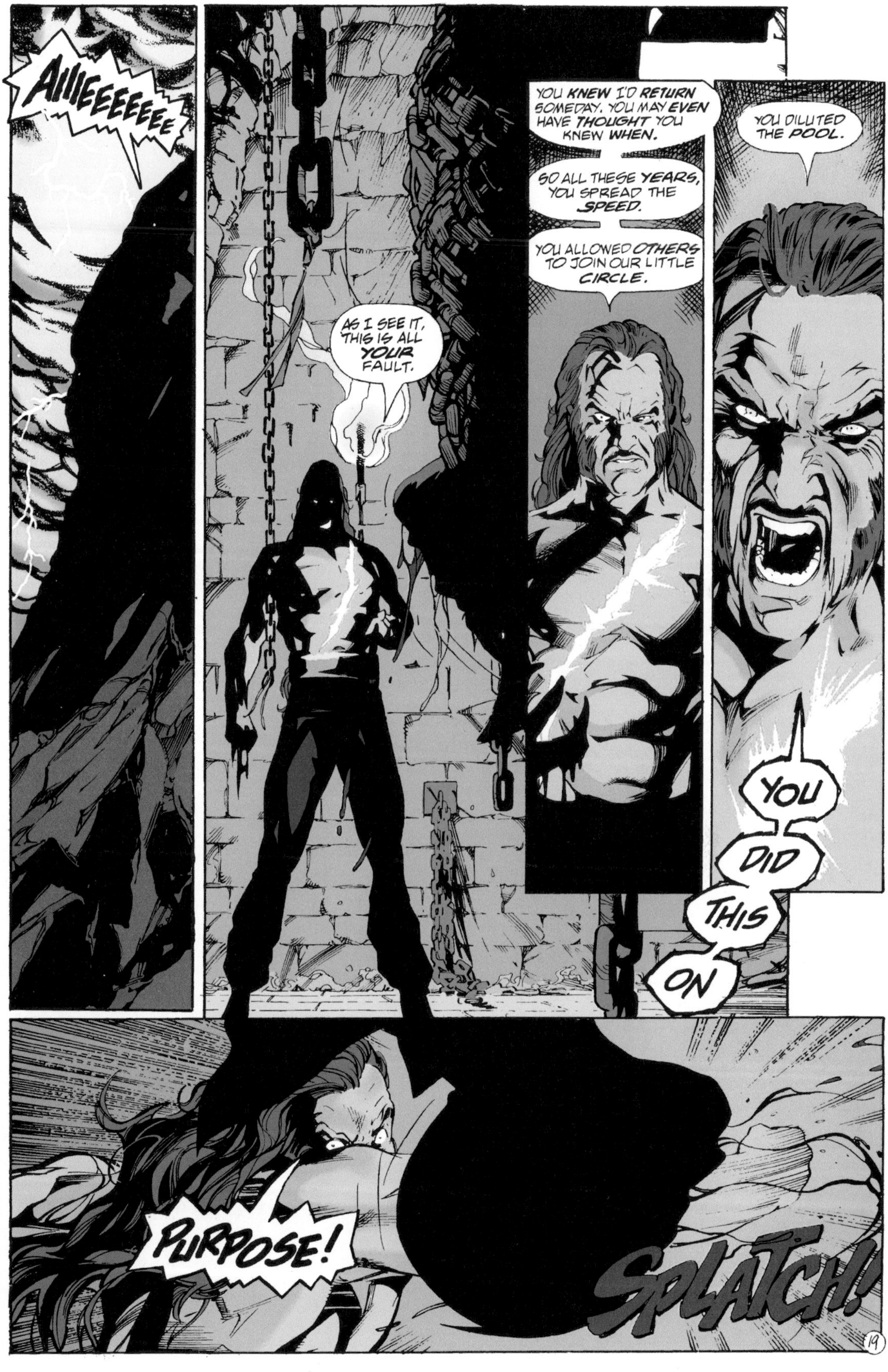
AIIIEEEEEEEE
AS I SEE IT, THIS IS ALL YOUR FAULT.
YOU KNEW I'D RETURN SOMEDAY. YOU MAY EVEN HAVE THOUGHT YOU KNEW WHEN.
SO ALL THESE YEARS, YOU SPREAD THE SPEED.
YOU ALLOWED OTHERS TO JOIN OUR LITTLE CIRCLE.
YOU DILUTED THE POOL.
YOU
DID
THIS
ON
PURPOSE!
SPLATCH!

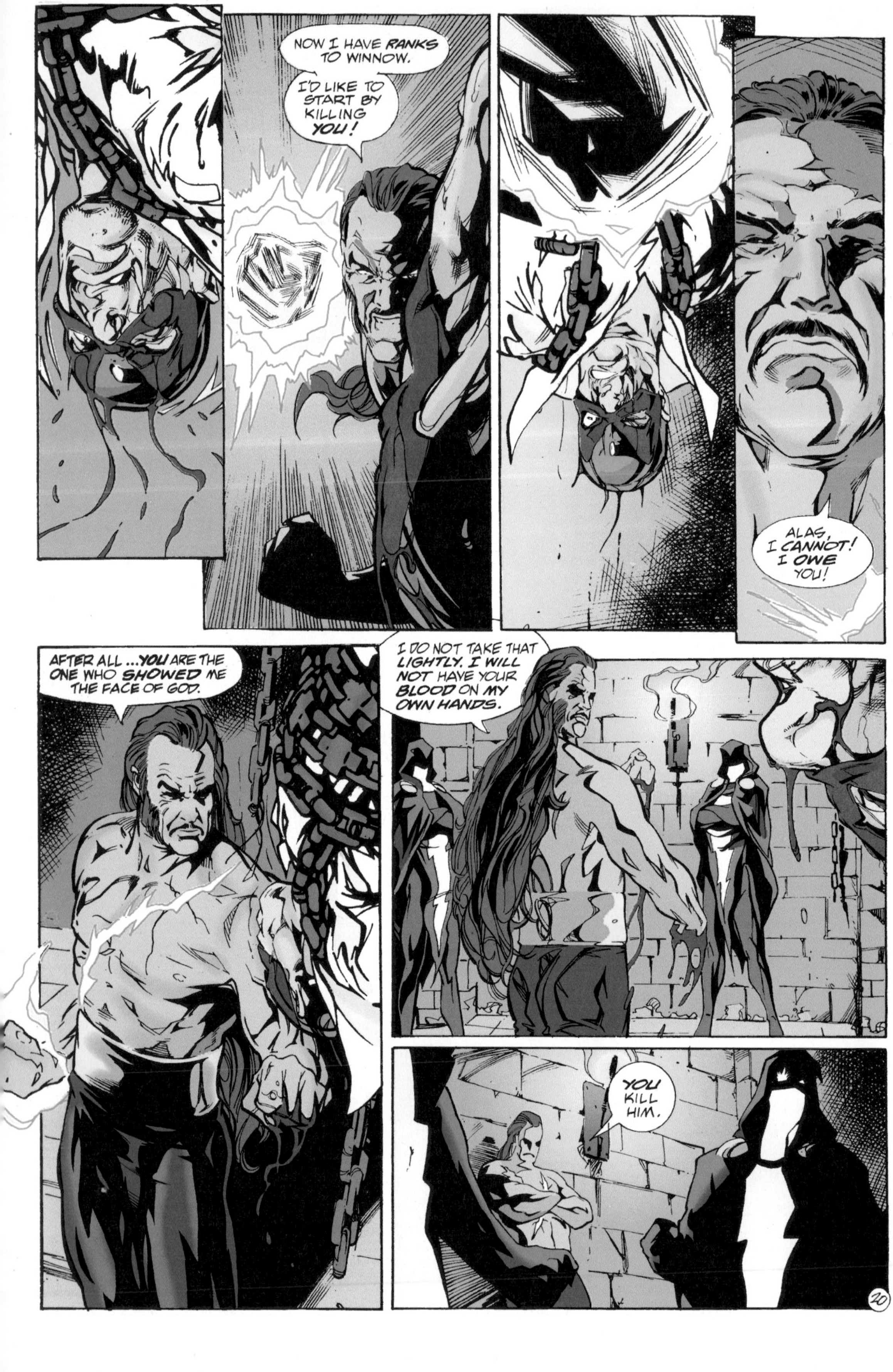
NOW I HAVE RANKS TO WINNOW.
I'D LIKE TO START BY KILLING YOU!
ALAS, I CANNOT! I OWE YOU!
AFTER ALL ...YOU ARE THE ONE WHO SHOWED ME THE FACE OF GOD.
I DO NOT TAKE THAT LIGHTLY. I WILL NOT HAVE YOUR BLOOD ON MY OWN HANDS.
YOU KILL HIM.

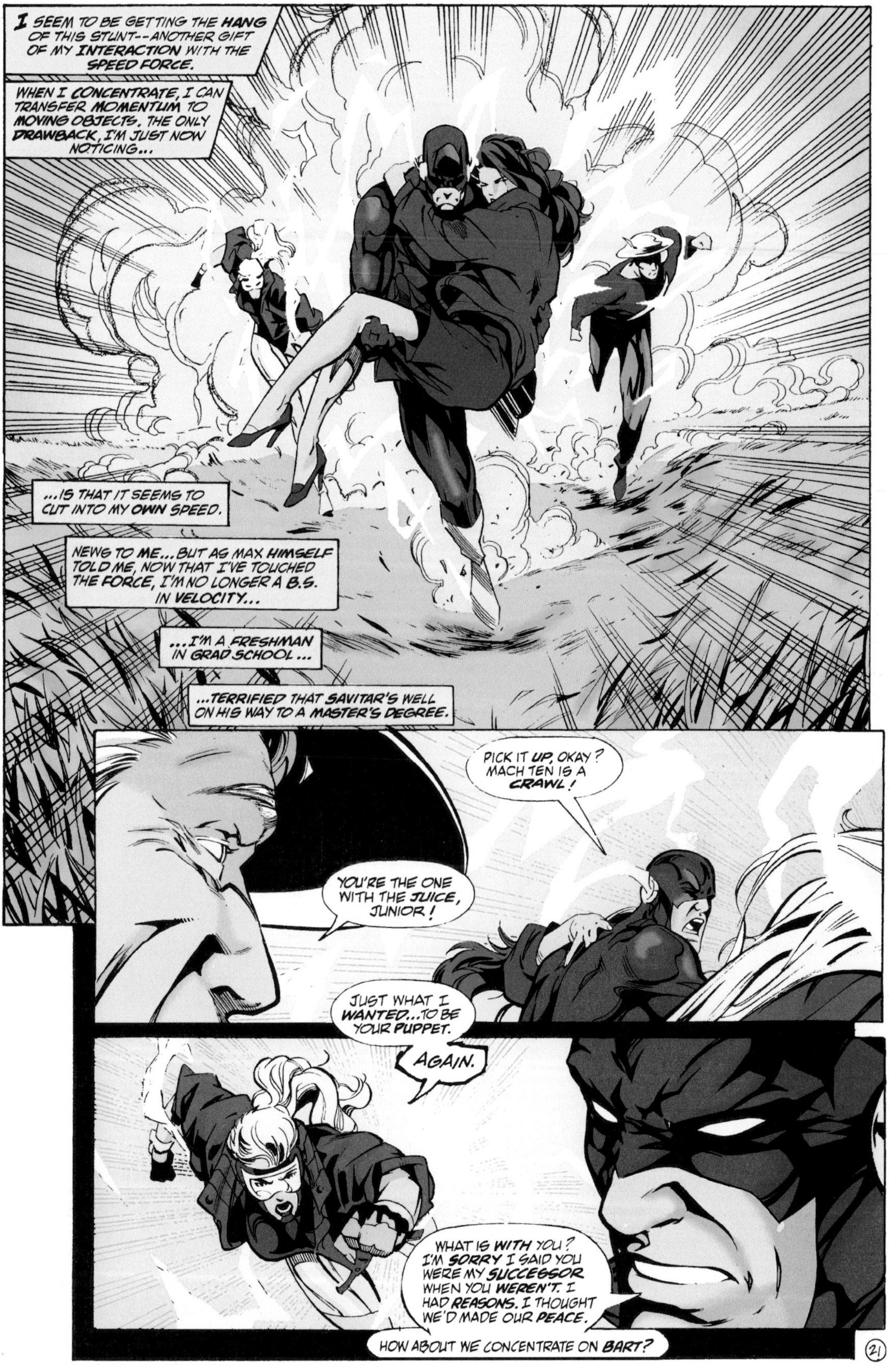
I SEEM TO BE GETTING THE HANG OF THIS STUNT--ANOTHER GIFT OF MY INTERACTION WITH THE SPEED FORCE.
WHEN I CONCENTRATE, I CAN TRANSFER MOMENTUM TO MOVING OBJECTS. THE ONLY DRAWBACK, I'M JUST NOW NOTICING...
...IS THAT IT SEEMS TO CUT INTO MY OWN SPEED.
NEWS TO ME...BUT AS MAX HIMSELF TOLD ME, NOW THAT I'VE TOUCHED THE FORCE, I'M NO LONGER A B.S. IN VELOCITY...
...I'M A FRESHMAN IN GRAD SCHOOL...
...TERRIFIED THAT SAVITAR'S WELL ON HIS WAY TO A MASTER'S DEGREE.
PICK IT UP, OKAY? MACH TEN IS A CRAWL!
YOU'RE THE ONE WITH THE JUICE, JUNIOR!
JUST WHAT I WANTED...TO BE YOUR PUPPET.
AGAIN.
WHAT IS WITH YOU? I'M SORRY I SAID YOU WERE MY SUCCESSOR WHEN YOU WEREN'T. I HAD REASONS. I THOUGHT WE'D MADE OUR PEACE.
HOW ABOUT WE CONCENTRATE ON BART?

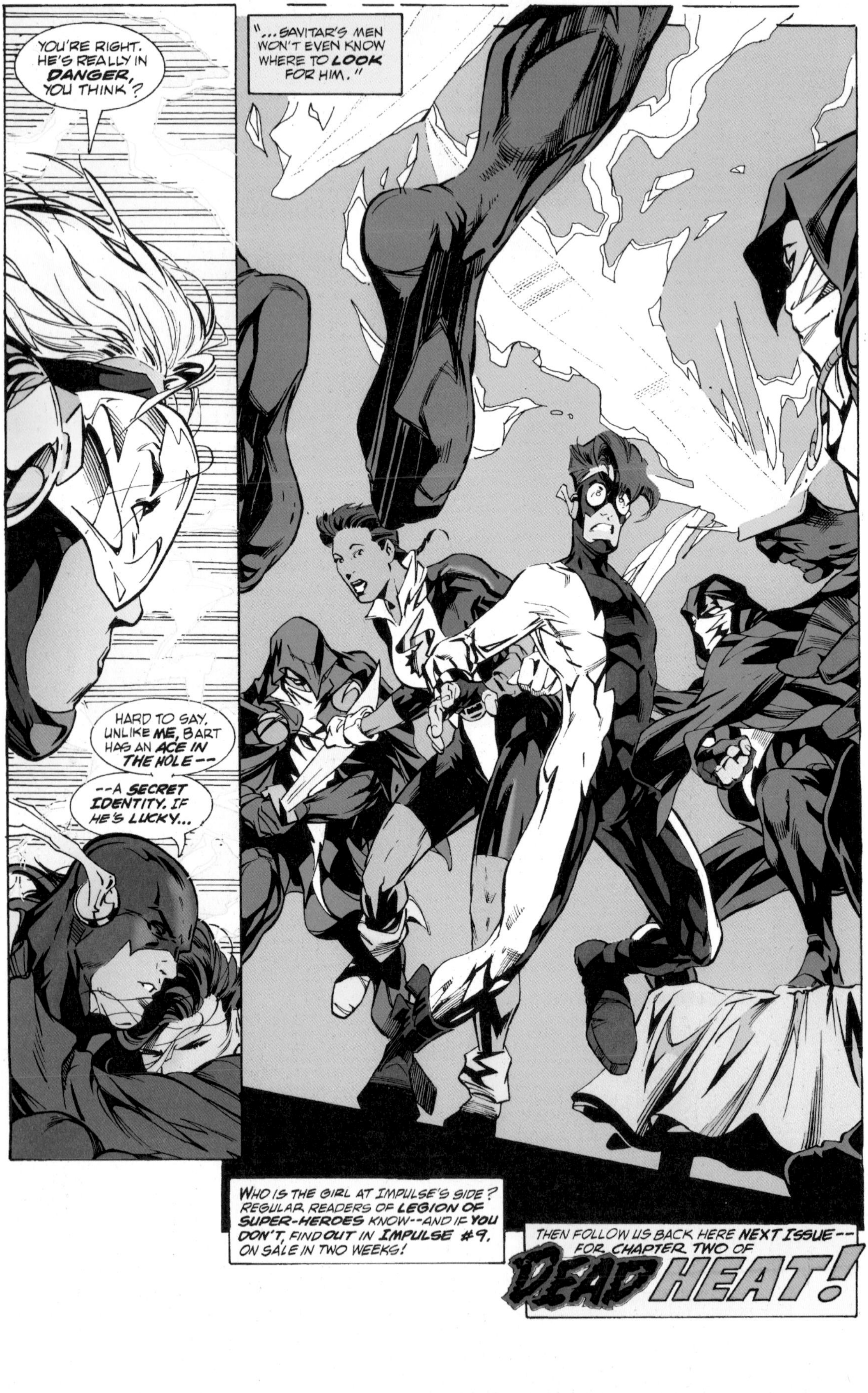
YOU'RE RIGHT. HE'S REALLY IN DANGER, YOU THINK?
HARD TO SAY. UNLIKE ME, BART HAS AN ACE IN THE HOLE--
--A SECRET IDENTITY. IF HE'S LUCKY...
"...SAVITAR'S MEN WON'T EVEN KNOW WHERE TO LOOK FOR HIM."
WHO IS THE GIRL AT IMPULSE'S SIDE? REGULAR READERS OF LEGION OF SUPER-HEROES KNOW--AND IF YOU DON'T, FIND OUT IN IMPULSE #9, ON SALE IN TWO WEEKS!
THEN FOLLOW US BACK HERE NEXT ISSUE--FOR CHAPTER TWO OF
DEAD HEAT!

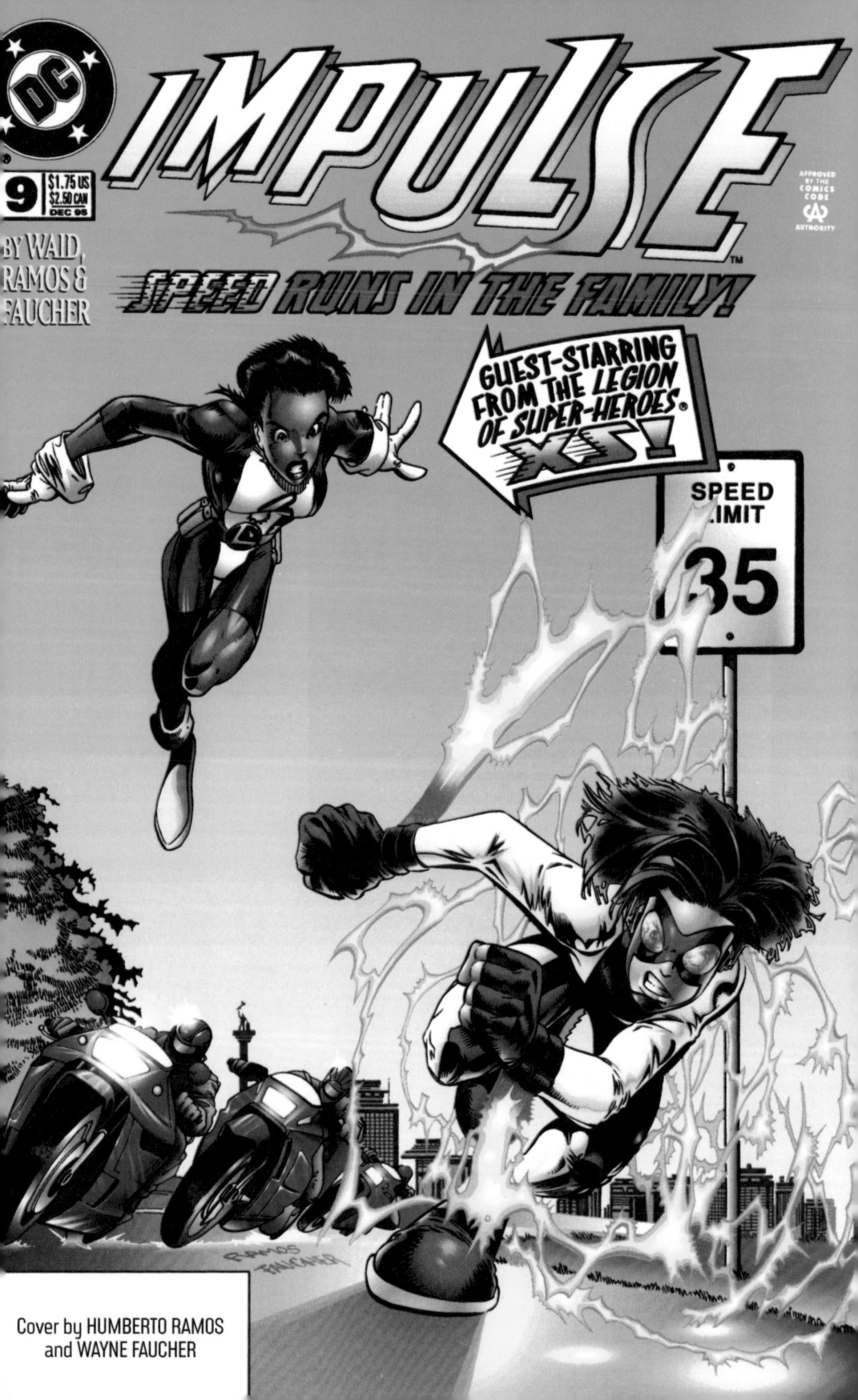
DC
IMPULSE
9
$1.75 US
$2.50 CAN
DEC 95
BY WAID, RAMOS & FAUCHER
APPROVED BY THE COMICS CODE AUTHORITY
SPEED RUNS IN THE FAMILY!
GUEST-STARRING FROM THE LEGION OF SUPER-HEROES® XS!
SPEED
35
RAMOS FAUCHER

Cover by HUMBERTO RAMOS and WAYNE FAUCHER

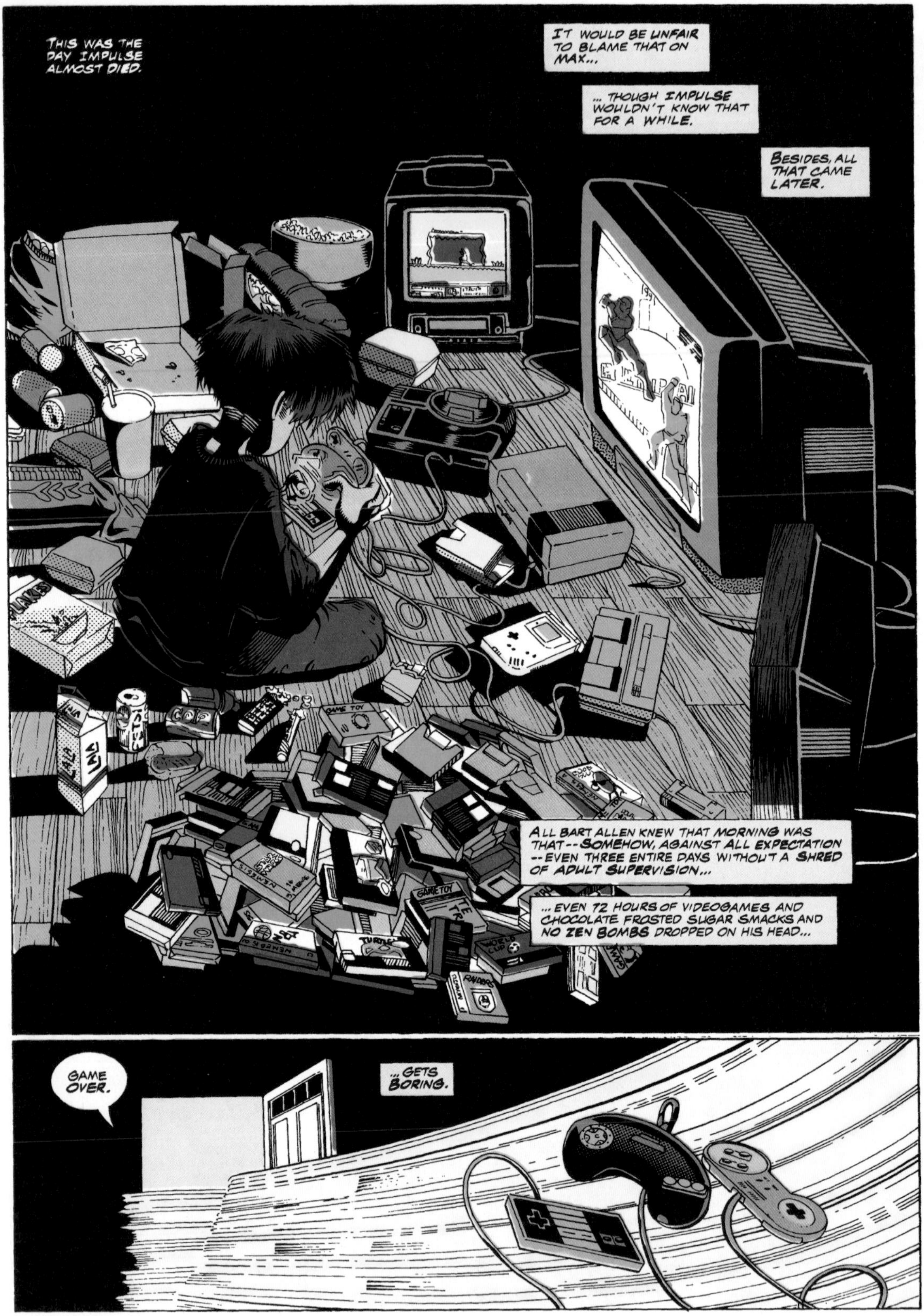
THIS WAS THE DAY IMPULSE ALMOST DIED.
IT WOULD BE UNFAIR TO BLAME THAT ON MAX...
... THOUGH IMPULSE WOULDN'T KNOW THAT FOR A WHILE.
BESIDES, ALL THAT CAME LATER.
ALL BART ALLEN KNEW THAT MORNING WAS THAT--SOMEHOW, AGAINST ALL EXPECTATION --EVEN THREE ENTIRE DAYS WITHOUT A SHRED OF ADULT SUPERVISION...
...EVEN 72 HOURS OF VIDEOGAMES AND CHOCOLATE FROSTED SUGAR SMACKS AND NO ZEN BOMBS DROPPED ON HIS HEAD...
GAME OVER.
...GETS BORING.

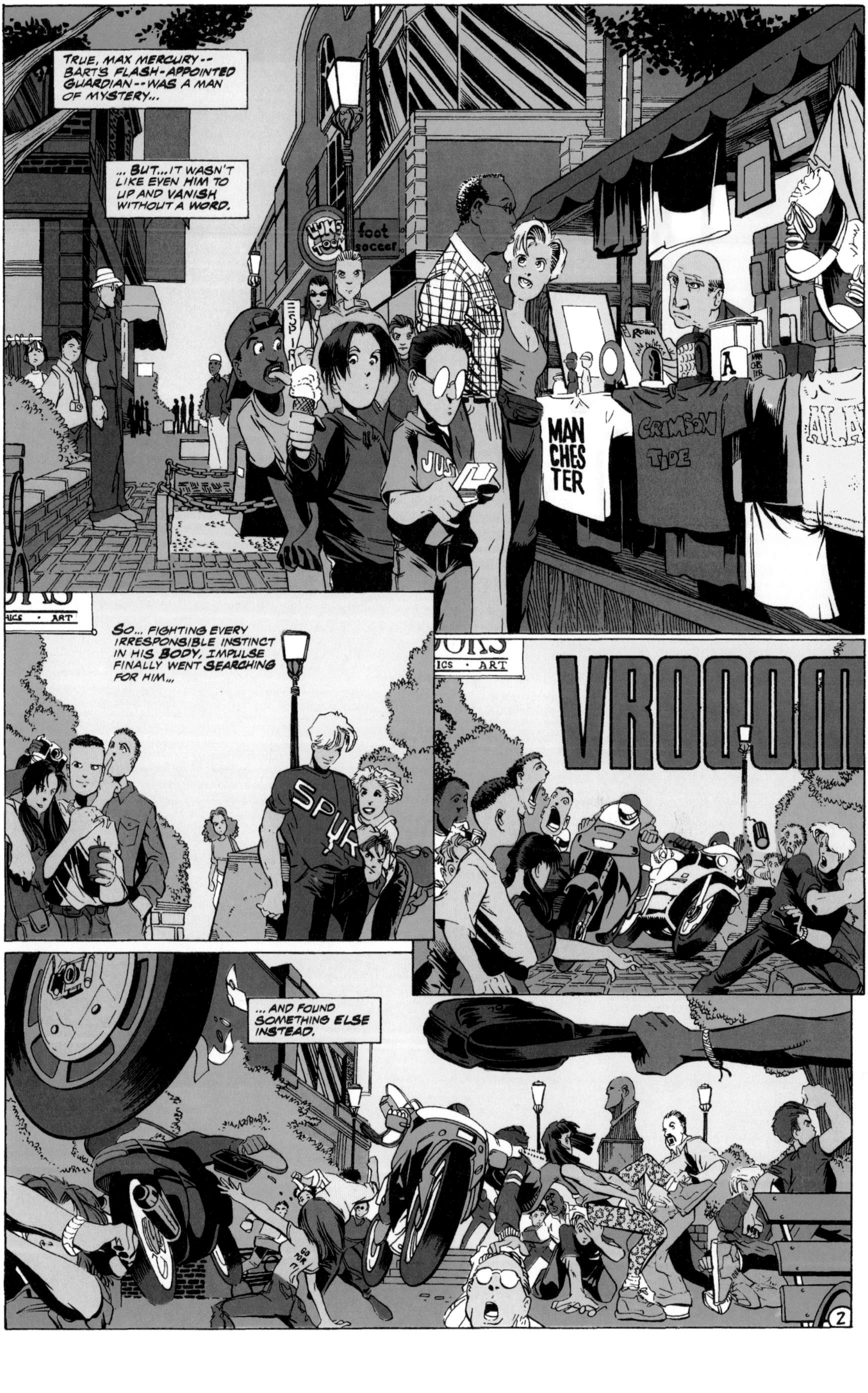

TRUE, MAX MERCURY--BART'S FLASH-APPOINTED GUARDIAN--WAS A MAN OF MYSTERY...
...BUT...IT WASN'T LIKE EVEN HIM TO UP AND VANISH WITHOUT A WORD.
foot soccer
MAN CHES TER
CRIMSON TIDE
SO... FIGHTING EVERY IRRESPONSIBLE INSTINCT IN HIS BODY, IMPULSE FINALLY WENT SEARCHING FOR HIM...
VROOOM
...AND FOUND SOMETHING ELSE INSTEAD.

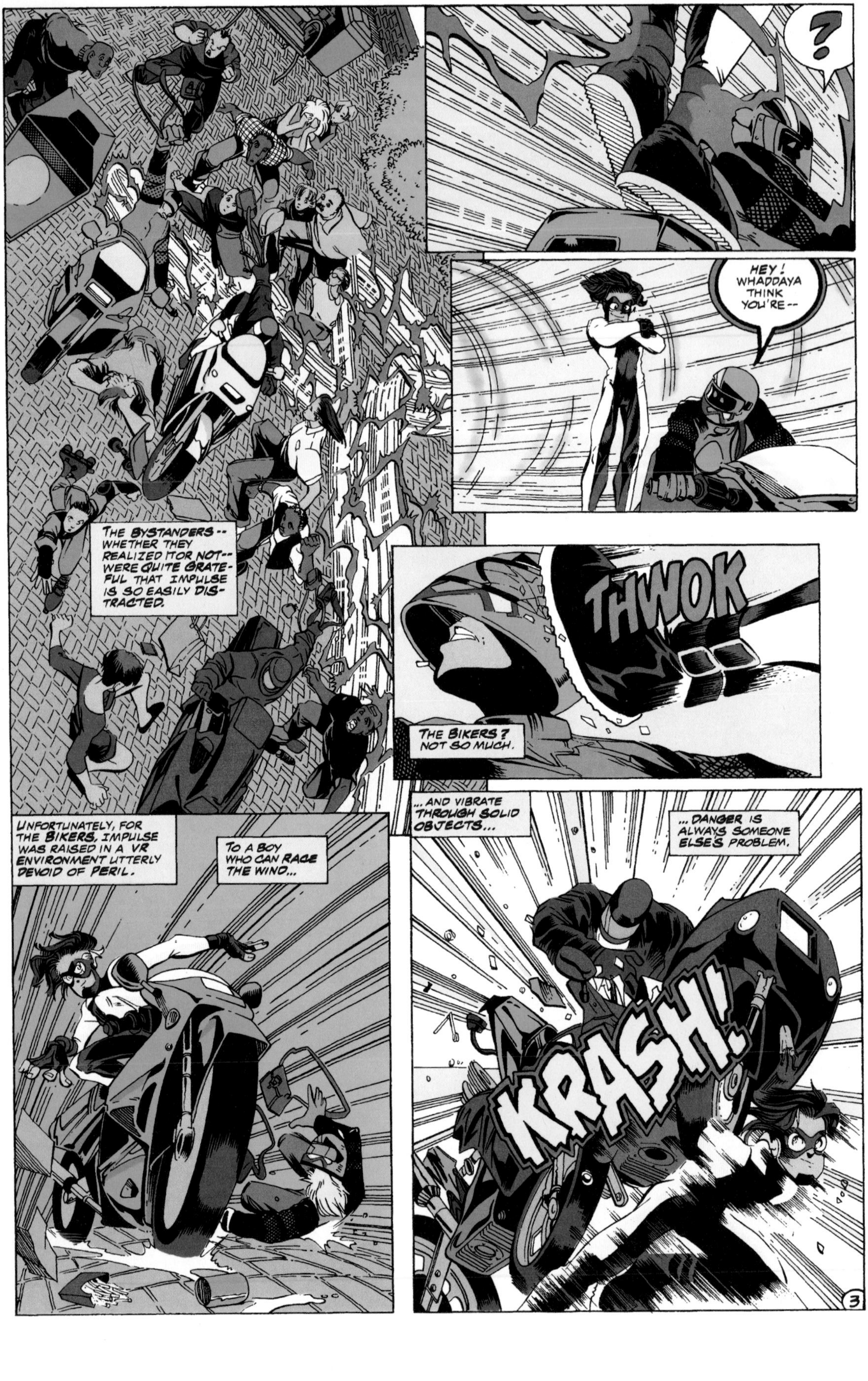
?
THE BYSTANDERS -- WHETHER THEY REALIZED IT OR NOT-- WERE QUITE GRATEFUL THAT IMPULSE IS SO EASILY DISTRACTED.
HEY! WHADDAYA THINK YOU'RE--
THWOK
THE BIKERS? NOT SO MUCH.
UNFORTUNATELY, FOR THE BIKERS, IMPULSE WAS RAISED IN A VR ENVIRONMENT UTTERLY DEVOID OF PERIL.
TO A BOY WHO CAN RACE THE WIND...
...AND VIBRATE THROUGH SOLID OBJECTS...
...DANGER IS ALWAYS SOMEONE ELSE'S PROBLEM.
KRASH!
3

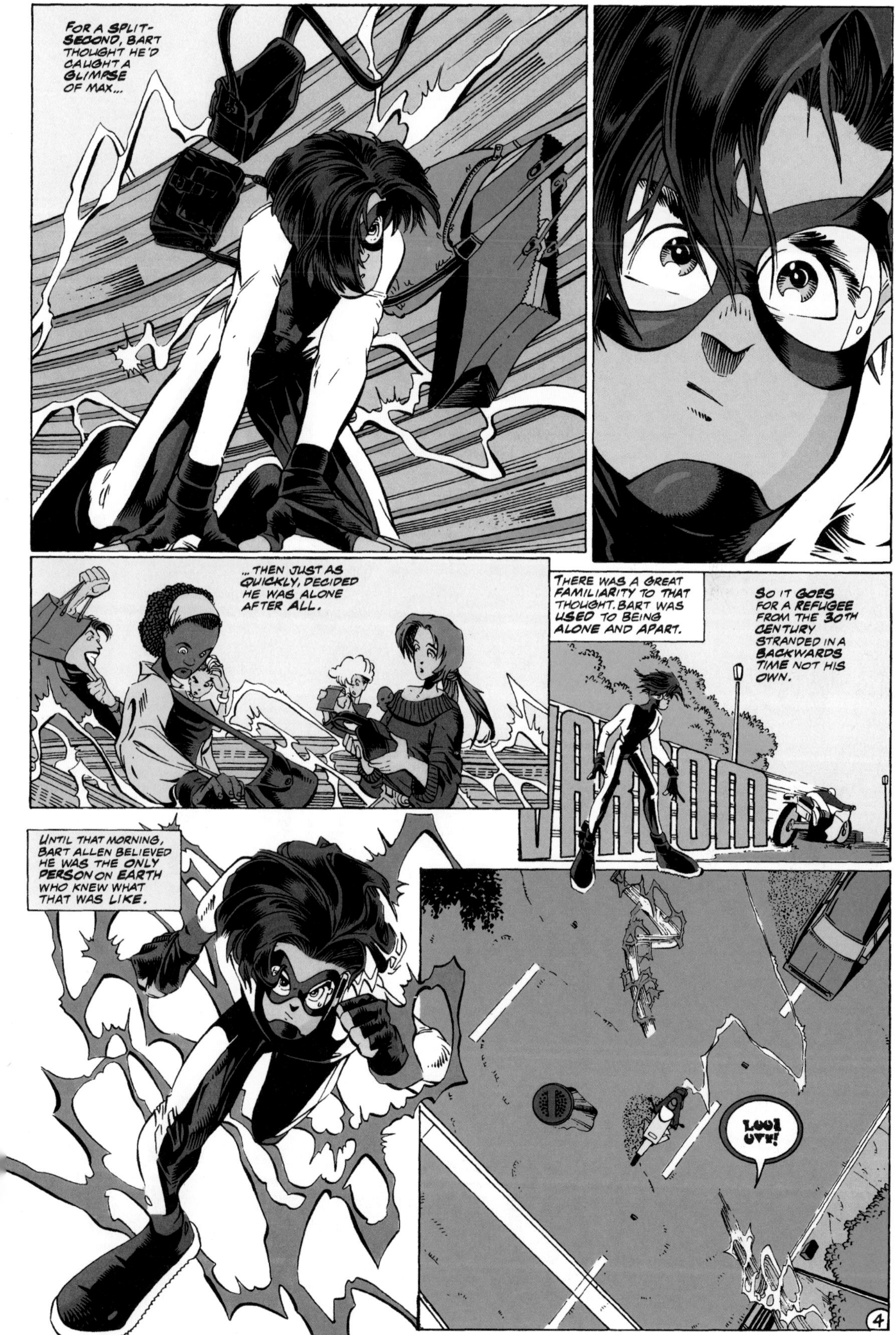
FOR A SPLIT-SECOND, BART THOUGHT HE'D CAUGHT A GLIMPSE OF MAX...
...THEN JUST AS QUICKLY, DECIDED HE WAS ALONE AFTER ALL.
THERE WAS A GREAT FAMILIARITY TO THAT THOUGHT. BART WAS USED TO BEING ALONE AND APART.
SO IT GOES FOR A REFUGEE FROM THE 30TH CENTURY STRANDED IN A BACKWARDS TIME NOT HIS OWN.
UNTIL THAT MORNING, BART ALLEN BELIEVED HE WAS THE ONLY PERSON ON EARTH WHO KNEW WHAT THAT WAS LIKE.

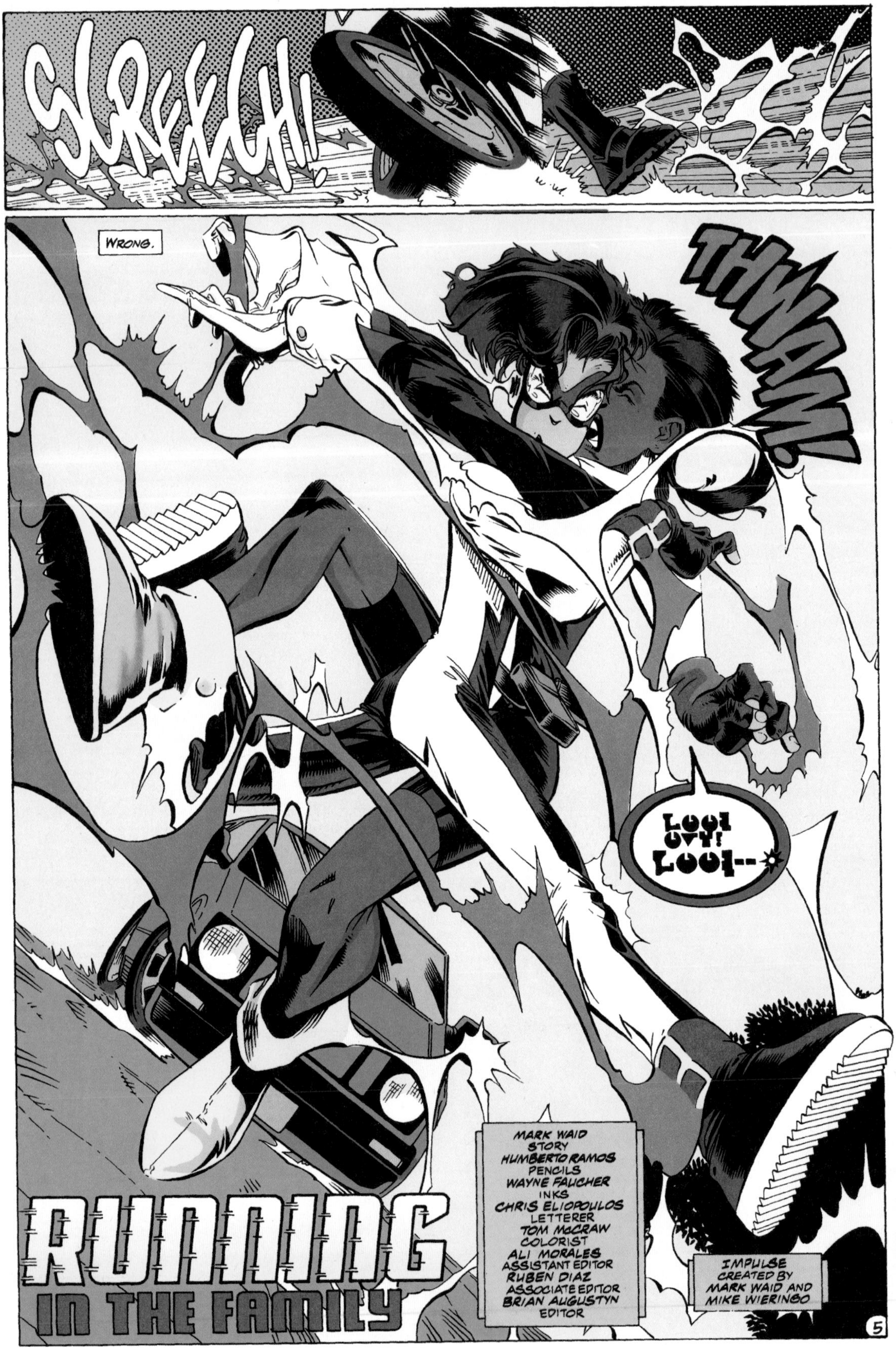
SKREECH!
WRONG.
THWAM!
LOOK OUT! LOOK--
RUNNING IN THE FAMILY
MARK WAID STORY
HUMBERTO RAMOS PENCILS
WAYNE FAUCHER INKS
CHRIS ELIOPOULOS LETTERER
TOM McCRAW COLORIST
ALI MORALES ASSISTANT EDITOR
RUBEN DIAZ ASSOCIATE EDITOR
BRIAN AUGUSTYN EDITOR
IMPULSE CREATED BY MARK WAID AND MIKE WIERINGO

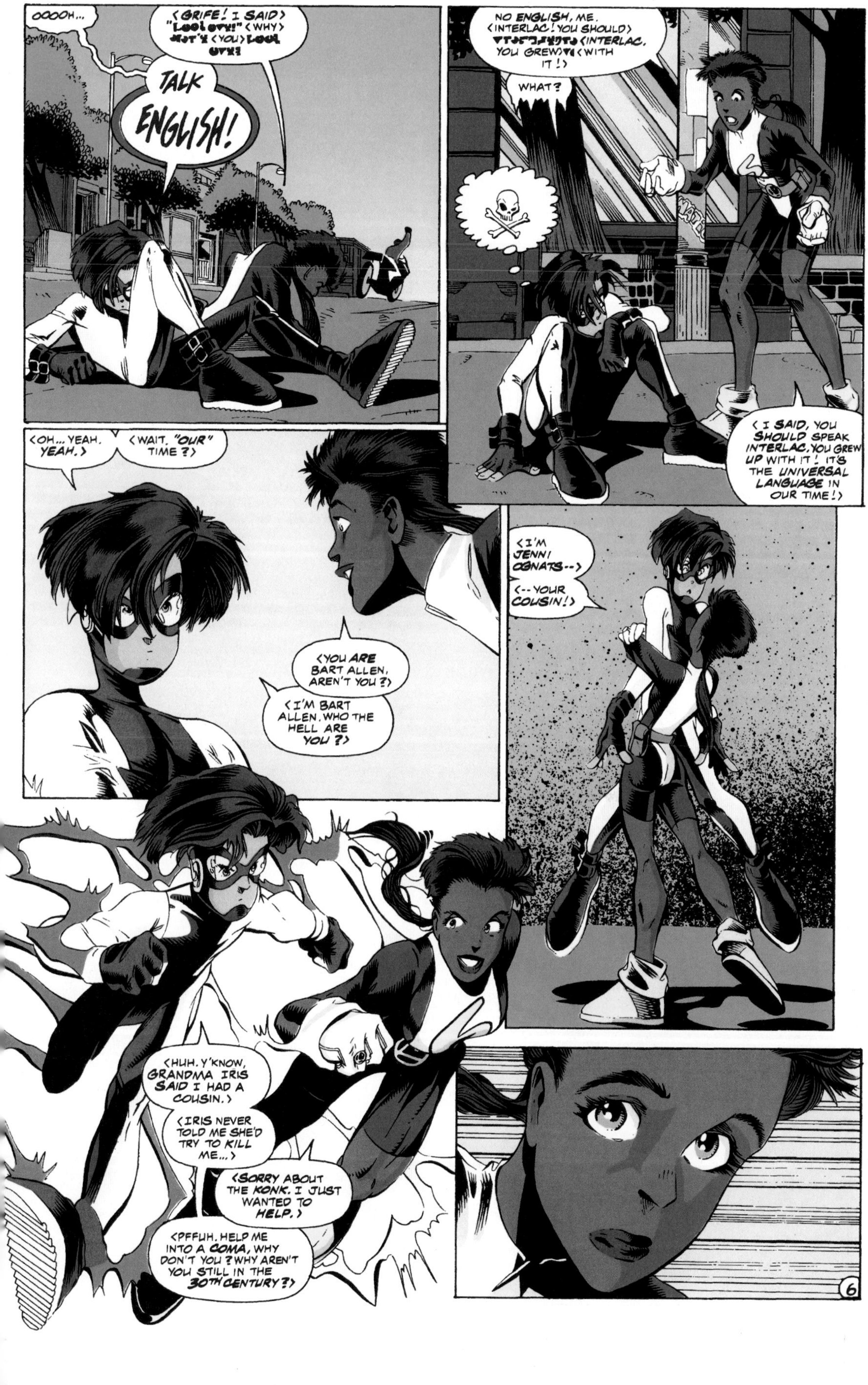
OOOOH...
<GRIFE! I SAID> <WHY> <YOU>
TALK ENGLISH!
NO ENGLISH, ME. <INTERLAC! YOU SHOULD> <INTERLAC, YOU GREW> <WITH IT!>
WHAT?
<I SAID, YOU SHOULD SPEAK INTERLAC. YOU GREW UP WITH IT! IT'S THE UNIVERSAL LANGUAGE IN OUR TIME!>
<OH... YEAH. YEAH.>
<WAIT. "OUR" TIME?>
<YOU ARE BART ALLEN, AREN'T YOU?>
<I'M BART ALLEN. WHO THE HELL ARE YOU?>
<I'M JENNI OGNATS-->
<--YOUR COUSIN!>
<HUH. Y'KNOW, GRANDMA IRIS SAID I HAD A COUSIN.>
<IRIS NEVER TOLD ME SHE'D TRY TO KILL ME...>
<SORRY ABOUT THE KONK. I JUST WANTED TO HELP.>
<PFFUH. HELP ME INTO A COMA, WHY DON'T YOU? WHY AREN'T YOU STILL IN THE 30TH CENTURY?>

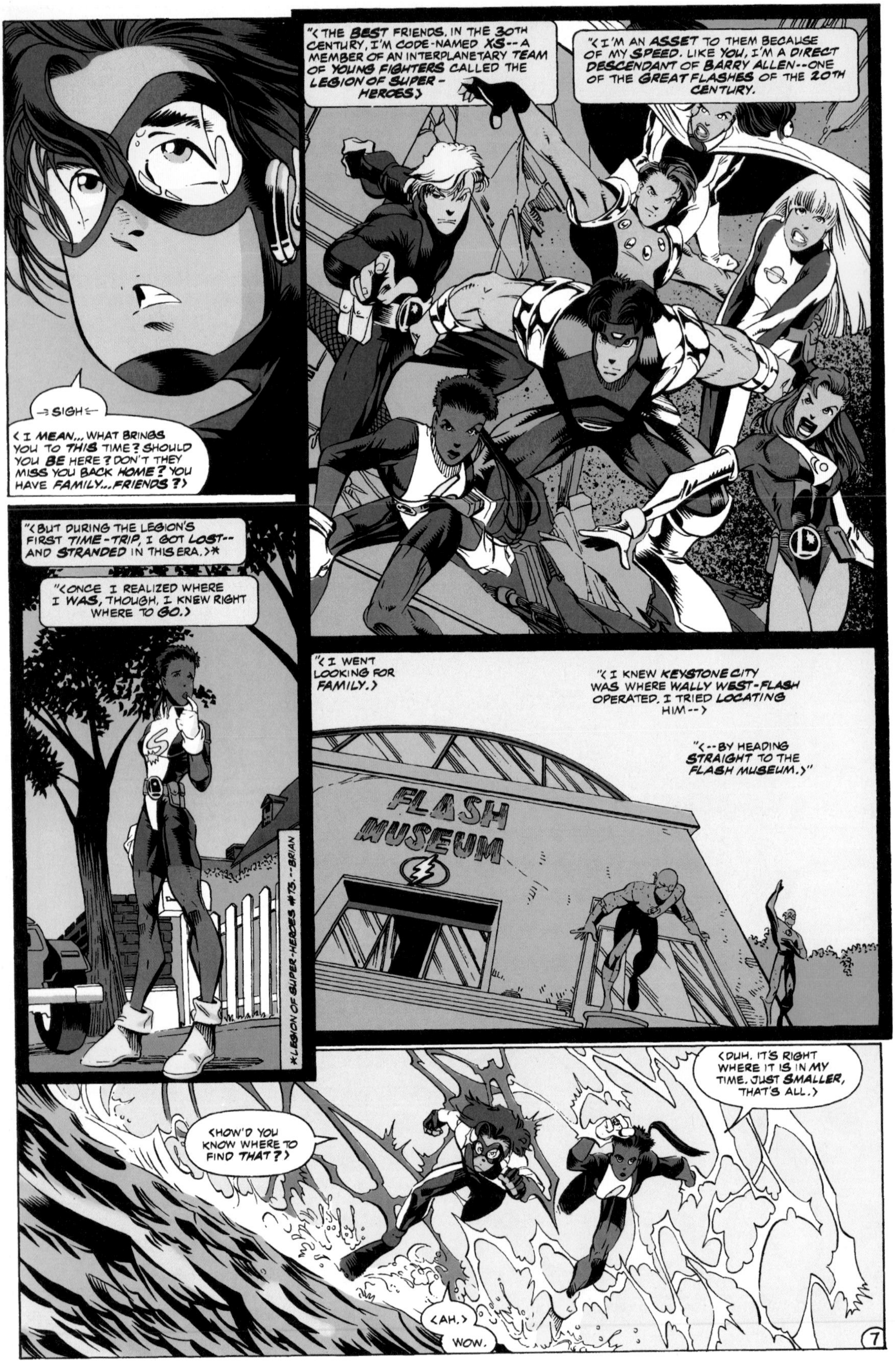

—SIGH—
< I MEAN... WHAT BRINGS YOU TO THIS TIME? SHOULD YOU BE HERE? DON'T THEY MISS YOU BACK HOME? YOU HAVE FAMILY... FRIENDS? >
"< THE BEST FRIENDS. IN THE 30TH CENTURY, I'M CODE-NAMED XS-- A MEMBER OF AN INTERPLANETARY TEAM OF YOUNG FIGHTERS CALLED THE LEGION OF SUPER-HEROES. >
"< I'M AN ASSET TO THEM BECAUSE OF MY SPEED. LIKE YOU, I'M A DIRECT DESCENDANT OF BARRY ALLEN--ONE OF THE GREAT FLASHES OF THE 20TH CENTURY.
"< BUT DURING THE LEGION'S FIRST TIME-TRIP, I GOT LOST-- AND STRANDED IN THIS ERA. >*
"< ONCE I REALIZED WHERE I WAS, THOUGH, I KNEW RIGHT WHERE TO GO. >
*LEGION OF SUPER-HEROES #73. --BRIAN
"< I WENT LOOKING FOR FAMILY. >
"< I KNEW KEYSTONE CITY WAS WHERE WALLY WEST-FLASH OPERATED. I TRIED LOCATING HIM-- >
"< --BY HEADING STRAIGHT TO THE FLASH MUSEUM. >"
FLASH MUSEUM
< HOW'D YOU KNOW WHERE TO FIND THAT? >
< DUH. IT'S RIGHT WHERE IT IS IN MY TIME. JUST SMALLER, THAT'S ALL. >
< AH. >
WOW.

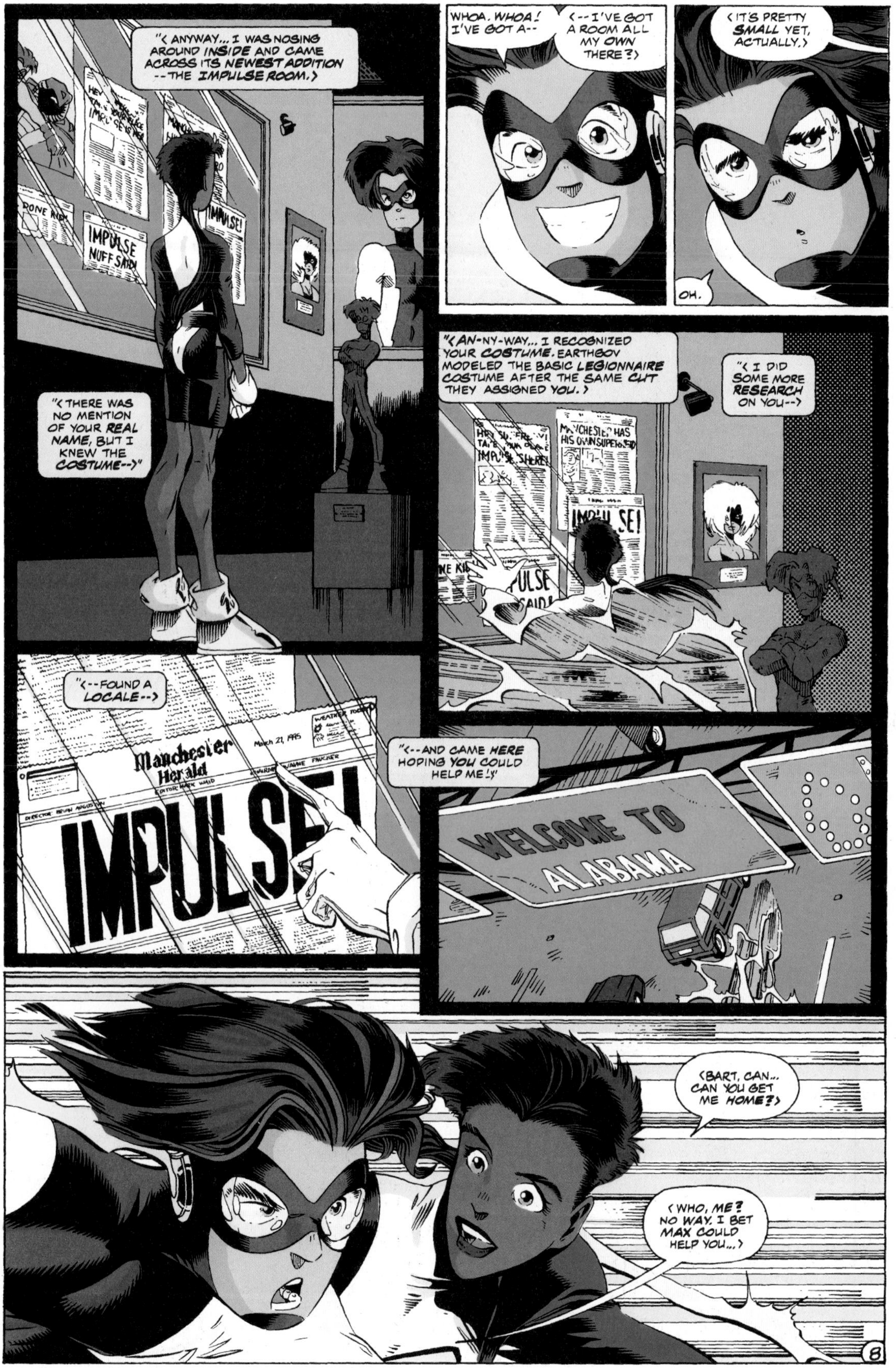

"< ANYWAY... I WAS NOSING AROUND INSIDE AND CAME ACROSS ITS NEWEST ADDITION --THE IMPULSE ROOM. >
IMPULSE NUFF SAID!
IMPULSE!
"< THERE WAS NO MENTION OF YOUR REAL NAME, BUT I KNEW THE COSTUME-- >"
WHOA. WHOA! I'VE GOT A--
< --I'VE GOT A ROOM ALL MY OWN THERE? >
< IT'S PRETTY SMALL YET, ACTUALLY. >
OH.
"< AN-NY-WAY... I RECOGNIZED YOUR COSTUME. EARTHGOV MODELED THE BASIC LEGIONNAIRE COSTUME AFTER THE SAME CUT THEY ASSIGNED YOU. >
"< I DID SOME MORE RESEARCH ON YOU-- >
MANCHESTER HAS HIS OWN SUPERHERO
"< --FOUND A LOCALE-- >
Manchester Herald
March 21, 1995
IMPULSE!
"< --AND CAME HERE HOPING YOU COULD HELP ME! >"
WELCOME TO ALABAMA
< BART, CAN... CAN YOU GET ME HOME? >
< WHO, ME? NO WAY. I BET MAX COULD HELP YOU... >

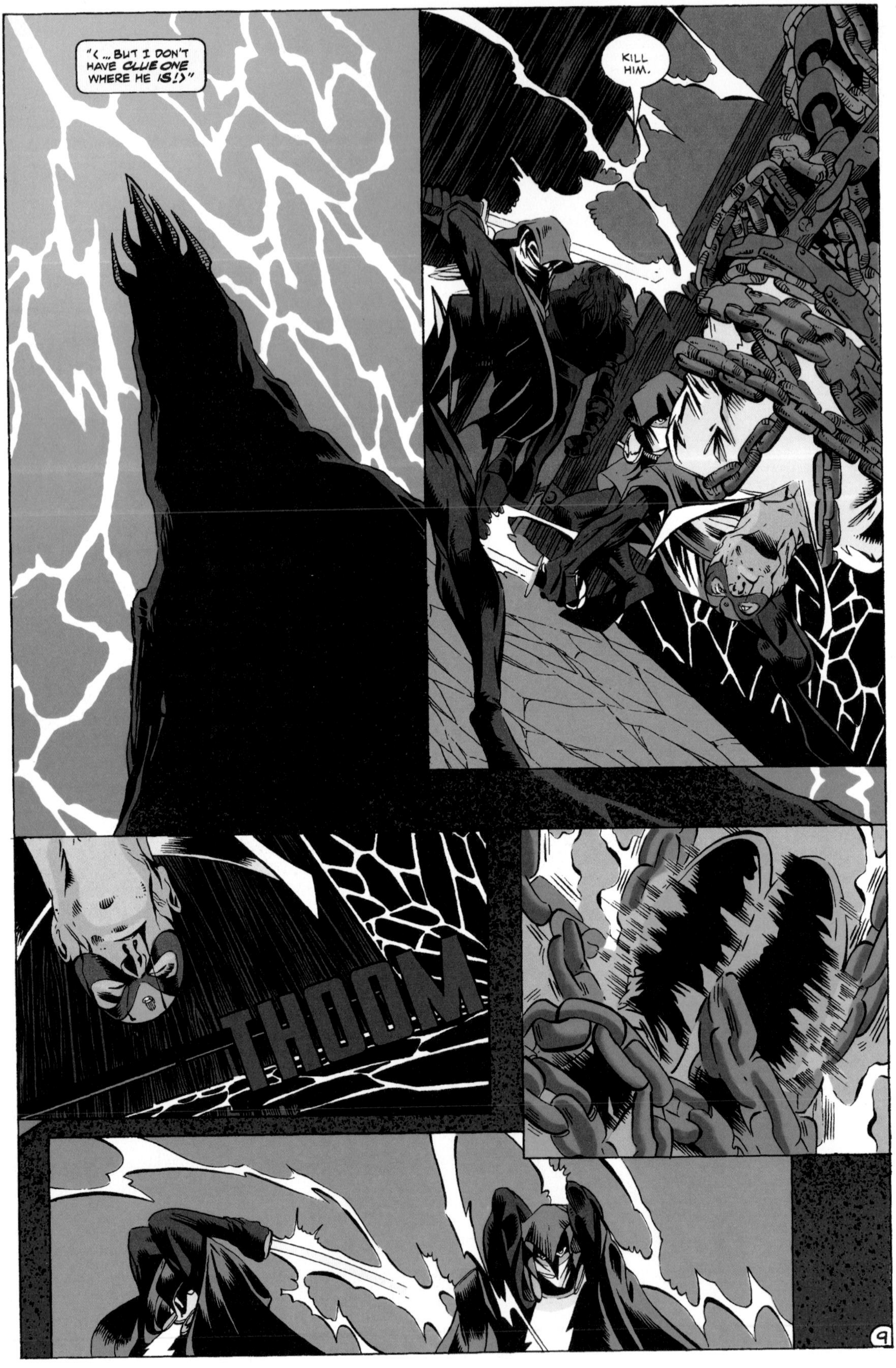
"< ... BUT I DON'T HAVE CLUE ONE WHERE HE IS!>"
KILL HIM.
THOOM

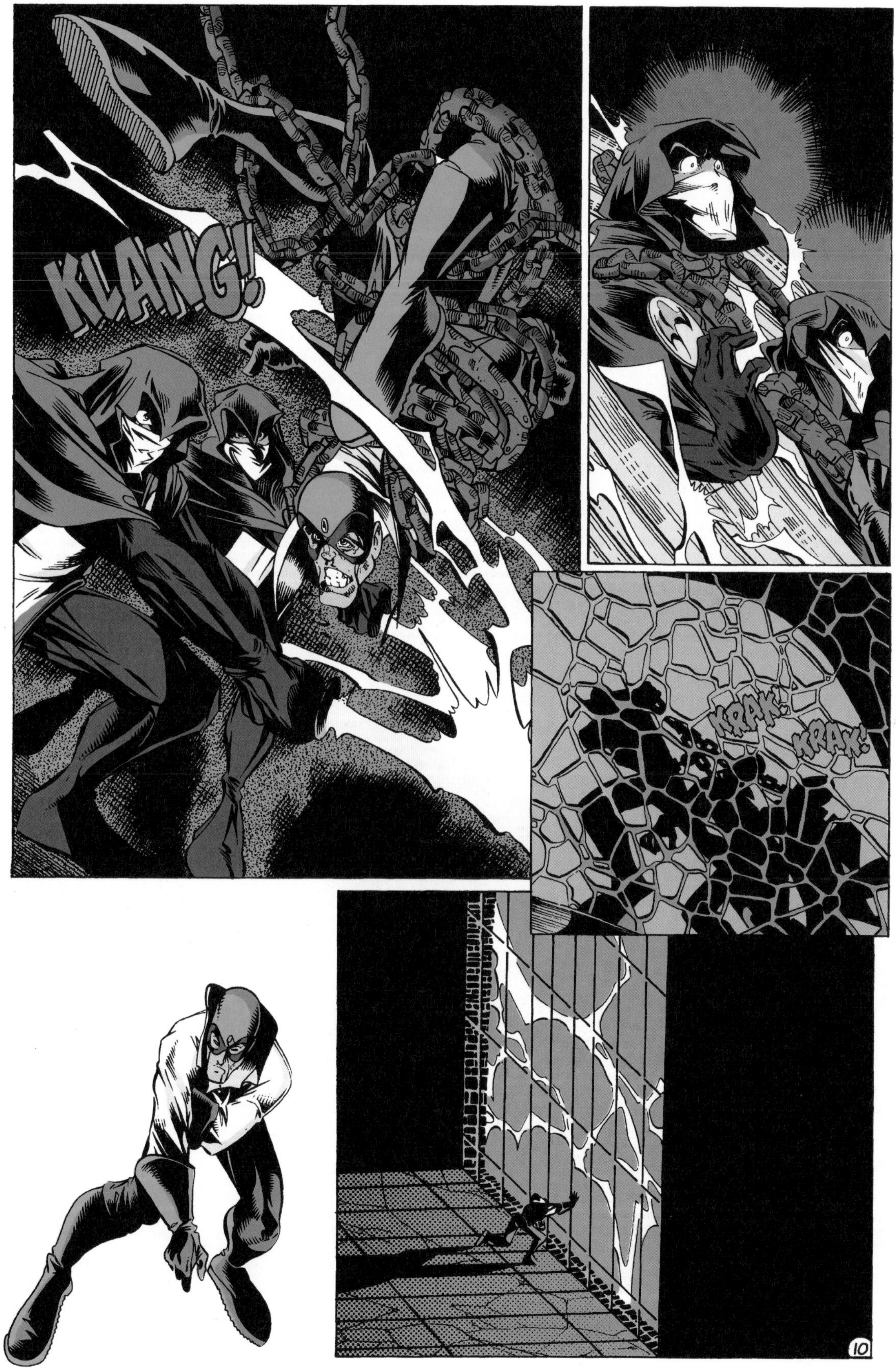
KLANG!
KRAK!
KRAK!

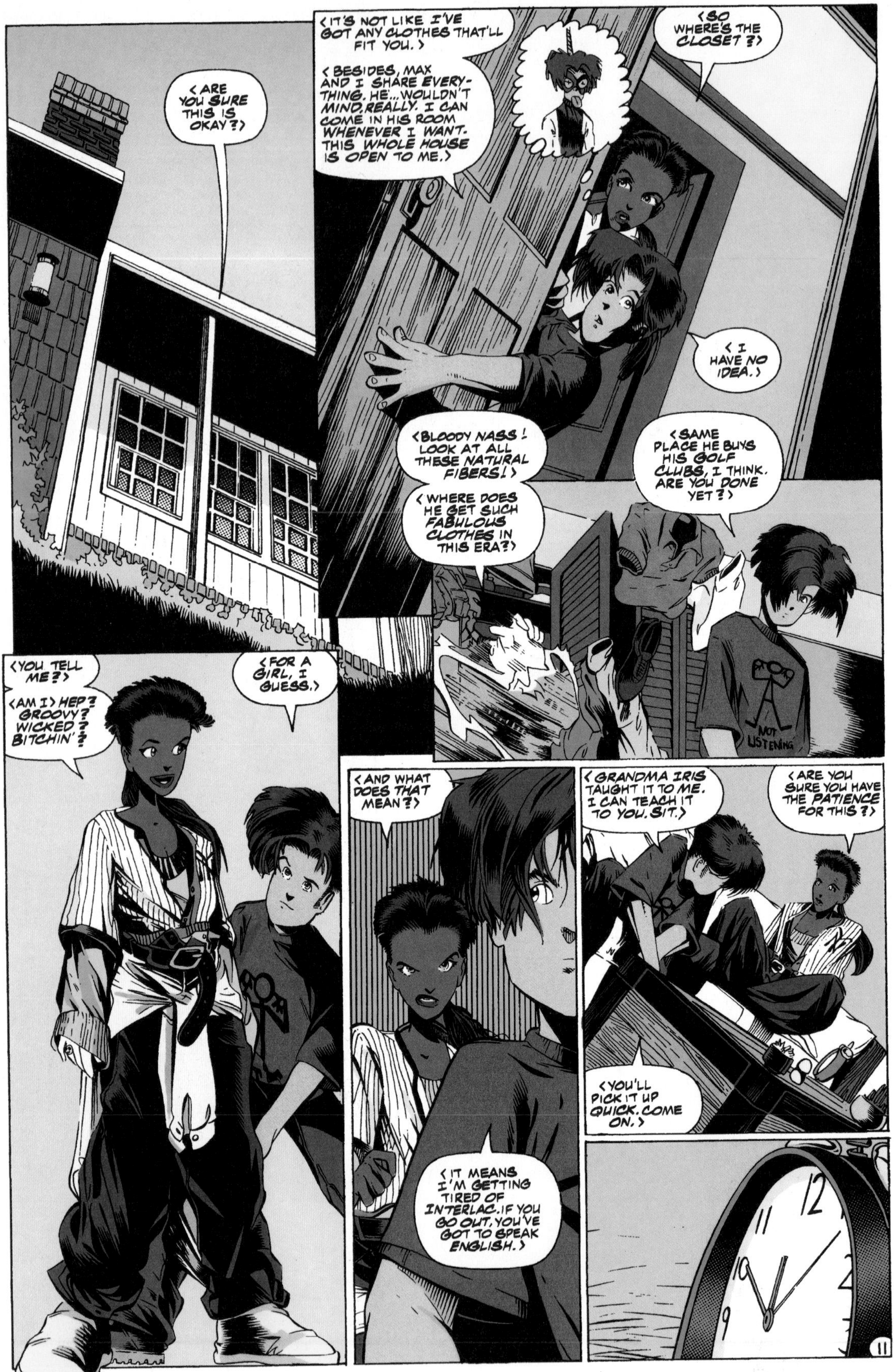

<ARE YOU SURE THIS IS OKAY?>
<IT'S NOT LIKE I'VE GOT ANY CLOTHES THAT'LL FIT YOU.>
<BESIDES, MAX AND I SHARE EVERYTHING. HE... WOULDN'T MIND, REALLY. I CAN COME IN HIS ROOM WHENEVER I WANT. THIS WHOLE HOUSE IS OPEN TO ME.>
<SO WHERE'S THE CLOSET?>
<I HAVE NO IDEA.>
<BLOODY NASS! LOOK AT ALL THESE NATURAL FIBERS!>
<WHERE DOES HE GET SUCH FABULOUS CLOTHES IN THIS ERA?>
<SAME PLACE HE BUYS HIS GOLF CLUBS, I THINK. ARE YOU DONE YET?>
NOT LISTENING
<YOU TELL ME?>
<AM I> HEP? GROOVY? WICKED? BITCHIN'?
<FOR A GIRL, I GUESS.>
<AND WHAT DOES THAT MEAN?>
<IT MEANS I'M GETTING TIRED OF INTERLAC. IF YOU GO OUT, YOU'VE GOT TO SPEAK ENGLISH.>
<GRANDMA IRIS TAUGHT IT TO ME. I CAN TEACH IT TO YOU. SIT.>
<ARE YOU SURE YOU HAVE THE PATIENCE FOR THIS?>
<YOU'LL PICK IT UP QUICK. COME ON.>

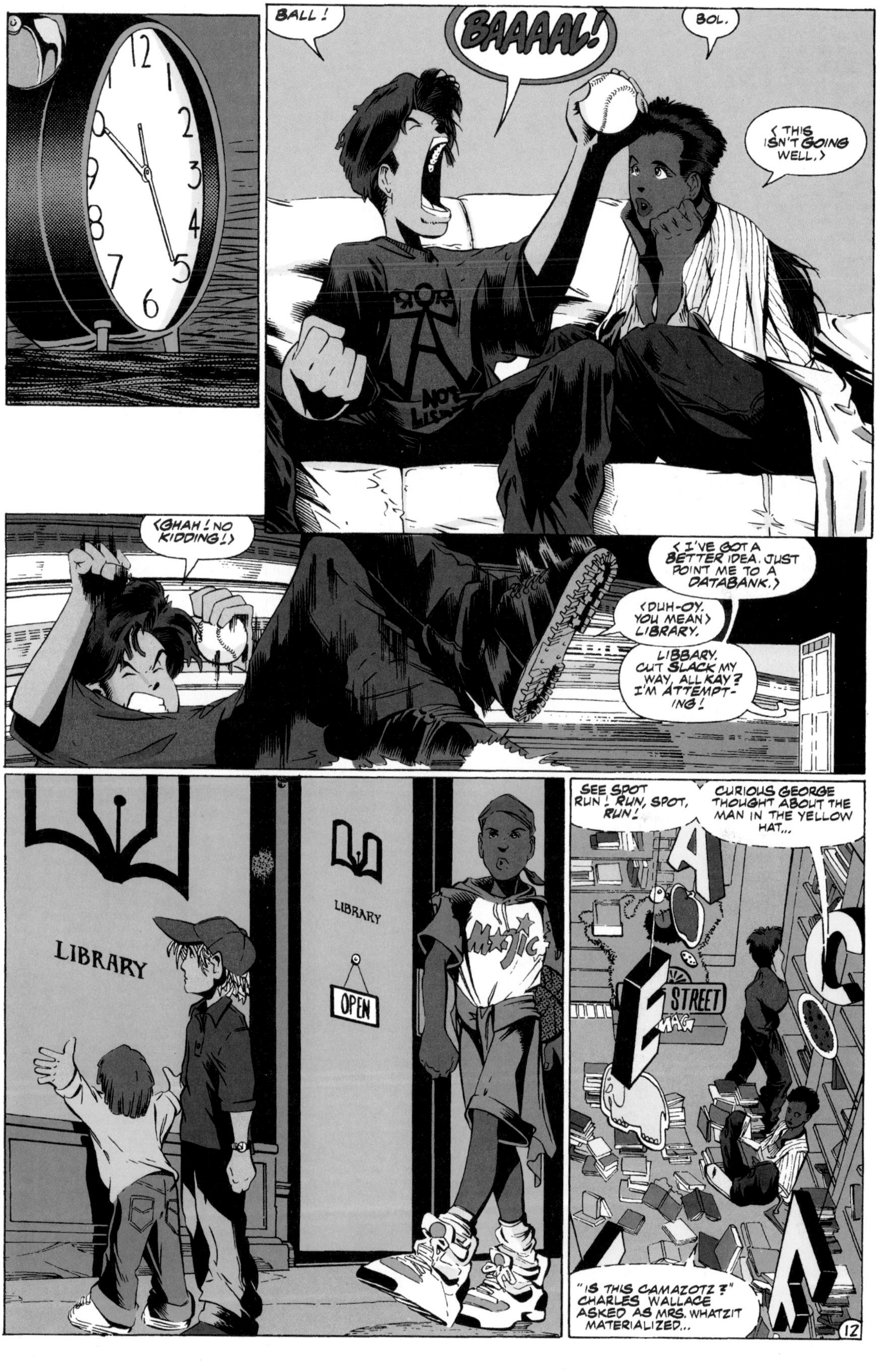
BALL!
BAAAAL!
BOL.
‹ THIS ISN'T GOING WELL. ›
‹GHAH! NO KIDDING!›
‹ I'VE GOT A BETTER IDEA. JUST POINT ME TO A DATABANK. ›
‹DUH-OY. YOU MEAN› LIBRARY.
LIBBARY. CUT SLACK MY WAY, ALL KAY? I'M ATTEMPT-ING!
LIBRARY
LIBRARY
OPEN
SEE SPOT RUN! RUN, SPOT, RUN!
CURIOUS GEORGE THOUGHT ABOUT THE MAN IN THE YELLOW HAT...
STREET
"IS THIS CAMAZOTZ?" CHARLES WALLACE ASKED AS MRS. WHATZIT MATERIALIZED...

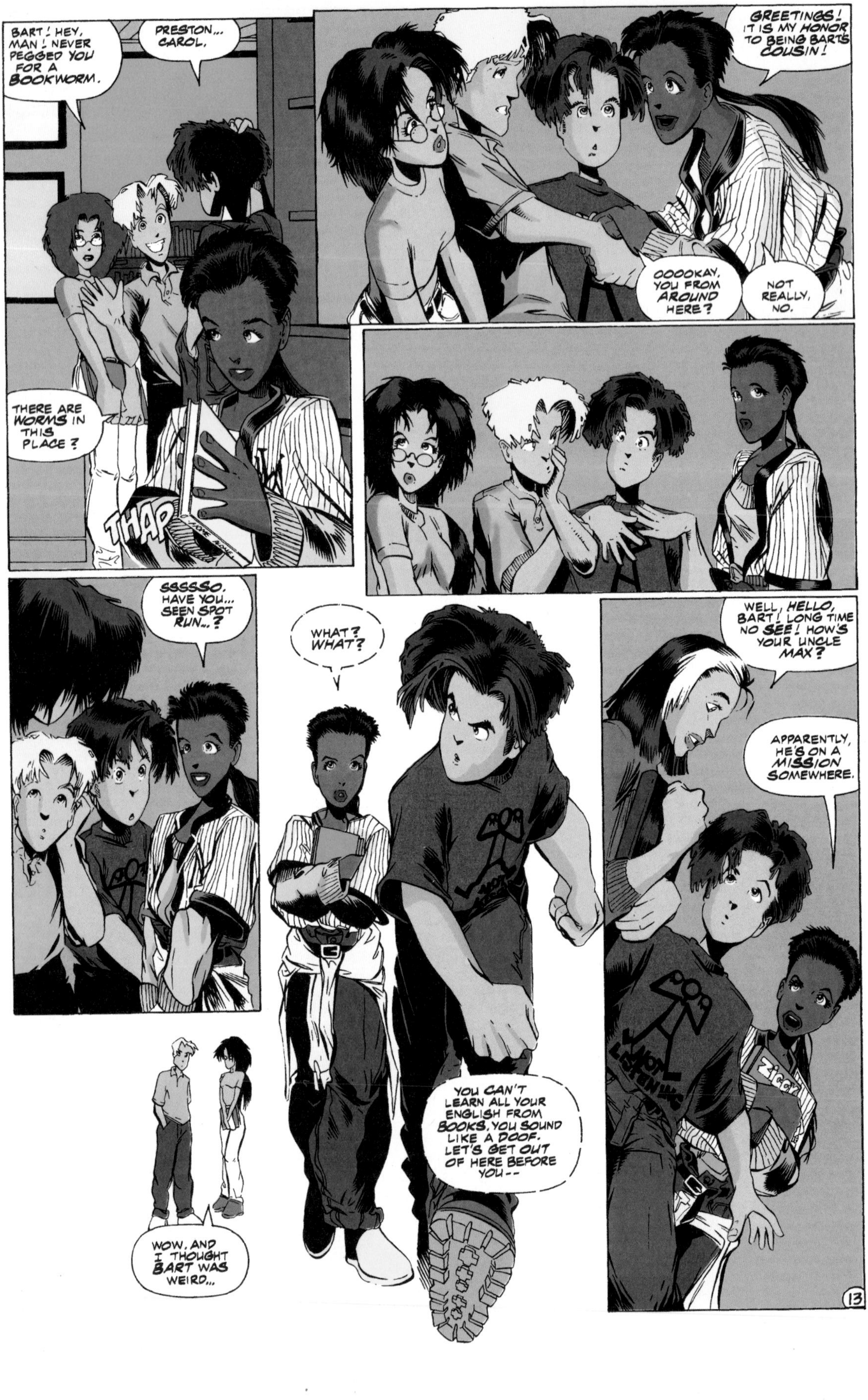
BART! HEY, MAN! NEVER PEGGED YOU FOR A BOOKWORM.
PRESTON... CAROL.
GREETINGS! IT IS MY HONOR TO BEING BART'S COUSIN!
OOOOKAY, YOU FROM AROUND HERE?
NOT REALLY, NO.
THERE ARE WORMS IN THIS PLACE?
THAP
SSSSSO. HAVE YOU... SEEN SPOT RUN...?
WHAT? WHAT?
WELL, HELLO, BART! LONG TIME NO SEE! HOW'S YOUR UNCLE MAX?
APPARENTLY, HE'S ON A MISSION SOMEWHERE.
YOU CAN'T LEARN ALL YOUR ENGLISH FROM BOOKS. YOU SOUND LIKE A DOOF. LET'S GET OUT OF HERE BEFORE YOU--
WOW. AND I THOUGHT BART WAS WEIRD...
ZIGGY

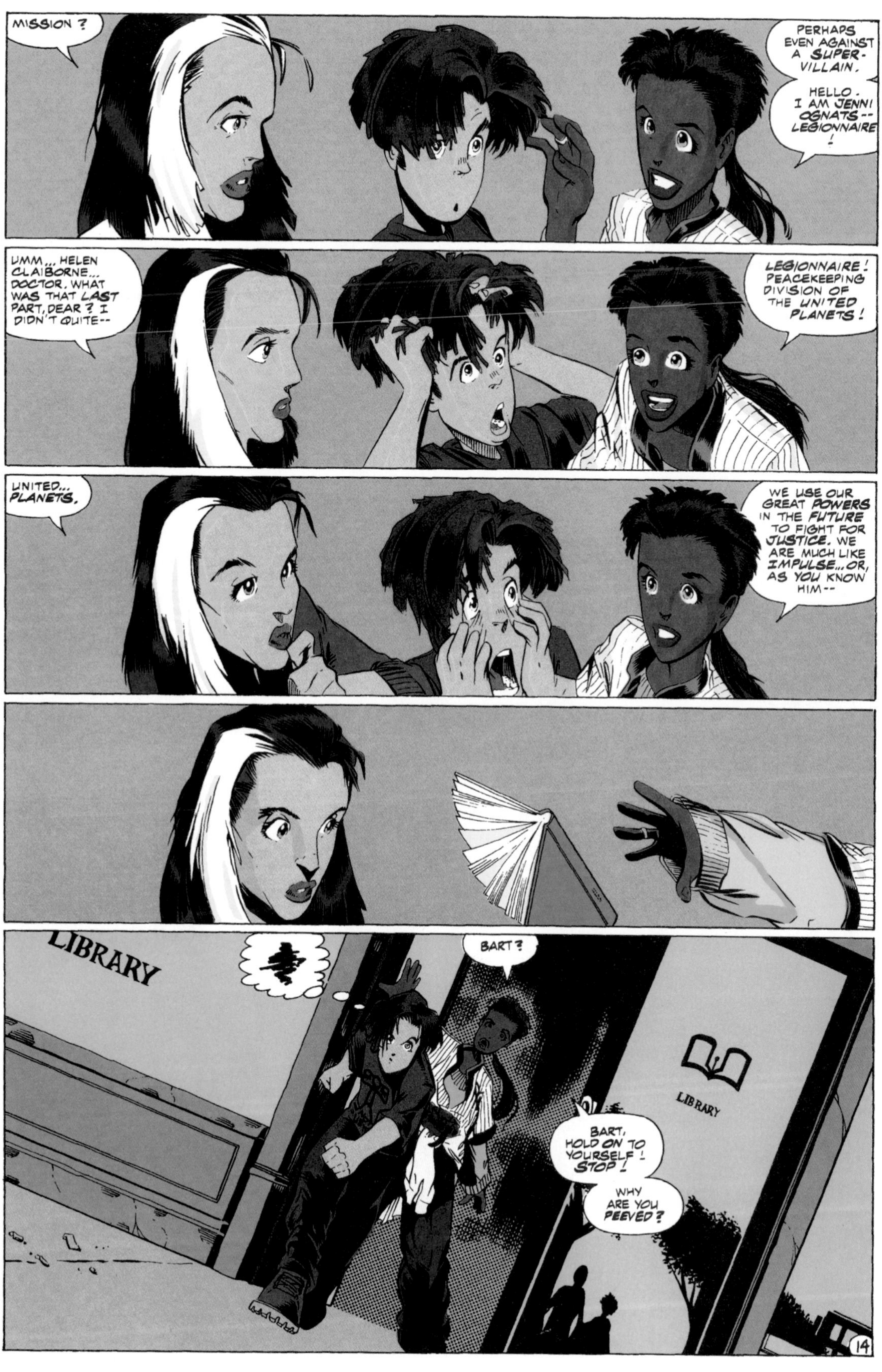
MISSION ?
PERHAPS EVEN AGAINST A SUPER-VILLAIN.
HELLO. I AM JENNI OGNATS-- LEGIONNAIRE!
UMM... HELEN CLAIBORNE... DOCTOR. WHAT WAS THAT LAST PART, DEAR? I DIDN'T QUITE--
LEGIONNAIRE! PEACEKEEPING DIVISION OF THE UNITED PLANETS!
UNITED... PLANETS.
WE USE OUR GREAT POWERS IN THE FUTURE TO FIGHT FOR JUSTICE. WE ARE MUCH LIKE IMPULSE... OR, AS YOU KNOW HIM--
LIBRARY
BART?
LIBRARY
BART, HOLD ON TO YOURSELF! STOP!
WHY ARE YOU PEEVED?
14

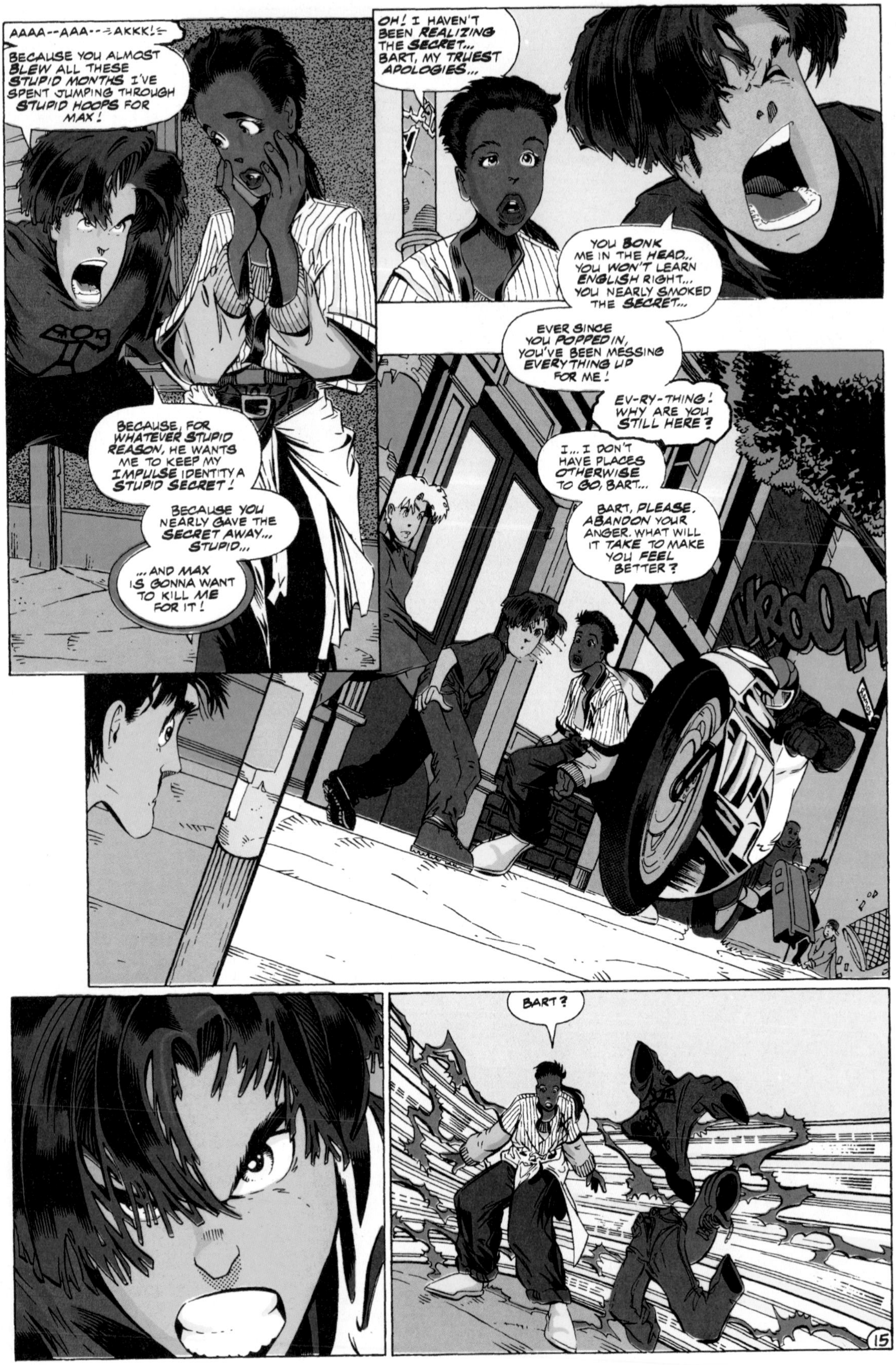
AAAA--AAA--AKKK!
BECAUSE YOU ALMOST BLEW ALL THESE STUPID MONTHS I'VE SPENT JUMPING THROUGH STUPID HOOPS FOR MAX!
BECAUSE, FOR WHATEVER STUPID REASON, HE WANTS ME TO KEEP MY IMPULSE IDENTITY A STUPID SECRET!
BECAUSE YOU NEARLY GAVE THE SECRET AWAY... STUPID...
...AND MAX IS GONNA WANT TO KILL ME FOR IT!
OH! I HAVEN'T BEEN REALIZING THE SECRET... BART, MY TRUEST APOLOGIES...
YOU BONK ME IN THE HEAD... YOU WON'T LEARN ENGLISH RIGHT... YOU NEARLY SMOKED THE SECRET...
EVER SINCE YOU POPPED IN, YOU'VE BEEN MESSING EVERYTHING UP FOR ME!
EV-RY-THING! WHY ARE YOU STILL HERE?
I... I DON'T HAVE PLACES OTHERWISE TO GO, BART...
BART, PLEASE. ABANDON YOUR ANGER. WHAT WILL IT TAKE TO MAKE YOU FEEL BETTER?
VROOM
BART?

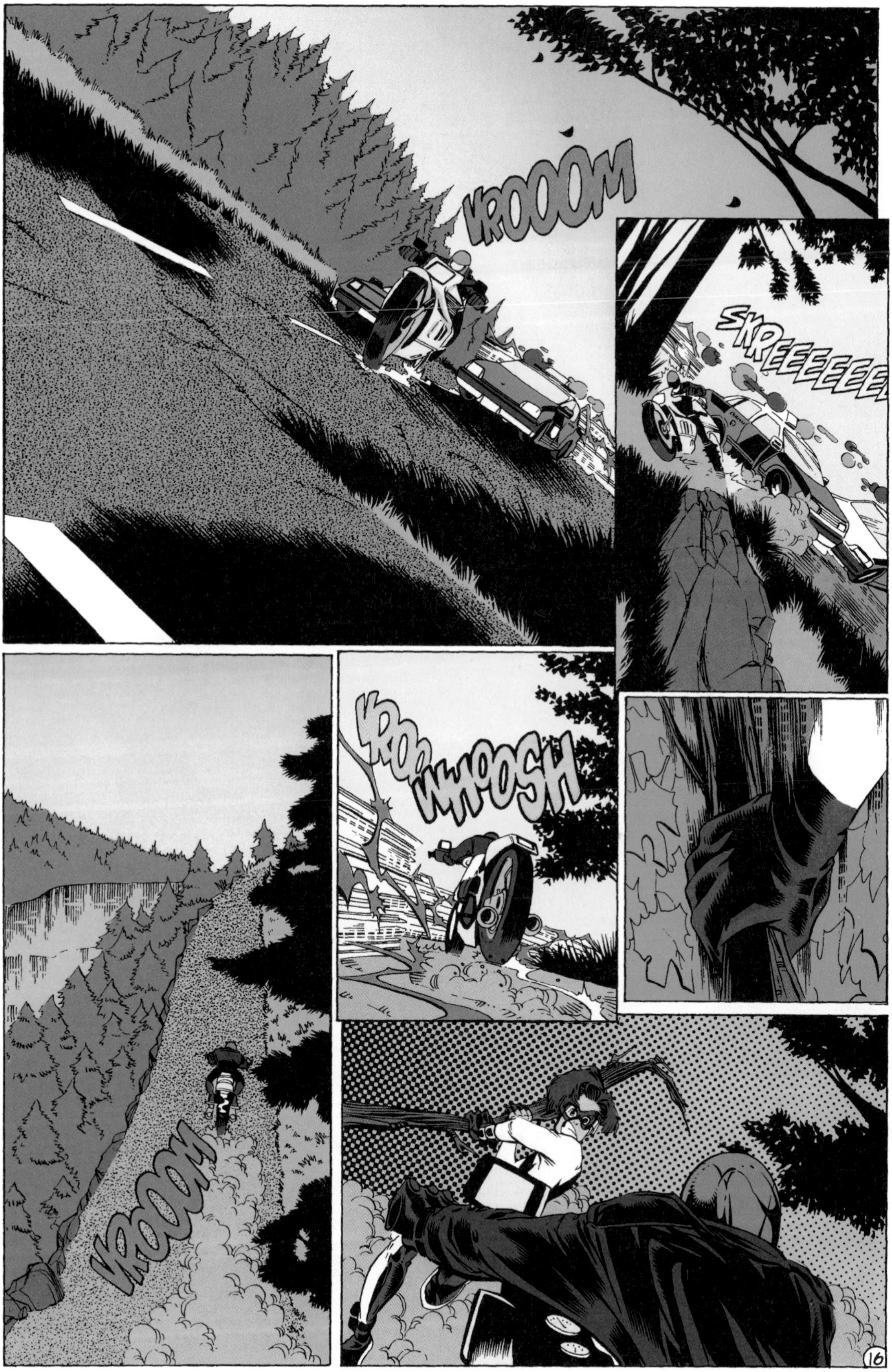
VROOOM
SKREEEEEEEL
VROOM
WHOOSH
VROOOM

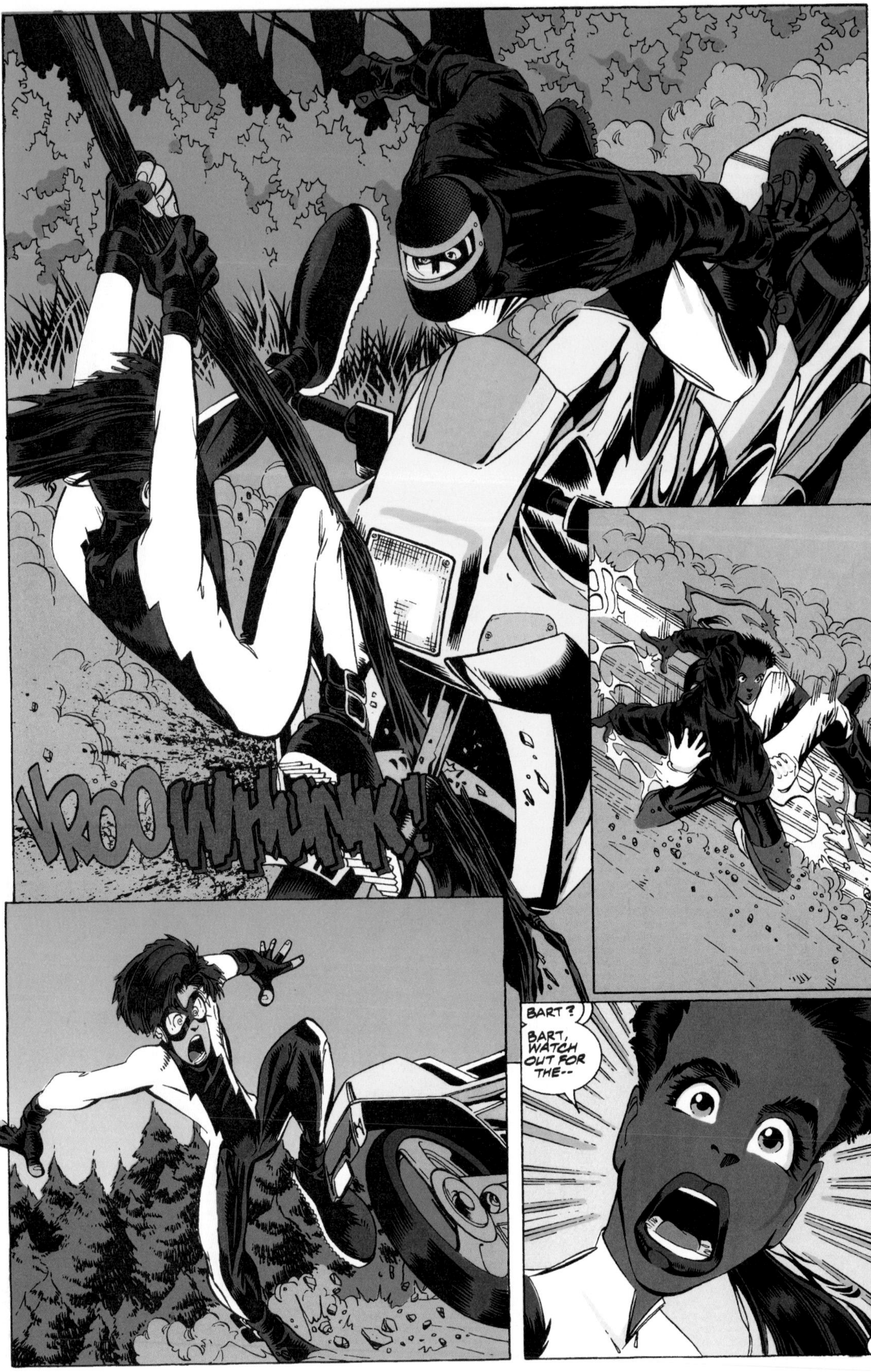
VROOWHUNK!
BART?
BART, WATCH OUT FOR THE--
17

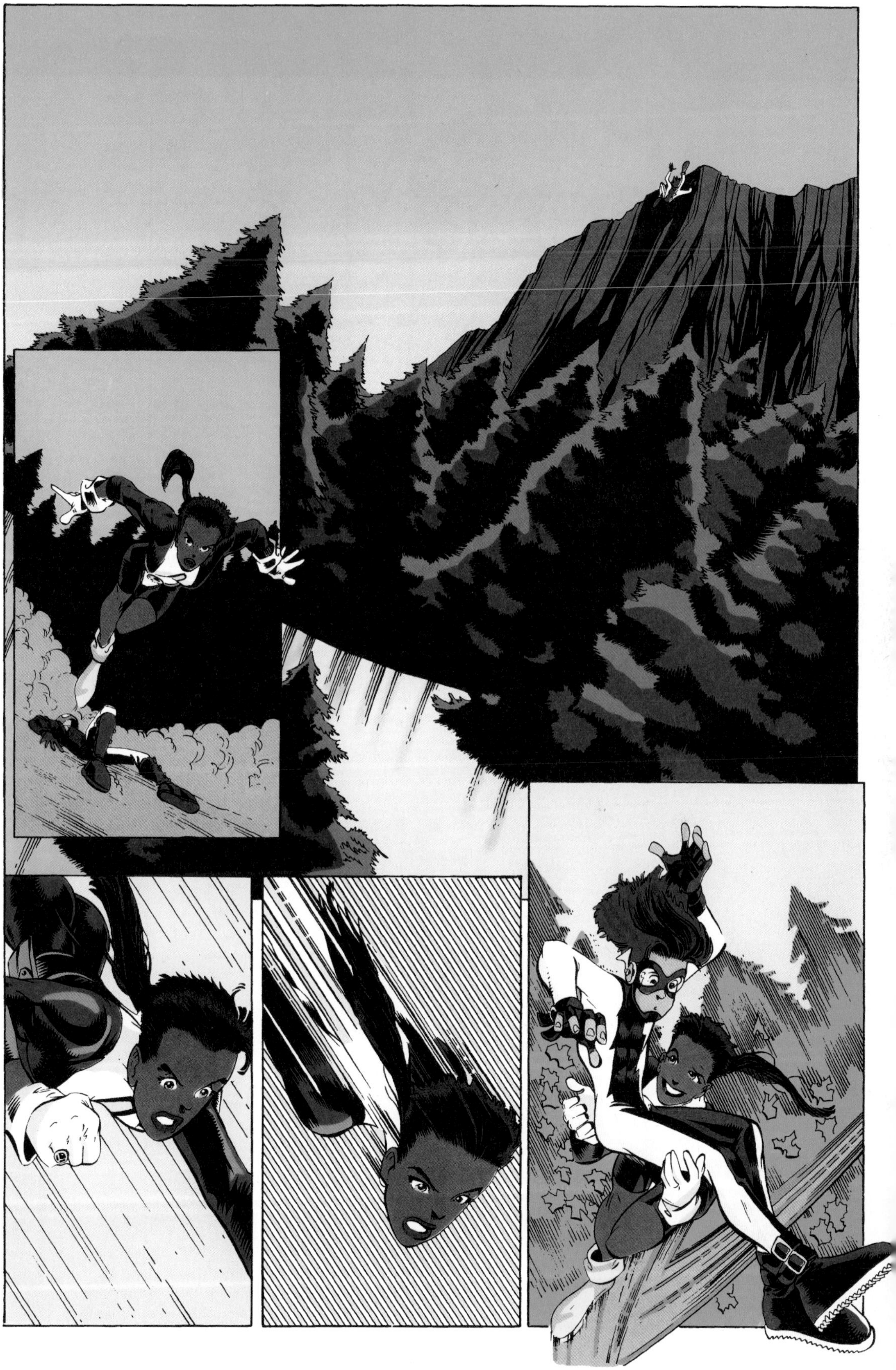

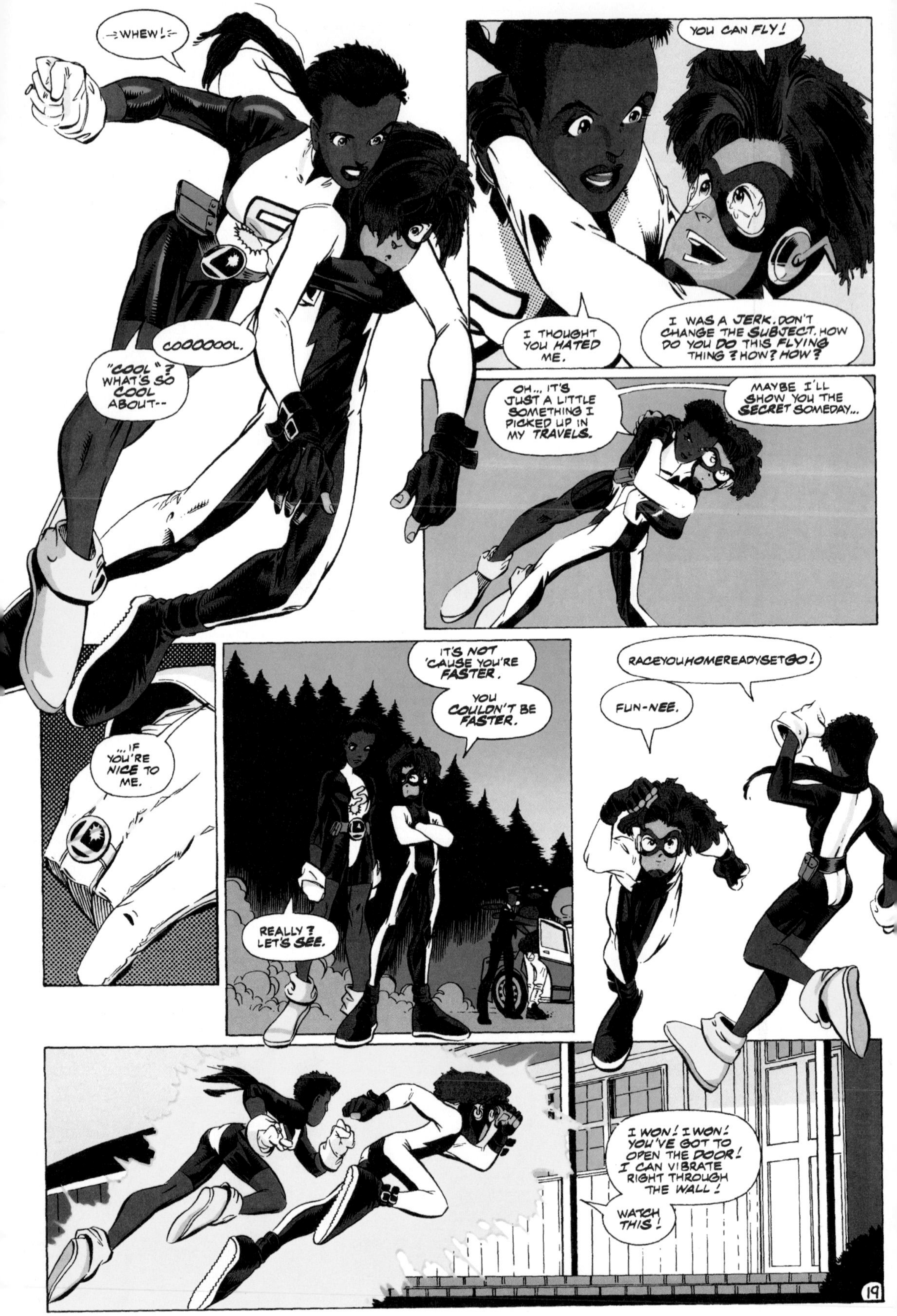
WHEW!
COOOOOOL.
"COOL"? WHAT'S SO COOL ABOUT--
YOU CAN FLY!
I THOUGHT YOU HATED ME.
I WAS A JERK. DON'T CHANGE THE SUBJECT. HOW DO YOU DO THIS FLYING THING? HOW? HOW?
OH... IT'S JUST A LITTLE SOMETHING I PICKED UP IN MY TRAVELS.
MAYBE I'LL SHOW YOU THE SECRET SOMEDAY...
...IF YOU'RE NICE TO ME.
IT'S NOT 'CAUSE YOU'RE FASTER.
YOU COULDN'T BE FASTER.
REALLY? LET'S SEE.
RACEYOUHOMEREADYSETGO!
FUN-NEE.
I WON! I WON! YOU'VE GOT TO OPEN THE DOOR! I CAN VIBRATE RIGHT THROUGH THE WALL!
WATCH THIS!

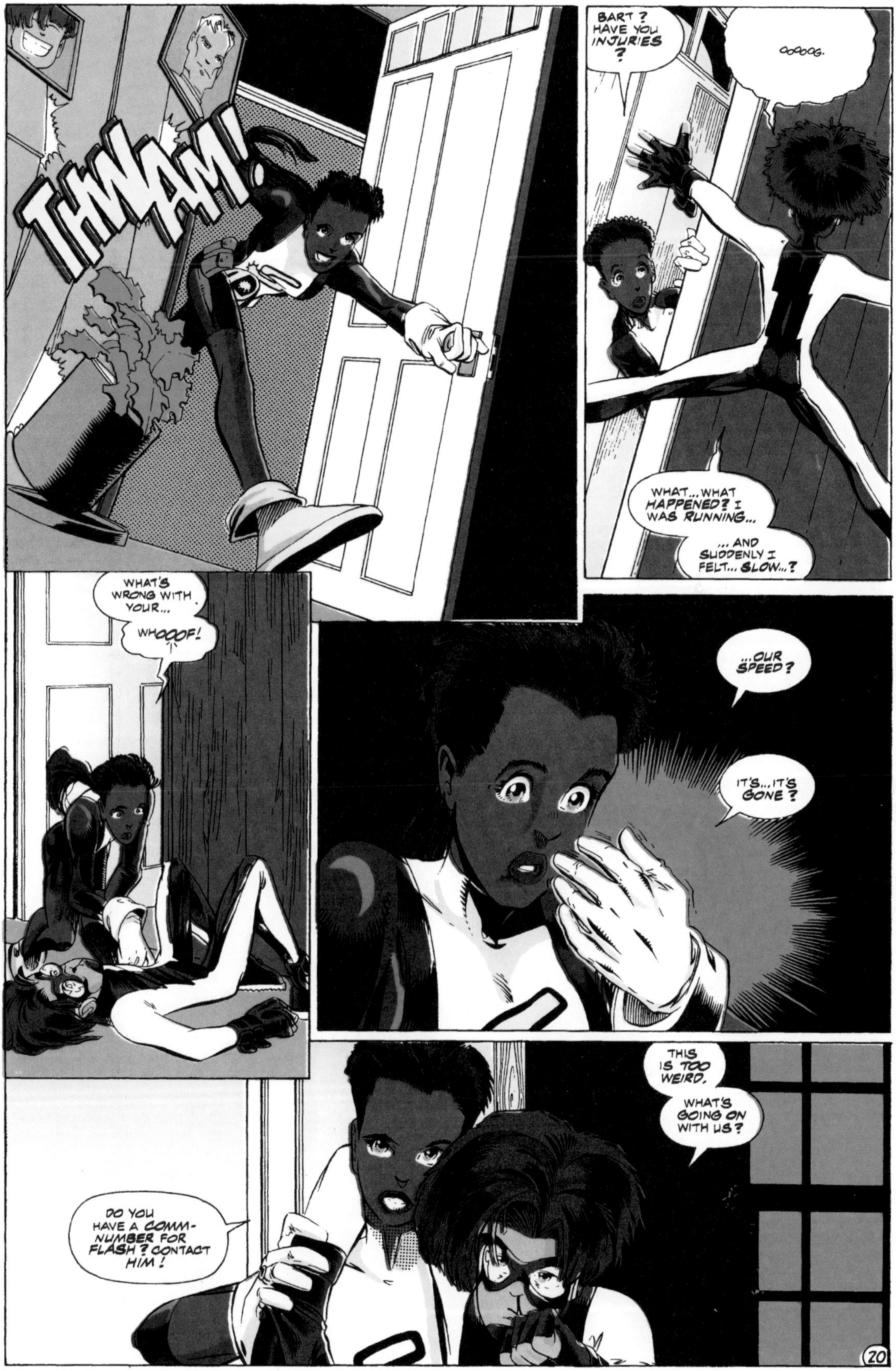
THWAM!
BART? HAVE YOU INJURIES?
OOPOOG.
WHAT... WHAT HAPPENED? I WAS RUNNING...
...AND SUDDENLY I FELT... SLOW...?
WHAT'S WRONG WITH YOUR...
WHOOOF!
...OUR SPEED?
IT'S... IT'S GONE?
THIS IS TOO WEIRD.
WHAT'S GOING ON WITH US?
DO YOU HAVE A COMM-NUMBER FOR FLASH? CONTACT HIM!

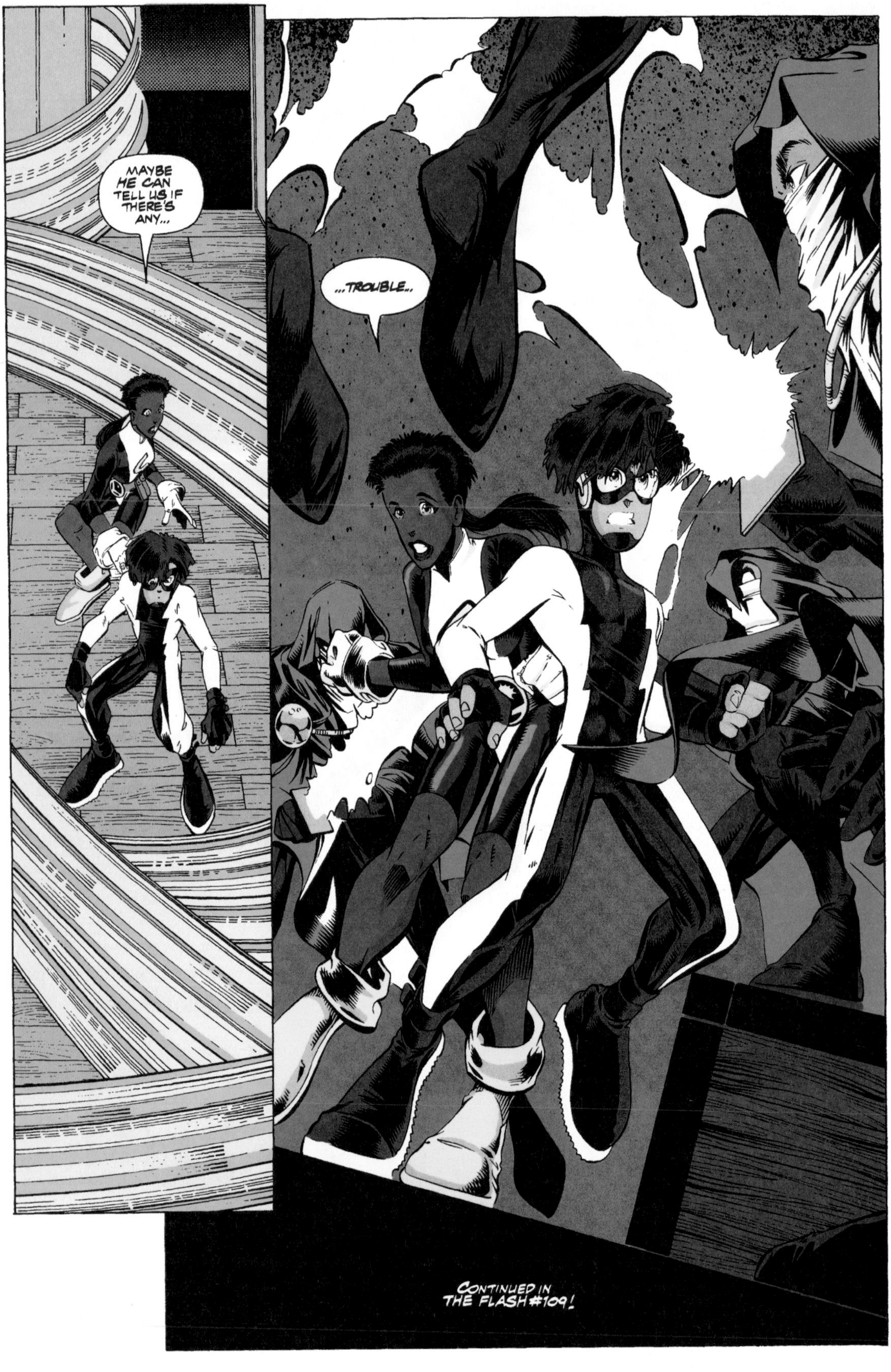
MAYBE HE CAN TELL US IF THERE'S ANY...
...TROUBLE...

CONTINUED IN THE FLASH #109!

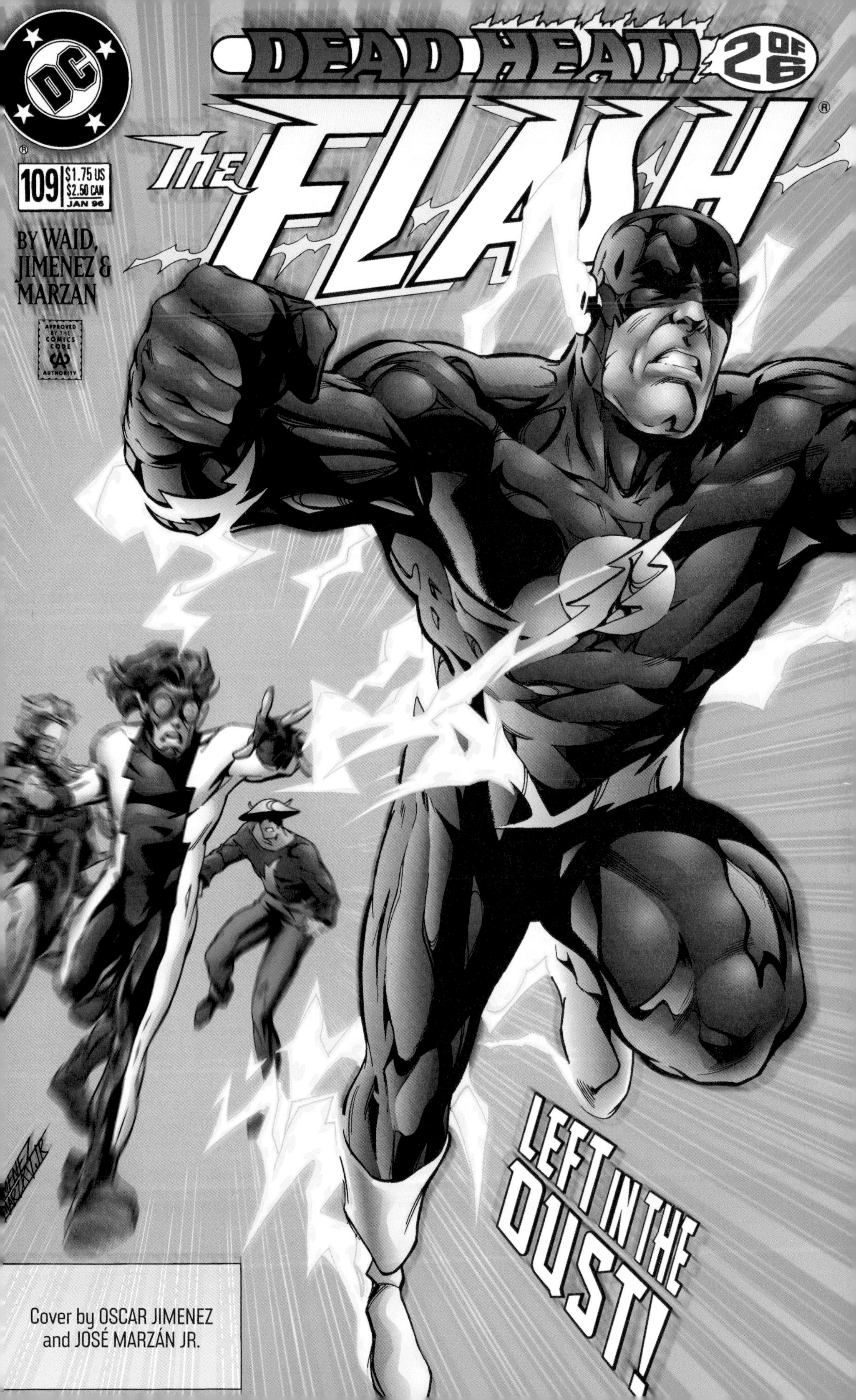
DEAD HEAT! 2 OF 6
DC
THE FLASH
109 $1.75 US $2.50 CAN JAN 96
BY WAID, JIMENEZ & MARZAN
APPROVED BY THE COMICS CODE AUTHORITY
LEFT IN THE DUST!

Cover by OSCAR JIMENEZ
and JOSÉ MARZÁN JR.

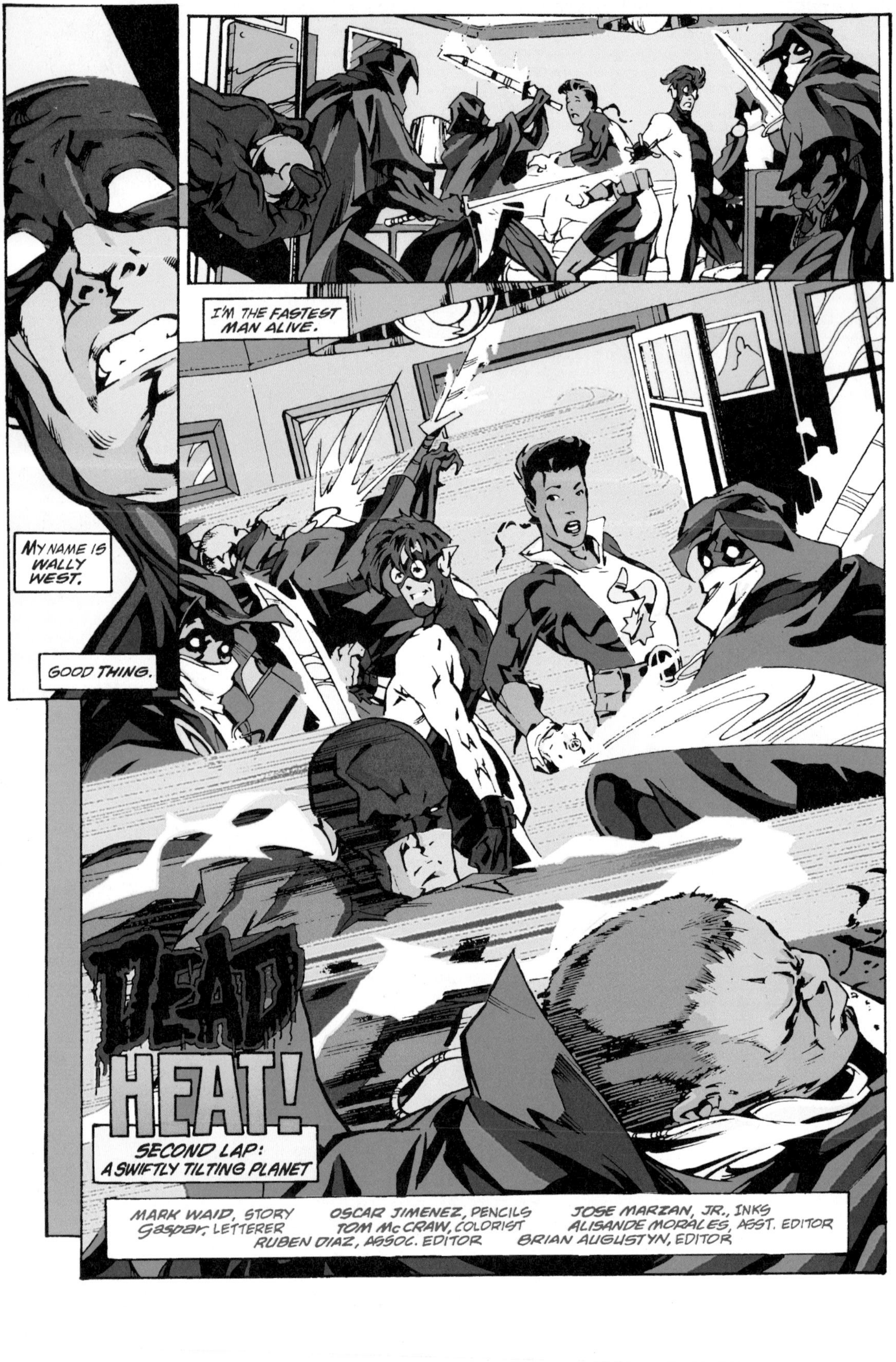
I'M THE FASTEST MAN ALIVE.
MY NAME IS WALLY WEST.
GOOD THING.
DEAD HEAT!
SECOND LAP: A SWIFTLY TILTING PLANET
MARK WAID, STORY
OSCAR JIMENEZ, PENCILS
JOSE MARZAN, JR., INKS
Gaspar, LETTERER
TOM McCRAW, COLORIST
ALISANDE MORALES, ASST. EDITOR
RUBEN DIAZ, ASSOC. EDITOR
BRIAN AUGUSTYN, EDITOR

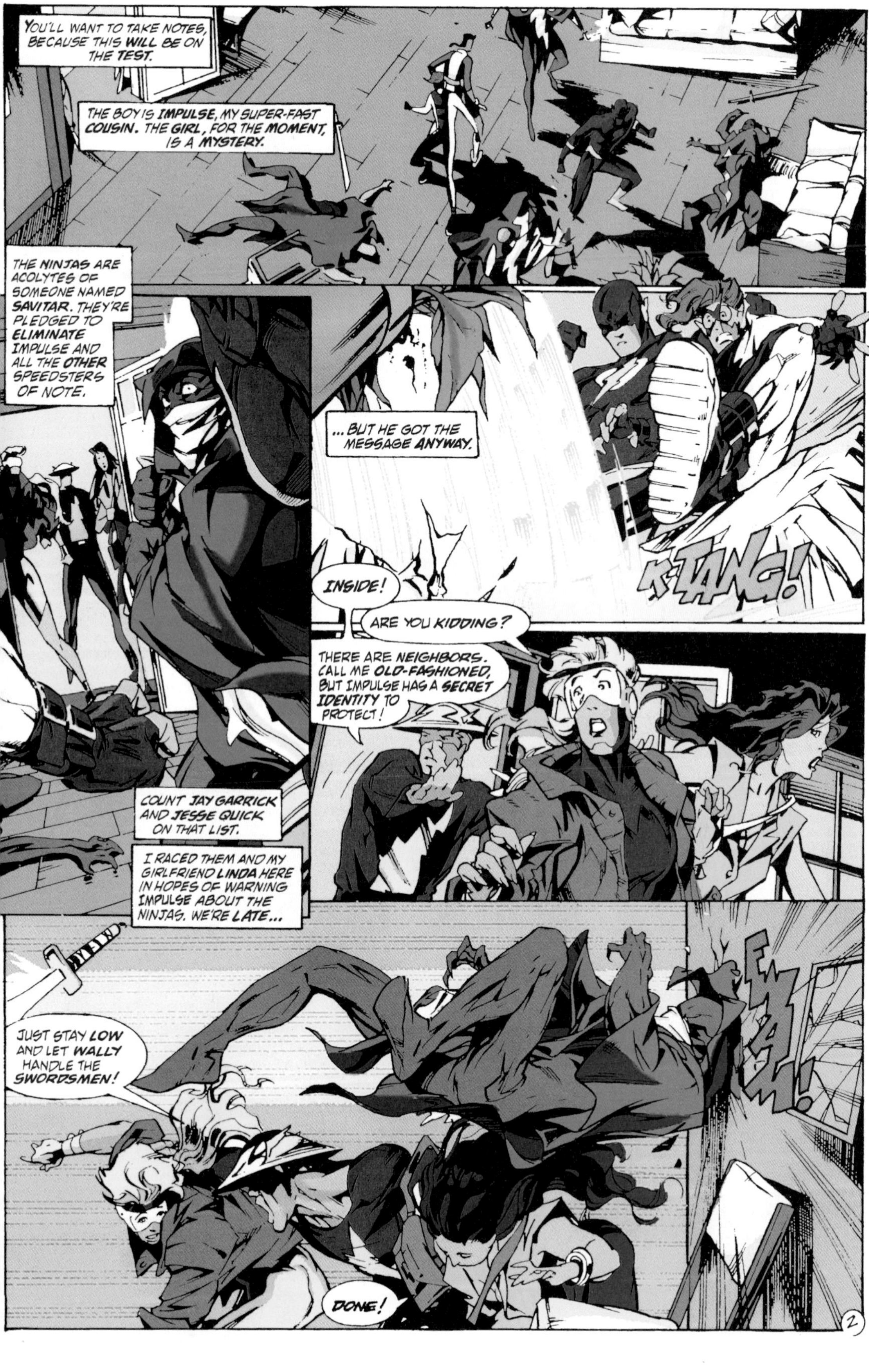

YOU'LL WANT TO TAKE NOTES, BECAUSE THIS WILL BE ON THE TEST.
THE BOY IS IMPULSE, MY SUPER-FAST COUSIN. THE GIRL, FOR THE MOMENT, IS A MYSTERY.
THE NINJAS ARE ACOLYTES OF SOMEONE NAMED SAVITAR. THEY'RE PLEDGED TO ELIMINATE IMPULSE AND ALL THE OTHER SPEEDSTERS OF NOTE.
COUNT JAY GARRICK AND JESSE QUICK ON THAT LIST.
I RACED THEM AND MY GIRLFRIEND LINDA HERE IN HOPES OF WARNING IMPULSE ABOUT THE NINJAS. WE'RE LATE...
...BUT HE GOT THE MESSAGE ANYWAY.
K-TANG!
INSIDE!
ARE YOU KIDDING?
THERE ARE NEIGHBORS. CALL ME OLD-FASHIONED, BUT IMPULSE HAS A SECRET IDENTITY TO PROTECT!
JUST STAY LOW AND LET WALLY HANDLE THE SWORDSMEN!
DONE!

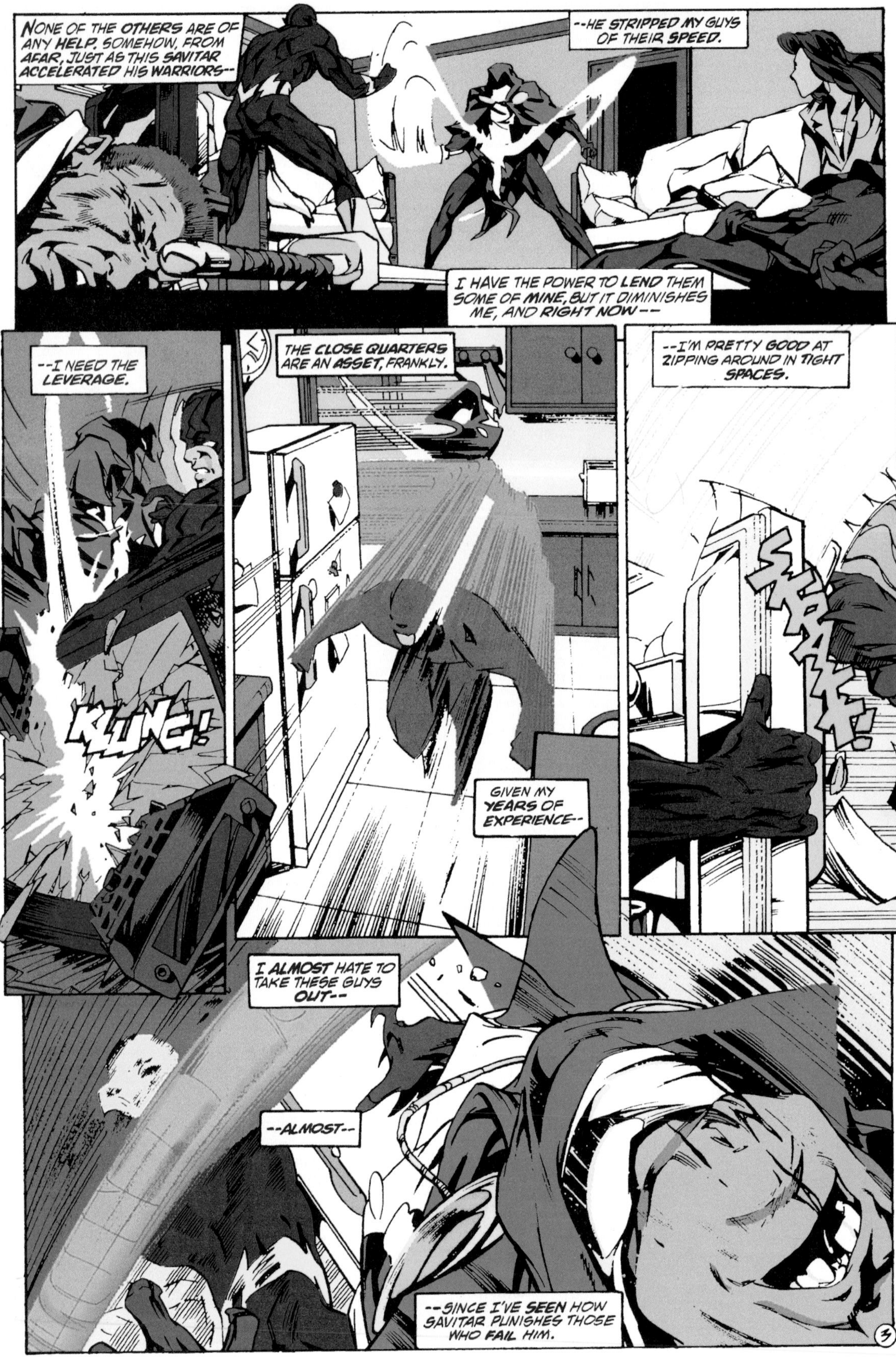
NONE OF THE OTHERS ARE OF ANY HELP. SOMEHOW, FROM AFAR, JUST AS THIS SAVITAR ACCELERATED HIS WARRIORS--
--HE STRIPPED MY GUYS OF THEIR SPEED.
I HAVE THE POWER TO LEND THEM SOME OF MINE, BUT IT DIMINISHES ME, AND RIGHT NOW--
--I NEED THE LEVERAGE.
KLUNG!
THE CLOSE QUARTERS ARE AN ASSET, FRANKLY.
GIVEN MY YEARS OF EXPERIENCE--
--I'M PRETTY GOOD AT ZIPPING AROUND IN TIGHT SPACES.
I ALMOST HATE TO TAKE THESE GUYS OUT--
--ALMOST--
--SINCE I'VE SEEN HOW SAVITAR PUNISHES THOSE WHO FAIL HIM.

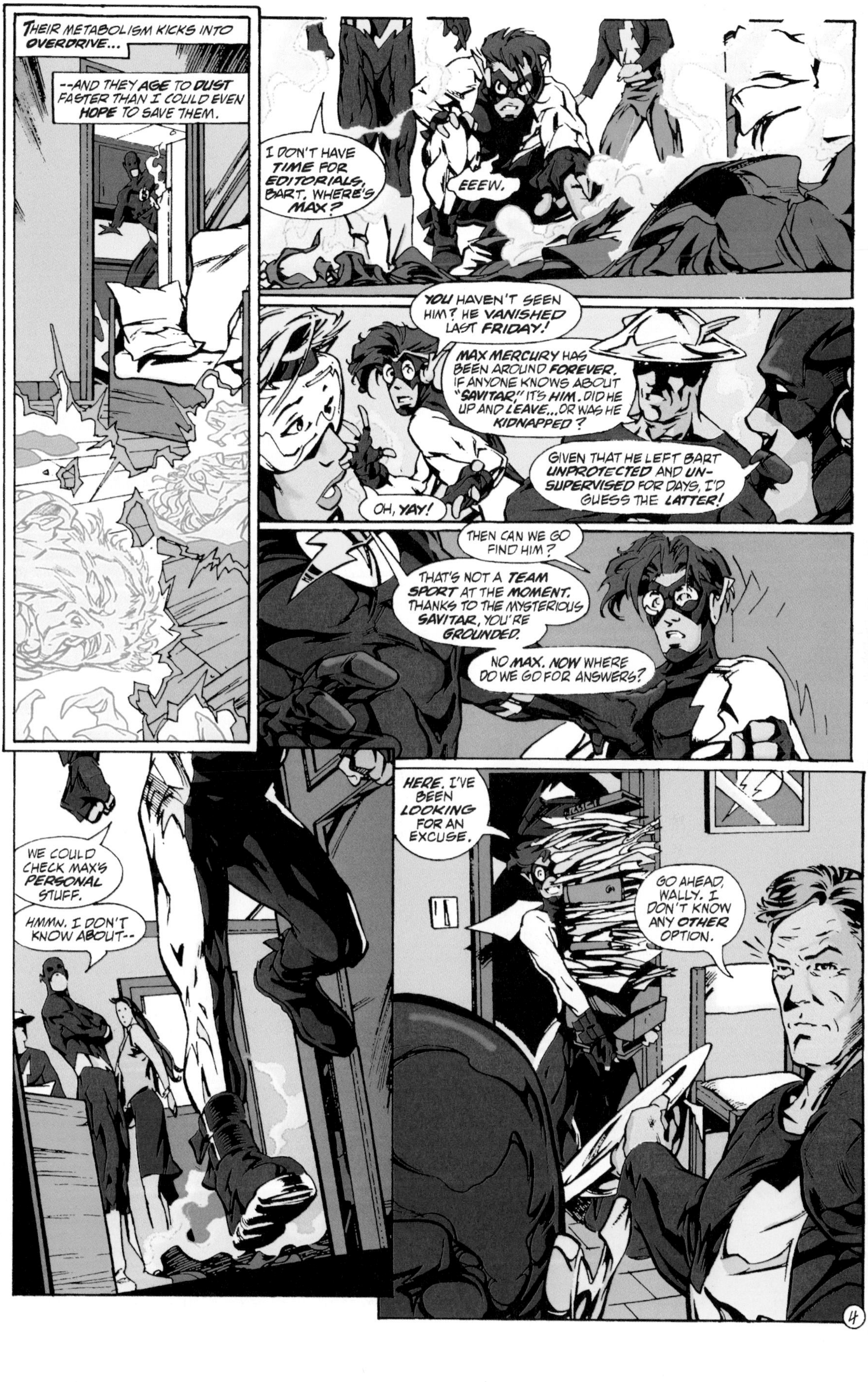
THEIR METABOLISM KICKS INTO OVERDRIVE...
--AND THEY AGE TO DUST FASTER THAN I COULD EVEN HOPE TO SAVE THEM.
I DON'T HAVE TIME FOR EDITORIALS, BART. WHERE'S MAX?
EEEW.
YOU HAVEN'T SEEN HIM? HE VANISHED LAST FRIDAY!
MAX MERCURY HAS BEEN AROUND FOREVER. IF ANYONE KNOWS ABOUT "SAVITAR," IT'S HIM. DID HE UP AND LEAVE...OR WAS HE KIDNAPPED?
GIVEN THAT HE LEFT BART UNPROTECTED AND UNSUPERVISED FOR DAYS, I'D GUESS THE LATTER!
OH, YAY!
THEN CAN WE GO FIND HIM?
THAT'S NOT A TEAM SPORT AT THE MOMENT. THANKS TO THE MYSTERIOUS SAVITAR, YOU'RE GROUNDED.
NO MAX. NOW WHERE DO WE GO FOR ANSWERS?
WE COULD CHECK MAX'S PERSONAL STUFF.
HMMN. I DON'T KNOW ABOUT--
HERE. I'VE BEEN LOOKING FOR AN EXCUSE.
GO AHEAD, WALLY. I DON'T KNOW ANY OTHER OPTION.
4

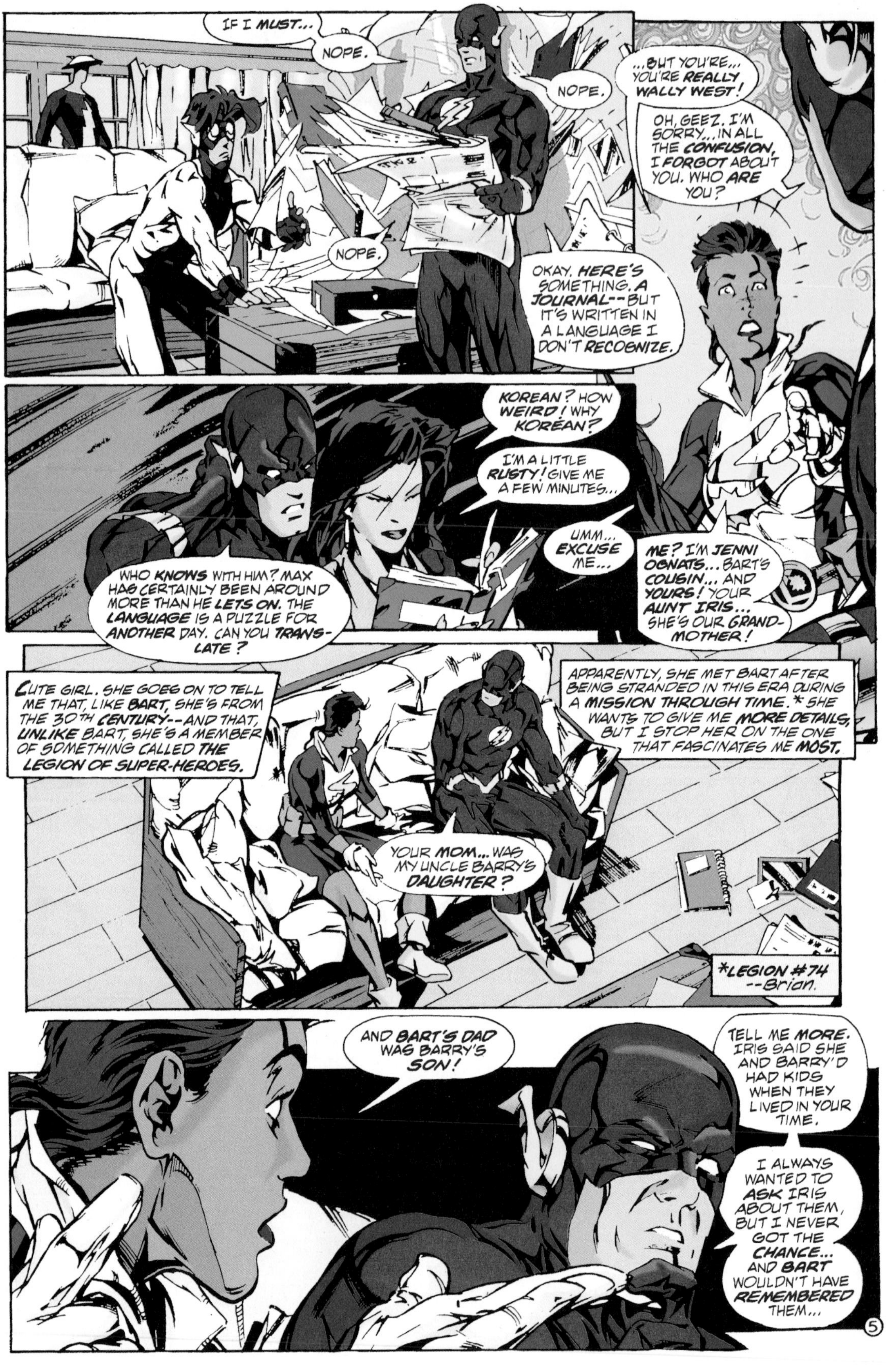
IF I MUST...
NOPE.
NOPE.
NOPE.
OKAY. HERE'S SOMETHING. A JOURNAL--BUT IT'S WRITTEN IN A LANGUAGE I DON'T RECOGNIZE.
...BUT YOU'RE... YOU'RE REALLY WALLY WEST!
OH, GEEZ. I'M SORRY... IN ALL THE CONFUSION, I FORGOT ABOUT YOU. WHO ARE YOU?
KOREAN? HOW WEIRD! WHY KOREAN?
I'M A LITTLE RUSTY! GIVE ME A FEW MINUTES...
WHO KNOWS WITH HIM? MAX HAS CERTAINLY BEEN AROUND MORE THAN HE LETS ON. THE LANGUAGE IS A PUZZLE FOR ANOTHER DAY. CAN YOU TRANSLATE?
UMM... EXCUSE ME...
ME? I'M JENNI OGNATS... BART'S COUSIN... AND YOURS! YOUR AUNT IRIS... SHE'S OUR GRANDMOTHER!
CUTE GIRL. SHE GOES ON TO TELL ME THAT, LIKE BART, SHE'S FROM THE 30TH CENTURY--AND THAT, UNLIKE BART, SHE'S A MEMBER OF SOMETHING CALLED THE LEGION OF SUPER-HEROES.
APPARENTLY, SHE MET BART AFTER BEING STRANDED IN THIS ERA DURING A MISSION THROUGH TIME.* SHE WANTS TO GIVE ME MORE DETAILS, BUT I STOP HER ON THE ONE THAT FASCINATES ME MOST.
YOUR MOM... WAS MY UNCLE BARRY'S DAUGHTER?
*LEGION #74 --Brian.
AND BART'S DAD WAS BARRY'S SON!
TELL ME MORE. IRIS SAID SHE AND BARRY'D HAD KIDS WHEN THEY LIVED IN YOUR TIME.
I ALWAYS WANTED TO ASK IRIS ABOUT THEM, BUT I NEVER GOT THE CHANCE... AND BART WOULDN'T HAVE REMEMBERED THEM...
5

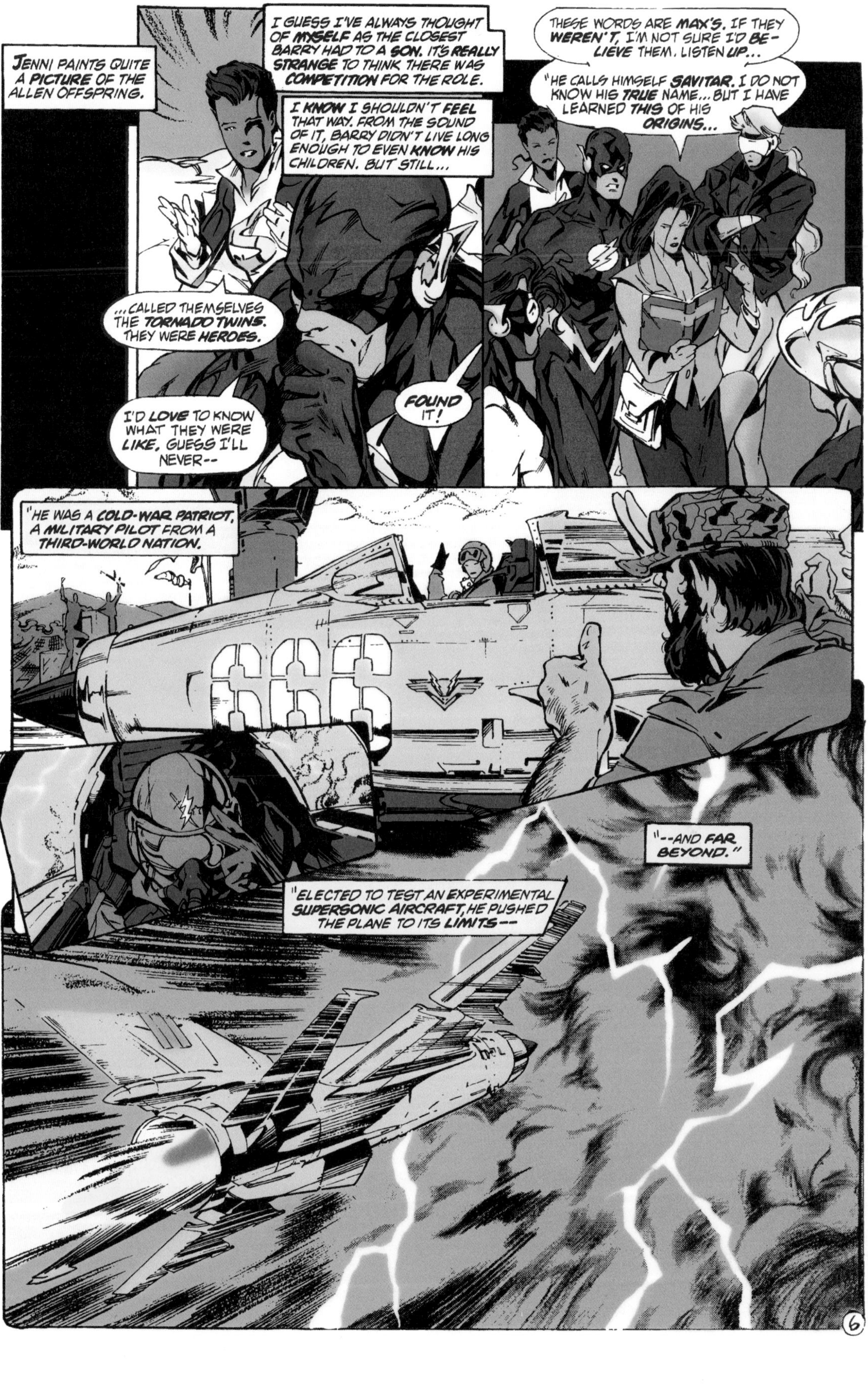
JENNI PAINTS QUITE A PICTURE OF THE ALLEN OFFSPRING.
I GUESS I'VE ALWAYS THOUGHT OF MYSELF AS THE CLOSEST BARRY HAD TO A SON. IT'S REALLY STRANGE TO THINK THERE WAS COMPETITION FOR THE ROLE.
I KNOW I SHOULDN'T FEEL THAT WAY. FROM THE SOUND OF IT, BARRY DIDN'T LIVE LONG ENOUGH TO EVEN KNOW HIS CHILDREN. BUT STILL...
...CALLED THEMSELVES THE TORNADO TWINS. THEY WERE HEROES.
I'D LOVE TO KNOW WHAT THEY WERE LIKE. GUESS I'LL NEVER--
FOUND IT!
THESE WORDS ARE MAX'S. IF THEY WEREN'T, I'M NOT SURE I'D BE-LIEVE THEM. LISTEN UP...
"HE CALLS HIMSELF SAVITAR. I DO NOT KNOW HIS TRUE NAME... BUT I HAVE LEARNED THIS OF HIS ORIGINS...
"HE WAS A COLD-WAR PATRIOT, A MILITARY PILOT FROM A THIRD-WORLD NATION.
"ELECTED TO TEST AN EXPERIMENTAL SUPERSONIC AIRCRAFT, HE PUSHED THE PLANE TO ITS LIMITS--
"--AND FAR BEYOND."
6

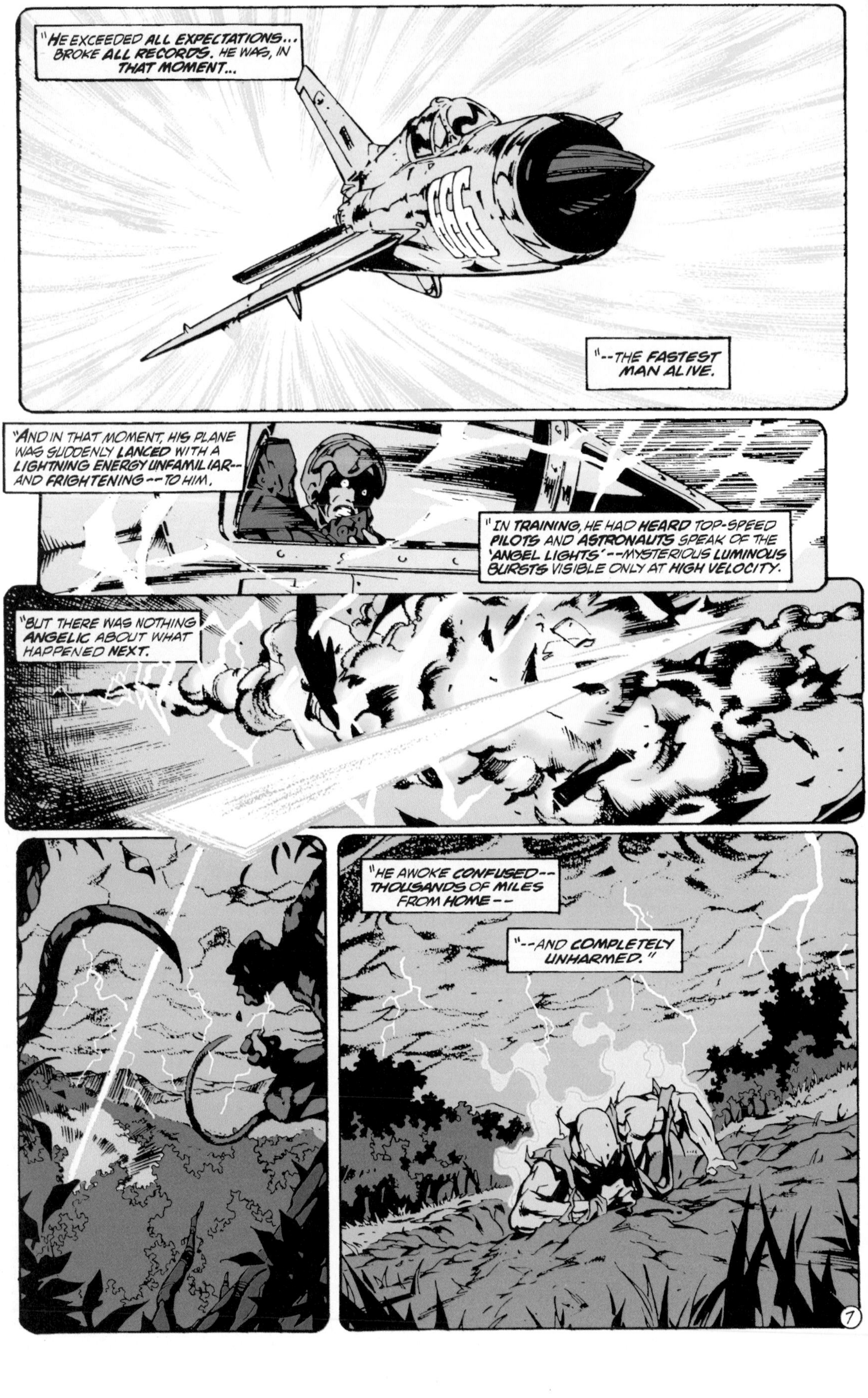
"HE EXCEEDED ALL EXPECTATIONS... BROKE ALL RECORDS. HE WAS, IN THAT MOMENT...
"--THE FASTEST MAN ALIVE.
"AND IN THAT MOMENT, HIS PLANE WAS SUDDENLY LANCED WITH A LIGHTNING ENERGY UNFAMILIAR-- AND FRIGHTENING--TO HIM.
"IN TRAINING, HE HAD HEARD TOP-SPEED PILOTS AND ASTRONAUTS SPEAK OF THE 'ANGEL LIGHTS'--MYSTERIOUS LUMINOUS BURSTS VISIBLE ONLY AT HIGH VELOCITY.
"BUT THERE WAS NOTHING ANGELIC ABOUT WHAT HAPPENED NEXT.
"HE AWOKE CONFUSED-- THOUSANDS OF MILES FROM HOME--
"--AND COMPLETELY UNHARMED."

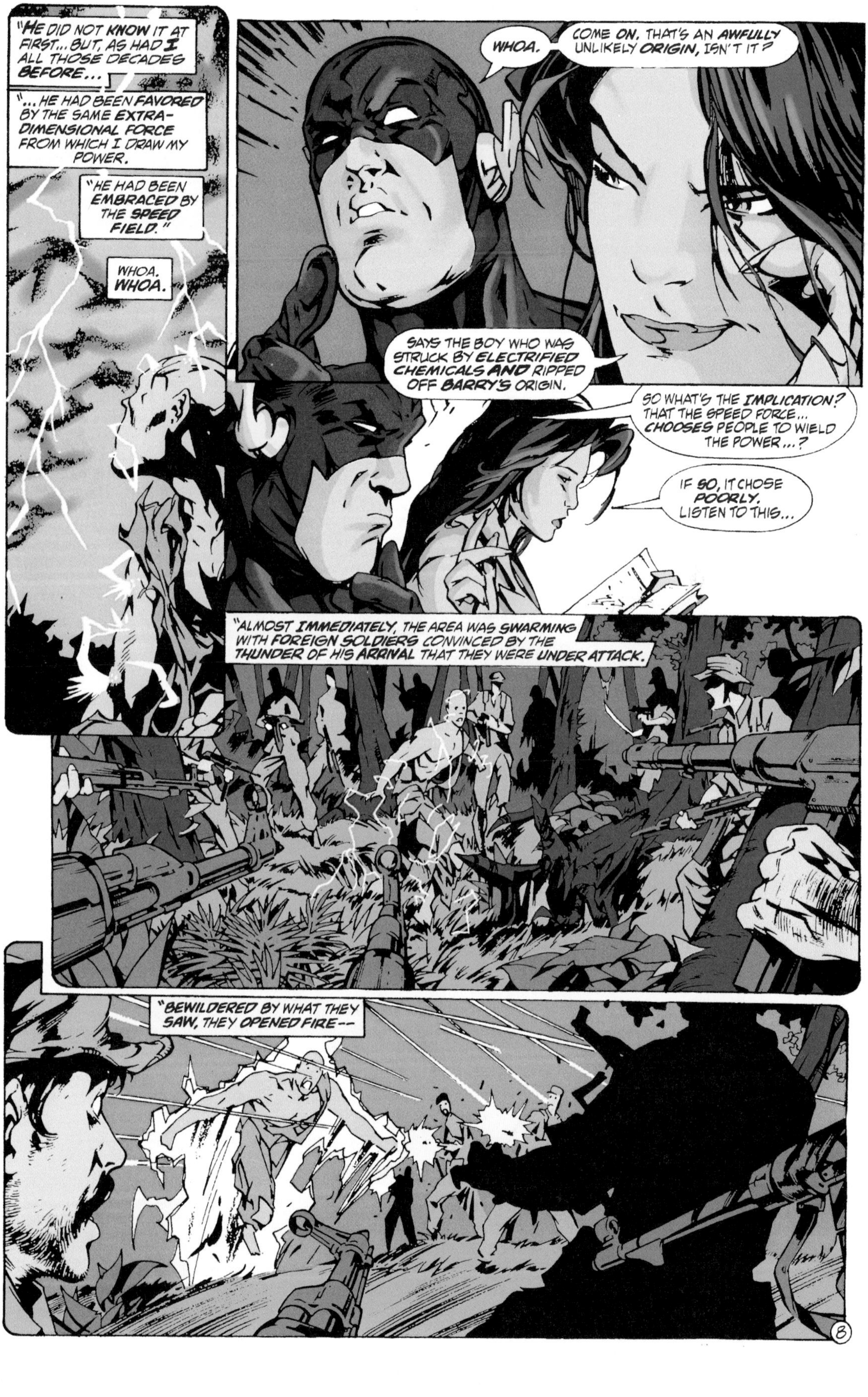
"HE DID NOT KNOW IT AT FIRST... BUT, AS HAD I ALL THOSE DECADES BEFORE...
"...HE HAD BEEN FAVORED BY THE SAME EXTRA-DIMENSIONAL FORCE FROM WHICH I DRAW MY POWER.
"HE HAD BEEN EMBRACED BY THE SPEED FIELD."
WHOA. WHOA.
WHOA.
COME ON. THAT'S AN AWFULLY UNLIKELY ORIGIN, ISN'T IT?
SAYS THE BOY WHO WAS STRUCK BY ELECTRIFIED CHEMICALS AND RIPPED OFF BARRY'S ORIGIN.
SO WHAT'S THE IMPLICATION? THAT THE SPEED FORCE... CHOOSES PEOPLE TO WIELD THE POWER...?
IF SO, IT CHOSE POORLY. LISTEN TO THIS...
"ALMOST IMMEDIATELY, THE AREA WAS SWARMING WITH FOREIGN SOLDIERS CONVINCED BY THE THUNDER OF HIS ARRIVAL THAT THEY WERE UNDER ATTACK.
"BEWILDERED BY WHAT THEY SAW, THEY OPENED FIRE--

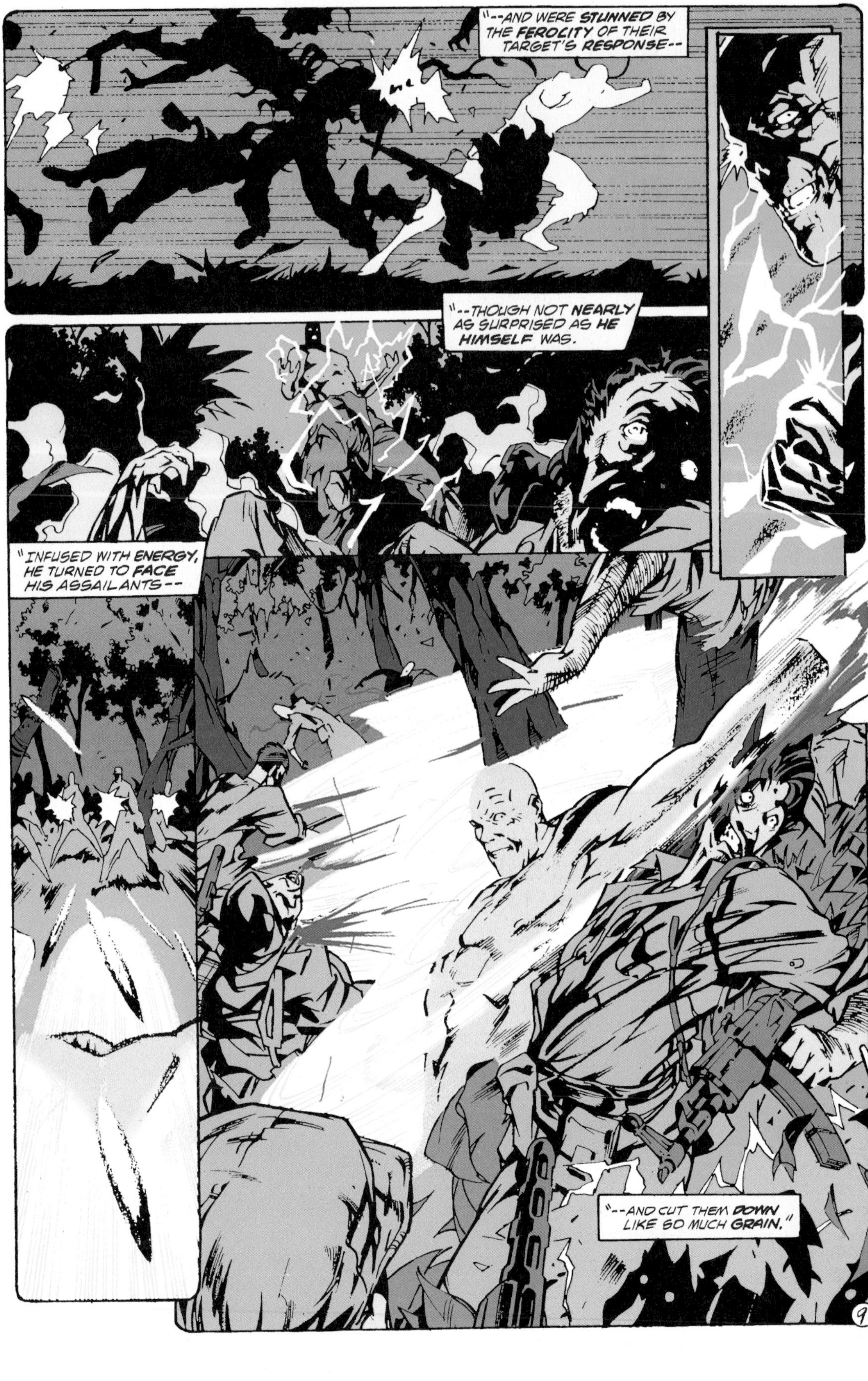
"--AND WERE STUNNED BY THE FEROCITY OF THEIR TARGET'S RESPONSE--
"--THOUGH NOT NEARLY AS SURPRISED AS HE HIMSELF WAS.
"INFUSED WITH ENERGY, HE TURNED TO FACE HIS ASSAILANTS--
"--AND CUT THEM DOWN LIKE SO MUCH GRAIN."

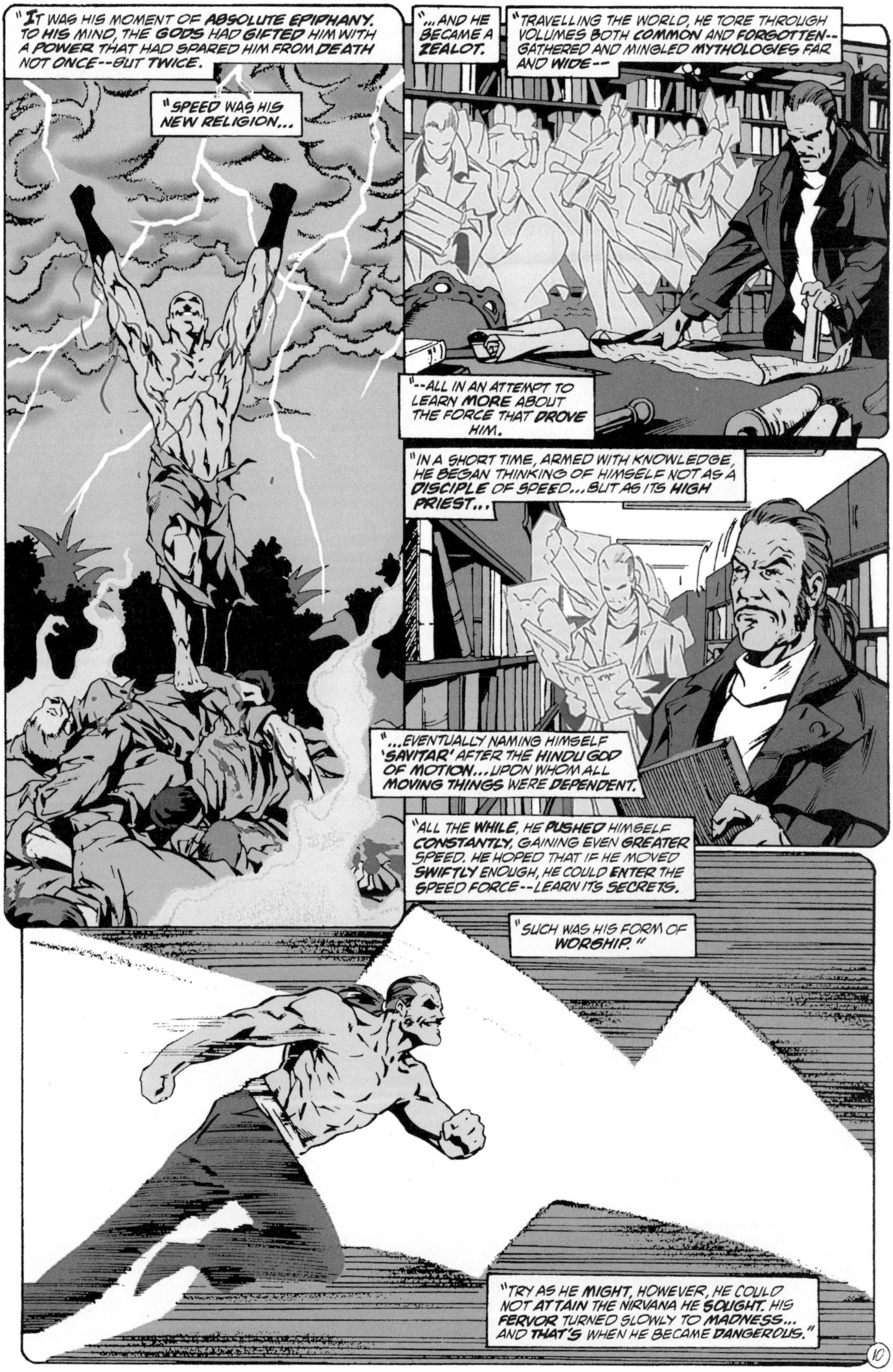
"IT WAS HIS MOMENT OF ABSOLUTE EPIPHANY. TO HIS MIND, THE GODS HAD GIFTED HIM WITH A POWER THAT HAD SPARED HIM FROM DEATH NOT ONCE--BUT TWICE.
"SPEED WAS HIS NEW RELIGION...
"...AND HE BECAME A ZEALOT.
"TRAVELLING THE WORLD, HE TORE THROUGH VOLUMES BOTH COMMON AND FORGOTTEN--GATHERED AND MINGLED MYTHOLOGIES FAR AND WIDE--
"--ALL IN AN ATTEMPT TO LEARN MORE ABOUT THE FORCE THAT DROVE HIM.
"IN A SHORT TIME, ARMED WITH KNOWLEDGE, HE BEGAN THINKING OF HIMSELF NOT AS A DISCIPLE OF SPEED...BUT AS ITS HIGH PRIEST...
"...EVENTUALLY NAMING HIMSELF 'SAVITAR' AFTER THE HINDU GOD OF MOTION...UPON WHOM ALL MOVING THINGS WERE DEPENDENT.
"ALL THE WHILE, HE PUSHED HIMSELF CONSTANTLY, GAINING EVEN GREATER SPEED. HE HOPED THAT IF HE MOVED SWIFTLY ENOUGH, HE COULD ENTER THE SPEED FORCE--LEARN ITS SECRETS.
"SUCH WAS HIS FORM OF WORSHIP."
"TRY AS HE MIGHT, HOWEVER, HE COULD NOT ATTAIN THE NIRVANA HE SOUGHT. HIS FERVOR TURNED SLOWLY TO MADNESS... AND THAT'S WHEN HE BECAME DANGEROUS."

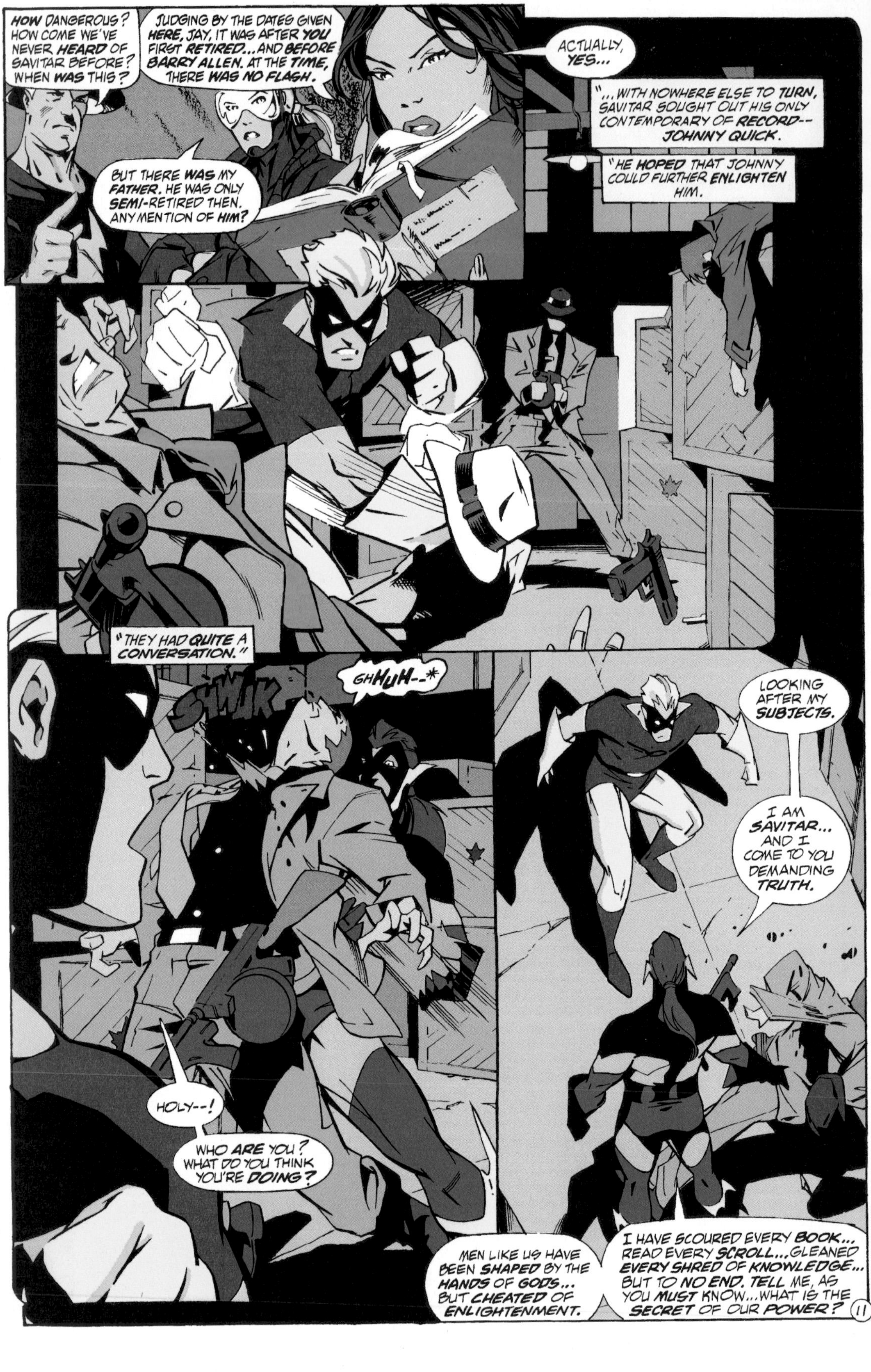
HOW DANGEROUS? HOW COME WE'VE NEVER HEARD OF SAVITAR BEFORE? WHEN WAS THIS?
JUDGING BY THE DATES GIVEN HERE, JAY, IT WAS AFTER YOU FIRST RETIRED... AND BEFORE BARRY ALLEN. AT THE TIME, THERE WAS NO FLASH.
BUT THERE WAS MY FATHER. HE WAS ONLY SEMI-RETIRED THEN. ANY MENTION OF HIM?
ACTUALLY, YES...
"...WITH NOWHERE ELSE TO TURN, SAVITAR SOUGHT OUT HIS ONLY CONTEMPORARY OF RECORD-- JOHNNY QUICK.
"HE HOPED THAT JOHNNY COULD FURTHER ENLIGHTEN HIM.
"THEY HAD QUITE A CONVERSATION."
SHWUK
GHHUH--*
HOLY--!
WHO ARE YOU? WHAT DO YOU THINK YOU'RE DOING?
LOOKING AFTER MY SUBJECTS.
I AM SAVITAR... AND I COME TO YOU DEMANDING TRUTH.
MEN LIKE US HAVE BEEN SHAPED BY THE HANDS OF GODS... BUT CHEATED OF ENLIGHTENMENT.
I HAVE SCOURED EVERY BOOK... READ EVERY SCROLL... GLEANED EVERY SHRED OF KNOWLEDGE... BUT TO NO END. TELL ME, AS YOU MUST KNOW... WHAT IS THE SECRET OF OUR POWER?

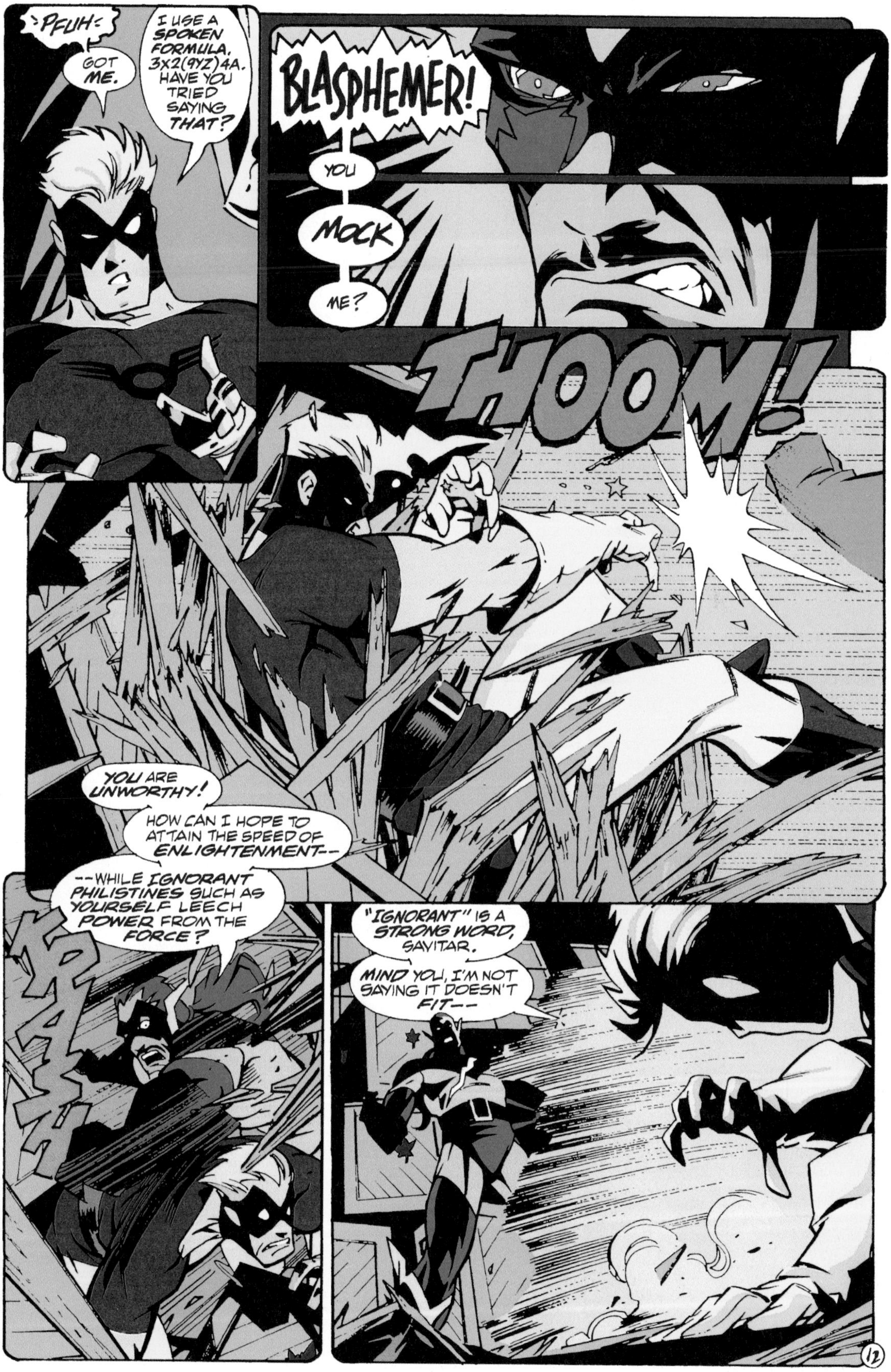

:PFUH:
GOT ME.
I USE A SPOKEN FORMULA. 3X2(9YZ)4A. HAVE YOU TRIED SAYING THAT?
BLASPHEMER!
YOU
MOCK
ME?
THOOM!
YOU ARE UNWORTHY!
HOW CAN I HOPE TO ATTAIN THE SPEED OF ENLIGHTENMENT--
--WHILE IGNORANT PHILISTINES SUCH AS YOURSELF LEECH POWER FROM THE FORCE?
"IGNORANT" IS A STRONG WORD, SAVITAR.
MIND YOU, I'M NOT SAYING IT DOESN'T FIT--

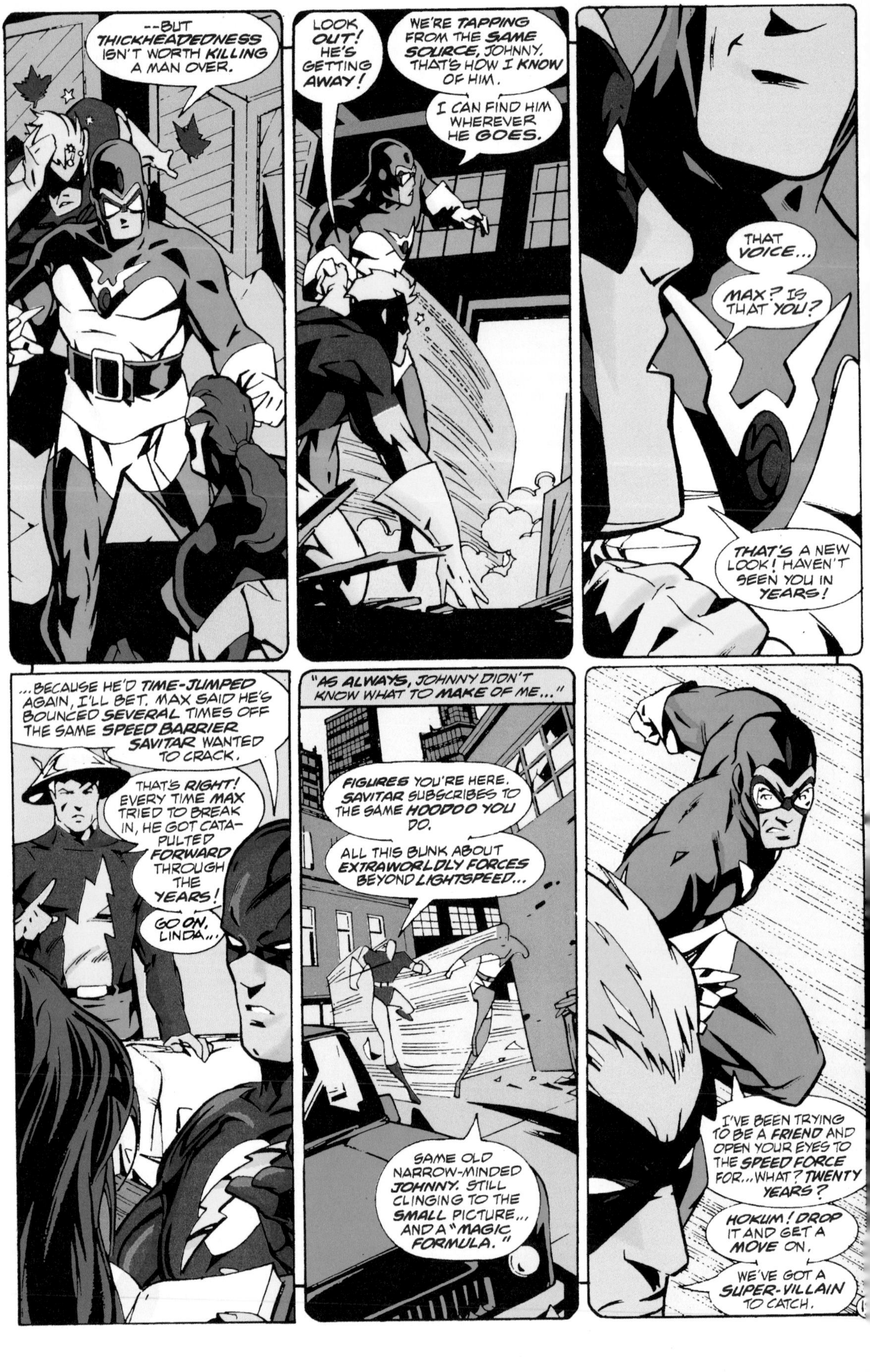
--BUT THICKHEADEDNESS ISN'T WORTH KILLING A MAN OVER.
LOOK OUT! HE'S GETTING AWAY!
WE'RE TAPPING FROM THE SAME SOURCE, JOHNNY. THAT'S HOW I KNOW OF HIM.
I CAN FIND HIM WHEREVER HE GOES.
THAT VOICE...
MAX? IS THAT YOU?
THAT'S A NEW LOOK! HAVEN'T SEEN YOU IN YEARS!
...BECAUSE HE'D TIME-JUMPED AGAIN, I'LL BET. MAX SAID HE'S BOUNCED SEVERAL TIMES OFF THE SAME SPEED BARRIER SAVITAR WANTED TO CRACK.
THAT'S RIGHT! EVERY TIME MAX TRIED TO BREAK IN, HE GOT CATA-PULTED FORWARD THROUGH THE YEARS!
GO ON, LINDA...
"AS ALWAYS, JOHNNY DIDN'T KNOW WHAT TO MAKE OF ME..."
FIGURES YOU'RE HERE. SAVITAR SUBSCRIBES TO THE SAME HOODOO YOU DO.
ALL THIS BUNK ABOUT EXTRAWORLDLY FORCES BEYOND LIGHTSPEED...
SAME OLD NARROW-MINDED JOHNNY. STILL CLINGING TO THE SMALL PICTURE... AND A "MAGIC FORMULA."
I'VE BEEN TRYING TO BE A FRIEND AND OPEN YOUR EYES TO THE SPEED FORCE FOR... WHAT? TWENTY YEARS?
HOKUM! DROP IT AND GET A MOVE ON.
WE'VE GOT A SUPER-VILLAIN TO CATCH.

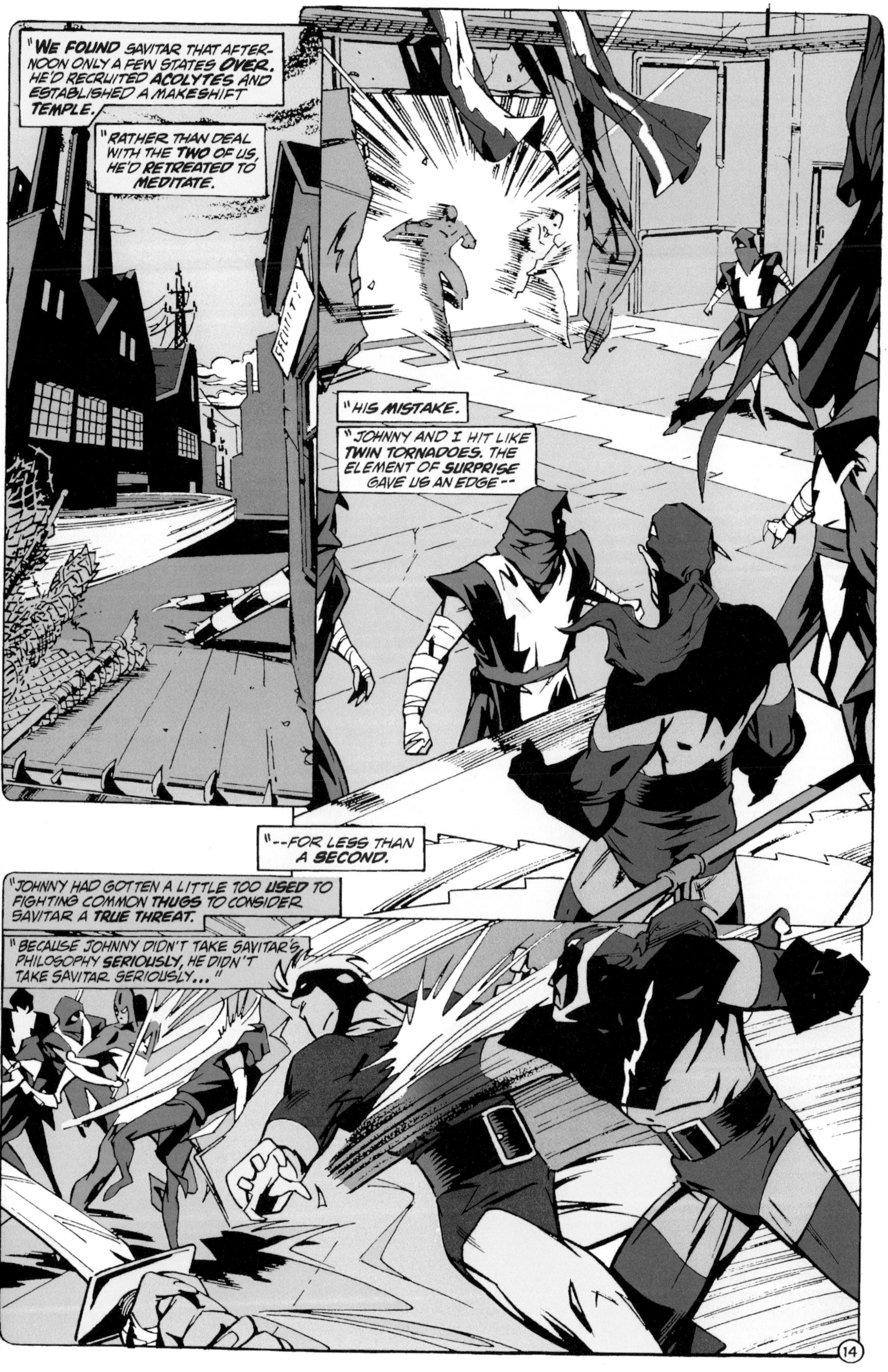
"WE FOUND SAVITAR THAT AFTERNOON ONLY A FEW STATES OVER. HE'D RECRUITED ACOLYTES AND ESTABLISHED A MAKESHIFT TEMPLE.
"RATHER THAN DEAL WITH THE TWO OF US, HE'D RETREATED TO MEDITATE.
"HIS MISTAKE.
"JOHNNY AND I HIT LIKE TWIN TORNADOES. THE ELEMENT OF SURPRISE GAVE US AN EDGE--
"--FOR LESS THAN A SECOND.
"JOHNNY HAD GOTTEN A LITTLE TOO USED TO FIGHTING COMMON THUGS TO CONSIDER SAVITAR A TRUE THREAT.
"BECAUSE JOHNNY DIDN'T TAKE SAVITAR'S PHILOSOPHY SERIOUSLY, HE DIDN'T TAKE SAVITAR SERIOUSLY..."

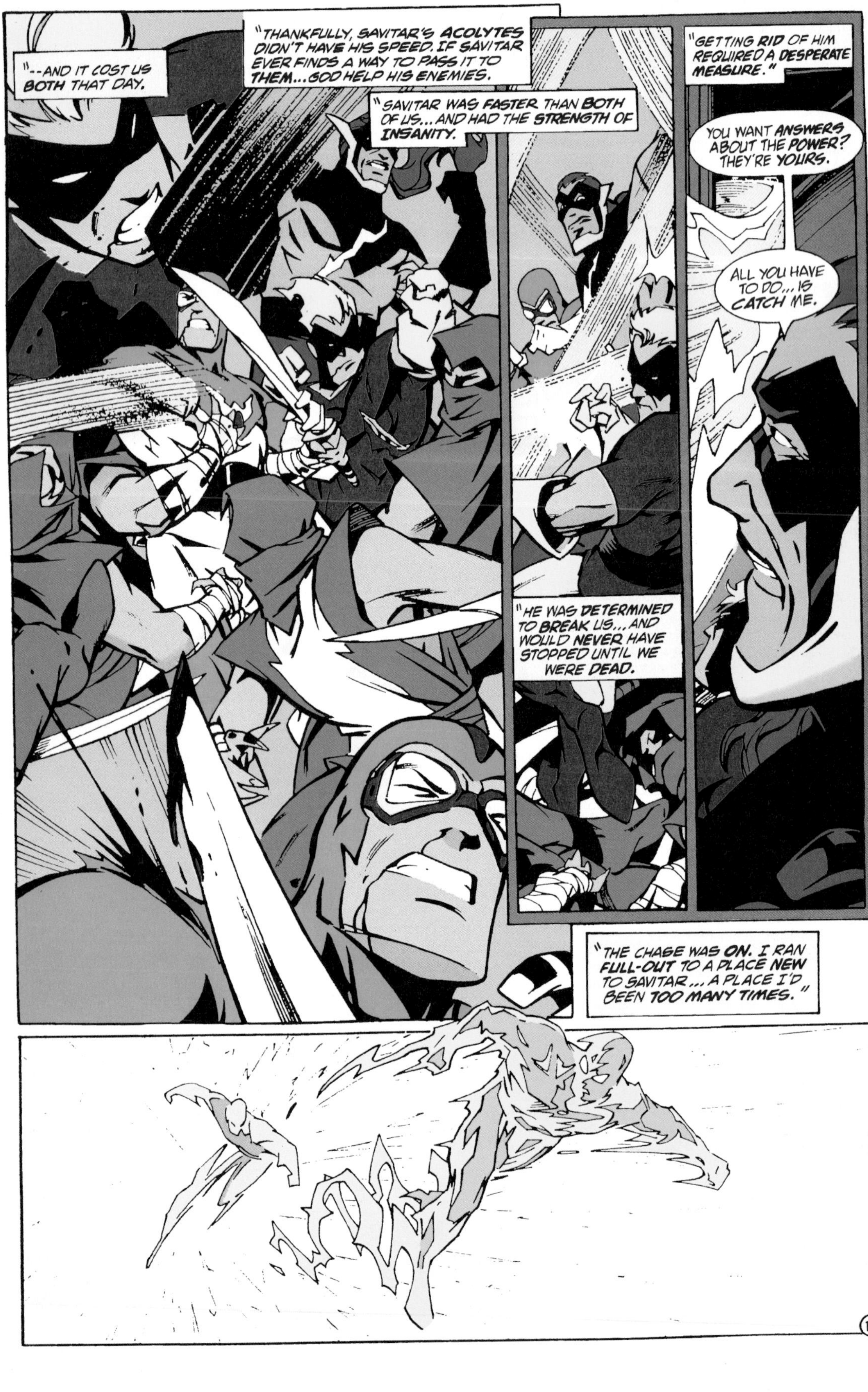

"--AND IT COST US BOTH THAT DAY.
"THANKFULLY, SAVITAR'S ACOLYTES DIDN'T HAVE HIS SPEED. IF SAVITAR EVER FINDS A WAY TO PASS IT TO THEM... GOD HELP HIS ENEMIES.
"SAVITAR WAS FASTER THAN BOTH OF US... AND HAD THE STRENGTH OF INSANITY.
"HE WAS DETERMINED TO BREAK US... AND WOULD NEVER HAVE STOPPED UNTIL WE WERE DEAD.
"GETTING RID OF HIM REQUIRED A DESPERATE MEASURE."
YOU WANT ANSWERS ABOUT THE POWER? THEY'RE YOURS.
ALL YOU HAVE TO DO... IS CATCH ME.
"THE CHASE WAS ON. I RAN FULL-OUT TO A PLACE NEW TO SAVITAR... A PLACE I'D BEEN TOO MANY TIMES."

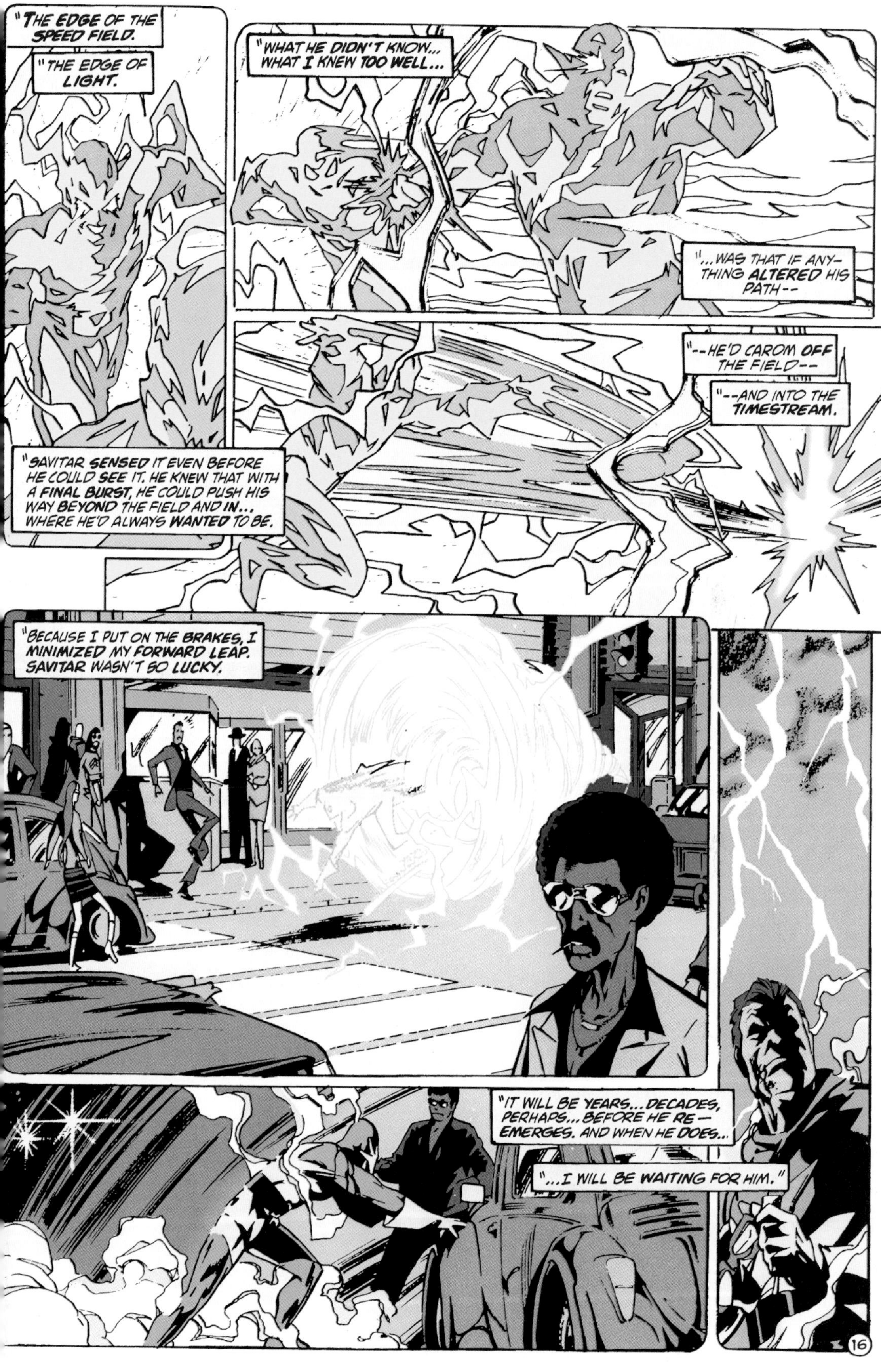
"THE EDGE OF THE SPEED FIELD.
"THE EDGE OF LIGHT.
"SAVITAR SENSED IT EVEN BEFORE HE COULD SEE IT. HE KNEW THAT WITH A FINAL BURST, HE COULD PUSH HIS WAY BEYOND THE FIELD AND IN... WHERE HE'D ALWAYS WANTED TO BE.
"WHAT HE DIDN'T KNOW... WHAT I KNEW TOO WELL...
"...WAS THAT IF ANYTHING ALTERED HIS PATH--
"--HE'D CAROM OFF THE FIELD--
"--AND INTO THE TIMESTREAM.
"BECAUSE I PUT ON THE BRAKES, I MINIMIZED MY FORWARD LEAP. SAVITAR WASN'T SO LUCKY.
"IT WILL BE YEARS... DECADES, PERHAPS... BEFORE HE RE-EMERGES. AND WHEN HE DOES...
"...I WILL BE WAITING FOR HIM."

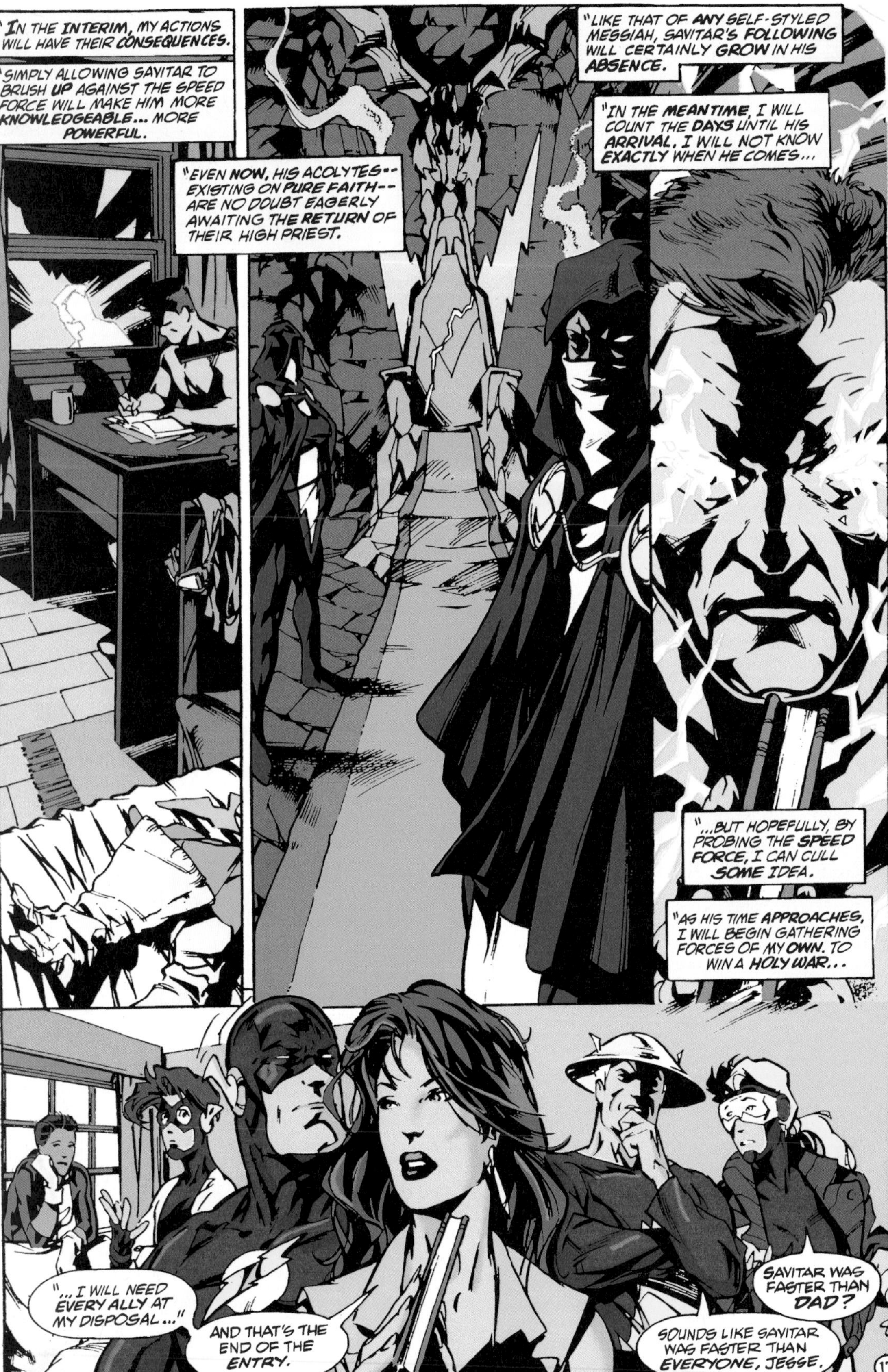
"IN THE INTERIM, MY ACTIONS WILL HAVE THEIR CONSEQUENCES.
"SIMPLY ALLOWING SAVITAR TO BRUSH UP AGAINST THE SPEED FORCE WILL MAKE HIM MORE KNOWLEDGEABLE... MORE POWERFUL.
"EVEN NOW, HIS ACOLYTES--EXISTING ON PURE FAITH--ARE NO DOUBT EAGERLY AWAITING THE RETURN OF THEIR HIGH PRIEST.
"LIKE THAT OF ANY SELF-STYLED MESSIAH, SAVITAR'S FOLLOWING WILL CERTAINLY GROW IN HIS ABSENCE.
"IN THE MEANTIME, I WILL COUNT THE DAYS UNTIL HIS ARRIVAL. I WILL NOT KNOW EXACTLY WHEN HE COMES...
"...BUT HOPEFULLY, BY PROBING THE SPEED FORCE, I CAN CULL SOME IDEA.
"AS HIS TIME APPROACHES, I WILL BEGIN GATHERING FORCES OF MY OWN. TO WIN A HOLY WAR...
"...I WILL NEED EVERY ALLY AT MY DISPOSAL..."
AND THAT'S THE END OF THE ENTRY.
SAVITAR WAS FASTER THAN DAD?
SOUNDS LIKE SAVITAR WAS FASTER THAN EVERYONE, JESSE.

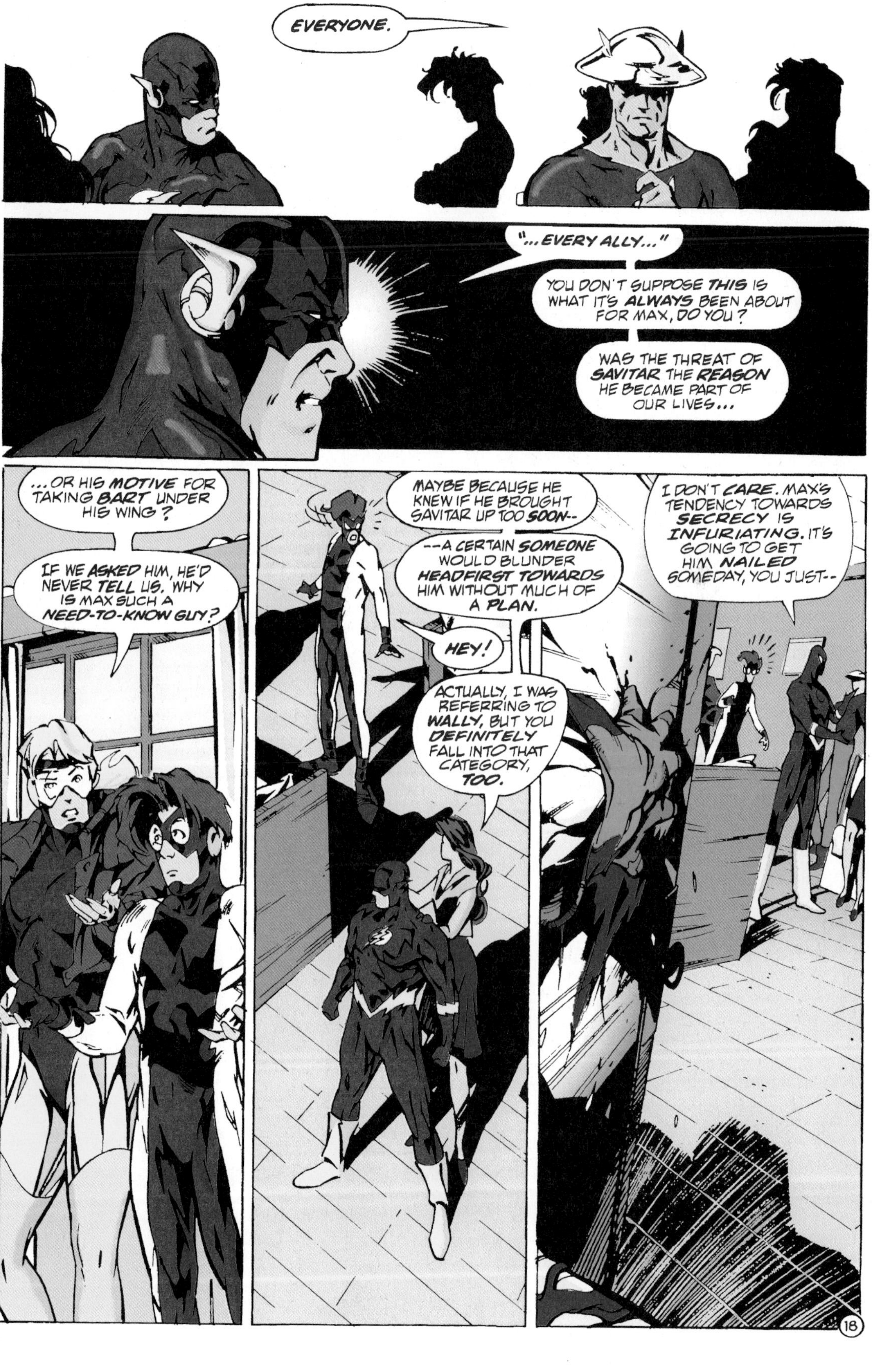
EVERYONE.
"...EVERY ALLY..."
YOU DON'T SUPPOSE THIS IS WHAT IT'S ALWAYS BEEN ABOUT FOR MAX, DO YOU?
WAS THE THREAT OF SAVITAR THE REASON HE BECAME PART OF OUR LIVES...
...OR HIS MOTIVE FOR TAKING BART UNDER HIS WING?
IF WE ASKED HIM, HE'D NEVER TELL US. WHY IS MAX SUCH A NEED-TO-KNOW GUY?
MAYBE BECAUSE HE KNEW IF HE BROUGHT SAVITAR UP TOO SOON--
--A CERTAIN SOMEONE WOULD BLUNDER HEADFIRST TOWARDS HIM WITHOUT MUCH OF A PLAN.
HEY!
ACTUALLY, I WAS REFERRING TO WALLY, BUT YOU DEFINITELY FALL INTO THAT CATEGORY, TOO.
I DON'T CARE. MAX'S TENDENCY TOWARDS SECRECY IS INFURIATING. IT'S GOING TO GET HIM NAILED SOMEDAY, YOU JUST--

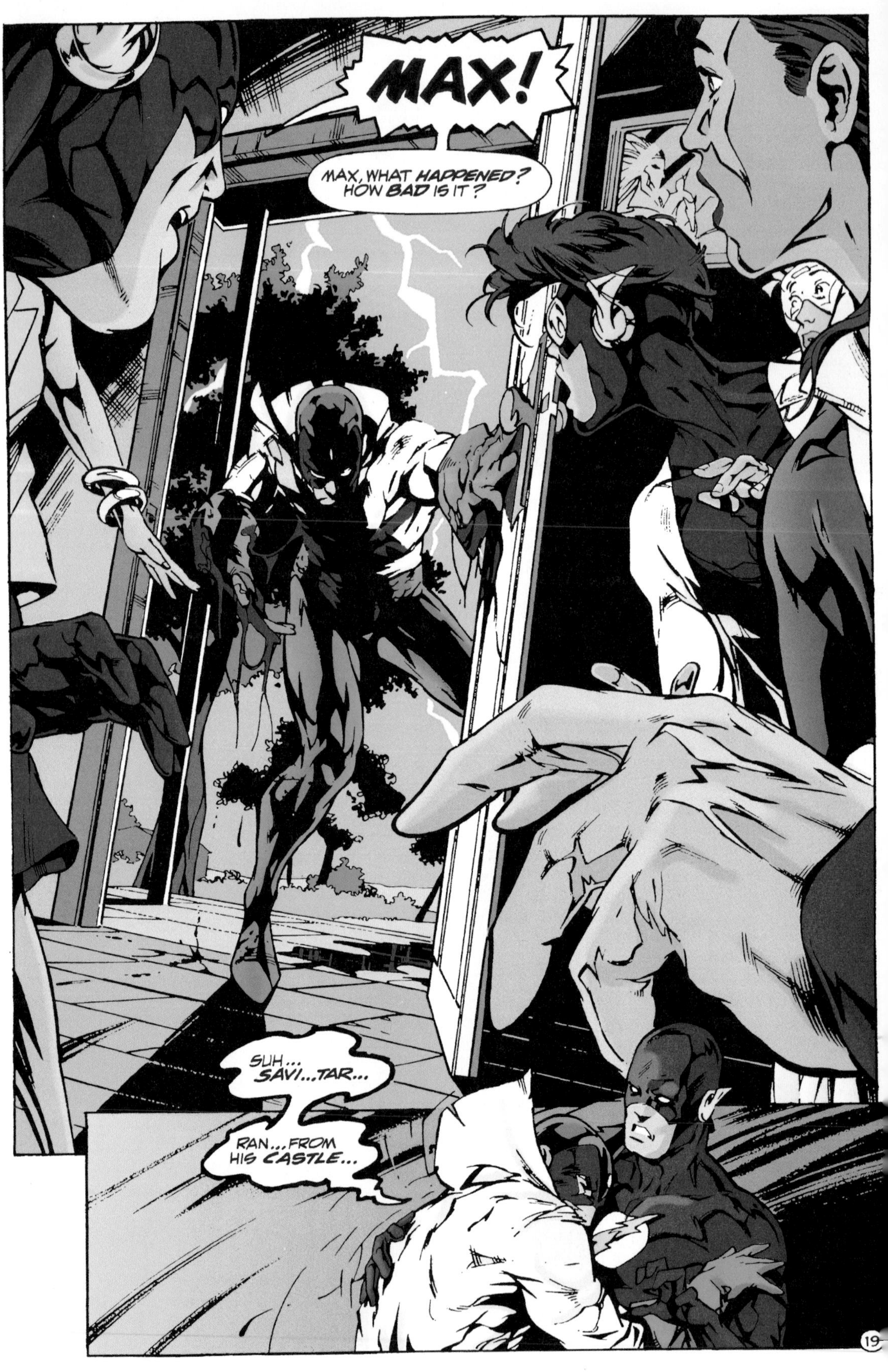
MAX!
MAX, WHAT HAPPENED? HOW BAD IS IT?
SUH... SAVI...TAR...
RAN...FROM HIS CASTLE...

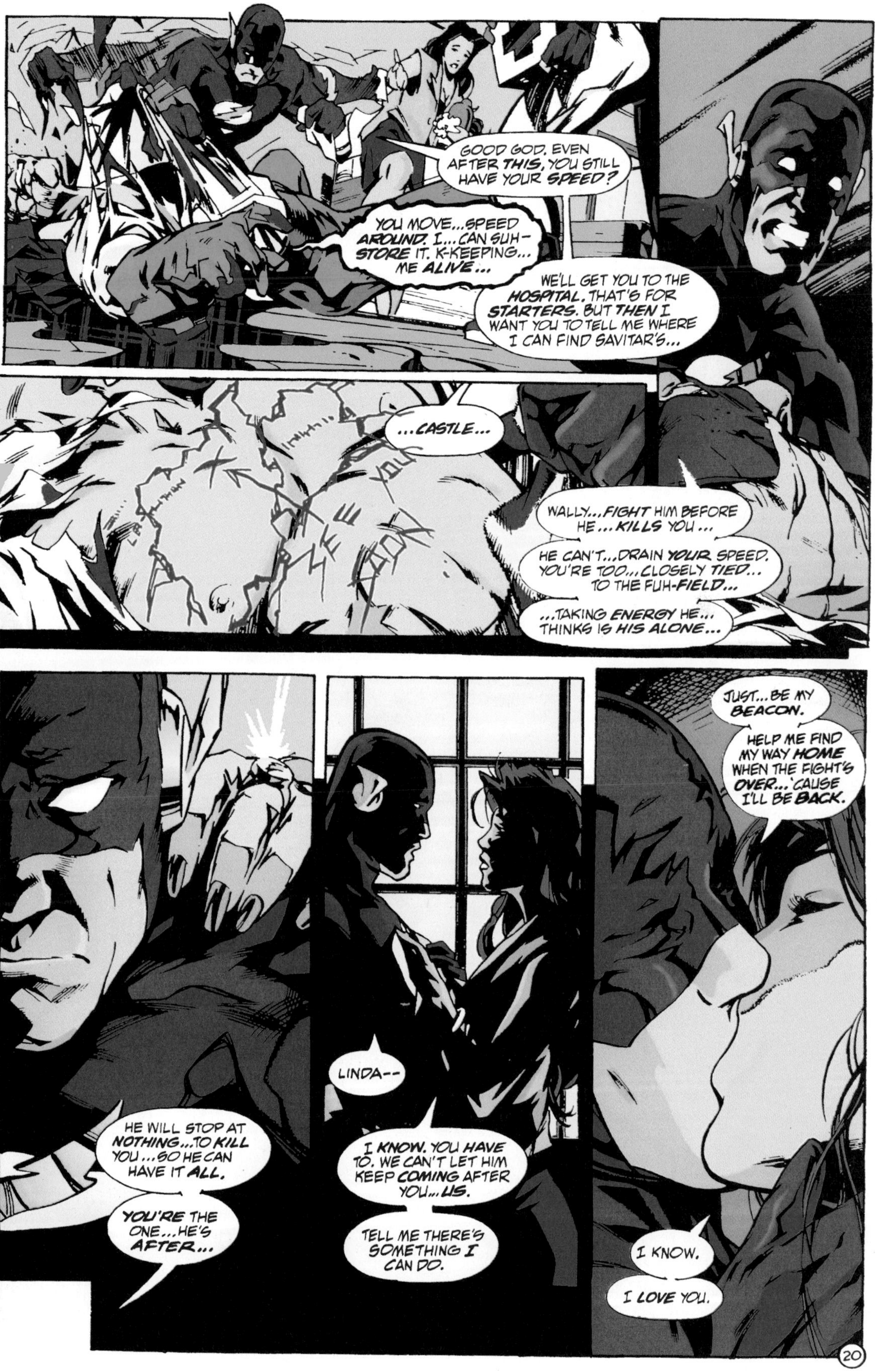
GOOD GOD. EVEN AFTER THIS, YOU STILL HAVE YOUR SPEED?
YOU MOVE...SPEED AROUND. I...CAN SUH-STORE IT. K-KEEPING... ME ALIVE...
WE'LL GET YOU TO THE HOSPITAL. THAT'S FOR STARTERS. BUT THEN I WANT YOU TO TELL ME WHERE I CAN FIND SAVITAR'S...
...CASTLE...
WALLY...FIGHT HIM BEFORE HE...KILLS YOU...
HE CAN'T...DRAIN YOUR SPEED. YOU'RE TOO...CLOSELY TIED... TO THE FUH-FIELD...
...TAKING ENERGY HE... THINKS IS HIS ALONE...
HE WILL STOP AT NOTHING...TO KILL YOU...SO HE CAN HAVE IT ALL.
YOU'RE THE ONE...HE'S AFTER...
LINDA--
I KNOW. YOU HAVE TO. WE CAN'T LET HIM KEEP COMING AFTER YOU...US.
TELL ME THERE'S SOMETHING I CAN DO.
JUST...BE MY BEACON.
HELP ME FIND MY WAY HOME WHEN THE FIGHT'S OVER...'CAUSE I'LL BE BACK.
I KNOW.
I LOVE YOU.

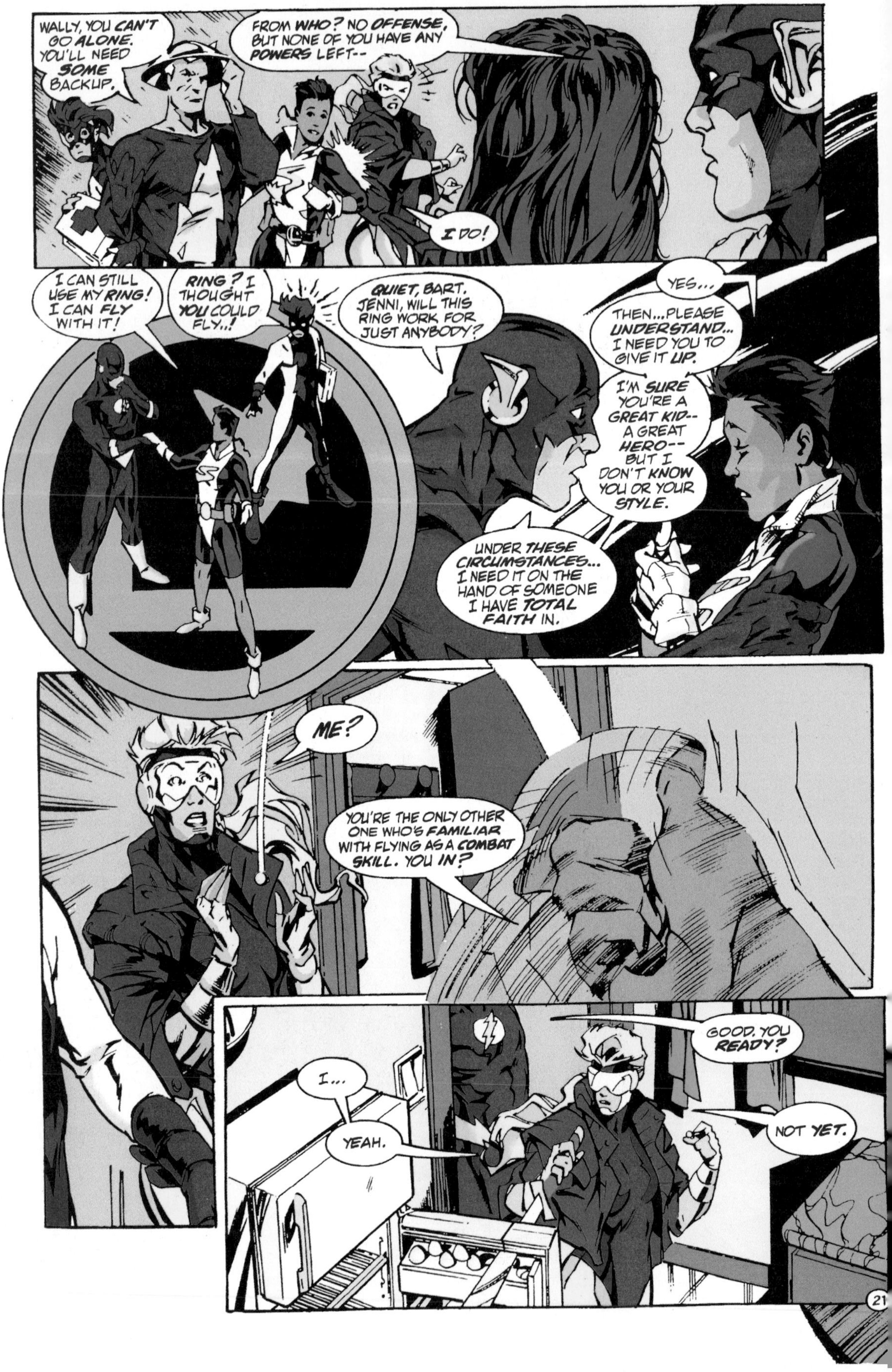
WALLY, YOU CAN'T GO ALONE. YOU'LL NEED SOME BACKUP.
FROM WHO? NO OFFENSE, BUT NONE OF YOU HAVE ANY POWERS LEFT--
I DO!
I CAN STILL USE MY RING! I CAN FLY WITH IT!
RING? I THOUGHT YOU COULD FLY..!
QUIET, BART. JENNI, WILL THIS RING WORK FOR JUST ANYBODY?
YES...
THEN...PLEASE UNDERSTAND... I NEED YOU TO GIVE IT UP.
I'M SURE YOU'RE A GREAT KID-- A GREAT HERO-- BUT I DON'T KNOW YOU OR YOUR STYLE.
UNDER THESE CIRCUMSTANCES... I NEED IT ON THE HAND OF SOMEONE I HAVE TOTAL FAITH IN.
ME?
YOU'RE THE ONLY OTHER ONE WHO'S FAMILIAR WITH FLYING AS A COMBAT SKILL. YOU IN?
GOOD. YOU READY?
I...
YEAH.
NOT YET.

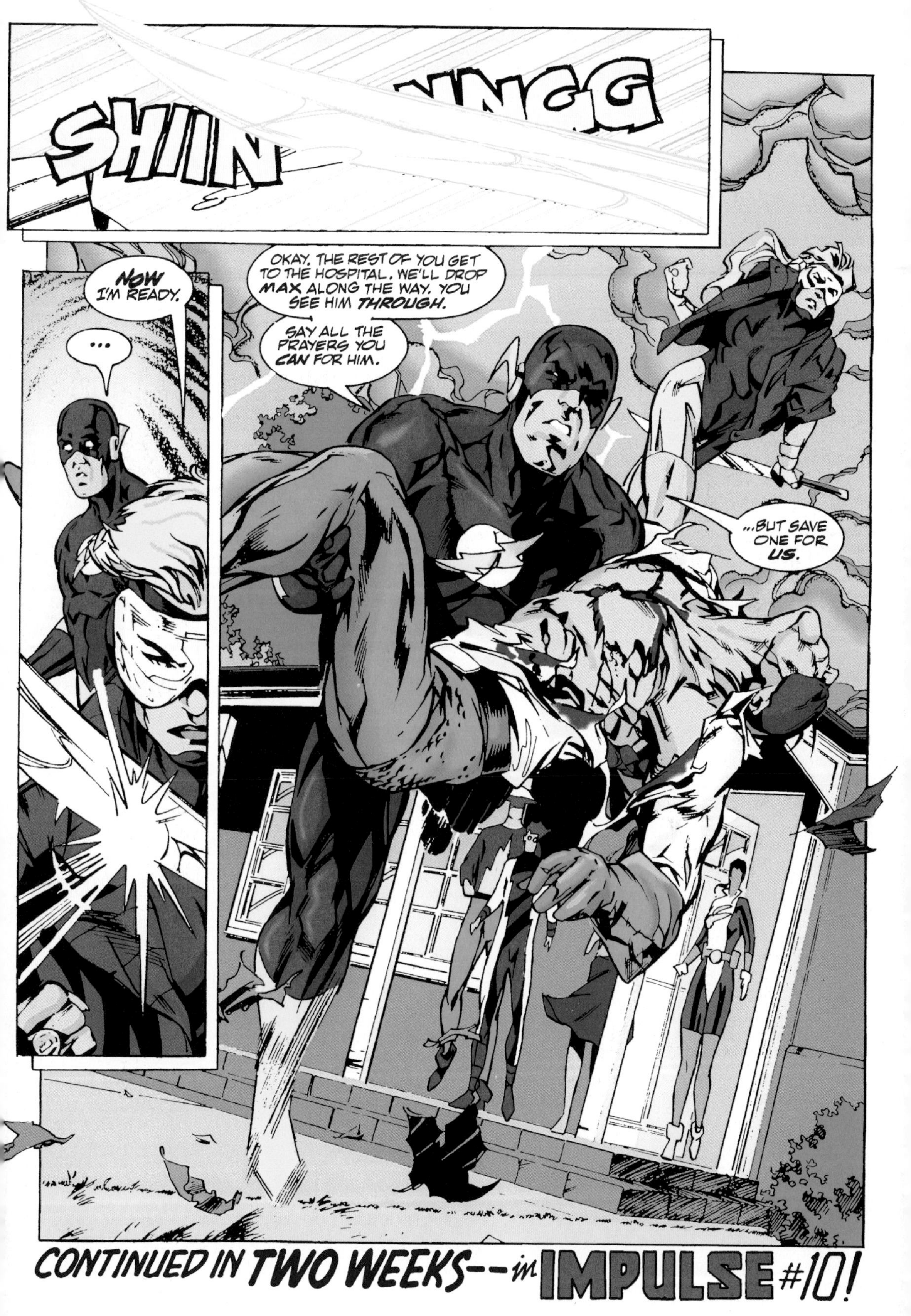
SHIIN NGG
NOW I'M READY.
...
OKAY. THE REST OF YOU GET TO THE HOSPITAL. WE'LL DROP MAX ALONG THE WAY. YOU SEE HIM THROUGH.
SAY ALL THE PRAYERS YOU CAN FOR HIM.
...BUT SAVE ONE FOR US.

CONTINUED IN TWO WEEKS--in IMPULSE #10!

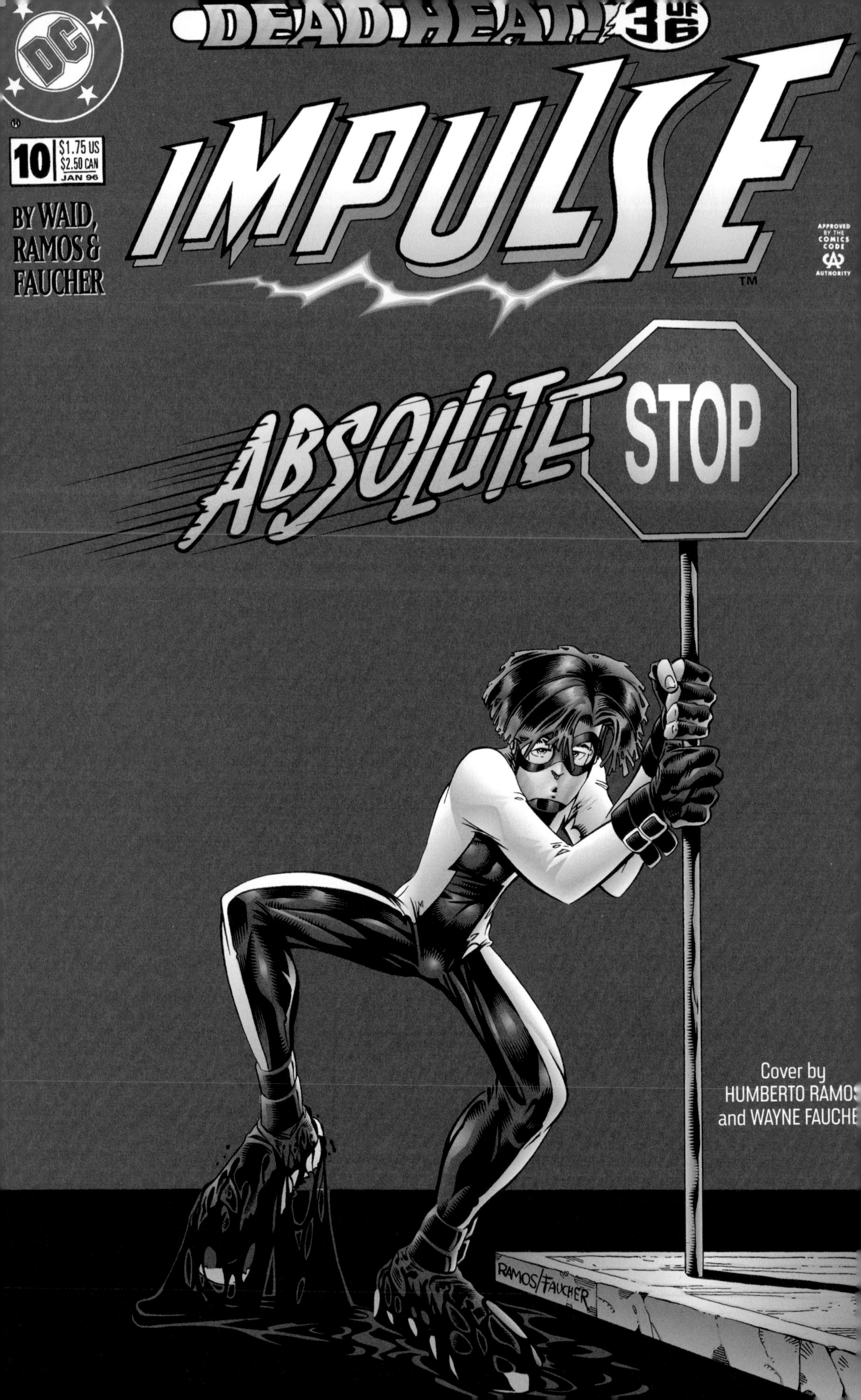

DEAD HEAT! 3 OF 6
DC
10
$1.75 US
$2.50 CAN
JAN 96
BY WAID, RAMOS & FAUCHER
IMPULSE
APPROVED BY THE COMICS CODE AUTHORITY
ABSOLUTE
STOP
Cover by
HUMBERTO RAMOS
and WAYNE FAUCHER
RAMOS/FAUCHER

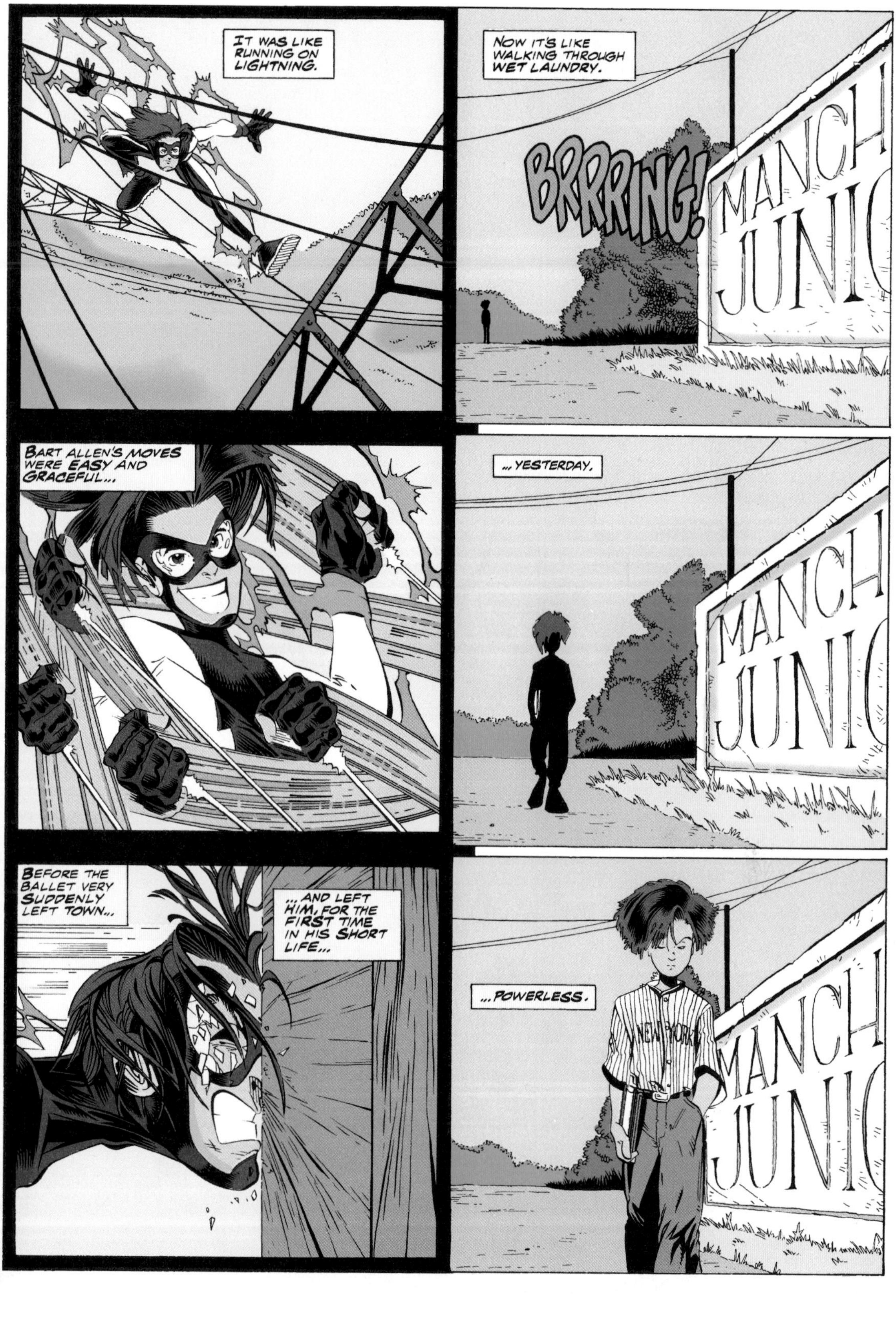
IT WAS LIKE RUNNING ON LIGHTNING.
NOW IT'S LIKE WALKING THROUGH WET LAUNDRY.
BRRRING!
MANCH
JUNIO
BART ALLEN'S MOVES WERE EASY AND GRACEFUL...
...YESTERDAY.
MANCH
JUNIO
BEFORE THE BALLET VERY SUDDENLY LEFT TOWN...
...AND LEFT HIM, FOR THE FIRST TIME IN HIS SHORT LIFE...
...POWERLESS.
NEW YORK
MANCH
JUNIO

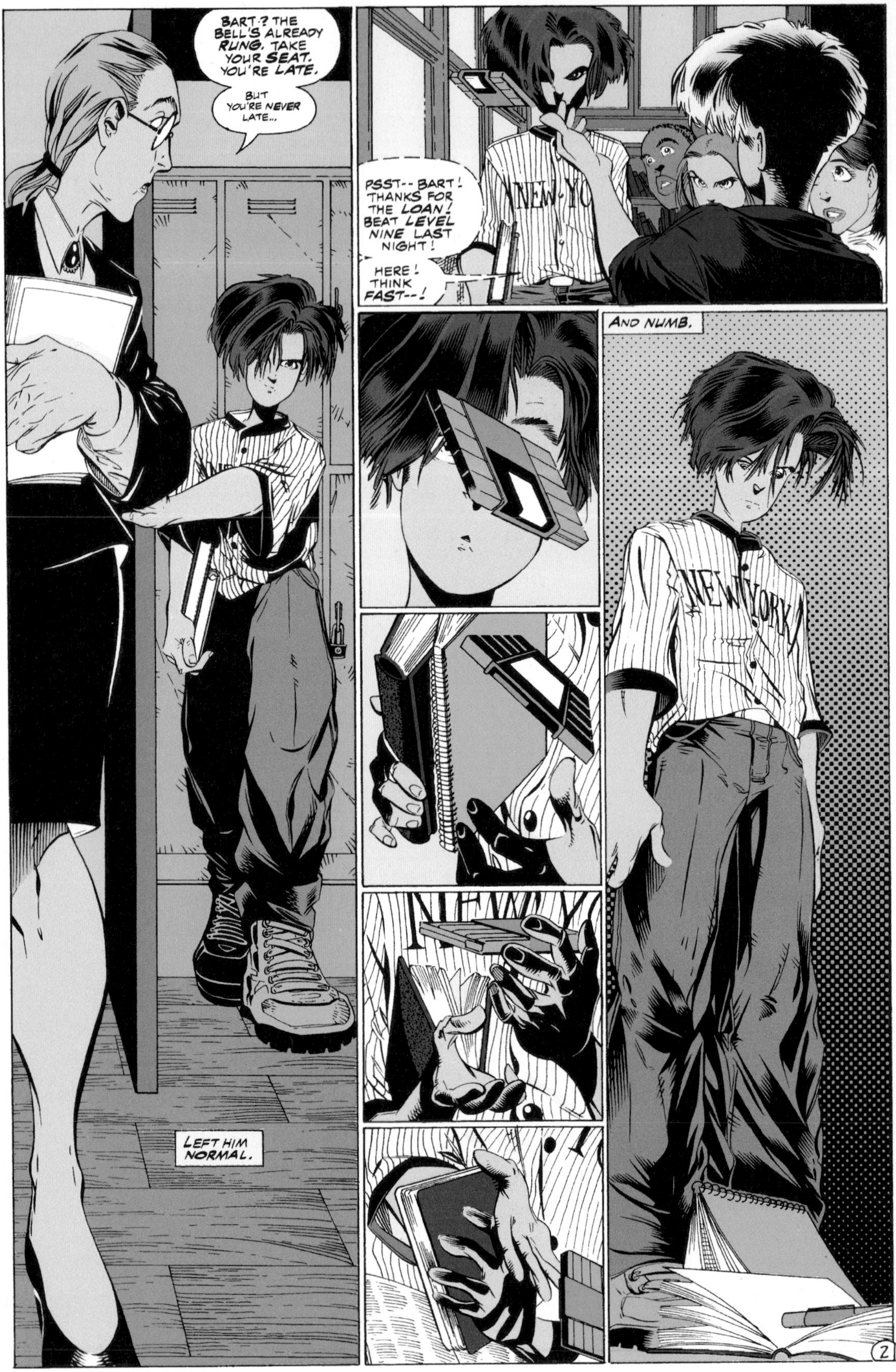

BART? THE BELL'S ALREADY RUNG. TAKE YOUR SEAT. YOU'RE LATE.
BUT YOU'RE NEVER LATE...
LEFT HIM NORMAL.
PSST-- BART! THANKS FOR THE LOAN! BEAT LEVEL NINE LAST NIGHT!
HERE! THINK FAST--!
AND NUMB.

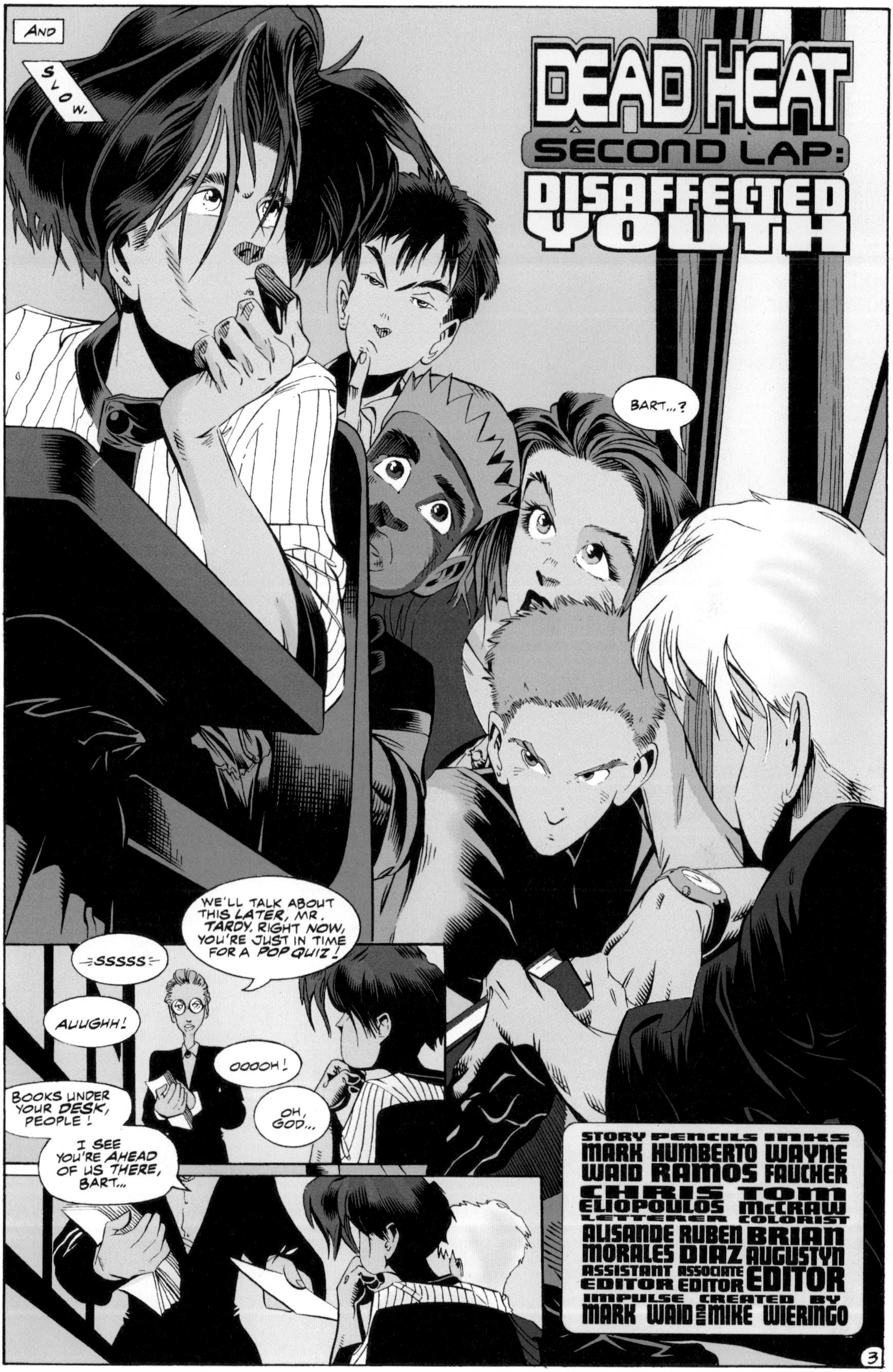
AND
SLOW.
DEAD HEAT
SECOND LAP:
DISAFFECTED YOUTH
BART...?
WE'LL TALK ABOUT THIS LATER, MR. TARDY. RIGHT NOW, YOU'RE JUST IN TIME FOR A POP QUIZ!
SSSSS
AUUGHH!
OOOOH!
BOOKS UNDER YOUR DESK, PEOPLE!
OH, GOD...
I SEE YOU'RE AHEAD OF US THERE, BART...
STORY MARK WAID PENCILS HUMBERTO RAMOS INKS WAYNE FAUCHER
CHRIS ELIOPOULOS LETTERER TOM McCRAW COLORIST
ALISANDE MORALES ASSISTANT EDITOR RUBEN DIAZ ASSOCIATE EDITOR BRIAN AUGUSTYN EDITOR
IMPULSE CREATED BY MARK WAID AND MIKE WIERINGO

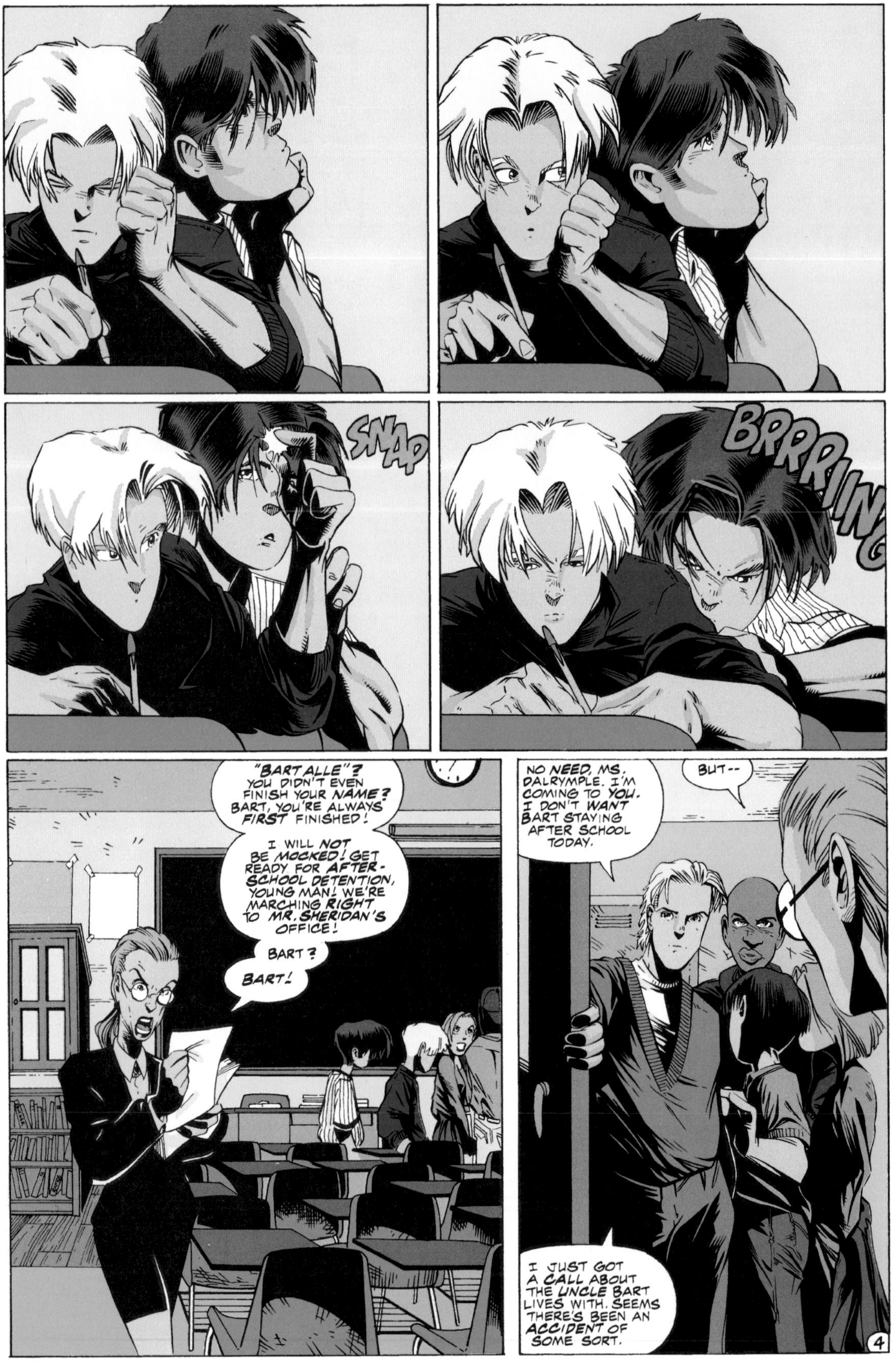

SNAP
BRRRRING
"BARTALLE"? YOU DIDN'T EVEN FINISH YOUR NAME? BART, YOU'RE ALWAYS FIRST FINISHED!
I WILL NOT BE MOCKED! GET READY FOR AFTER-SCHOOL DETENTION, YOUNG MAN! WE'RE MARCHING RIGHT TO MR. SHERIDAN'S OFFICE!
BART?
BART!
NO NEED, MS. DALRYMPLE. I'M COMING TO YOU. I DON'T WANT BART STAYING AFTER SCHOOL TODAY.
BUT--
I JUST GOT A CALL ABOUT THE UNCLE BART LIVES WITH. SEEMS THERE'S BEEN AN ACCIDENT OF SOME SORT.

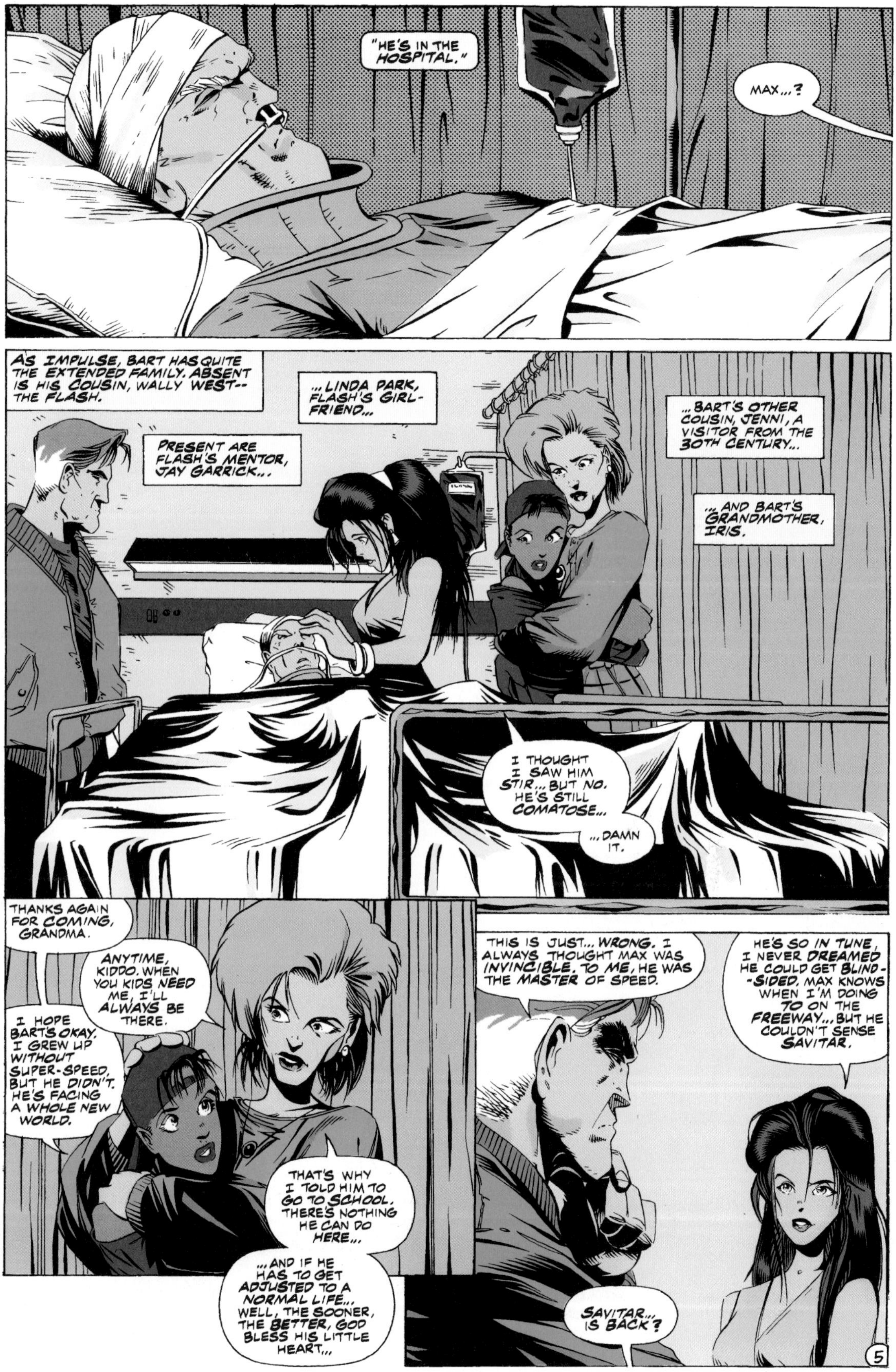
"HE'S IN THE HOSPITAL."
MAX...?
AS IMPULSE, BART HAS QUITE THE EXTENDED FAMILY. ABSENT IS HIS COUSIN, WALLY WEST-- THE FLASH.
PRESENT ARE FLASH'S MENTOR, JAY GARRICK...
...LINDA PARK, FLASH'S GIRL-FRIEND...
...BART'S OTHER COUSIN, JENNI, A VISITOR FROM THE 30TH CENTURY...
...AND BART'S GRANDMOTHER, IRIS.
I THOUGHT I SAW HIM STIR... BUT NO. HE'S STILL COMATOSE...
...DAMN IT.
THANKS AGAIN FOR COMING, GRANDMA.
ANYTIME, KIDDO. WHEN YOU KIDS NEED ME, I'LL ALWAYS BE THERE.
I HOPE BART'S OKAY. I GREW UP WITHOUT SUPER-SPEED, BUT HE DIDN'T. HE'S FACING A WHOLE NEW WORLD.
THAT'S WHY I TOLD HIM TO GO TO SCHOOL. THERE'S NOTHING HE CAN DO HERE...
...AND IF HE HAS TO GET ADJUSTED TO A NORMAL LIFE... WELL, THE SOONER, THE BETTER, GOD BLESS HIS LITTLE HEART...
THIS IS JUST... WRONG. I ALWAYS THOUGHT MAX WAS INVINCIBLE. TO ME, HE WAS THE MASTER OF SPEED.
HE'S SO IN TUNE, I NEVER DREAMED HE COULD GET BLIND-SIDED. MAX KNOWS WHEN I'M DOING 70 ON THE FREEWAY... BUT HE COULDN'T SENSE SAVITAR.
SAVITAR... IS BACK?
5

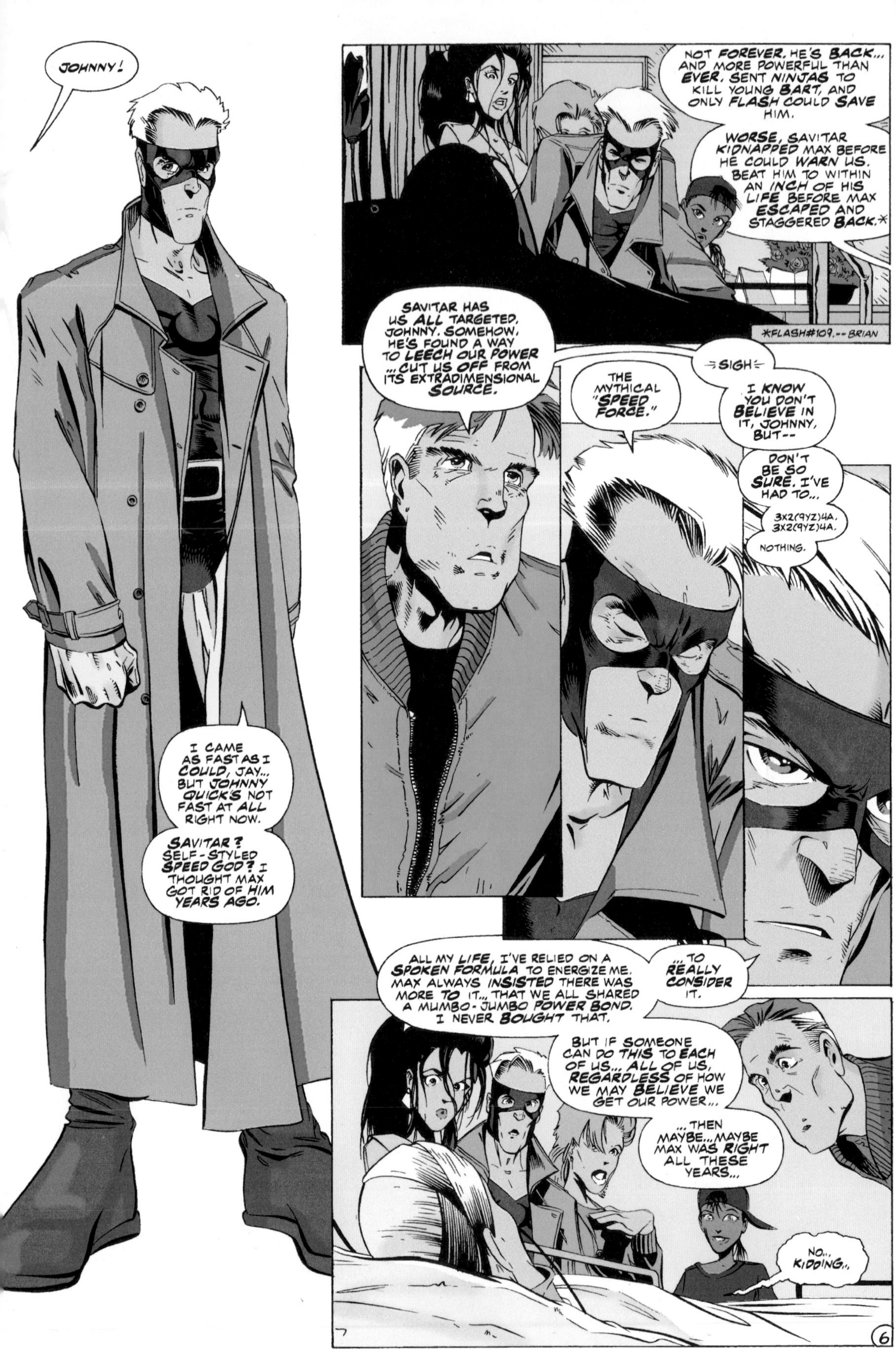

JOHNNY!
NOT FOREVER. HE'S BACK... AND MORE POWERFUL THAN EVER. SENT NINJAS TO KILL YOUNG BART, AND ONLY FLASH COULD SAVE HIM.
WORSE, SAVITAR KIDNAPPED MAX BEFORE HE COULD WARN US. BEAT HIM TO WITHIN AN INCH OF HIS LIFE BEFORE MAX ESCAPED AND STAGGERED BACK.*
*FLASH #109. --BRIAN
I CAME AS FAST AS I COULD, JAY... BUT JOHNNY QUICK'S NOT FAST AT ALL RIGHT NOW.
SAVITAR? SELF-STYLED SPEED GOD? I THOUGHT MAX GOT RID OF HIM YEARS AGO.
SAVITAR HAS US ALL TARGETED, JOHNNY. SOMEHOW, HE'S FOUND A WAY TO LEECH OUR POWER ...CUT US OFF FROM ITS EXTRADIMENSIONAL SOURCE.
THE MYTHICAL "SPEED FORCE."
=SIGH=
I KNOW YOU DON'T BELIEVE IN IT, JOHNNY, BUT--
DON'T BE SO SURE. I'VE HAD TO...
3X2(9YZ)4A. 3X2(9YZ)4A.
NOTHING.
ALL MY LIFE, I'VE RELIED ON A SPOKEN FORMULA TO ENERGIZE ME. MAX ALWAYS INSISTED THERE WAS MORE TO IT... THAT WE ALL SHARED A MUMBO-JUMBO POWER BOND. I NEVER BOUGHT THAT.
...TO REALLY CONSIDER IT.
BUT IF SOMEONE CAN DO THIS TO EACH OF US... ALL OF US, REGARDLESS OF HOW WE MAY BELIEVE WE GET OUR POWER...
...THEN MAYBE... MAYBE MAX WAS RIGHT ALL THESE YEARS...
NO... KIDDING..
6

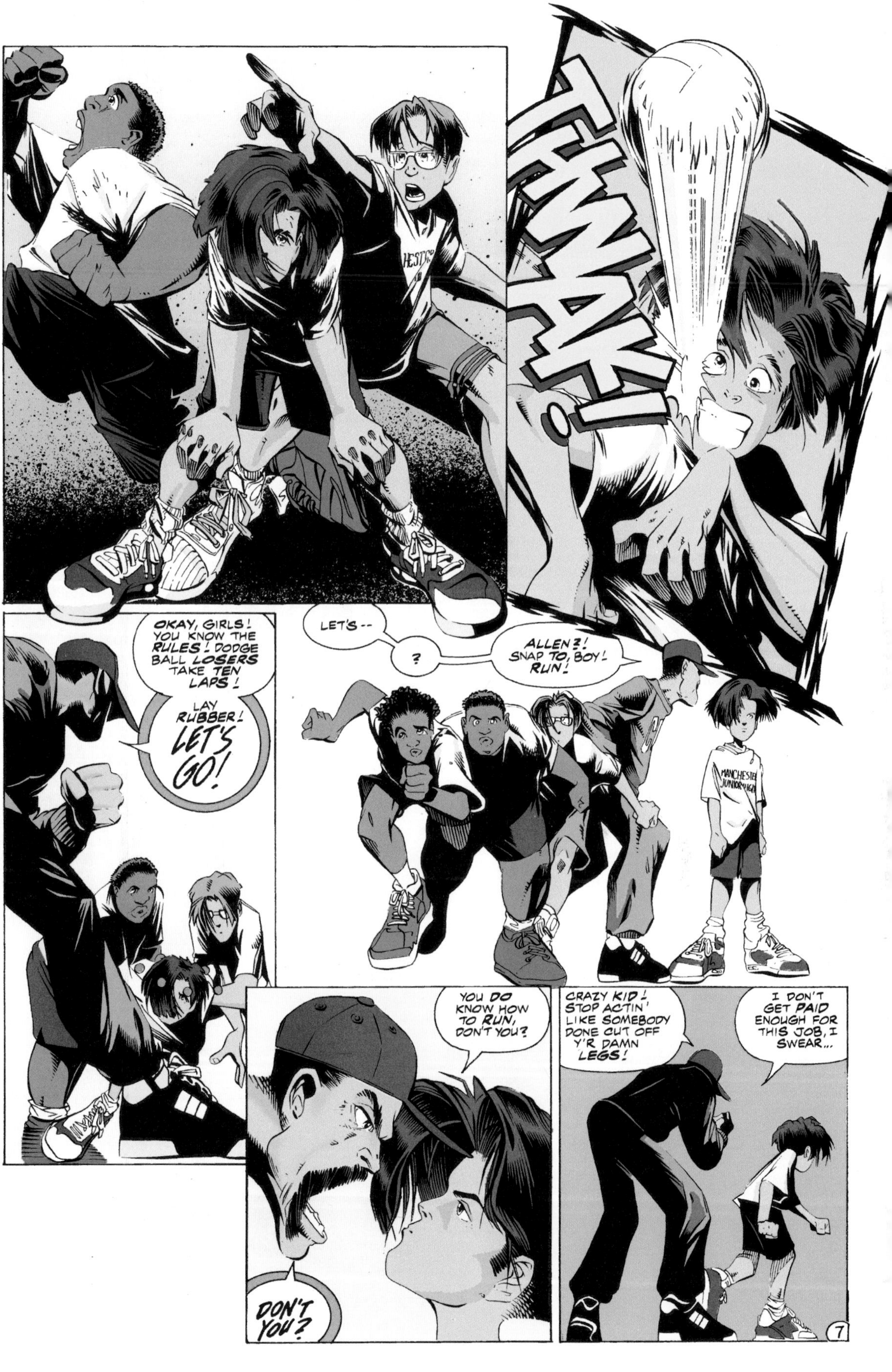
THWAK!
OKAY, GIRLS! YOU KNOW THE RULES! DODGE BALL LOSERS TAKE TEN LAPS!
LAY RUBBER! LET'S GO!
LET'S --
?
ALLEN?! SNAP TO, BOY! RUN!
MANCHESTER JUNIOR HIGH
YOU DO KNOW HOW TO RUN, DON'T YOU?
DON'T YOU?
CRAZY KID! STOP ACTIN' LIKE SOMEBODY DONE CUT OFF Y'R DAMN LEGS!
I DON'T GET PAID ENOUGH FOR THIS JOB, I SWEAR...
7

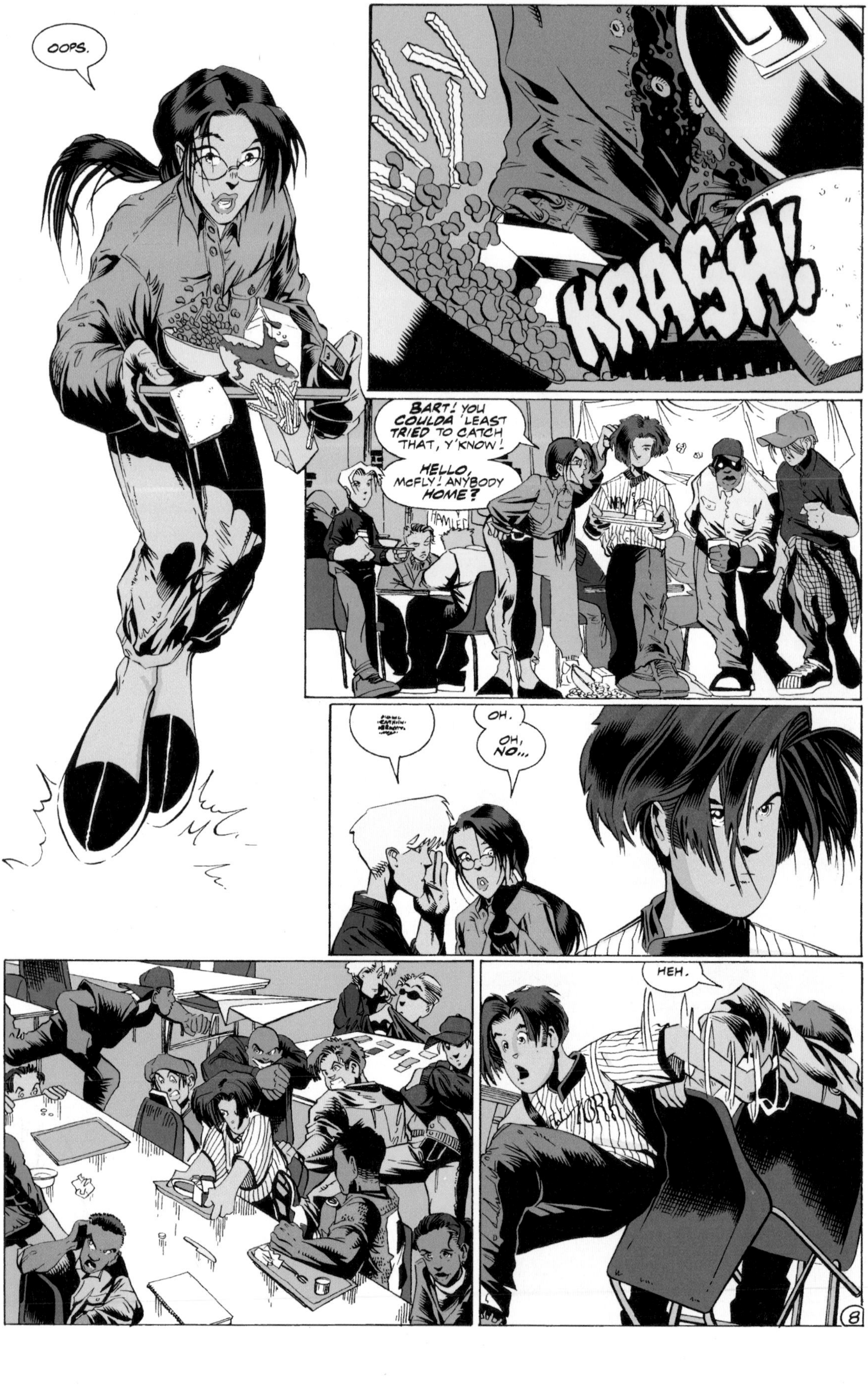
OOPS.
KRASH!
BART! YOU COULDA 'LEAST TRIED TO CATCH THAT, Y'KNOW!
HELLO, McFLY! ANYBODY HOME?
OH.
OH, NO...
HEH.
8

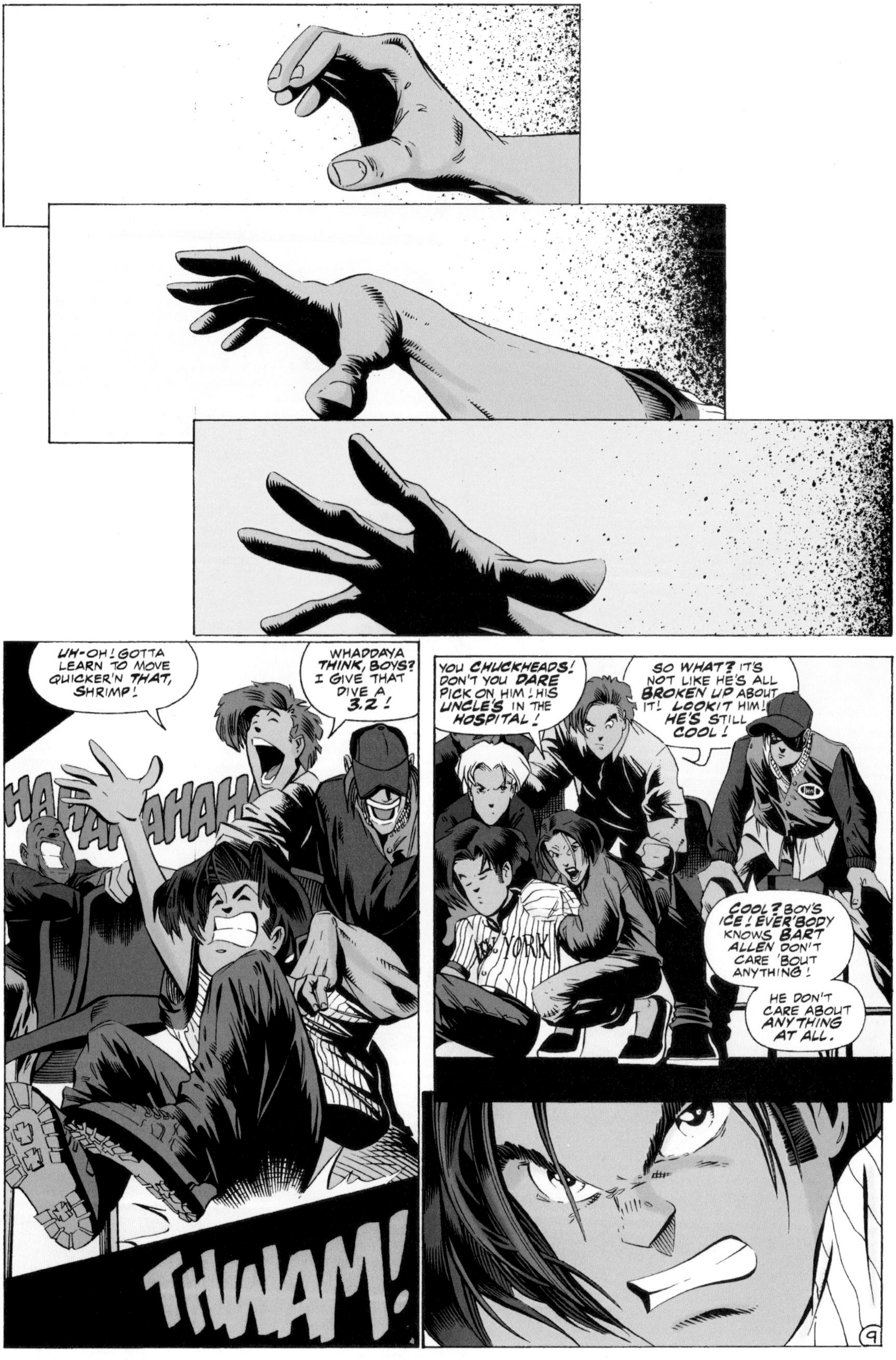
UH-OH! GOTTA LEARN TO MOVE QUICKER'N THAT, SHRIMP!
WHADDAYA THINK, BOYS? I GIVE THAT DIVE A 3.2!
HAHAHAHAH
THWAM!
YOU CHUCKHEADS! DON'T YOU DARE PICK ON HIM! HIS UNCLE'S IN THE HOSPITAL!
SO WHAT? IT'S NOT LIKE HE'S ALL BROKEN UP ABOUT IT! LOOKIT HIM! HE'S STILL COOL!
COOL? BOY'S ICE! EVER'BODY KNOWS BART ALLEN DON'T CARE 'BOUT ANYTHING!
HE DON'T CARE ABOUT ANYTHING AT ALL.
9

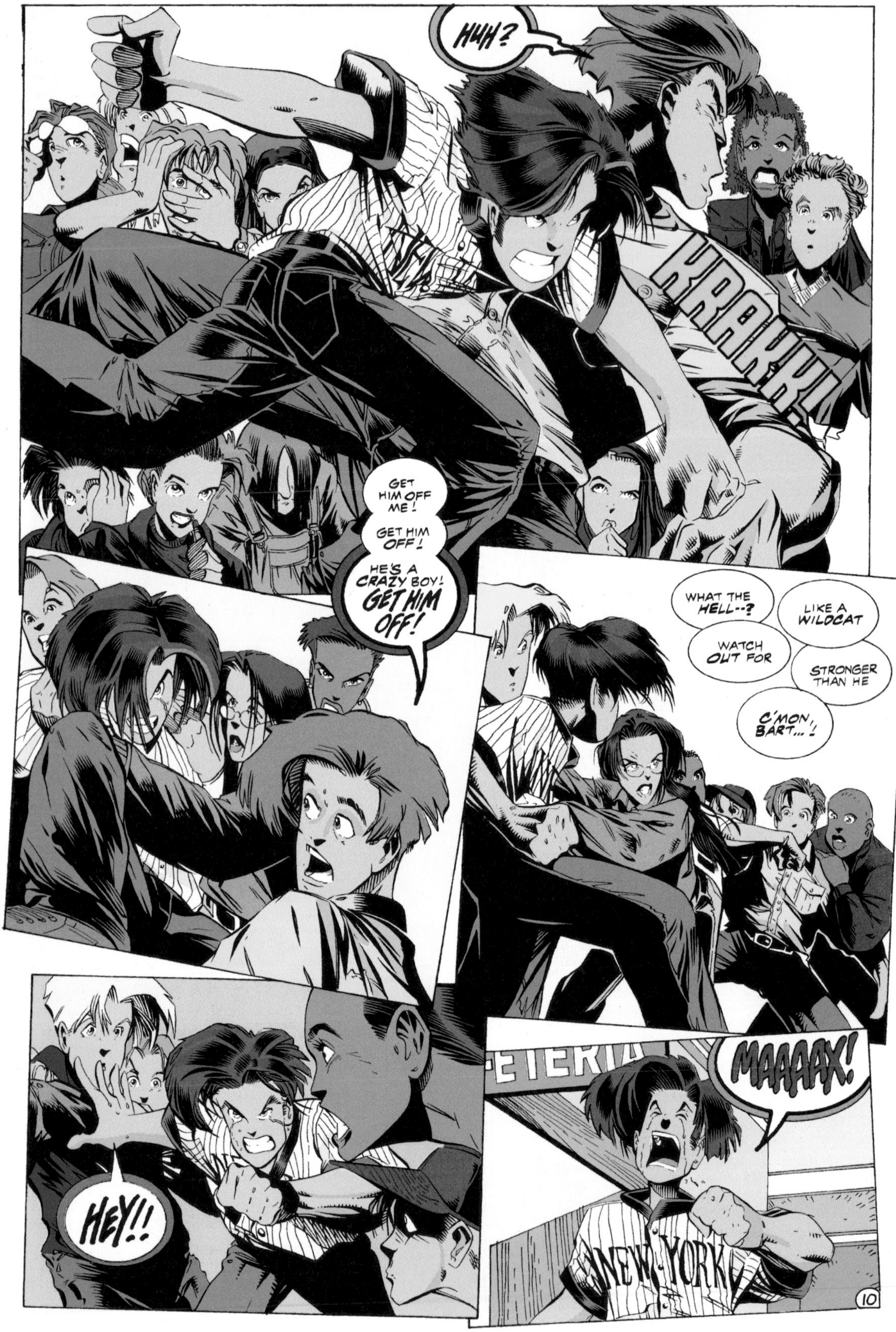
HUH?
KRAKK!
GET HIM OFF ME!
GET HIM OFF!
HE'S A CRAZY BOY! GET HIM OFF!
WHAT THE HELL--?
LIKE A WILDCAT
WATCH OUT FOR
STRONGER THAN HE
C'MON, BART...!
HEY!!
FETERIA
MAAAAX!
NEW YORK
10

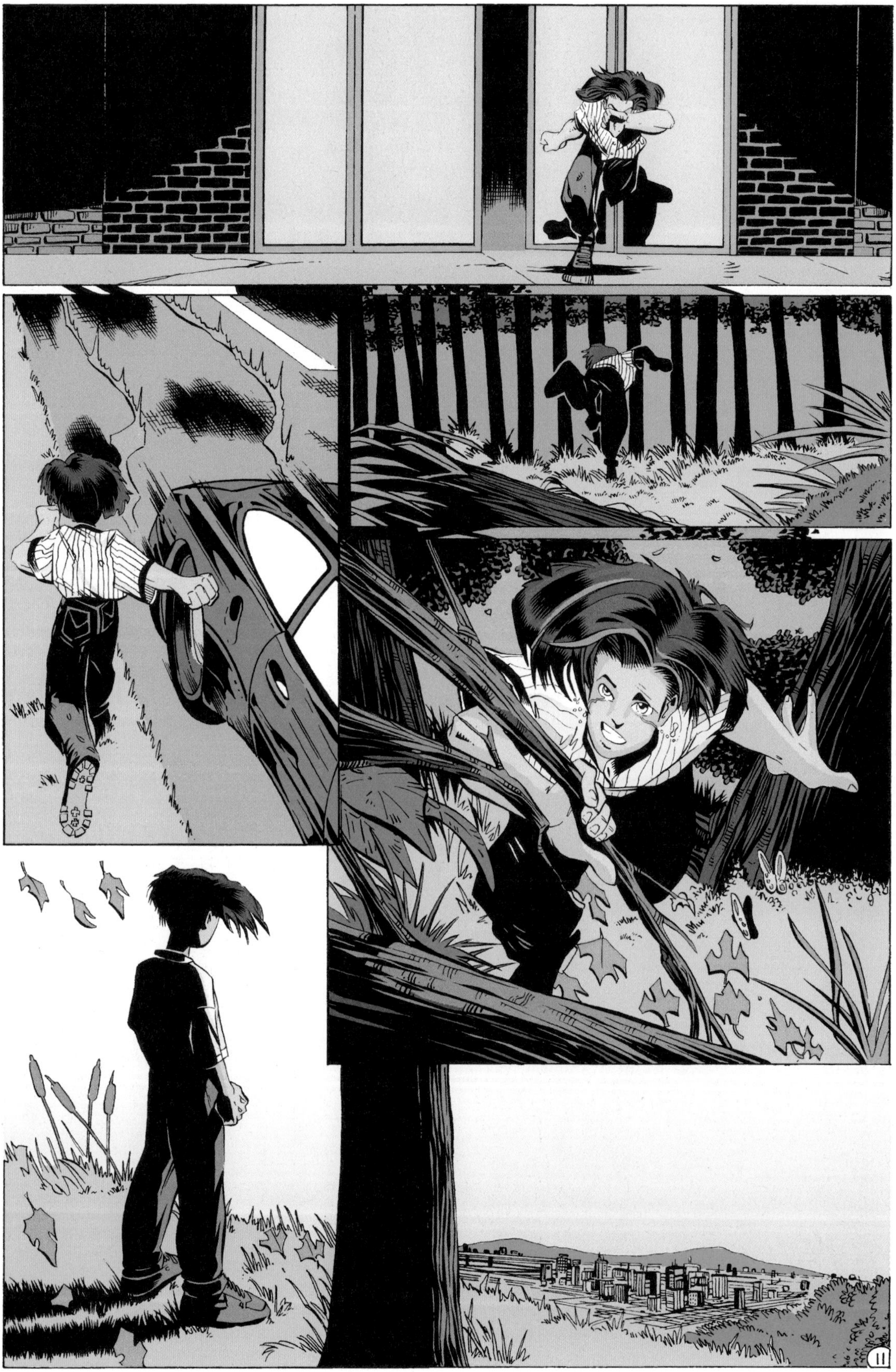

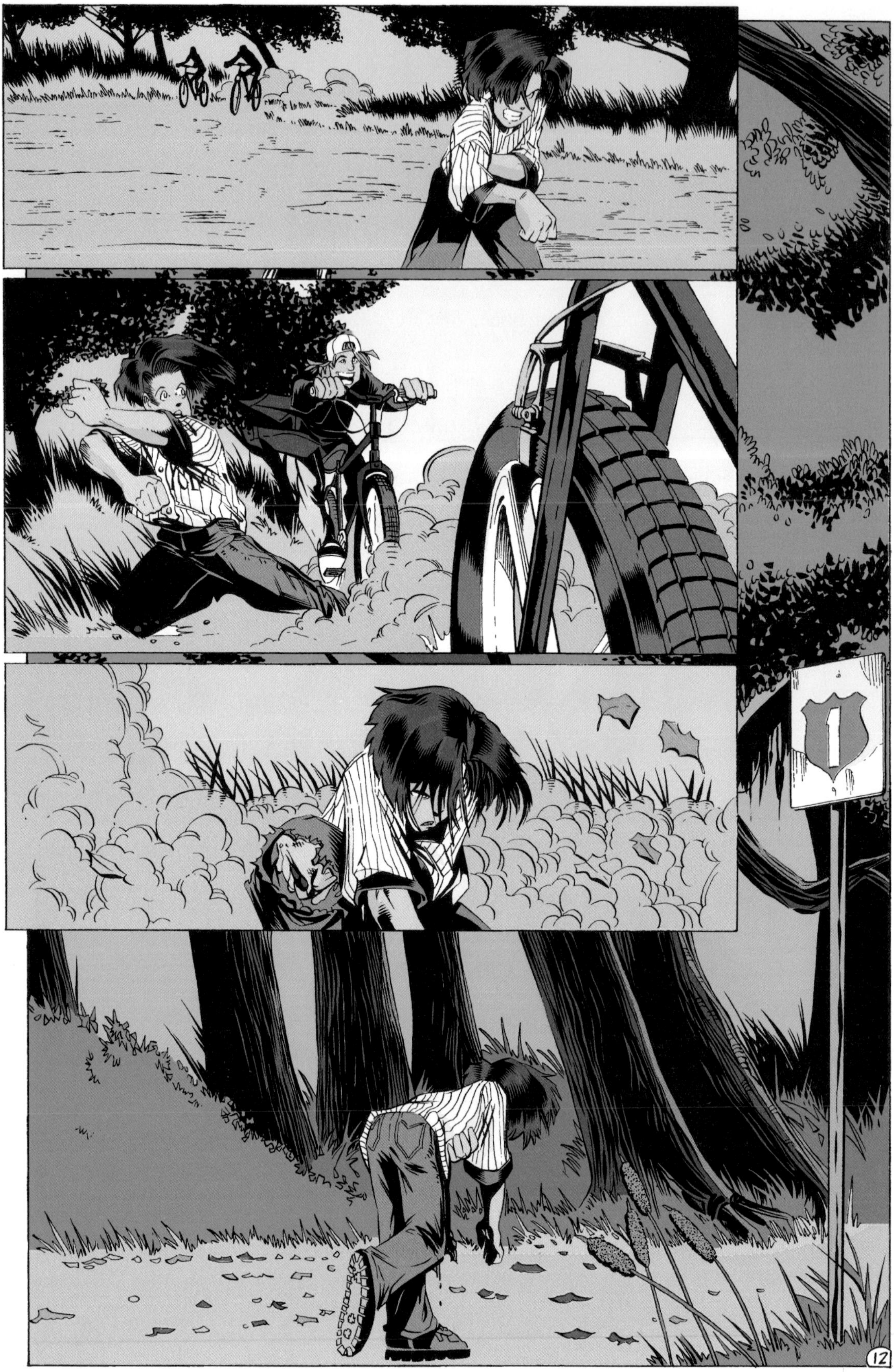
1

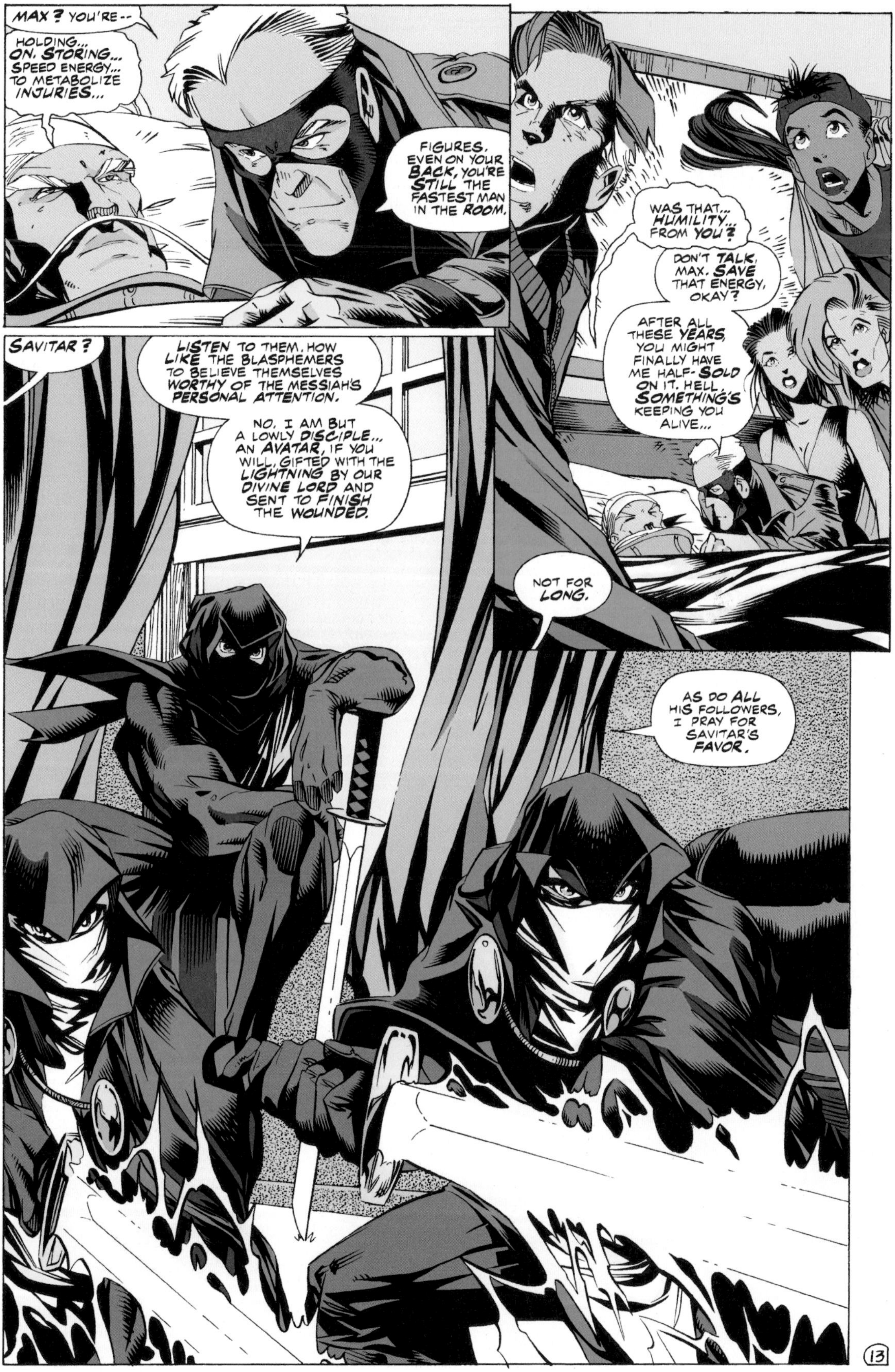

MAX? YOU'RE--
HOLDING... ON. STORING... SPEED ENERGY... TO METABOLIZE INJURIES...
FIGURES. EVEN ON YOUR BACK, YOU'RE STILL THE FASTEST MAN IN THE ROOM.
WAS THAT... HUMILITY... FROM YOU?
DON'T TALK, MAX. SAVE THAT ENERGY, OKAY?
AFTER ALL THESE YEARS, YOU MIGHT FINALLY HAVE ME HALF-SOLD ON IT. HELL, SOMETHING'S KEEPING YOU ALIVE...
NOT FOR LONG.
SAVITAR?
LISTEN TO THEM. HOW LIKE THE BLASPHEMERS TO BELIEVE THEMSELVES WORTHY OF THE MESSIAH'S PERSONAL ATTENTION.
NO. I AM BUT A LOWLY DISCIPLE... AN AVATAR, IF YOU WILL, GIFTED WITH THE LIGHTNING BY OUR DIVINE LORD AND SENT TO FINISH THE WOUNDED.
AS DO ALL HIS FOLLOWERS, I PRAY FOR SAVITAR'S FAVOR.

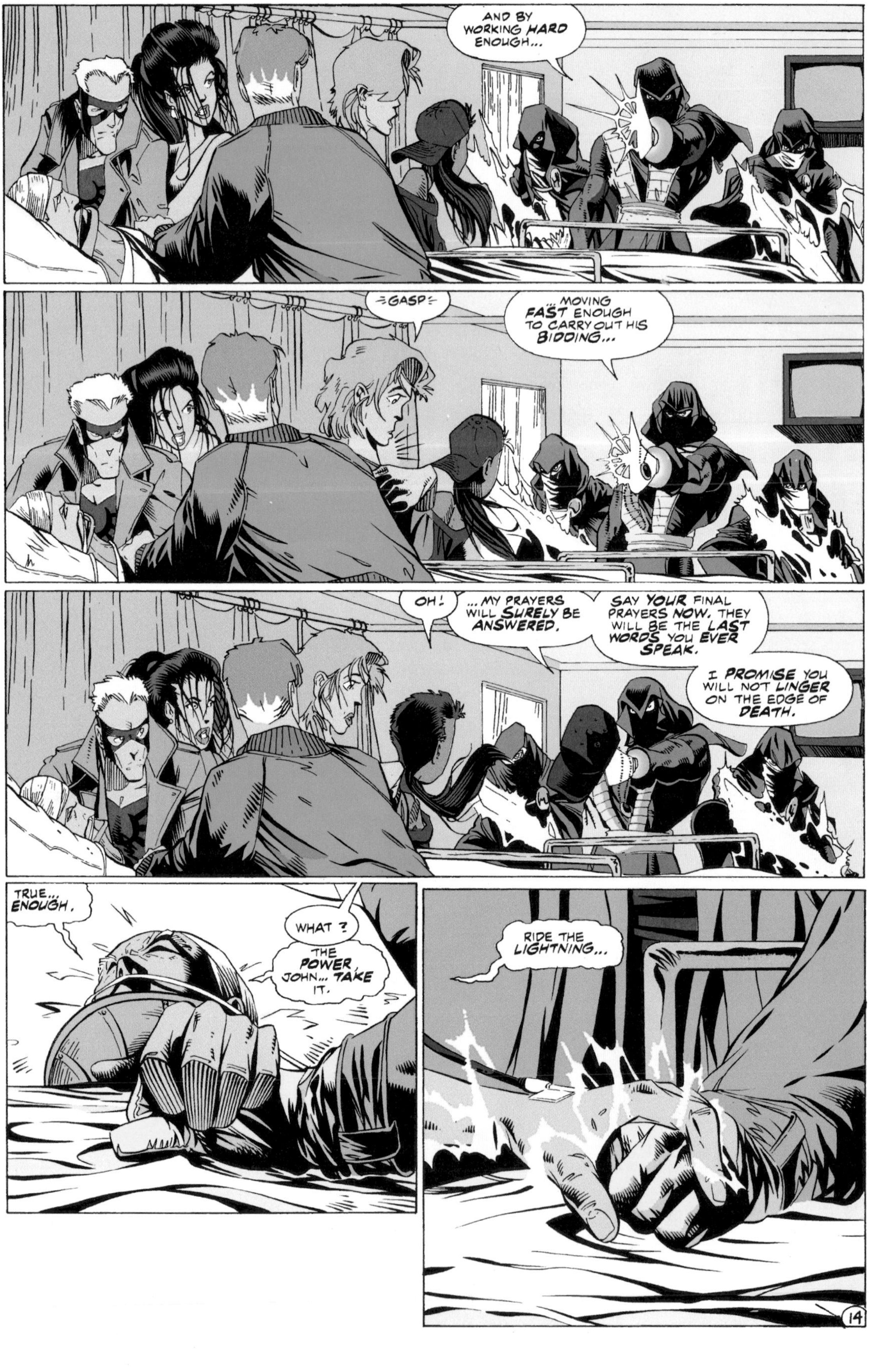
AND BY WORKING HARD ENOUGH...
GASP
...MOVING FAST ENOUGH TO CARRY OUT HIS BIDDING...
OH!
...MY PRAYERS WILL SURELY BE ANSWERED.
SAY YOUR FINAL PRAYERS NOW. THEY WILL BE THE LAST WORDS YOU EVER SPEAK.
I PROMISE YOU WILL NOT LINGER ON THE EDGE OF DEATH.
TRUE... ENOUGH.
WHAT?
THE POWER, JOHN... TAKE IT.
RIDE THE LIGHTNING...

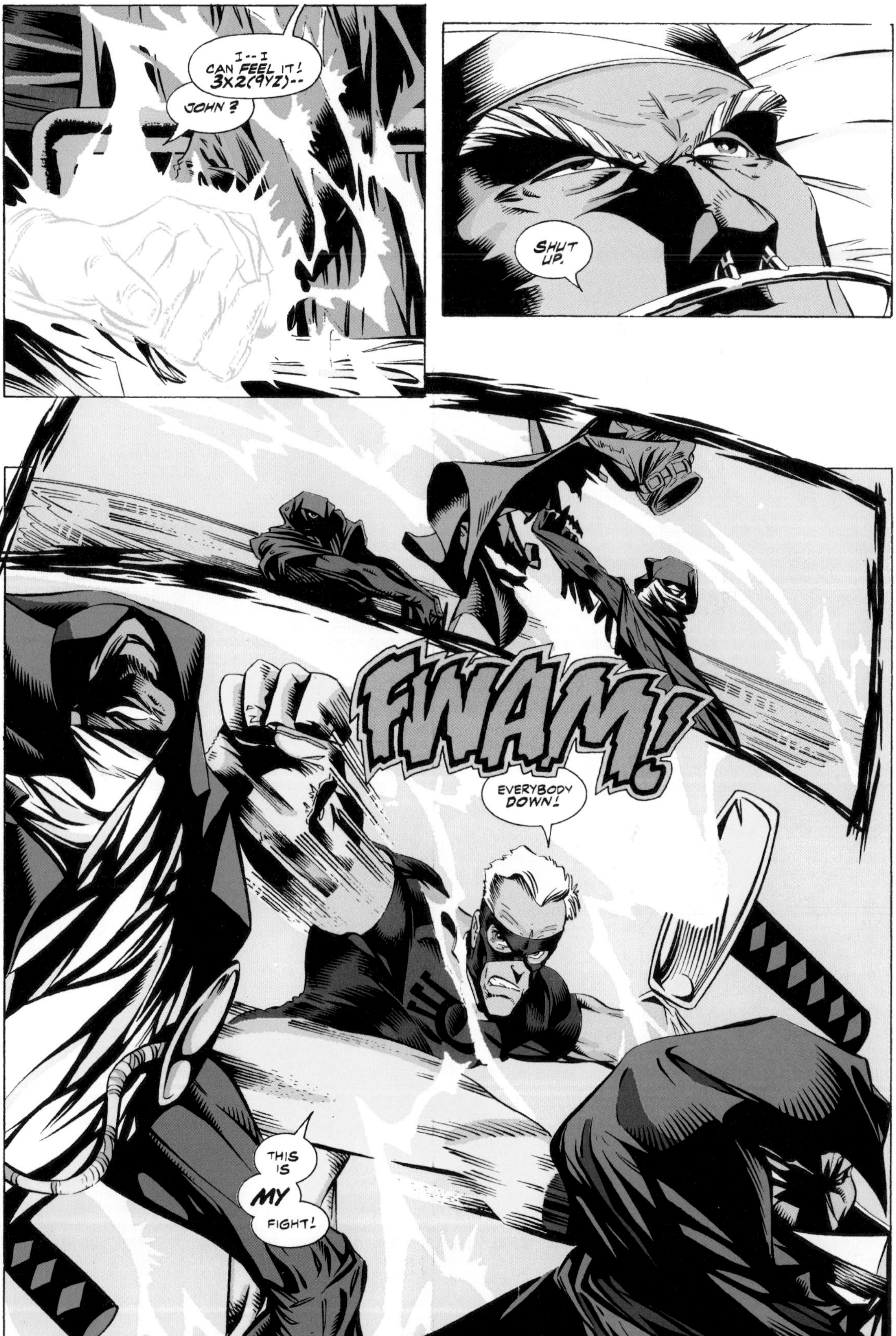

I-- I CAN FEEL IT! 3X2(9YZ)--
JOHN ?
SHUT UP.
FWAM!
EVERYBODY DOWN!
THIS IS MY FIGHT!

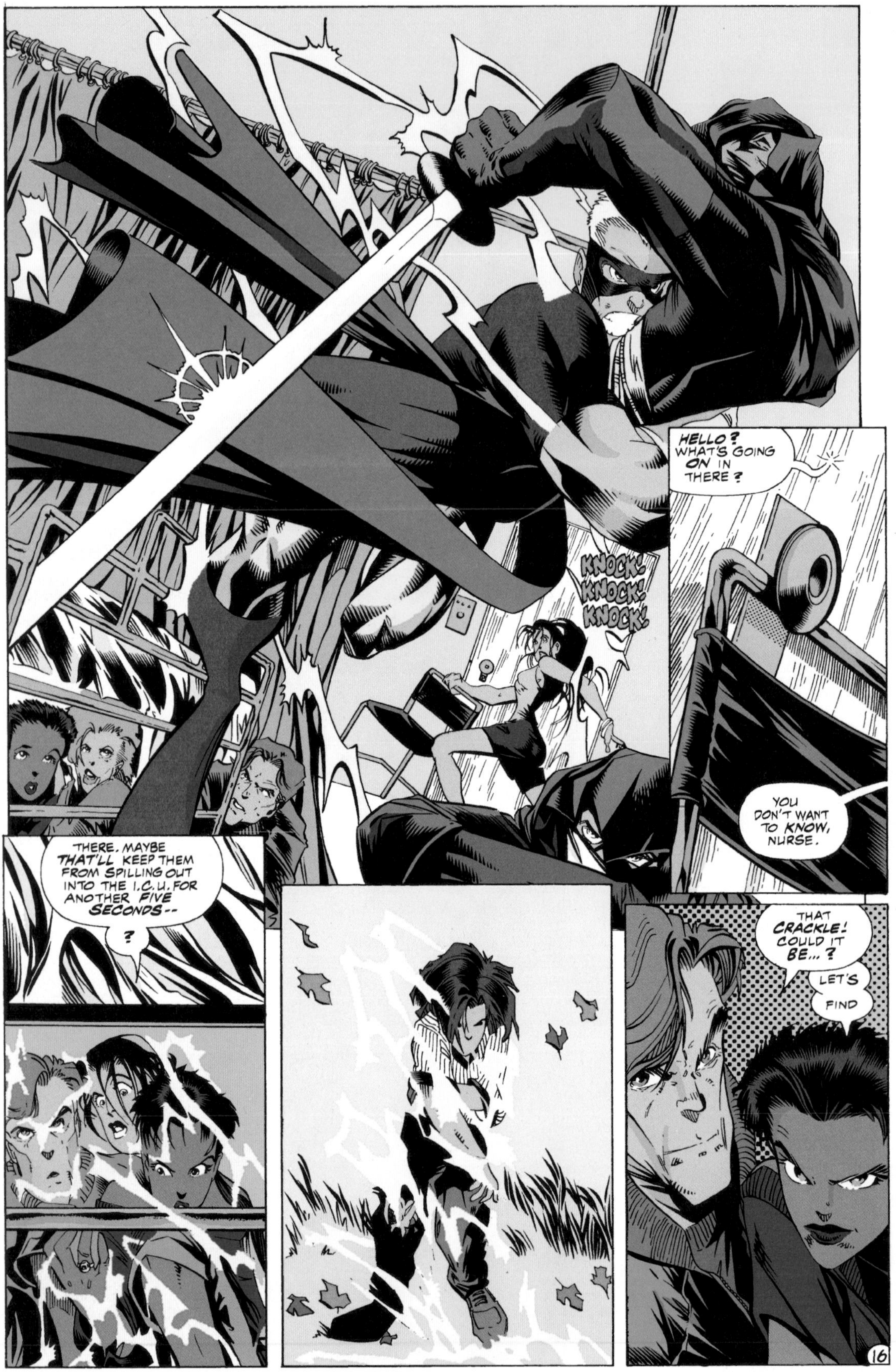
HELLO? WHAT'S GOING ON IN THERE?
KNOCK! KNOCK! KNOCK!
YOU DON'T WANT TO KNOW, NURSE.
THERE. MAYBE THAT'LL KEEP THEM FROM SPILLING OUT INTO THE I.C.U. FOR ANOTHER FIVE SECONDS--
?
THAT CRACKLE! COULD IT BE...?
LET'S
FIND

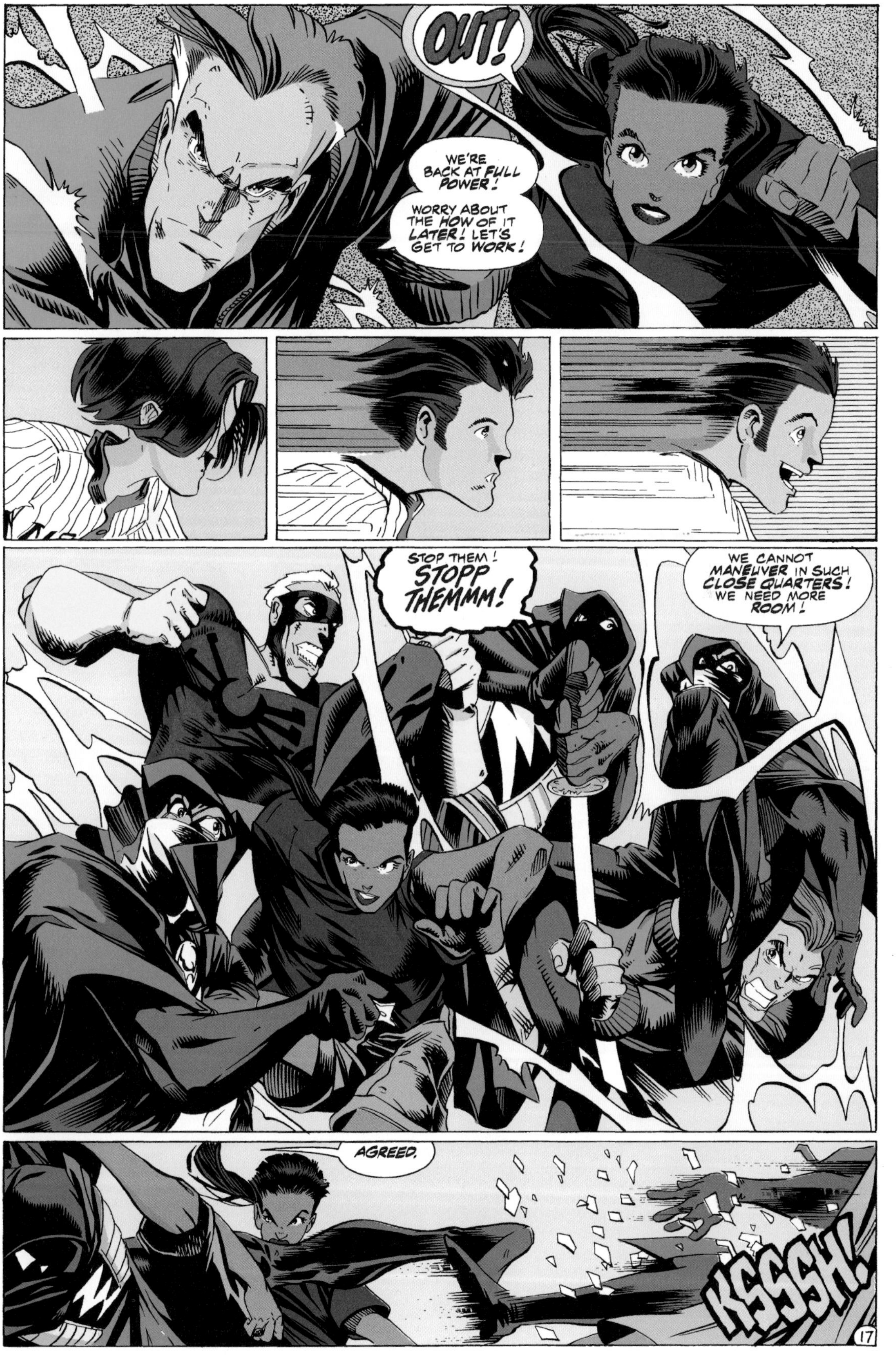
OUT!
WE'RE BACK AT FULL POWER!
WORRY ABOUT THE HOW OF IT LATER! LET'S GET TO WORK!
STOP THEM! STOPP THEMMM!
WE CANNOT MANEUVER IN SUCH CLOSE QUARTERS! WE NEED MORE ROOM!
AGREED.
KSSSH!

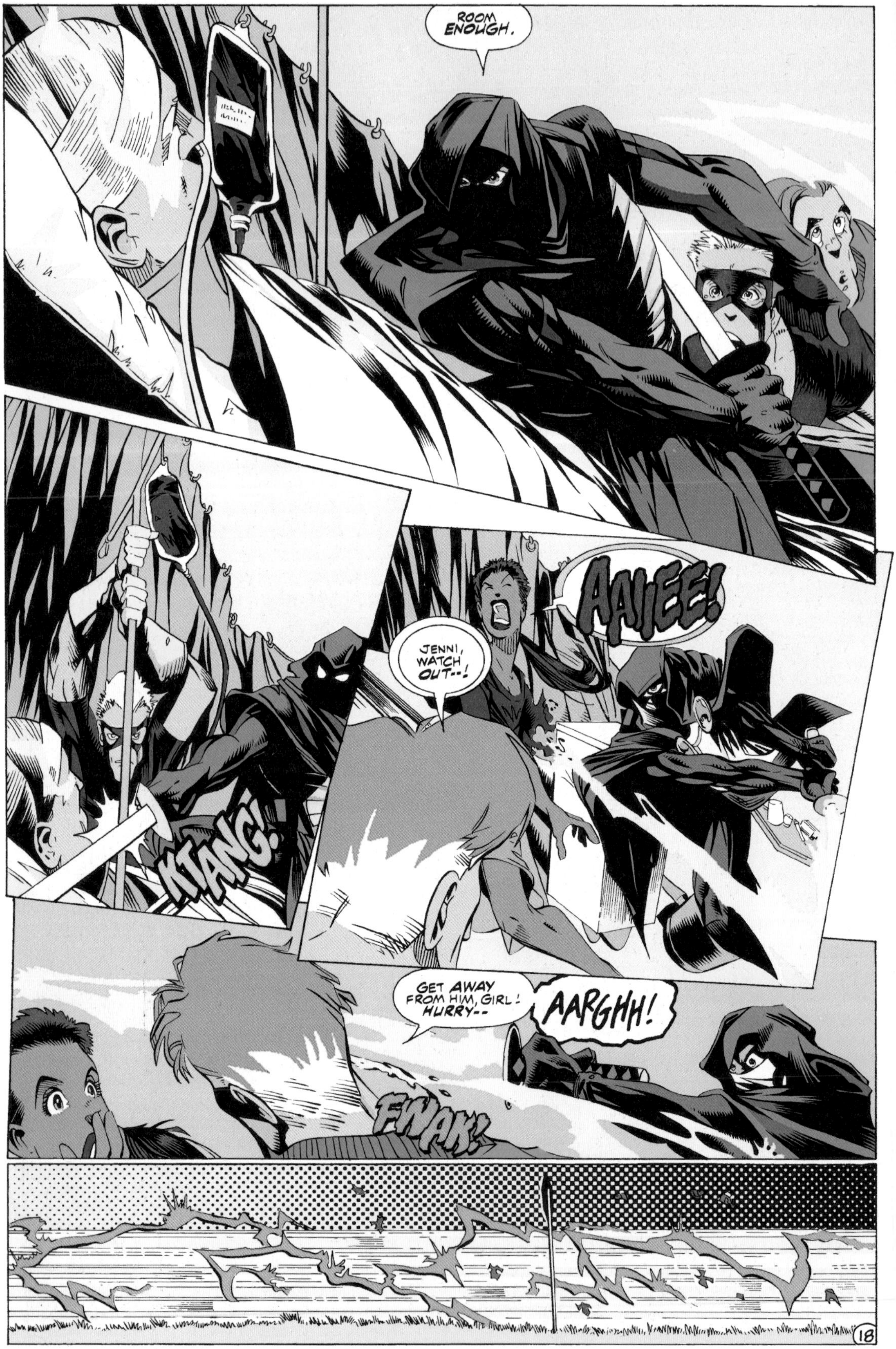
ROOM ENOUGH.
KTANG!
JENNI, WATCH OUT--!
AAIEE!
GET AWAY FROM HIM, GIRL! HURRY--
AARGHH!
FWAK!

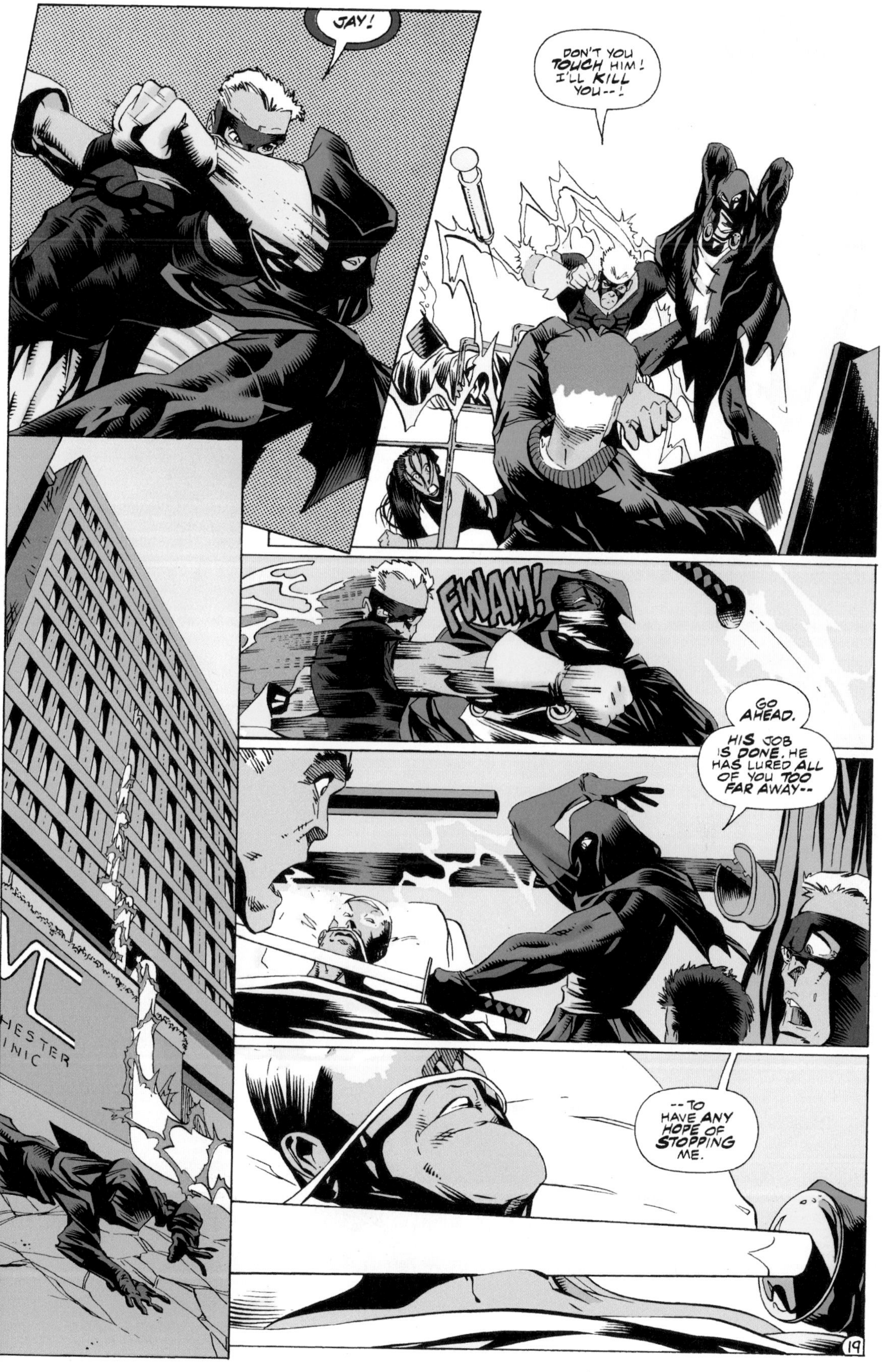
JAY!
DON'T YOU TOUCH HIM! I'LL KILL YOU--!
FWAM!
GO AHEAD.
HIS JOB IS DONE. HE HAS LURED ALL OF YOU TOO FAR AWAY--
--TO HAVE ANY HOPE OF STOPPING ME.
HESTER
INIC

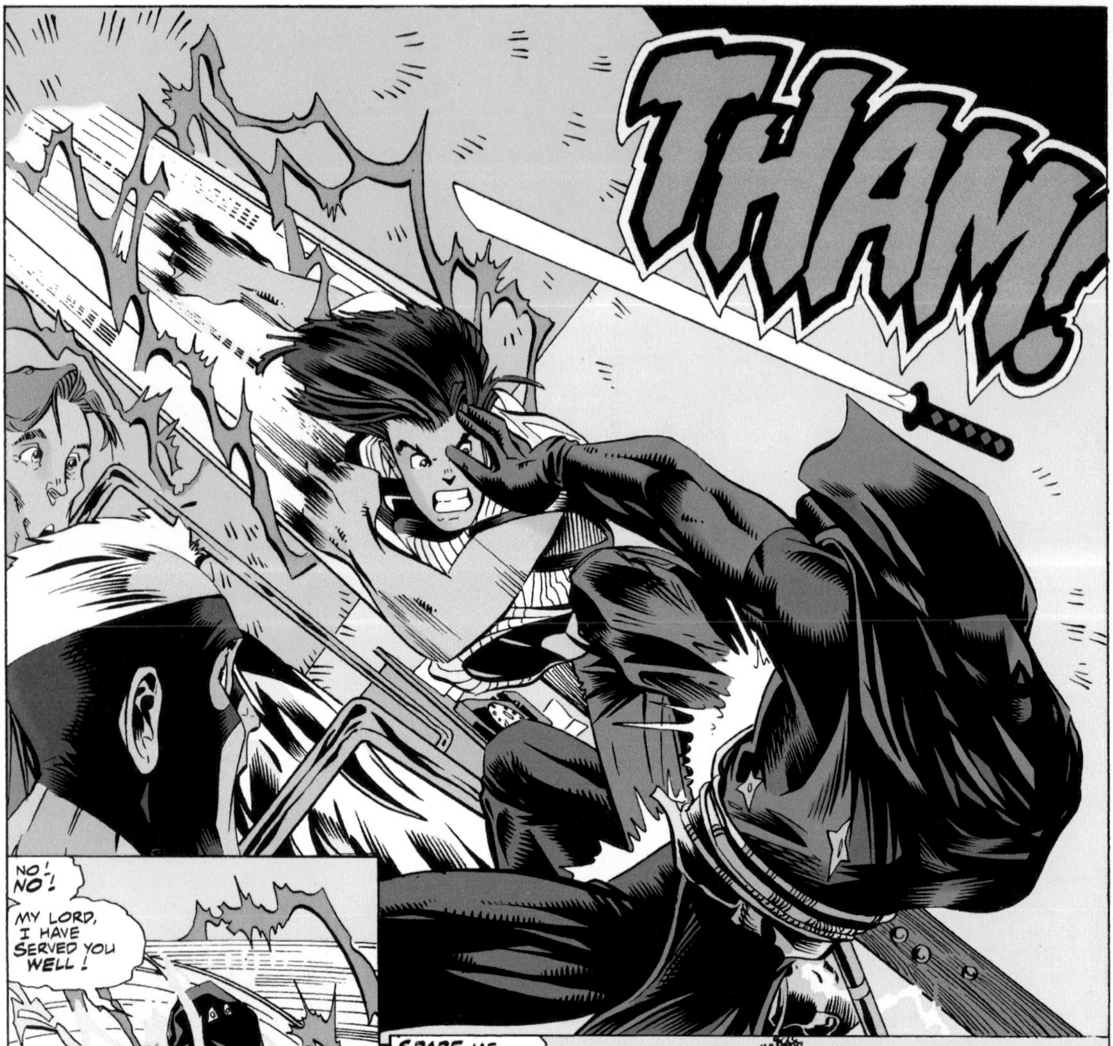
THAM!
NO! NO!
MY LORD, I HAVE SERVED YOU WELL!
SPARE ME, MY LORD! GIVE ME ANOTHER CHANCE!
SPARE MEEEE--

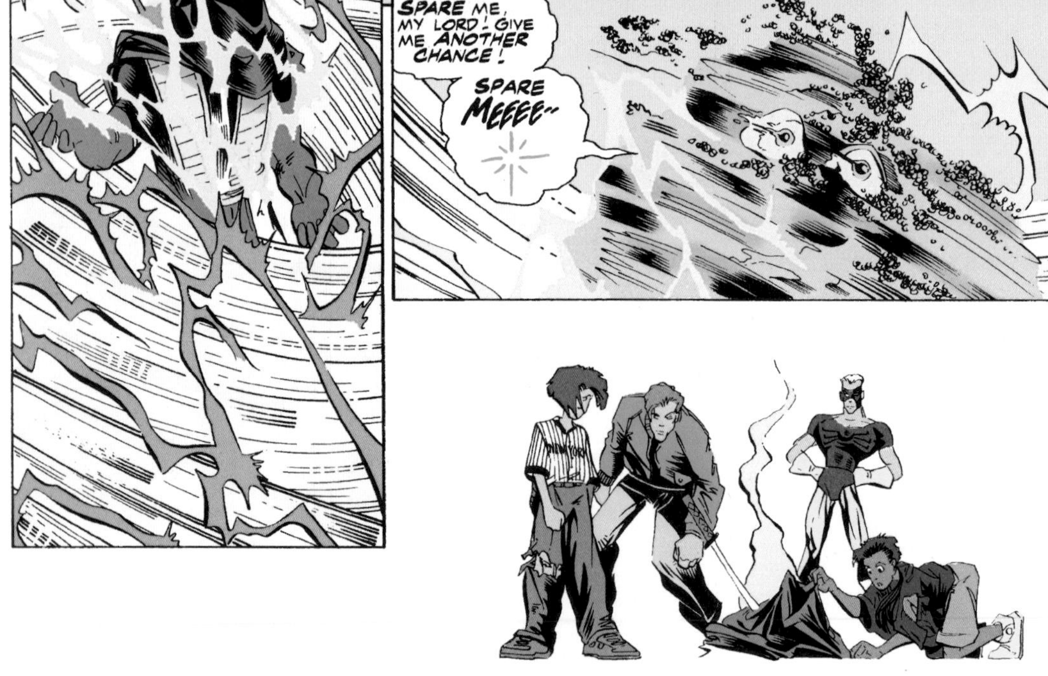

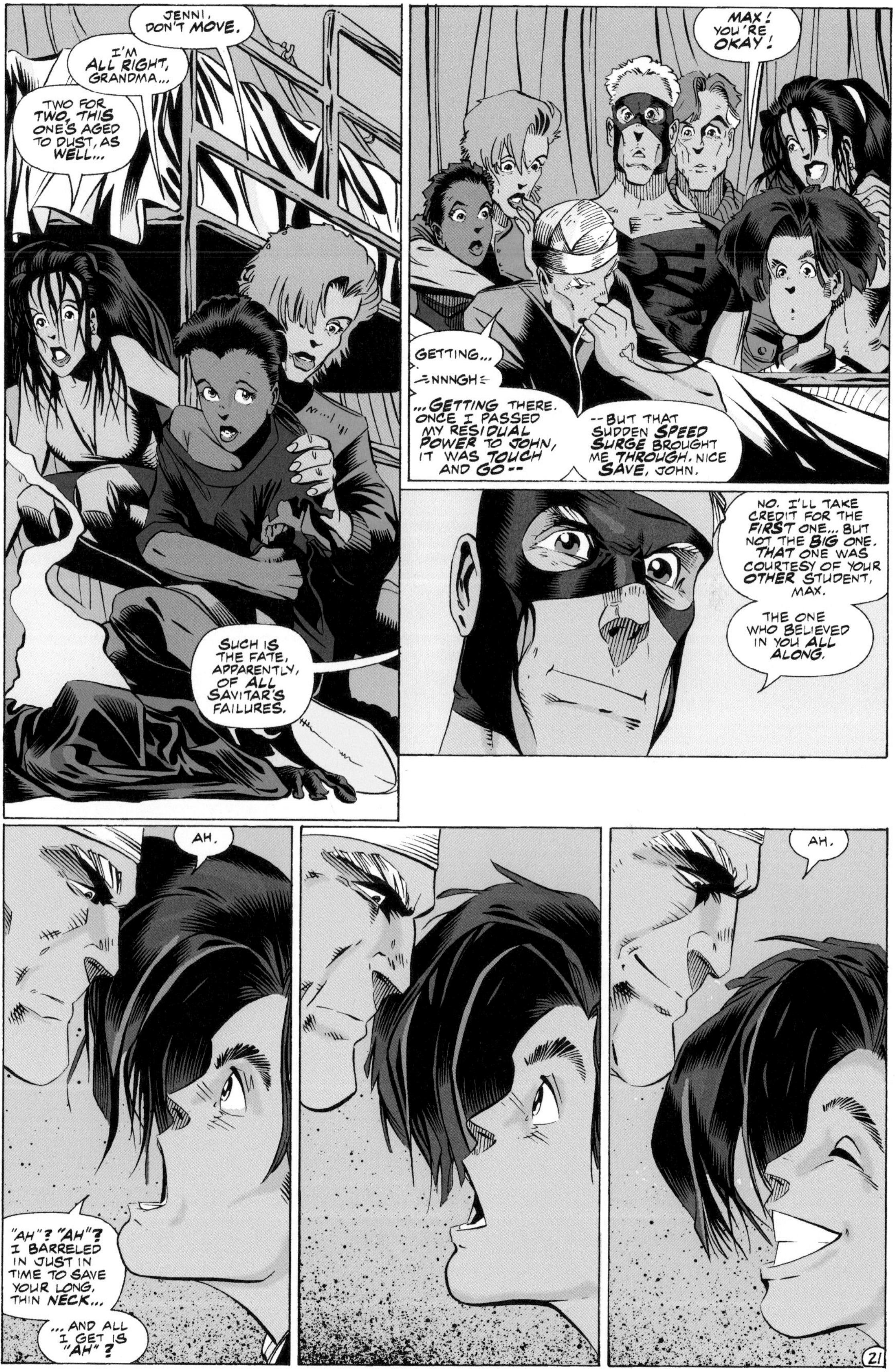
JENNI, DON'T MOVE.
I'M ALL RIGHT, GRANDMA...
TWO FOR TWO, THIS ONE'S AGED TO DUST, AS WELL...
SUCH IS THE FATE, APPARENTLY, OF ALL SAVITAR'S FAILURES.
MAX! YOU'RE OKAY!
GETTING...
NNNGH
...GETTING THERE. ONCE I PASSED MY RESIDUAL POWER TO JOHN, IT WAS TOUCH AND GO--
--BUT THAT SUDDEN SPEED SURGE BROUGHT ME THROUGH. NICE SAVE, JOHN.
NO. I'LL TAKE CREDIT FOR THE FIRST ONE... BUT NOT THE BIG ONE. THAT ONE WAS COURTESY OF YOUR OTHER STUDENT, MAX.
THE ONE WHO BELIEVED IN YOU ALL ALONG.
AH.
"AH"? "AH"? I BARRELED IN JUST IN TIME TO SAVE YOUR LONG, THIN NECK...
...AND ALL I GET IS "AH"?
AH.
21

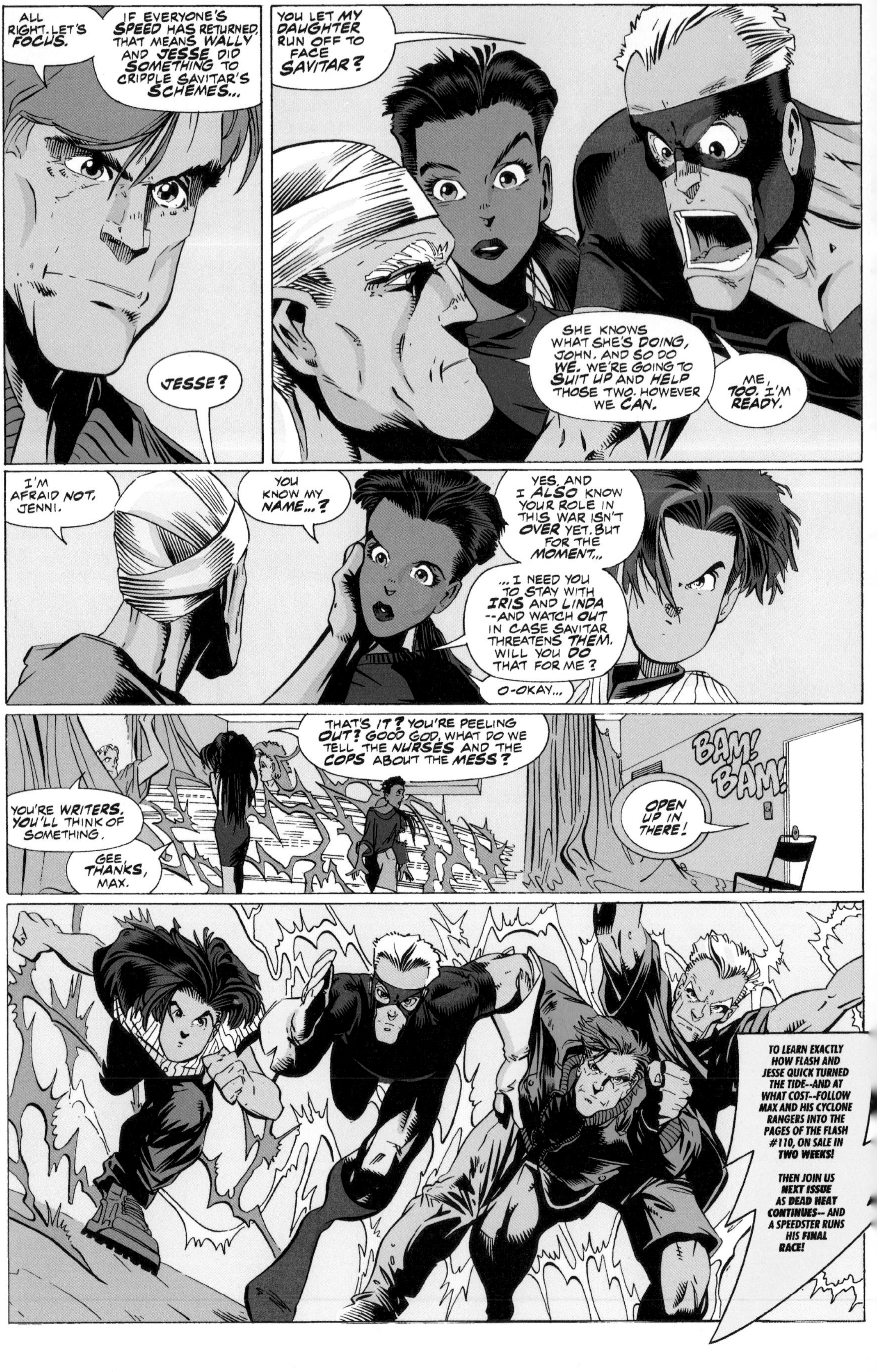
ALL RIGHT. LET'S FOCUS.
IF EVERYONE'S SPEED HAS RETURNED, THAT MEANS WALLY AND JESSE DID SOMETHING TO CRIPPLE SAVITAR'S SCHEMES...
JESSE?
YOU LET MY DAUGHTER RUN OFF TO FACE SAVITAR?
SHE KNOWS WHAT SHE'S DOING, JOHN. AND SO DO WE. WE'RE GOING TO SUIT UP AND HELP THOSE TWO. HOWEVER WE CAN.
ME, TOO. I'M READY.
I'M AFRAID NOT, JENNI.
YOU KNOW MY NAME...?
YES, AND I ALSO KNOW YOUR ROLE IN THIS WAR ISN'T OVER YET. BUT FOR THE MOMENT...
...I NEED YOU TO STAY WITH IRIS AND LINDA --AND WATCH OUT IN CASE SAVITAR THREATENS THEM. WILL YOU DO THAT FOR ME?
O-OKAY...
THAT'S IT? YOU'RE PEELING OUT? GOOD GOD, WHAT DO WE TELL THE NURSES AND THE COPS ABOUT THE MESS?
YOU'RE WRITERS. YOU'LL THINK OF SOMETHING.
GEE, THANKS, MAX.
BAM! BAM!
OPEN UP IN THERE!
TO LEARN EXACTLY HOW FLASH AND JESSE QUICK TURNED THE TIDE--AND AT WHAT COST--FOLLOW MAX AND HIS CYCLONE RANGERS INTO THE PAGES OF THE FLASH #110, ON SALE IN TWO WEEKS!
THEN JOIN US NEXT ISSUE AS DEAD HEAT CONTINUES-- AND A SPEEDSTER RUNS HIS FINAL RACE!

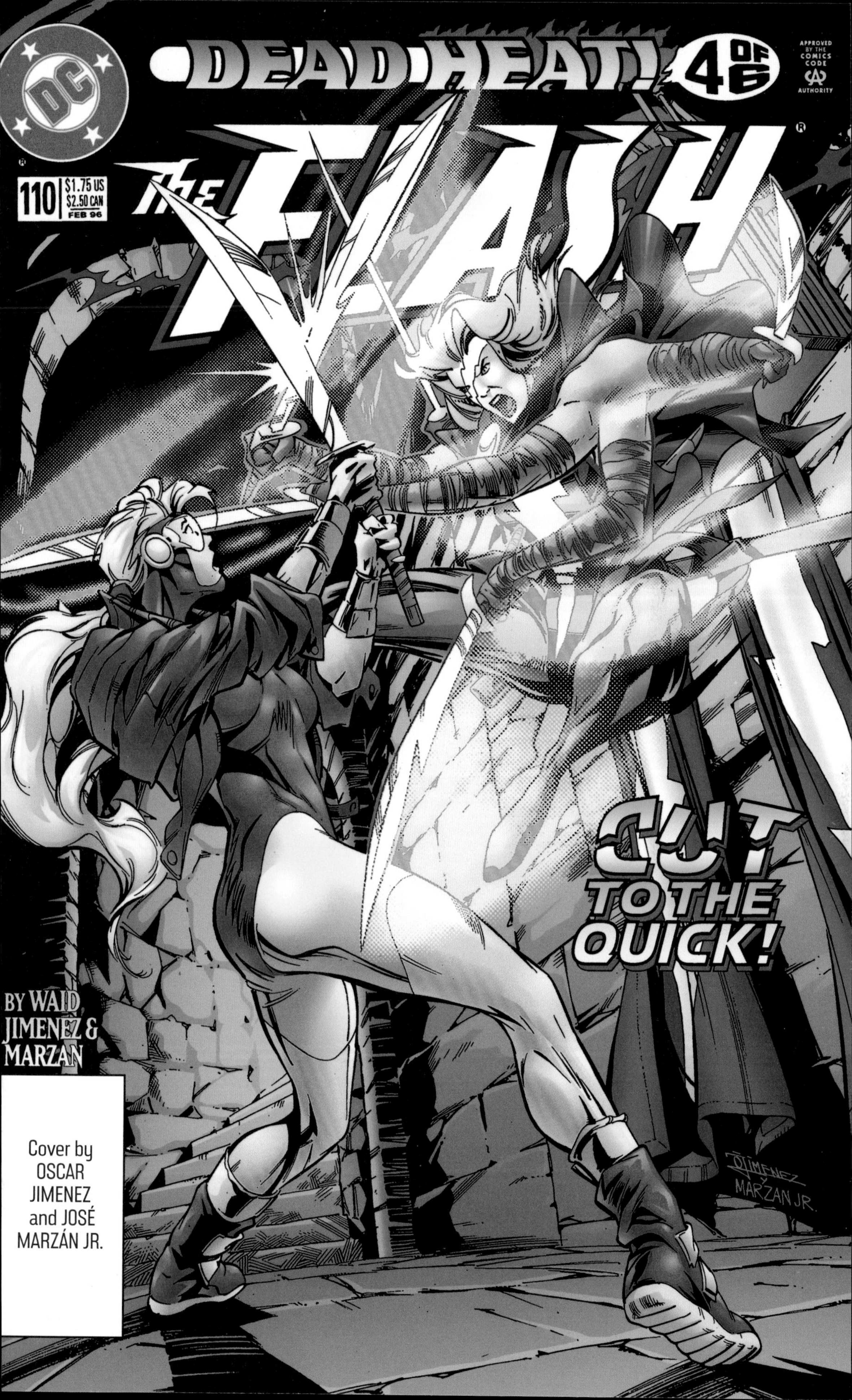
DC
DEAD HEAT! 4 OF 6
APPROVED BY THE COMICS CODE AUTHORITY
THE FLASH
110 $1.75 US $2.50 CAN FEB 96
CUT TO THE QUICK!
BY WAID JIMENEZ & MARZAN
O. JIMENEZ y MARZAN JR.

Cover by OSCAR JIMENEZ and JOSÉ MARZÁN JR.

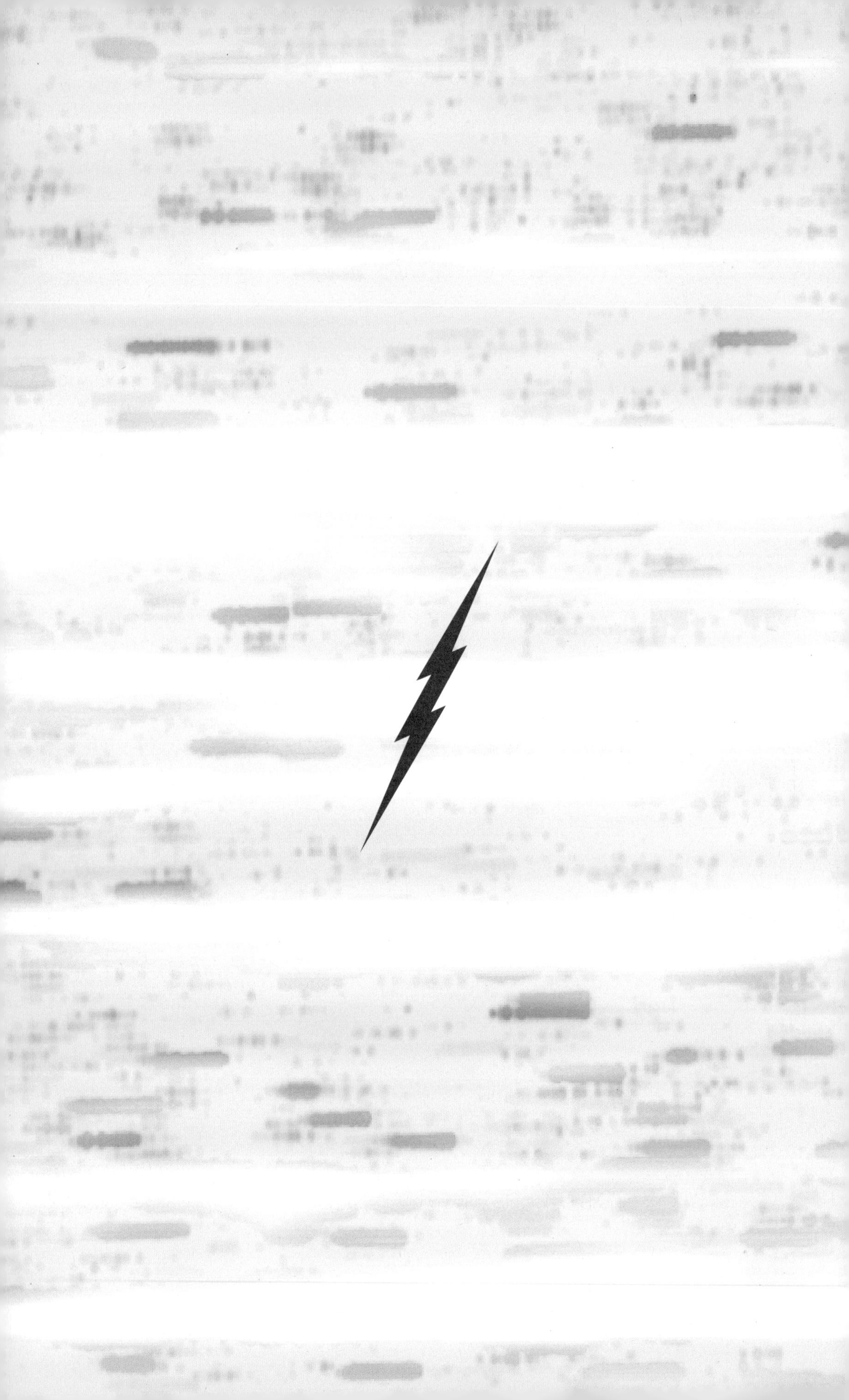

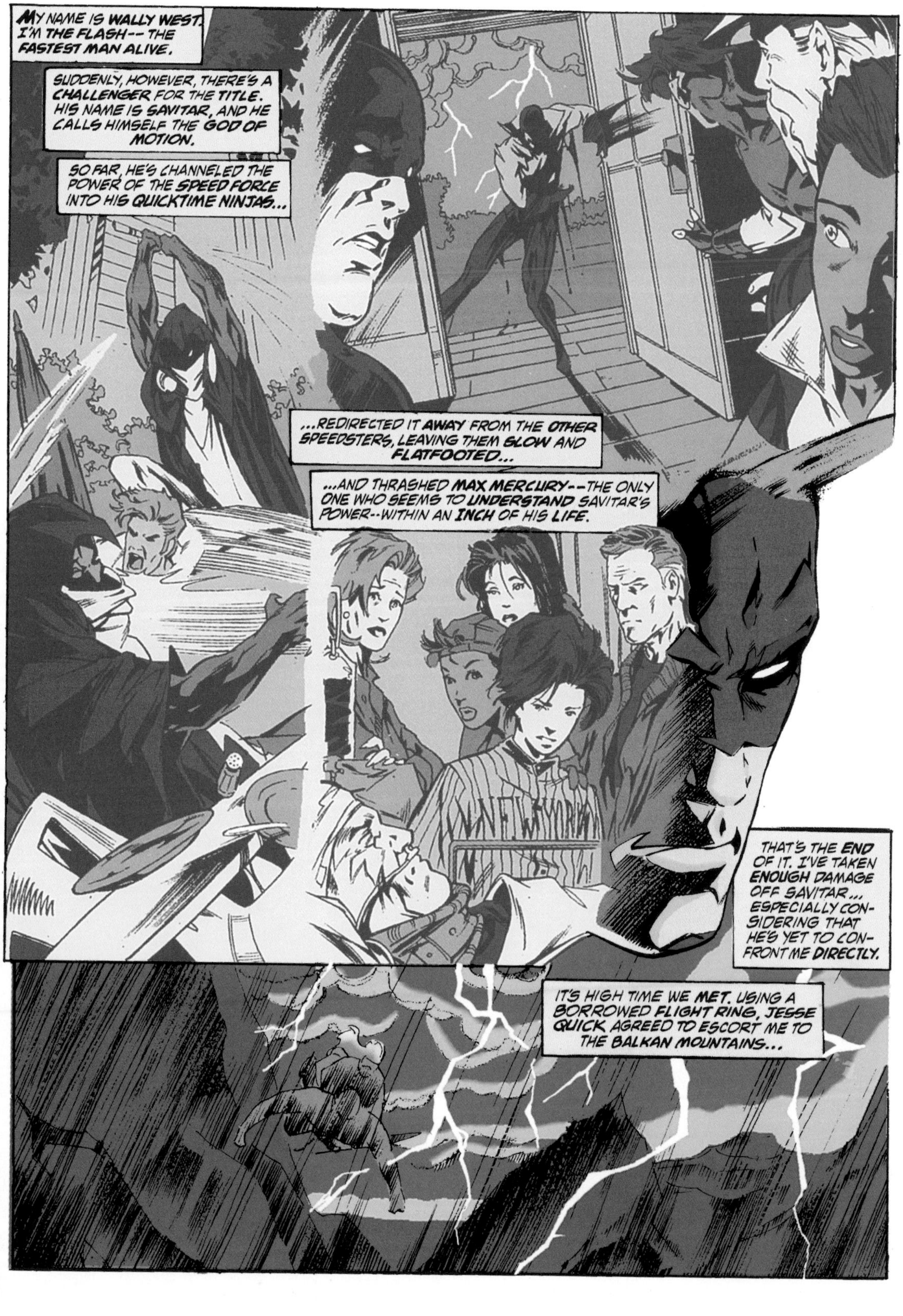
MY NAME IS WALLY WEST. I'M THE FLASH-- THE FASTEST MAN ALIVE.
SUDDENLY, HOWEVER, THERE'S A CHALLENGER FOR THE TITLE. HIS NAME IS SAVITAR, AND HE CALLS HIMSELF THE GOD OF MOTION.
SO FAR, HE'S CHANNELED THE POWER OF THE SPEED FORCE INTO HIS QUICKTIME NINJAS...
...REDIRECTED IT AWAY FROM THE OTHER SPEEDSTERS, LEAVING THEM SLOW AND FLATFOOTED...
...AND THRASHED MAX MERCURY--THE ONLY ONE WHO SEEMS TO UNDERSTAND SAVITAR'S POWER--WITHIN AN INCH OF HIS LIFE.
THAT'S THE END OF IT. I'VE TAKEN ENOUGH DAMAGE OFF SAVITAR... ESPECIALLY CONSIDERING THAT HE'S YET TO CONFRONT ME DIRECTLY.
IT'S HIGH TIME WE MET. USING A BORROWED FLIGHT RING, JESSE QUICK AGREED TO ESCORT ME TO THE BALKAN MOUNTAINS...

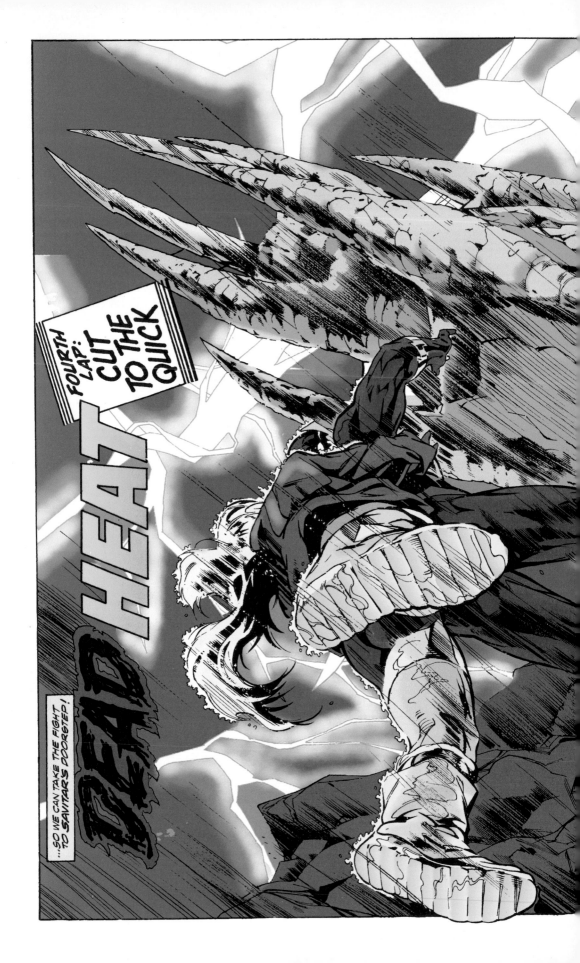

DEAD HEAT

FOURTH LAP: CUT TO THE QUICK

...SO WE CAN TAKE THE FIGHT TO SAVITAR'S DOORSTEP!

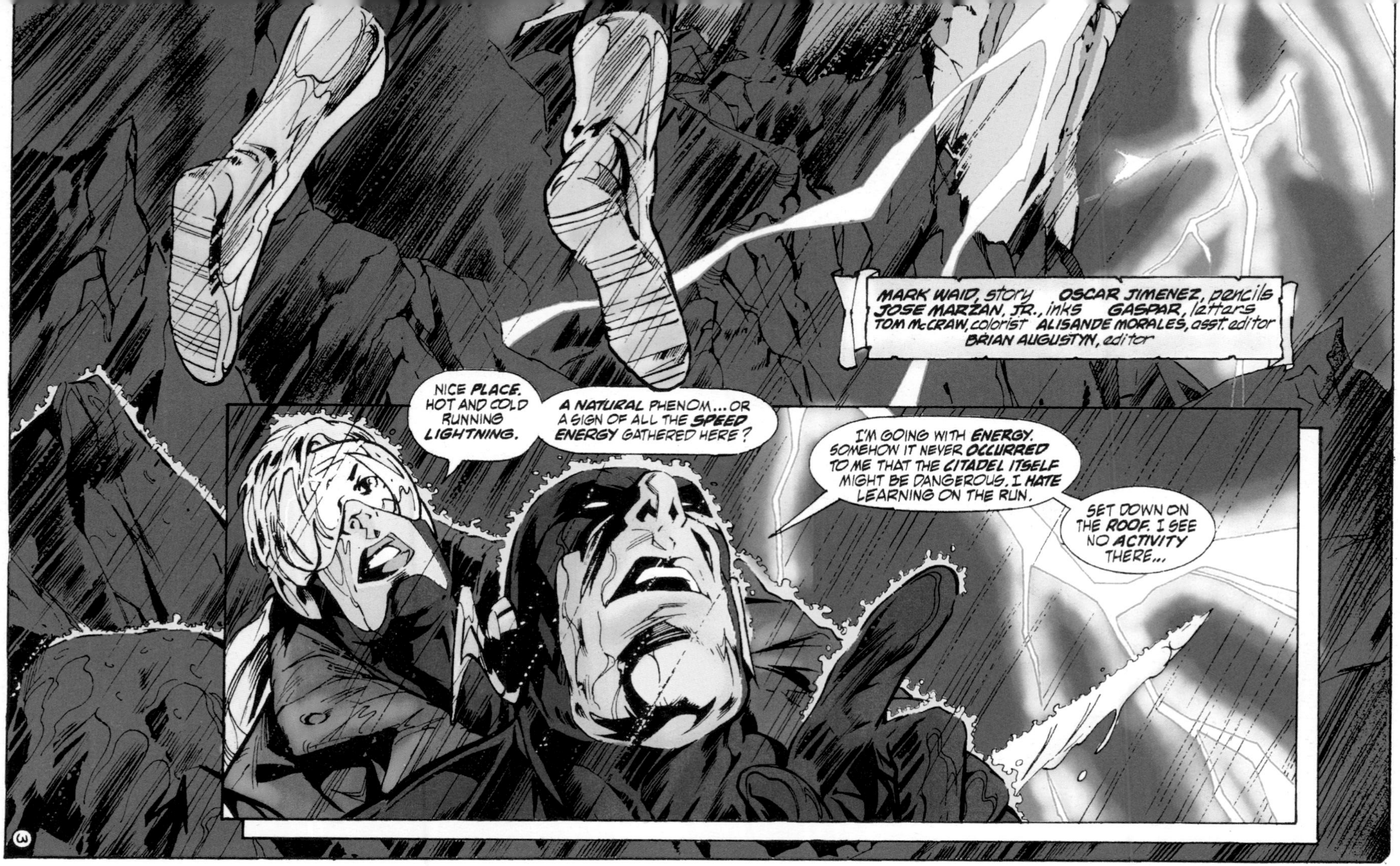
MARK WAID, story OSCAR JIMENEZ, pencils
JOSE MARZAN, JR., inks GASPAR, letters
TOM McCRAW, colorist ALISANDE MORALES, asst. editor
BRIAN AUGUSTYN, editor
NICE PLACE. HOT AND COLD RUNNING LIGHTNING.
A NATURAL PHENOM... OR A SIGN OF ALL THE SPEED ENERGY GATHERED HERE?
I'M GOING WITH ENERGY. SOMEHOW IT NEVER OCCURRED TO ME THAT THE CITADEL ITSELF MIGHT BE DANGEROUS. I HATE LEARNING ON THE RUN.
SET DOWN ON THE ROOF. I SEE NO ACTIVITY THERE...
3

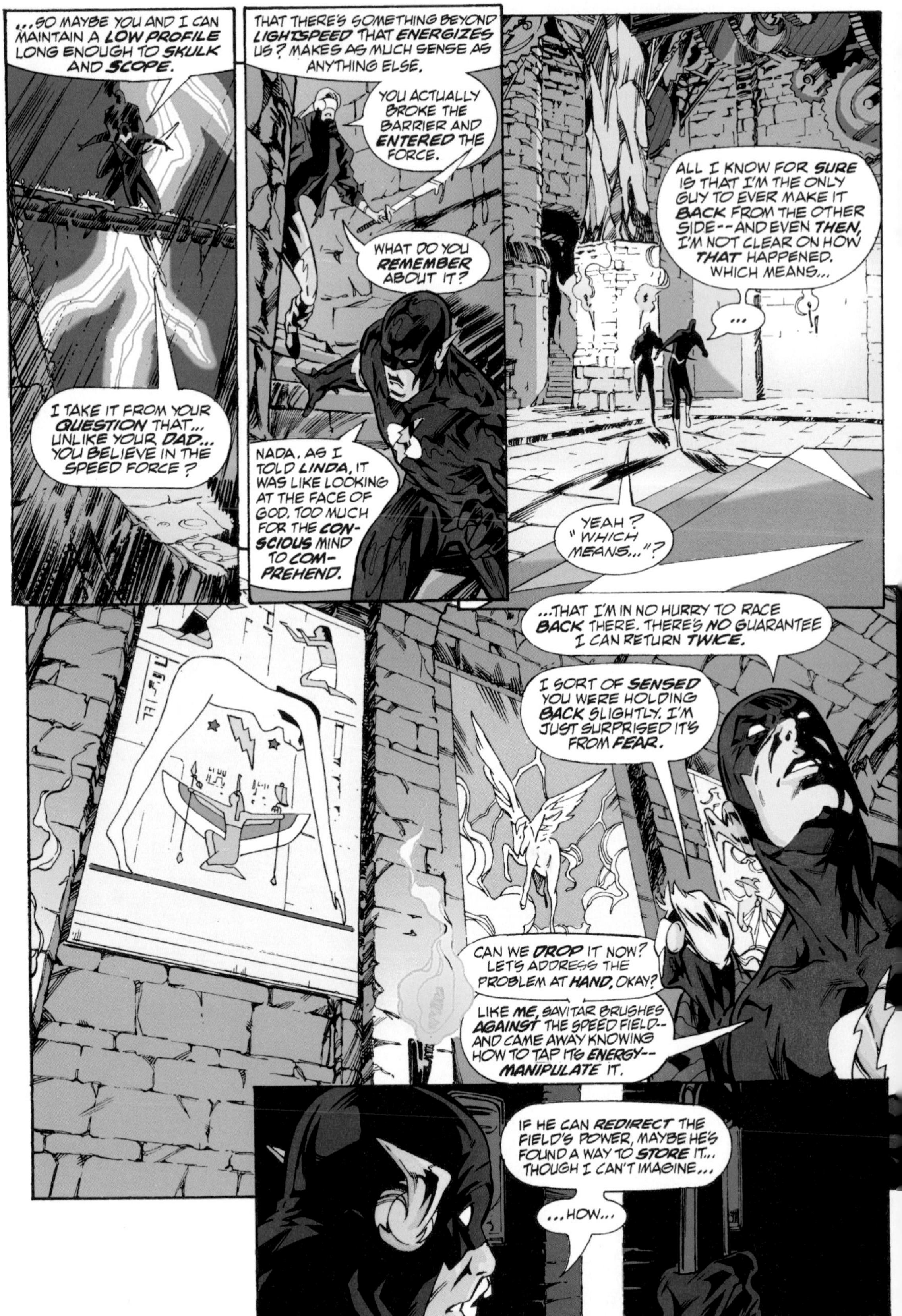
...SO MAYBE YOU AND I CAN MAINTAIN A LOW PROFILE LONG ENOUGH TO SKULK AND SCOPE.
I TAKE IT FROM YOUR QUESTION THAT... UNLIKE YOUR DAD... YOU BELIEVE IN THE SPEED FORCE?
THAT THERE'S SOMETHING BEYOND LIGHTSPEED THAT ENERGIZES US? MAKES AS MUCH SENSE AS ANYTHING ELSE.
YOU ACTUALLY BROKE THE BARRIER AND ENTERED THE FORCE.
WHAT DO YOU REMEMBER ABOUT IT?
NADA. AS I TOLD LINDA, IT WAS LIKE LOOKING AT THE FACE OF GOD. TOO MUCH FOR THE CONSCIOUS MIND TO COMPREHEND.
ALL I KNOW FOR SURE IS THAT I'M THE ONLY GUY TO EVER MAKE IT BACK FROM THE OTHER SIDE--AND EVEN THEN, I'M NOT CLEAR ON HOW THAT HAPPENED. WHICH MEANS...
...
YEAH? "WHICH MEANS..."?
...THAT I'M IN NO HURRY TO RACE BACK THERE. THERE'S NO GUARANTEE I CAN RETURN TWICE.
I SORT OF SENSED YOU WERE HOLDING BACK SLIGHTLY. I'M JUST SURPRISED IT'S FROM FEAR.
CAN WE DROP IT NOW? LET'S ADDRESS THE PROBLEM AT HAND, OKAY?
LIKE ME, SAVITAR BRUSHES AGAINST THE SPEED FIELD--AND CAME AWAY KNOWING HOW TO TAP ITS ENERGY--MANIPULATE IT.
IF HE CAN REDIRECT THE FIELD'S POWER, MAYBE HE'S FOUND A WAY TO STORE IT... THOUGH I CAN'T IMAGINE...
...HOW...

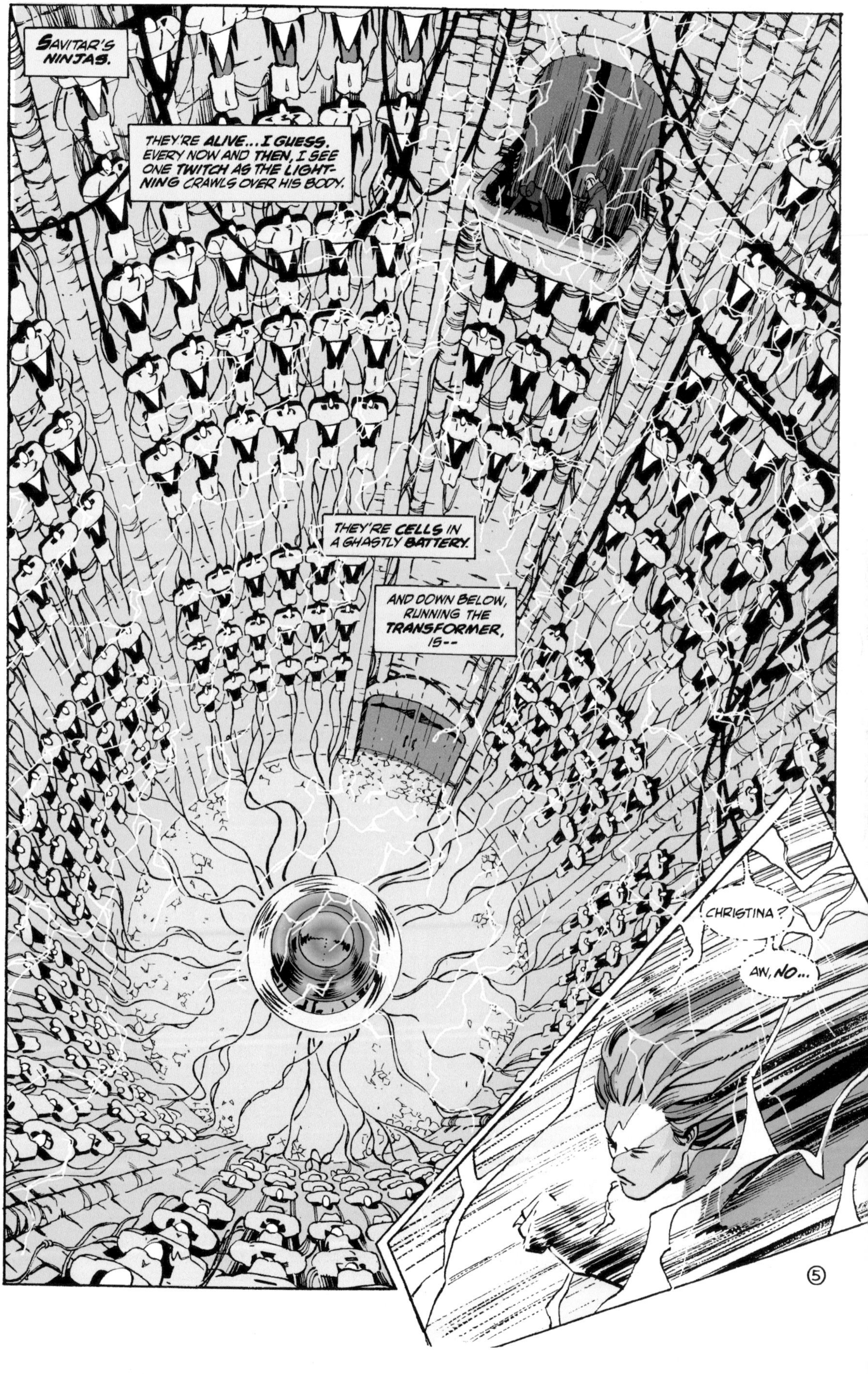
SAVITAR'S NINJAS.
THEY'RE ALIVE... I GUESS. EVERY NOW AND THEN, I SEE ONE TWITCH AS THE LIGHTNING CRAWLS OVER HIS BODY.
THEY'RE CELLS IN A GHASTLY BATTERY.
AND DOWN BELOW, RUNNING THE TRANSFORMER, IS--
CHRISTINA?
AW, NO...

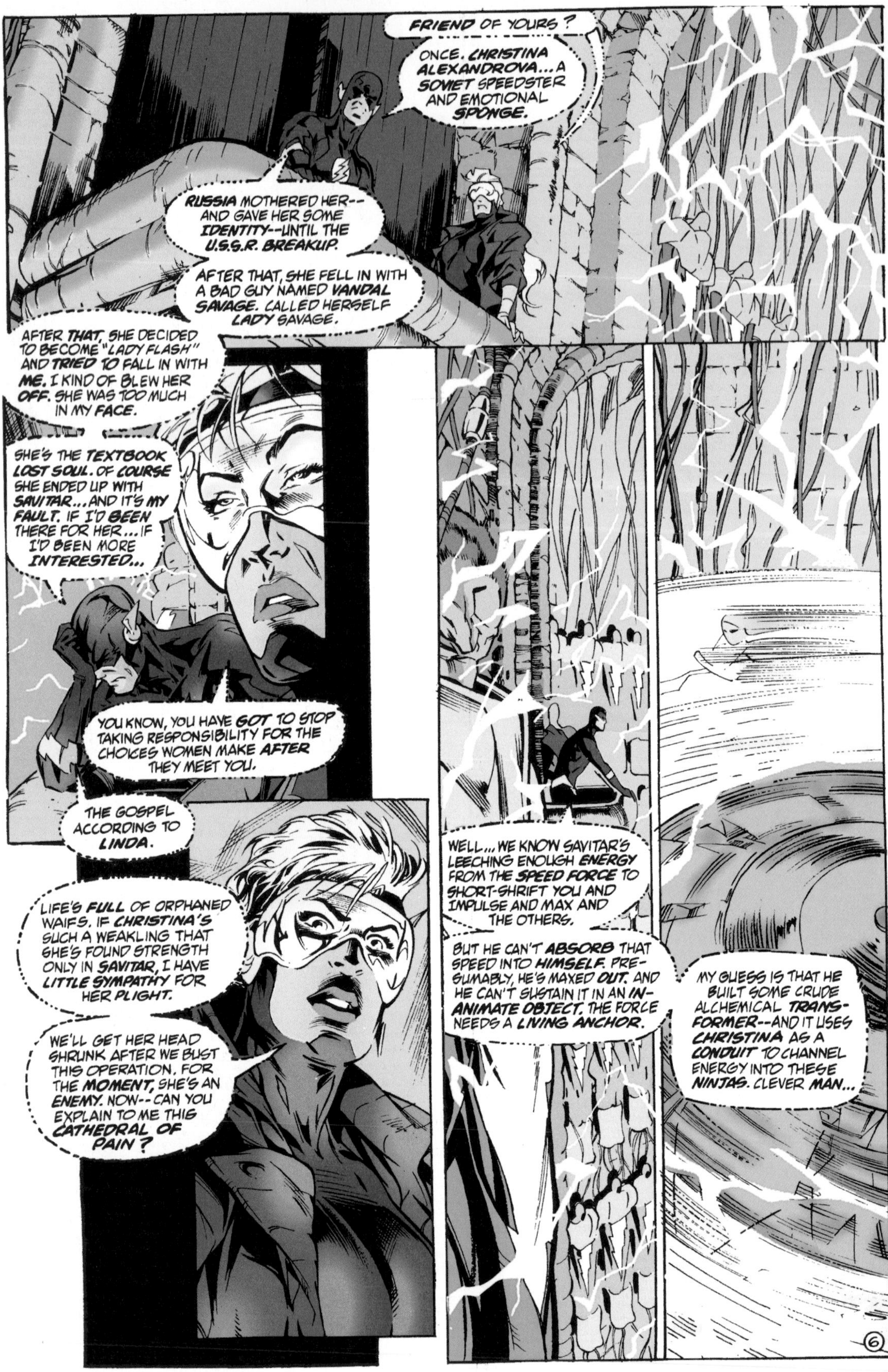
FRIEND OF YOURS?
ONCE. CHRISTINA ALEXANDROVA... A SOVIET SPEEDSTER AND EMOTIONAL SPONGE.
RUSSIA MOTHERED HER-- AND GAVE HER SOME IDENTITY--UNTIL THE U.S.S.R. BREAKUP.
AFTER THAT, SHE FELL IN WITH A BAD GUY NAMED VANDAL SAVAGE. CALLED HERSELF LADY SAVAGE.
AFTER THAT, SHE DECIDED TO BECOME "LADY FLASH" AND TRIED TO FALL IN WITH ME. I KIND OF BLEW HER OFF. SHE WAS TOO MUCH IN MY FACE.
SHE'S THE TEXTBOOK LOST SOUL. OF COURSE SHE ENDED UP WITH SAVITAR... AND IT'S MY FAULT. IF I'D BEEN THERE FOR HER... IF I'D BEEN MORE INTERESTED...
YOU KNOW, YOU HAVE GOT TO STOP TAKING RESPONSIBILITY FOR THE CHOICES WOMEN MAKE AFTER THEY MEET YOU.
THE GOSPEL ACCORDING TO LINDA.
LIFE'S FULL OF ORPHANED WAIFS. IF CHRISTINA'S SUCH A WEAKLING THAT SHE'S FOUND STRENGTH ONLY IN SAVITAR, I HAVE LITTLE SYMPATHY FOR HER PLIGHT.
WE'LL GET HER HEAD SHRUNK AFTER WE BUST THIS OPERATION. FOR THE MOMENT, SHE'S AN ENEMY. NOW-- CAN YOU EXPLAIN TO ME THIS CATHEDRAL OF PAIN?
WELL... WE KNOW SAVITAR'S LEECHING ENOUGH ENERGY FROM THE SPEED FORCE TO SHORT-SHRIFT YOU AND IMPULSE AND MAX AND THE OTHERS.
BUT HE CAN'T ABSORB THAT SPEED INTO HIMSELF. PRE-SUMABLY, HE'S MAXED OUT. AND HE CAN'T SUSTAIN IT IN AN IN-ANIMATE OBJECT. THE FORCE NEEDS A LIVING ANCHOR.
MY GUESS IS THAT HE BUILT SOME CRUDE ALCHEMICAL TRANS-FORMER--AND IT USES CHRISTINA AS A CONDUIT TO CHANNEL ENERGY INTO THESE NINJAS. CLEVER MAN...
6

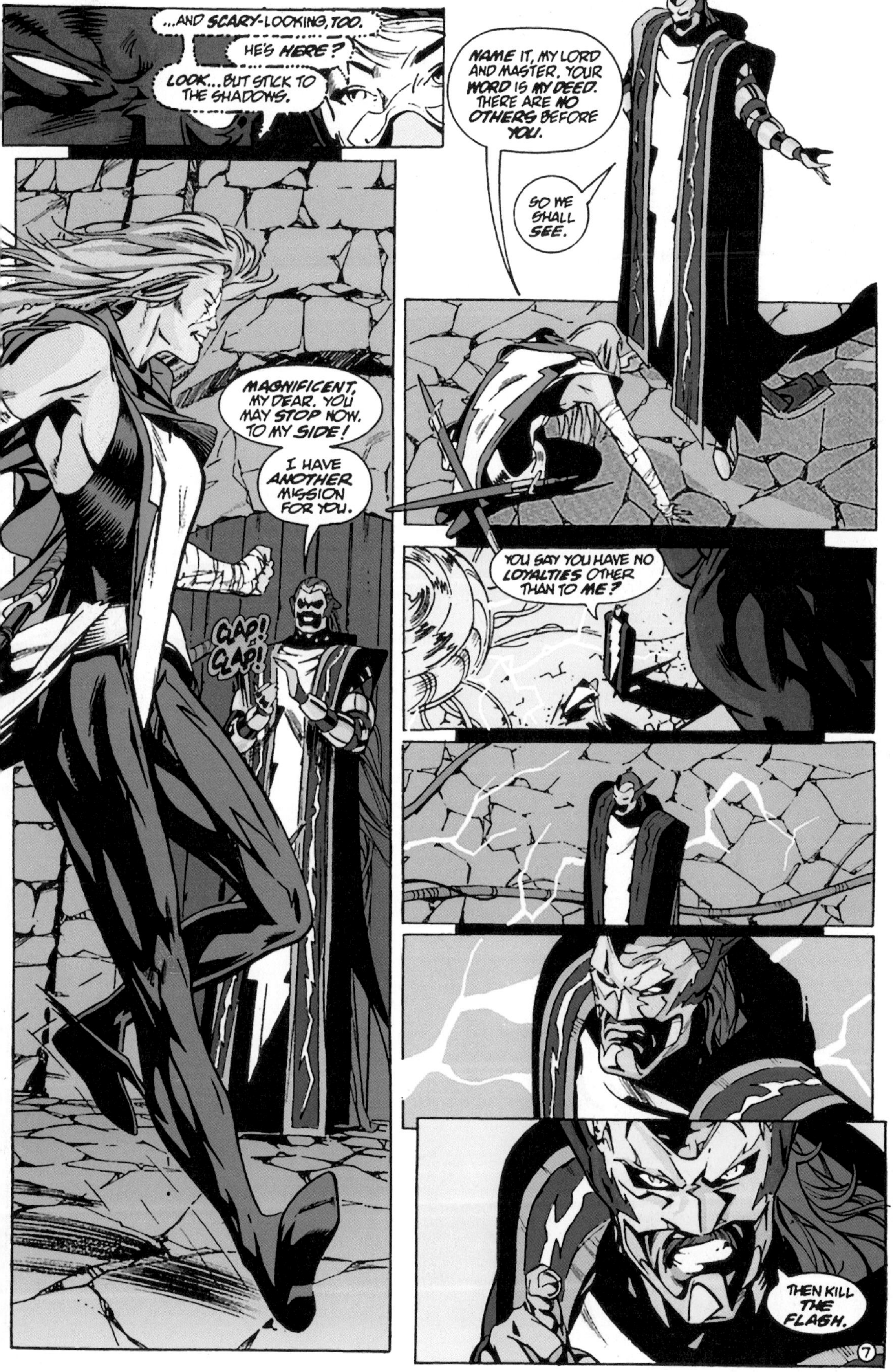

...AND SCARY-LOOKING, TOO.
HE'S HERE?
LOOK...BUT STICK TO THE SHADOWS.
MAGNIFICENT, MY DEAR. YOU MAY STOP NOW. TO MY SIDE!
I HAVE ANOTHER MISSION FOR YOU.
CLAP! CLAP!
NAME IT, MY LORD AND MASTER. YOUR WORD IS MY DEED. THERE ARE NO OTHERS BEFORE YOU.
SO WE SHALL SEE.
YOU SAY YOU HAVE NO LOYALTIES OTHER THAN TO ME?
THEN KILL THE FLASH.

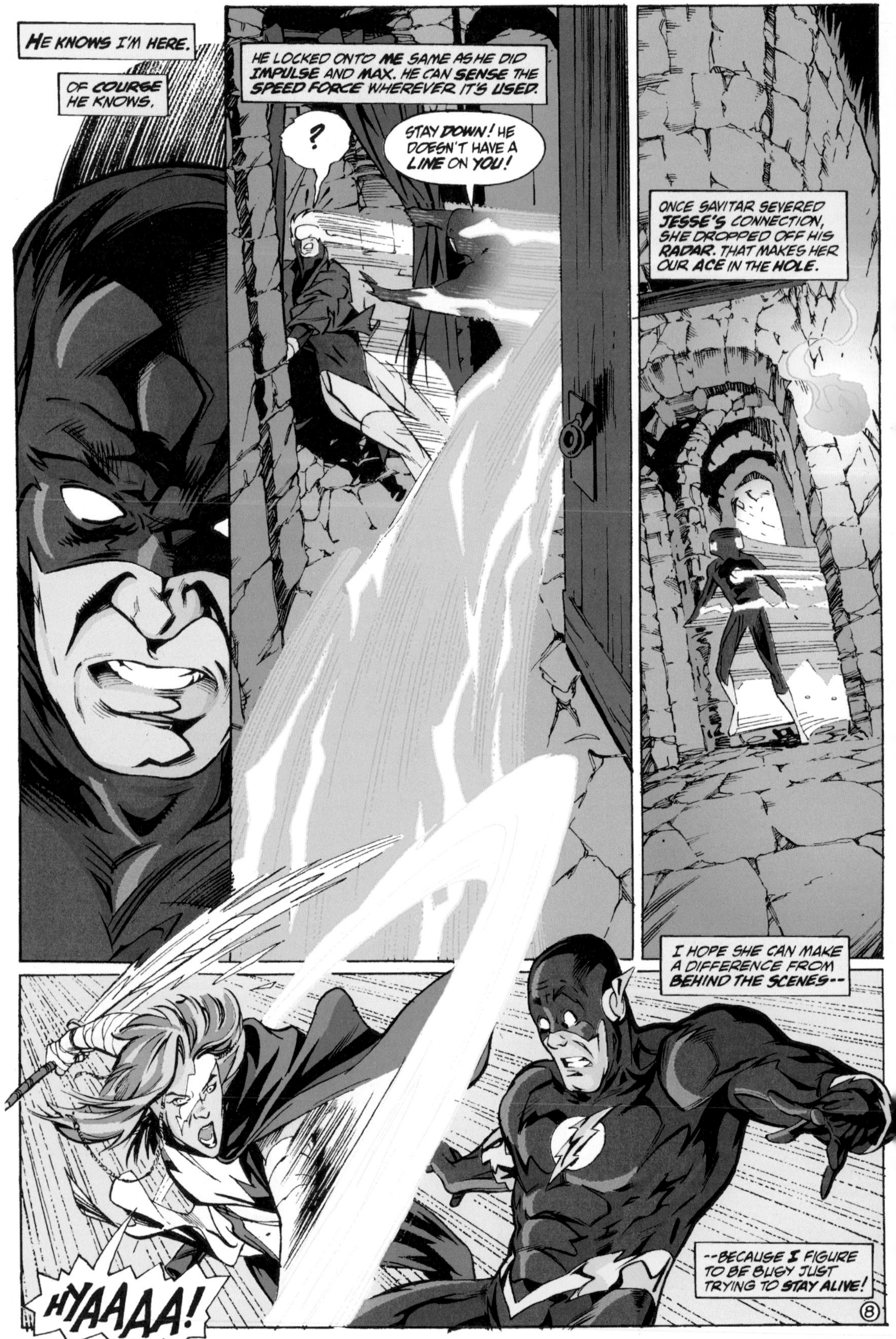
HE KNOWS I'M HERE.
OF COURSE HE KNOWS.
HE LOCKED ONTO ME SAME AS HE DID IMPULSE AND MAX. HE CAN SENSE THE SPEED FORCE WHEREVER IT'S USED.
?
STAY DOWN! HE DOESN'T HAVE A LINE ON YOU!
ONCE SAVITAR SEVERED JESSE'S CONNECTION, SHE DROPPED OFF HIS RADAR. THAT MAKES HER OUR ACE IN THE HOLE.
I HOPE SHE CAN MAKE A DIFFERENCE FROM BEHIND THE SCENES--
--BECAUSE I FIGURE TO BE BUSY JUST TRYING TO STAY ALIVE!
HYAAAA!

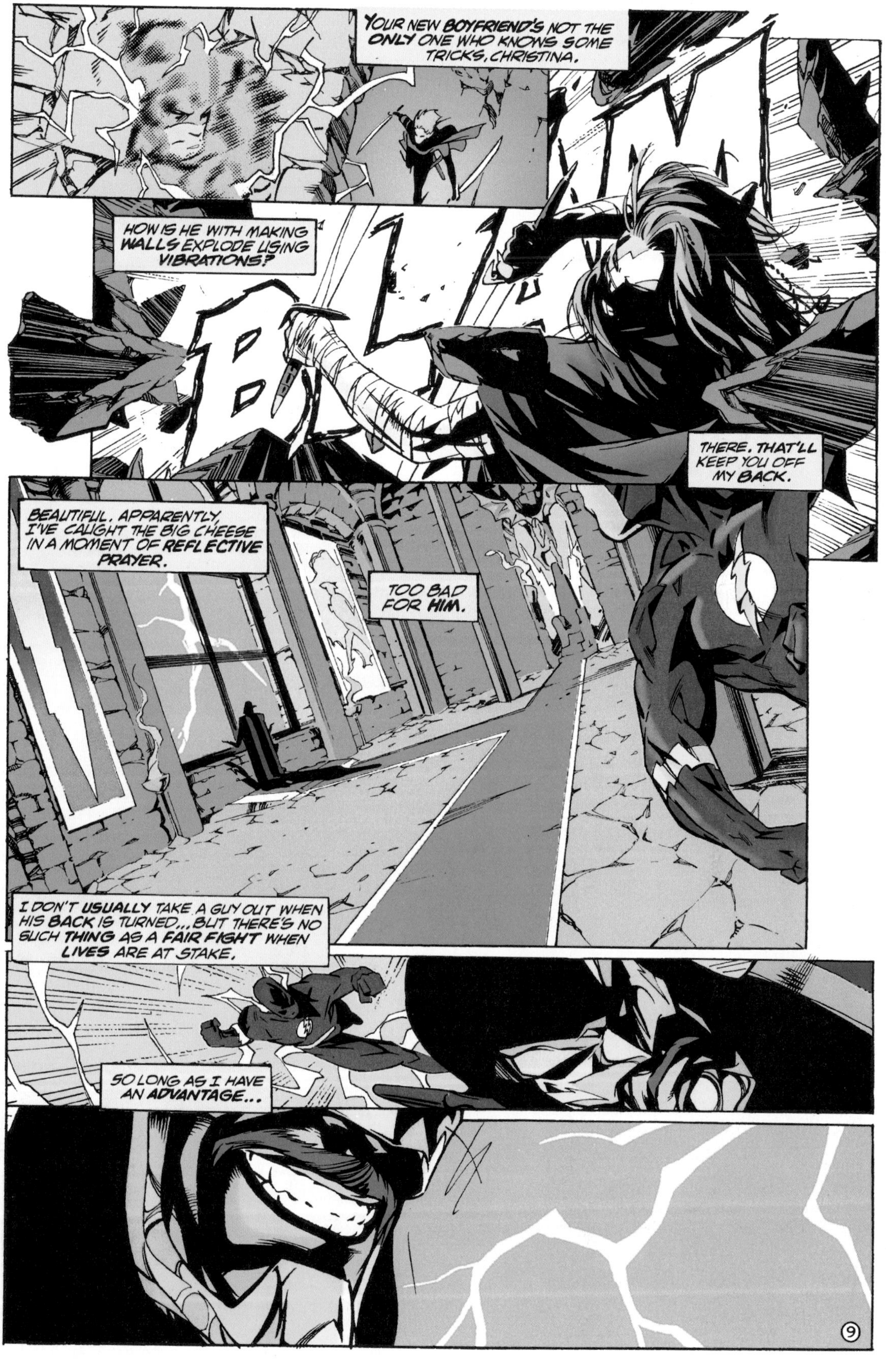
YOUR NEW BOYFRIEND'S NOT THE ONLY ONE WHO KNOWS SOME TRICKS, CHRISTINA.
HOW IS HE WITH MAKING WALLS EXPLODE USING VIBRATIONS?
BLAM
THERE. THAT'LL KEEP YOU OFF MY BACK.
BEAUTIFUL. APPARENTLY, I'VE CAUGHT THE BIG CHEESE IN A MOMENT OF REFLECTIVE PRAYER.
TOO BAD FOR HIM.
I DON'T USUALLY TAKE A GUY OUT WHEN HIS BACK IS TURNED... BUT THERE'S NO SUCH THING AS A FAIR FIGHT WHEN LIVES ARE AT STAKE.
SO LONG AS I HAVE AN ADVANTAGE...

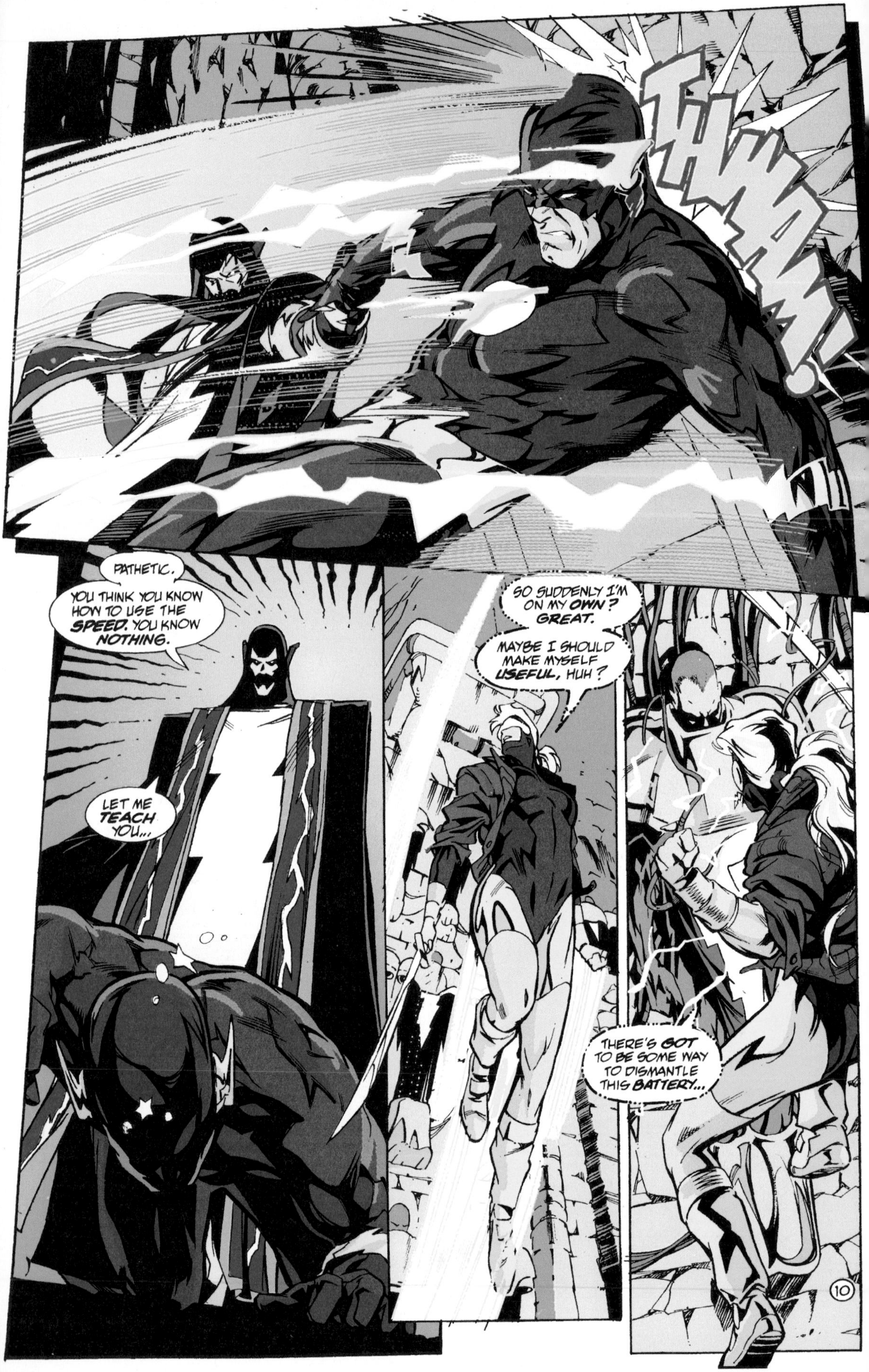
THWAM!
PATHETIC.
YOU THINK YOU KNOW HOW TO USE THE **SPEED.** YOU KNOW **NOTHING.**
LET ME **TEACH** YOU...
SO SUDDENLY I'M ON MY **OWN**? **GREAT.**
MAYBE I SHOULD MAKE MYSELF **USEFUL**, HUH?
THERE'S **GOT** TO BE SOME WAY TO DISMANTLE THIS **BATTERY**...
10

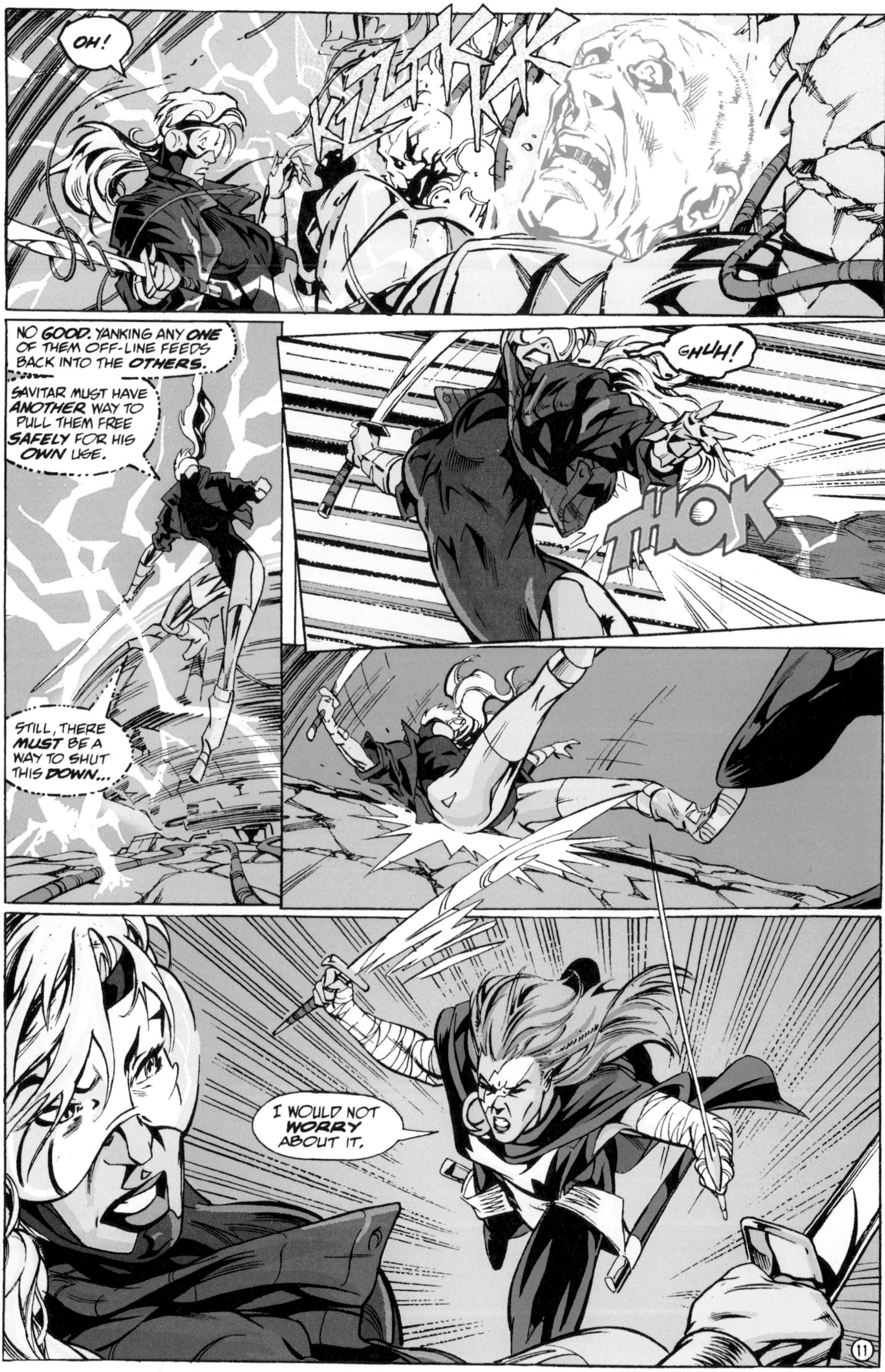
OH!
KZZKKK
NO GOOD. YANKING ANY ONE OF THEM OFF-LINE FEEDS BACK INTO THE OTHERS.
SAVITAR MUST HAVE ANOTHER WAY TO PULL THEM FREE SAFELY FOR HIS OWN USE.
GHUH!
THOK
STILL, THERE MUST BE A WAY TO SHUT THIS DOWN...
I WOULD NOT WORRY ABOUT IT.

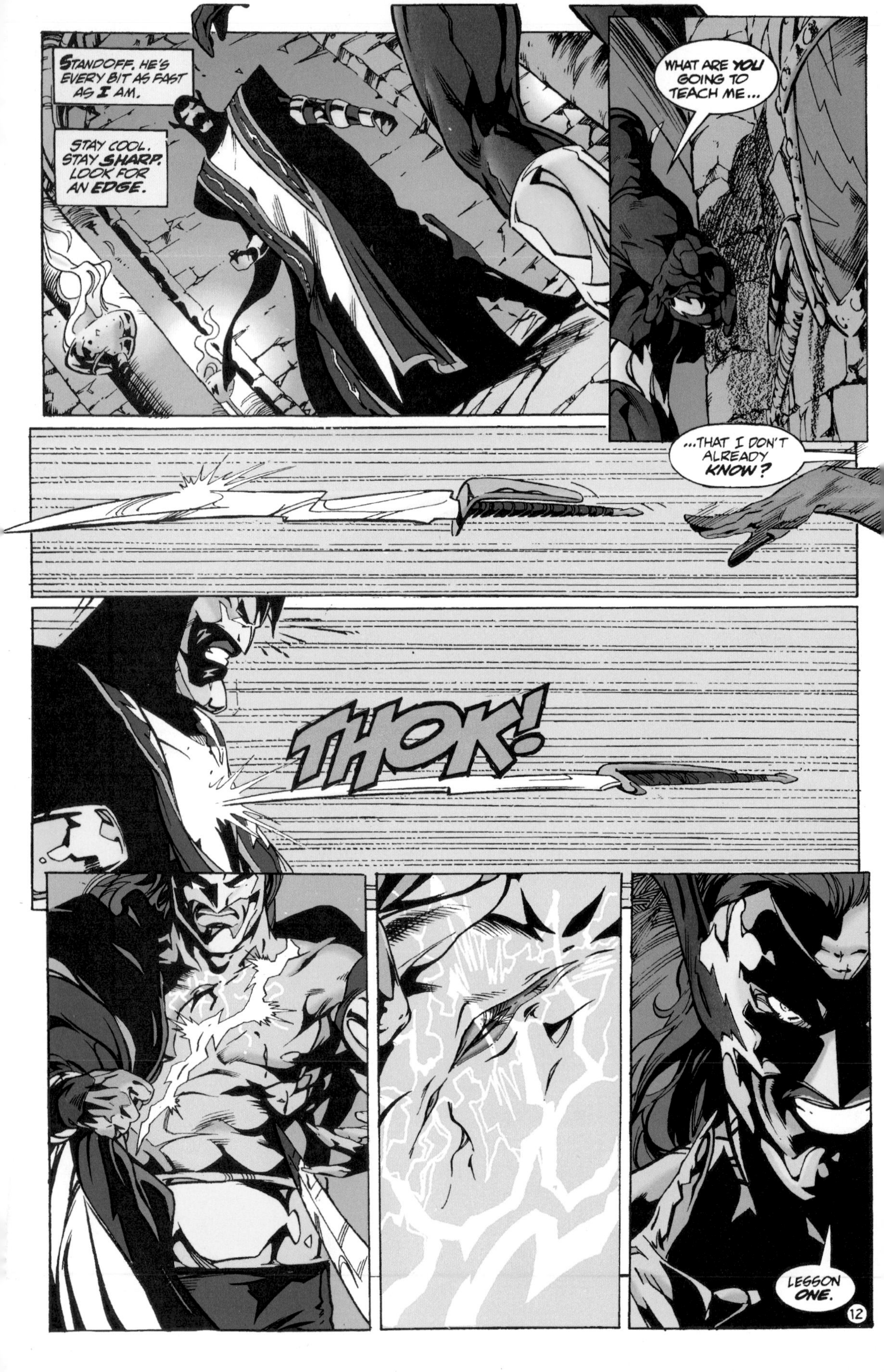
STANDOFF. HE'S EVERY BIT AS FAST AS I AM.
STAY COOL. STAY SHARP. LOOK FOR AN EDGE.
WHAT ARE YOU GOING TO TEACH ME...
...THAT I DON'T ALREADY KNOW?
THOK!
LESSON ONE.

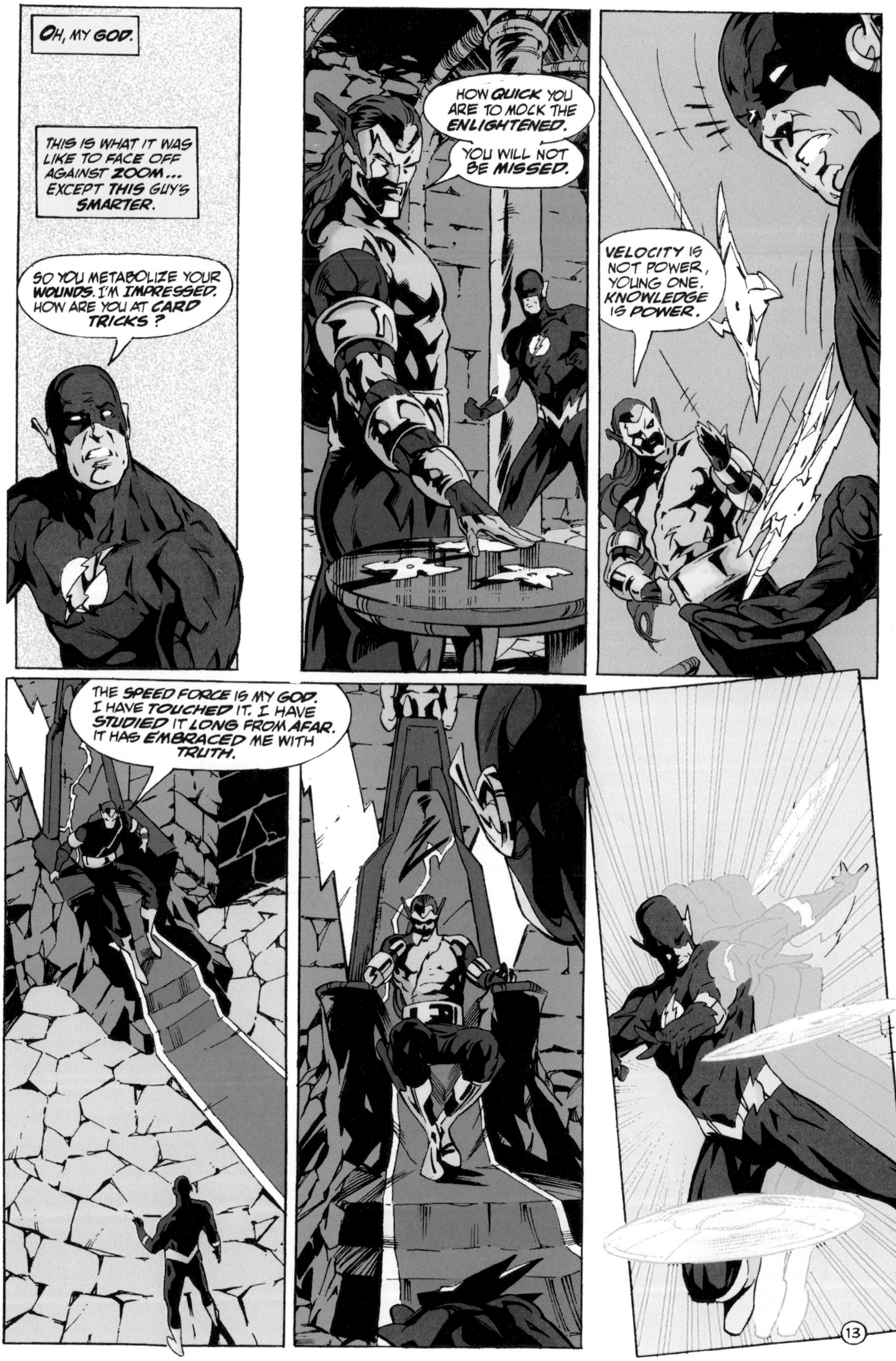

OH, MY GOD.
THIS IS WHAT IT WAS LIKE TO FACE OFF AGAINST ZOOM... EXCEPT THIS GUY'S SMARTER.
SO YOU METABOLIZE YOUR WOUNDS. I'M IMPRESSED. HOW ARE YOU AT CARD TRICKS?
HOW QUICK YOU ARE TO MOCK THE ENLIGHTENED.
YOU WILL NOT BE MISSED.
VELOCITY IS NOT POWER, YOUNG ONE. KNOWLEDGE IS POWER.
THE SPEED FORCE IS MY GOD. I HAVE TOUCHED IT. I HAVE STUDIED IT LONG FROM AFAR. IT HAS EMBRACED ME WITH TRUTH.

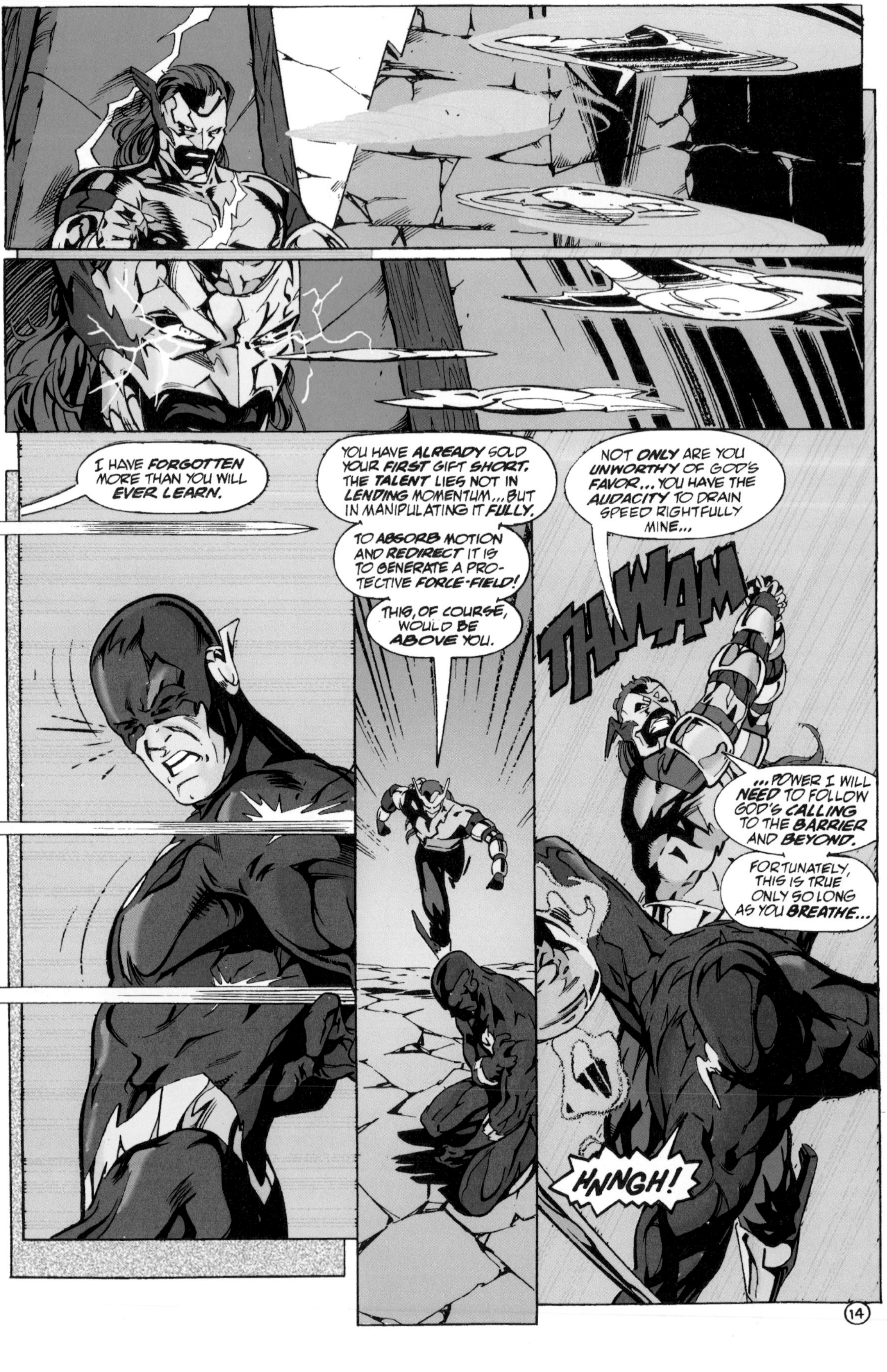
I HAVE FORGOTTEN MORE THAN YOU WILL EVER LEARN.
YOU HAVE ALREADY SOLD YOUR FIRST GIFT SHORT. THE TALENT LIES NOT IN LENDING MOMENTUM... BUT IN MANIPULATING IT FULLY.
TO ABSORB MOTION AND REDIRECT IT IS TO GENERATE A PROTECTIVE FORCE-FIELD!
THIS, OF COURSE, WOULD BE ABOVE YOU.
NOT ONLY ARE YOU UNWORTHY OF GOD'S FAVOR... YOU HAVE THE AUDACITY TO DRAIN SPEED RIGHTFULLY MINE...
THWAM
...POWER I WILL NEED TO FOLLOW GOD'S CALLING TO THE BARRIER AND BEYOND.
FORTUNATELY, THIS IS TRUE ONLY SO LONG AS YOU BREATHE...
HNNGH!

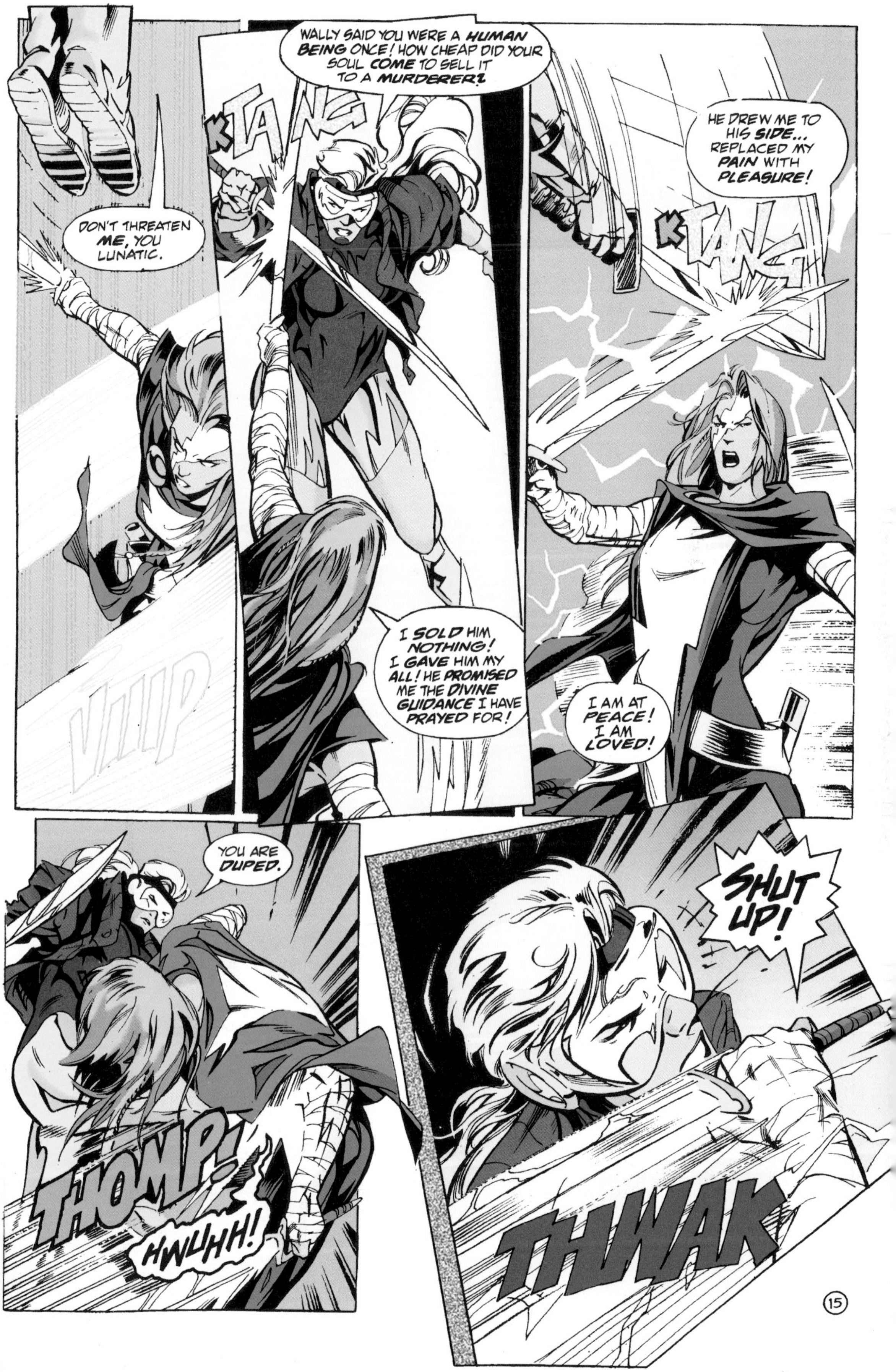

DON'T THREATEN ME, YOU LUNATIC.
VHIP
WALLY SAID YOU WERE A HUMAN BEING ONCE! HOW CHEAP DID YOUR SOUL COME TO SELL IT TO A MURDERER?
KTANG
I SOLD HIM NOTHING! I GAVE HIM MY ALL! HE PROMISED ME THE DIVINE GUIDANCE I HAVE PRAYED FOR!
HE DREW ME TO HIS SIDE... REPLACED MY PAIN WITH PLEASURE!
KTANG
I AM AT PEACE! I AM LOVED!
YOU ARE DUPED.
THOMP!
HWUHH!
SHUT UP!
THWAK

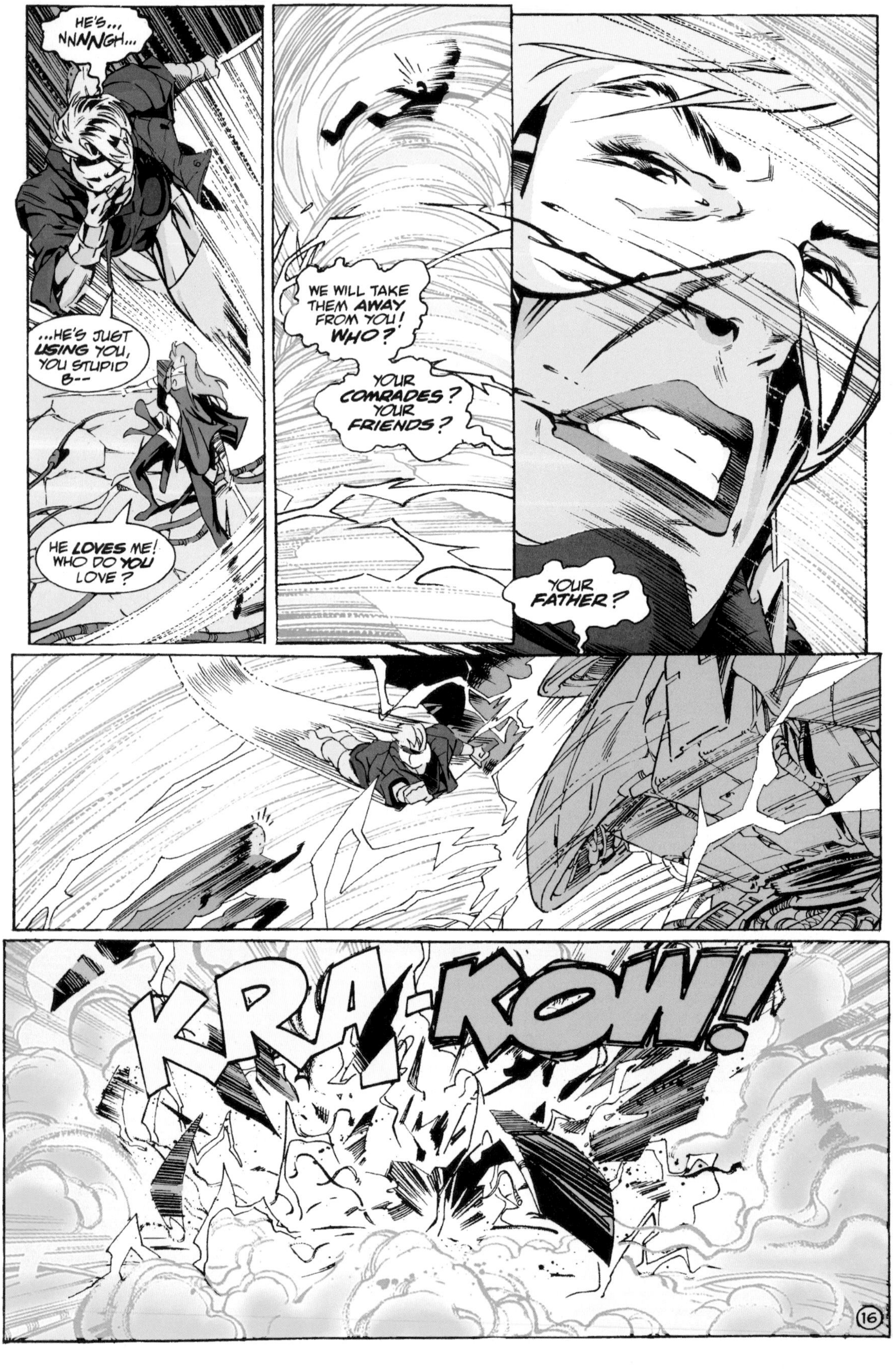

HE'S... NNNNGH...
...HE'S JUST USING YOU, YOU STUPID B--
HE LOVES ME! WHO DO YOU LOVE?
WE WILL TAKE THEM AWAY FROM YOU! WHO?
YOUR COMRADES? YOUR FRIENDS?
YOUR FATHER?
KRA-KOW!

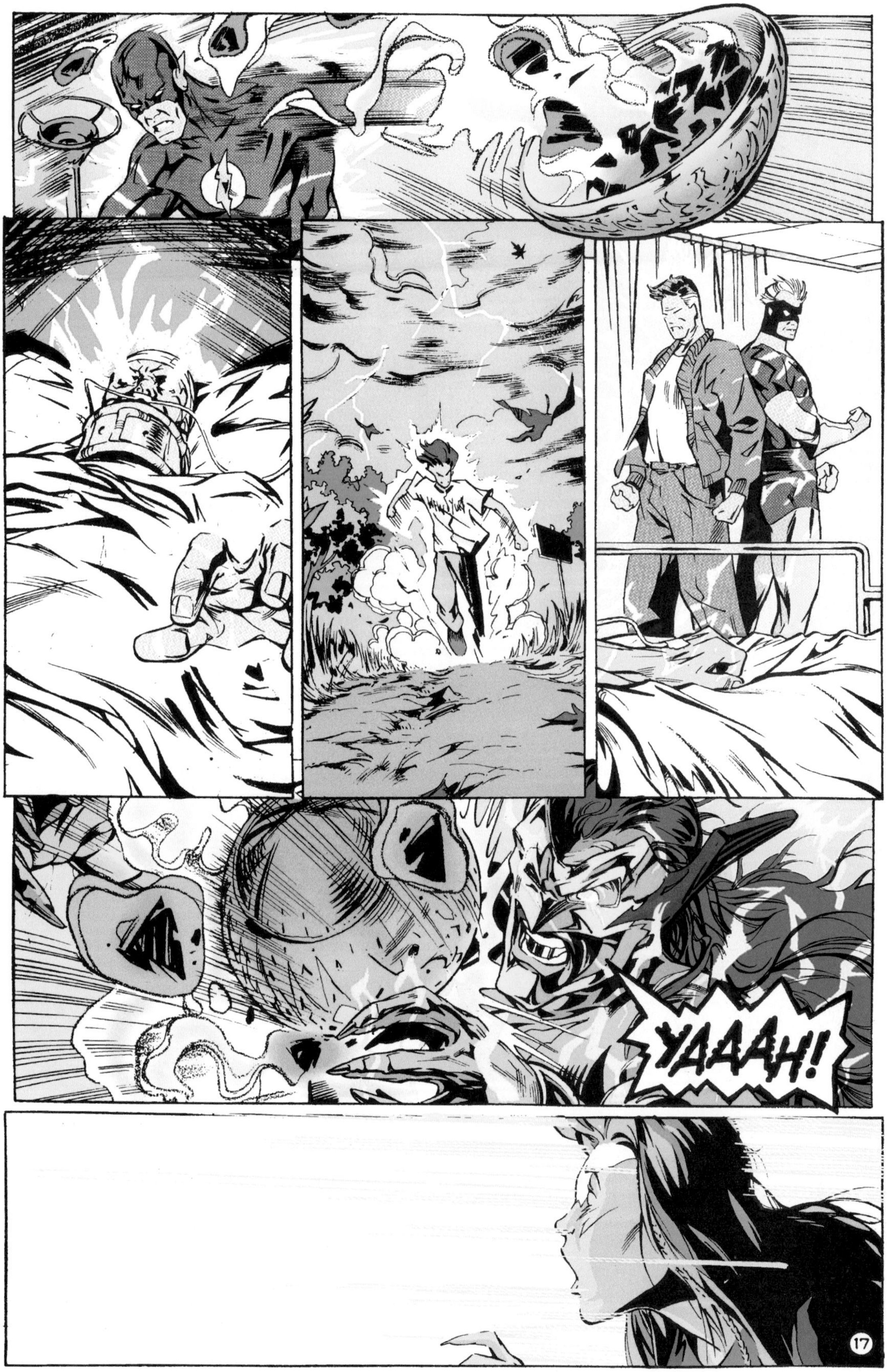
YAAAH!

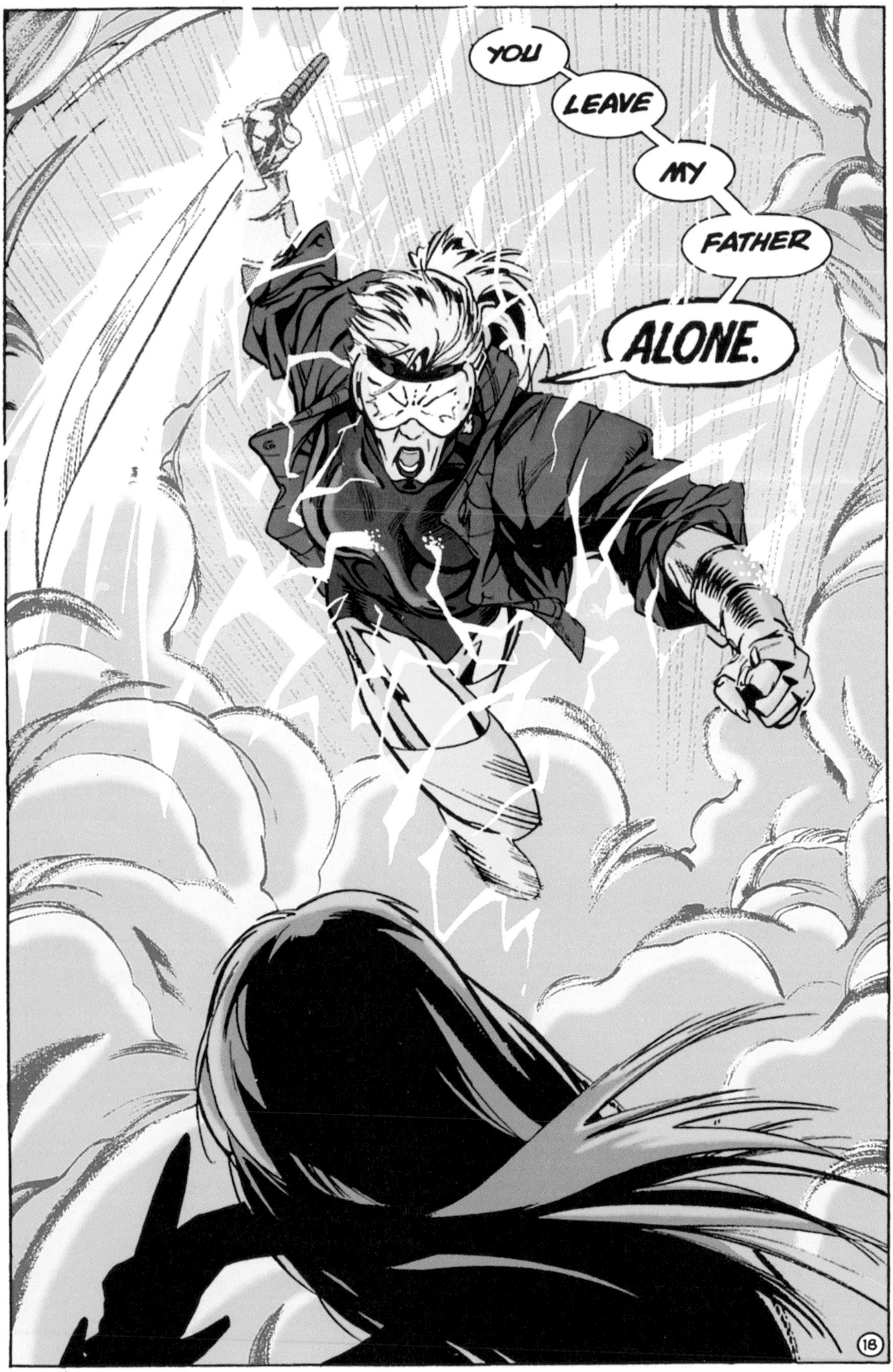
YOU
LEAVE
MY
FATHER
ALONE.

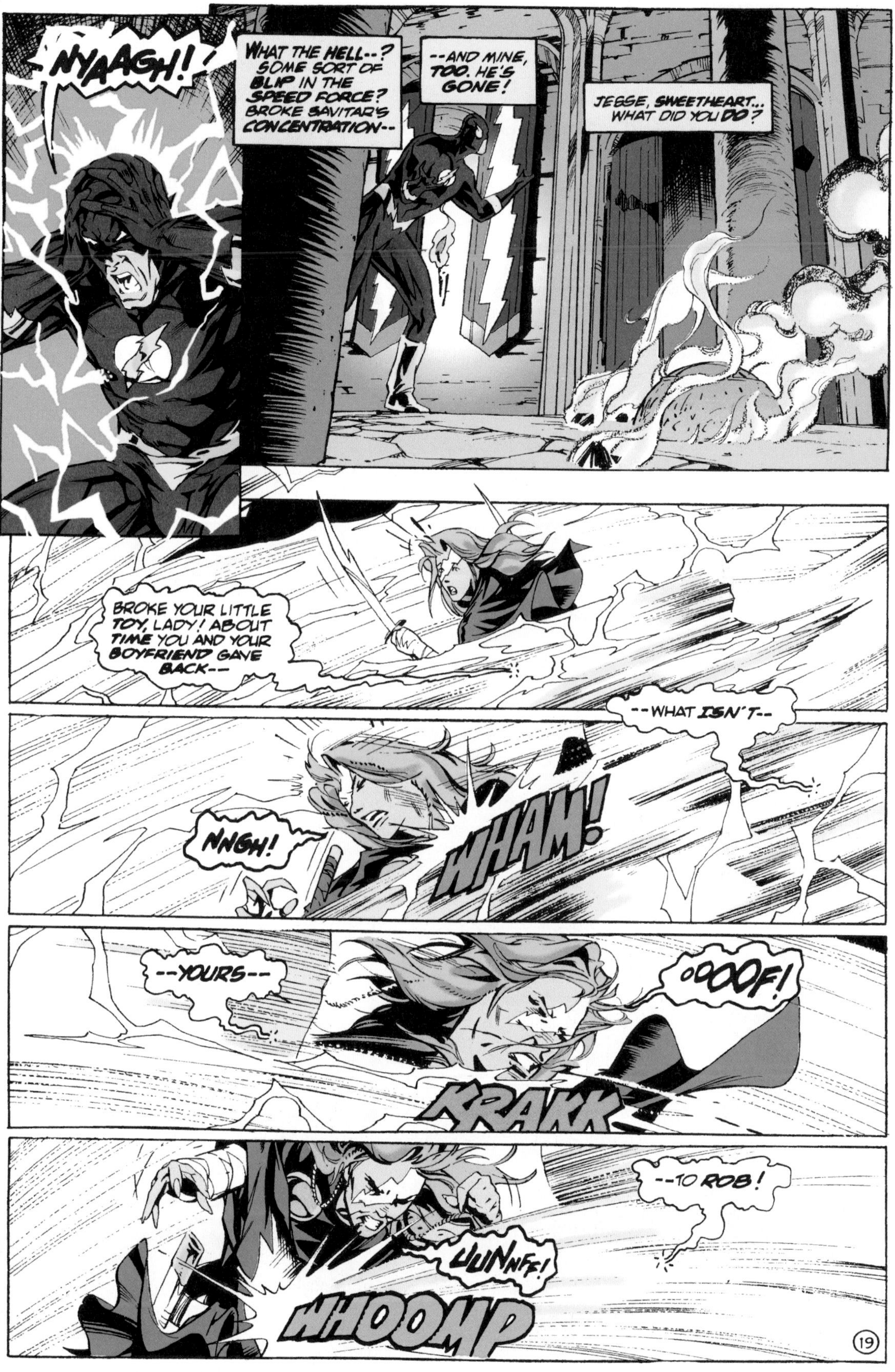

NYAAGH!
WHAT THE HELL--? SOME SORT OF BLIP IN THE SPEED FORCE? BROKE SAVITAR'S CONCENTRATION--
--AND MINE, TOO. HE'S GONE!
JESSE, SWEETHEART... WHAT DID YOU DO?
BROKE YOUR LITTLE TOY, LADY! ABOUT TIME YOU AND YOUR BOYFRIEND GAVE BACK--
--WHAT ISN'T--
NNGH!
WHAM!
--YOURS--
OOOOF!
KRAKK
--TO ROB!
UUNNFF!
WHOOMP

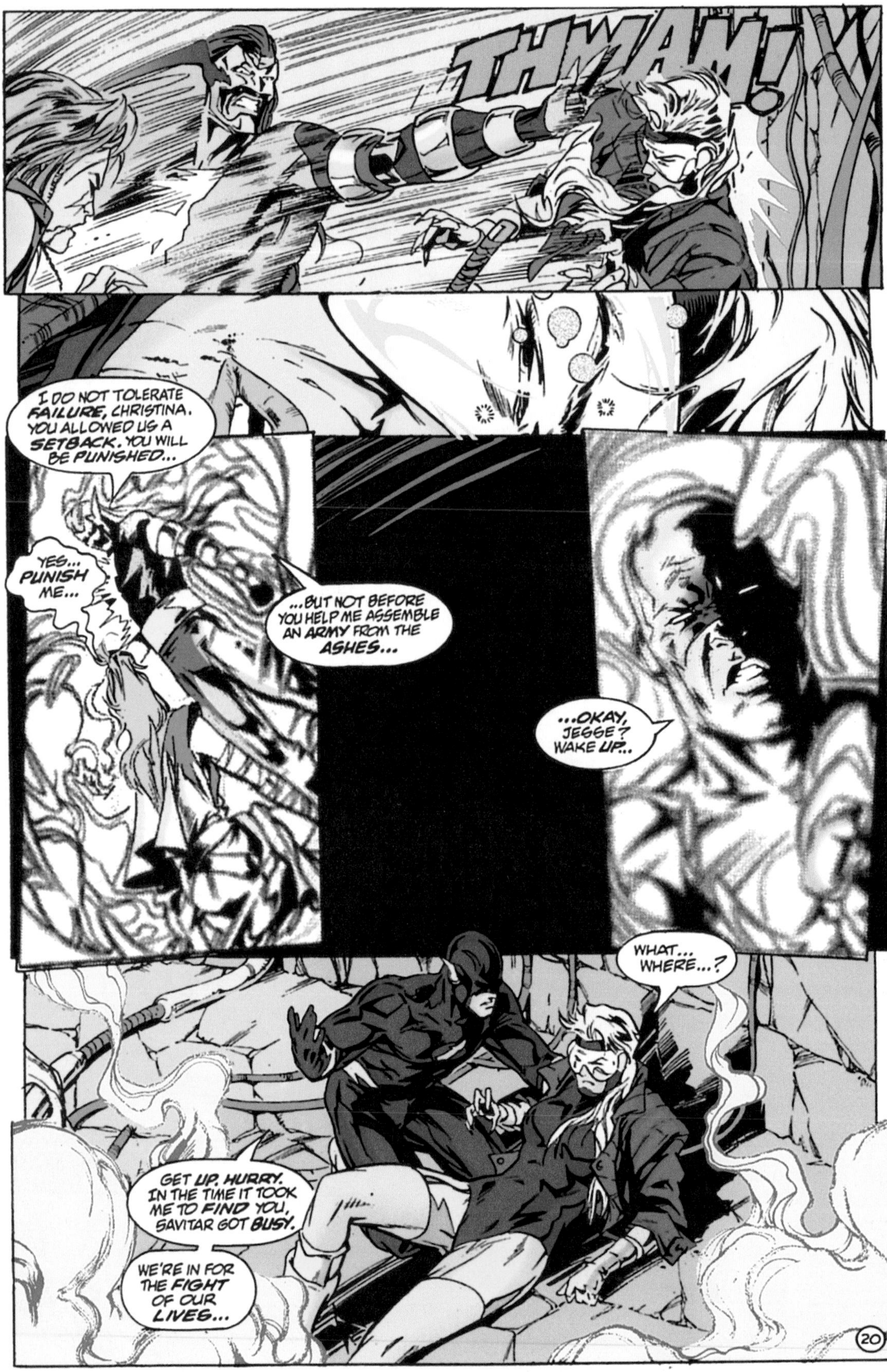
THMAM!
I DO NOT TOLERATE FAILURE, CHRISTINA. YOU ALLOWED US A SETBACK. YOU WILL BE PUNISHED...
YES... PUNISH ME...
...BUT NOT BEFORE YOU HELP ME ASSEMBLE AN ARMY FROM THE ASHES...
...OKAY, JESSE? WAKE UP...
WHAT... WHERE...?
GET UP, HURRY. IN THE TIME IT TOOK ME TO FIND YOU, SAVITAR GOT BUSY.
WE'RE IN FOR THE FIGHT OF OUR LIVES...

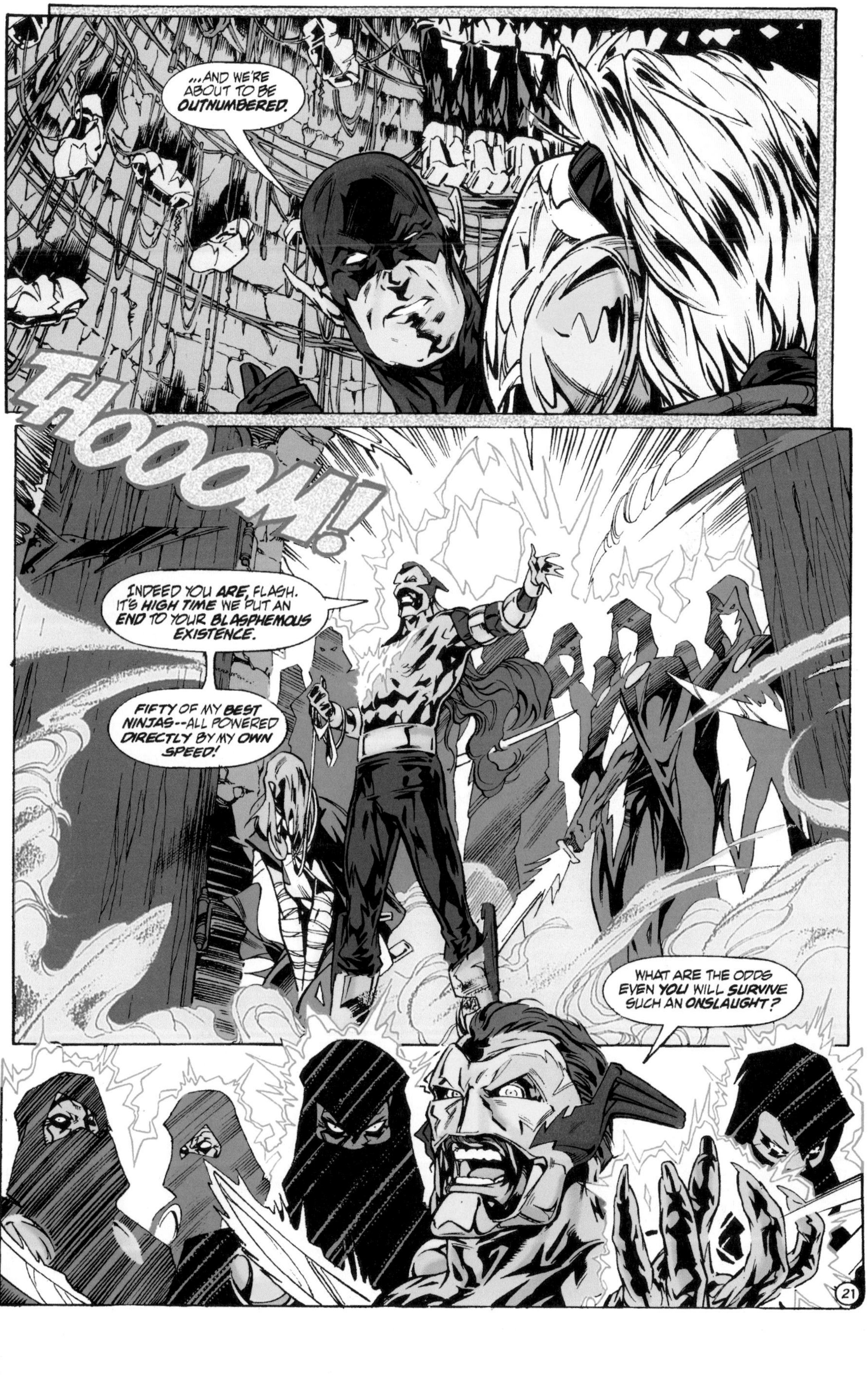
...AND WE'RE ABOUT TO BE OUTNUMBERED.
THOOOM!
INDEED YOU ARE, FLASH. IT'S HIGH TIME WE PUT AN END TO YOUR BLASPHEMOUS EXISTENCE.
FIFTY OF MY BEST NINJAS--ALL POWERED DIRECTLY BY MY OWN SPEED!
WHAT ARE THE ODDS EVEN YOU WILL SURVIVE SUCH AN ONSLAUGHT?

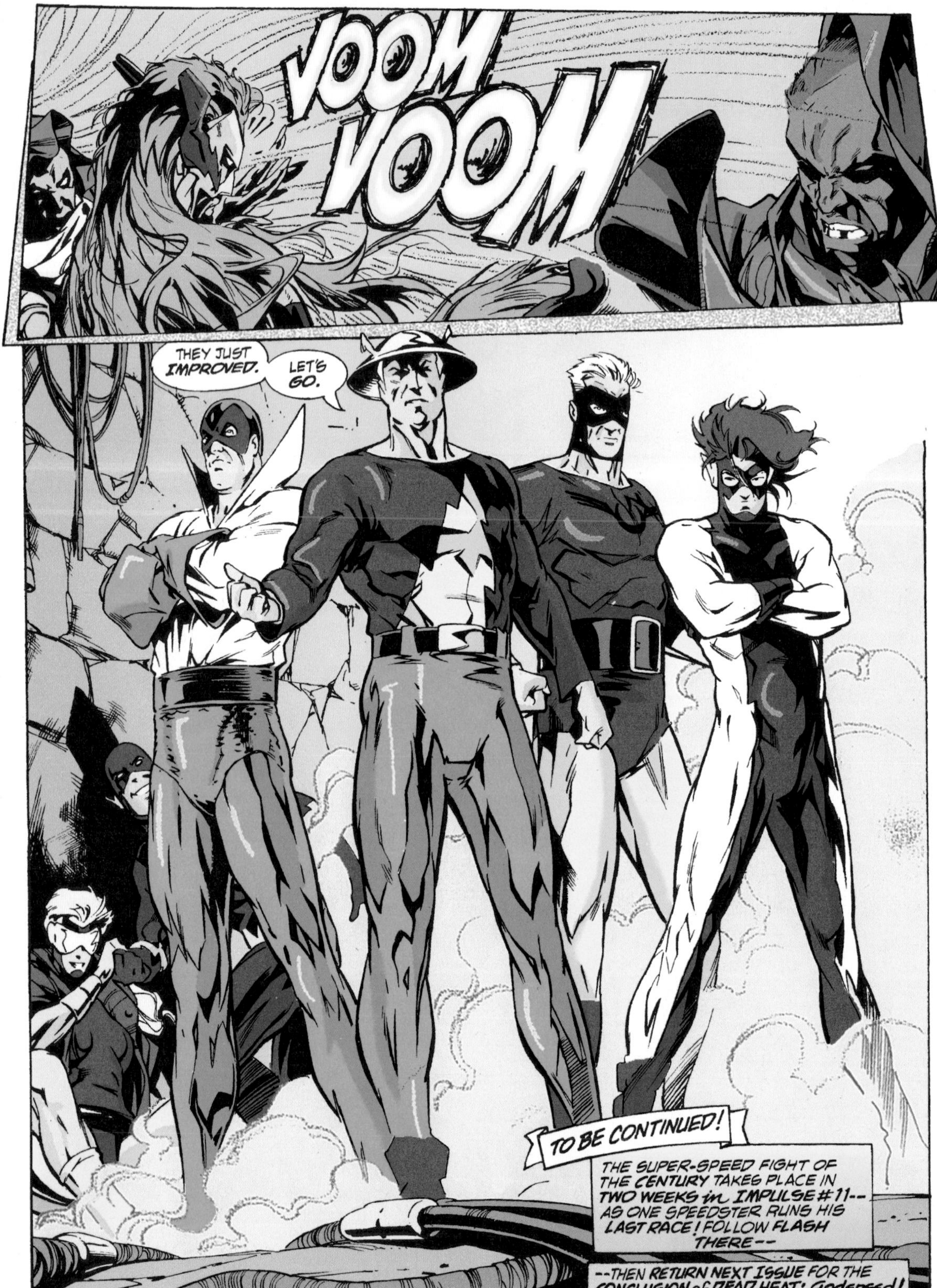

VOOM VOOM
THEY JUST IMPROVED.
LET'S GO.
TO BE CONTINUED!
THE SUPER-SPEED FIGHT OF THE CENTURY TAKES PLACE IN TWO WEEKS in IMPULSE #11-- AS ONE SPEEDSTER RUNS HIS LAST RACE! FOLLOW FLASH THERE--
--THEN RETURN NEXT ISSUE FOR THE CONCLUSION of DEAD HEAT: Godspeed!

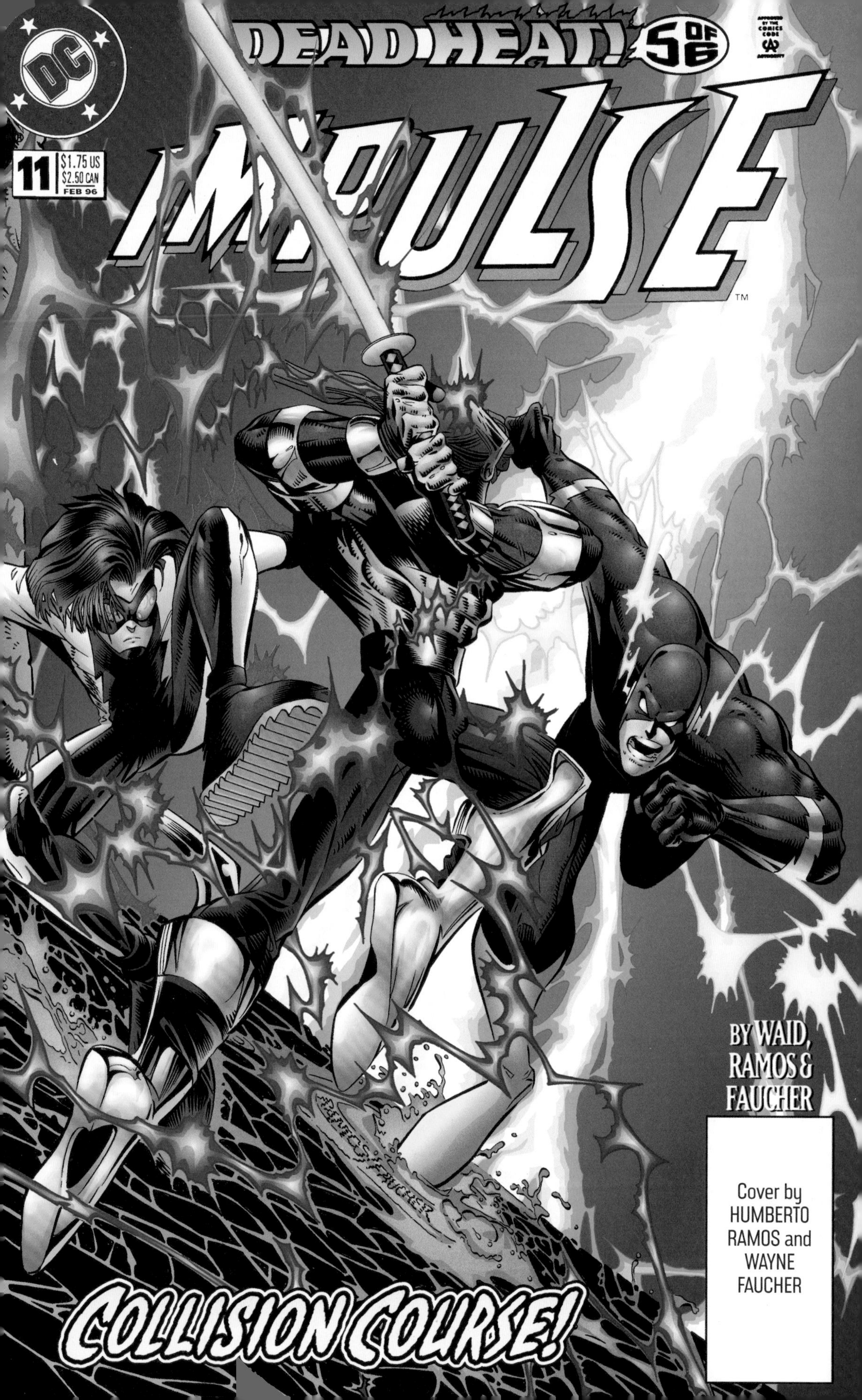
DC
DEAD HEAT! 5 OF 6
APPROVED BY THE COMICS CODE AUTHORITY
11
$1.75 US
$2.50 CAN
FEB 96
IMPULSE ™
BY WAID, RAMOS & FAUCHER
Cover by HUMBERTO RAMOS and WAYNE FAUCHER
COLLISION COURSE!

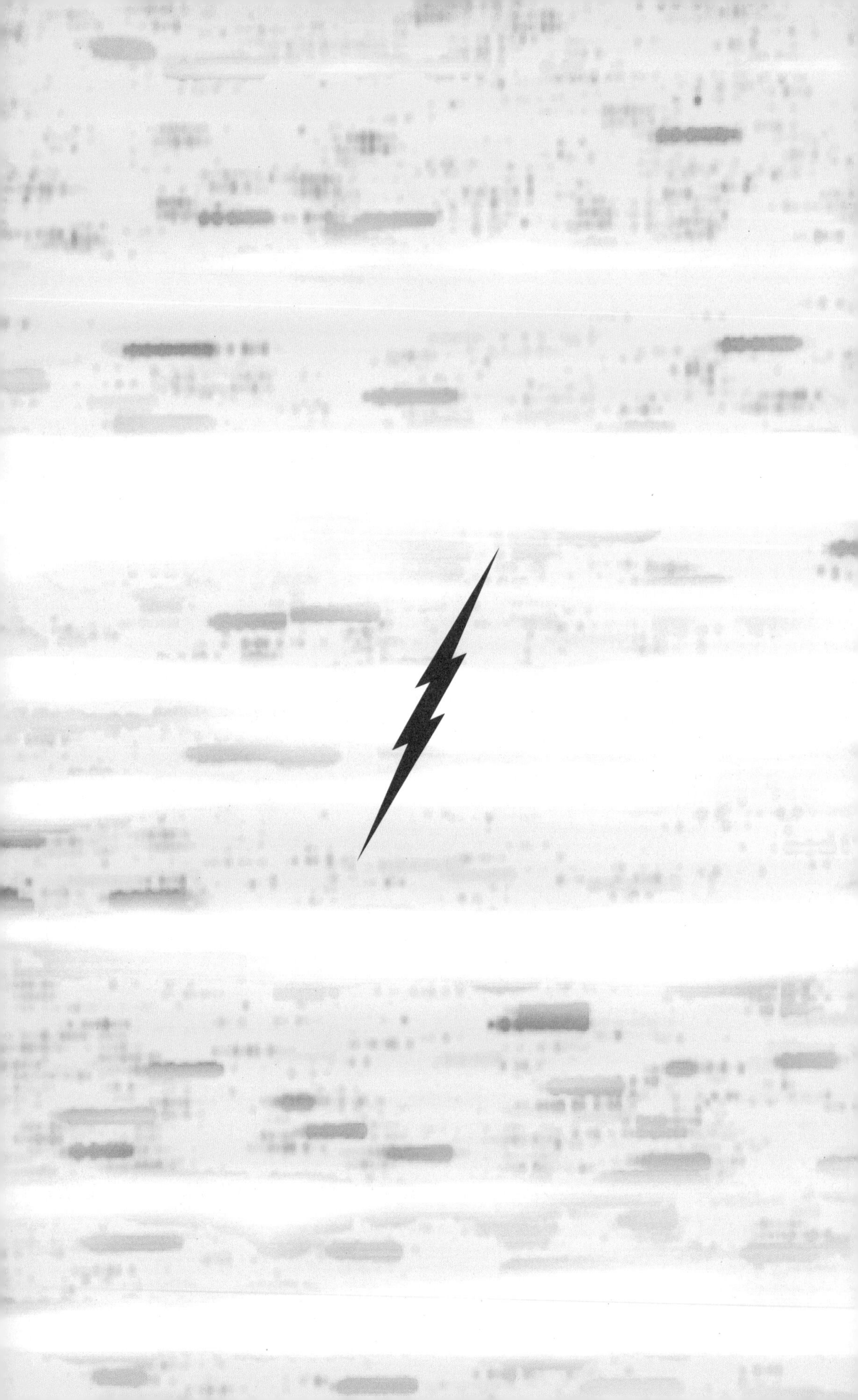

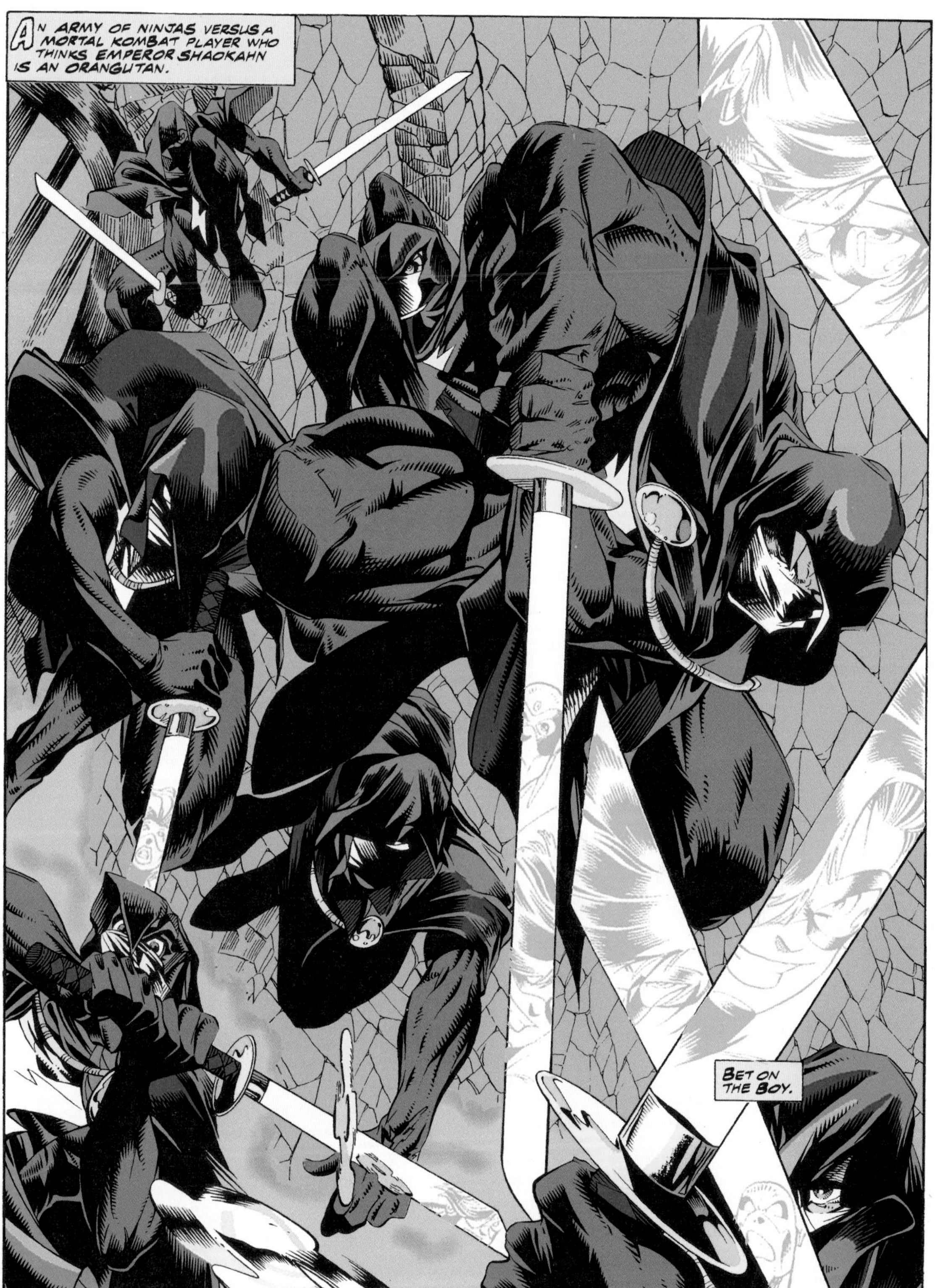
AN ARMY OF NINJAS VERSUS A MORTAL KOMBAT PLAYER WHO THINKS EMPEROR SHAOKAHN IS AN ORANGUTAN.
BET ON THE BOY.

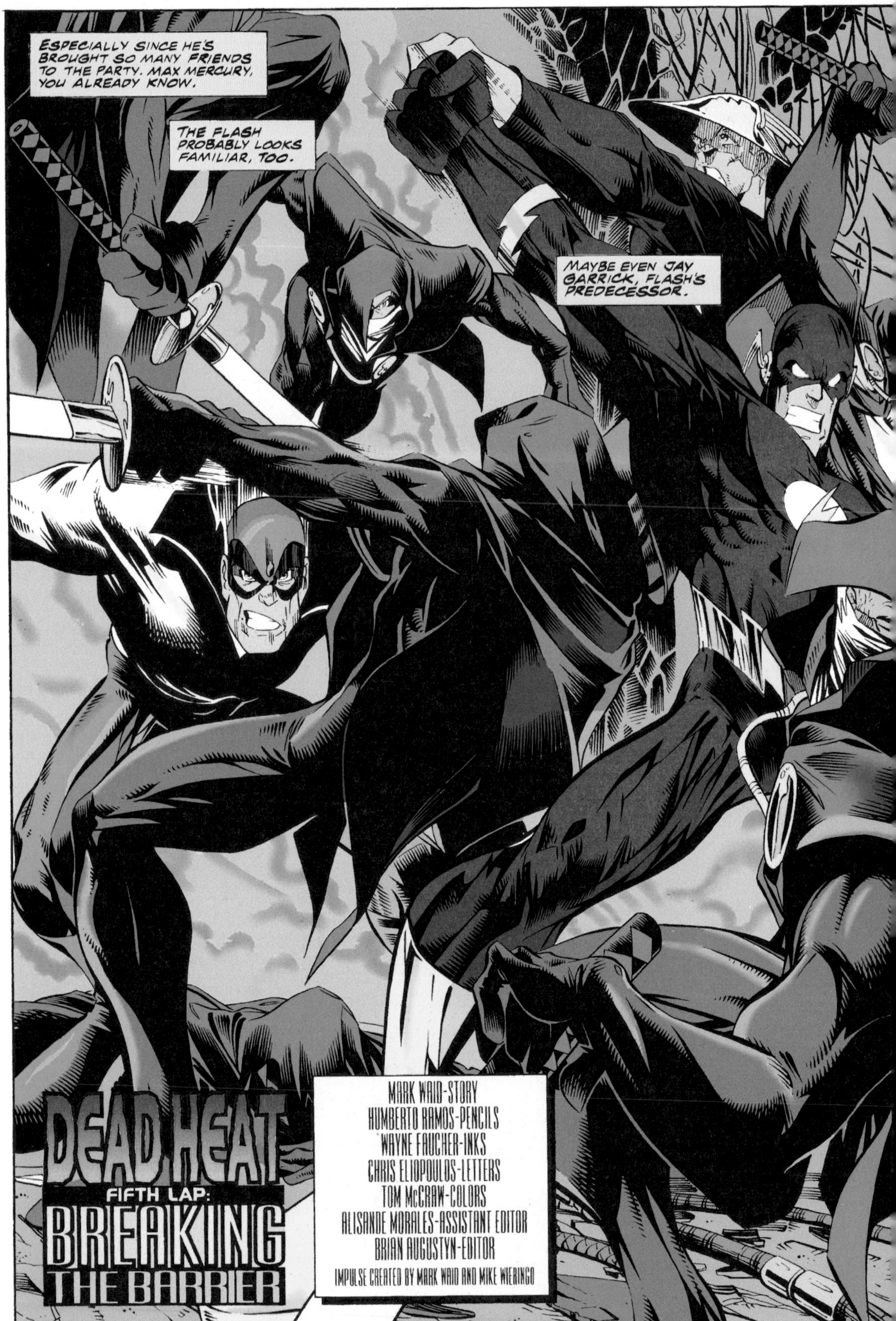
ESPECIALLY SINCE HE'S BROUGHT SO MANY FRIENDS TO THE PARTY. MAX MERCURY, YOU ALREADY KNOW.
THE FLASH PROBABLY LOOKS FAMILIAR, TOO.
MAYBE EVEN JAY GARRICK, FLASH'S PREDECESSOR.
DEAD HEAT
FIFTH LAP:
BREAKING THE BARRIER
MARK WAID-STORY
HUMBERTO RAMOS-PENCILS
WAYNE FAUCHER-INKS
CHRIS ELIOPOULOS-LETTERS
TOM McCRAW-COLORS
ALISANDE MORALES-ASSISTANT EDITOR
BRIAN AUGUSTYN-EDITOR
IMPULSE CREATED BY MARK WAID AND MIKE WIERINGO

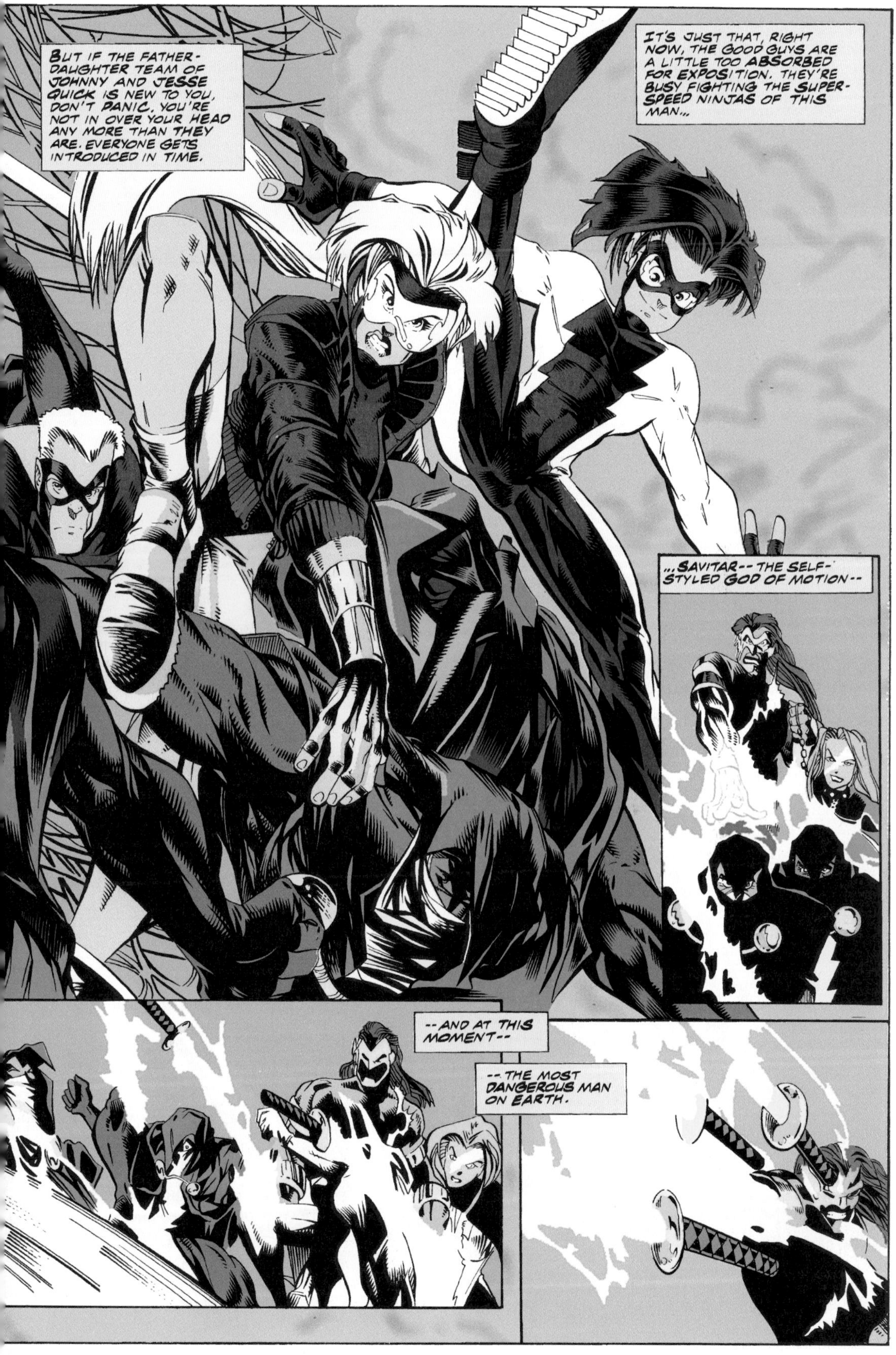
BUT IF THE FATHER-DAUGHTER TEAM OF JOHNNY AND JESSE QUICK IS NEW TO YOU, DON'T PANIC. YOU'RE NOT IN OVER YOUR HEAD ANY MORE THAN THEY ARE. EVERYONE GETS INTRODUCED IN TIME.
IT'S JUST THAT, RIGHT NOW, THE GOOD GUYS ARE A LITTLE TOO ABSORBED FOR EXPOSITION. THEY'RE BUSY FIGHTING THE SUPER-SPEED NINJAS OF THIS MAN...
...SAVITAR-- THE SELF-STYLED GOD OF MOTION--
--AND AT THIS MOMENT--
--THE MOST DANGEROUS MAN ON EARTH.

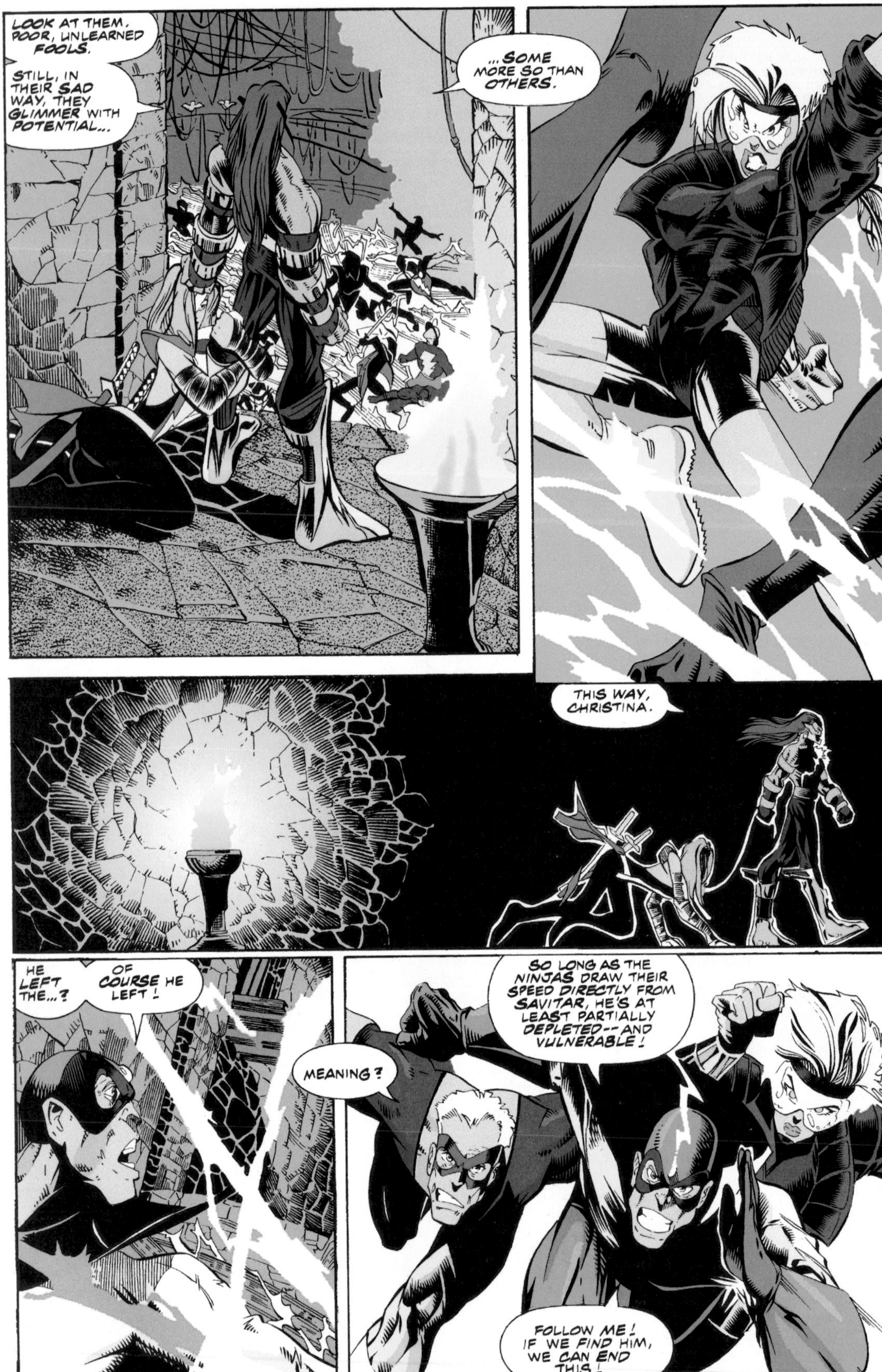
LOOK AT THEM. POOR, UNLEARNED FOOLS.
STILL, IN THEIR SAD WAY, THEY GLIMMER WITH POTENTIAL...
...SOME MORE SO THAN OTHERS.
THIS WAY, CHRISTINA.
HE LEFT THE...?
OF COURSE HE LEFT!
MEANING?
SO LONG AS THE NINJAS DRAW THEIR SPEED DIRECTLY FROM SAVITAR, HE'S AT LEAST PARTIALLY DEPLETED--AND VULNERABLE!
FOLLOW ME! IF WE FIND HIM, WE CAN END THIS!

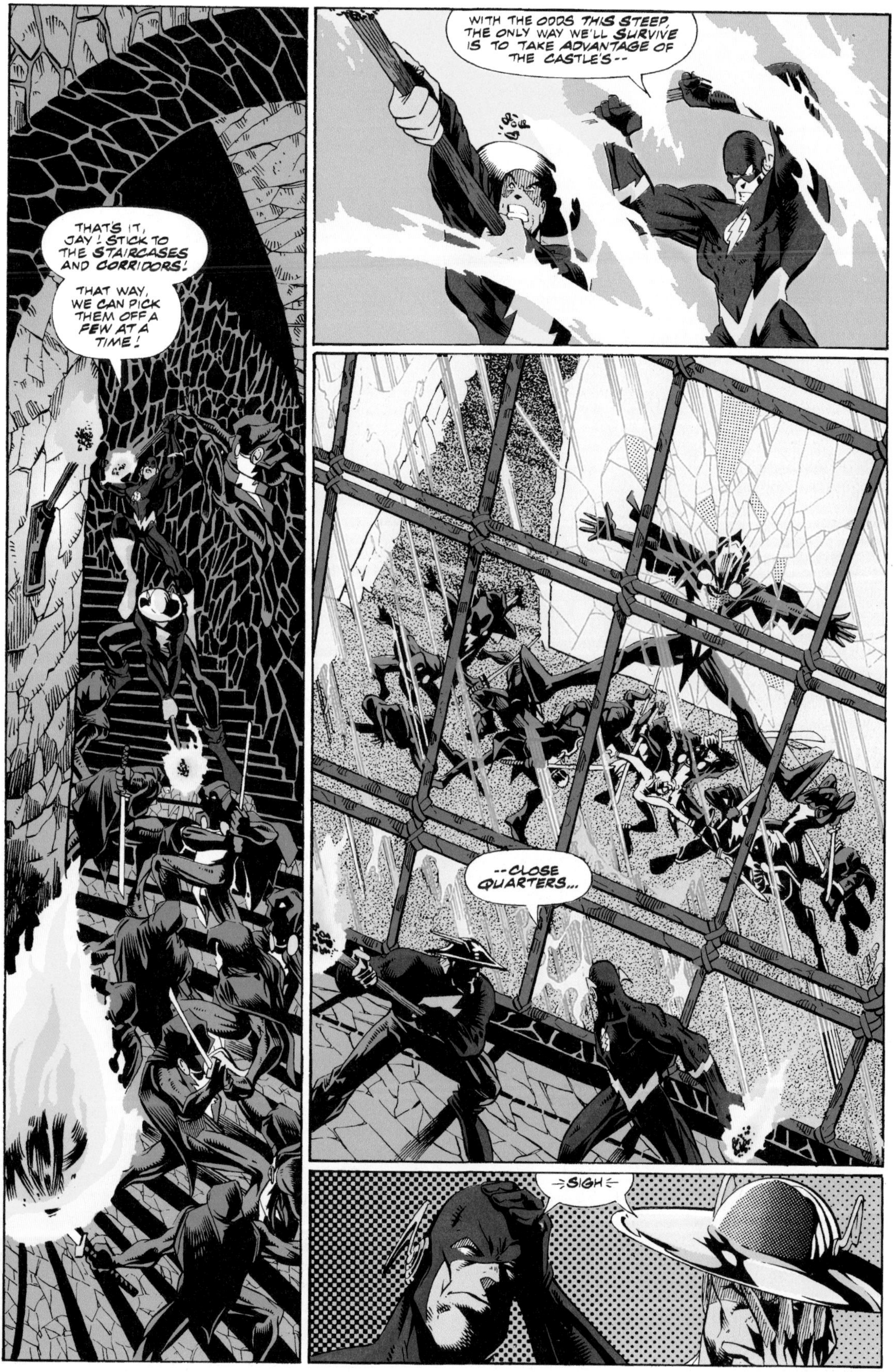
THAT'S IT, JAY! STICK TO THE STAIRCASES AND CORRIDORS!
THAT WAY, WE CAN PICK THEM OFF A FEW AT A TIME!
WITH THE ODDS THIS STEEP, THE ONLY WAY WE'LL SURVIVE IS TO TAKE ADVANTAGE OF THE CASTLE'S--
--CLOSE QUARTERS...
SIGH

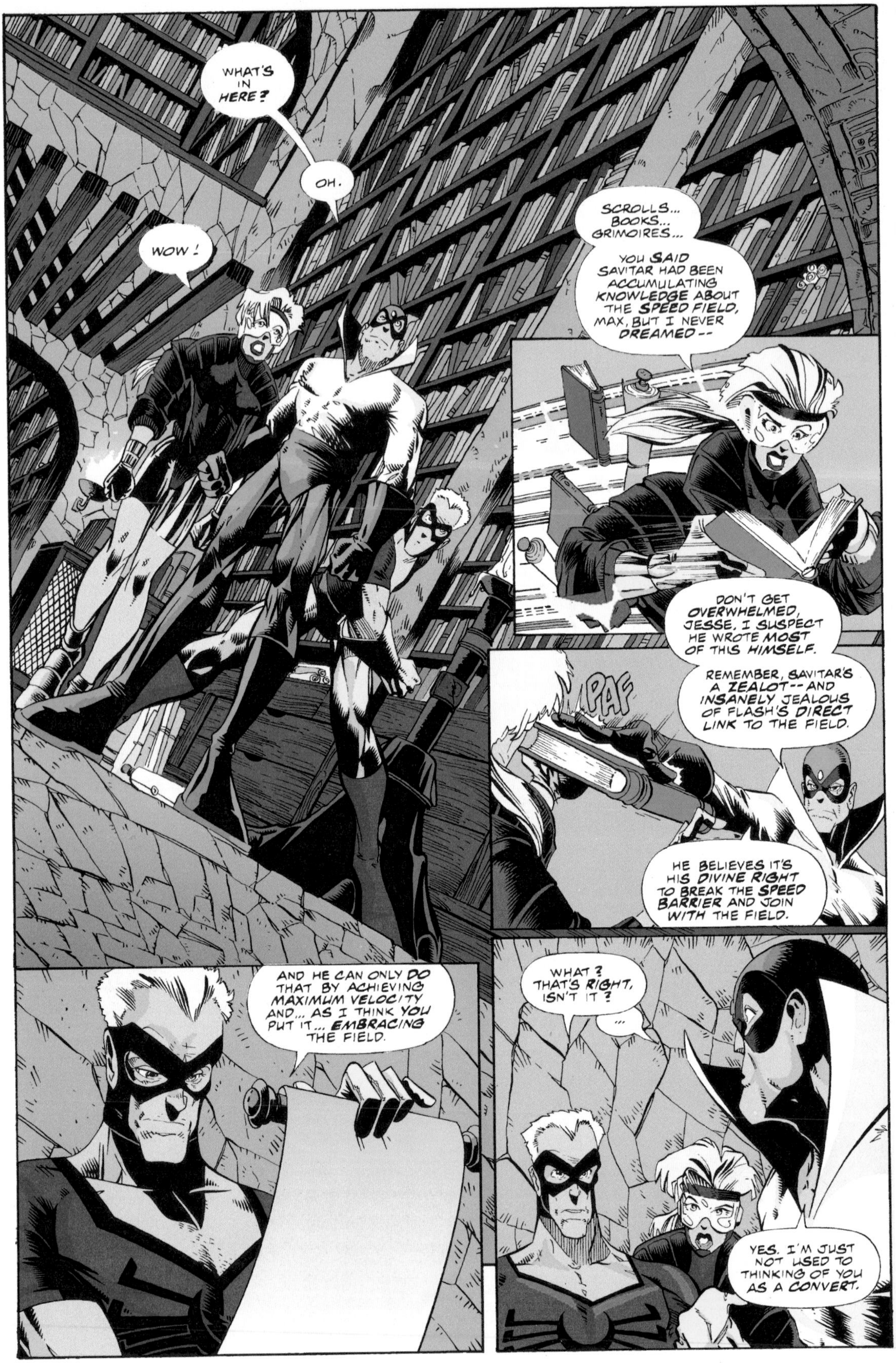
WHAT'S IN HERE?
OH.
WOW!
SCROLLS... BOOKS... GRIMOIRES...
YOU SAID SAVITAR HAD BEEN ACCUMULATING KNOWLEDGE ABOUT THE SPEED FIELD, MAX, BUT I NEVER DREAMED--
DON'T GET OVERWHELMED, JESSE. I SUSPECT HE WROTE MOST OF THIS HIMSELF.
REMEMBER, SAVITAR'S A ZEALOT--AND INSANELY JEALOUS OF FLASH'S DIRECT LINK TO THE FIELD.
PAF
HE BELIEVES IT'S HIS DIVINE RIGHT TO BREAK THE SPEED BARRIER AND JOIN WITH THE FIELD.
AND HE CAN ONLY DO THAT BY ACHIEVING MAXIMUM VELOCITY AND... AS I THINK YOU PUT IT... EMBRACING THE FIELD.
WHAT? THAT'S RIGHT, ISN'T IT?
...
YES. I'M JUST NOT USED TO THINKING OF YOU AS A CONVERT.

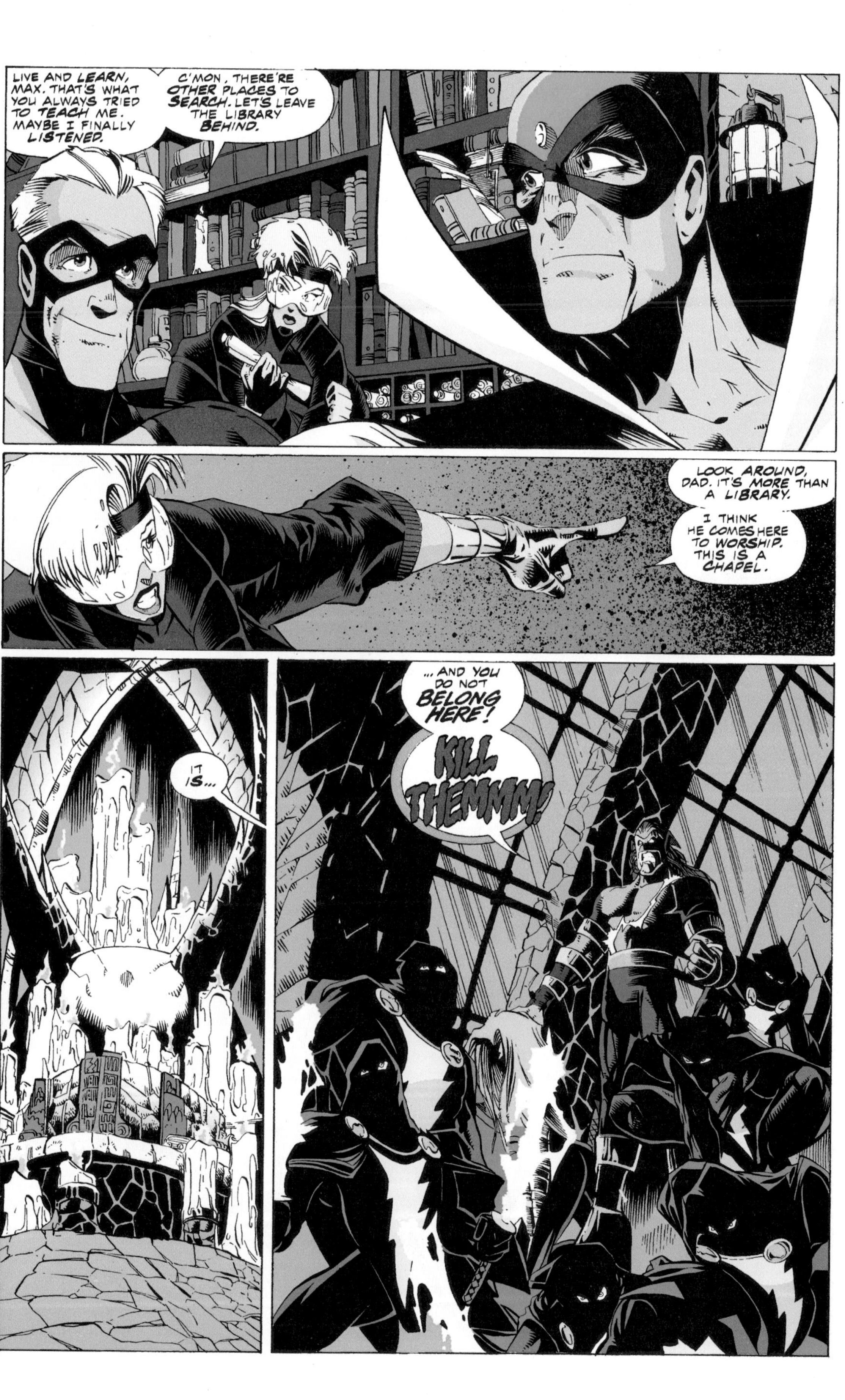

LIVE AND LEARN, MAX. THAT'S WHAT YOU ALWAYS TRIED TO TEACH ME. MAYBE I FINALLY LISTENED.
C'MON, THERE'RE OTHER PLACES TO SEARCH. LET'S LEAVE THE LIBRARY BEHIND.
LOOK AROUND, DAD. IT'S MORE THAN A LIBRARY.
I THINK HE COMES HERE TO WORSHIP. THIS IS A CHAPEL.
IT IS...
...AND YOU DO NOT BELONG HERE!
KILL THEMMM!

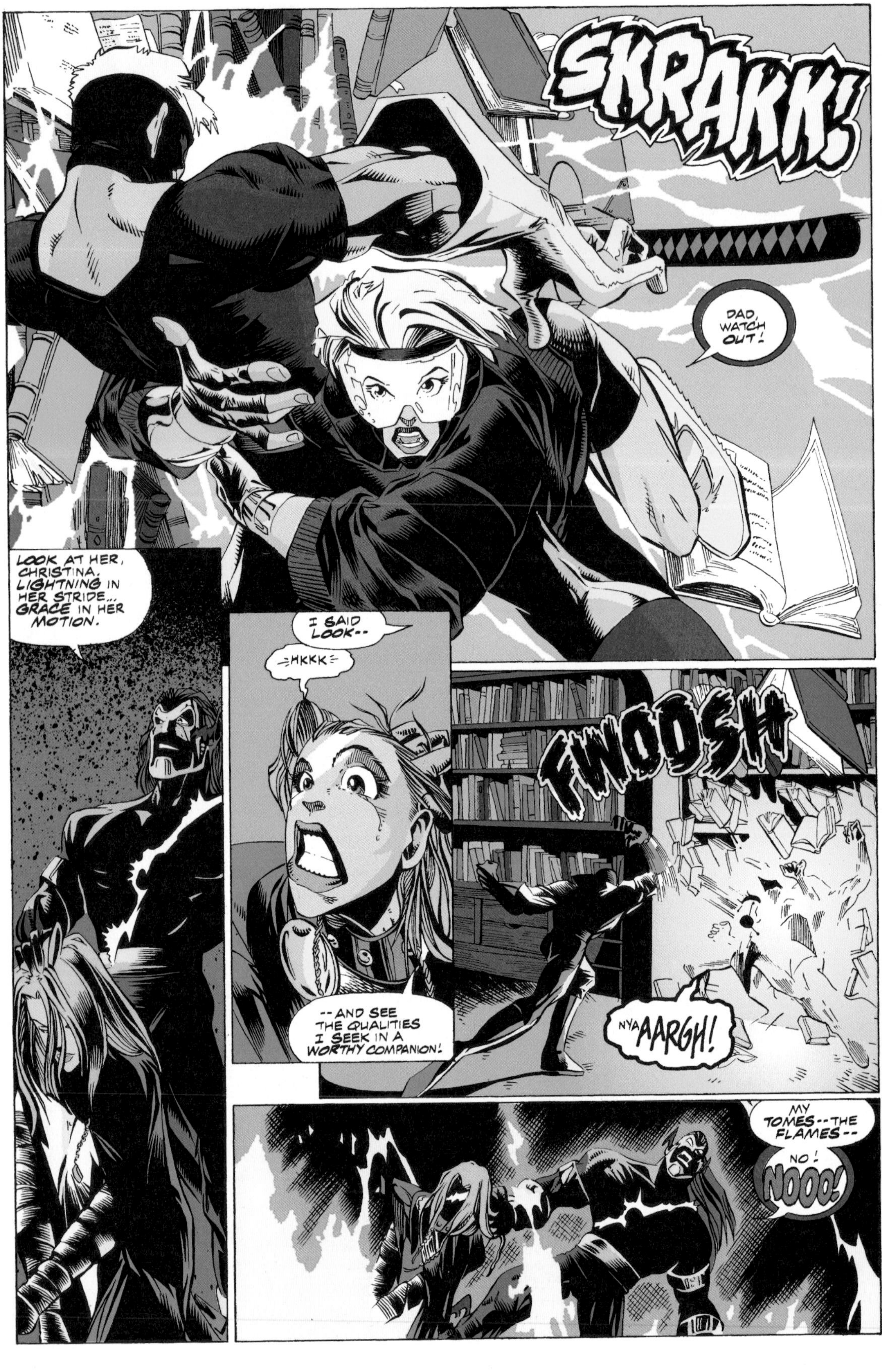
SKRAKK!
DAD, WATCH OUT!
LOOK AT HER, CHRISTINA. LIGHTNING IN HER STRIDE... GRACE IN HER MOTION.
I SAID LOOK--
HKKK
--AND SEE THE QUALITIES I SEEK IN A WORTHY COMPANION!
FWOOSH
NYAAARGH!
MY TOMES--THE FLAMES--
NO! NOOO!

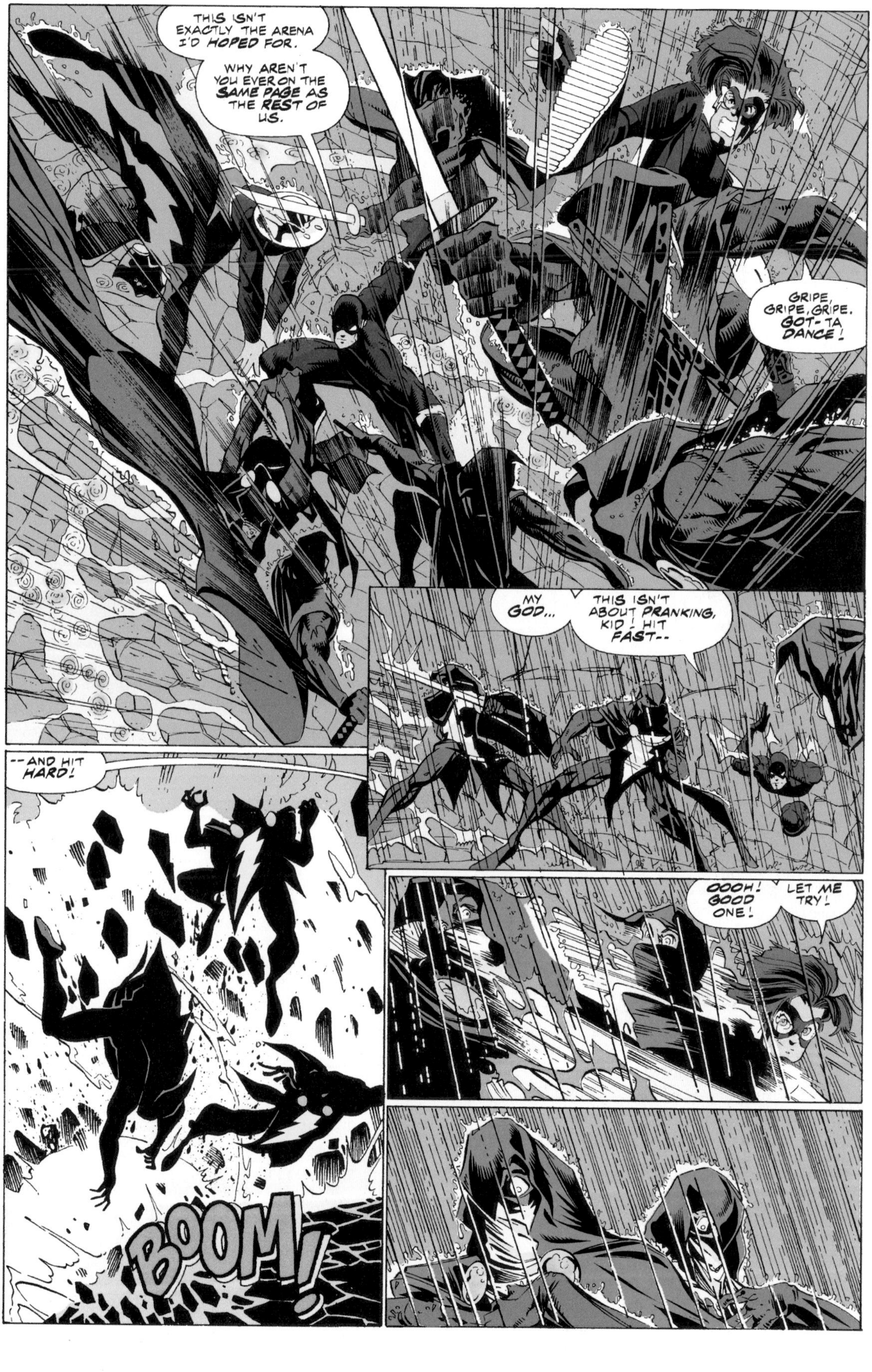

THIS ISN'T EXACTLY THE ARENA I'D HOPED FOR.
WHY AREN'T YOU EVER ON THE SAME PAGE AS THE REST OF US.
GRIPE, GRIPE, GRIPE. GOT-TA DANCE!
MY GOD...
THIS ISN'T ABOUT PRANKING, KID! HIT FAST--
--AND HIT HARD!
BOOM!
OOOH! GOOD ONE!
LET ME TRY!

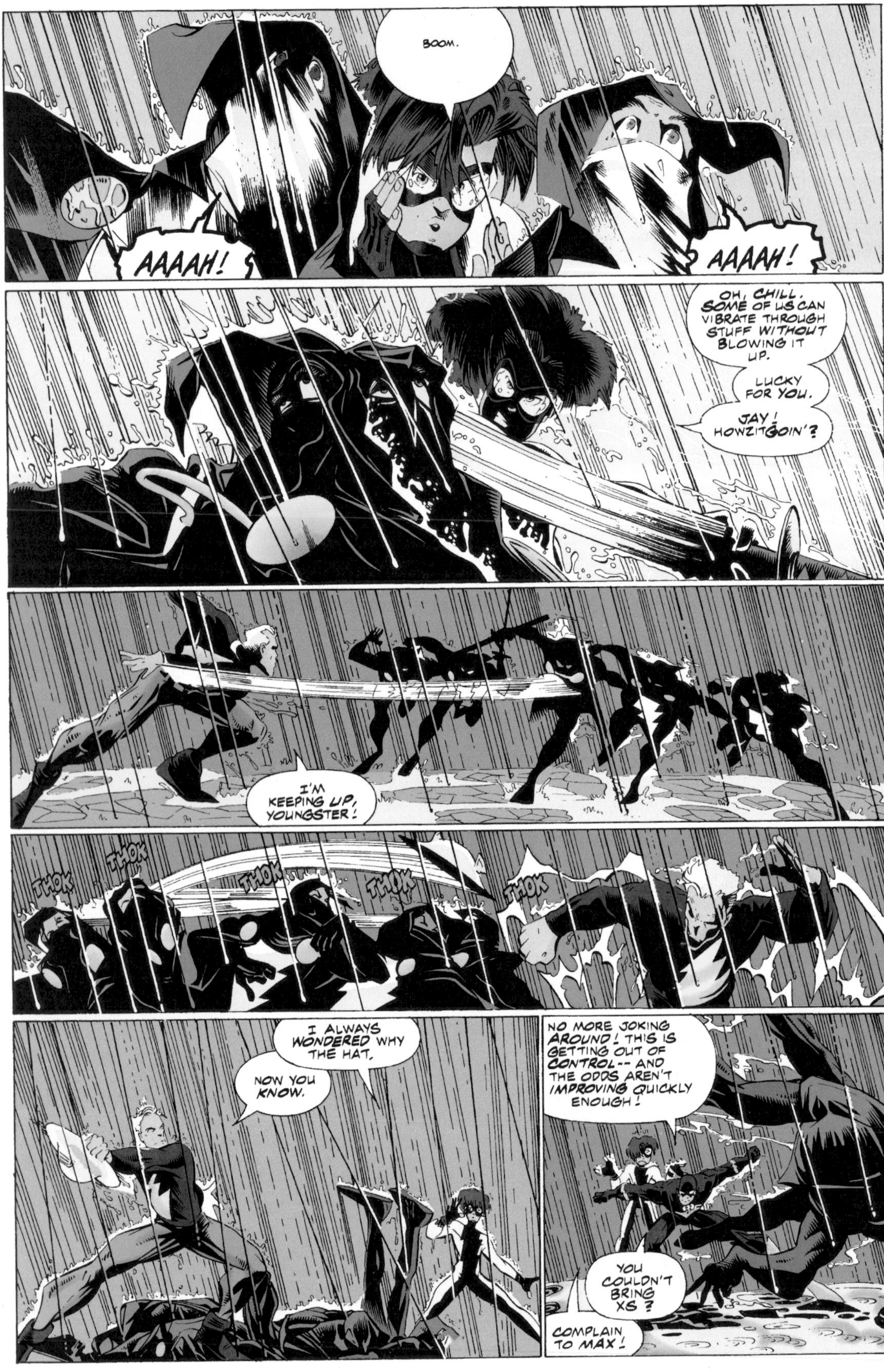
BOOM.
AAAAH!
AAAAH!
OH, CHILL. SOME OF US CAN VIBRATE THROUGH STUFF WITHOUT BLOWING IT UP.
LUCKY FOR YOU.
JAY! HOWZITGOIN'?
I'M KEEPING UP, YOUNGSTER!
THOK
THOK
THOK
THOK
THOK
I ALWAYS WONDERED WHY THE HAT.
NOW YOU KNOW.
NO MORE JOKING AROUND! THIS IS GETTING OUT OF CONTROL-- AND THE ODDS AREN'T IMPROVING QUICKLY ENOUGH!
YOU COULDN'T BRING XS?
COMPLAIN TO MAX!

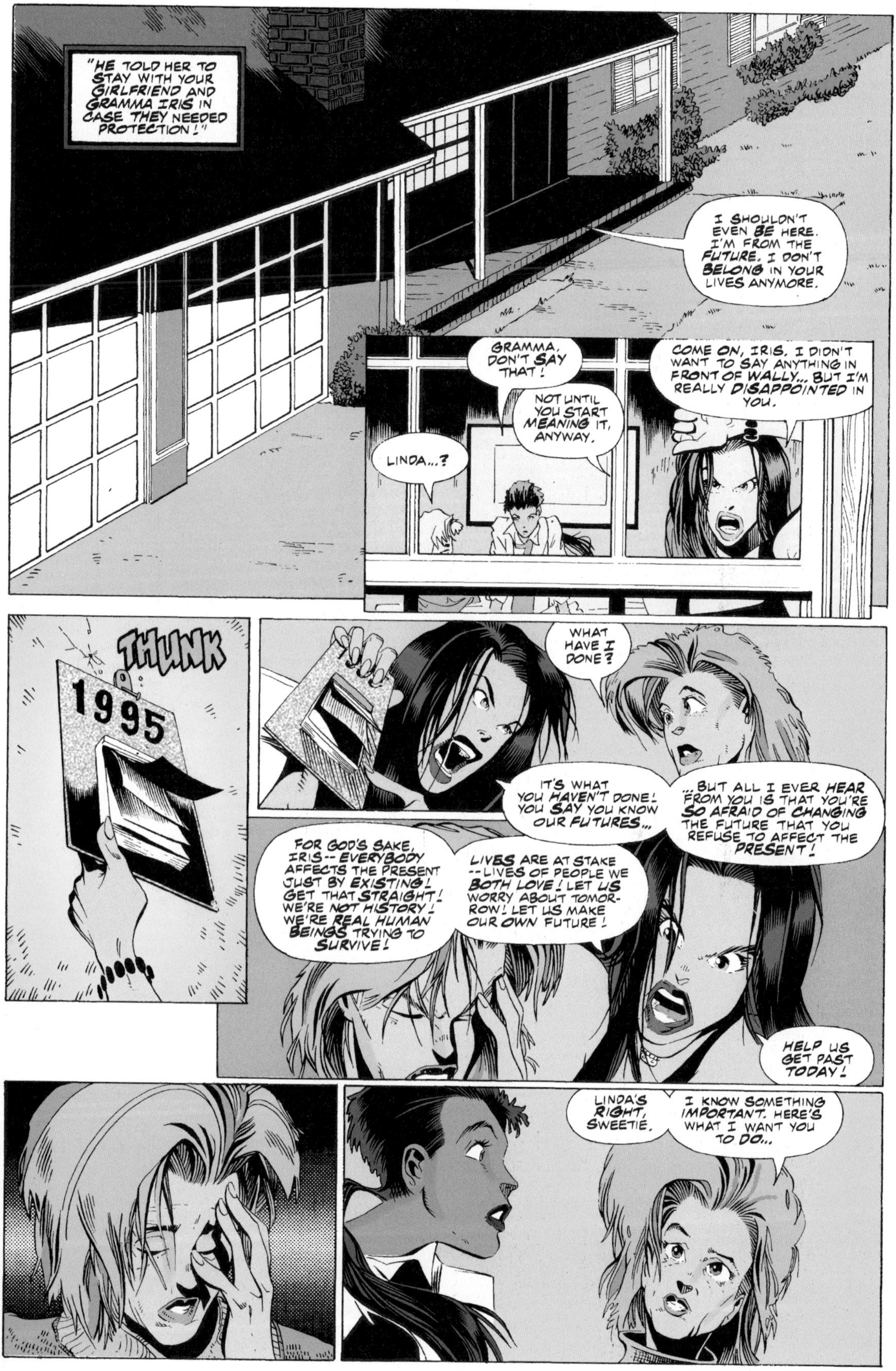
"HE TOLD HER TO STAY WITH YOUR GIRLFRIEND AND GRAMMA IRIS IN CASE THEY NEEDED PROTECTION!"
I SHOULDN'T EVEN BE HERE. I'M FROM THE FUTURE. I DON'T BELONG IN YOUR LIVES ANYMORE.
GRAMMA, DON'T SAY THAT!
NOT UNTIL YOU START MEANING IT, ANYWAY.
LINDA...?
COME ON, IRIS. I DIDN'T WANT TO SAY ANYTHING IN FRONT OF WALLY... BUT I'M REALLY DISAPPOINTED IN YOU.
THUNK
1995
WHAT HAVE I DONE?
IT'S WHAT YOU HAVEN'T DONE! YOU SAY YOU KNOW OUR FUTURES...
...BUT ALL I EVER HEAR FROM YOU IS THAT YOU'RE SO AFRAID OF CHANGING THE FUTURE THAT YOU REFUSE TO AFFECT THE PRESENT!
FOR GOD'S SAKE, IRIS-- EVERYBODY AFFECTS THE PRESENT JUST BY EXISTING! GET THAT STRAIGHT! WE'RE NOT HISTORY! WE'RE REAL HUMAN BEINGS TRYING TO SURVIVE!
LIVES ARE AT STAKE --LIVES OF PEOPLE WE BOTH LOVE! LET US WORRY ABOUT TOMORROW! LET US MAKE OUR OWN FUTURE!
HELP US GET PAST TODAY!
LINDA'S RIGHT, SWEETIE.
I KNOW SOMETHING IMPORTANT. HERE'S WHAT I WANT YOU TO DO...

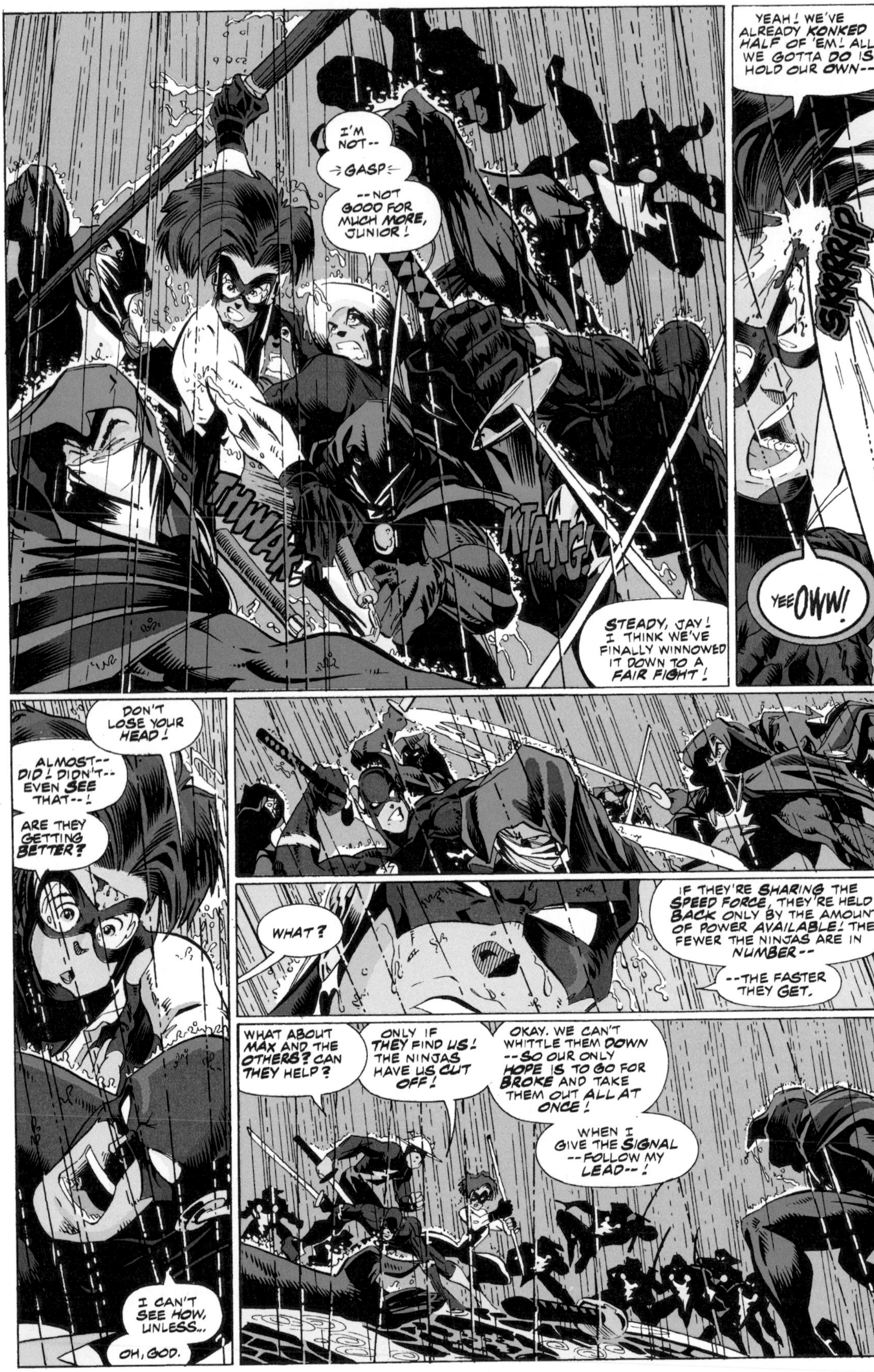
I'M NOT--
GASP
--NOT GOOD FOR MUCH MORE, JUNIOR!
THWAK
KTANG!
STEADY, JAY! I THINK WE'VE FINALLY WINNOWED IT DOWN TO A FAIR FIGHT!
YEAH! WE'VE ALREADY KONKED HALF OF 'EM! ALL WE GOTTA DO IS HOLD OUR OWN--
SKRRRIP
YEEOWW!
DON'T LOSE YOUR HEAD!
ALMOST-- DID! DIDN'T-- EVEN SEE THAT--!
ARE THEY GETTING BETTER?
I CAN'T SEE HOW, UNLESS...
OH, GOD.
WHAT?
IF THEY'RE SHARING THE SPEED FORCE, THEY'RE HELD BACK ONLY BY THE AMOUNT OF POWER AVAILABLE! THE FEWER THE NINJAS ARE IN NUMBER--
--THE FASTER THEY GET.
WHAT ABOUT MAX AND THE OTHERS? CAN THEY HELP?
ONLY IF THEY FIND US! THE NINJAS HAVE US CUT OFF!
OKAY. WE CAN'T WHITTLE THEM DOWN --SO OUR ONLY HOPE IS TO GO FOR BROKE AND TAKE THEM OUT ALL AT ONCE!
WHEN I GIVE THE SIGNAL --FOLLOW MY LEAD--!

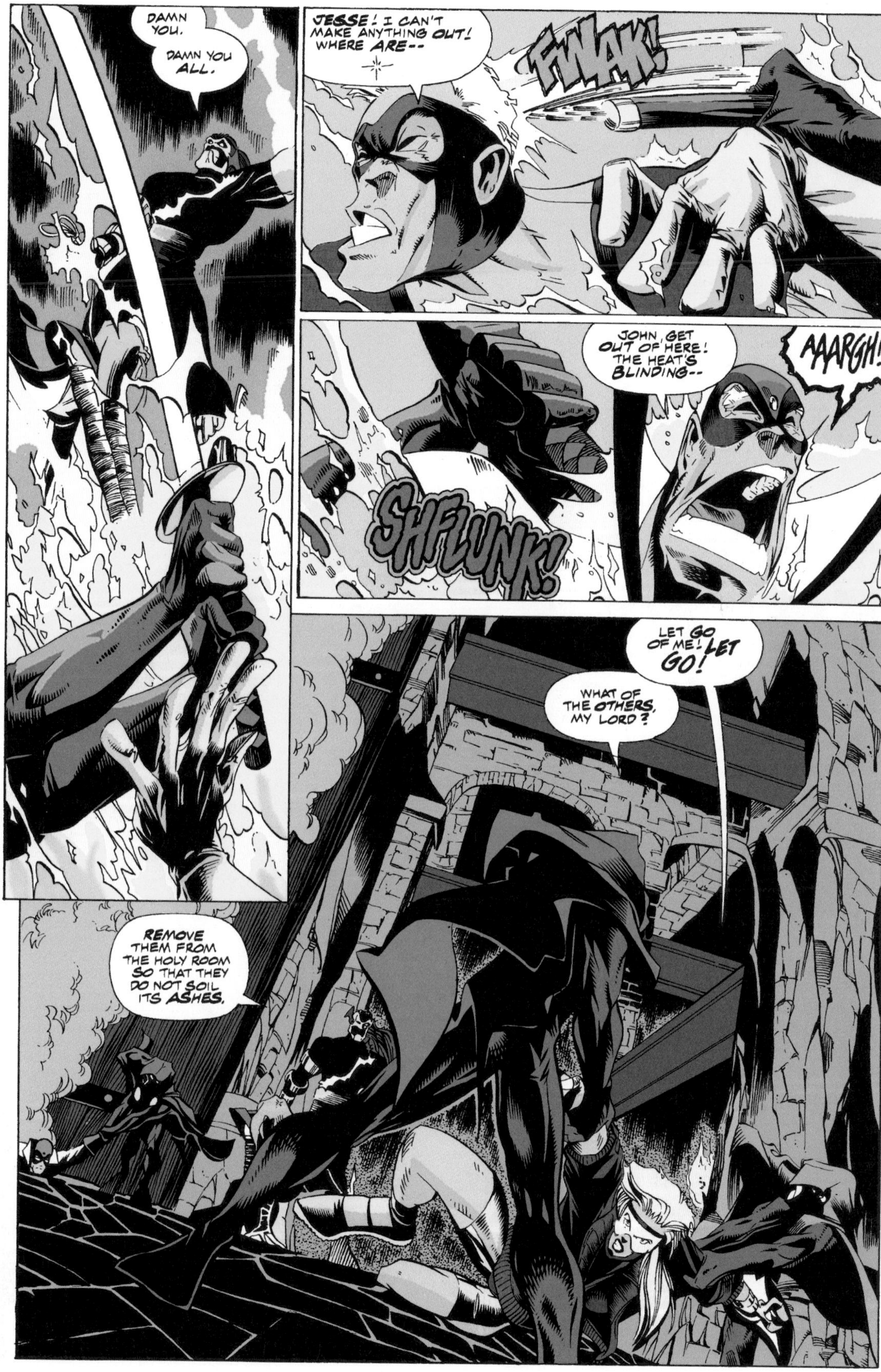
DAMN YOU.
DAMN YOU ALL.
JESSE! I CAN'T MAKE ANYTHING OUT! WHERE ARE--
FWAK!
JOHN, GET OUT OF HERE! THE HEAT'S BLINDING--
AAARGH!
SHFLUNK!
LET GO OF ME! LET GO!
WHAT OF THE OTHERS, MY LORD?
REMOVE THEM FROM THE HOLY ROOM SO THAT THEY DO NOT SOIL ITS ASHES.

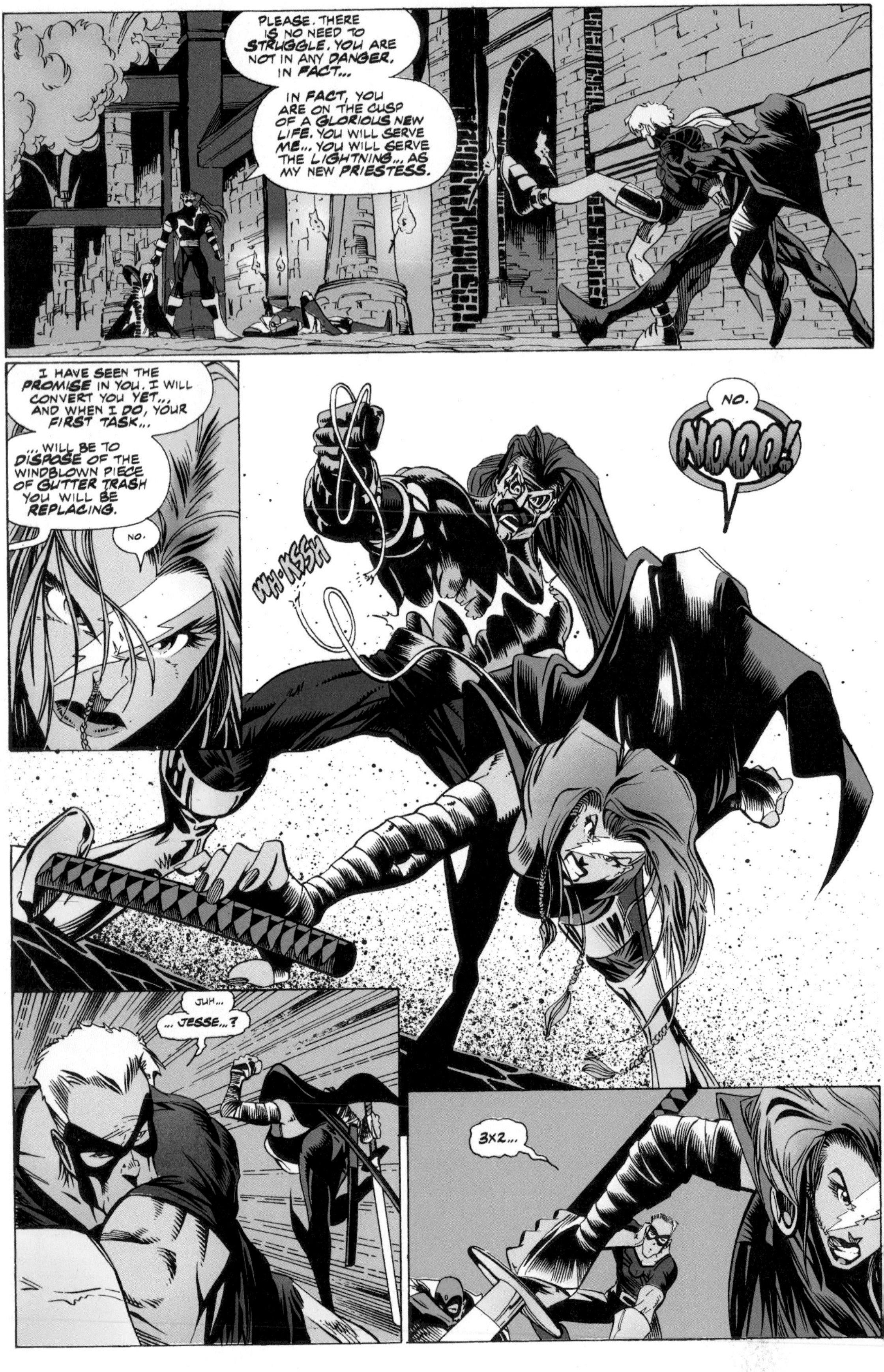

PLEASE. THERE IS NO NEED TO STRUGGLE. YOU ARE NOT IN ANY DANGER. IN FACT...
IN FACT, YOU ARE ON THE CUSP OF A GLORIOUS NEW LIFE. YOU WILL SERVE ME... YOU WILL SERVE THE LIGHTNING... AS MY NEW PRIESTESS.
I HAVE SEEN THE PROMISE IN YOU. I WILL CONVERT YOU YET... AND WHEN I DO, YOUR FIRST TASK...
...WILL BE TO DISPOSE OF THE WINDBLOWN PIECE OF GUTTER TRASH YOU WILL BE REPLACING.
NO.
NO.
NOOO!
WH-KSSH
JUH...
...JESSE...?
3X2...

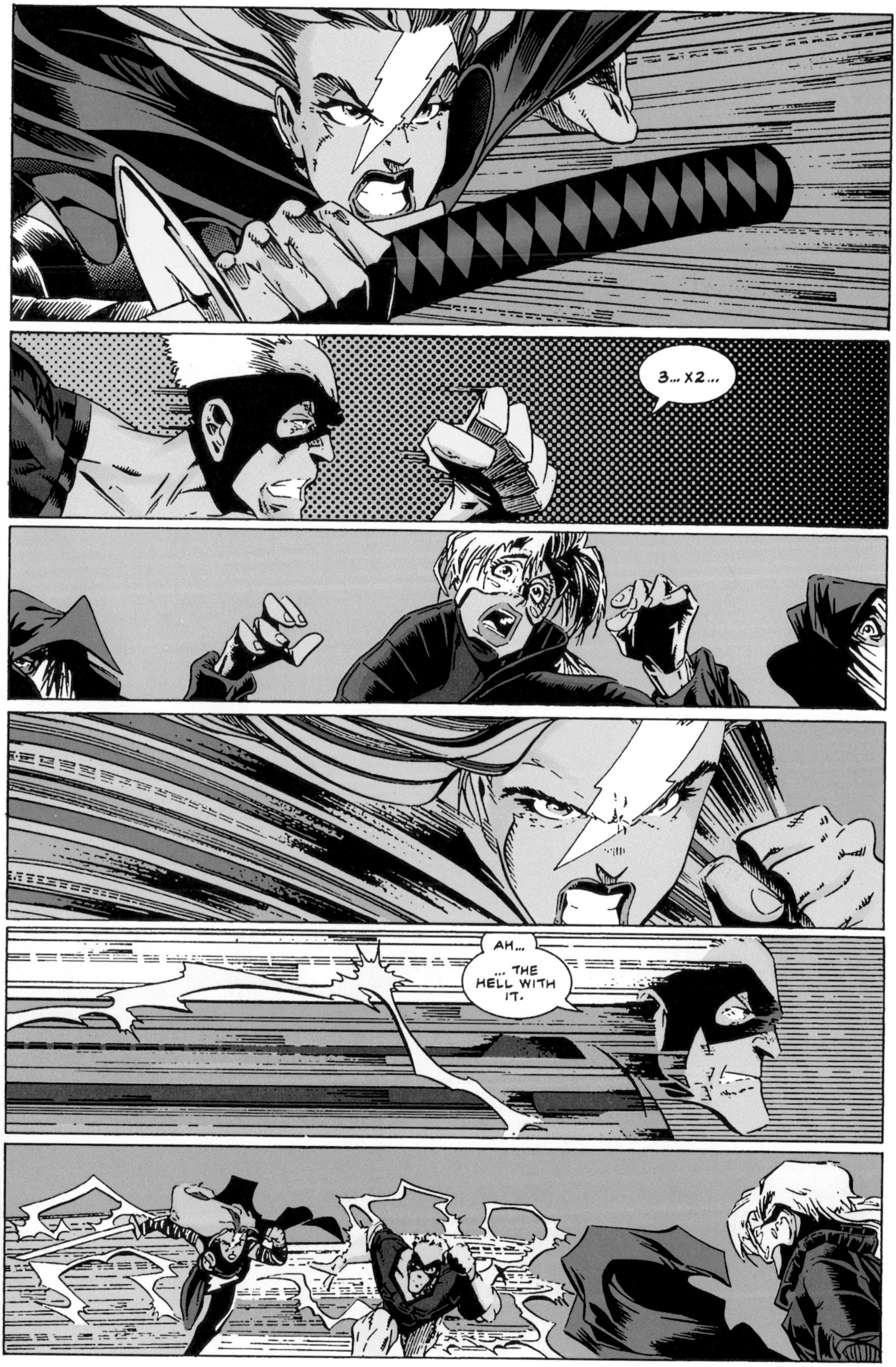
3... X2...
AH...
... THE HELL WITH IT.

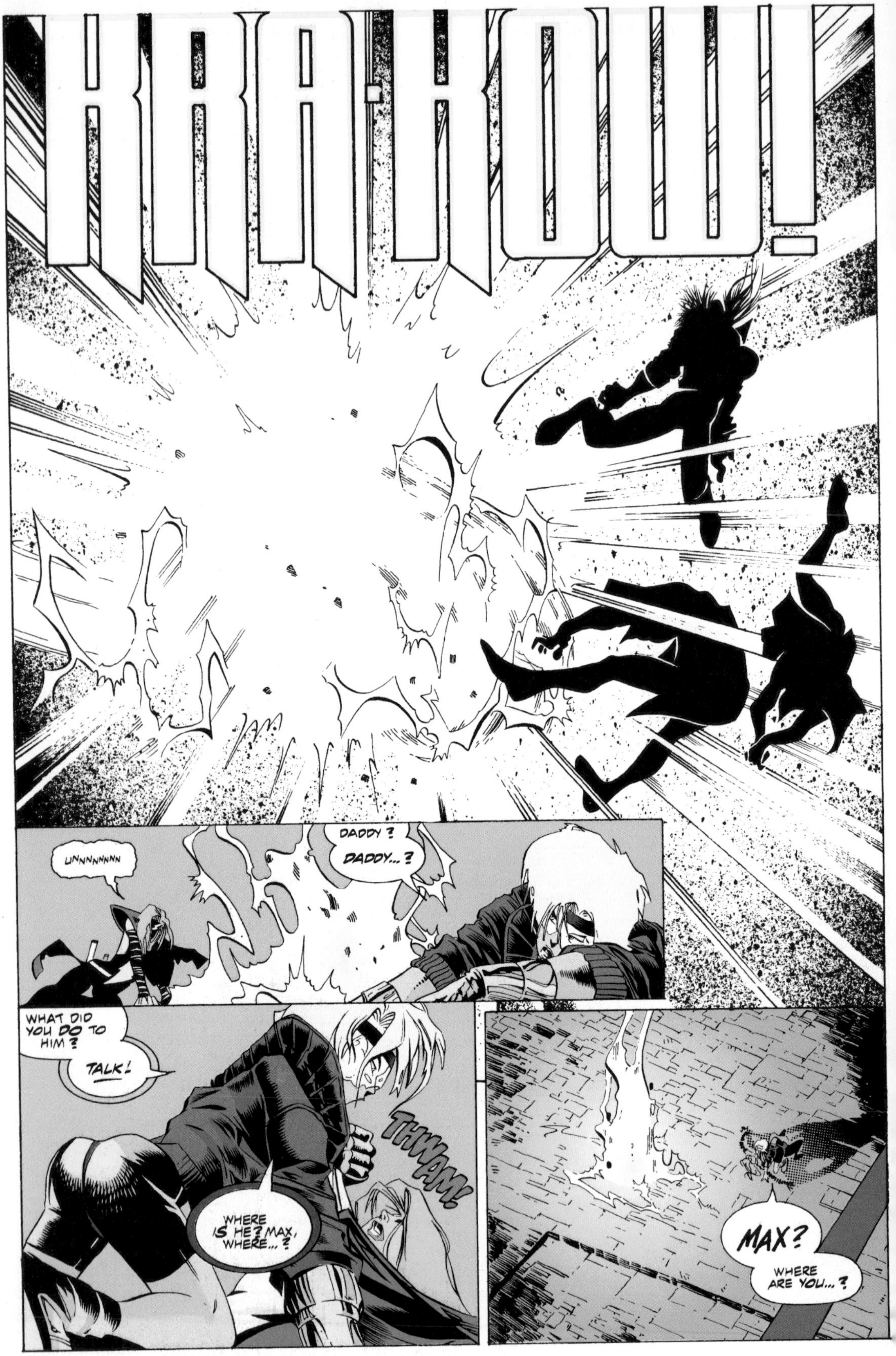
KRA-KOOM!
UNNNNNNNN
DADDY?
DADDY...?
WHAT DID YOU DO TO HIM?
TALK!
THWAM!
WHERE IS HE? MAX, WHERE...?
MAX?
WHERE ARE YOU...?

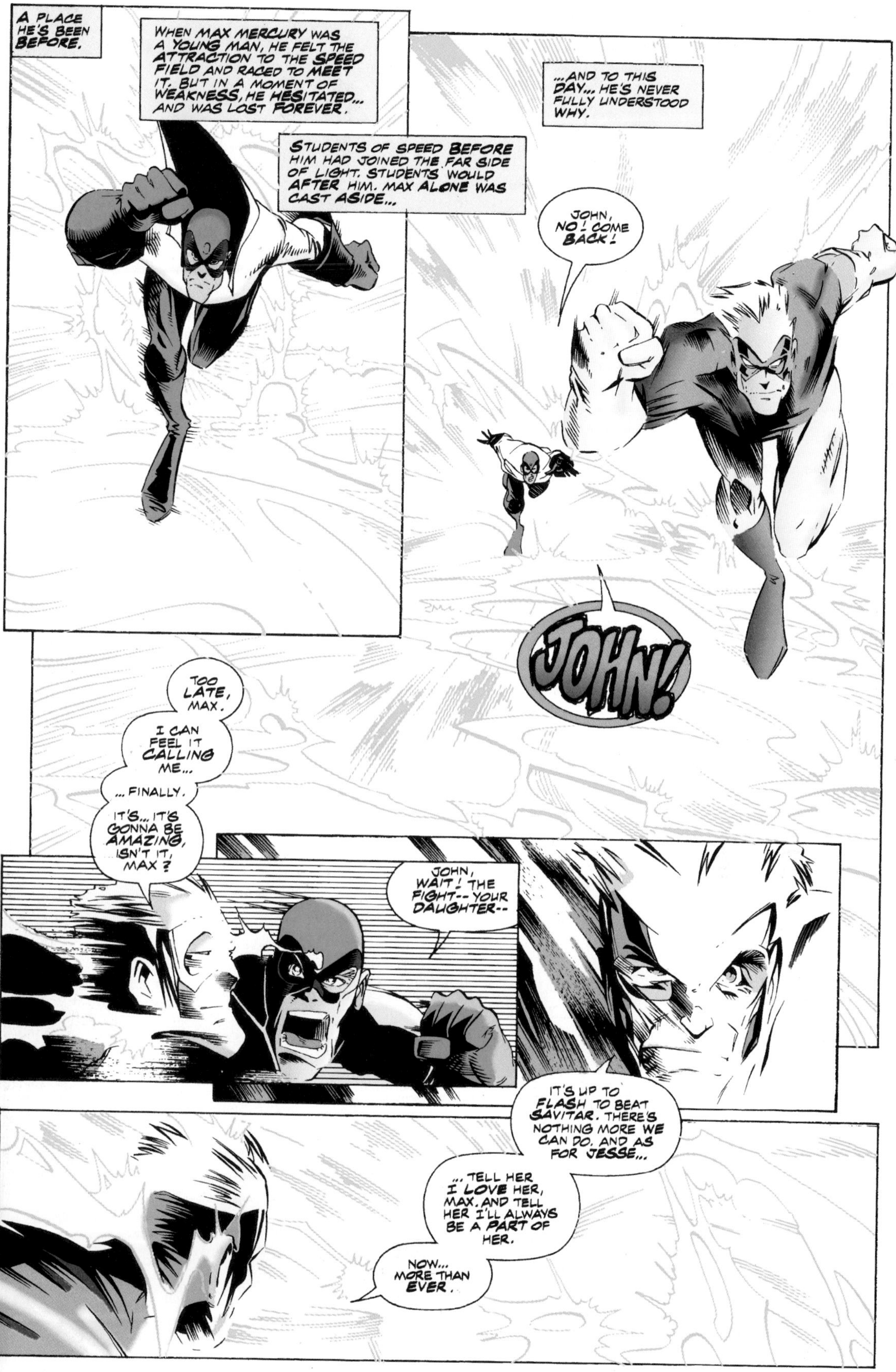

A PLACE HE'S BEEN BEFORE.
WHEN MAX MERCURY WAS A YOUNG MAN, HE FELT THE ATTRACTION TO THE SPEED FIELD AND RACED TO MEET IT. BUT IN A MOMENT OF WEAKNESS, HE HESITATED... AND WAS LOST FOREVER.
STUDENTS OF SPEED BEFORE HIM HAD JOINED THE FAR SIDE OF LIGHT. STUDENTS WOULD AFTER HIM. MAX ALONE WAS CAST ASIDE...
...AND TO THIS DAY... HE'S NEVER FULLY UNDERSTOOD WHY.
JOHN, NO! COME BACK!
JOHN!
TOO LATE, MAX.
I CAN FEEL IT CALLING ME...
...FINALLY.
IT'S... IT'S GONNA BE AMAZING, ISN'T IT, MAX?
JOHN, WAIT! THE FIGHT-- YOUR DAUGHTER--
IT'S UP TO FLASH TO BEAT SAVITAR. THERE'S NOTHING MORE WE CAN DO. AND AS FOR JESSE...
...TELL HER I LOVE HER, MAX. AND TELL HER I'LL ALWAYS BE A PART OF HER.
NOW... MORE THAN EVER.

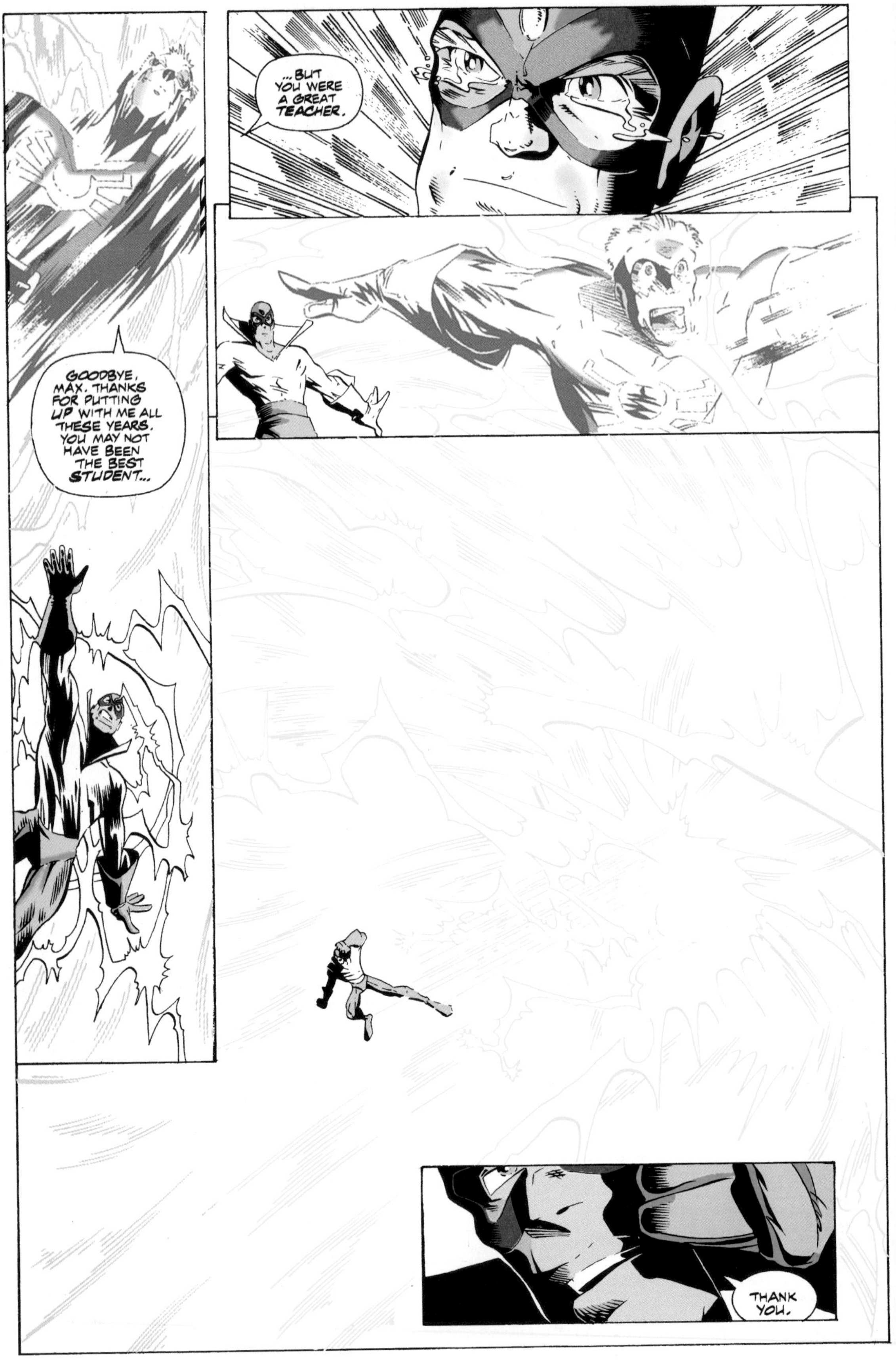
GOODBYE, MAX. THANKS FOR PUTTING UP WITH ME ALL THESE YEARS. YOU MAY NOT HAVE BEEN THE BEST STUDENT...
...BUT YOU WERE A GREAT TEACHER.
THANK YOU.

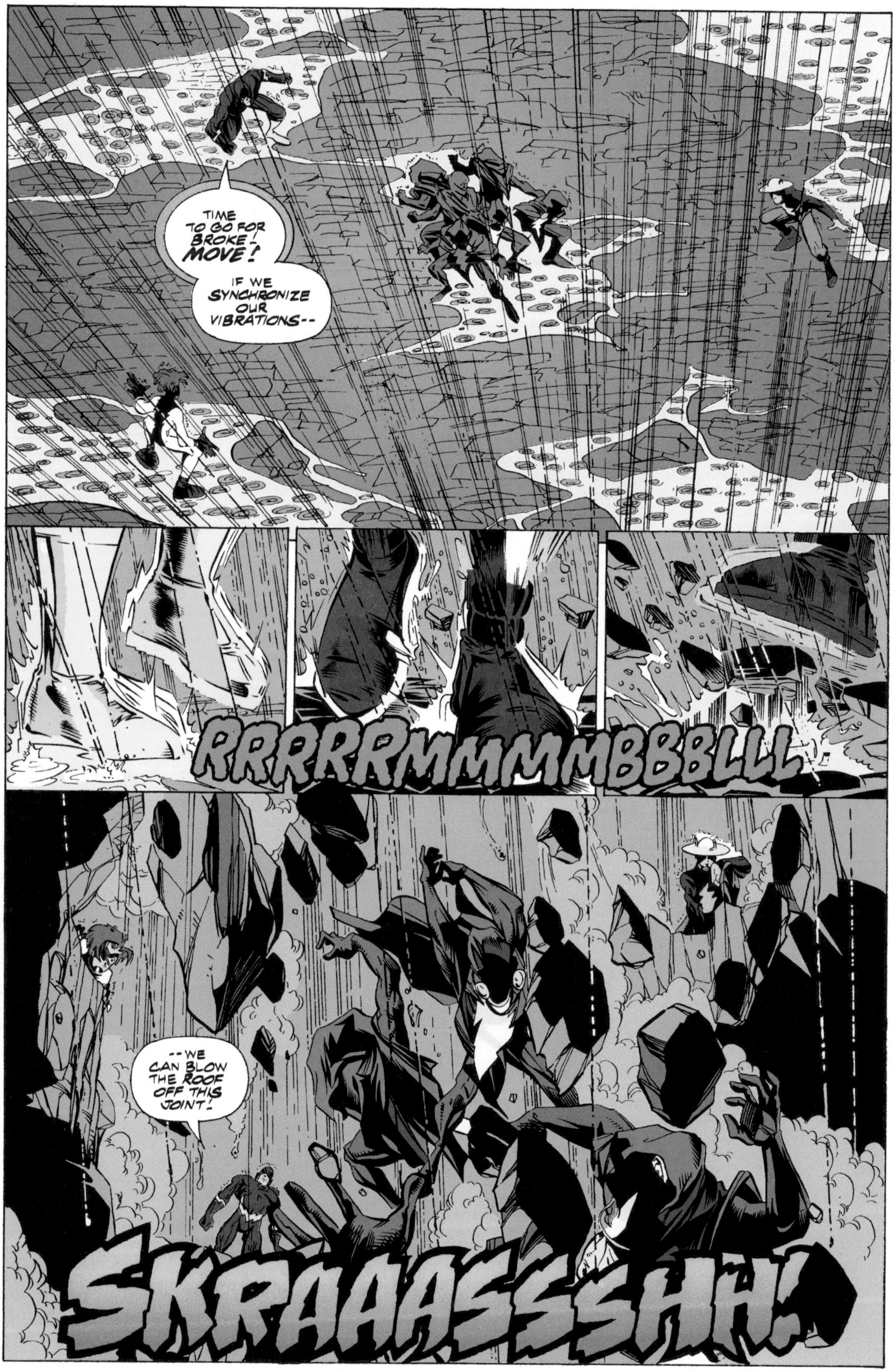
TIME TO GO FOR BROKE! MOVE!
IF WE SYNCHRONIZE OUR VIBRATIONS--
RRRRRMMMMMBBBLLL
--WE CAN BLOW THE ROOF OFF THIS JOINT!
SKRAAASSSHH!

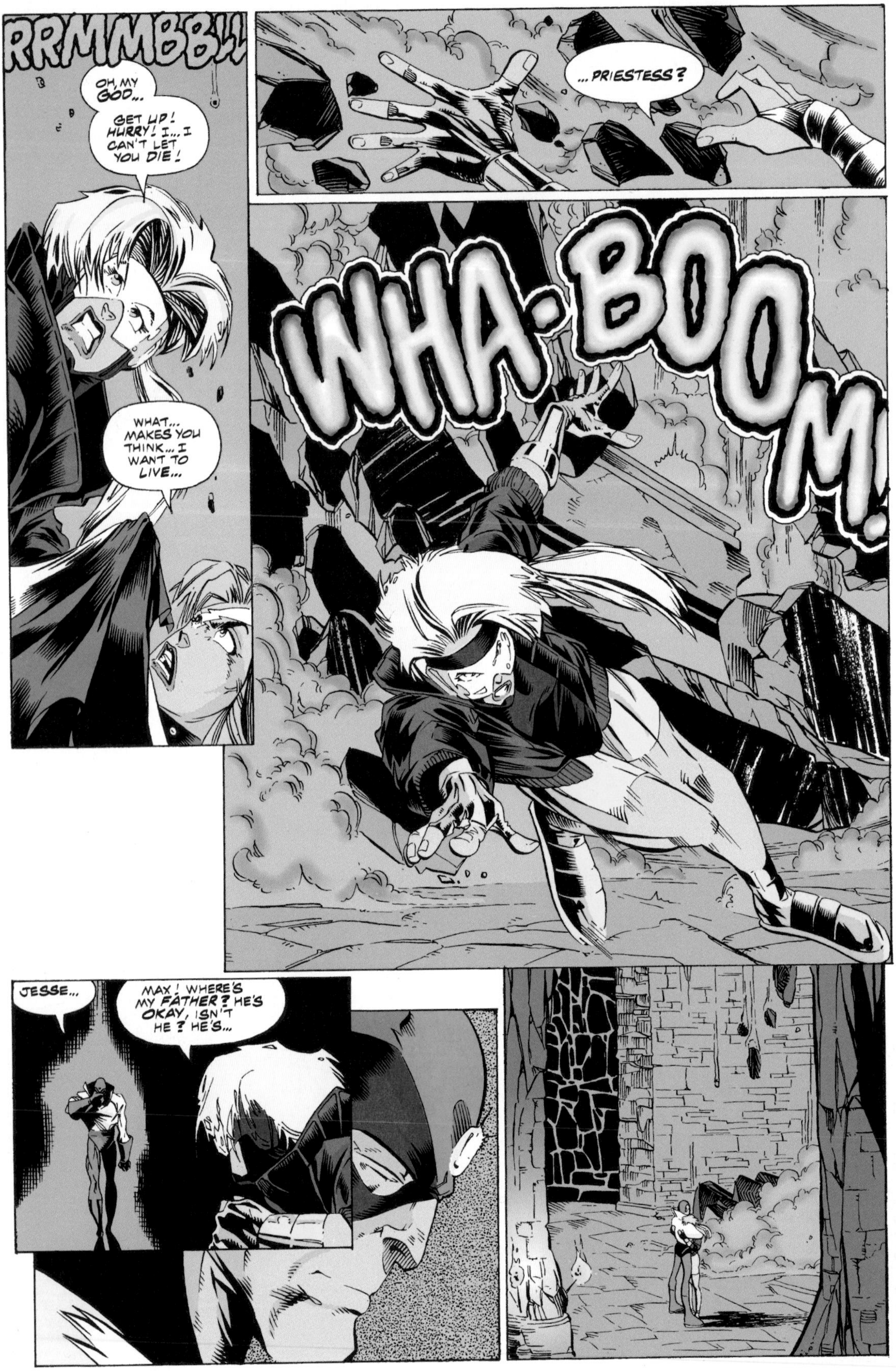
RRMMBB!!
OH, MY GOD...
GET UP! HURRY! I... I CAN'T LET YOU DIE!
...PRIESTESS?
WHA-BOOM!
WHAT... MAKES YOU THINK... I WANT TO LIVE...
JESSE...
MAX! WHERE'S MY FATHER? HE'S OKAY, ISN'T HE? HE'S...

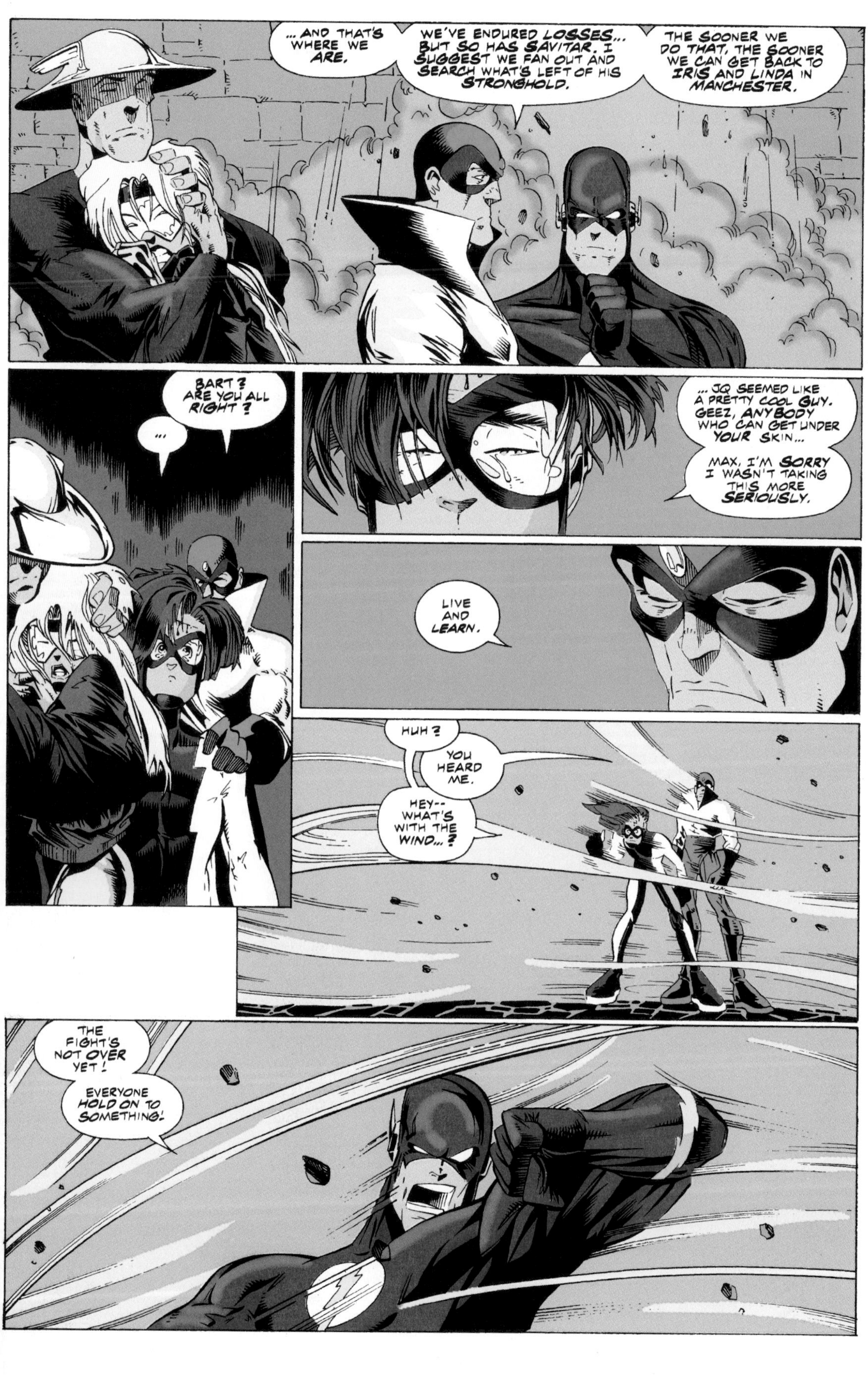
...AND THAT'S WHERE WE ARE.
WE'VE ENDURED LOSSES... BUT SO HAS SAVITAR. I SUGGEST WE FAN OUT AND SEARCH WHAT'S LEFT OF HIS STRONGHOLD.
THE SOONER WE DO THAT, THE SOONER WE CAN GET BACK TO IRIS AND LINDA IN MANCHESTER.
BART? ARE YOU ALL RIGHT?
...
...JQ SEEMED LIKE A PRETTY COOL GUY. GEEZ, ANYBODY WHO CAN GET UNDER YOUR SKIN...
MAX, I'M SORRY I WASN'T TAKING THIS MORE SERIOUSLY.
LIVE AND LEARN.
HUH?
YOU HEARD ME.
HEY--WHAT'S WITH THE WIND...?
THE FIGHT'S NOT OVER YET!
EVERYONE HOLD ON TO SOMETHING!

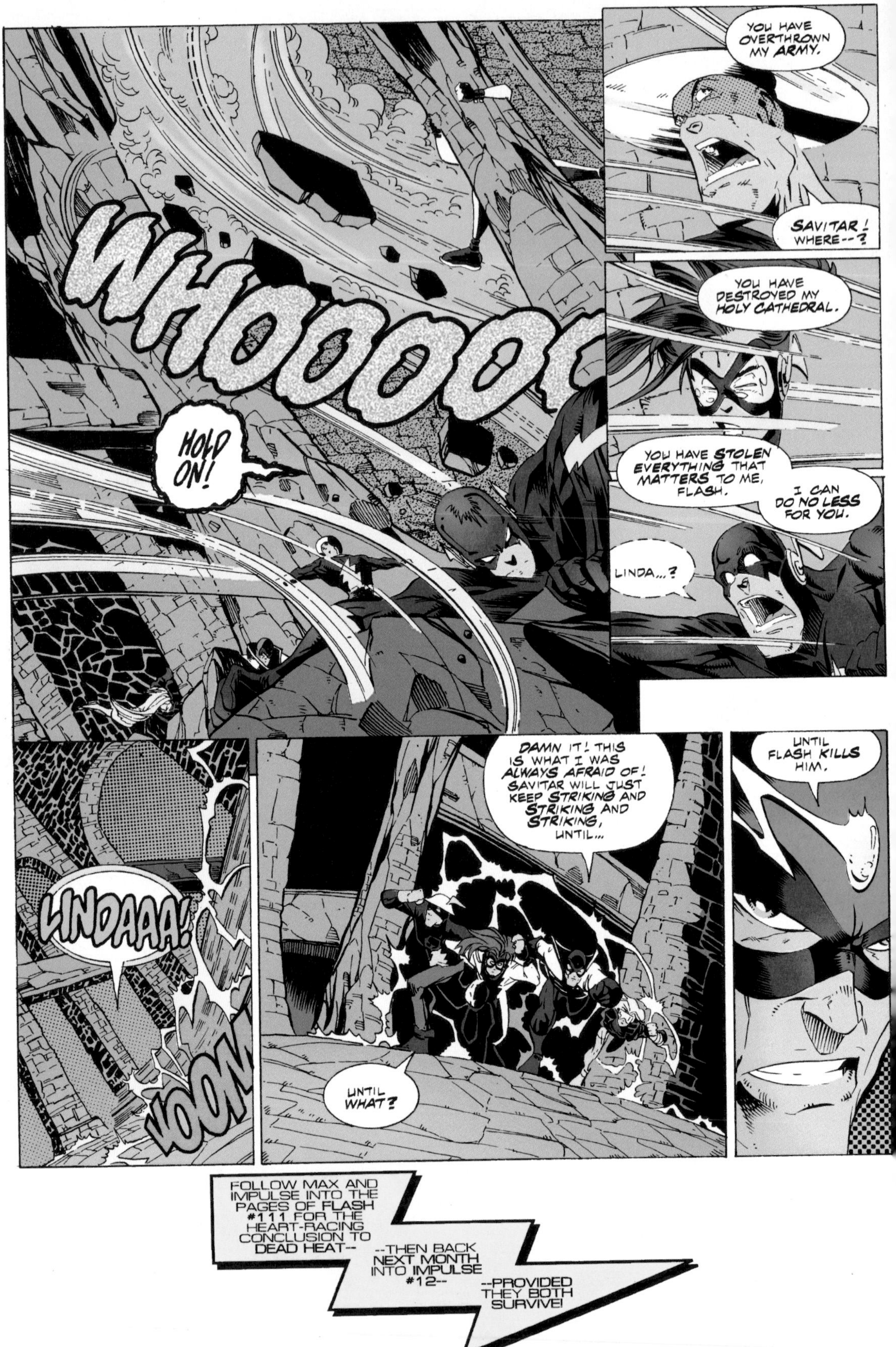
WHOOOOO
HOLD ON!
YOU HAVE OVERTHROWN MY ARMY.
SAVITAR! WHERE--?
YOU HAVE DESTROYED MY HOLY CATHEDRAL.
YOU HAVE STOLEN EVERYTHING THAT MATTERS TO ME, FLASH.
I CAN DO NO LESS FOR YOU.
LINDA...?
LINDAAA!
VOOM
DAMN IT! THIS IS WHAT I WAS ALWAYS AFRAID OF! SAVITAR WILL JUST KEEP STRIKING AND STRIKING AND STRIKING, UNTIL...
UNTIL WHAT?
UNTIL FLASH KILLS HIM.
FOLLOW MAX AND IMPULSE INTO THE PAGES OF FLASH #111 FOR THE HEART-RACING CONCLUSION TO DEAD HEAT--
--THEN BACK NEXT MONTH INTO IMPULSE #12--
--PROVIDED THEY BOTH SURVIVE!

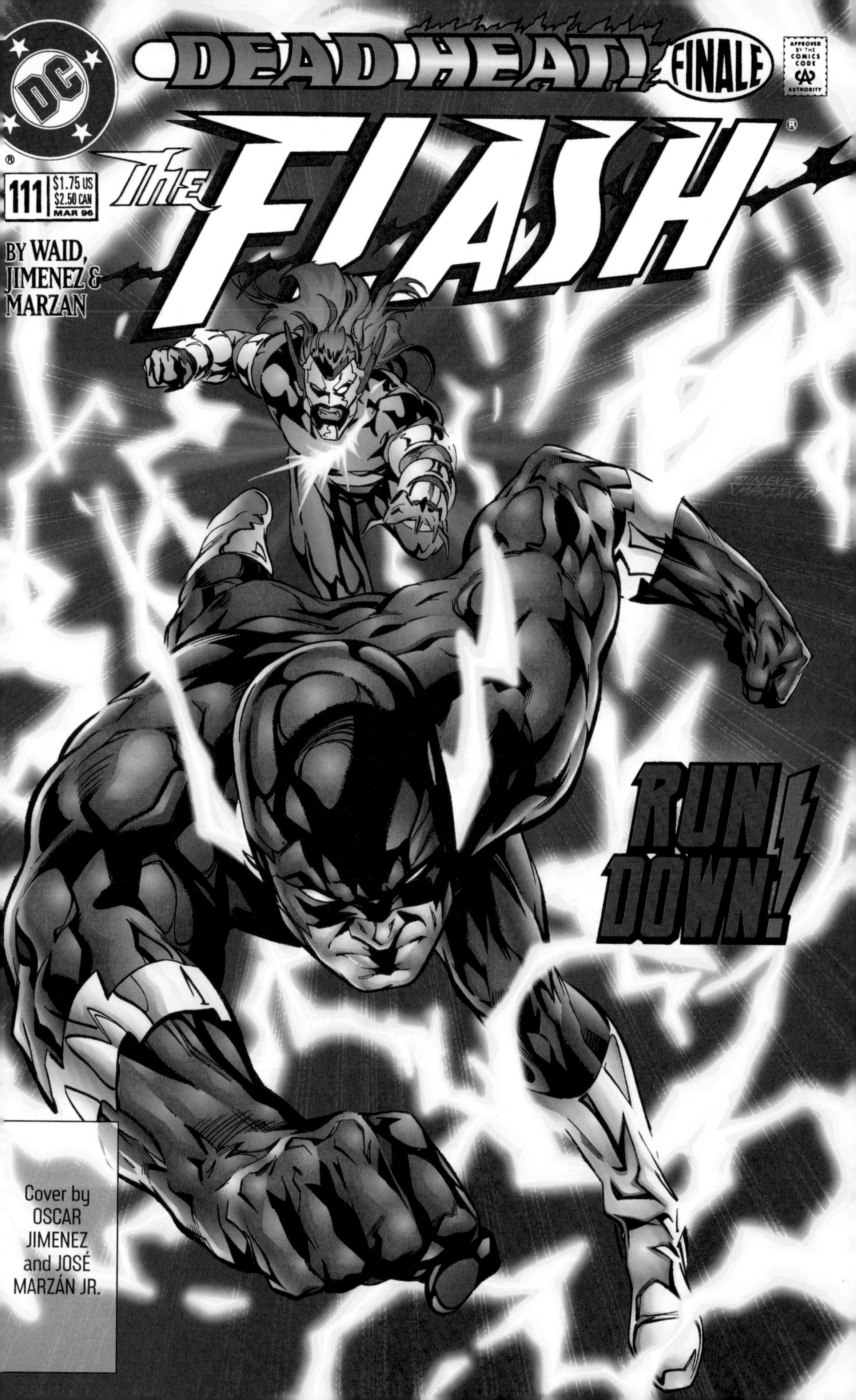
DEAD HEAT! FINALE
APPROVED BY THE COMICS CODE AUTHORITY
DC
THE FLASH
111 $1.75 US $2.50 CAN MAR 96
BY WAID, JIMENEZ & MARZAN
RUN DOWN!
Cover by OSCAR JIMENEZ and JOSÉ MARZÁN JR.

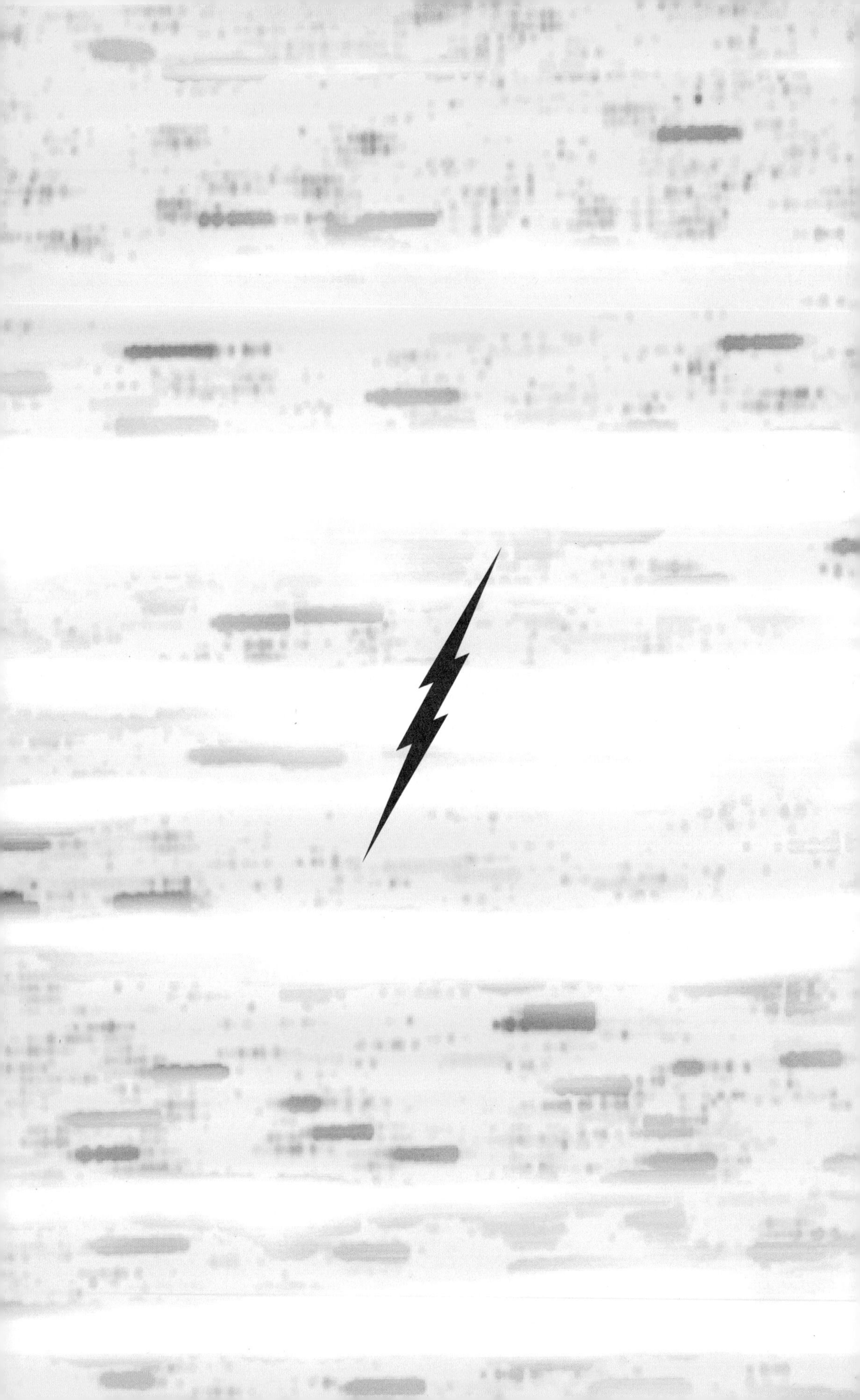

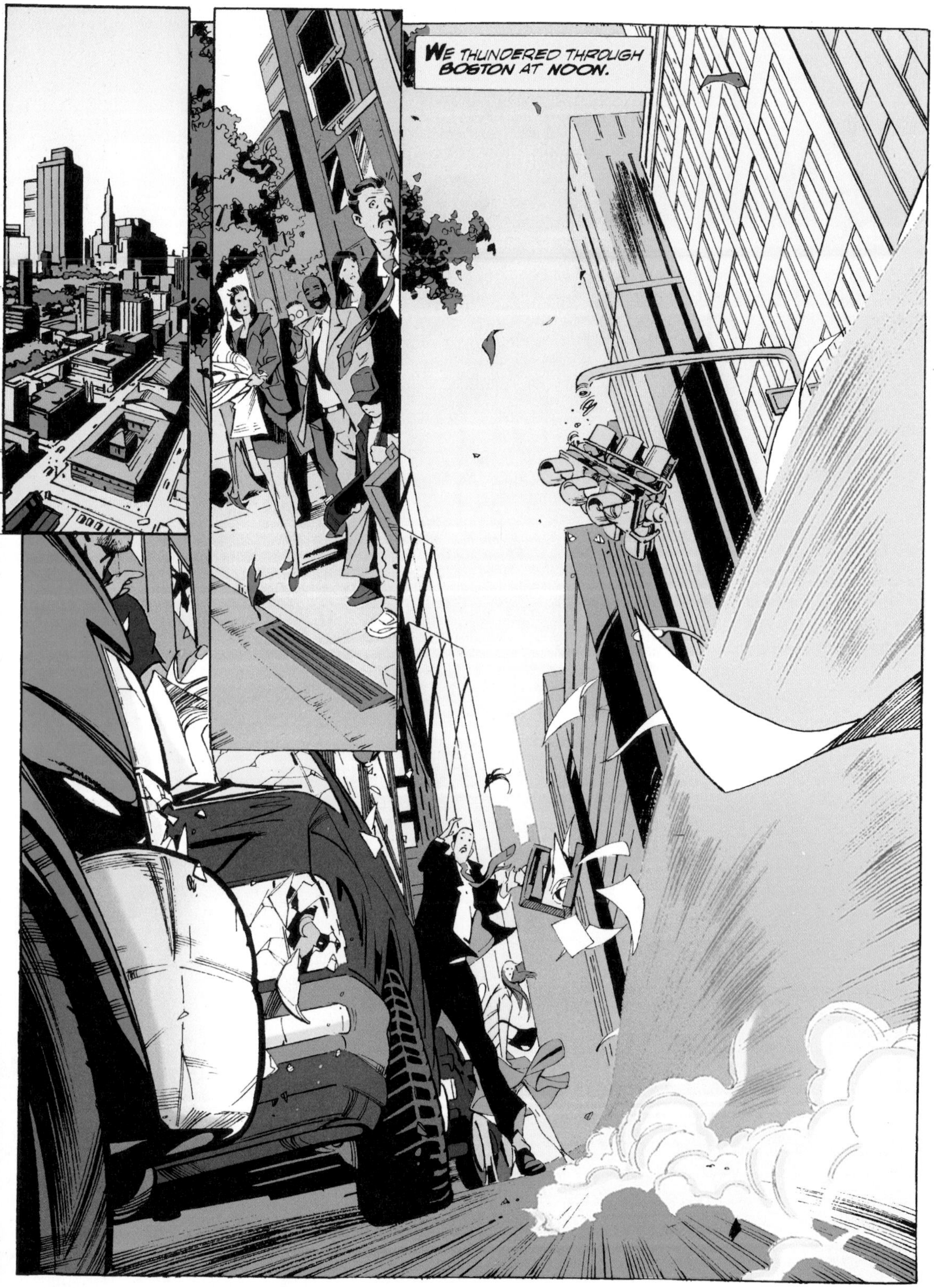
WE THUNDERED THROUGH BOSTON AT NOON.

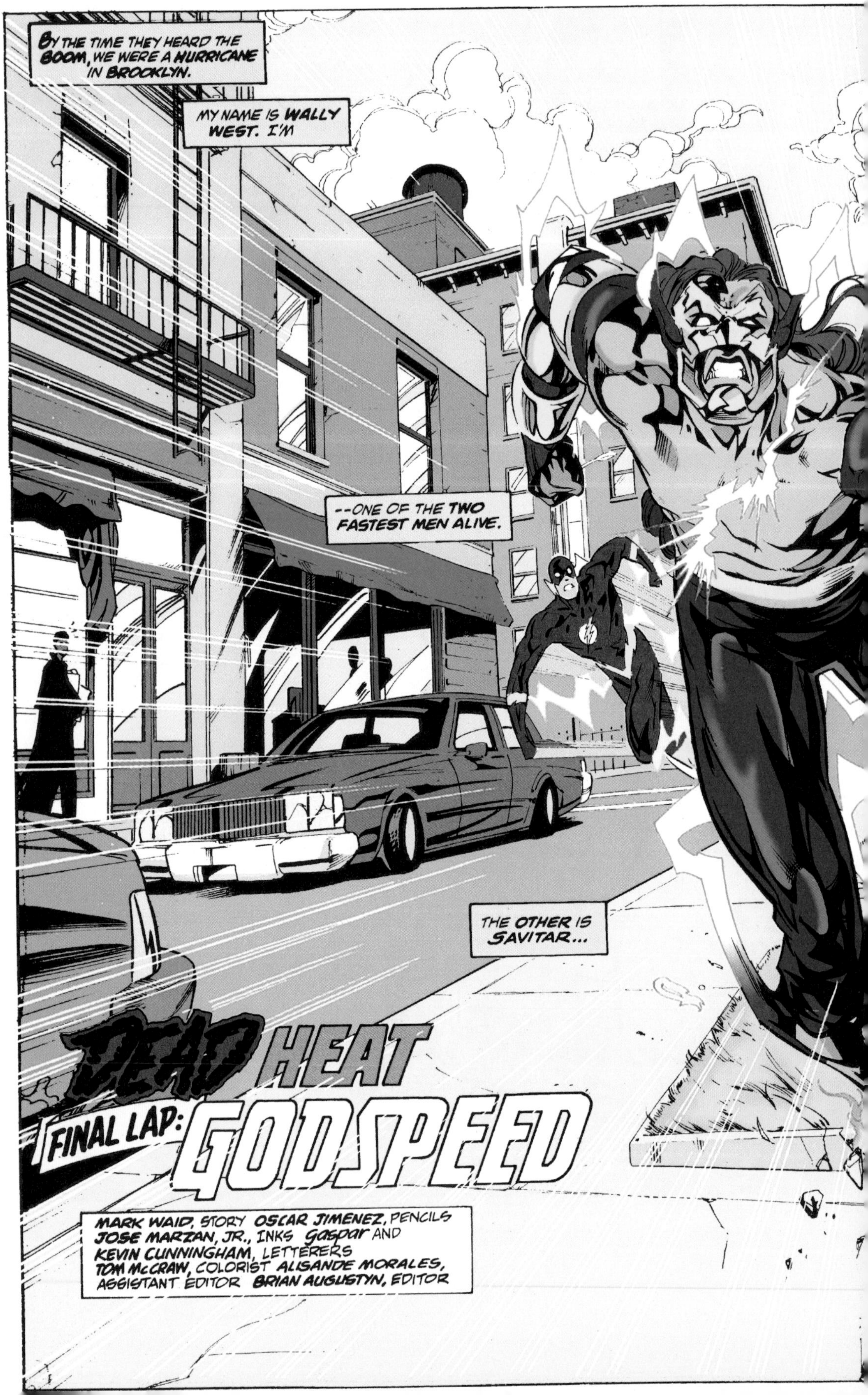

BY THE TIME THEY HEARD THE BOOM, WE WERE A HURRICANE IN BROOKLYN.
MY NAME IS WALLY WEST. I'M
--ONE OF THE TWO FASTEST MEN ALIVE.
THE OTHER IS SAVITAR...
DEAD HEAT
FINAL LAP: GODSPEED
MARK WAID, STORY OSCAR JIMENEZ, PENCILS JOSE MARZAN, JR., INKS Gaspar AND KEVIN CUNNINGHAM, LETTERERS TOM McCRAW, COLORIST ALISANDE MORALES, ASSISTANT EDITOR BRIAN AUGUSTYN, EDITOR

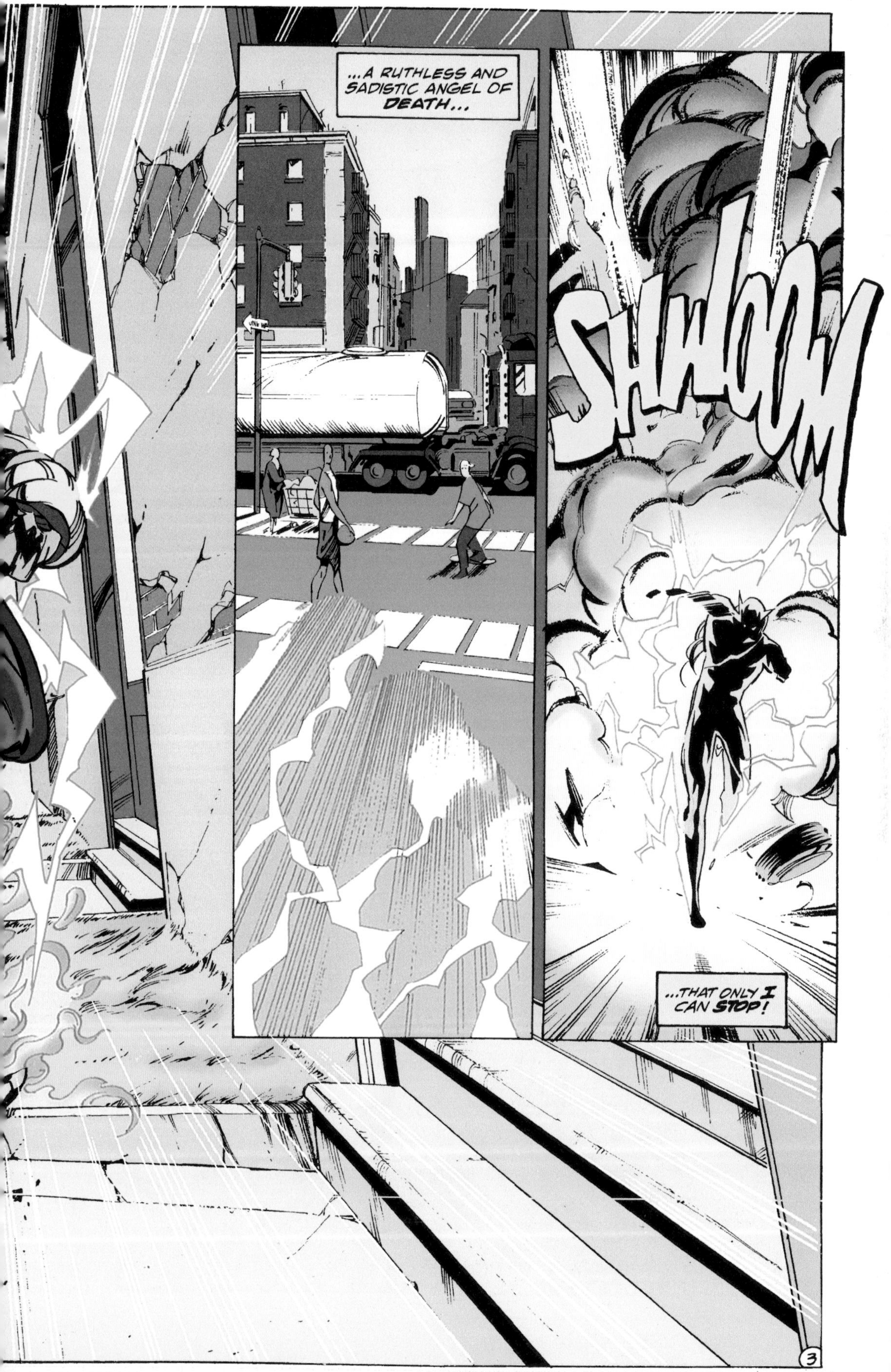
...A RUTHLESS AND SADISTIC ANGEL OF DEATH...
SHWOOM
...THAT ONLY I CAN STOP!

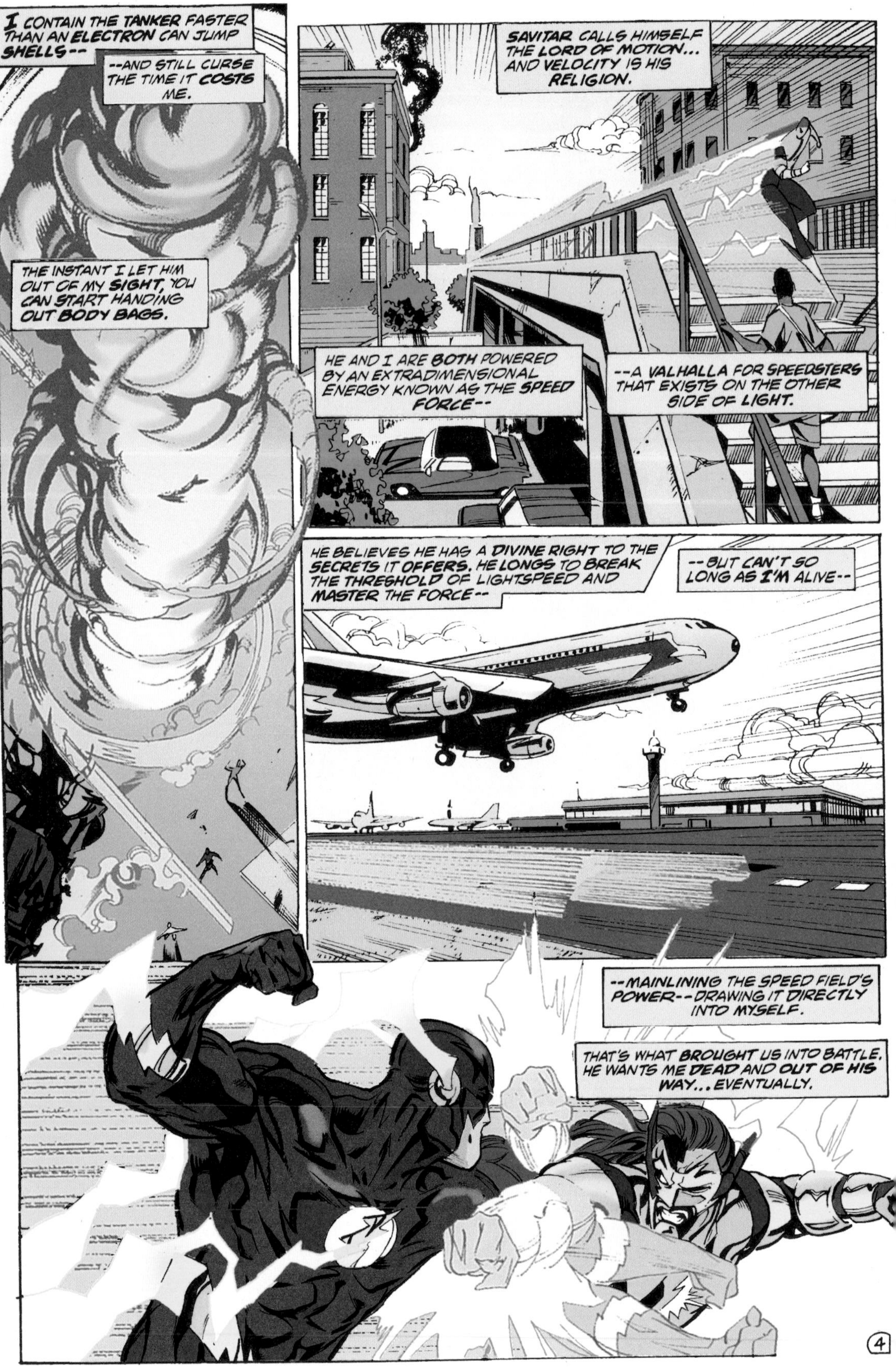
I CONTAIN THE TANKER FASTER THAN AN ELECTRON CAN JUMP SHELLS--
--AND STILL CURSE THE TIME IT COSTS ME.
THE INSTANT I LET HIM OUT OF MY SIGHT, YOU CAN START HANDING OUT BODY BAGS.
SAVITAR CALLS HIMSELF THE LORD OF MOTION... AND VELOCITY IS HIS RELIGION.
HE AND I ARE BOTH POWERED BY AN EXTRADIMENSIONAL ENERGY KNOWN AS THE SPEED FORCE--
--A VALHALLA FOR SPEEDSTERS THAT EXISTS ON THE OTHER SIDE OF LIGHT.
HE BELIEVES HE HAS A DIVINE RIGHT TO THE SECRETS IT OFFERS. HE LONGS TO BREAK THE THRESHOLD OF LIGHTSPEED AND MASTER THE FORCE--
--BUT CAN'T SO LONG AS I'M ALIVE--
--MAINLINING THE SPEED FIELD'S POWER--DRAWING IT DIRECTLY INTO MYSELF.
THAT'S WHAT BROUGHT US INTO BATTLE. HE WANTS ME DEAD AND OUT OF HIS WAY... EVENTUALLY.

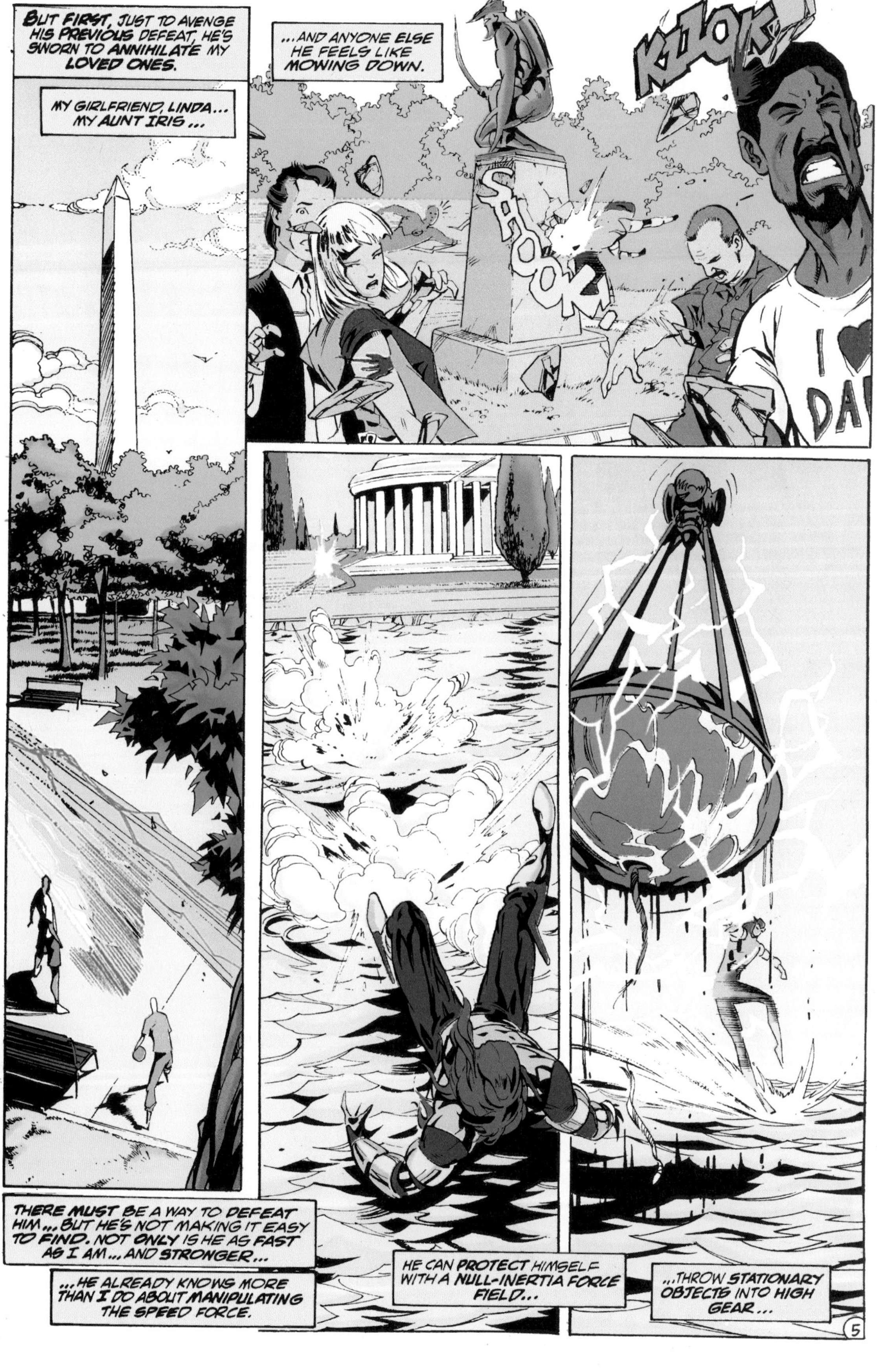
BUT FIRST, JUST TO AVENGE HIS PREVIOUS DEFEAT, HE'S SWORN TO ANNIHILATE MY LOVED ONES.
MY GIRLFRIEND, LINDA... MY AUNT IRIS...
...AND ANYONE ELSE HE FEELS LIKE MOWING DOWN.
KLOK!
SHOOOK!
I ♥ DA
THERE MUST BE A WAY TO DEFEAT HIM... BUT HE'S NOT MAKING IT EASY TO FIND. NOT ONLY IS HE AS FAST AS I AM... AND STRONGER...
...HE ALREADY KNOWS MORE THAN I DO ABOUT MANIPULATING THE SPEED FORCE.
HE CAN PROTECT HIMSELF WITH A NULL-INERTIA FORCE FIELD...
...THROW STATIONARY OBJECTS INTO HIGH GEAR...

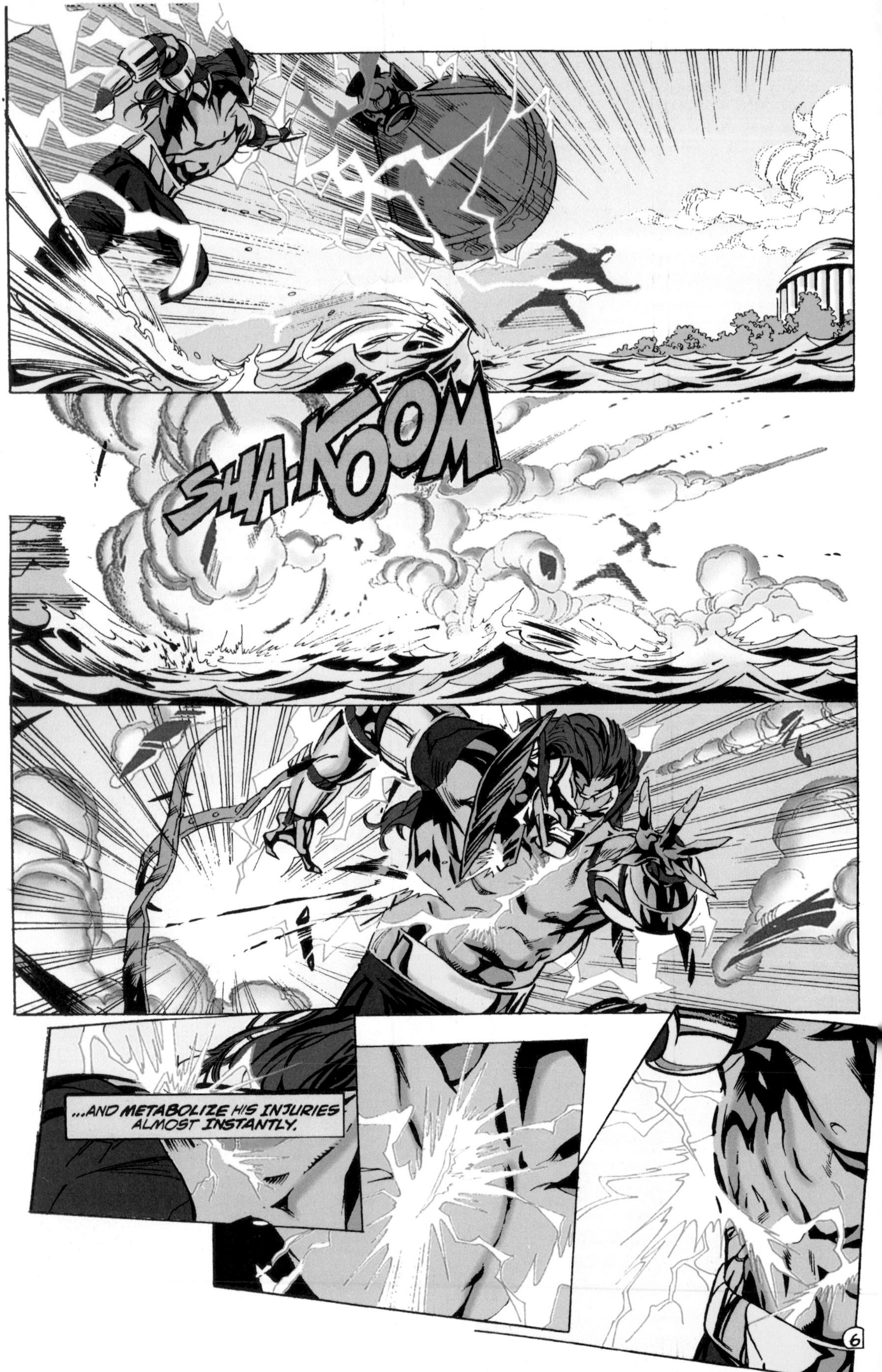
SHA-KOOM
...AND METABOLIZE HIS INJURIES ALMOST INSTANTLY.

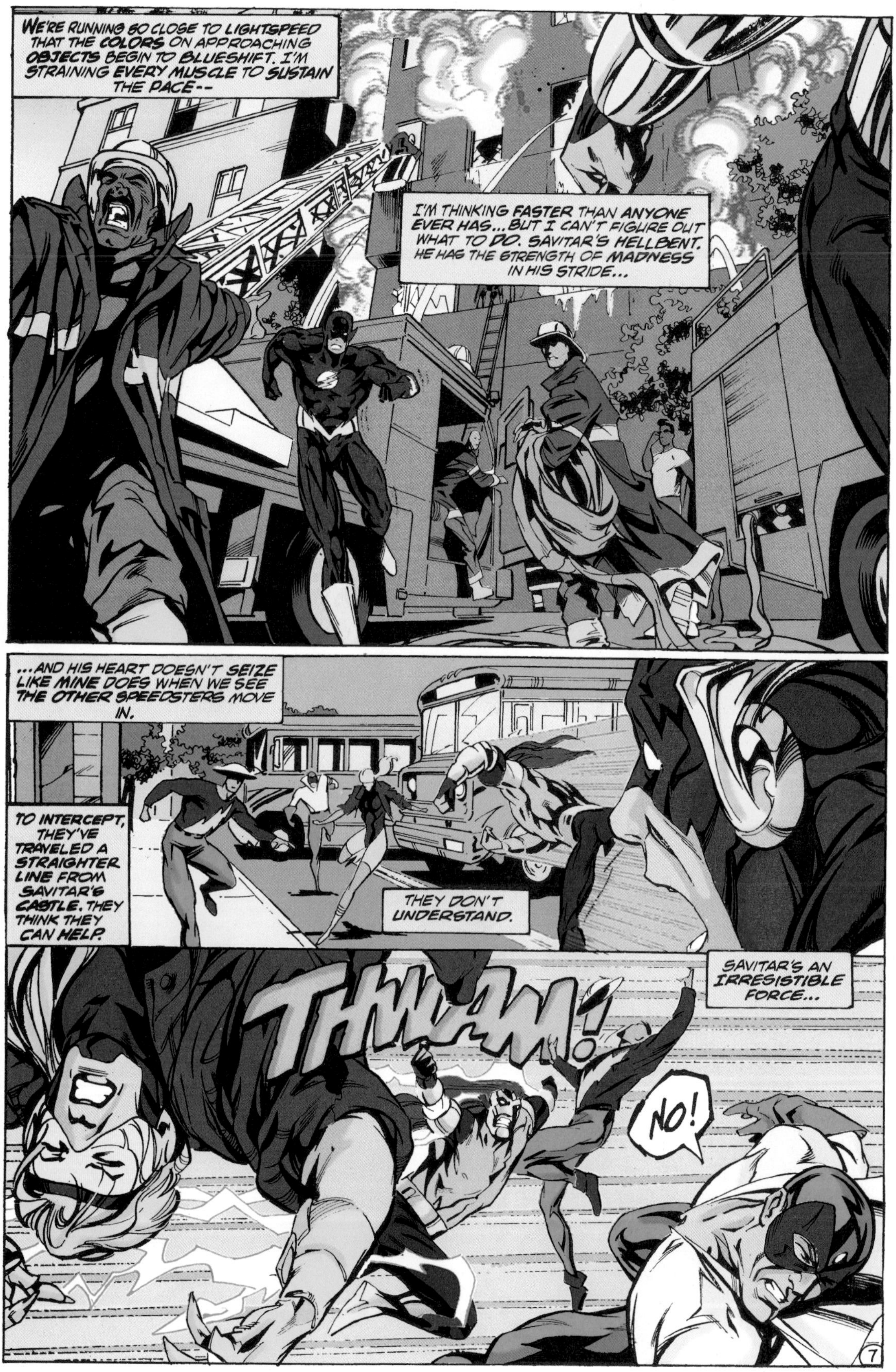
WE'RE RUNNING SO CLOSE TO LIGHTSPEED THAT THE COLORS ON APPROACHING OBJECTS BEGIN TO BLUESHIFT. I'M STRAINING EVERY MUSCLE TO SUSTAIN THE PACE--
I'M THINKING FASTER THAN ANYONE EVER HAS... BUT I CAN'T FIGURE OUT WHAT TO DO. SAVITAR'S HELLBENT. HE HAS THE STRENGTH OF MADNESS IN HIS STRIDE...
...AND HIS HEART DOESN'T SEIZE LIKE MINE DOES WHEN WE SEE THE OTHER SPEEDSTERS MOVE IN.
TO INTERCEPT, THEY'VE TRAVELED A STRAIGHTER LINE FROM SAVITAR'S CASTLE. THEY THINK THEY CAN HELP.
THEY DON'T UNDERSTAND.
SAVITAR'S AN IRRESISTIBLE FORCE...
THWAM!
NO!

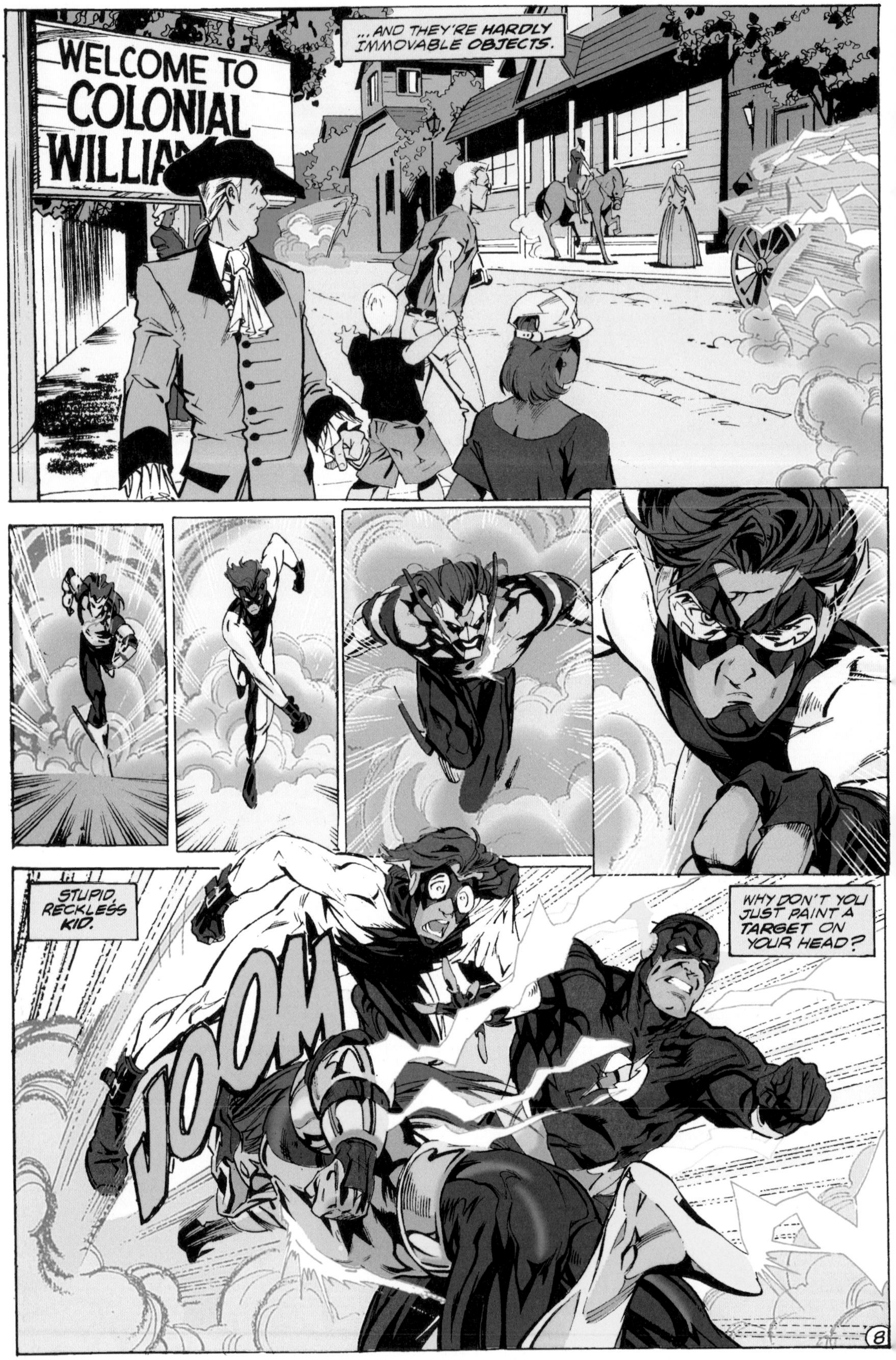
WELCOME TO
COLONIAL
WILLIA
...AND THEY'RE HARDLY IMMOVABLE OBJECTS.
STUPID, RECKLESS KID.
WHY DON'T YOU JUST PAINT A TARGET ON YOUR HEAD?
ZOOM
8

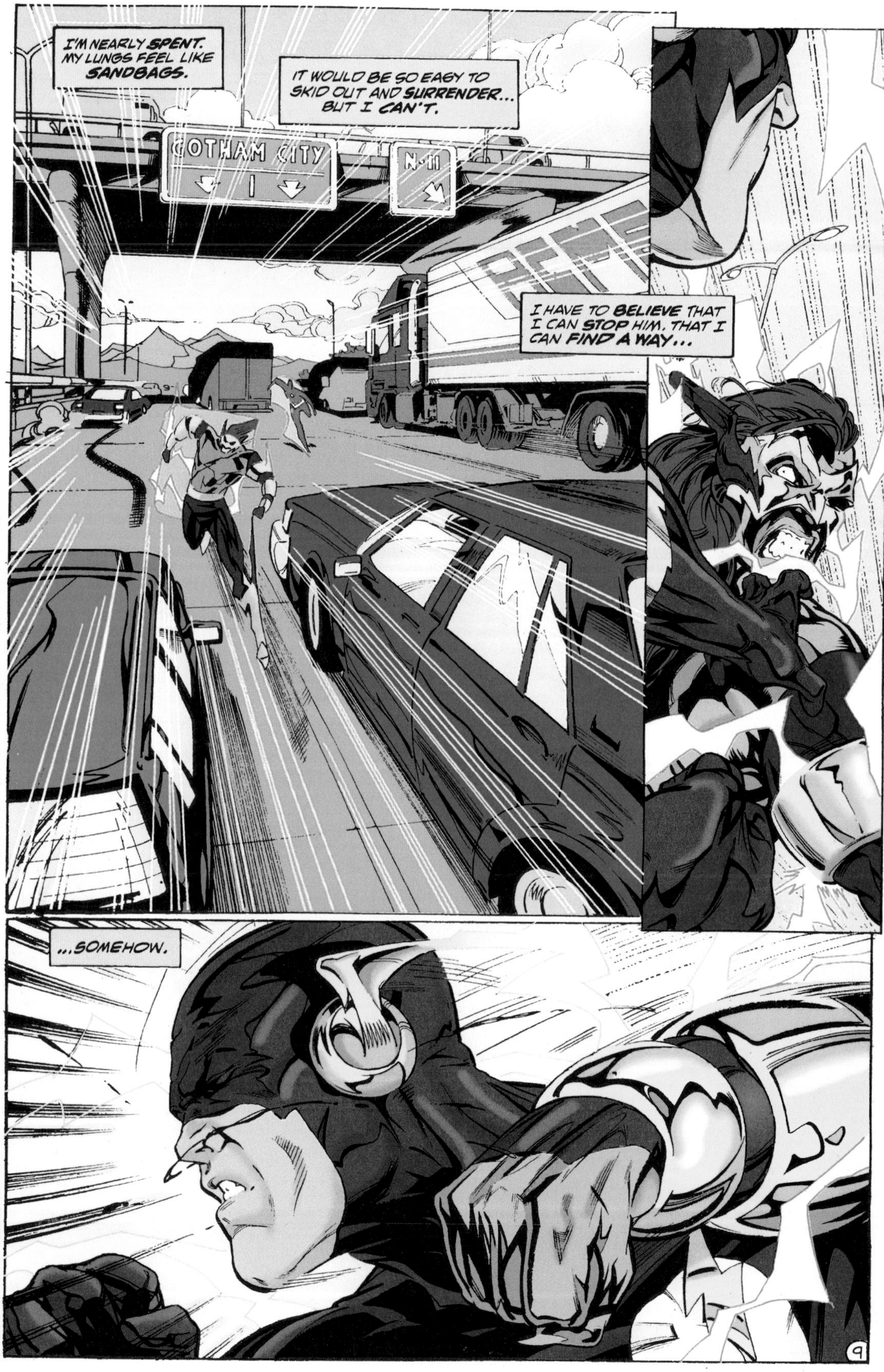

I'M NEARLY SPENT. MY LUNGS FEEL LIKE SANDBAGS.
IT WOULD BE SO EASY TO SKID OUT AND SURRENDER... BUT I CAN'T.
GOTHAM CITY 1
N-11
I HAVE TO BELIEVE THAT I CAN STOP HIM. THAT I CAN FIND A WAY...
...SOMEHOW.

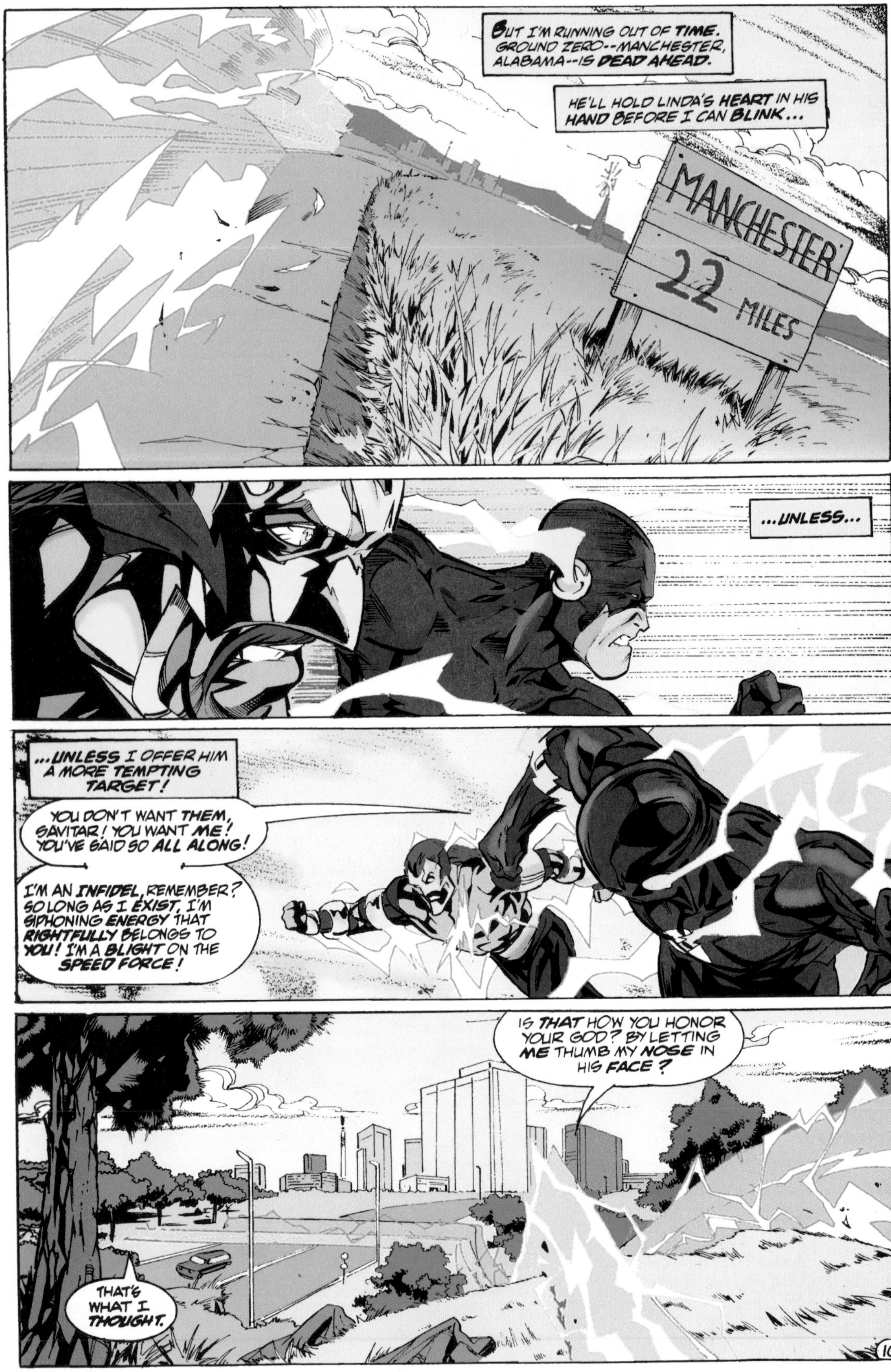
BUT I'M RUNNING OUT OF TIME. GROUND ZERO--MANCHESTER, ALABAMA--IS DEAD AHEAD.
HE'LL HOLD LINDA'S HEART IN HIS HAND BEFORE I CAN BLINK...
MANCHESTER 22 MILES
...UNLESS...
...UNLESS I OFFER HIM A MORE TEMPTING TARGET!
YOU DON'T WANT THEM, SAVITAR! YOU WANT ME! YOU'VE SAID SO ALL ALONG!
I'M AN INFIDEL, REMEMBER? SO LONG AS I EXIST, I'M SIPHONING ENERGY THAT RIGHTFULLY BELONGS TO YOU! I'M A BLIGHT ON THE SPEED FORCE!
IS THAT HOW YOU HONOR YOUR GOD? BY LETTING ME THUMB MY NOSE IN HIS FACE?
THAT'S WHAT I THOUGHT.
10

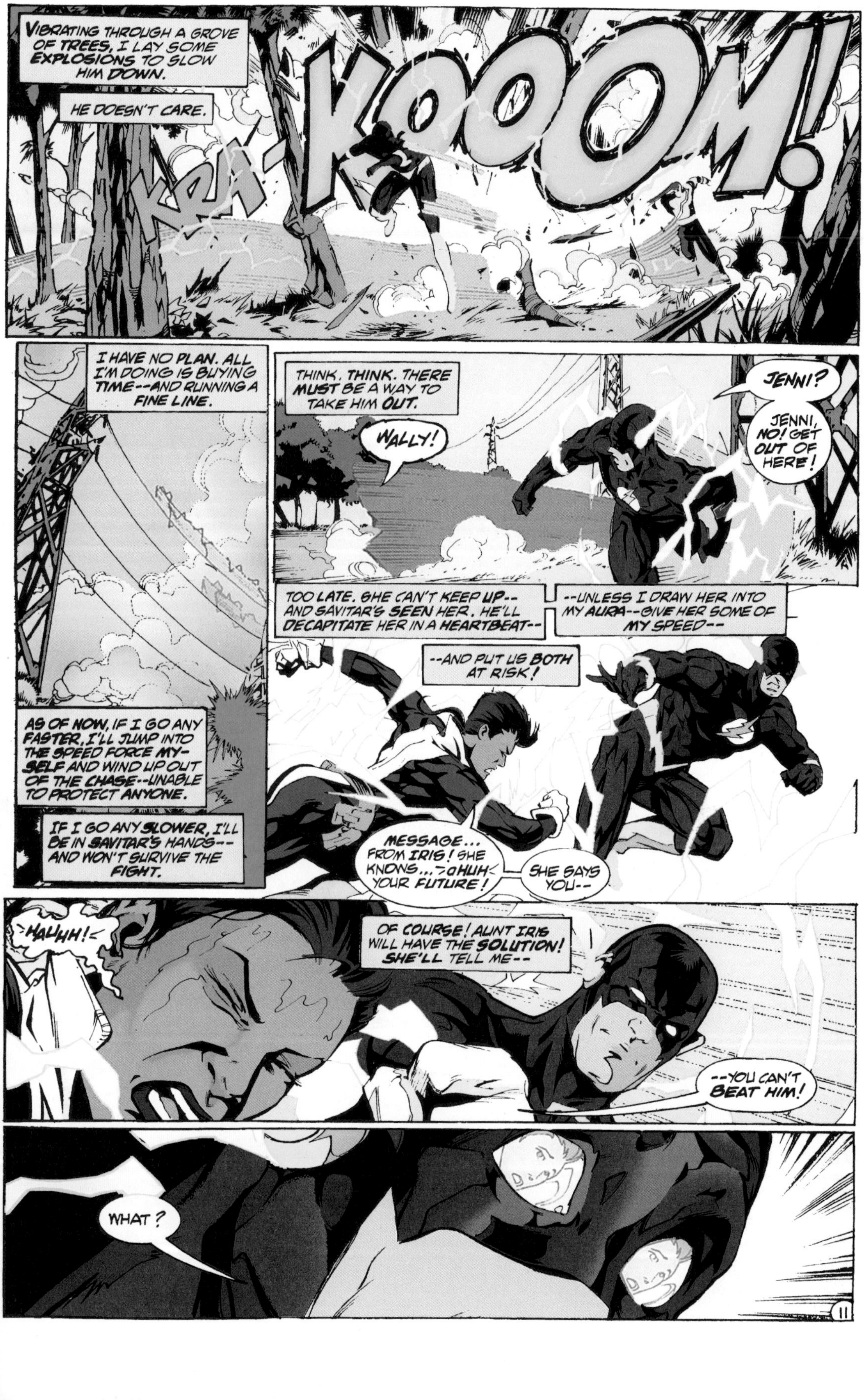
VIBRATING THROUGH A GROVE OF TREES, I LAY SOME EXPLOSIONS TO SLOW HIM DOWN.
HE DOESN'T CARE.
KRA-KOOOOM!
I HAVE NO PLAN. ALL I'M DOING IS BUYING TIME--AND RUNNING A FINE LINE.
THINK. THINK. THERE MUST BE A WAY TO TAKE HIM OUT.
WALLY!
JENNI?
JENNI, NO! GET OUT OF HERE!
TOO LATE. SHE CAN'T KEEP UP--AND SAVITAR'S SEEN HER. HE'LL DECAPITATE HER IN A HEARTBEAT--
--UNLESS I DRAW HER INTO MY AURA--GIVE HER SOME OF MY SPEED--
--AND PUT US BOTH AT RISK!
AS OF NOW, IF I GO ANY FASTER, I'LL JUMP INTO THE SPEED FORCE MYSELF AND WIND UP OUT OF THE CHASE--UNABLE TO PROTECT ANYONE.
IF I GO ANY SLOWER, I'LL BE IN SAVITAR'S HANDS--AND WON'T SURVIVE THE FIGHT.
MESSAGE... FROM IRIS! SHE KNOWS... HUH YOUR FUTURE!
SHE SAYS YOU--
HAUHH!
OF COURSE! AUNT IRIS WILL HAVE THE SOLUTION! SHE'LL TELL ME--
--YOU CAN'T BEAT HIM!
WHAT?
11

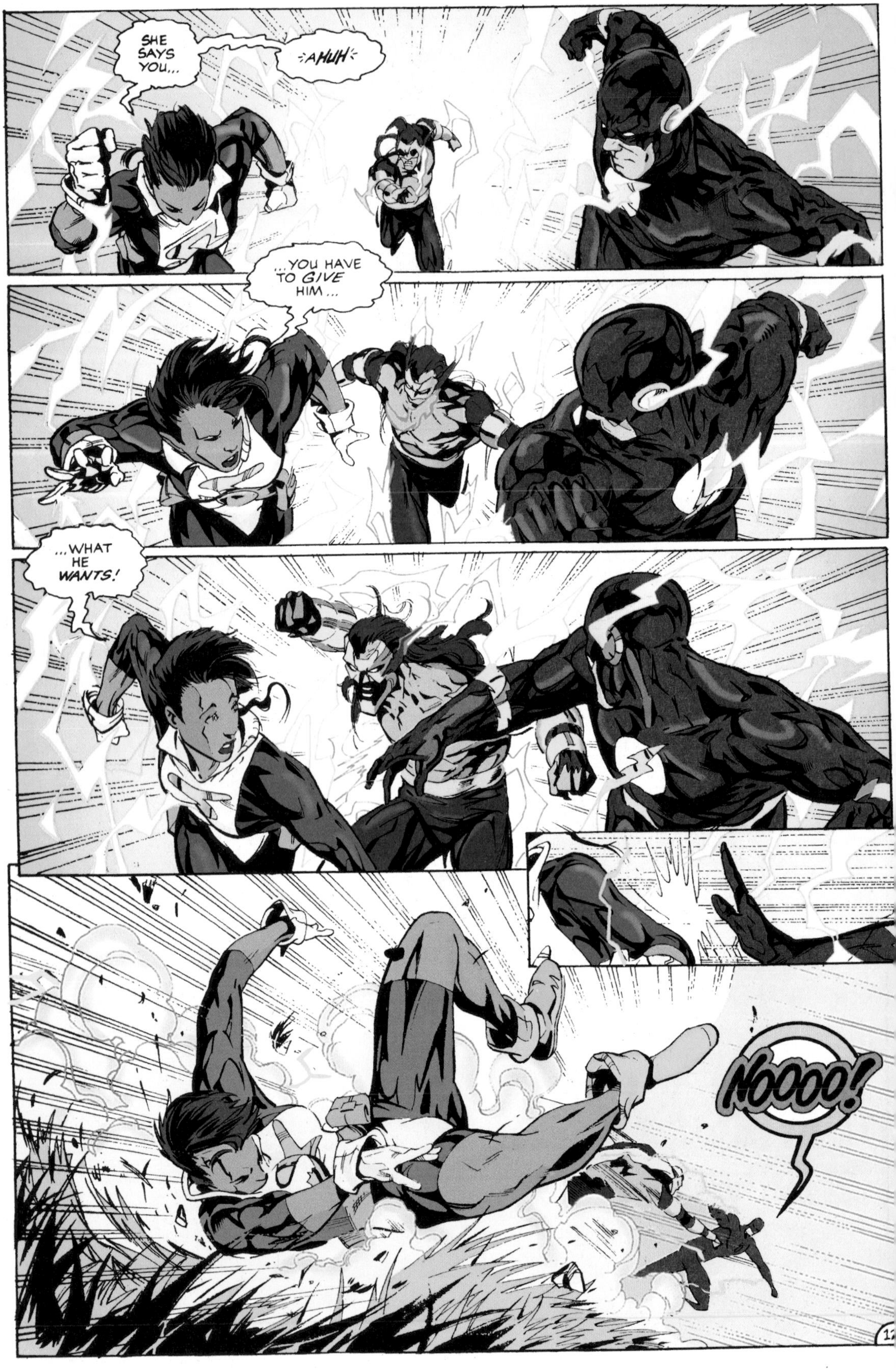
SHE SAYS YOU...
AHUH
...YOU HAVE TO GIVE HIM...
...WHAT HE WANTS!
NOOOO!

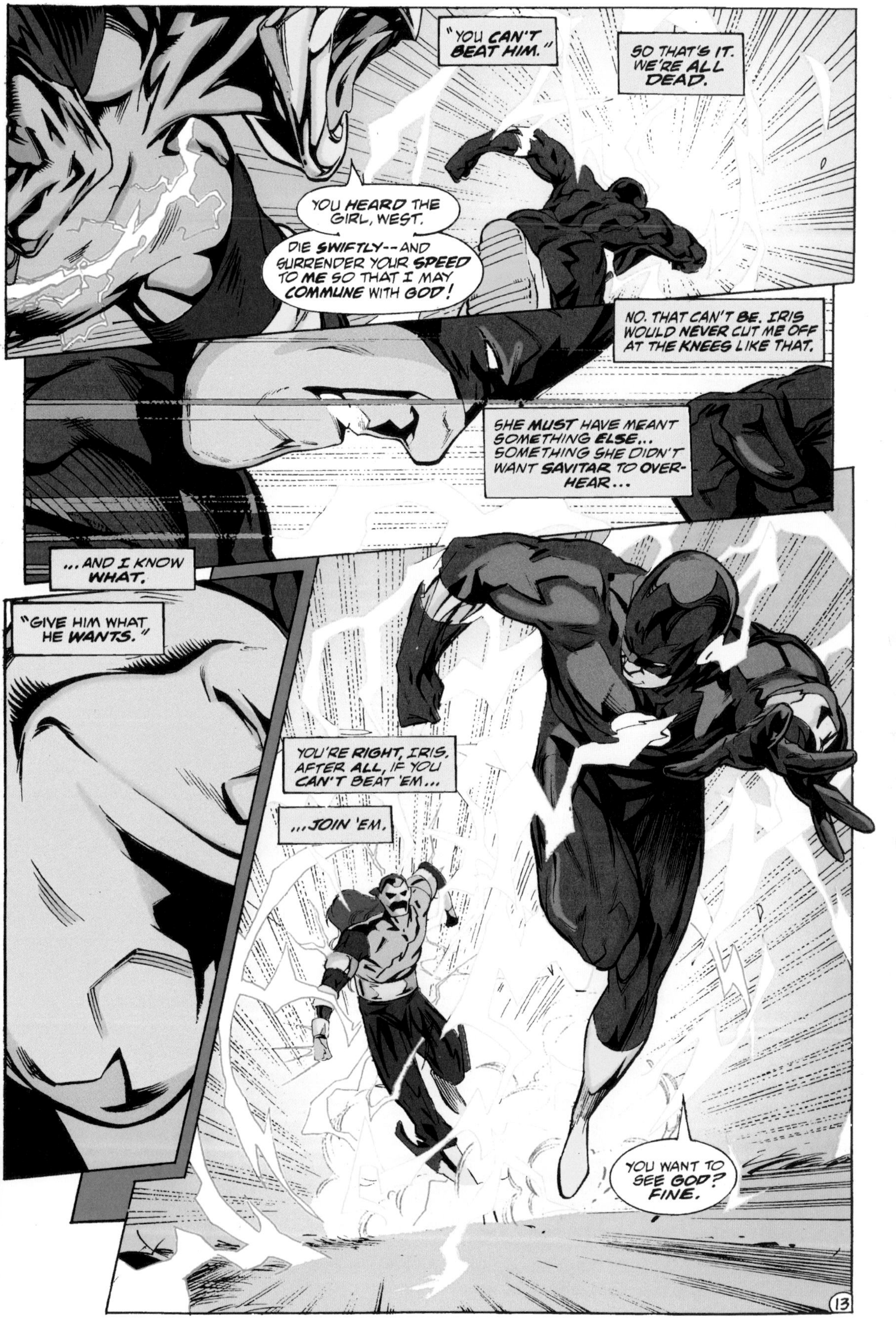
"YOU CAN'T BEAT HIM."
SO THAT'S IT. WE'RE ALL DEAD.
YOU HEARD THE GIRL, WEST.
DIE SWIFTLY--AND SURRENDER YOUR SPEED TO ME SO THAT I MAY COMMUNE WITH GOD!
NO. THAT CAN'T BE. IRIS WOULD NEVER CUT ME OFF AT THE KNEES LIKE THAT.
SHE MUST HAVE MEANT SOMETHING ELSE... SOMETHING SHE DIDN'T WANT SAVITAR TO OVER-HEAR...
...AND I KNOW WHAT.
"GIVE HIM WHAT HE WANTS."
YOU'RE RIGHT, IRIS. AFTER ALL, IF YOU CAN'T BEAT 'EM...
...JOIN 'EM.
YOU WANT TO SEE GOD? FINE.
13

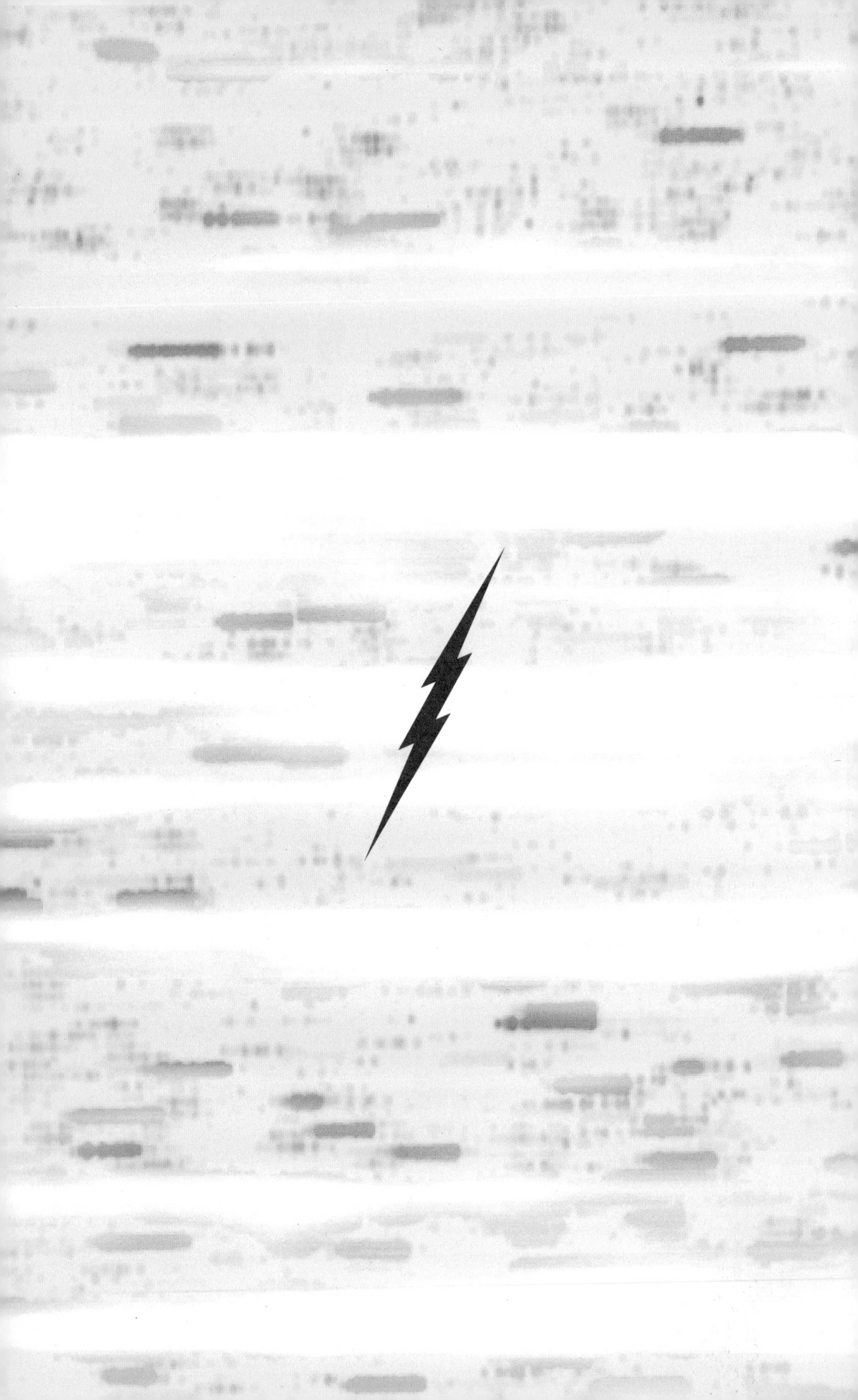

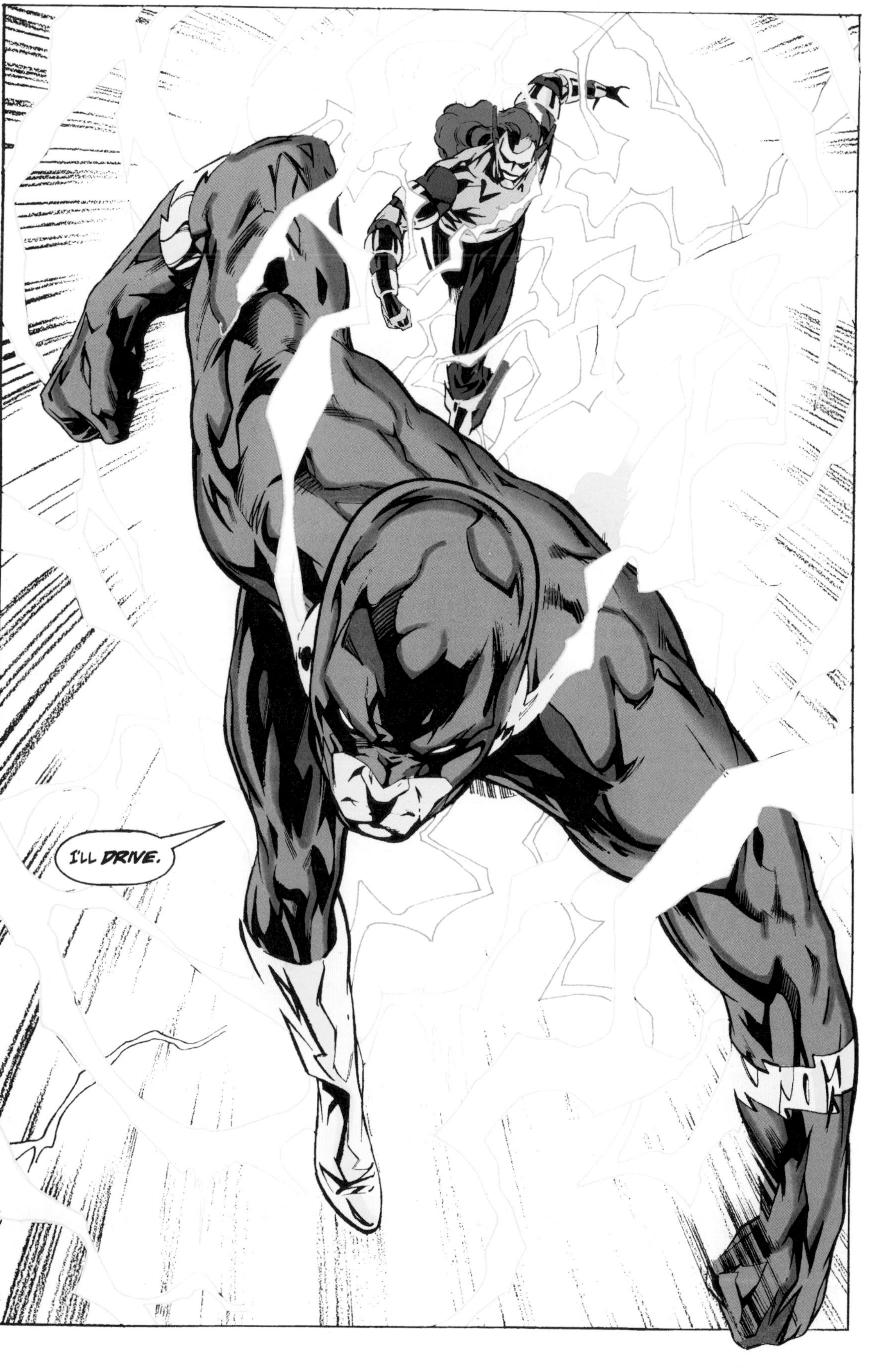
I'LL DRIVE.

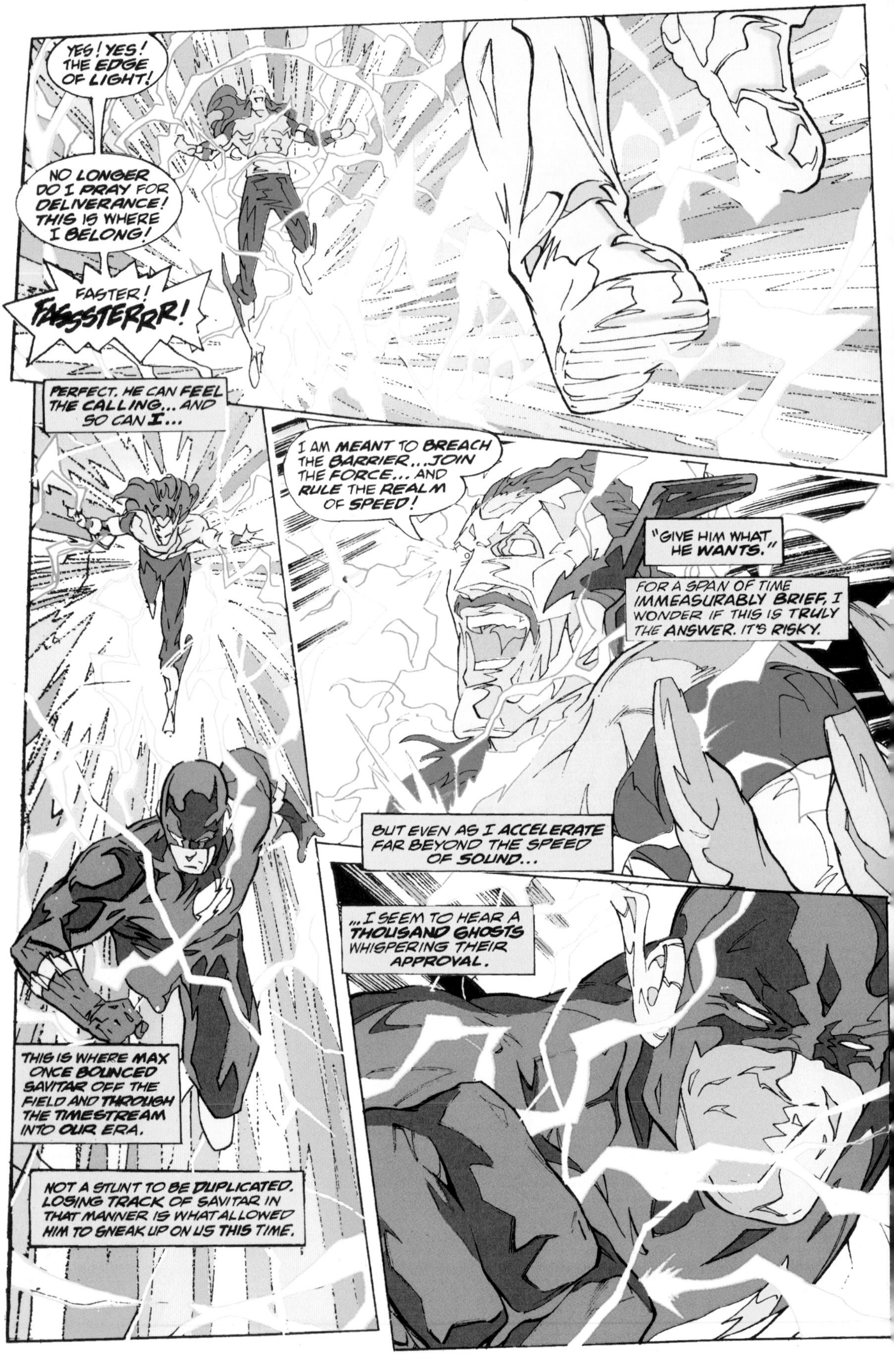
YES! YES! THE EDGE OF LIGHT!
NO LONGER DO I PRAY FOR DELIVERANCE! THIS IS WHERE I BELONG!
FASTER! FASSSTERRR!
PERFECT. HE CAN FEEL THE CALLING... AND SO CAN I...
I AM MEANT TO BREACH THE BARRIER... JOIN THE FORCE... AND RULE THE REALM OF SPEED!
"GIVE HIM WHAT HE WANTS."
FOR A SPAN OF TIME IMMEASURABLY BRIEF, I WONDER IF THIS IS TRULY THE ANSWER. IT'S RISKY.
THIS IS WHERE MAX ONCE BOUNCED SAVITAR OFF THE FIELD AND THROUGH THE TIMESTREAM INTO OUR ERA.
NOT A STUNT TO BE DUPLICATED. LOSING TRACK OF SAVITAR IN THAT MANNER IS WHAT ALLOWED HIM TO SNEAK UP ON US THIS TIME.
BUT EVEN AS I ACCELERATE FAR BEYOND THE SPEED OF SOUND...
...I SEEM TO HEAR A THOUSAND GHOSTS WHISPERING THEIR APPROVAL.

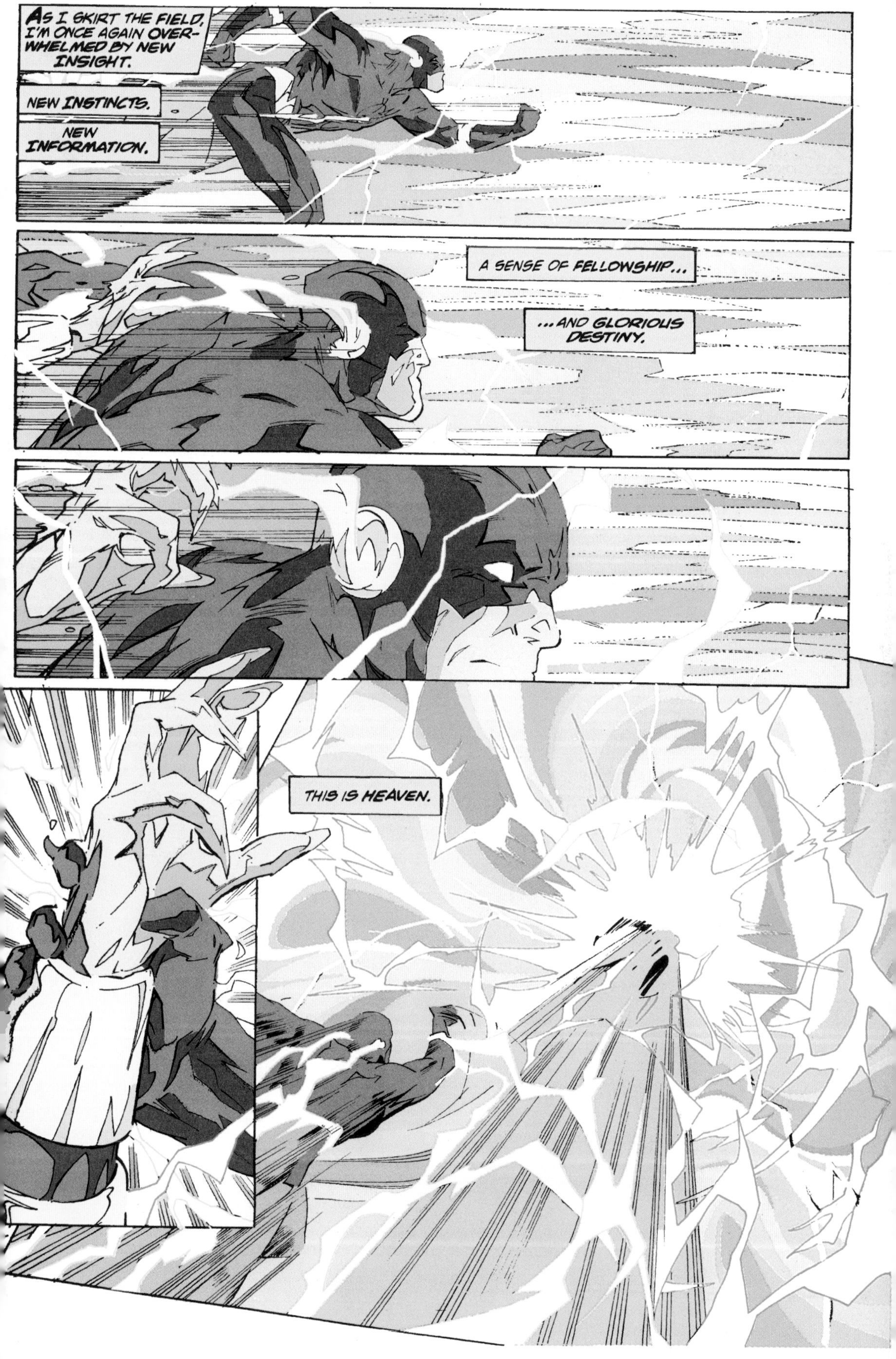
AS I SKIRT THE FIELD, I'M ONCE AGAIN OVERWHELMED BY NEW INSIGHT.
NEW INSTINCTS.
NEW INFORMATION.
A SENSE OF FELLOWSHIP...
...AND GLORIOUS DESTINY.
THIS IS HEAVEN.

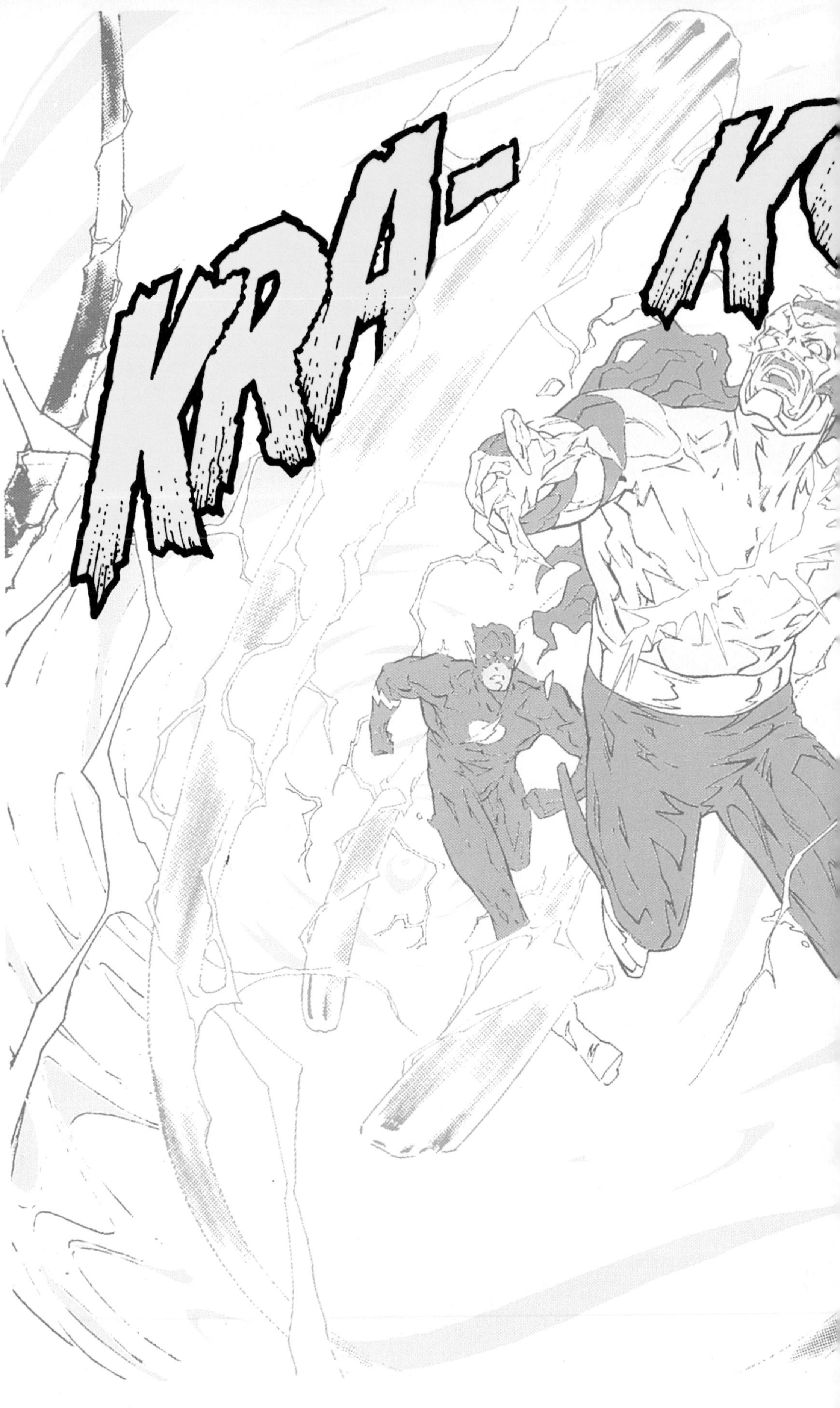
KRA- K

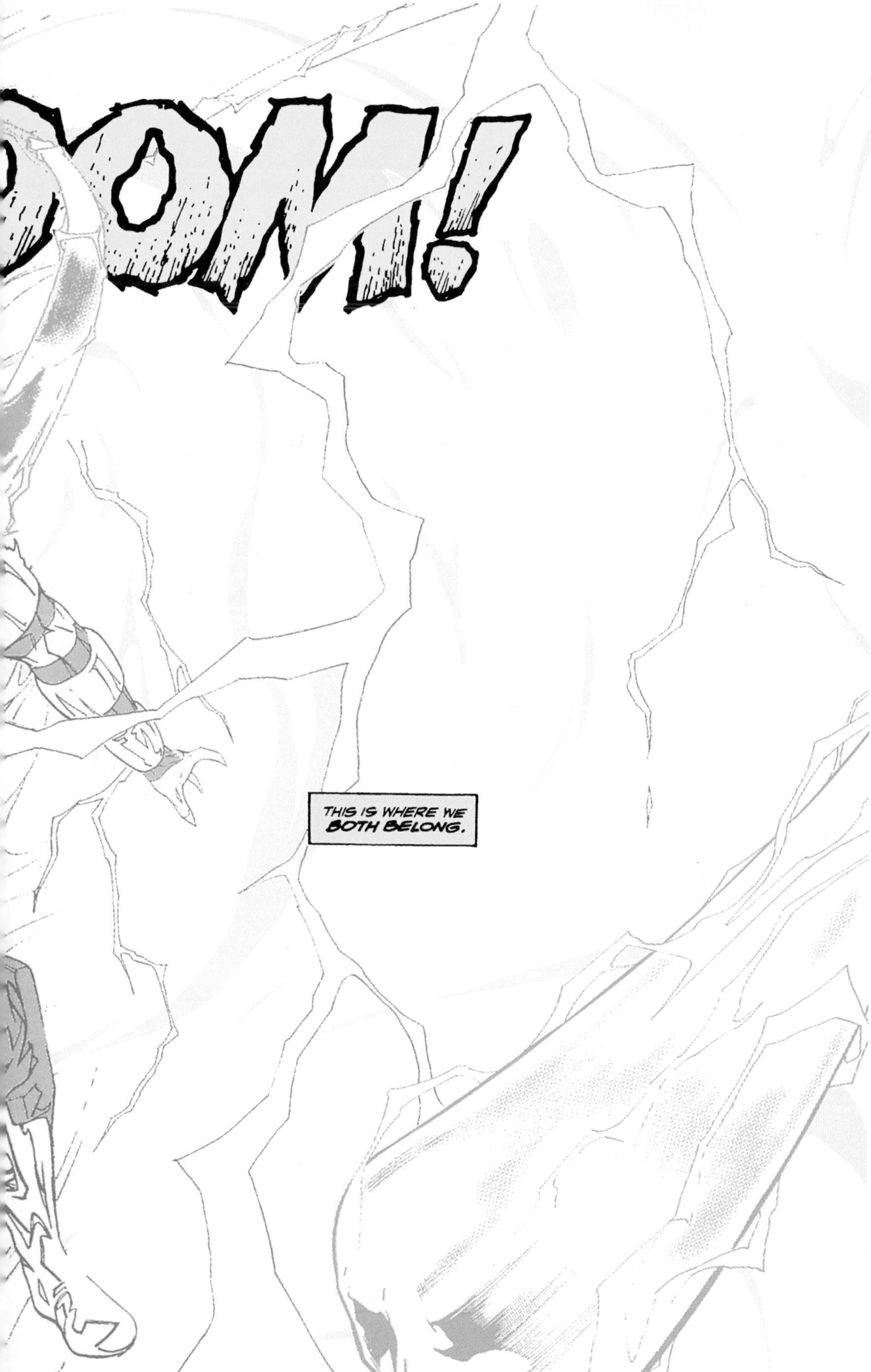
OOM!
THIS IS WHERE WE BOTH BELONG.

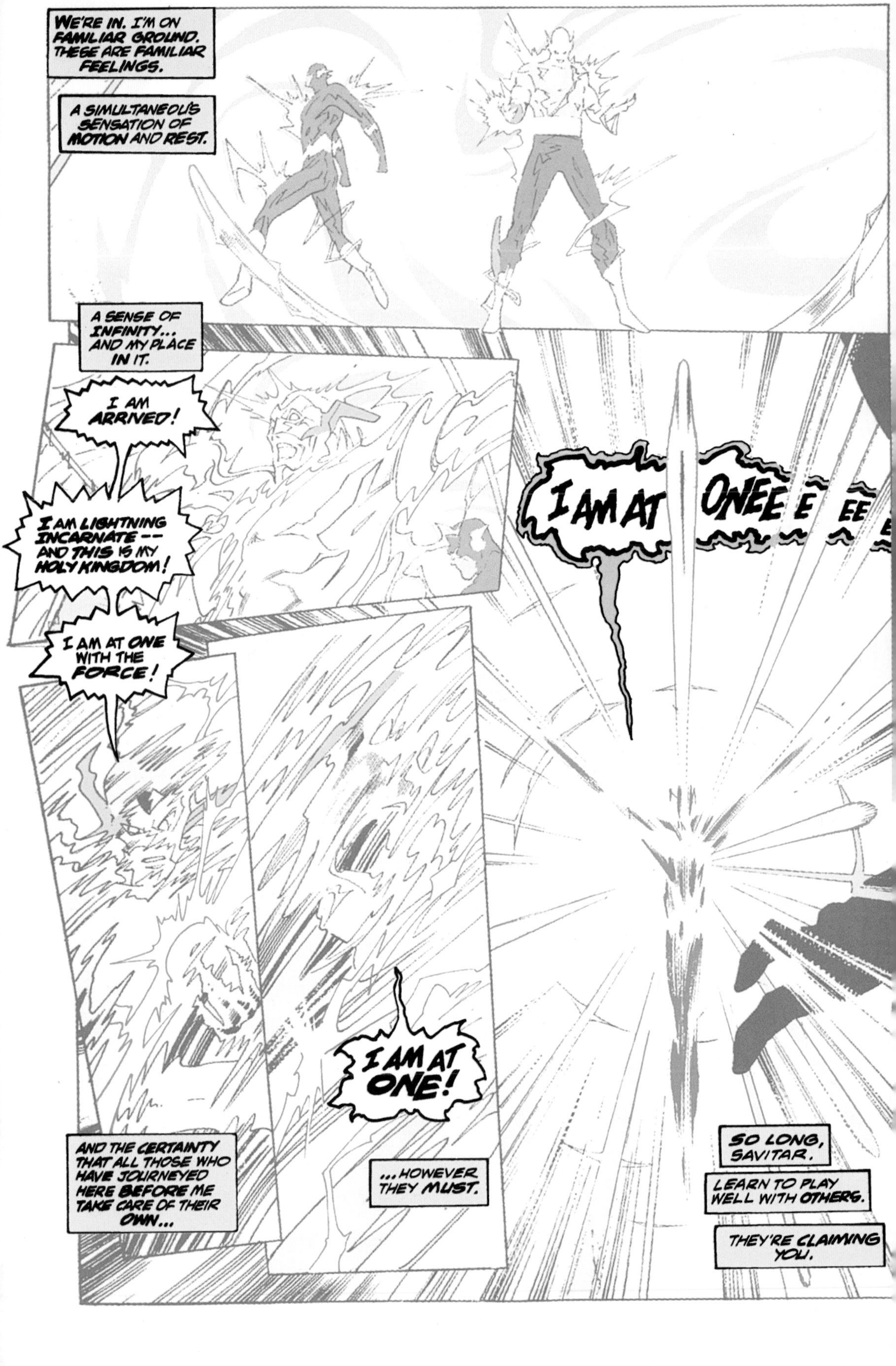
WE'RE IN. I'M ON FAMILIAR GROUND. THESE ARE FAMILIAR FEELINGS.
A SIMULTANEOUS SENSATION OF MOTION AND REST.
A SENSE OF INFINITY... AND MY PLACE IN IT.
I AM ARRIVED!
I AM LIGHTNING INCARNATE -- AND THIS IS MY HOLY KINGDOM!
I AM AT ONE WITH THE FORCE!
I AM AT ONEEE E EE E
I AM AT ONE!
AND THE CERTAINTY THAT ALL THOSE WHO HAVE JOURNEYED HERE BEFORE ME TAKE CARE OF THEIR OWN...
...HOWEVER THEY MUST.
SO LONG, SAVITAR.
LEARN TO PLAY WELL WITH OTHERS.
THEY'RE CLAIMING YOU.

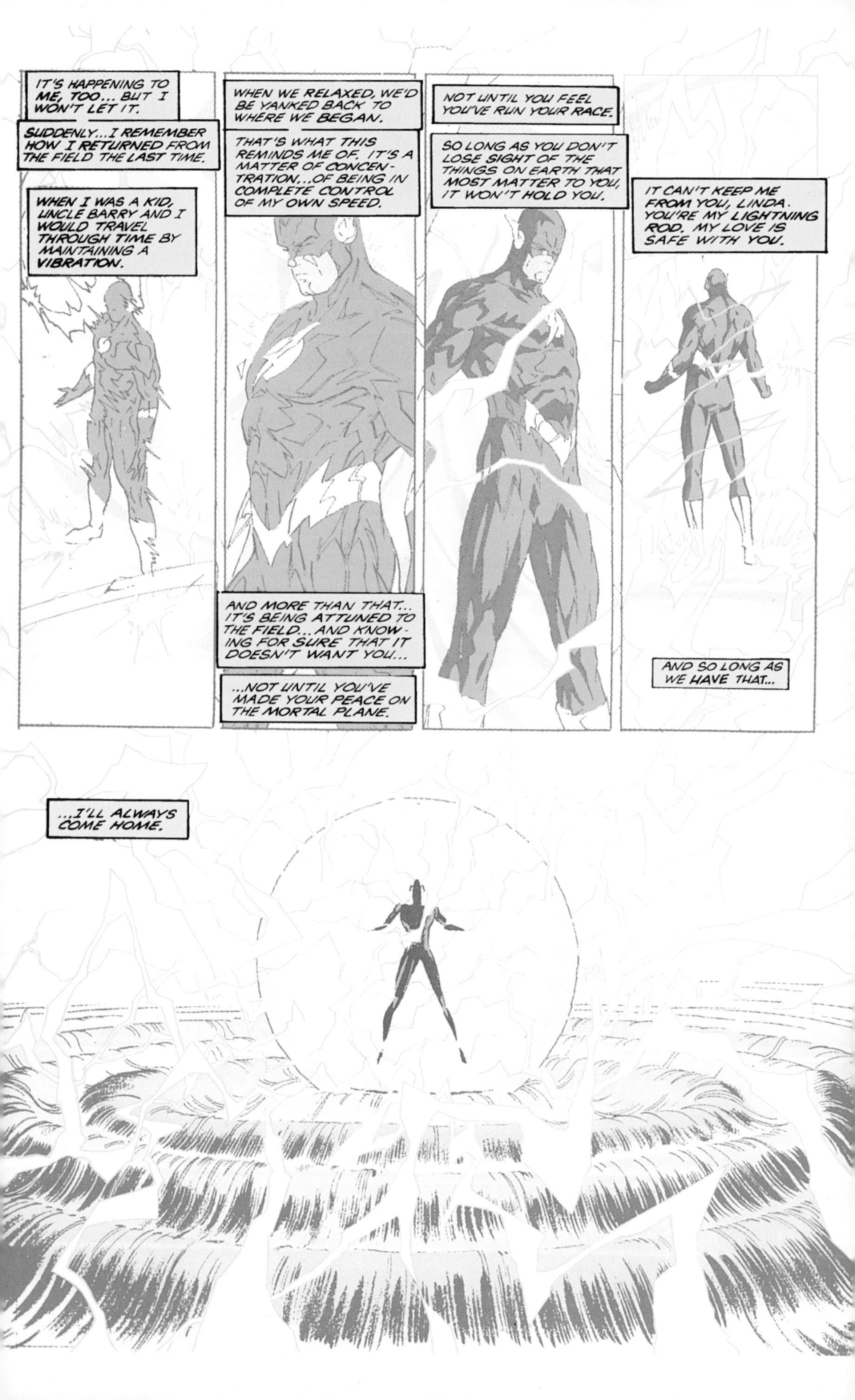
IT'S HAPPENING TO ME, TOO... BUT I WON'T LET IT.
SUDDENLY...I REMEMBER HOW I RETURNED FROM THE FIELD THE LAST TIME.
WHEN I WAS A KID, UNCLE BARRY AND I WOULD TRAVEL THROUGH TIME BY MAINTAINING A VIBRATION.
WHEN WE RELAXED, WE'D BE YANKED BACK TO WHERE WE BEGAN.
THAT'S WHAT THIS REMINDS ME OF. IT'S A MATTER OF CONCENTRATION...OF BEING IN COMPLETE CONTROL OF MY OWN SPEED.
AND MORE THAN THAT... IT'S BEING ATTUNED TO THE FIELD... AND KNOWING FOR SURE THAT IT DOESN'T WANT YOU...
...NOT UNTIL YOU'VE MADE YOUR PEACE ON THE MORTAL PLANE.
NOT UNTIL YOU FEEL YOU'VE RUN YOUR RACE.
SO LONG AS YOU DON'T LOSE SIGHT OF THE THINGS ON EARTH THAT MOST MATTER TO YOU, IT WON'T HOLD YOU.
IT CAN'T KEEP ME FROM YOU, LINDA. YOU'RE MY LIGHTNING ROD. MY LOVE IS SAFE WITH YOU.
AND SO LONG AS WE HAVE THAT...
...I'LL ALWAYS COME HOME.

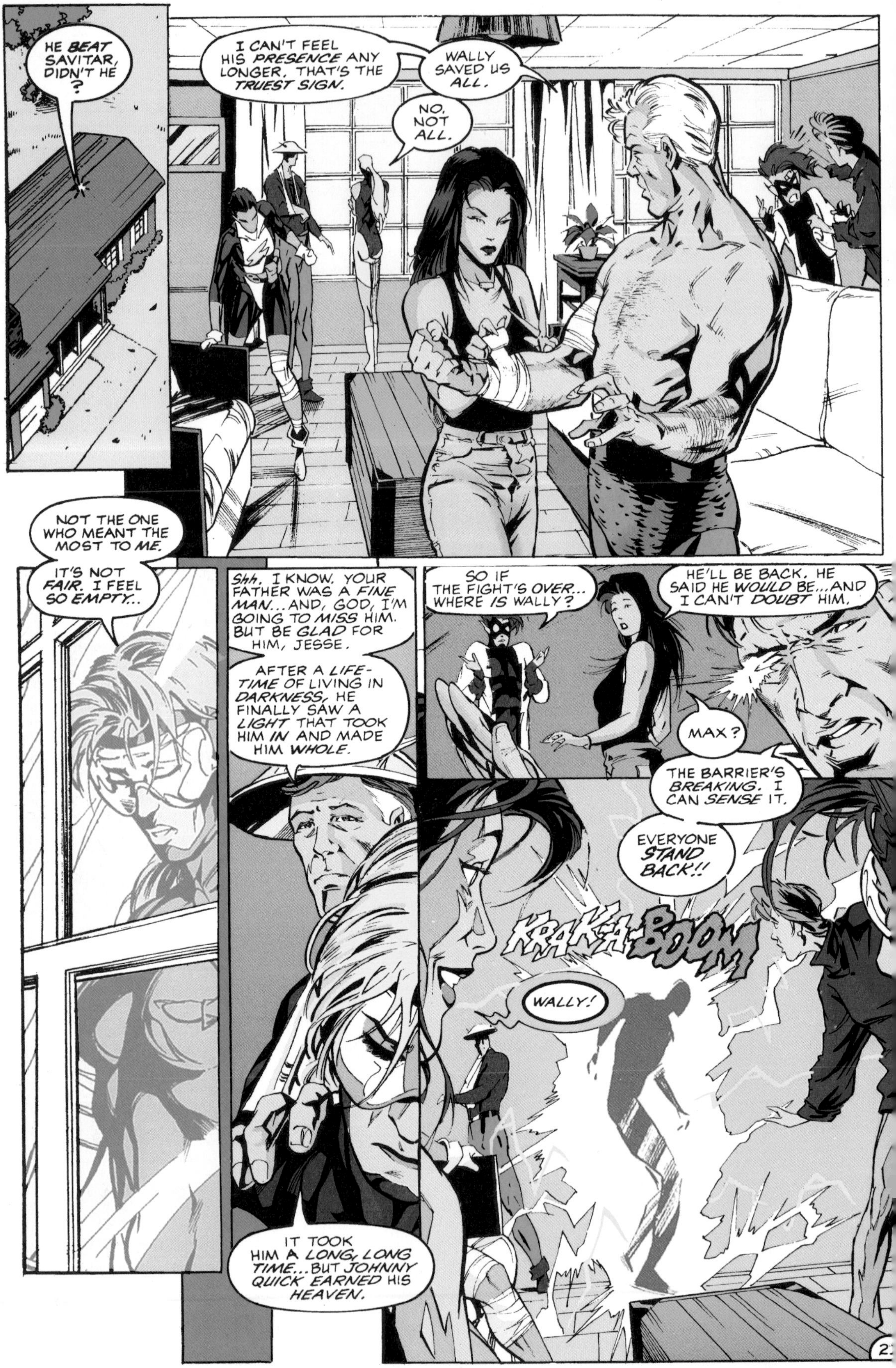
HE BEAT SAVITAR, DIDN'T HE?
I CAN'T FEEL HIS PRESENCE ANY LONGER. THAT'S THE TRUEST SIGN.
WALLY SAVED US ALL.
NO, NOT ALL.
NOT THE ONE WHO MEANT THE MOST TO ME.
IT'S NOT FAIR. I FEEL SO EMPTY...
Shh. I KNOW. YOUR FATHER WAS A FINE MAN... AND, GOD, I'M GOING TO MISS HIM. BUT BE GLAD FOR HIM, JESSE.
AFTER A LIFE-TIME OF LIVING IN DARKNESS, HE FINALLY SAW A LIGHT THAT TOOK HIM IN AND MADE HIM WHOLE.
IT TOOK HIM A LONG, LONG TIME... BUT JOHNNY QUICK EARNED HIS HEAVEN.
SO IF THE FIGHT'S OVER... WHERE IS WALLY?
HE'LL BE BACK. HE SAID HE WOULD BE... AND I CAN'T DOUBT HIM.
MAX?
THE BARRIER'S BREAKING. I CAN SENSE IT.
EVERYONE STAND BACK!!
KRAKA-BOOM
WALLY!

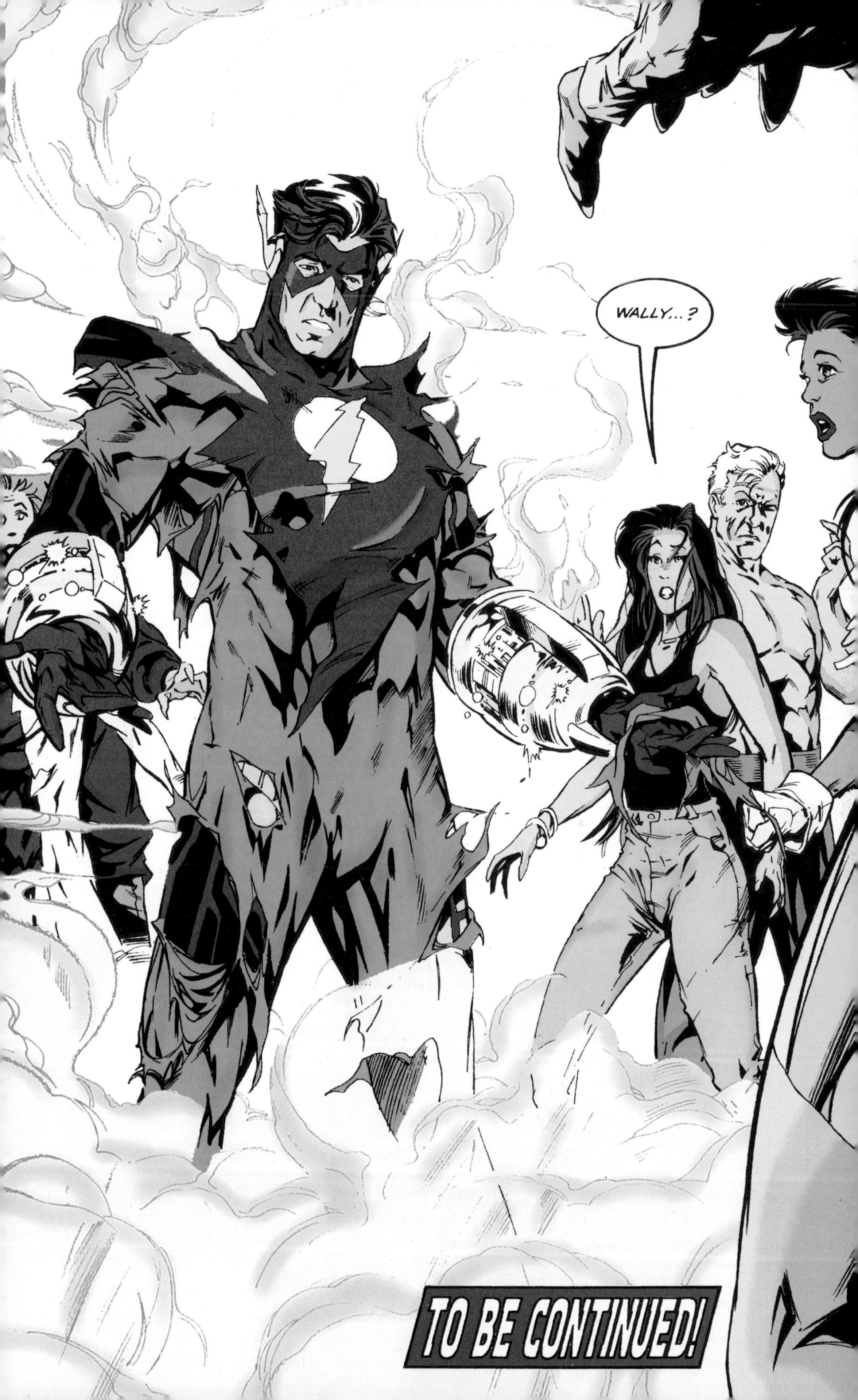
WALLY...?
TO BE CONTINUED!

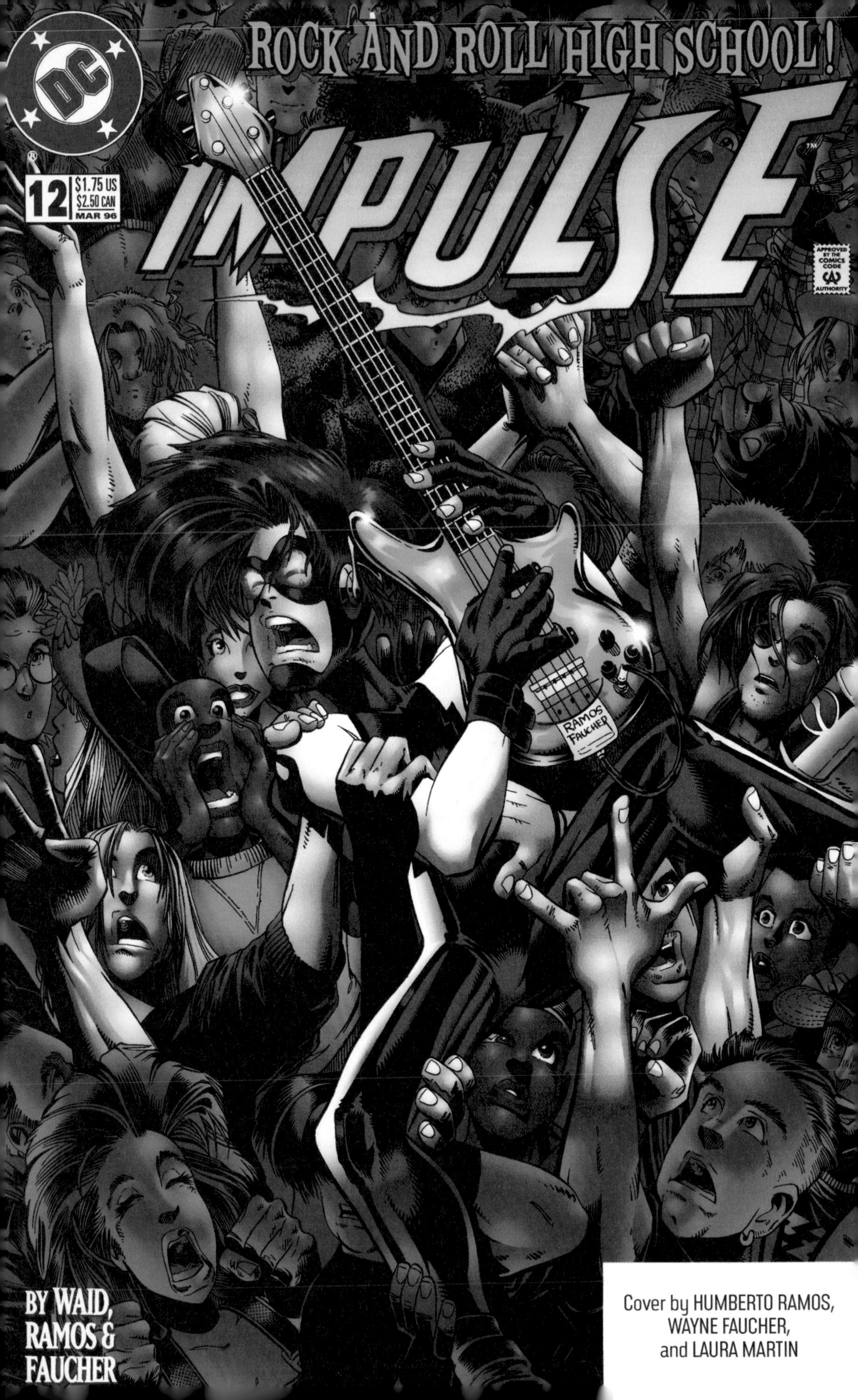
DC
ROCK AND ROLL HIGH SCHOOL!
IMPULSE
12
$1.75 US
$2.50 CAN
MAR 96
APPROVED BY THE COMICS CODE AUTHORITY
RAMOS FAUCHER
BY WAID, RAMOS & FAUCHER

Cover by HUMBERTO RAMOS, WAYNE FAUCHER, and LAURA MARTIN

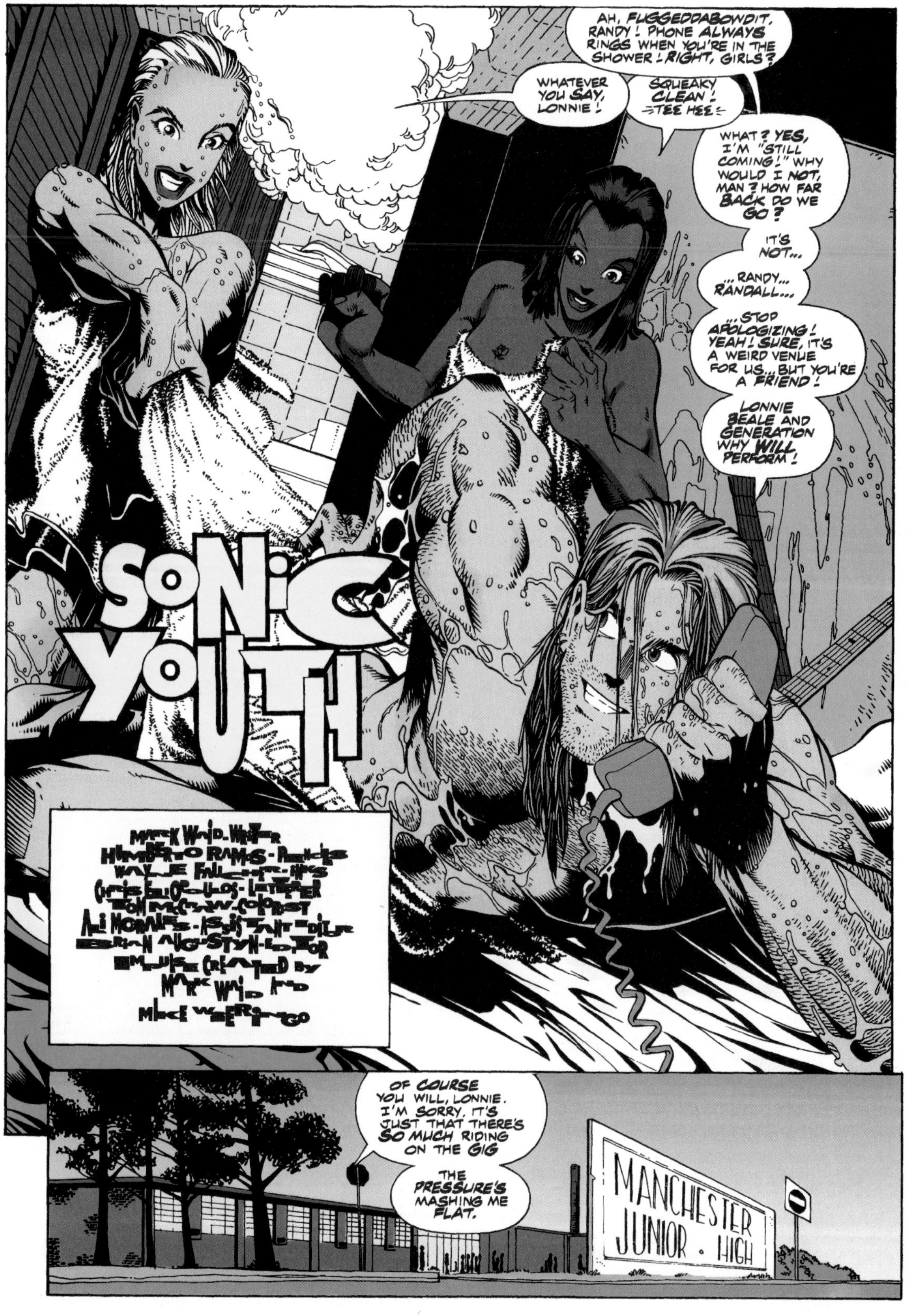
AH, FUGGEDDABOWDIT, RANDY! PHONE ALWAYS RINGS WHEN YOU'RE IN THE SHOWER! RIGHT, GIRLS?
WHATEVER YOU SAY, LONNIE!
SQUEAKY CLEAN! TEE HEE
WHAT? YES, I'M "STILL COMING!" WHY WOULD I NOT, MAN? HOW FAR BACK DO WE GO?
IT'S NOT...
...RANDY... RANDALL...
...STOP APOLOGIZING! YEAH! SURE, IT'S A WEIRD VENUE FOR US... BUT YOU'RE A FRIEND!
LONNIE BEALE AND GENERATION WHY WILL PERFORM!
SONIC YOUTH
OF COURSE YOU WILL, LONNIE. I'M SORRY. IT'S JUST THAT THERE'S SO MUCH RIDING ON THE GIG
THE PRESSURE'S MASHING ME FLAT.
MANCHESTER JUNIOR · HIGH

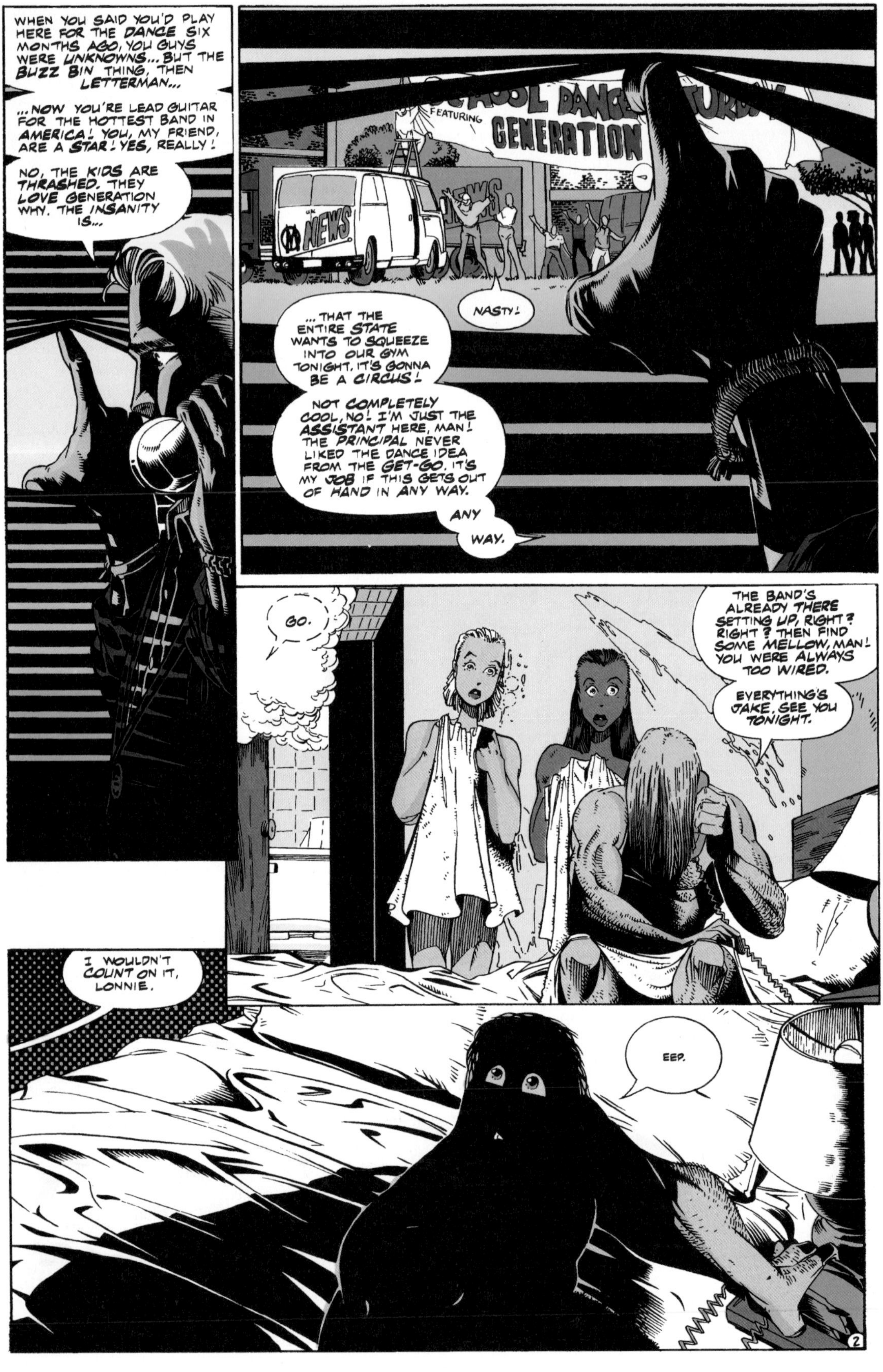
WHEN YOU SAID YOU'D PLAY HERE FOR THE DANCE SIX MONTHS AGO, YOU GUYS WERE UNKNOWNS... BUT THE BUZZ BIN THING, THEN LETTERMAN...
...NOW YOU'RE LEAD GUITAR FOR THE HOTTEST BAND IN AMERICA! YOU, MY FRIEND, ARE A STAR! YES, REALLY!
NO, THE KIDS ARE THRASHED. THEY LOVE GENERATION WHY. THE INSANITY IS...
FEATURING
GENERATION
NEWS
NASTY!
...THAT THE ENTIRE STATE WANTS TO SQUEEZE INTO OUR GYM TONIGHT. IT'S GONNA BE A CIRCUS!
NOT COMPLETELY COOL, NO! I'M JUST THE ASSISTANT HERE, MAN! THE PRINCIPAL NEVER LIKED THE DANCE IDEA FROM THE GET-GO. IT'S MY JOB IF THIS GETS OUT OF HAND IN ANY WAY.
ANY
WAY.
GO.
THE BAND'S ALREADY THERE SETTING UP, RIGHT? RIGHT? THEN FIND SOME MELLOW, MAN! YOU WERE ALWAYS TOO WIRED.
EVERYTHING'S JAKE. SEE YOU TONIGHT.
I WOULDN'T COUNT ON IT, LONNIE.
EEP.

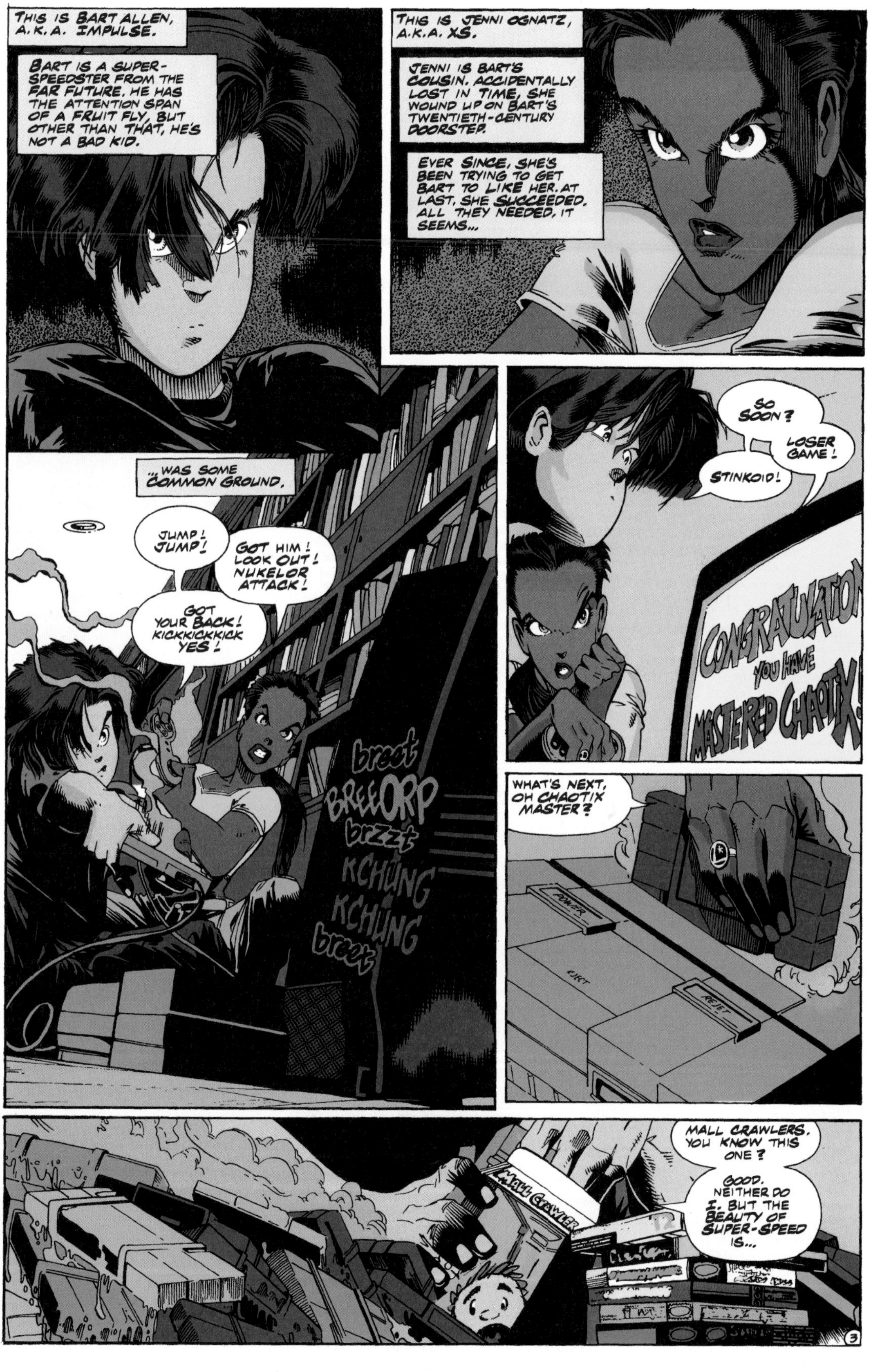

THIS IS BART ALLEN, A.K.A. IMPULSE.
BART IS A SUPER-SPEEDSTER FROM THE FAR FUTURE. HE HAS THE ATTENTION SPAN OF A FRUIT FLY, BUT OTHER THAN THAT, HE'S NOT A BAD KID.
THIS IS JENNI OGNATZ, A.K.A. XS.
JENNI IS BART'S COUSIN. ACCIDENTALLY LOST IN TIME, SHE WOUND UP ON BART'S TWENTIETH-CENTURY DOORSTEP.
EVER SINCE, SHE'S BEEN TRYING TO GET BART TO LIKE HER. AT LAST, SHE SUCCEEDED. ALL THEY NEEDED, IT SEEMS...
...WAS SOME COMMON GROUND.
JUMP! JUMP!
GOT HIM! LOOK OUT! NUKELOR ATTACK!
GOT YOUR BACK! KICKKICKKICK YES!
breet
BREEORP
brzzt
KCHUNG
KCHUNG
breet
SO SOON?
LOSER GAME!
STINKOID!
CONGRATULATIONS YOU HAVE MASTERED CHAOTIX!
WHAT'S NEXT, OH CHAOTIX MASTER?
POWER
EJECT
RESET
MALL CRAWLERS. YOU KNOW THIS ONE?
GOOD. NEITHER DO I. BUT THE BEAUTY OF SUPER-SPEED IS...
MALL CRAWLER

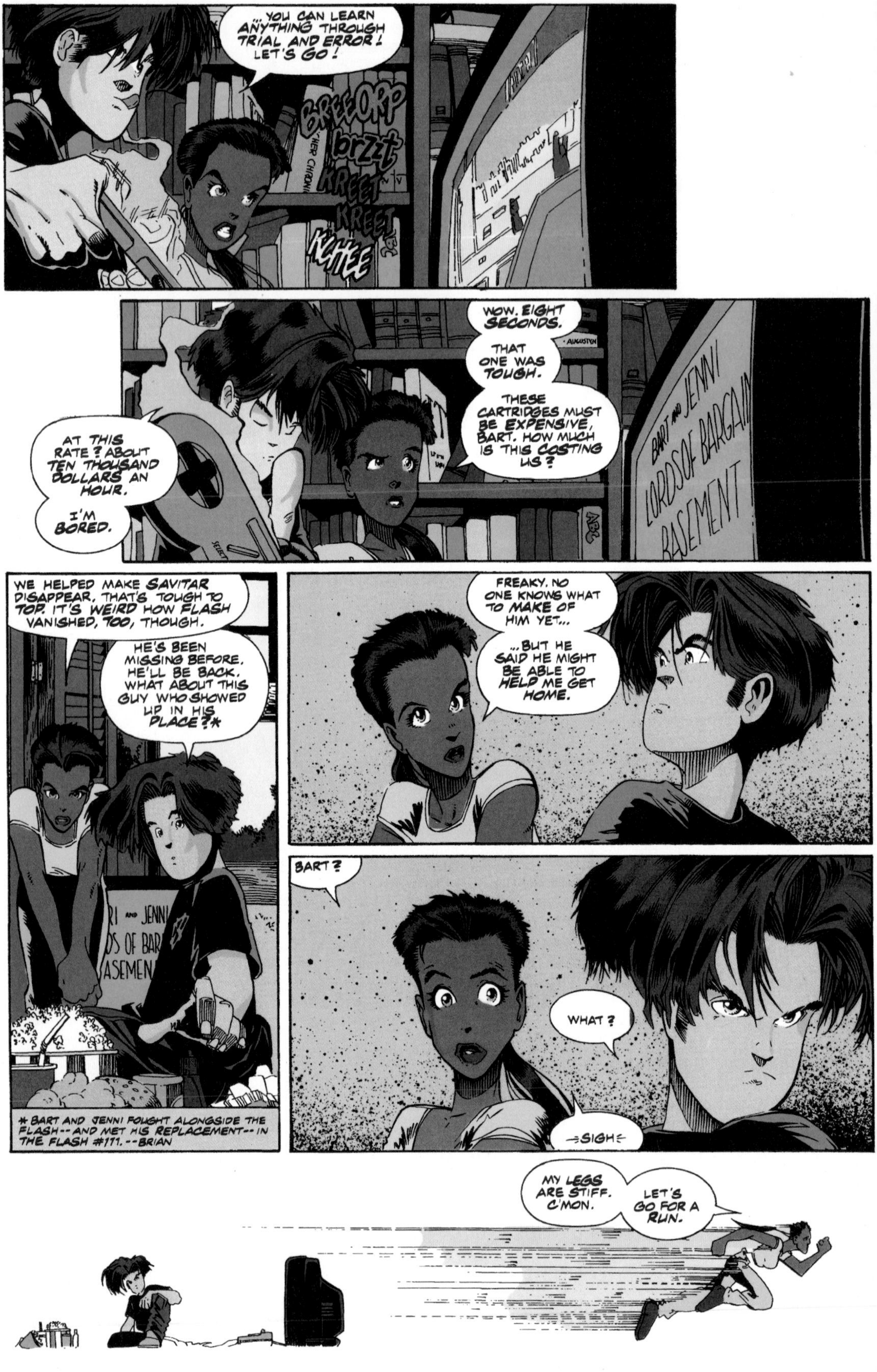
...YOU CAN LEARN ANYTHING THROUGH TRIAL AND ERROR! LET'S GO!
BREEORP
brZzt
KREET
KREET
KCHEE
WOW. EIGHT SECONDS.
THAT ONE WAS TOUGH.
THESE CARTRIDGES MUST BE EXPENSIVE, BART. HOW MUCH IS THIS COSTING US?
AT THIS RATE? ABOUT TEN THOUSAND DOLLARS AN HOUR.
I'M BORED.
BART AND JENNI
LORDS OF BARGAIN
BASEMENT
WE HELPED MAKE SAVITAR DISAPPEAR, THAT'S TOUGH TO TOP. IT'S WEIRD HOW FLASH VANISHED, TOO, THOUGH.
HE'S BEEN MISSING BEFORE. HE'LL BE BACK. WHAT ABOUT THIS GUY WHO SHOWED UP IN HIS PLACE?*
* BART AND JENNI FOUGHT ALONGSIDE THE FLASH--AND MET HIS REPLACEMENT--IN THE FLASH #171. --BRIAN
FREAKY. NO ONE KNOWS WHAT TO MAKE OF HIM YET...
...BUT HE SAID HE MIGHT BE ABLE TO HELP ME GET HOME.
BART?
WHAT?
SIGH
MY LEGS ARE STIFF. C'MON.
LET'S GO FOR A RUN.

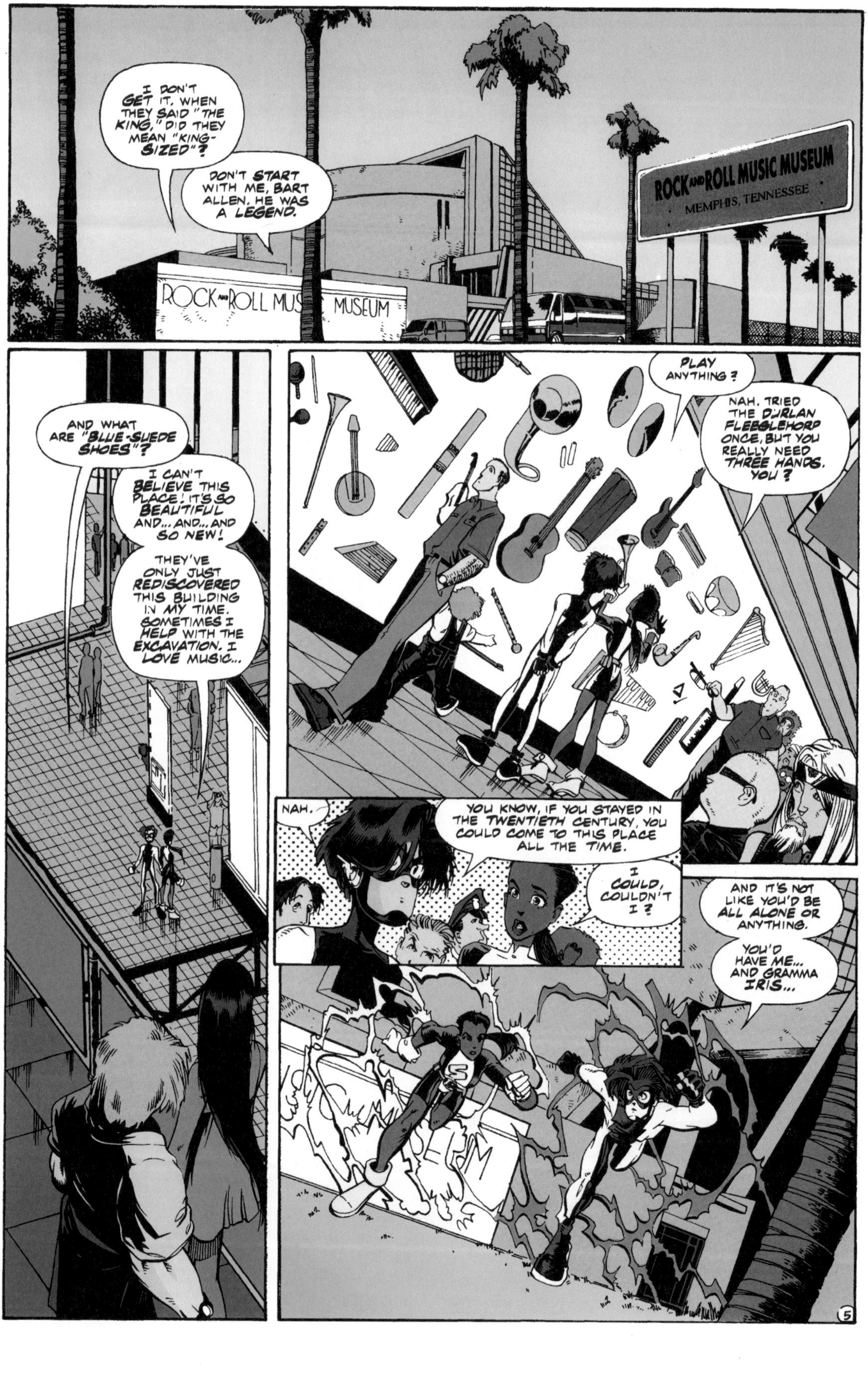

I DON'T GET IT. WHEN THEY SAID "THE KING," DID THEY MEAN "KING-SIZED"?
DON'T START WITH ME, BART ALLEN. HE WAS A LEGEND.
ROCK AND ROLL MUSIC MUSEUM
MEMPHIS, TENNESSEE
ROCK AND ROLL MUS MUSEUM
AND WHAT ARE "BLUE-SUEDE SHOES"?
I CAN'T BELIEVE THIS PLACE! IT'S SO BEAUTIFUL AND... AND... AND SO NEW!
THEY'VE ONLY JUST REDISCOVERED THIS BUILDING IN MY TIME. SOMETIMES I HELP WITH THE EXCAVATION. I LOVE MUSIC...
PLAY ANYTHING?
NAH. TRIED THE DJRLAN FLEEGLEHORP ONCE, BUT YOU REALLY NEED THREE HANDS. YOU?
NAH.
YOU KNOW, IF YOU STAYED IN THE TWENTIETH CENTURY, YOU COULD COME TO THIS PLACE ALL THE TIME.
I COULD, COULDN'T I?
AND IT'S NOT LIKE YOU'D BE ALL ALONE OR ANYTHING.
YOU'D HAVE ME... AND GRAMMA IRIS...

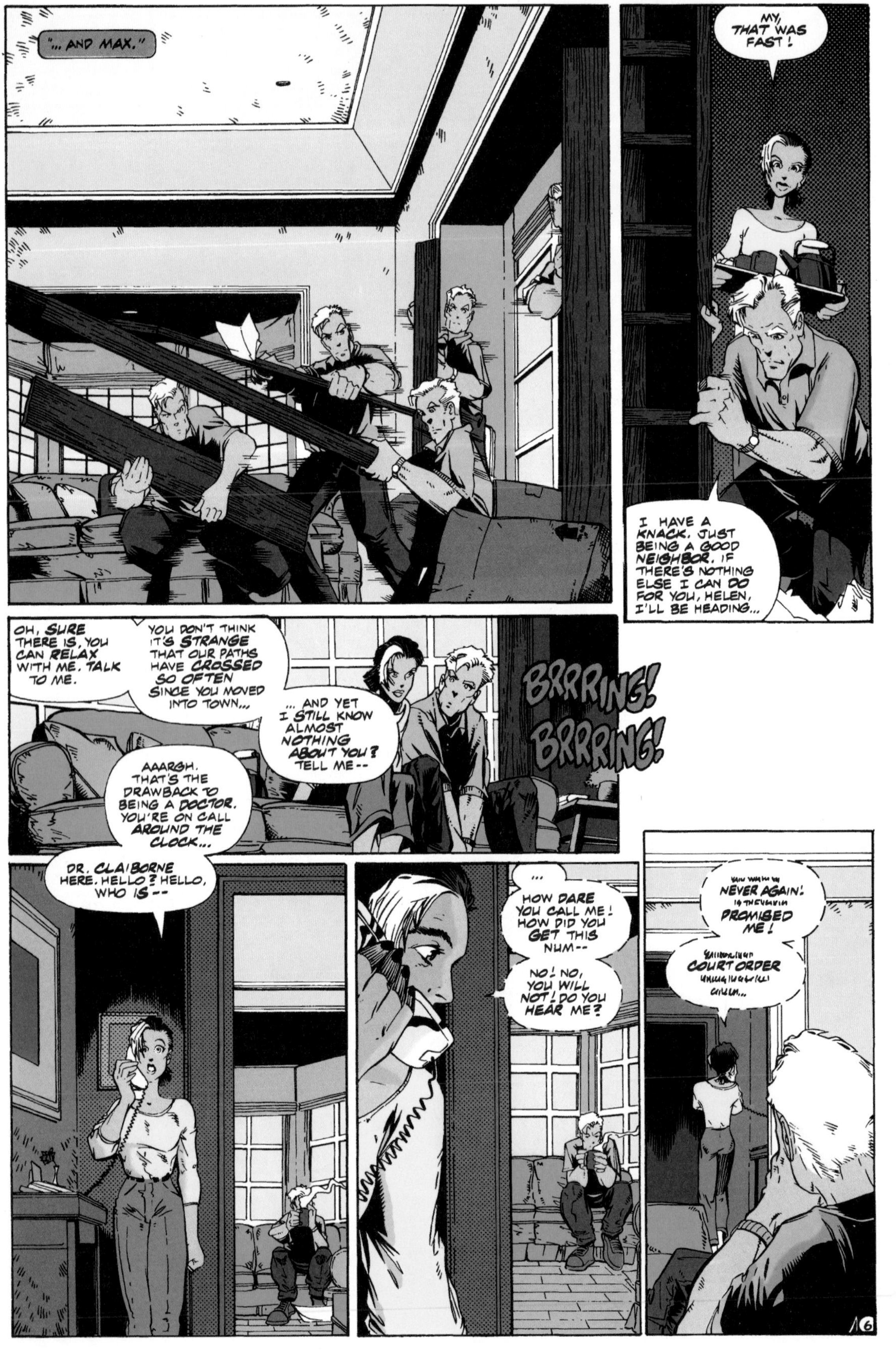
"... AND MAX."
MY, THAT WAS FAST!
I HAVE A KNACK. JUST BEING A GOOD NEIGHBOR. IF THERE'S NOTHING ELSE I CAN DO FOR YOU, HELEN, I'LL BE HEADING...
OH, SURE THERE IS. YOU CAN RELAX WITH ME. TALK TO ME.
YOU DON'T THINK IT'S STRANGE THAT OUR PATHS HAVE CROSSED SO OFTEN SINCE YOU MOVED INTO TOWN...
... AND YET I STILL KNOW ALMOST NOTHING ABOUT YOU? TELL ME--
BRRRING! BRRRING!
AAARGH. THAT'S THE DRAWBACK TO BEING A DOCTOR. YOU'RE ON CALL AROUND THE CLOCK...
DR. CLAIBORNE HERE. HELLO? HELLO, WHO IS--
...
HOW DARE YOU CALL ME! HOW DID YOU GET THIS NUM--
NO! NO, YOU WILL NOT! DO YOU HEAR ME?
NEVER AGAIN!
PROMISED ME!
COURT ORDER

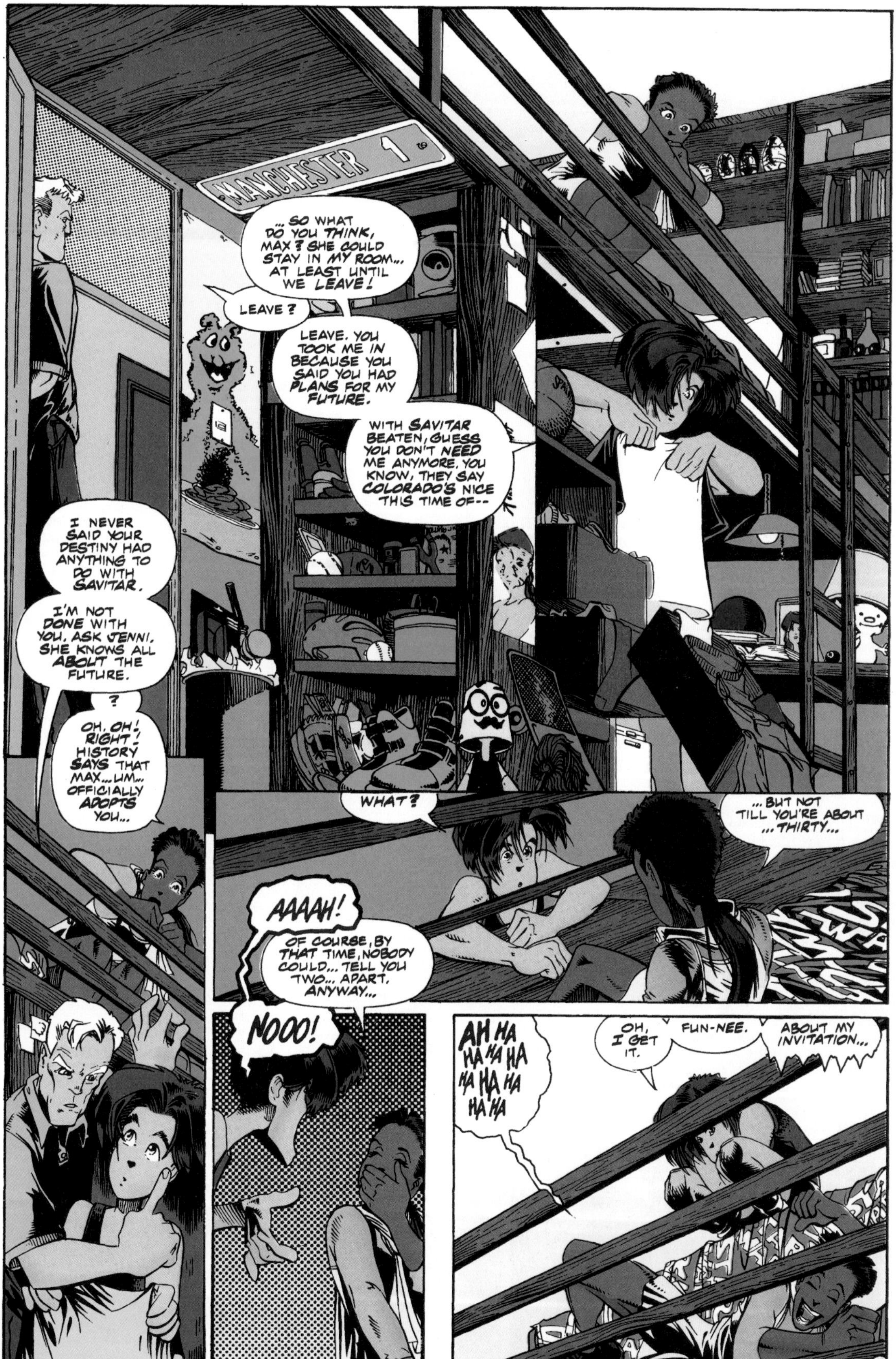

MANCHESTER 1
...SO WHAT DO YOU THINK, MAX? SHE COULD STAY IN MY ROOM... AT LEAST UNTIL WE LEAVE!
LEAVE?
LEAVE. YOU TOOK ME IN BECAUSE YOU SAID YOU HAD PLANS FOR MY FUTURE.
WITH SAVITAR BEATEN, GUESS YOU DON'T NEED ME ANYMORE. YOU KNOW, THEY SAY COLORADO'S NICE THIS TIME OF--
I NEVER SAID YOUR DESTINY HAD ANYTHING TO DO WITH SAVITAR.
I'M NOT DONE WITH YOU. ASK JENNI. SHE KNOWS ALL ABOUT THE FUTURE.
?
OH. OH! RIGHT! HISTORY SAYS THAT MAX... UM... OFFICIALLY ADOPTS YOU...
WHAT?
...BUT NOT TILL YOU'RE ABOUT ...THIRTY...
AAAAH!
OF COURSE, BY THAT TIME, NOBODY COULD... TELL YOU TWO... APART, ANYWAY...
NOOO!
AH HA HA HA HA HA HA HA HA HA HA HA HA
OH, I GET IT.
FUN-NEE.
ABOUT MY INVITATION...

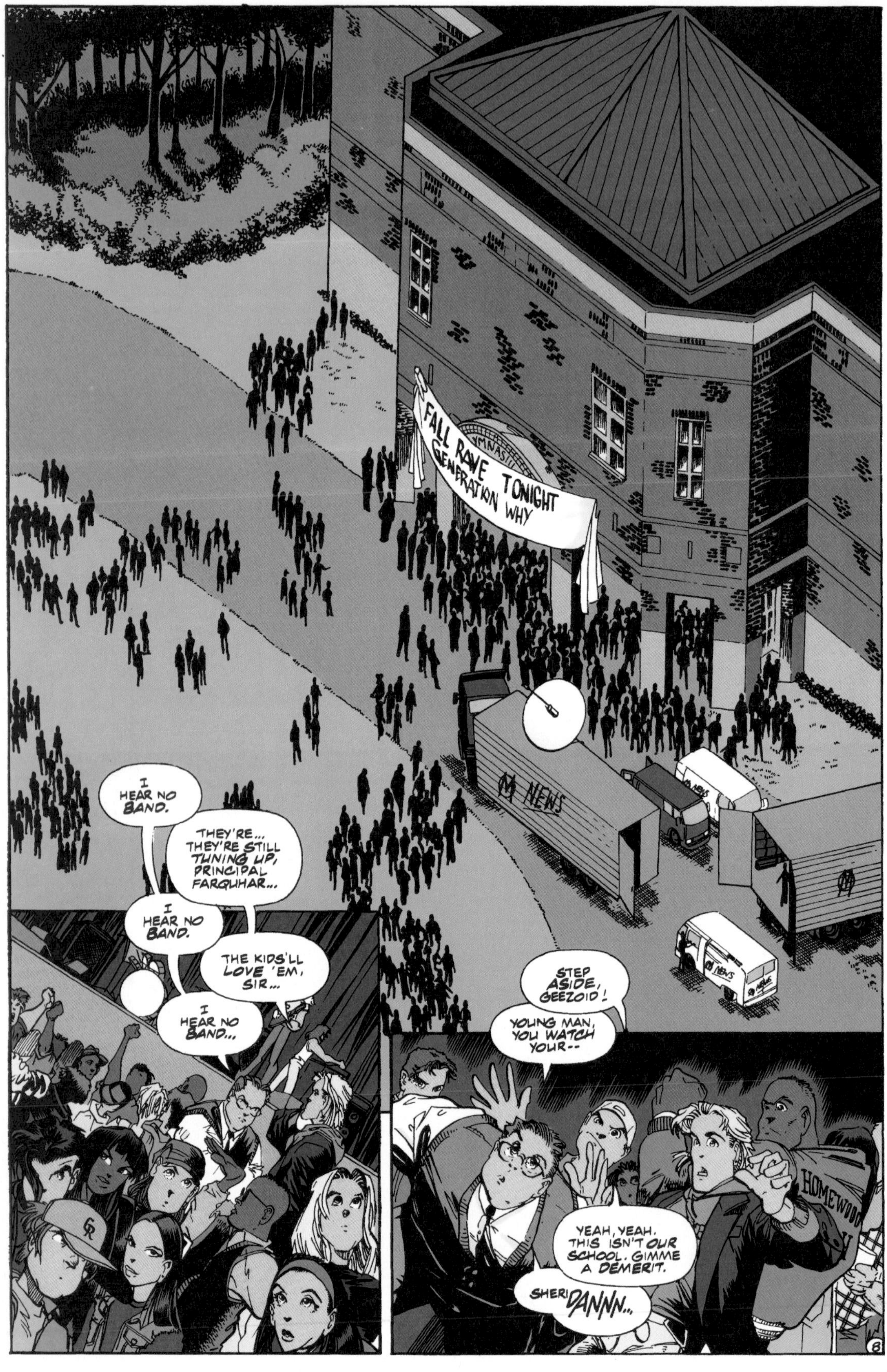
FALL RAVE TONIGHT
GENERATION WHY
GYMNASI
NEWS
I HEAR NO BAND.
THEY'RE... THEY'RE STILL TUNING UP, PRINCIPAL FARQUHAR...
I HEAR NO BAND.
THE KIDS'LL LOVE 'EM, SIR...
I HEAR NO BAND...
STEP ASIDE, GEEZOID!
YOUNG MAN, YOU WATCH YOUR--
YEAH, YEAH. THIS ISN'T OUR SCHOOL. GIMME A DEMERIT.
SHERIDANNN...
HOMEWOOD
8

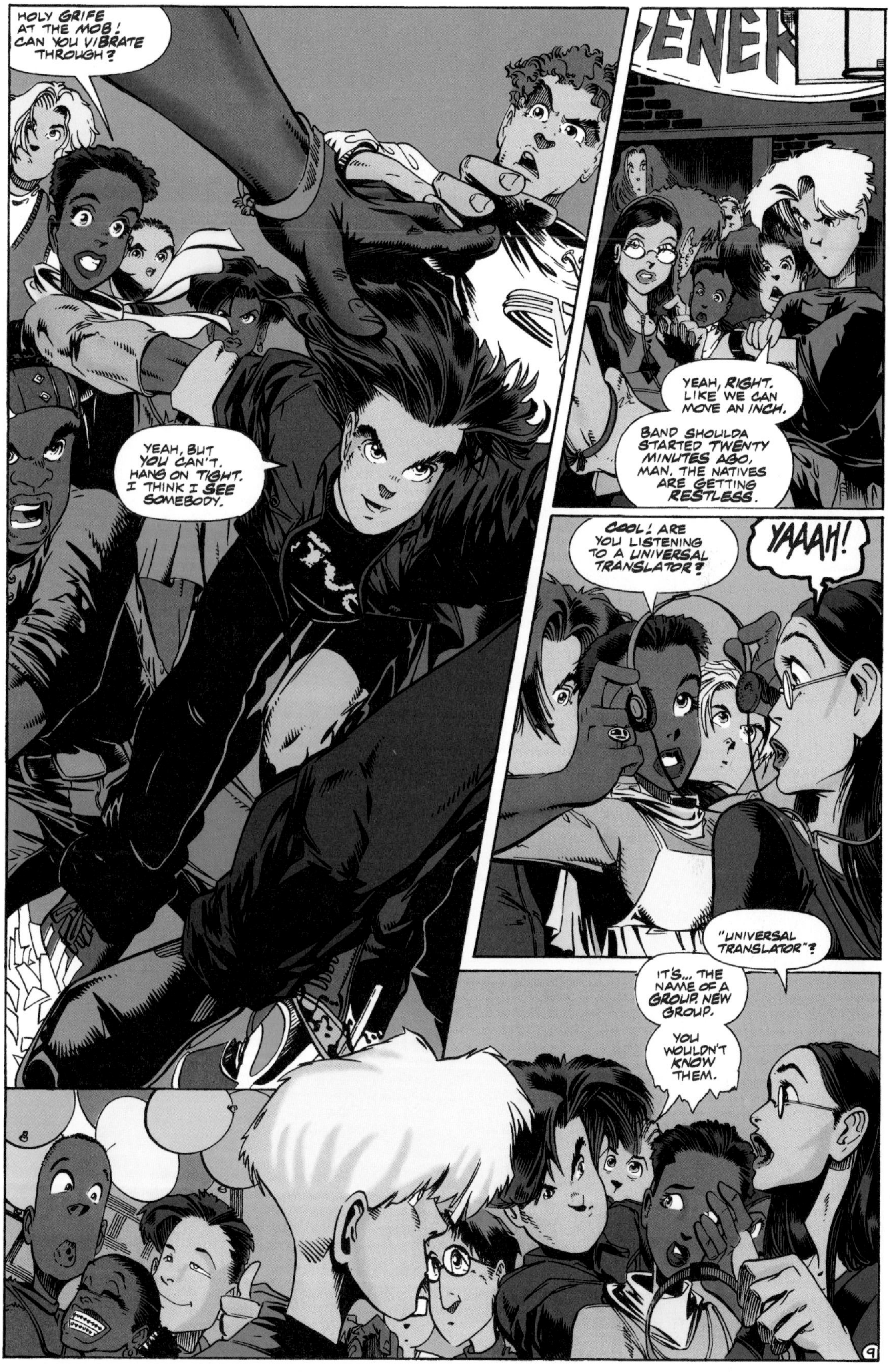
HOLY GRIFE AT THE MOB! CAN YOU VIBRATE THROUGH?
YEAH, BUT YOU CAN'T. HANG ON TIGHT. I THINK I SEE SOMEBODY.
GENER
YEAH, RIGHT. LIKE WE CAN MOVE AN INCH.
BAND SHOULDA STARTED TWENTY MINUTES AGO, MAN. THE NATIVES ARE GETTING RESTLESS.
COOL! ARE YOU LISTENING TO A UNIVERSAL TRANSLATOR?
YAAAH!
"UNIVERSAL TRANSLATOR"?
IT'S... THE NAME OF A GROUP. NEW GROUP.
YOU WOULDN'T KNOW THEM.
9

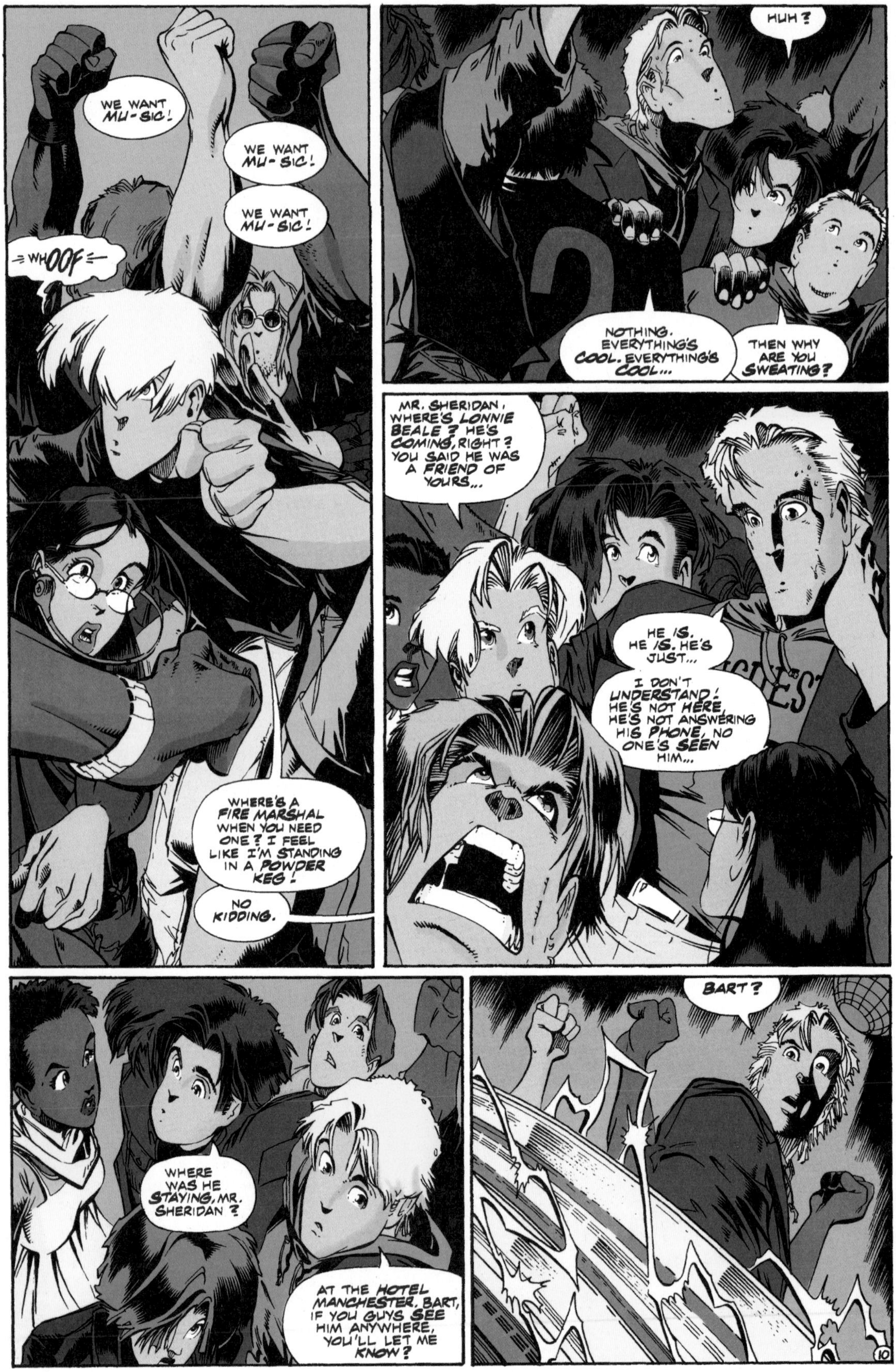
WE WANT MU-SIC!
WE WANT MU-SIC!
WE WANT MU-SIC!
WHOOF
WHERE'S A FIRE MARSHAL WHEN YOU NEED ONE? I FEEL LIKE I'M STANDING IN A POWDER KEG!
NO KIDDING.
HUH?
NOTHING. EVERYTHING'S COOL. EVERYTHING'S COOL...
THEN WHY ARE YOU SWEATING?
MR. SHERIDAN, WHERE'S LONNIE BEALE? HE'S COMING, RIGHT? YOU SAID HE WAS A FRIEND OF YOURS...
HE IS. HE IS. HE'S JUST...
I DON'T UNDERSTAND! HE'S NOT HERE, HE'S NOT ANSWERING HIS PHONE, NO ONE'S SEEN HIM...
WHERE WAS HE STAYING, MR. SHERIDAN?
AT THE HOTEL MANCHESTER. BART, IF YOU GUYS SEE HIM ANYWHERE, YOU'LL LET ME KNOW?
BART?
10

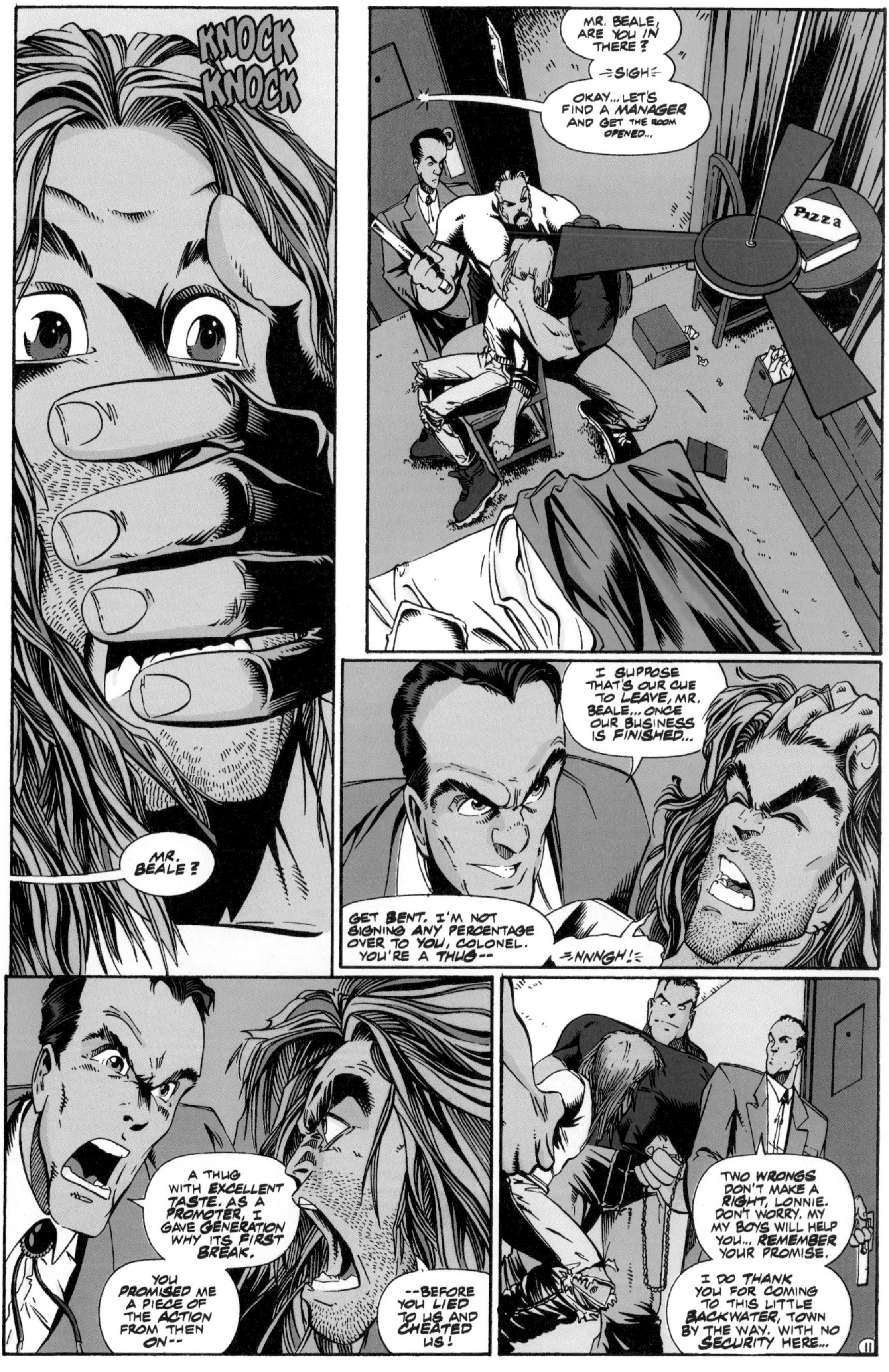
KNOCK KNOCK
MR. BEALE ?
MR. BEALE, ARE YOU IN THERE ?
SIGH
OKAY... LET'S FIND A MANAGER AND GET THE ROOM OPENED...
Pizza
I SUPPOSE THAT'S OUR CUE TO LEAVE, MR. BEALE... ONCE OUR BUSINESS IS FINISHED...
GET BENT. I'M NOT SIGNING ANY PERCENTAGE OVER TO YOU, COLONEL. YOU'RE A THUG--
NNNGH!
A THUG WITH EXCELLENT TASTE. AS A PROMOTER, I GAVE GENERATION WHY ITS FIRST BREAK.
YOU PROMISED ME A PIECE OF THE ACTION FROM THEN ON--
--BEFORE YOU LIED TO US AND CHEATED US!
TWO WRONGS DON'T MAKE A RIGHT, LONNIE. DON'T WORRY. MY MY BOYS WILL HELP YOU... REMEMBER YOUR PROMISE.
I DO THANK YOU FOR COMING TO THIS LITTLE BACKWATER, TOWN BY THE WAY. WITH NO SECURITY HERE...
11

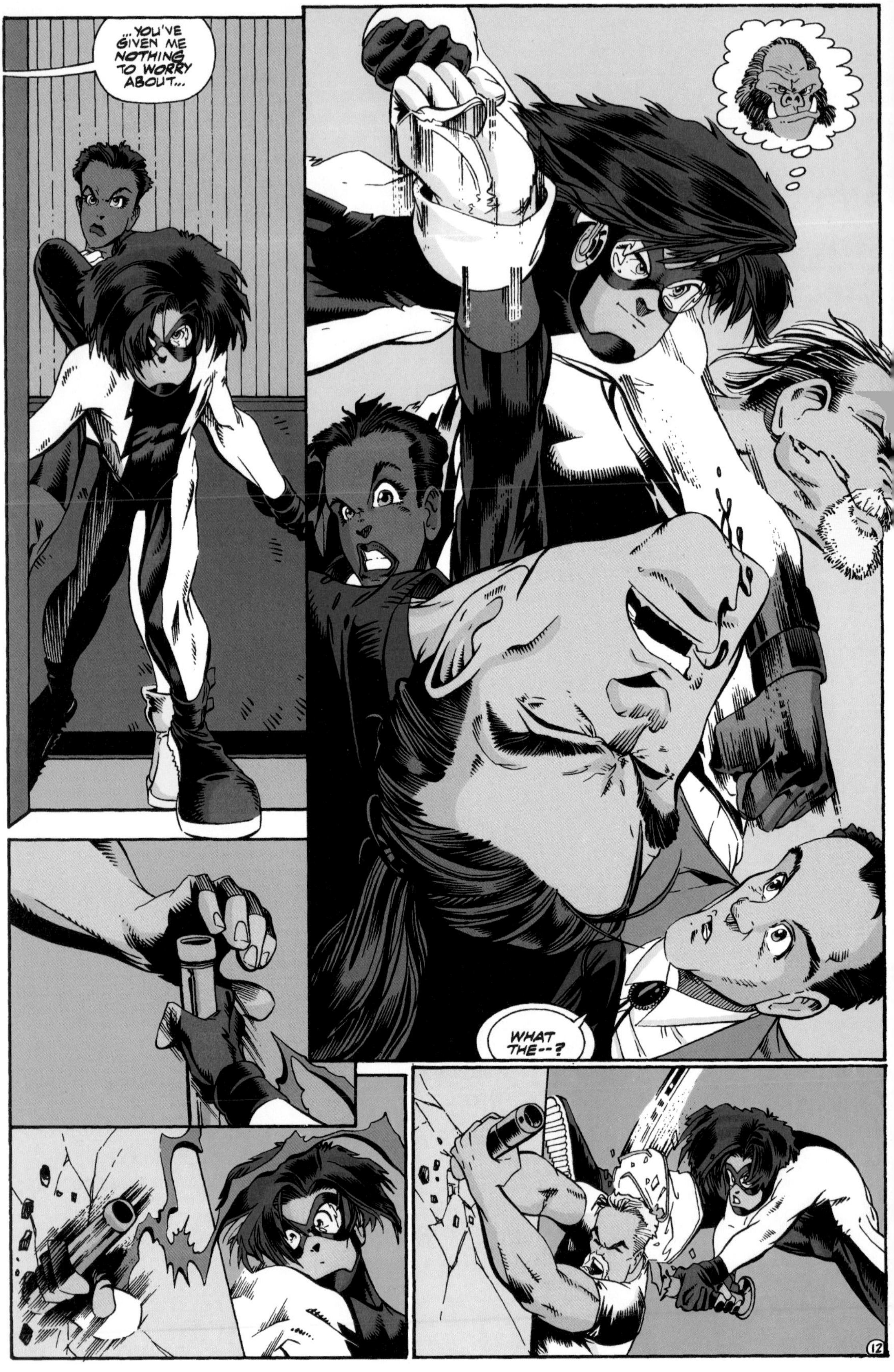
...YOU'VE GIVEN ME NOTHING TO WORRY ABOUT...
WHAT THE--?
12

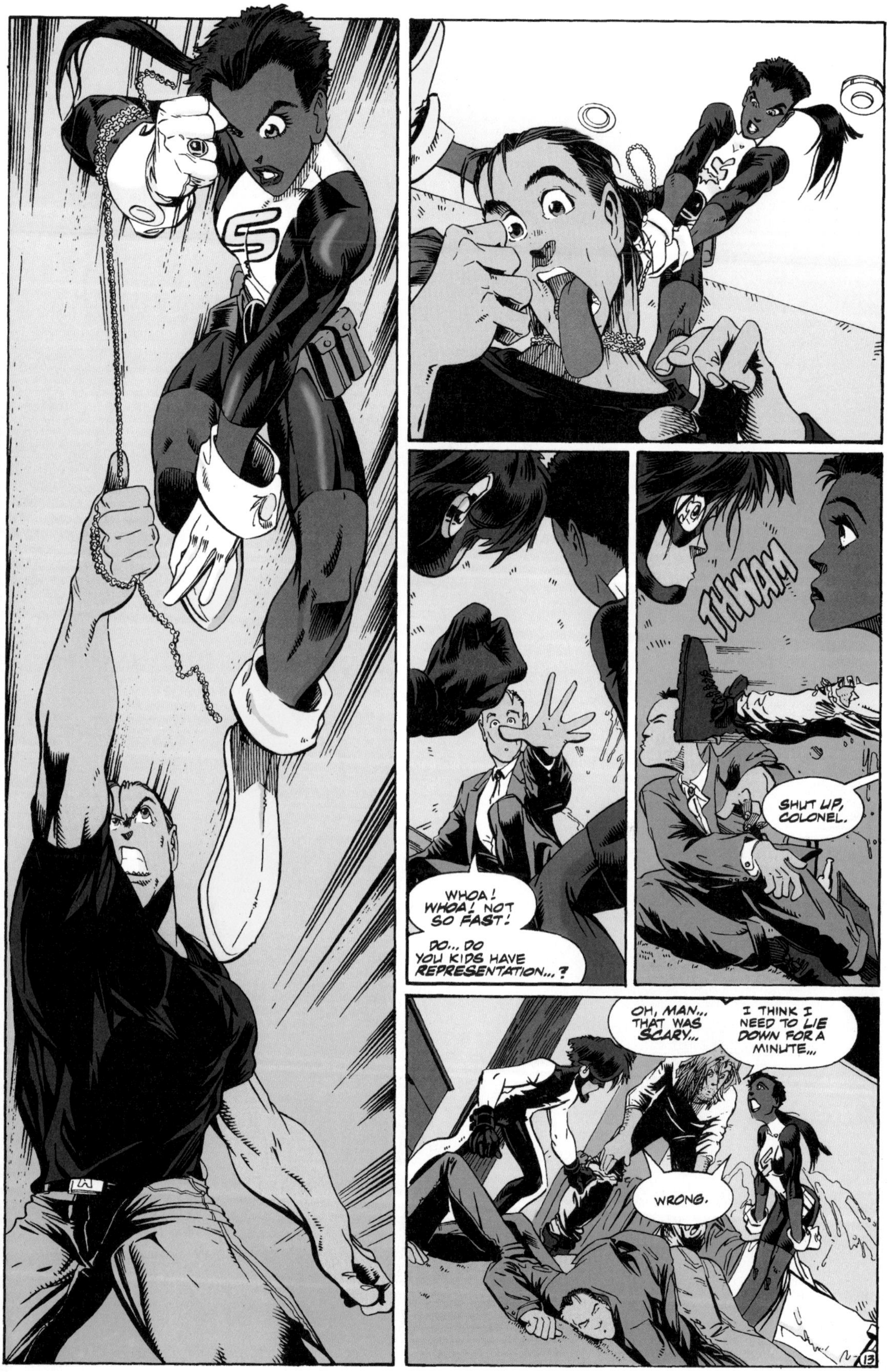

THWAM
WHOA! WHOA! NOT SO FAST!
DO... DO YOU KIDS HAVE REPRESENTATION...?
SHUT UP, COLONEL.
OH, MAN... THAT WAS SCARY...
I THINK I NEED TO LIE DOWN FOR A MINUTE...
WRONG.

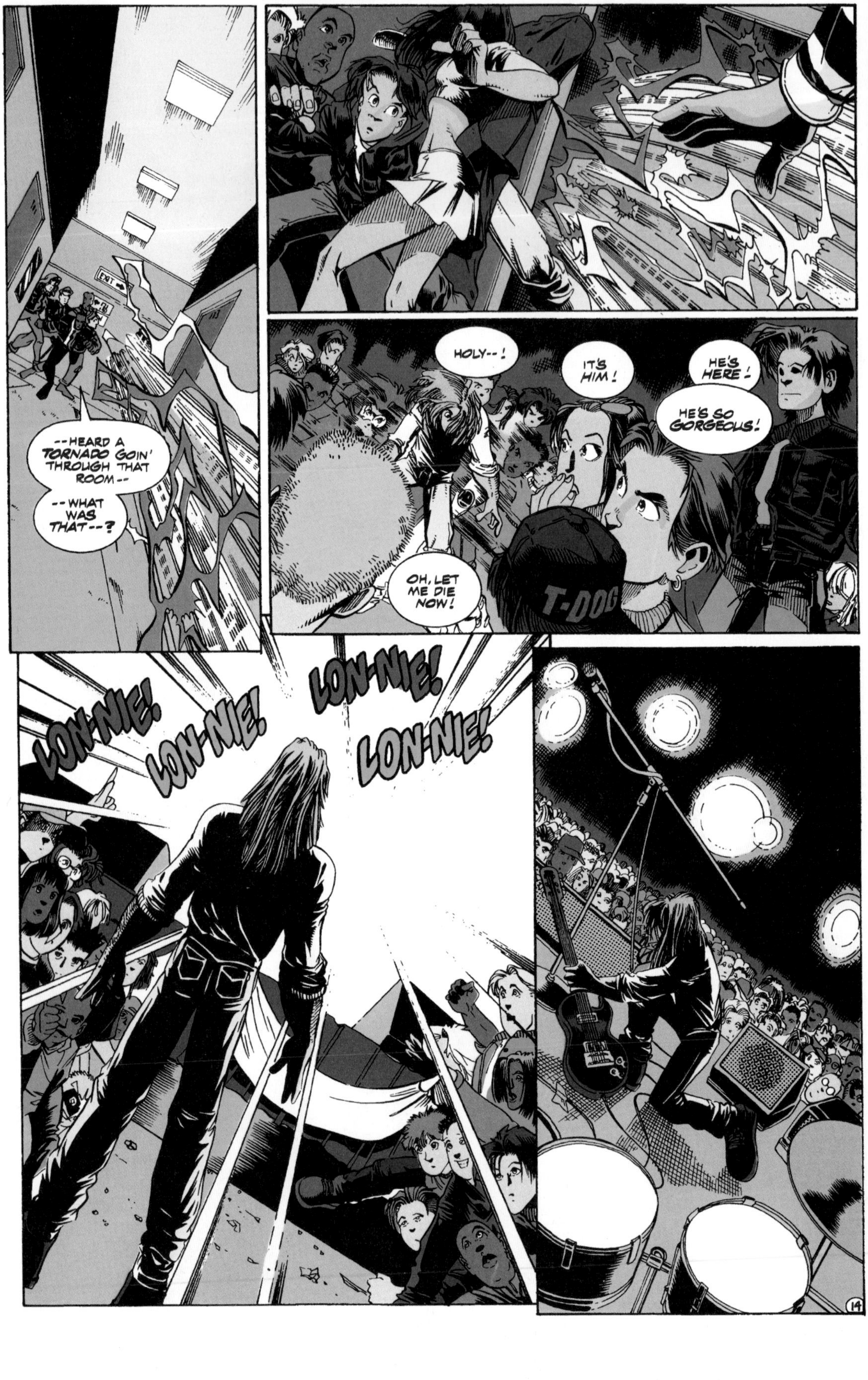
--HEARD A TORNADO GOIN' THROUGH THAT ROOM--
--WHAT WAS THAT--?
HOLY--!
IT'S HIM!
HE'S HERE!
HE'S SO GORGEOUS!
OH, LET ME DIE NOW!
T-DOG
LON-NIE!
LON-NIE!
LON-NIE!
LON-NIE!

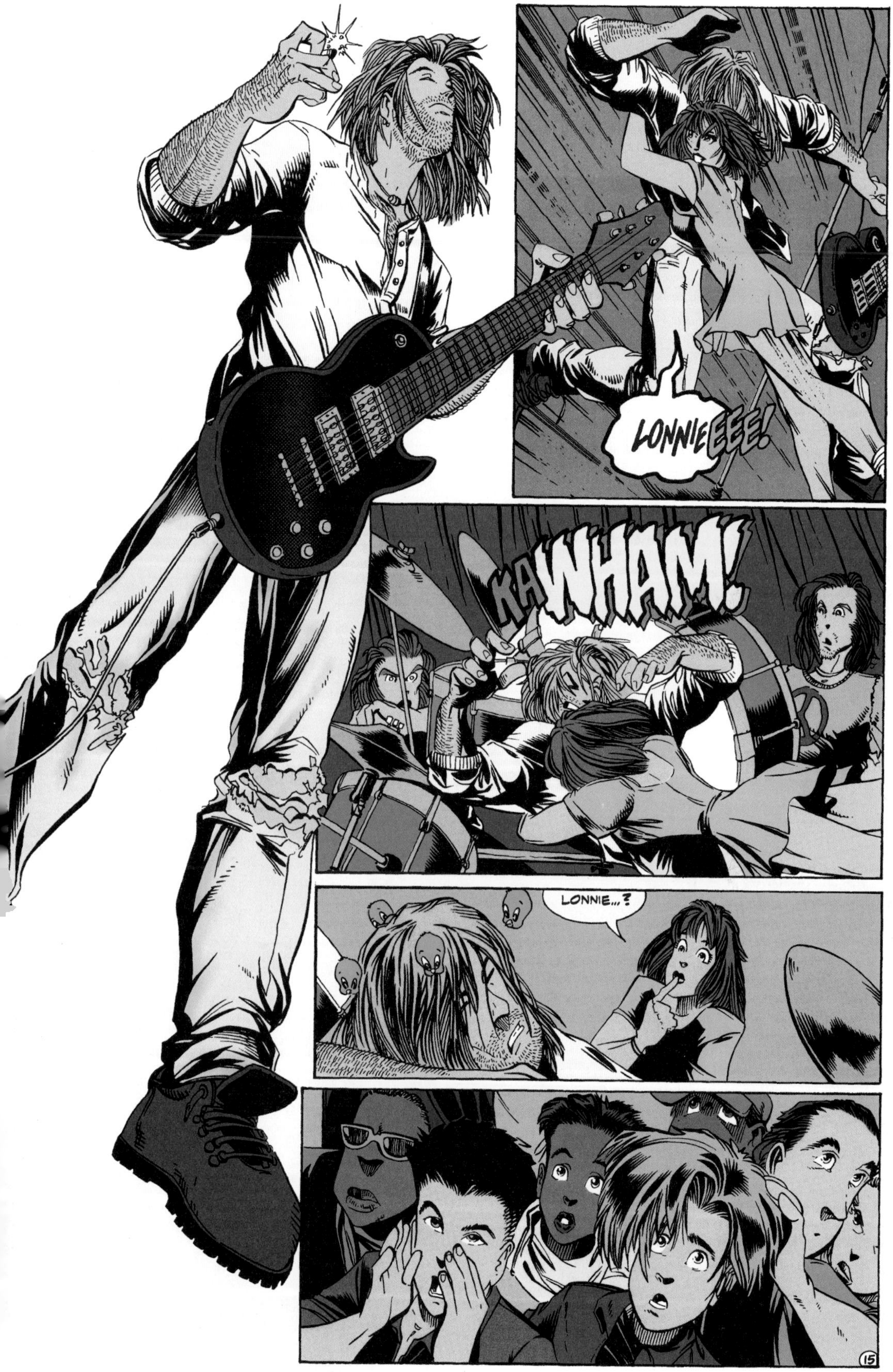
LONNIEEEE!
KAWHAM!
LONNIE...?

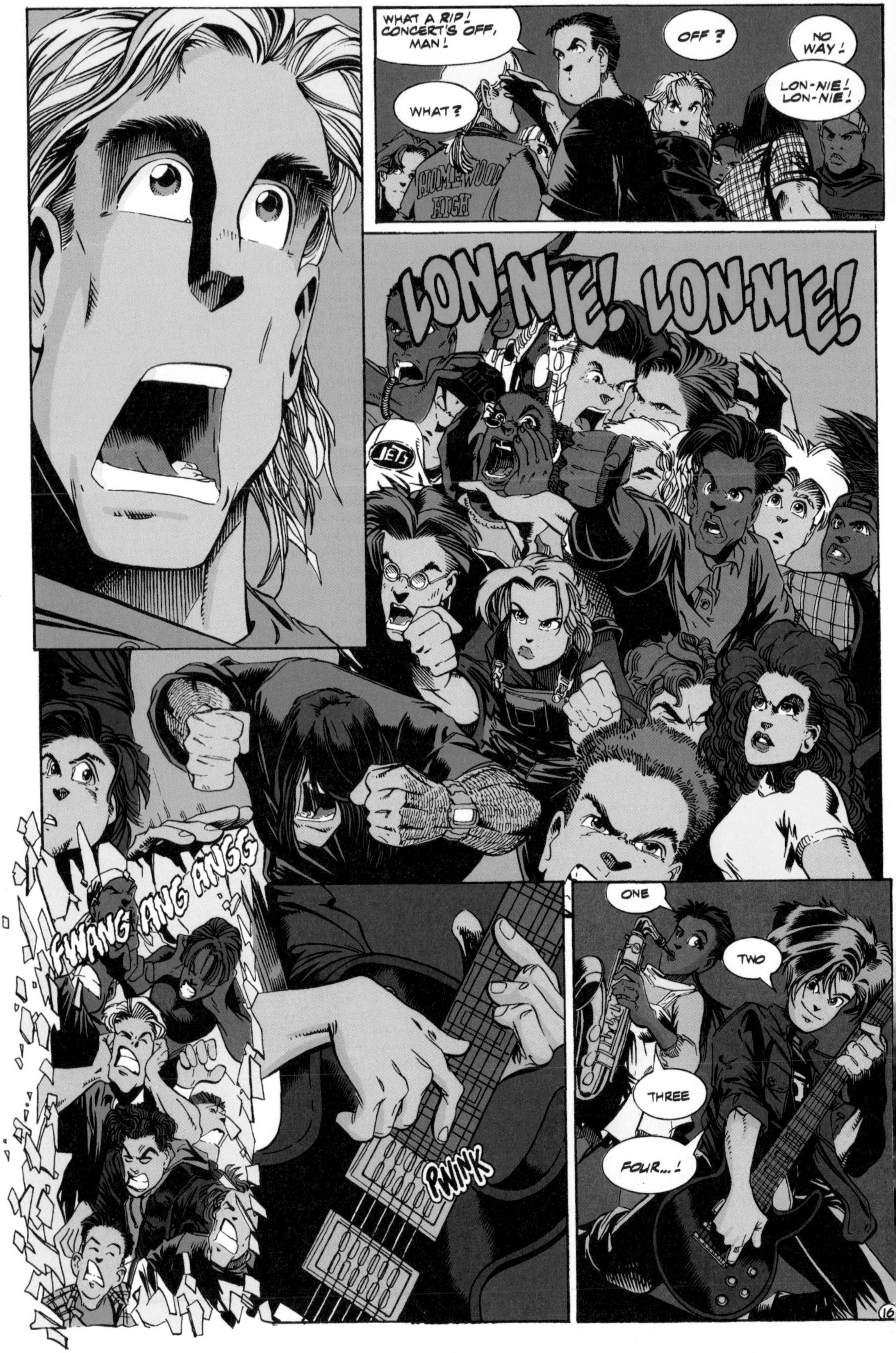

WHAT A RIP! CONCERT'S OFF, MAN!
WHAT?
OFF?
NO WAY!
LON-NIE! LON-NIE!
HOMEWOOD HIGH
LON-NIE! LON-NIE!
FWANG ANG ANGG
PWINK
ONE
TWO
THREE
FOUR...!

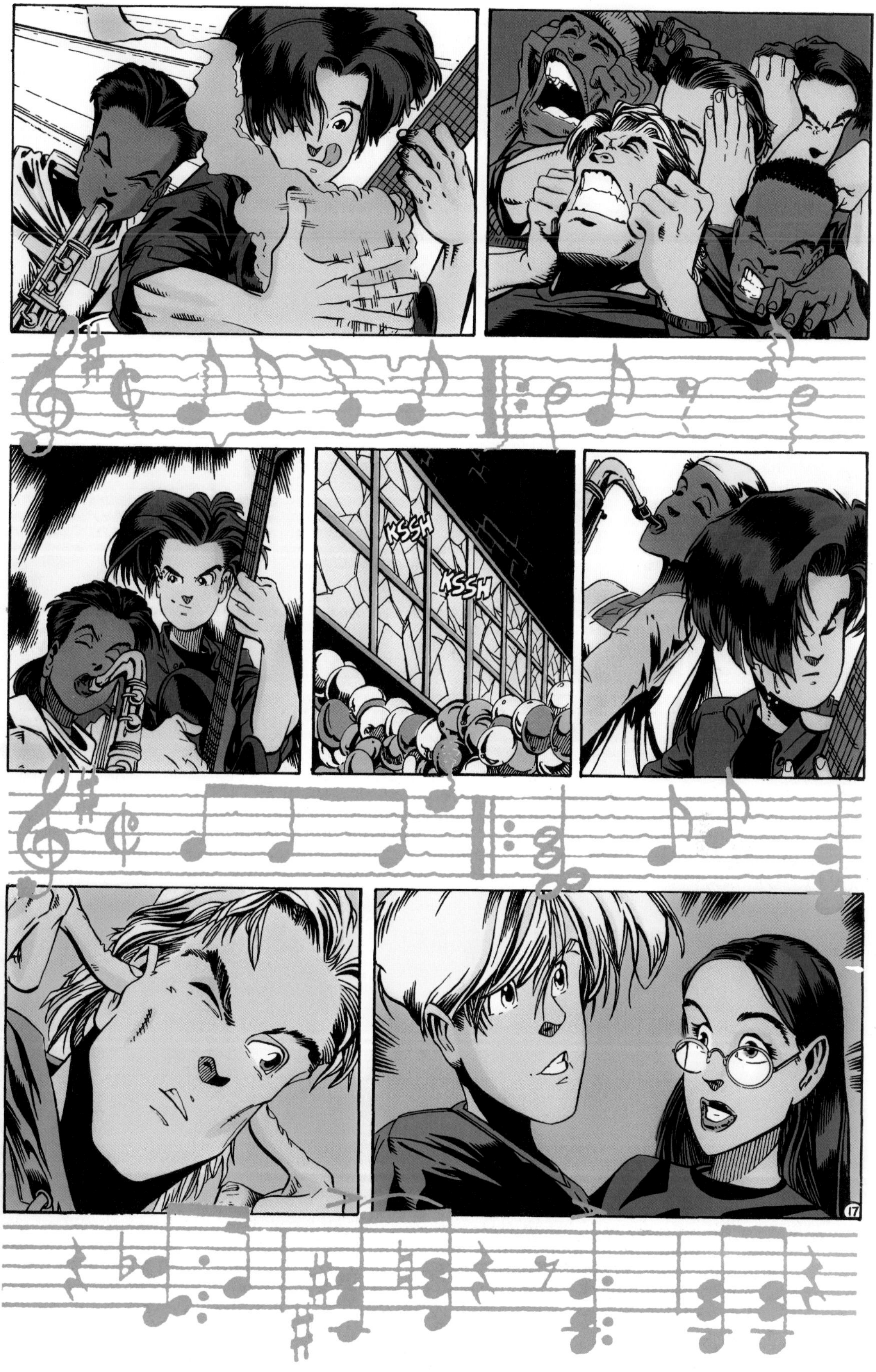
KSSH
KSSH
17

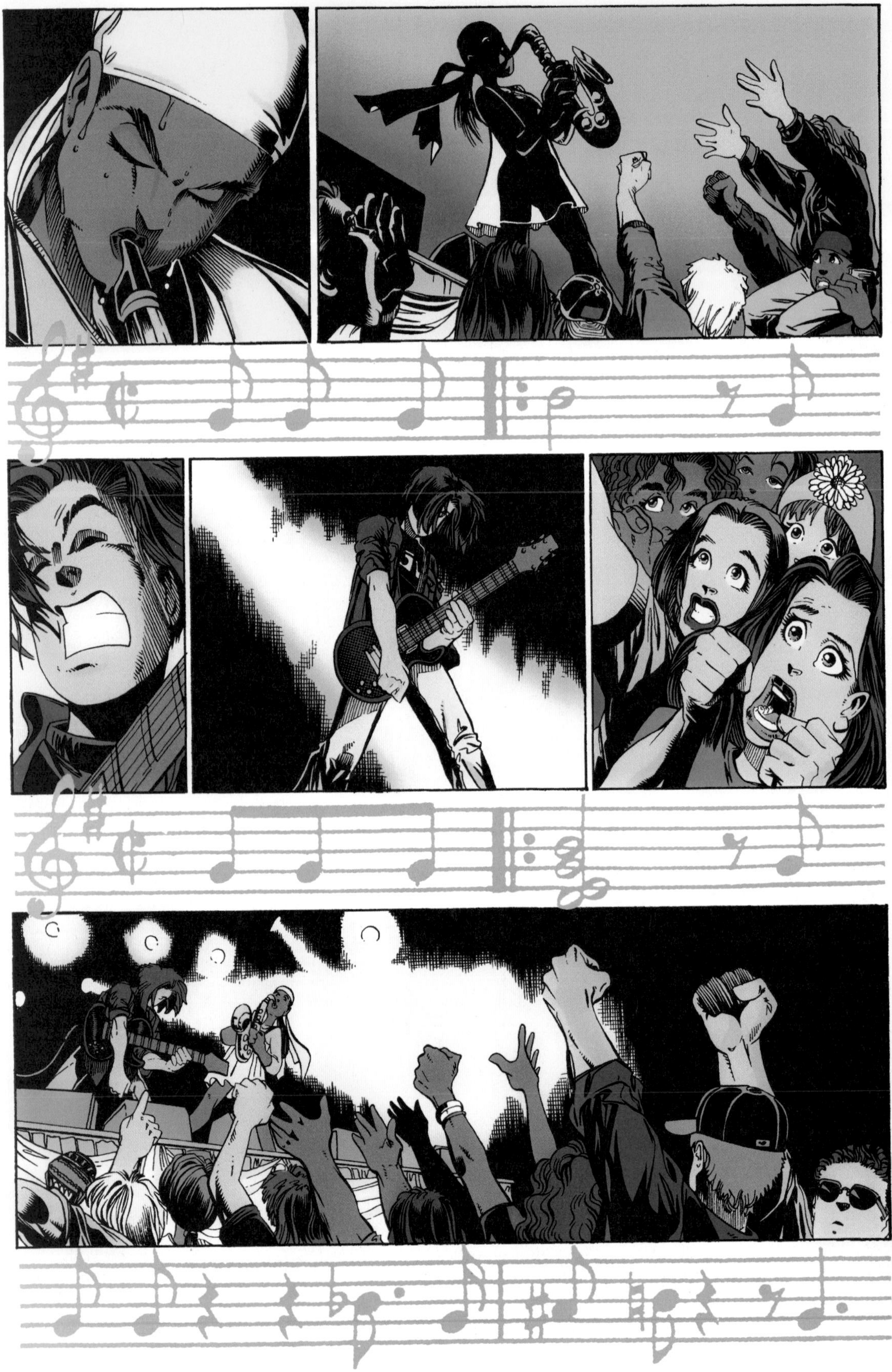

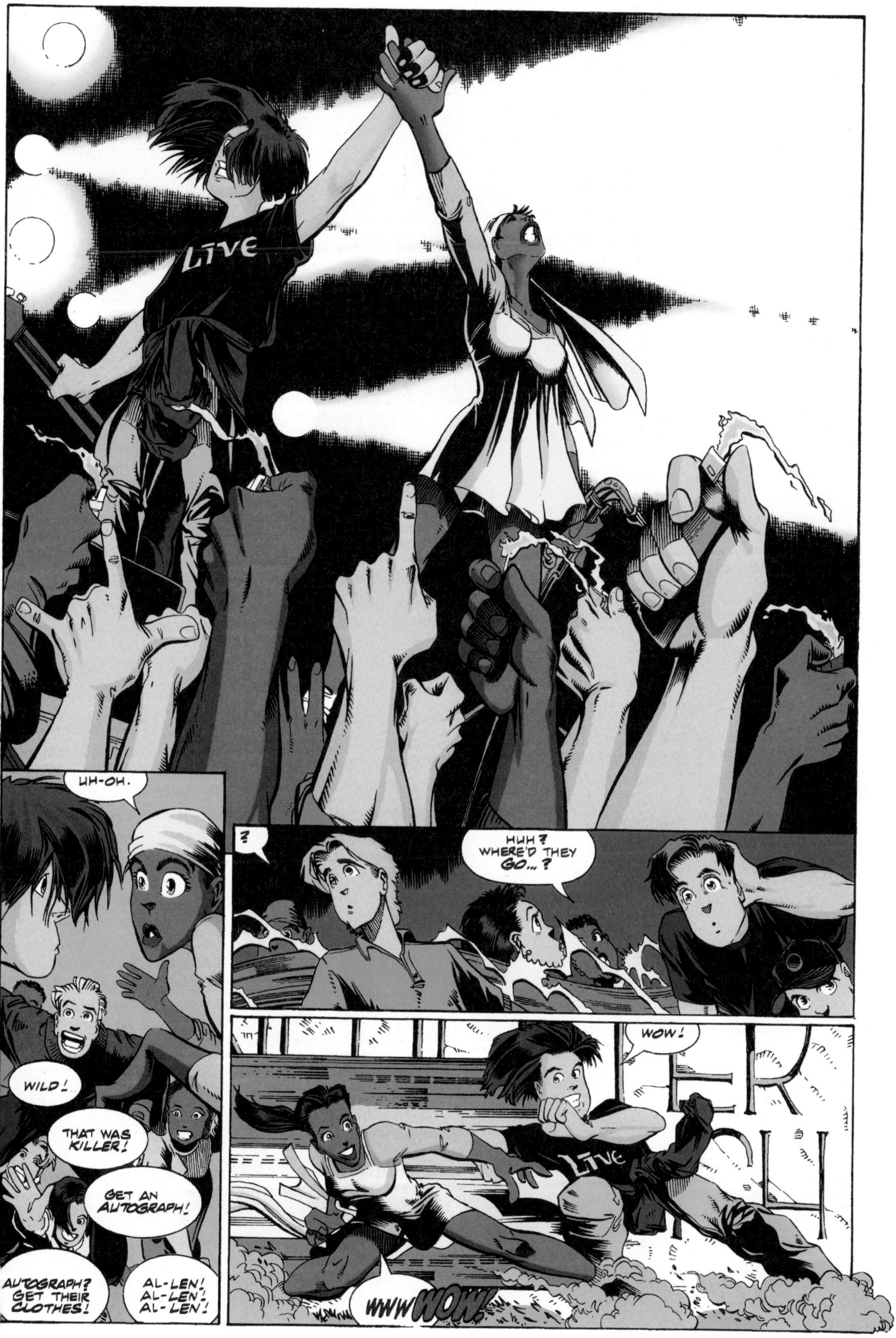
LIVE
UH-OH.
WILD!
THAT WAS KILLER!
GET AN AUTOGRAPH!
AUTOGRAPH? GET THEIR CLOTHES!
AL-LEN! AL-LEN! AL-LEN!
?
HUH? WHERE'D THEY GO...?
WOW!
LIVE
WWWWOW!

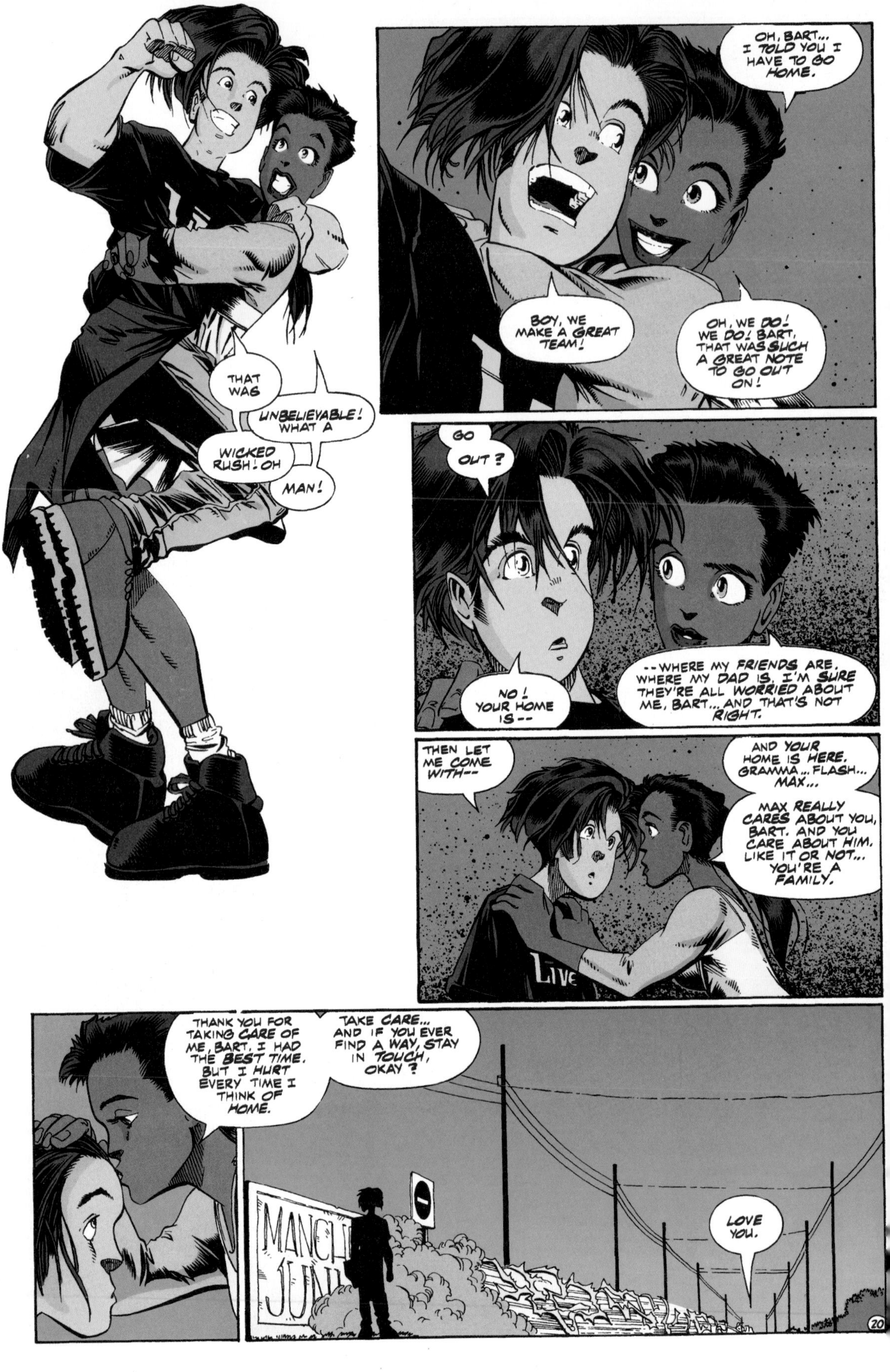
THAT WAS
UNBELIEVABLE! WHAT A
WICKED RUSH! OH
MAN!
OH, BART... I TOLD YOU I HAVE TO GO HOME.
BOY, WE MAKE A GREAT TEAM!
OH, WE DO! WE DO! BART, THAT WAS SUCH A GREAT NOTE TO GO OUT ON!
GO
OUT?
NO! YOUR HOME IS--
--WHERE MY FRIENDS ARE. WHERE MY DAD IS. I'M SURE THEY'RE ALL WORRIED ABOUT ME, BART... AND THAT'S NOT RIGHT.
THEN LET ME COME WITH--
AND YOUR HOME IS HERE. GRAMMA... FLASH... MAX...
MAX REALLY CARES ABOUT YOU, BART. AND YOU CARE ABOUT HIM. LIKE IT OR NOT... YOU'RE A FAMILY.
LIVE
THANK YOU FOR TAKING CARE OF ME, BART. I HAD THE BEST TIME. BUT I HURT EVERY TIME I THINK OF HOME.
TAKE CARE... AND IF YOU EVER FIND A WAY, STAY IN TOUCH, OKAY?
LOVE YOU.
20

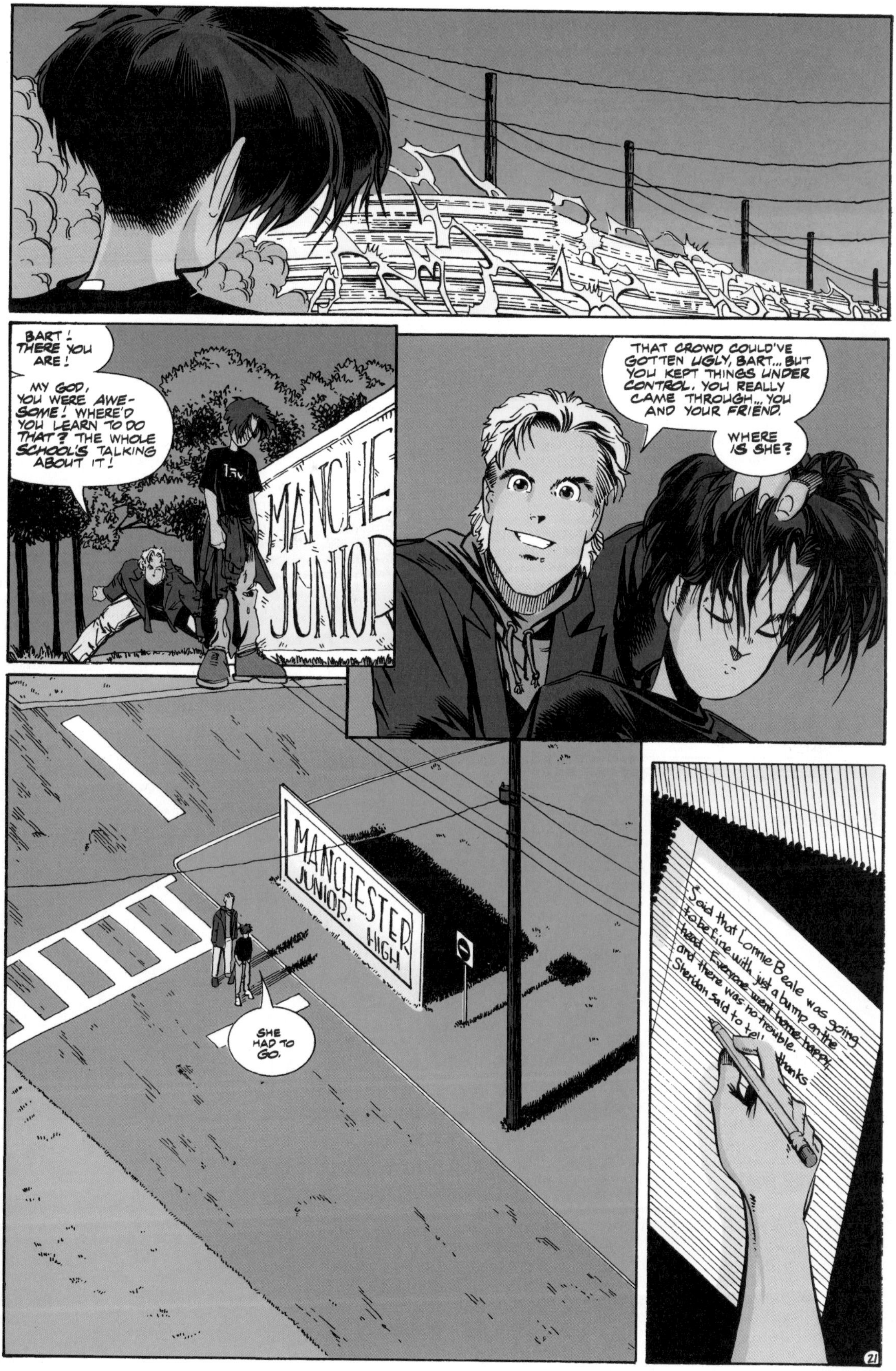
BART! THERE YOU ARE!
MY GOD, YOU WERE AWESOME! WHERE'D YOU LEARN TO DO THAT? THE WHOLE SCHOOL'S TALKING ABOUT IT!
MANCHE JUNIOR
THAT CROWD COULD'VE GOTTEN UGLY, BART... BUT YOU KEPT THINGS UNDER CONTROL. YOU REALLY CAME THROUGH... YOU AND YOUR FRIEND.
WHERE IS SHE?
MANCHESTER JUNIOR HIGH
SHE HAD TO GO.
Said that Lonnie Beale was going to be fine with just a bump on the head. Everyone went home happy and there was no trouble. Sheridan said to tell thanks

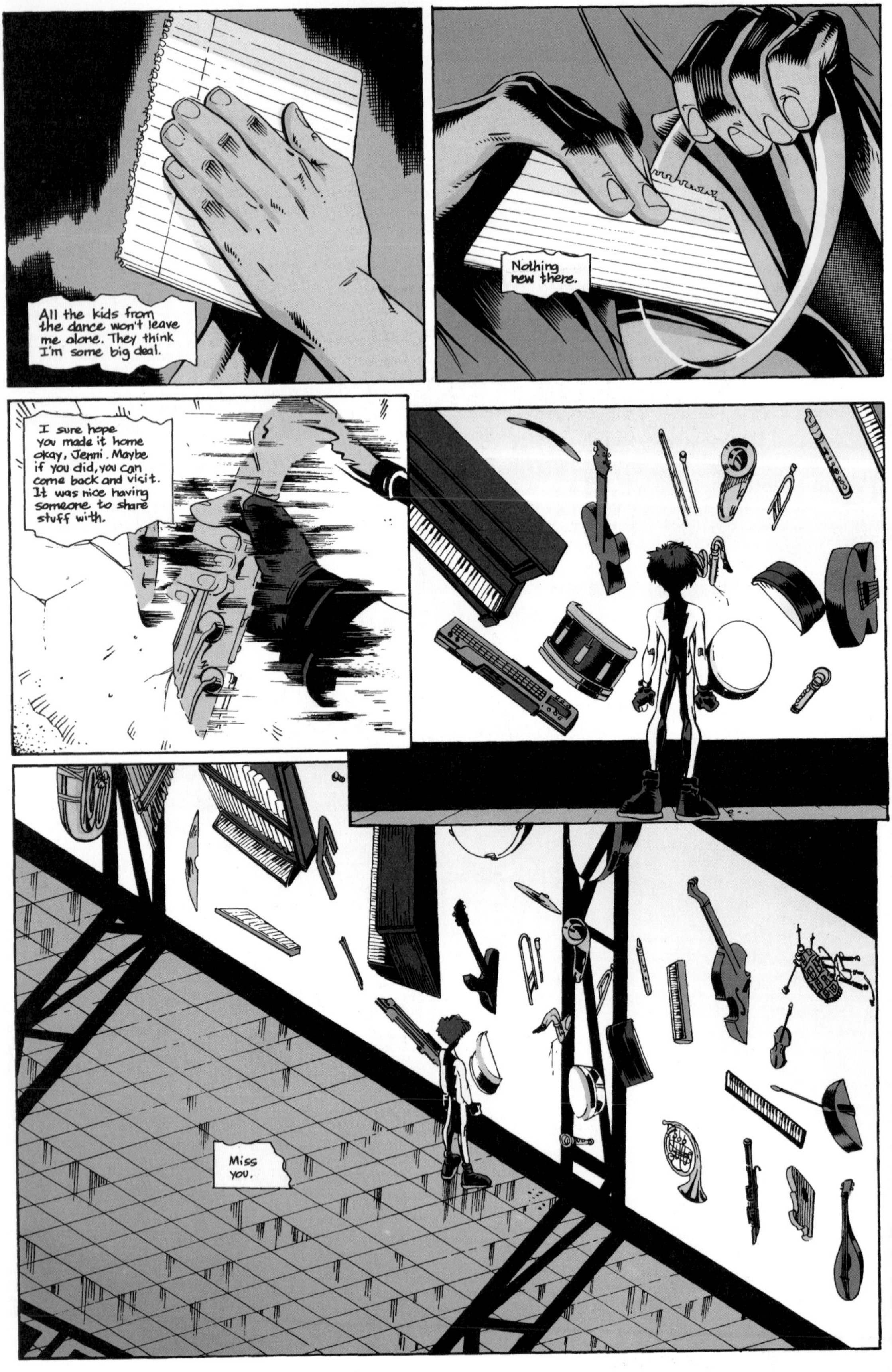
All the kids from the dance won't leave me alone. They think I'm some big deal.
Nothing new there.
I sure hope you made it home okay, Jenni. Maybe if you did, you can come back and visit. It was nice having someone to share stuff with.
Miss you.